THE CHURCH OF CHRIST

The Church of Christ

A BIBLICAL ECCLESIOLOGY FOR TODAY

Everett Ferguson

WILLIAM B. EERDMANS PUBLISHING COMPANY
GRAND RAPIDS, MICHIGAN / CAMBRIDGE, U.K.

© 1996 Wm. B. Eerdmans Publishing Co.
255 Jefferson Ave. S.E., Grand Rapids, Michigan 49503 /
P.O. Box 163, Cambridge, CB3 9PU U.K.
All rights reserved

Printed in the United States of America

07 06 05 04 03 02   10 9 8 7 6 5

Library of Congress Cataloging-in-Publication Data

Ferguson, Everett, 1933-
   The church of Christ : a biblical ecclesiology for today /
Everett Ferguson.
      p.   cm.
   Includes bibliographical references.
   ISBN 0-8028-4189-9 (paper : alk. paper)
   1. Church. 2. Church — Biblical teaching. I. Title.
BV600.2.F46 1996
262 — dc20   96-16701
                                                        CIP

To my children and grandchildren —

may they exemplify the church as it should be,

today and tomorrow

Contents

Preface

ECCLESIOLOGY may be regarded as the organizing theme for twentieth-century theology.[1] The ecumenical movement gave new stimulus in the mid-twentieth century to the doctrine of the church. A large number of studies of the church or some aspect of it have resulted. I will not often enter directly into dialogue with these studies, but will develop a positive exposition of the material from the New Testament.

Recent scholarship has emphasized the diversity of theologies within the New Testament. This has made the question of unity and diversity an acute problem.[2] Ecclesiology is not exempt from this concern.[3] It may seem rather old-fashioned to do this study systematically, when modern studies emphasize the plurality of ecclesiologies in the New Testament. The approach taken is not intended as a denial of diversity and does not indicate a neglect of the distinctive emphases of different writers in my preparation. I have tried to be sensitive to the different emphases represented by different New Testament authors. Bo Reicke compares the different portrayals of Christ in the New Testament to different musical instruments playing a melody;[4] that analogy

---

1. Jaroslav Pelikan, *The Christian Tradition: A History of the Development of Doctrine,* Vol. 5: *Christian Doctrine and Modern Culture (since 1700)* (Chicago: University of Chicago Press, 1989), p. 282.

2. James D. G. Dunn, *Unity and Diversity in the New Testament: An Inquiry into the Character of Earliest Christianity,* 2nd ed. (London: SCM, 1990); John Reumann, *Variety and Unity in New Testament Thought* (Oxford: University Press, 1991).

3. E. Käsemann, "Unity and Multiplicity in the New Testament Doctrine of the Church," *New Testament Questions of Today* (Philadelphia: Fortress, 1969), pp. 252-259; E. Käsemann and Raymond Brown, "Unity and Diversity in New Testament Ecclesiology," *Novum Testamentum* 6 (1963): 293-297, 298-308.

4. Bo Reicke, "Unity and Diversity in the Theology of the New Testament,"

may apply to the different expressions of ecclesiology in the New Testament. I have chosen to pay more attention in this study to the melody than to the individual instruments.

Although the synthetic approach adopted in this book may be out of fashion, the recognition of the authority of a canon of scripture (see Introduction) justifies the effort to bring together the teaching of the various New Testament documents on the relevant topics. A canon has the effect of unifying any disparate elements by bringing the hills and valleys into one picture. When authors are read and interpreted in relation to one another the sharp edges are blunted. This kind of reading does not serve the purposes of historians well, but it is a necessary task for theologians.[5]

The book is written by one whose academic training is primarily that of a historian, but a historian interested in theology who has used history as a way of understanding theological questions. I have set my hand in this work to a book that is completely theological and systematic. In doing that, I trust I have not forgotten my historical discipline, but the intention is to stay within the biblical text and construct a doctrinal exposition.

This study will limit itself to the New Testament, with its diversity, but with the New Testament against the background of the Old Testament.

The aim is to present a biblical theology of the church. The author, however, is quite conscious that no one can claim to encompass all of biblical teaching. At the same time, the "Today" in the subtitle does not mean a tailoring of biblical ecclesiology to the interests of the present but is meant to emphasize that biblical ecclesiology is viable today. The "Today" is also an acknowledgment that the questions addressed are in part shaped by contemporary as well as historical issues in ecclesiology. Even in these cases an effort is made to treat these secondary matters in the light of biblical theology.

Much of the material and insights developed in this book first appeared in a Bible class study book *The New Testament Church* (now

---

in Ed. L. Miller, ed., *Good News in History: Essays in Honor of Bo Reicke* (Atlanta: Scholars Press, 1993), pp. 173-192.

5. Without identifying myself with "canonical criticism," that development does represent the move away from an atomizing criticism to a reading of documents as a whole in the context of canon. Brevard S. Childs, *The New Testament as Canon*, new ed. (Valley Forge: Trinity Press International, 1994).

published by ACU Press) and is used here by permission. That material is often recast in form and context.

Almost every sentence could be footnoted. It would defeat the purpose of this book to attempt such complete documentation. Moreover, some things through repetition in the classroom and other settings have become so much a part of me that I do not remember where I got them. I apologize to those for whom footnotes and bibliographies do not give credit for ideas and wording that did not originate with me. The selected bibliographies include not only books to which I am especially indebted but also important works from different ecclesiastical traditions in order to inform the reader of alternative interpretations.

The book has been greatly improved by the comments and suggestions of Allan McNicol, Abraham J. Malherbe, Thomas H. Olbricht, and John Willis. I have learned much from them, as well as from many others; they could wish that I had learned more. Recording my indebtedness to them does not mean that this is the book any of them would write, nor does it even imply that this is the book any of them would have wanted me to write.

Biblical quotations are based on the New Revised Standard Version, but modified on occasion according to the Greek or to fit the context of my discussion.

Introduction

GOD gave a _person_, then a _proclamation_, and then a _people_. This is the historical and theological order.

God gave first a _person_, Jesus Christ. He gave a person and not a creed as the object of faith and basis of salvation. God the Father of the Lord Jesus Christ is always a God of personal presence and a God who expects a personal response.

The _proclamation_ centers in the person. He is the content of the message preached. The early church proclaimed "this Jesus" and declared what God had done through him. That preached word was soon written and collected into what we call the "New Testament" and added to the "Old Testament" to form the Christian Bible. The Bible is the written form of the proclamation of what God had done. God gave a Bible and not a catechism. The proclamation calls for a response.

The proclaimed word calls and gathers a _people_. The people respond to the proclamation of the person. The church is derived from the word of the gospel and from the Christ, who is the Word. God gave a word before he gave a church. This book studies the people, the church. As such it is concerned with what is derivative and in third position. The reader should keep this perspective in mind, as the author has tried to do in the writing. I seek to relate every aspect of the doctrine about the church to Christ. While stressing the church for the purposes of this study, we must remember that it is not itself part of the proclamation, but is the result of the proclamation.

The oral message about Jesus Christ gathered a people and so created a church. That message was put in written form for the use of the people and to aid them in their proclamation. Eventually the church had to distinguish its authoritative documents from other writings and so recognized a "canon" of scripture.[1] In a historical sense, one may say that "the church gave us the Bible." There was no individual or group otherwise to be the means of the formation of the scriptures. The church brought together and preserved the Bible. It did so in acknowledgment that these writings were its authority and the source of its life. Although the church was historically prior to the Bible as a given collection of books, the word contained in the Bible was theologically prior to the church. The recognition of a canon of scripture was an acknowledgment by the church that it was not its own authority and was an act of submission to the authority of apostolic preaching inscripturated in the apostolic writings.[2]

Hence, the standpoint of this study is the normativeness of the apostolic word (the teaching of apostles and other apostolic persons) contained in the scriptures accepted by the church. Later historical developments may throw light on that word (and such is another story) but are not themselves normative and must be judged by that word. This is so because the witness of the first generations of Christians about what was authoritative for them is an irreversible decision and remains determinative of what the essence of Christianity is. This does not mean that age alone makes something authoritative. Other teachings besides those accepted as genuinely apostolic were present in the churches of the first century. In fact, much of what was written in the New Testament was written to correct false interpretations of the gospel or improper responses to it. The corrections made by the apostolic writers remain authoritative, not simply because they make corrections, but because those corrections are set forth from the standpoint of the true nature of the Christian revelation. That fact lifts the corrections out of the realm of the temporal and temporary and into the realm of what is normative and abiding. Knowledge of the history of the times is necessary in order to understand properly and fully the apostolic teaching. Nevertheless, the historical circumstances of the first century are not normative for Christians in later centuries, but the apostolic teaching given in those historical circumstances is normative.

1. My perspective on the historical sequence is set forth briefly in the introduction to Everett Ferguson, ed., *Studies in Early Christianity,* Vol. 3, *The Bible in the Early Church* (New York: Garland, 1993), pp. xi-xiii.

2. Oscar Cullmann, "The Tradition," *The Early Church: Studies in Early Christian History and Theology* (Philadelphia: Westminster, 1956), pp. 59-99; reprinted in Everett Ferguson, *Studies in Early Christianity,* Vol. 3, *The Bible in the Early Church* (New York: Garland, 1993), pp. 109-149.

The argument of this book, therefore, seeks to take seriously the implications of canon, namely that there is a certain normativeness for the church in the written word of the Bible. History as history has no authority for the church of a later day. However, since God has always revealed himself in history, the historical context is caught up in the message that is God's word for the church. The apostolic message itself, as related to and illumined by a particular historical period and set of circumstances, is normative for the church.

This book is limited to a consideration of biblical teaching about the church. The intention is to let the biblical text speak its own word on the subjects brought up for consideration, and insofar as possible to let the biblical text determine these subjects. However, a study of ecclesiology requires a consideration of some of the topics that have recurred through Christian history in regard to the nature and activities of the church. This book takes up these traditional topics in ecclesiology (but not necessarily in their usual order in systematic theology) and studies the biblical passages relevant to these topics. Thus some of the questions addressed to the biblical text in this study are questions that have arisen later in Christian history and were not of primary concern to the biblical writers. Even where the questions that have confronted the church as it reflected on itself in later times were not those of the church in the first century, the biblical text will be found to offer guidance in dealing with these later questions.

The effort to find an authoritative word in scripture on the matters discussed does not mean adopting the kind of "proof-text" approach that often takes verses out of context. The effort has been made to show the interconnectedness of themes. Although the author seeks to be aware of historical developments in the presentation, this is not a historical study but a doctrinal study. A doctrinal approach does not mean imposing a doctrinal scheme on the text; the effort rather is to let the doctrinal teaching arise out of the text itself.

There is such an interrelatedness of themes that this book could almost be considered a New Testament theology organized with reference to ecclesiology. It is not that; there are too many aspects of New Testament theology that are not included. However, the doctrine of the church does touch many important biblical themes, and the intention in this work is to place the doctrine of the church in a broad perspective.

It was popular a few years ago to say, "Jesus, yes; the church, no!" Or, in other words, "Give me *Christ*ianity, not *church*ianity." The author felt a certain sympathy for that expression, and in many ways still does.

The person of Jesus is more attractive than those who claim to follow him are. But, from another perspective, one cannot have Jesus without the church. We hope to show that Christ *or* the church is a false alternative. On the very practical level, without the Bible preserved and promoted by the church, and without a believing group of people teaching about Jesus, he would not be known. On a more theological level, one cannot have Jesus without the church. Jesus died for the church; his whole mission was directed toward gathering a saved community. Christ is not complete without his people. To take Jesus means taking also his teachings and taking the people who are joined to him. To emphasize Christ is to make his church important.

Sometimes people, finding the heart of the gospel, want to treat the rest of biblical teaching as irrelevant. It may be secondary, but it is not irrelevant. The proper procedure is to work out from the center of the gospel to other things and apply the gospel to other aspects of doctrine. On our topic, that means working from Christ to the nature of the church and to its activities. That will be what we try to do in this book. Matters of worship and polity are not as central as the saving work of Christ, but in their own sphere the biblical materials on these topics are normative.

Perhaps the problem for many has been in taking the church too much in an institutional sense and not sufficiently in terms of a people, a redeemed community. In other quarters, there has been more emphasis on a set of specific church characteristics than on a crucified Christ. The demands are thereby considerably reduced. For whatever reason, too often the church in its attitudes and in the perceptions of others has been divorced from the Christ. The church may often have been presented in such a way as to obscure Christ. If this book can take some steps toward correcting misconceptions about the church, it will have served a worthwhile purpose.

The church is a result of and response to God's action in Christ. The first three chapters of this book develop the theological axiom that Christology and soteriology determine ecclesiology. The last three chapters then apply this insight to the ministry, worship, and life of the church. We want to take seriously that this study concerns the church *of Christ*. He gives existence, meaning, and purpose to the church. Christology is the norm for ecclesiology, and that is what justifies the title of the book.[3]

3. See the twelve theses on the church in relation to Christology by E. Schlink, "Christ and the Church," *Scottish Journal of Theology* 10 (1957): 1-23.

1. The People and the Messiah: History and Eschatology

"I will build my church."   (MATT. 16:18)

THIS study is concerned with the New Testament doctrine of the church. A proper understanding of the New Testament, however, requires the whole biblical context. Therefore, this first chapter offers an exploration of some topics from the Old Testament and Jewish background which are important for understanding the Christian church and then a discussion of the New Testament development of these themes.[1] The concepts of *covenant, kingdom,* and *messiah* provide the framework for the New Testament understandings of history and eschatology and so of the place of the *community* of the Christ in God's purpose and plan. As detailed aspects of the church are taken up in later chapters, there will be further attention to the Old Testament background of these aspects as appropriate.

These topics emphasize something of the theological perspective important for understanding the biblical doctrine of the church. God initiates the covenant relationship in calling a people; God rules in the affairs of human beings for the redemptive purpose of saving a people; God anoints (selects and empowers) his chosen representatives to lead his people; and God's goal is to build a community of people who

---

1. F. F. Bruce, *New Testament Development of Old Testament Themes* (Grand Rapids: Eerdmans, 1968), exemplifies the approach over a different and broader range of topics.

1

acknowledge him as their God. In the New Testament, these items are related to Jesus Christ. The new covenant is in Christ; the authority of kingship is now given to Christ; he is the anointed king; and the church is the community of Christ.

COVENANT

> *"I will make a new covenant with the*
> *house of Israel and the house of Judah."*   (JER. 31:31; HEB. 8:8)

Meaning of Covenant

Biblical religion is covenant religion.[2] Biblical history is punctuated by God's covenants with individuals and peoples, and the teachings of the Old and New Testaments are set in a covenant framework. *Covenant* may be defined as a relationship based on promises or sworn oaths. Different kinds of covenants were known in the world of ancient Israel.[3]

The parity covenant was a contract or mutual agreement between individuals who were in certain respects equals, as the covenants between Laban and Jacob (Gen. 31:43-54) and between David and Jonathan (1 Sam. 18:3; 23:18). No covenant in which God is a partner is conceived in this way, for human beings never initiate the covenant with God or draw up the conditions of the relationship. A partial exception is marriage, for God describes his relationship with Israel as a marriage (Hos. 1–3; Ezek. 16), and marriage is one of the social institutions in the Old Testament described as a covenant (Mal. 2:14-15). But husband and wife were not fully equals in Israelite society, and the initiative and requirements of the relationship between God and Israel remained with God.

Most often, covenant language in the ancient Near East referred to actions by sovereigns and relations between nations. The different

---

2. Walter Eichrodt takes covenant as the organizing principle of his *Theology of the Old Testament*, 2 vols. (Philadelphia: Westminster, 1961, 1967). Cf. also W. J. Dumbrell, *Covenant and Creation: An Old Testament Covenantal Theology* (Exeter: Paternoster, 1984; reprint, Grand Rapids: Baker, 1993).

3. See G. E. Mendenhall and G. A. Herion, "Covenant," *Anchor Bible Dictionary*, ed. D. N. Freedman (New York: Doubleday, 1992), Vol. 1, pp. 1179-1202 and their bibliography; Steven L. McKenzie, *Covenant* (St. Louis: Chalice, 2000).

types of documents involved may be classified as charters, treaties, and loyalty oaths. The first two, at least, offer significant parallels to God's covenants in the Old Testament.

God's Covenants

God's covenants with Noah, Abraham, and David may be termed *charters,* in which God bound himself by oath to grant certain favors to a chosen person and the people descended from or joined to that person. The first reference to a covenant in the Bible occurs in the story of Noah and the flood (Gen. 6:18; 9:8-17). Here God gave his unconditional promise not to destroy again the world and its inhabitants by water and placed the rainbow in the sky as the sign and reminder of his covenant with the earth and all flesh. Even this unilateral covenant was accompanied by laws of conduct for Noah and his descendants (Gen. 9:1-7).

An unconditional promise by which God bound himself is exemplified in the covenant with Abraham. God's call of Abraham carried the promise that God would bless him and through him all the families of the earth (Gen. 12:1-3). God further promised to Abraham numerous descendants and made a grant of land to them (Gen. 15:18; 17:1-21). The sign of this covenant was circumcision, and so important did this sign become that the covenant itself was called "the covenant of circumcision" (Acts 7:8). The covenant promise was continued through Isaac and Jacob (Israel), as affirmed in 1 Chronicles 16:14-17.

> He is the LORD our God; his judgments are in all the earth.
> Remember his covenant forever,
>   the word that he commanded, for a thousand generations,
> the covenant that he made with Abraham,
>   his sworn promise to Isaac,
> which he confirmed to Jacob as a statute,
>   to Israel as an everlasting covenant.

The parallelism of Hebrew poetry in this passage (also found in Ps. 105:7-11) concerning God's covenant with Abraham and his descendants gives an indication of the meaning of the word *covenant* by the terms used in parallel with it: "judgments," "word commanded," "sworn promise" (oath), and "statute." The emphasis is clearly on

God's initiative — his promises, decrees, and ordinances. (One may compare Luke 1:72-73, where God's covenant with Abraham is a "sworn oath.")

God promised to Phinehas, grandson of Aaron, and his descendants "a covenant of perpetual priesthood" (Num. 25:13; cf. Neh. 13:29) because of his zeal for the purity of Israel.

Another unilateral covenant was God's oath to preserve the throne for David's descendants (2 Sam. 23:5; 2 Chron. 13:5; Ps. 89:3-4, 29, 34-36; based on the promise in 2 Sam. 7:11-16). Some passages do add the condition of keeping God's commandments in order for individual descendants to share in the blessings of God (1 Kings 6:12; 8:25: Pss. 89:30-32, 38-39; 132:12). The covenant with David became an important part of the prophetic hope of Israel (Isa. 55:3-5; Jer. 33:20-21).[4]

God's initiative also lies behind the Sinai, or Mosaic, covenant. It differs from God's covenants with individuals and their descendants by being entered into with a nation, or a people, and by being expressly accompanied by stipulations. On the basis of God's deliverance of Israel from Egyptian bondage at the Red Sea (the Exodus), God offered a covenant relationship to the people and added the requirement that they obey his voice (Exod. 19:1-6). God had done for Israel what Israel could not do for herself: he saved the people from slavery and oppression. God's action in Egypt and at the Red Sea was followed by the giving of the Torah, setting forth in narrative that action and the codification of God's required response. The people, out of gratitude and out of their experience of God as gracious, bound themselves to keep the words of God before they even knew what those commands were (Exod. 19:7-8). Obedience is connected with the covenant as the faithful response of those to whom the gracious promises are given. The Sinai covenant was a conditional covenant, the conditions being spelled out in the law delivered through Moses. The law and the covenant are not the same, but are related. The covenant was the basis of the relationship, and the law constituted the stipulations of the covenant.

In the Sinai covenant (Exod. 19–24, esp. 19:5-8 and 24:7-8), it was human beings and not God who were bound by oath. Hence, some scholars see the background to the Mosaic covenant in ancient Near

---

4. F. F. Bruce, *New Testament Development of Old Testament Themes* (Grand Rapids: Eerdmans, 1968), p. 79, esp. n. 3.

Eastern loyalty oaths.[5] The extensive parallels to Near Eastern suzerainty treaties, nevertheless, are impressive. The form of these treaties emphasized the benevolent action of the suzerain and the dependence of the continuation of the relationship on his graciousness. The elements of the suzerainty treaties found in connection with the Sinai covenant, although not in one place in the biblical text, include the following: identification of the superior power who initiates the treaty and the historical prologue that is its basis (Exod. 20:1); the stipulations (Exod. 20:3-17); provision for deposit (Josh. 24:26) and periodic public reading (Deut. 17:18-19; 27:11-26); a list of witnesses (not the gods but heaven, earth, and the people — Exod. 20:18-22; Deut. 32:1, 46: Josh. 24:22, 27; Mic. 6:1-2); blessings of keeping the treaty and curses for violating it (Deut. 28); and the ratification ceremony (Exod. 24:5-8). Many of these elements appear in Joshua 24.

Even with the emphasis in the Sinai covenant on the stipulations of the covenant, Israel's relationship with God was dependent on God's grace:

> It was not because you were more numerous than any other people that the LORD set his heart on you and chose you — for you were the fewest of all people. It was because the LORD loved you and kept the oath that he swore to your ancestors, that the LORD has brought you out with a mighty hand, and redeemed you from the house of slavery, from the hand of Pharaoh king of Egypt. Know therefore that the LORD your God is God, the faithful God who maintains covenant loyalty with those who love him and keep his commandments, to a thousand generations. (Deut. 7:7-9)

Because of the covenant with Abraham, Israel was not completely cast off when she failed to live by the covenant. God's grace continued to find a remnant among the people. Thus, even for Israel, the situation was not a matter of keeping the law in order to be justified. God established the relationship at the Exodus. Disobedience could cause a person to be cut out of the covenant, but keeping the law was not the basis of the relationship and the covenant itself remained because of God's faithfulness even in the face of human unfaithfulness. The people obligated themselves because of what God

5. D. McCarthy, *Old Testament Covenant: A Survey of Current Opinions* (Richmond: John Knox, 1973); E. W. Nicholson, *God and His People: Covenant Theology in the Old Testament* (Oxford: University Press, 1986).

had done, which they could not have done by themselves and which was unmerited by them.

The Mosaic covenant established a people as God's own special possession (Exod. 19:5). That the covenant constituted the nation as God's people is brought out in Deuteronomy 29:12-13.

> [T]o enter into the covenant of the LORD your God, sworn by an oath, which the LORD your God is making with you today; in order that he may establish you today as his people, and that he may be your God, as he promised you and as he swore to your ancestors.

The Promise of a New Covenant

The New Testament use of the covenant idea is particularly influenced by the promise of a new covenant made by the prophet Jeremiah. Because of the constant failures by the people and their resulting punishment, God would act in a new way to accomplish what human beings had failed to do:

> The days are surely coming, says the LORD, when I will make a new covenant with the house of Israel and the house of Judah. It will not be like the covenant that I made with their ancestors when I took them by the hand to bring them out of the land of Egypt — a covenant that they broke, though I was their husband, says the LORD. But this is the covenant that I will make with the house of Israel after those days, says the LORD: I will put my law within them, and I will write it on their hearts; and I will be their God, and they shall be my people. No longer shall they teach one another, or say to each other, "Know the LORD," for they shall all know me, from the least of them to the greatest, says the LORD; for I will forgive their iniquity, and remember their sin no more. (Jer. 31:31-34)

Several items in this text should be noted as significant for New Testament teaching. The new covenant will not be like the covenant made at the time of the Exodus and mediated by Moses. Although the result of the Lord being their God and they his people was the same (cf. Lev. 26:12), the nature of the relationship was different in two important respects. (1) The law would be written within — on the hearts of the people — instead of on tablets of stone, so that they would all know the Lord. (2) The basis of this relationship would be that the

Lord would pardon their iniquities and remember their sins no more. The differences, therefore, are not in what God requires, but in the internalizing of his law and in the means of forgiveness for violation. The consequence of everyone knowing the Lord indicates that instead of coming into a covenant relationship by natural birth one would enter the new covenant by a conscious choice based on personal knowledge of the Lord.

Other passages from the prophets expand on what would be involved in the law being written on the heart. Jeremiah himself says the Lord would give the people "one heart and one way" when he made an "everlasting covenant" with his people (Jer. 32:37-41). Isaiah used the phrase "everlasting covenant" for God's "steadfast, sure love for David" (Isa. 55:3). He identified God's covenant in this way: "My Spirit that is upon you, and my words that I have put in your mouth" (Isa. 59:21), showing by the parallelism the association of God's Spirit and God's words. When Paul cites this passage in Romans 11:26-27, he substitutes "When I take away their sins" for "My Spirit that is upon you," either interpreting the removal of sins as the significance of God's Spirit being upon his people or conflating this prophecy with the new covenant prophecy of Jeremiah 31:34. In either case, he shows that for him there is an equivalence, or at least close association, between the forgiveness of sins and the gift of the Holy Spirit.

Ezekiel, too, speaks of an "everlasting covenant," a "covenant of peace" (Ezek. 37:26; cf. 34:25), but the most significant association of ideas is found in Ezekiel 36:25-27, where he speaks of a new empowerment to keep the law of God:

> I will sprinkle clean water upon you, and you shall be clean from all your uncleannesses, and from all your idols I will cleanse you. A new heart I will give you, and a new spirit I will put within you; and I will remove from your body the heart of stone and give you a heart of flesh. I will put my Spirit within you, and make you follow my statutes and be careful to observe my ordinances.

Instead of using the terminology of forgiveness, Ezekiel speaks of purification according to the priestly ritual of sprinkling clean water.[6] The

---

6. Ezekiel draws on the practice of ceremonial cleansing as known from the law of Moses. The association of water with purification is repeated in the New Testament, but it would be a mistake to conclude from his reference to sprinkling the mode of the application of water observed in the New Testament (Chap. 3).

new heart and spirit given by God enable the people to observe his ordinances (cf. Ezek. 11:19-20). To have the law written in the heart and to be taught of God in Jeremiah may be seen as equivalent to having God's Spirit and a new heart so as to be able to keep God's statutes in Ezekiel. Ezekiel 37:27 contains the same promise as Jeremiah 31:33, "I will be their God, and they shall be my people." Here again the association is shown by Paul, for he combines in 1 Thessalonians 4:8-9 allusions to Ezekiel 36:27 (God's giving his Holy Spirit) and Jeremiah 31:34 (taught of God).[7]

From these prophetic passages, it may be seen that the essence of the promise of a new covenant is the forgiveness of sins and the indwelling of the Holy Spirit. The result was to be the people of God (Jer. 31:31; Heb. 8:10; see further Chap. 2, pp. 73ff.).

Covenant in the New Testament

When the Jews translated their Bible into Greek, they faced the problem of how to express the Hebrew word for "covenant": *berith*. One possibility was *synthēkē*, which expressed the idea of mutuality, a compact or treaty. This word preserved one aspect of the Hebrew covenant, an agreement, but did not do justice to the predominant emphasis on God's initiative, so the translators chose *diathēkē*, a word meaning "disposition" or "arrangement." In view of the Hebrew background, the emphasis was on the dispensation of God. The common Hellenistic usage of *diathēkē* was for a testament or last will. This was a particular kind of disposition and provides the imagery for Galatians 3:15 and Hebrews 9:17.[8] Otherwise, the New Testament uses "covenant" according to the Jewish background, in every case keeping the emphasis on the divine disposition, a laying down, whether of promises or of conditions.

The covenants (sworn promises) of God with Abraham and David are of particular importance for the New Testament, because both are affirmed as being fulfilled in Christ. The connection of Jesus

---

7. This becomes the theological basis for the treatment of *New Covenant Morality in Paul* by T. J. Deidun (Rome: Biblical Institute Press, 1981), pp. 1-43.

8. John J. Hughes, "Hebrews 9:15ff. and Galatians 3:15ff.: A Study in Covenant Practice and Procedure," *Novum Testamentum* 21 (1979): 27-96, argues that even in these passages the translation should be covenant and not will.

with both Abraham and David is signalled in the first verse of the New Testament, "Jesus the Messiah, the son of David, the son of Abraham" (Matt. 1:1).

The resurrected Christ is declared to occupy the throne of David in fulfillment of God's promises to David. Peter in Acts 2:30-32 — drawing on Psalm 132:11, 2 Samuel 7:12-13, and Psalm 16:10 — interprets God's oath that he would set one of David's descendants on his throne as referring to the resurrection of Jesus. In Acts 13:32-35 — quoting the Greek of Psalm 2:7, Isaiah 55:3, and Psalm 16:10 — Paul similarly understands the everlasting covenant of kingship with David (a leader and commander of the peoples) as referring to the resurrection of Jesus. The prophecy of Amos 9:11-12 that God "will raise up the booth of David that is fallen," that is, his dynasty, so that "they may possess . . . all the nations that are called by my name," is quoted in Acts 15:16-17 according to the Septuagint translation in order to make the association of Christ's kingship with the bringing of Gentiles into covenant relationship with God. The resurrected Christ now occupies the throne of David and rules over the new people of God made up of Gentiles as well as Jews (see further below on kingdom). The promises of the Lord to build a house (that is, a family) for David, maintaining his line and his throne forever (Ps. 89:28-29), and that his son would build a house (that is, a temple) for the Lord (2 Sam. 7:11-13) are presented in the New Testament as having their ultimate fulfillment not in Solomon but in Jesus as the "son of David" who built the new temple of the church.[9] Already in Isaiah 55:3 the covenant with David was related to the whole people, so the way was prepared for the New Testament application of the Davidic covenant not only to his descendant, the Christ, but also to the people of the Christ.

Paul connects the Christians' relationship to God with the Abrahamic covenant, in contrast to the Mosaic covenant.[10] God's promise to Abraham still stands. The definition of his descendants, however,

9. F. F. Bruce, *New Testament Development of Old Testament Themes* (Grand Rapids: Eerdmans, 1968), p. 79. Robert F. O'Toole, "Acts 2:30 and the Davidic Covenant of Pentecost," *Journal of Biblical Literature* 102 (1983): 245-258, concludes that Luke used "covenant," "oath," "mercy," and "promise" as virtually equivalent and saw the promises made to Abraham and the fathers as all caught up in the covenant with David.

10. Morna D. Hooker, "Paul and 'Covenantal Nomism,'" *Paul and Paulinism: Essays in Honour of C. K. Barrett*, ed. Morna D. Hooker and S. G. Wilson (London: SPCK, 1982), pp. 47-56.

is no longer limited to his fleshly descendants. The promise that Abraham and his descendants would "inherit the world" (Rom. 4:13) and he would be the "father of many nations" (Rom. 4:17 = Gen. 17:5) "depends on faith, in order that the promise may rest on grace and be guaranteed to all his descendants, not only to the adherents of the law but also to those who share the faith of Abraham" (Rom. 4:16). Those who have the faith of Abraham are as much (or more) his children as those descended from him by the flesh. Abraham's faith was reckoned as righteousness (Rom. 4:3, 22). That same righteousness is reckoned now on the same basis, faith. And that faith is in the same God, the God who raised Jesus from the dead (Rom. 4:23-25).

How this works Paul explains in Galatians 3. The promise to Abraham is not abrogated by the law given to Moses (Gal. 3:17). The promises made to Abraham and his descendants apply to Christ, who is the true offspring (seed) of Abraham (Gal. 3:16). Everyone who is in Christ (a principle elaborated in the next chapter) and who belongs to Christ shares Christ's status, so what is said of Christ in Galatians 3:16 is said of the church in 3:29: "If you belong to Christ, then you are Abraham's offspring, heirs according to the promise" (Gal. 3:29). Those who have been baptized into Christ have put on Christ (Gal. 3:27) and become one people in him (Gal. 3:28), the spiritual children of Abraham (Gal. 3:29). God accounts as his people all who are in Christ in fulfillment of the promise to Abraham. This is all a matter of promise, without reference to merit.

The remembrance of the Abrahamic covenant and its relevance for the unfolding of God's purposes in the events associated with the coming of Jesus is evident in other New Testament writers. The father of John the Baptist refers to it in speaking of the salvation God has raised up in the house of David (Luke 1:69-73), and Acts 3:25-26 and Hebrews 6:13-20 recall it especially in connection with Jesus' resurrection, even as other texts connect the Davidic covenant with that event.[11]

A central use of the language of covenant in the New Testament occurs in reference to the death of Christ and what was effected by it. At the last supper, Jesus identified the cup with his "blood of the covenant, which is poured out for many for the forgiveness of sins" (Matt. 26:28; Mark 14:24; Luke 22:20; 1 Cor. 11:25). The reference in

---

11. Also notable is that Acts 3:25-26 connects the Abrahamic covenant with the promise that in his descendants all the families of the earth would be blessed.

Matthew to the "forgiveness of sins" alludes to Jeremiah's prophecy of a new covenant with its new basis for forgiveness.

The book of Hebrews quotes Jeremiah's prophecy of a new covenant (Heb. 8:8-12), and the author is particularly concerned to connect this covenant to Christ and his sacrificial death. He is the mediator (Heb. 9:15; 12:24) and guarantor (Heb. 7:22) of a new and better covenant (Heb. 8:6-10; cf. 2 Cor. 3:6) by his blood (Heb. 9:15-23). The defect of the old law, as the author of Hebrews argues, was that it had no adequate basis for once-for-all forgiveness (Heb. 9:12-15; 10:4), but God has remedied that, and he reestablished and sustains the covenant relationship (Heb. 8:8-13). The sacrifices of the Mosaic law brought forgiveness up to the time of the sacrifice, but Christ's death covers all future sins so no new sacrifice is required. The new covenant is sealed with the blood of Christ that makes an eternal atonement (Heb. 9:12), so it is an "eternal covenant" (Heb. 13:20).

This new covenant brings the Holy Spirit, who writes the law of God on the heart (2 Cor. 3:2, 6, 8; Gal. 3:14).

The Old Covenant Obsolete

Unlike the note of continuity sounded by the New Testament about the Abrahamic and Davidic covenants, the Sinai covenant is placed in contrast to the "new covenant" in Christ Jesus. Many passages affirm that Christians, or at least Gentile Christians, are not under the Mosaic covenant as the basis of their relationship with God and, therefore, are not bound by its ceremonial and ritual stipulations.[12] There is a new covenant based on a new means of forgiveness and of appropriation of that forgiveness.

Romans 7:1-7 contrasts "the old written code" of the Mosaic law with "the new life of the Spirit" (vs. 6). In order to show the temporary validity of the law of Moses, Paul compares the marital relationship. A "married woman is bound by the law to her husband as long as he

12. For recent discussion of Paul's teaching on the Christian's relationship to the law of Moses, see Morna D. Hooker, "Paul and 'Covenantal Nomism,'" *Paul and Paulinism: Essays in Honour of C. K. Barrett*, ed. M. D. Hooker and S. G. Wilson (London: SCM, 1982), pp. 47-56; E. P. Sanders, *Paul, the Law, and the Jewish People* (Philadelphia: Fortress, 1983); Heikki Räisänen, *Paul and the Law*, 2nd ed. (Tübingen: J. C. B. Mohr, 1987); Frank Thielman, *Paul and the Law: A Contextual Approach* (Downers Grove: InterVarsity Press, 1994).

lives," but the death of the husband breaks that bond (vss. 2-3). Changing the point of reference but maintaining the principle that death discharges a person from the obligation to a law, Paul proceeds to declare that the one who has died to the law through the body of Christ can be married to Christ (vs. 4), and presumably only someone who has so died to the law can be. "Now we are discharged from the law" (vs. 6). Verse 7's reference to the last of the Ten Commandments makes clear that it is the law of Moses that Paul has been discussing.

The note of contrast between the Mosaic law and the new dispensation of the Spirit is particularly strong in 2 Corinthians 3: between tablets of stone and tablets of human hearts (vs. 3), between the letter and the Spirit (vs. 6), between the ministry of death (condemnation) and ministry of the Spirit (justification) (vss. 7-9), between what was set aside and what is permanent (vss. 10-11), between reading the old covenant with a veil and seeing the glory of the Lord face to face (vss. 12-18). Turning to the Lord (vs. 16) removes the veil, since only Christ permits one to read the "old covenant" correctly (vs. 14). This passage shows the importance of the new covenant for Paul, since he defines Christian existence and his own apostolate in terms of it.[13]

Galatians argues at length for the freedom of Gentiles from the requirements of the "works of the law," specifically circumcision. Paul's argument appears in capsule form in 3:23-25:

> Now before faith [in Christ] came, we were imprisoned and guarded under the law until faith would be revealed. Therefore the law was our disciplinarian until Christ came, so that we might be justified by faith. But now that faith has come, we are no longer subject to a disciplinarian.

There is a history-of-salvation approach set forth here. The law of Moses had a purpose for a time. Now after the coming of Christ "we are no longer subject" to it.[14] The "disciplinarian" (NRSV) is the Greek peda-

---

13. T. J. Deidun, *New Covenant Morality in Paul* (Rome: Biblical Institute Press, 1981), pp. 33-35.

14. J. W. MacGorman, "The Law as Paidagogos: A Study in Pauline Analogy," in H. L. Drumwright and Curtis Vaughan, *New Testament Studies: Essays in Honor of Ray Summers* (Waco: Markham Press Fund, 1975), pp. 99-111, concludes that the use of *paidagogos* ("disciplinarian" — NRSV) in this passage is custodial, not educative. See also James D. G. Dunn, *The Theology of Paul's Letter to the Galatians* (Cambridge: University Press, 1993), pp. 76-85.

gogue, a slave who accompanied the child to school and was responsible for moral discipline. To draw out Paul's analogy, we can say that a child needs a disciplinarian to instill the right habits, but when one becomes an adult and the proper habits are formed the disciplinarian is no longer needed. The law has become internalized through faith in Christ; the forgiveness of sins by him and the empowerment by the Spirit remove the pedagogical place of the law.

Paul uses the analogy of children to make the history-of-salvation point even more emphatically in his "allegory" of Sarah and Hagar with their children in Galatians 4:21-31.[15] "These women are two covenants" (vs. 24) — Hagar is the covenant at Mount Sinai, "bearing children for slavery," and Sarah is the "Jerusalem above," whose children are free-born (vss. 25-26). Christians "are the children of the promise, like Isaac" and are "born according to the Spirit" (vss. 28-29). The quotation of Genesis 21:10, according to the allegory, has the consequence, "Drive out" the old covenant and its children of slavery (vs. 30).

Ephesians 2:11-17 contrasts the previous condition of Gentiles with their status in Christ. The Gentiles formerly were "strangers to the covenants of promise" (vs. 12). The Mosaic law provided a wall of separation between Jews and Gentiles. "Commandments and ordinances" (vs. 15) is the language for the Old Testament laws. Jesus has abolished this law that separated Jews and Gentiles (vs. 15) in order to bring them together as one new people.

The fullest use in the New Testament of the theme of the new covenant is found in Hebrews. The book reiterates some of the points found above in Paul and adds its own distinctive thrust. One of these new motifs is the priesthood of Christ. He did not qualify as a priest under the Mosaic law (Heb. 7:14), so the author argues that he belongs to a different order of priests, that of Melchizedek (Heb. 7:1-28). A consequence of the change in priesthood is that the law has been changed (Heb. 7:12). To accept the priesthood of Christ requires one to acknowledge a change in the law as well. The earlier commandment was abrogated (Heb. 7:18) so that there might be introduced a better hope (Heb. 7:19); "accordingly Jesus has also become the guarantee of a better covenant" (Heb. 7:22). The faults the writer of Hebrews finds with the

---

15. F. F. Bruce, " 'Abraham Had Two Sons' — A Study in Pauline Hermeneutics," in H. L. Drumwright and Curtis Vaughan, *New Testament Studies: Essays in Honor of Ray Summers* (Waco: Markham Press Fund, 1975), pp. 71-84.

old arrangement were that the priests kept on dying (Heb. 7:23) and had to keep on making atonement for their own sins (Heb. 7:27). In contrast, the covenant basis is now new, for the sacrificer (Heb. 7:15-17) and the sacrifice (Heb. 7:25; 9:25-27) are forever.

The historical sequence of covenants is more fully expressed in Hebrews 8, which is built around Jeremiah 31:31-34 (also quoted in Heb. 10:16-17). Jesus "is the mediator of a better covenant, which has been enacted through better promises" (Heb. 8:6). This covenant corrects the faults of the first covenant (through Moses) (Heb. 8:7); the new covenant "has made the first one obsolete," so that it is now passing away (Heb. 8:13). As a result of the old covenant becoming obsolete, all its institutions likewise became obsolete — priesthood, sacrifice, and sanctuary. Hebrews 10:1-10 specifies that the imperfection of the old covenant had to do with its sacrificial system. The law was only the shadow, not the substance (Heb. 10:1). It was unable to make the worshippers perfect (Heb. 10:2), for its sacrifices had to be repeated (Heb. 10:2-3) and were inferior, bringing no final remission of sins (Heb. 10:4). Hence, Christ "abolishes the first [the cultic system of atonement] in order to establish the second [the principle of obedience to God's will]" (Heb. 10:9).[16] The replacement of the institutions of old Israel through Christ's once-for-all action did not, however, remove for the writer of Hebrews the authority of the message of the Old Testament, for he bases his whole argument on it.

For the Christian, the Old Testament remains the "word of God" (see the next section), but the basis of the relationship with God now is different — what God has done in Jesus and the new covenant of forgiveness in him. The Old Testament as a system of religion does not regulate the activities of the church, that is, the people of Christ. The church of Christ is a new covenant community. Hence, this study will concentrate on the church as set forth in the New Testament.

Value of the Old Testament for Christians

In spite of the negative words in the above passages (often due to the polemical context), the Old Testament is the word of God. The biblical message occurs in a narrative framework; hence it is necessary to have

16. Harold W. Attridge, *The Epistle to the Hebrews* (Philadelphia: Fortress, 1989), pp. 275-76.

the total biblical story. One does not place the early parts of the narrative on an equal footing with the climax of the story; nor does one neglect the early parts of the narrative. The New Testament perspective is that God had a plan of salvation throughout history leading up to the coming of Christ, a plan to be consummated at his return. It is absolutely essential, in order to grasp the full drama, to read the whole story. The New Testament writers make frequent, almost constant, use of the Old Testament and repeatedly affirm its value for Christians.[17]

(1) The Old Testament law reveals sin (Rom. 7:7). It shows human nature (see pp. 137ff.) and sets forth the will of God and his moral law. The hearer of the scriptures learns what sin is and comes to realize weakness and needs.

(2) The Old Testament warns of disobedience and its results (Heb. 2:1-4; 1 Cor. 10:6-11). Sin carries consequences. Punishment follows sin.

(3) The Old Testament scriptures point to Christ (John 5:39). This is their principal function for Christians. Christ is the answer to the problem of sin and punishment. This function of witness to Christ is both the Old Testament's usefulness and the reason why it is not the final authority. As a testimony to Christ, it can never be given up by Christians. Now that Christ has come, he is the norm for conduct and for the interpretation of scripture.

(4) The Old Testament scriptures instruct in salvation; this comes about when they are joined with faith in Christ Jesus (2 Tim. 3:15). Their pointing to Christ comes to fruition when the salvation in him is received through faith and results in righteous living. They provide teaching, reproof, correction, and training in righteousness, so that one may be equipped for every good work (2 Tim. 3:16-17).

(5) The Old Testament provides examples of righteousness (Heb. 11:1–12:2). Not only does it reveal sin and show the consequences of disobedience, but it also gives positive encouragement by showing the lives of those faithful to God. Even the greatest heroes of the Old Testament are shown in their weaknesses and sin, but this too can be an encouragement by showing how God can work through the life of anyone who puts trust in him and seeks to do his will.

(6) The Old Testament gives hope (Rom. 15:4). Biblical religion is

<hr>

17. Everett Ferguson, "The Christian Use of the Old Testament," in *The World and Literature of the Old Testament*, ed. John T. Willis (Abilene: ACU Press, 1979), pp. 357-373.

a religion of hope. It reveals the faithfulness of God and points his people to the future and the blessings God will bestow.

(7) The Old Testament reveals the nature of God. He declared his nature to Moses:

> The LORD, the LORD, a God merciful and gracious, slow to anger, and abounding in steadfast love and faithfulness, keeping steadfast love for the thousandth generation, forgiving iniquity and transgression and sin, yet by no means clearing the guilty. (Exod. 34:6-7).

The substance of this statement is repeated seven other times (Num. 14:18; Neh. 9:17; Pss. 86:15; 103:8; 145:8; Joel 2:13; Jon. 4:2). This God was the Creator of all things (Gen. 1). New Testament references to the "one God, Father, from whom are all things and for whom we exist" (1 Cor. 8:6) assume the nature of God spelled out in the prior revelation.

(8) The Old Testament shows the unfolding purpose of this God (1 Pet. 1:10-12). It not only reveals the character of God but it also provides a philosophy of history and of the natural world. The Old Testament gives the grand sweep of the history of salvation. There is no proper understanding of Jesus and his church except in continuity with this story. The nature of God is always the same. Truth about him, his creation, and his people remains true. It is this God revealed in the Old Testament whose Son Jesus is. The Old Testament thus provides a biblical understanding of history and of the created order as well as testifying to God's saving activity.

New Testament writers appeal to the Old Testament as authoritative for Christians. A typical instance of the way Paul supports his reasoning is this appeal: "Do I say this on human authority? Does not the law also say the same?" (1 Cor. 9:8). One way of expressing the relationship of the two parts of the Christian Bible is to say that the Old Testament is still authoritative for God's people in its theology but not in its institutions.[18] In other words, as a "system of religion," the Mosaic law (at least for Gentile Christians) has been superseded. Another way might be to say that for Christians the basis of the relationship with God is different now; but God's word, whenever expressed, remains valid. The New Testament is the fulfillment of the Old Testament promise.

For all their indebtedness to the Old Testament, New Testament writers express the conviction that God has spoken definitively now

---

18. John Bright, *The Authority of the Old Testament* (Nashville: Abingdon, 1967).

through Christ (Heb. 1:1-2), that this revelation represents a permanent (2 Cor. 3:11) and final word, the last dispensation (1 Cor. 10:11; 1 Pet. 1:20) and ultimate authority for today (Matt. 28:18). The redemptive history of the Old Testament has its significance for Christians as pointing to the Christ event and gains its fullness of meaning as related to him.[19]

The Covenant People

Inherent in the idea of a covenant is a community. The covenants with Noah, Abraham, and David included their descendants and so involved more than an individual. To be in covenant with God means to be his people (cf. Hos. 1:9 and 2:23). This community dimension is evident in the Mosaic covenant, for it was made with a people, Israel. Indeed, the covenant created the people (Deut. 29:13). According to Jeremiah 31:31-34, even as the Sinai covenant was made with a people, so too is the new covenant made with a people. The new covenant is a covenant of forgiveness; hence the new covenant people of God is a forgiven people, on whose hearts the laws of God are written (Heb. 8:7-13, quoting Jer. 31:31-34). The "two covenants," according to Paul's allegory in Galatians 4:21-31, are represented by two women, Hagar and Sarah, who each bear children and so represent a people. Christ makes a covenant with his disciples (Luke 22:29). The sign of this new covenant is the gift of the Holy Spirit to dwell in the hearts of the forgiven people (2 Cor. 1:22; Eph. 1:13; 4:30). The church of the Messiah is a new covenant people.

God, in bringing Israel out of Egypt, did for her what she could not do for herself. On the basis of that gracious historical act of deliverance, God entered into a covenant relationship with the nation. The new covenant community was formed by a new historical act of God. In the death and resurrection of Christ God did for humanity what we could not do for ourselves, in delivering us from sin and its power. Based on this mighty and gracious act of God, a covenant is offered and a people gathered. Our response is grateful obedience. Israel could have refused God's covenant, but it is hard to imagine her doing so. Human beings today can refuse the offer of salvation in Christ. It is hard to imagine one who really understands what is offered doing so,

19. This is the "mid-point" of salvation history according to Oscar Cullmann, *Christ and Time* (Philadelphia: Westminster, 1950), 121-137. N. T. Wright speaks of *The Climax of the Covenant* in his book of that title (Minneapolis: Fortress, 1991).

yet many do. Response to what God has done in Christ does not achieve salvation or establish the relationship with God (although disobedience, which is an expression of a lack of gratitude, as with Israel, deprives one of the blessings). Entering into the new covenant makes one a child of Abraham, a servant of the king, and a part of the Israel of God.

A covenant, based on the promises of God and requiring the appropriate conduct by the people in response, describes the relationship of God and his people. God's covenants are not so much legal relationships as love relationships, a fact shown by the marriage analogies employed by the prophets (Jer. 2:2; Ezek. 16:8-14; Hos. 2:1–3:1). A covenant requires a people with whom it is entered into, and that people may be characterized as a covenant people. The church is the new covenant community. Although honoring the Old Testament as a revelation from God, the church is a people who live by the new covenant.

Part of the background to the covenant language of the Old Testament was the practice of kings offering treaties to nations. God as king offered a covenant to Israel. Jesus "covenanted ["conferred" — NRSV] a kingdom" on his disciples (Luke 22:29). With these associations of covenant and kingdom, we turn to the kingship language in the Bible as an important component of the biblical concept of a people and consequently of the notion of "church."

KINGDOM

"The God of heaven will set up a kingdom
that shall never be destroyed."   (DAN. 2:44)

The "kingdom of God," which was the theme of Jesus' preaching (Mark 1:15), has received many different interpretations.[20] Bypassing an examination of these interpretations, I shall proceed to set forth my understanding of the biblical meaning of the kingdom.[21]

---

20. For an introductory survey, see Wendell Willis, ed., *The Kingdom of God in 20th-Century Interpretation* (Peabody, Mass.: Hendrickson, 1987).

21. I have done this more extensively in a popular format in *The Everlasting Kingdom* (Abilene: ACU, 1989). Out of the extensive bibliography there, I am most indebted to H. Kleinknecht, G. von Rad, K. L. Schmidt, *"Basileus, Basileia, et al.," Theological Dictionary of the New Testament,* ed. G. Kittel, tr. G. W. Bromiley (Grand Rapids: Eerdmans, 1964), 1.564-593; W. G. Kümmel, *Promise and Fulfilment* (Naper-

Meaning of Kingdom

In Hebrew, Aramaic, and Greek, the primary meaning of "kingdom" is "kingship," that is, royal power or kingly rule. The words more often refer to the "reign" than to the "realm" in which the rule is exercised, to the dominion rather than the domain. This meaning may be seen quite clearly in the story of the Babylonian king Nebuchadnezzar's madness in Daniel 4. While the king was boasting of the magnificent capital he had built and his power and majesty, "There came a voice from heaven: 'To you, King Nebuchadnezzar, the word is spoken: the kingdom has passed from you'" (Dan. 4:30-31, REB). Babylon as a realm, of course, remained; it was Nebuchadnezzar's exercise of kingship that was removed. The occasion was a period of insanity. Afterward, the king acknowledged God's sovereignty (Dan. 4:34), and, as the story proceeds in the words of Nebuchadnezzar, "At that very time I was restored to my right mind and, for the glory of my kingdom, my majesty and royal splendor returned to me . . . , and I was reestablished in my kingdom and my power was greatly increased" (Dan. 4:36, REB). The realm was not restored; it was Nebuchadnezzar's rule that was reestablished. A New Testament illustration is provided by Revelation 11:15: "The kingdom of the world has become the kingdom of our Lord and of his Messiah, and he will reign forever and ever." It is the rule, or sovereignty, that passes from the world to the Lord, so that, as expressed in the last clause by the verb form of the noun, "he will reign forever."

Of course, kingship does not operate in a void, so the word "kingdom" is often used in close connection with the people or territory living under a given reign. That usage gives the secondary meaning of "realm," a meaning evident in references to the "kingdom of Judah" (2 Chron. 11:17; 20:30), to Babylon (Dan. 1:20), and to Persia (Ezra 1:1). In the New Testament, this derivative meaning occurs in such passages as the temptation narrative, where the devil offers Jesus "all the king-

---

ville, Ill.: A. R. Allenson, 1957); R. Schnackenburg, *God's Rule and Kingdom* (New York: Herder and Herder, 1963); Oscar Cullmann, *Christ and Time* (London: SCM, 1967); G. E. Ladd, *The Presence of the Future: The Eschatology of Biblical Realism* (Grand Rapids: Eerdmans, 1974); B. D. Chilton, *God in Strength: Jesus' Announcement of the Kingdom* (Freistadt: F. Plöchl, 1979); G. R. Beasley-Murray, *Jesus and the Kingdom of God* (Grand Rapids: Eerdmans, 1986). My perspective is nearest to what is called "inaugurated eschatology," and I have sought to relate that view to the doctrine of the church.

doms of the world" (Matt. 4:8: Luke 4:5), and in Herod Antipas' offer
of half his kingdom to the daughter of Herodias (Mark 6:23).

The political/legal metaphor of a kingdom takes on distinctive
connotations when applied to God and his people. The kingdom of
God refers to his majesty and activity, more often than to his people.
The concept or symbol[22] indicates that God is at work, ruling and
accomplishing his purposes. The kingdom is active, not static. But
God's rule does involve a people. The rule of God presupposes a people
of God in whom it can be established (cf. Matt. 21:43).[23] God creates a
people and seeks a people over whom to exercise his rule, so sometimes
God's kingdom is his people.

The Kingdom of God and Israel

God as king and the effects of his sovereignty are common motifs in
the Old Testament,[24] even if the exact phrase "kingdom of God" does
not occur.[25] The event that lay at the basis of the covenant with Israel,
the deliverance from Egypt, was also the time when God's everlasting
reign was declared (Exod. 15:18). God is elsewhere described as ruling
over his people (Judg. 8:23), and he is often called "king" (e.g., Num.
23:21; Pss. 74:12; 95:3; Jer. 10:7, 10). He is king over the whole universe
and over all nations (Pss. 22:28; 29:3-4, 10; 47:2, 6-8; 96:10-13; 99:1-4),
but especially is he king over Israel (Deut. 33:5; Isa. 41:21; 43:15). Because God was their king, the prophet Samuel argued that Israel should
not have a human king (1 Sam. 12:12; cf. 8:7). That God is the universal
and everlasting king is reaffirmed in the New Testament, as in the
impressive doxology of 1 Timothy 1:17, "To the king of the ages, im-
mortal, invisible, the only God, be honor and glory for ever and ever."

Furthermore, different forms of the Hebrew word for kingdom

22. Norman Perrin, *Jesus and the Language of the Kingdom* (Philadelphia:
Fortress, 1980) objects to the language of "conception" or "idea," and argues for
"symbol" instead.

23. Gerhard Lohfink, *Jesus and Community* (London: SPCK, 1985), p. 27; Gerhard Lohfink, "Die Korrelation von Reich Gottes und Volk Gottes bei Jesus," *Theologische Quartalschrift* 165 (1985): 173-183.

24. John Bright took it as a unifying theme for biblical theology — *The Kingdom
of God* (New York: Abingdon-Cokesbury, 1953).

25. "Kingdom of Yahweh" occurs in 1 Chron. 28:5 in reference to Israel as
Solomon's realm; cf. 17:14.

occur in descriptions of God. Since God is always king, his kingdom is an ever-present reality. The dynamic, active sense of kingdom is particularly evident in the passages using kingdom (or kingship) about God. "The LORD has established his throne in the heavens, and his kingdom rules over all" (Ps. 103:19). The parallelism characteristic of Hebrew poetry helps to define the meaning of kingdom through associated words, and that feature should be observed in many of the passages to be cited. Note especially Psalm 145:11-13:

> They shall speak of the glory of your kingdom,
>   and tell of your power,
> to make known to all people your mighty deeds,
>   and the glorious splendor of your kingdom.
> Your kingdom is an everlasting kingdom,
>   and your dominion endures throughout all generations.

Kingdom is associated with power, mighty deeds, and dominion, and God's kingdom is everlasting. The cluster of words in 1 Chronicles 29:11 is significant: "Yours, O LORD, are the greatness, the power, the glory, the victory, and the majesty; for all that is in the heavens and on the earth is yours; yours is the kingdom, O LORD, and you are exalted as head above all." "For dominion belongs to the LORD, and he rules over the nations" (Ps. 22:28). The everlasting nature of God's kingdom contrasts with earthly kingdoms: "How great are his signs, how mighty his wonders! His kingdom is an everlasting kingdom, and his sovereignty is from generation to generation" (Dan. 4:3). "I blessed the Most High, and praised and honored the one who lives forever. For his sovereignty is an everlasting sovereignty, and his kingdom endures from generation to generation" (Dan. 4:34).

The manifestation of God's kingdom among the nations in the Old Testament was Israel. An example of the meaning "realm" is Exodus 19:6, where Israel is denominated as the Lord's "priestly kingdom"; look also at Psalm 114:2 for Israel as the Lord's "dominion" (NRSV). The human king was intended to be the representative and servant of God (Deut. 17:14-20; 2 Sam. 23:1-7; Ps. 61:6-7; and esp. Ps. 72:1-4). Hence, the king was said to be God's anointed (1 Sam. 24:6, 10; Pss. 45:7; 89:20) and God's "son" (2 Sam. 7:14; Pss. 2:7; 89:27).[26]

---

26. God's anointed (Messiah) will be studied later in this chapter (pp. 36ff.) and the title "Son" in Chap. 2, pp. 116ff.

The nation of Israel and her kings proved to be quite imperfect manifestations of the reign of God. So, the prophets looked forward to a time when God would invade the affairs of human beings, overthrow evil, and demonstrate his sovereignty. They speak of God's rule in the future tense. Although God is always king and always exercises kingship, there will be a time in the future when this will be manifested among his people in a special way. "The LORD of hosts will reign on Mount Zion and in Jerusalem, and before his elders he will manifest his glory" (Isa. 24:23).[27] "Those who have been saved shall go up to Mount Zion to rule Mount Esau; and the kingdom shall be the LORD's" (Obad. 21). "And the LORD will become king over all the earth" (Zech. 14:9). As a result of subjugation to foreign powers, this expectation of a future exercise of God's kingship was intensified during the intertestamental period.

The Kingdom of God and Jesus

In the ministry of Jesus as described in the Synoptic Gospels, we hear much about the kingdom and meet for the first time in the canonical writings the exact phrase "kingdom of God." Jesus, however, was clearly not introducing a new concept. The Old Testament passages referred to above, and others, as well as writings from the apocrypha, the pseudepigrapha, and Qumran make evident that the concept of God's kingdom was prominent and quite intelligible among Jesus' Jewish hearers. The topic of the kingdom of God in the preaching of Jesus and its relation to him is too large for complete treatment, but we want to call attention to certain features that correlate with themes in this book.

All three Synoptic Gospels characterize the central theme of Jesus' preaching as "the kingdom of God." "From that time [the arrest of John the Baptist] Jesus began to proclaim, 'Repent, for the kingdom of heaven has come near,'" or, "is at hand" (Matt. 4:17; cf. 4:23: "proclaiming the good news of the kingdom"). "Now after John was arrested, Jesus came to Galilee, proclaiming the good news of God, and saying, 'The time is fulfilled, and the kingdom of God has come near [or, is at hand]; repent and believe in the good news'" (Mark

27. Cf. Isa. 33:22: "For the LORD is our judge, the LORD is our ruler, the LORD is our king; he will save us."

1:14-15). Jesus "said to them, 'I must proclaim the good news of the kingdom of God to the other cities also; for I was sent for this purpose'" (Luke 4:43).

When Jesus declared "The time is fulfilled," he was saying that it was time for all God had said and done in Israel's history to be brought to completion. The universal reign of God was about to be manifested in a new and special way. The hopes expressed in the Old Testament prophets were ready to be realized. Jesus sums up that earlier message as "the kingdom of God" or "kingdom of heaven." The former phrase is used uniformly in Mark's and Luke's reports of Jesus' teaching; the latter, with a few exceptions, occurs in Matthew's reports. The phrases are equivalent. The Jews customarily used circumlocutions in order to avoid use of the divine name, and "heaven" was one of the common substitutes (cf. Matt. 21:25; Luke 15:21). What cannot be determined is whether Jesus commonly used "heaven," and Mark and Luke adapted the wording to their Gentile audiences, or whether Matthew accommodated Jewish sensibilities and adopted "heaven" for whatever term Jesus used.

The proximity of the kingdom is expressed by a word (*engiken*, "come near" or "at hand") that means to approach or draw near, either spatially or temporally. God was ready to act in a new way to overthrow his enemies and manifest his kingship. His kingdom was in the process of coming; it was nearby, even "breaking in." That nearness required that the people repent and prepare themselves for the rule of God. The imminence of the kingdom meant that all other concerns had become secondary (Luke 9:57-62). The age of fulfillment now dominated the scene and transcended all the normal activities of life.

As the phrase "at hand" indicates, Jesus normally spoke of the kingdom in the imminent future. However, he eschewed setting any timetable for the divine action (Matt. 24:36; Mark 13:32; cf. Acts 1:6-7). Sometimes he referred the kingdom to the heavenly bliss of the saved in contrast to the punishment of others (Matt. 8:11-12, which draws on the imagery of Ps. 107:3 and Isa. 25:6-9). As a consequence of the imminence of the kingdom, Jesus could also speak of it as present in his miracles (Matt. 12:28; Luke 11:20).[28] The verb *phthano* in these verses brings out the proleptic nature of the kingdom, for the verb suggests

28. The Lukan phrase "by the finger of God" picks up a Hebrew expression for God's mighty works: in creation (Ps. 8:3), the exodus (Exod. 8:19), and giving of the law (Exod. 31:18).

something that is present but not yet fully attained or realized (cf. Phil. 3:16; 1 Thess. 2:16). The kingdom was also present in his own proclamation (Luke 16:16; Matt. 11:12) and presence (Luke 17:20-21, "among you" or "within your reach"). The power of the kingdom was present in Jesus' ministry. In his teachings, he showed what was required by God's kingdom.

The phrase "kingdom of God" emphasizes the most important thing Jesus had to say about the kingdom: it is God's. And this coincides with the whole ministry of Jesus, which was God-centered. This kingdom is active, working to overthrow the forces of evil (Matt. 12:28). God gives the kingdom to whom he chooses (Luke 12:32). The kingdom must be received, and Jesus taught the qualities necessary to "receive" God's rule: the humble, teachable, receptive spirit of children (Mark 10:15). Similar teaching is found in Matthew 18:3-4, which uses the expression "to enter the kingdom," terminology associated in Matthew with righteousness (Matt. 5:20), doing the will of God (Matt. 7:21), and not trusting in riches (Matt. 19:23-24; cf. 5:3). An alternative expression is "to inherit the kingdom" (Matt. 25:34).

Jesus' teaching about the kingdom, its nature, and those who possess it, is summarized in the opening petitions of the Lord's Prayer:

> "Our Father in heaven,
>   your name be hallowed;
>   your kingdom come;
>   your will be done,
>   on earth as it is in heaven"   (Matt. 6:9-10).

The three central phrases are parallel in structure in Greek. They may be taken as equivalent in significance. For God's name to be sanctified and for his will to be done is for his kingdom (his rule) to come. "On earth as it is in heaven" modifies all three phrases, not just the last. The petition is for the holiness, kingship, and purposes of God to be realized on earth as they are in heaven.

There is implicit within Jesus' ministry a close association of himself with the kingdom. This is particularly evident in Luke's presentation. He interchanges "Jesus" with "the kingdom of God" in the sayings in Luke 14:26 and 18:29, and in Acts he associates the preaching of the kingdom of God with the name of Jesus Christ (Acts 8:12; 28:23, 31). To follow Jesus is to be a follower of the kingdom of God (Luke 9:60-62; 18:28-29). In the accounts of Jesus' triumphal entry into Jerusalem, Matthew parallels "Son of David" and "the one who comes in the name of the Lord" (Matt.

21:9);[29] Mark parallels the coming one with the "coming kingdom of David" (Mark 11:9-10); and Luke speaks of "the king who comes in the name of the Lord" (Luke 19:38; cf. John 12:13, "King of Israel"). Luke associates the kingdom with Jesus and the twelve disciples as well as with God (Luke 22:29-30). Luke shares with Matthew the motif of Jesus as king. Whereas Matthew traces this theme throughout his Gospel, from the birth (Matt. 2:2) to the triumphal entry (Matt. 21:5, quoting Zech. 9:9), crucifixion (Matt. 27:11, 29, 37, 42), and resurrection (Matt. 28:18, "all authority"), using the title "son of David" for Jesus nine times; Luke associates the kingship of Jesus with his occupying the throne of David at his resurrection (Luke 1:32-33; Acts 2:30-31, 34-35; 13:22-23, 34-35; cf. 17:7; see above on the covenant of David associated with Christ's resurrection). A text that may have encouraged this association of kingship with the resurrection was 2 Samuel 7:12, "I will raise up your [David's] offspring after you . . . , and I will establish his kingdom."

All three Synoptic Gospels relate that Jesus was tried on a charge of being a messianic pretender, a king (Matt. 27:11, 37; Mark 15:2, 26; Luke 23:2-3, 38).[30] (Note the interchange in the different accounts between "king of the Jews" [Matt 27:42], "Messiah of God" ["God's anointed one"] [Luke 23:35], and the combination of the two titles, "the Messiah, the king of Israel" [Mark 15:32].) John elaborates on the conversation between Pilate and Jesus. In response to Pilate's question, "Are you the King of the Jews?" Jesus declared, "My kingdom is not from this world. If my kingdom were from this world, my followers would be fighting to keep me from being handed over to the Jews" (John 18:33-36). After acknowledging that he was a king, Jesus identified his kingly work as testifying to the truth (John 18:37). His is a kingdom of truth.

One important text that appears to place some chronological limits on the expectation of the coming of the kingdom is Mark 9:1: "Truly I tell you, there are some standing here who will not taste death until they see the kingdom of God has come with power." The meaning of this statement is very controversial and serves to focus the conflicting interpretations of the kingdom in the preaching of Jesus. Four principal interpretations have been advanced.[31] (1) Perhaps the most common view is to see

29. Matt. 21:5's quotation of Zech. 9:9 highlights the different kind of kingship represented by Jesus.

30. Nils Dahl, "The Crucified Messiah," in *Jesus the Christ: The Historical Origins of Christological Doctrine* (Minneapolis: Fortress, 1991), pp. 27-47.

31. G. R. Beasley-Murray, *Jesus and the Kingdom of God* (Grand Rapids: Eerdmans, 1986), pp. 187-193.

in the declaration a reference to the eschatological kingdom at the end of the ages, as might be indicated by the preceding verse (Mark 8:38). The kingdom of which Jesus speaks clearly has something to do with the coming of the Son of Man (compare the wording in Mark 13:26 and Matt. 16:27-28; 24:29-30), and that is normally understood of the second coming of Christ. The fact that "the end" did not come within a generation may be explained by the "foreshortened perspective" characteristic of many declarations of the prophets and intensified in apocalyptic eschatology, whereby future expectations are telescoped into the immediate future (cf. Mark 13:30). Yet, the failure of an imminent Parousia remains a problem for many in accepting this interpretation. Even with an early dating of Mark (before A.D. 70), a generation would already have passed since Jesus spoke these words. Moreover, this view makes some false assumptions. Something in the future is not necessarily the absolute future, the End. If the Greek perfect tense is to be taken at face value ("the kingdom of God to have come with power"), then some of the bystanders will look back on the coming of the kingdom as a past event.[32] (2) Common in the ancient church but less common among modern interpreters is understanding the statement as a reference to the transfiguration, which follows in Mark's narrative (Mark 9:2-8). Some of the disciples saw the glory of Jesus, and this might be understood as a manifestation of the kingdom. The qualification of "tasting death," however, hardly seems necessary for an event only "six days" later. (3) Another possibility is to refer the words to the destruction of Jerusalem. Mark 13:26 gives some support to this interpretation, but this understanding does not conform to what would appear to be the consolatory intention of the words. (4) Some see the promise of Mark 9:1 in relation to Jesus' prediction of his death and resurrection that immediately precedes in Mark 8:31. Mark 9:9 connects the transfiguration with the resurrection. Although Mark does not use "kingdom" in reference to these events, there is other New Testament usage that would favor seeing the powerful manifestation of God's kingdom in relation to the resurrection and subsequent gift of the Holy Spirit.

The uses of the word "power" in the New Testament may be a clue to what is involved in the powerful coming of the kingdom. Those uses tend to cluster around certain ideas. It is a common word for

---

32. G. B. Caird, "Eschatology and Politics: Some Misconceptions," in J. R. McKay and J. F. Miller, eds., *Biblical Studies: Essays in Honor of William Barclay* (Philadelphia: Westminster, 1976), pp. 72-86, esp. p. 74.

miracles (e.g., Mark 6:2, 5; 9:39), notably for power over evil spirits (Luke 4:36; 9:1). Power is associated especially with resurrection (Mark 12:24; Rom. 1:4; 1 Cor. 6:14; Eph. 1:19-20; Phil. 3:10) and with the Holy Spirit (Luke 1:35; 4:14; 24:49 = Acts 1:8; 10:38; Rom. 15:13, 19; Eph. 3:16). Paul, too, associates power with the kingdom of God (1 Cor. 4:20) and with the gospel (Rom. 1:16; 1 Cor. 1:18).

The basic meaning of kingdom as kingship or reign means that any manifestation of God's activity could be associated with the kingdom idea, and a variety of applications of the terminology is reinforced by the Old Testament usage. Thus various manifestations of the kingdom might be in view in different texts. Regardless of the correct interpretation of Mark 9:1, the other passages cited in the preceding paragraph show that the resurrection of Jesus and the gift of the Holy Spirit can be understood as an expression of the kingdom of God. Moreover, they are events especially associated with the authority and rule of Christ (Matt. 28:18; Eph. 1:20-21; 5:5).

As noted above, according to Luke, Jesus' own kingship began at the resurrection and was signalled by the pouring forth of the Holy Spirit (Acts 2:25-35). After his resurrection, Jesus was given the kingly authority of God (Matt. 28:18; Eph. 1:20-22). The resurrected Jesus sits on the throne of David in fulfillment of Old Testament prophecy; at the time of his resurrection, he occupied the throne and so began his reign. Accordingly, Jesus has a present kingdom: God "has rescued us from the power of darkness and transferred us into the kingdom of his beloved Son, in whom we have redemption, the forgiveness of sins" (Col. 1:13-14). It is to be noted here that kingdom and power (or authority) are equivalent terms in the contrast of darkness with God's beloved Son. And the kingdom of God's Son is associated with redemption and the forgiveness of sins, blessings accomplished by his death and resurrection (cf. Col. 1:18, 22; 2:12-14). One text can speak of "the kingdom of Christ and of God" (Eph. 5:5).

The kingdom of Christ that began at his resurrection will come to an end at the general resurrection:

> Christ the first fruits [of the resurrection], then at his coming those who belong to Christ. Then comes the end, when he hands over the kingdom to God the Father, after he has destroyed every ruler and every authority and power. For he must reign until he has put all his enemies under his feet. The last enemy to be destroyed is death. (1 Cor. 15:23-26)

When Jesus comes again it will not be to set up a kingdom but to "deliver up" or "hand over" an already existing kingdom (his kingship). Jesus reigns until death is destroyed. That occurs at the general resurrection. Then his rule is returned to God, the one who subjected all things to him (1 Cor. 15:27-28). The passage not only does not refer to a millennial or interim kingdom of any duration between the return of Jesus and the final consummation, but the sequence of thought positively precludes it. Jesus is reigning now, and he reigns until all his enemies are defeated (1 Cor. 15:25). The last enemy to be destroyed is death (1 Cor. 15:26). Death is destroyed at his second coming and the general resurrection (1 Cor. 15:23). The reign of Christ is concluded at his second coming. "The end" and the handing over of the kingdom to God the Father follow the resurrection at his coming (1 Cor. 15:23-24). That resurrection marks the subjection of the last enemy and so the end of his reign, not its beginning.[33]

Jesus' proclamation of the kingdom of God and the experience of its dynamic presence in his ministry were the presupposition for the early church's understanding of the resurrection and outpouring of the Holy Spirit as the inauguration of the eschatological age.[34]

The Kingdom of God and the Church

The relation of the kingdom and the church has been expressed all the way from a complete identification of the two, so that the church is the kingdom, to a complete separation of the two, as expressed in the quip of the French scholar Loisy, "Jesus preached the kingdom, and the church came."[35] If the kingdom is defined primarily according to the word study above as the "rule of God," and the church is defined as "the people of God" (pp. 73ff.), then a basis is laid for explaining the

33. C. E. Hill, "Paul's Understanding of Christ's Kingdom in 1 Cor. 15:20-28," *Novum Testamentum* 30 (1988): 297-320. The modifications in the structure of the passage by J. Lambrecht, "Structure and Line of Thought in 1 Cor. 15:23-8," *Novum Testamentum* 32 (1990): 143-151, do not affect the point about the eschatological sequence.

34. Marinus De Jonge, *Jesus, The Servant-Messiah* (New Haven: Yale, 1991), p. 58, following Nils Dahl, "The Problem of the Historical Jesus," reprinted in *Jesus the Christ: Historical Origins of Christological Doctrine* (Minneapolis: Fortress, 1991), pp. 81-111.

35. Quoted in M. Goguel, *Le Problème de l'église* (Paris, 1947), p. 22.

difference yet the interrelationship of the church and the kingdom. The church may be defined as the people who come under the reign of God and accept his rule in their lives (Col. 1:12-14). That makes the church one manifestation, the present manifestation, of the kingdom of God, the kingdom in the secondary sense of realm, the sphere in which the kingship is exercised. The church is not the kingdom but is closely related to it.[36]

The kingdom in the sense of kingship was promised in the vision of Daniel 7 to the "one like a son of man" and to the "people of the holy ones of the Most High" (Dan. 7:14, 22, 27). Even as there was an earthly king representing God in the nation of Israel, so this passage uses the imagery of kingship for God's people and/or their representative. This usage may provide important background for the New Testament understanding of the church in relation to the kingdom.

Jesus during his earthly ministry related his disciples to the kingdom: "Do not be afraid, little flock, for it is your Father's good pleasure to give you the kingdom" (Luke 12:32). It is not immediately evident whether they were given the kingship or were given a place under God's kingship and so constituted his realm. In another passage where Luke connects the kingdom more particularly with the twelve, the idea is kingship: "I confer on you, just as my Father has conferred on me, a kingdom, so that you may eat and drink at my table in my kingdom, and you will sit on thrones judging the twelve tribes of Israel" (Luke 22:29-30). Literally translated, the statement is that Jesus covenanted (promised) a kingdom to the twelve even as the Father had covenanted a kingdom to him. Their royal position involved judging the twelve tribes of Israel (cf. Matt. 19:28). In view of Luke's general presentation of Jesus' kingship as beginning with his resurrection, this promise, too, should be seen as a statement of the disciples' present (not eschatological) place in the kingdom.

Three passages bring the kingdom and the church into proximity with each other. The first is Matthew 16:18-19, "I will build my church. . . . I will give you the keys of the kingdom of heaven." This passage will be explored in more detail below, but for now it may be noted that there is no indication of a change in subject, so the church

36. Without my agreeing with every interpretation he offers, this perspective is close to that of R. Newton Flew, *Jesus and His Church* (London: Epworth, 1956), pp. 17-29, 91; cf. also Hans Küng, *The Church* (London: Burns & Oates, 1968), pp. 74, 94-96.

and the kingdom must be related in some significant way.[37] Peter was given the function of granting or denying entrance to the kingdom. Those who entered formed Christ's assembly.

The second passage to be considered is Hebrews 12:23 and 28. Those who have come "to the assembly [church] of the firstborn who are enrolled in heaven" are said to receive "a kingdom that cannot be shaken." The kingdom as the eschatological reign of God is already possessed.[38] The description in verse 23, too, may be eschatological (see comments on pp. 120-121), but, even so, it is the people in the present who are being addressed. The association of a people in assembly (or who will be in assembly) with receiving in the present the unshakable kingdom of God connects the church and the kingdom.

A third passage connecting the church with the kingdom is the most explicit of all, Revelation 1:4, 6, and 9. John writes "to the seven churches that are in Asia" (Rev. 1:4) and says to them that Christ "made us to be a kingdom, priests serving his God" (Rev. 1:6; cf. 1 Pet. 2:9). Then he declares, "I, John, your brother who shares with you in Jesus the persecution and the kingdom and the patient endurance" (Rev. 1:9). The churches, by the activity of Christ, form a kingdom (realm) and share a kingdom (reign or realm), but like the kingdom of Jesus himself (John 18:36), not of this world nor according to the world's expectations, for it is a kingdom that involves the patient endurance of persecution and suffering.

Without using the word "church," another passage explicitly places the "saints and faithful brothers and sisters" (Col. 1:2) in the kingdom: "Giving thanks to the Father, who has enabled you to share in the inheritance of the saints in the light. He has rescued us from the power of darkness and transferred us into the kingdom of his beloved Son, in whom we have redemption, the forgiveness of sins" (Col. 1:12-14).[39] Two spheres of power and influence are presented: that of dark-

---

37. George Johnston, *The Doctrine of the Church in the New Testament* (Cambridge: University Press, 1943), p. 51 claims, on the basis of the parables of the tares and the dragnet (Matt. 13:24-30, 47-50), that Matthew identified the kingdom and the church.

38. Harold W. Attridge, *The Epistle to the Hebrews* (Philadelphia: Fortress, 1989), p. 382; N. A. Dahl, "A New and Living Way: The Approach to God According to Hebrews 10:19-25," *Interpretation* 5 (1951): 401-412, esp. 403-410.

39. Oscar Cullmann, although making a useful correlation between the rule of Christ and the church, distinguishes too sharply between the kingdom of Christ and the kingdom of God — "The Kingship of Christ and the Church in the New Testament," in *The Early Church* (London: SCM, 1966), pp. 105-137.

ness and that of God's beloved Son. Each person is under the sway of one or the other. Those who have received redemption and forgiveness in Christ are under his power and rule. They have the inheritance and belong to the realm of light. They are in the kingdom in the present.

The significance of this correlation of church and kingdom may be seen in the equivalent expressions used in the New Testament for, and in conjunction with, the kingdom. These equivalent terms show the significance of being under the rule of God in Christ.

One way of describing the kingdom hope of the Bible is in terms of God acting for the salvation of his people. The ideas of kingship and salvation occur together in the Old Testament (e.g., Ps. 74:12; Isa. 33:22; 44:6). This association is reflected in the accounts of the triumphal entry of Jesus into Jerusalem. The acclamation "Hosanna" means "Save!" (Matt. 21:9; Mark 11:9-10; John 12:13). Matthew and John make the royal connotations of the event explicit by including a quotation of Zechariah 9:9 (Matt. 21:5; John 12:15). John uses "King of Israel" in the crowd's acclamation, but Matthew uses "Son of David"; the latter introduces his quotation of Zechariah with a phrase from Isaiah 62:11, a phrase followed in Isaiah by "See your salvation comes," evidently understood by Matthew as the equivalent of "your king comes" in Zechariah 9:9.

An impressive New Testament declaration is the following: "Now have come the salvation and the power and the kingdom of our God and the authority of his Messiah, for the accuser of our comrades has been thrown down, who accuses them day and night before our God" (Rev. 12:10). Salvation, power, kingdom, and authority are associated, and they are realized because Satan has been conquered (Rev. 12:11). The nature of that salvation is further spelled out in other words associated with the kingdom.

For Luke, "To testify to the good news of God's grace" is to go about "proclaiming the kingdom" (Acts 20:24-25). Luke also parallels the terms "redemption" and "kingdom of God" (Luke 21:28, 31). God's goal for his people is righteousness, and kingdom and righteousness occur together: "But strive first for the kingdom of God and his righteousness" (Matt. 6:33). Furthermore, Jesus' teaching in Mark 9:42-48 (cf. Matt. 18:8-9) uses as parallel ideas "to enter life" (Mark 9:43, 45) and "to enter the kingdom of God" (Mark 9:47).

The doxology of the Lord's Prayer, even though not part of the original text, well expresses equivalent ideas in the Bible: "The kingdom and the power and the glory" are God's forever (Matt. 6:13 in later manuscripts). The association of God's kingdom with power has occurred in several texts already cited (e.g., Ps. 145:11; Rev. 12:10). The kingdom is also associated with glory, as in the equivalent versions of the request of James and John to sit at the right and left hand of Jesus "in your glory" (Mark 10:37) or "in your kingdom" (Matt. 20:21). To summarize thus far, the kingdom as God's power, authority, glory, and grace exercised through Christ brings the blessings of salvation, redemption, life, and righteousness to his people.

It is interesting to note that the same two ideas found to provide the content of the new covenant — forgiveness of sins and indwelling of the Holy Spirit — are associated with the kingdom. The relationship of the kingdom of Christ to forgiveness of sins (Col. 1:13-14) is anticipated in Jesus' parables, where he teaches that the kingdom is God's gracious gift by comparing it to a king who gave a marriage feast for his son (Matt. 22:2-10; cf. Luke 14:15-24) and that it brings forgiveness by comparing it to a king who forgave his slave's debt (Matt. 18:23-27). A similar association is found in Revelation: Those freed from their sins by the blood of Jesus Christ are made a kingdom (Rev. 1:5-6). The kingdom of God means, among other things, the forgiveness of sins. This present kingdom is also associated with the working of the Holy Spirit, who brings other blessings associated with the kingdom: "For the kingdom of God is not food and drink but righteousness and peace and joy in the Holy Spirit" (Rom. 14:17). The rule of God and of Christ is expressed in the victory over the forces of evil and by giving forgiveness and the Holy Spirit to those who enter the sphere of their sovereignty.

Matthew's account of Jesus' interview with the rich young ruler uses as parallel expressions "to have eternal life" (Matt. 19:16) ("inherit eternal life" in Matt. 19:29), "to enter into life" (Matt. 19:23), "to enter the kingdom of heaven" (Matt. 19:23) or "kingdom of God" (Matt. 19:24), and "be saved" (Matt. 19:25). Mark uses as parallels in the same story "eternal life" (Mark 10:17), "heaven" (Mark 10:21), "kingdom of God" (Mark 10:23, 24, 25), and "saved" (Mark 10:26). In Luke's account, the parallels are "to inherit eternal life," "to enter the kingdom of God," and to "be saved" (Luke 18:18, 24-25, 26, 29). The result of righteous living is the joy of heaven. The reward of the faithful servants in the parable of the talents is to "enter into the joy of your master" (Matt. 25:21, 23), surely an equivalent expression to the reward in the subsequent parable offered to the sheep on the right hand, "inherit the kingdom prepared for you from the foundation of the world" (Matt. 25:34). These equivalent terms and their eschatological connotations prepare us for the next dimension to be considered of the New Testament's kingdom teaching.

The Kingdom of God and the Future

The kingdom of God took a decisive step forward in the resurrection of Christ, the outpouring of the Holy Spirit, and the beginning of the church. God's sovereignty was more fully realized as a result of these events. Satan was conquered (Rev. 12:10). Nevertheless, God's rule was still imperfectly realized. Christians stand farther along in God's history of salvation, but in spite of the enthusiastic overreaction of some of the early converts, there was not a full consummation yet (1 Cor. 4:8). Even as the kingdom was both present and future for Israel and then for Jesus, so it remains for Christians living in the age of the church. The church exists between the "already" and the "not yet" of God's eschatological fulfillment. That duality is inherent in the meaning of kingdom as kingship. God is king in the present, but until all acknowledge and submit to his rule there is a future dimension to his kingdom.

Several passages in the New Testament reflect the duality of "already" but "not yet." The "angels, authorities, and powers" were made subject to Christ at his ascension to the right hand of God (1 Pet. 3:22), but from another perspective he waits at the right hand of God "until his enemies would be made a footstool for his feet" (Heb. 10:12-13). According to 2 Timothy 1:10, Christ Jesus at his appearing "abolished death and brought life and immortality to light through the gospel"; yet elsewhere that victory over death comes at his return (1 Cor. 15:26). In the imagery of Revelation, Satan has been thrown down from heaven but still attacks human beings on earth (Rev. 12:7-17); he is bound, but will be completely destroyed after the thousand years' reign of Christ and the saints (Rev. 20:1-10).[40]

Paul maintains the tension, or perhaps simply the multivalence, of different aspects of the rule of God. He speaks of an existing reign of Christ to be surrendered at the end of time (1 Cor. 15:24). He describes the present experience of the kingdom of God (Rom. 14:17) and its present power (1 Cor. 4:20). The admonition to "lead a life worthy of God, who calls you into his own kingdom and glory" (1 Thess. 2:12) could go either way or both ways. The calling and the kind of life

---

40. A present reign acccording to Rev. 1:6 and 5:10.

expected in response are in the present, but glory is usually associated with the heavenly or eschatological kingdom. The latter is clearly the reference when Paul speaks of the kind of conduct required to inherit the kingdom of God (1 Cor. 6:9-10; 15:50; Gal. 5:21).

Although 1 Corinthians 15:24-28 anticipates the surrender of the kingdom of Christ to God, Ephesians 5:5 speaks of an "inheritance in the kingdom of Christ and of God." Similarly 2 Peter 1:11 speaks of "the eternal kingdom of our Lord and Savior Jesus Christ." There is a tension also between 1 Corinthians 15:24 and the promise of Luke 1:33 that "of his kingdom there will be no end." The latter verse may speak in a relative sense, even as the Old Testament spoke of many things as "everlasting" or "forever" that were simply long lasting (Exod. 40:15; Josh. 14:9; 1 Kings 9:3); this explanation has some pertinence, because the promise in Luke 1:33 is couched in the language of the Davidic kingship to which the same promise of perpetuity was made in the Old Testament (2 Sam. 7:13-16; 1 Chron. 17:12-14). A theological explanation would interpret 1 Corinthians 15:24 as a reference to the humanity ("Son" in vs. 28) and so the earthly kingdom of Christ; in the same way Luke 1:33 would apply to the Davidic, earthly kingdom and not be a declaration about eternity. Ephesians 5:5 and 2 Peter 1:11 would then pertain to Christ's divine nature united with God the Father. Another explanation, and one that avoids the problems, is to take kingdom in the sense of realm in 1 Corinthians 15:24, so it is not Christ's kingship but his people who are delivered over to God. But I am inclined to think this meaning less likely both according to the context and according to the most frequent meaning of the word "kingdom."

In some passages "kingdom" clearly refers to the world to come, heaven, as in Paul's confidence that "The Lord will rescue me from every evil attack and save me for his heavenly kingdom" (2 Tim. 4:18). Similarly, there is the assurance that "entry into the eternal kingdom of our Lord and Savior Jesus Christ will be richly provided for you" (2 Pet. 1:11).

Christians through their union with Christ (see next chapter) in some sense share the kingship of Christ. "If we have died with him, we will also live with him; if we endure, we will also reign with him" (2 Tim. 2:11-12). As Christ by his resurrection was exalted to the right hand of God above all other rule (Eph. 1:20-21), so those raised in baptism with him are made to sit in the heavenly places in Christ Jesus (Eph. 2:6). Sharing in Christ's reign means sharing in his eschatological task of judging the world (1 Cor. 6:2, in fulfillment of Dan. 7:22). How this could work is perhaps indicated by Matthew 12:41-42.

There is already inaugurated in the Christian age a beginning, or foretaste, of the final heavenly condition. Christ "gave himself for our sins to set us free from the present evil age, according to the will of our God and Father" (Gal. 1:4). Christians "have tasted the heavenly gift, and have shared in the Holy Spirit, and have tasted the goodness of the word of God and the powers of the age to come" (Heb. 6:4-5). Although living temporally in this "present evil age," Christians already experience the "powers of the age to come." They already know the present kingdom of God. The resurrection of Christ, the forgiveness of sins, and the gift of the Holy Spirit are present expressions of the experience of the blessings of the End time. Christ's resurrection is "first fruits" (1 Cor. 15:23); so is the gift of the Holy Spirit (Rom. 8:23). Repentance brings "times of refreshing" in anticipation of the return of the Messiah (Acts 3:19-20). The gift of the Holy Spirit is a first installment, a guarantee or pledge, of the full eschatological blessings (2 Cor. 1:22; 5:5; Eph. 1:13-14).

Through Christ the End, or the beginning of the End, has come. Tomorrow is here today. Something of God's glory and power has reached down and called people for the coming age. The kingdom of God has created a new people, the church. But all this is only a down payment. Much more awaits the final consummation of God's purposes. Nevertheless, the imagery of first fruits and first installment indicates that life in the world to come and its blessings will be in continuity with the present. Those who share the kingdom now will be those to participate in it in the future.

Summary Points

(1) The kingdom is active. It refers to the kingly activity of God, the rule of God among people. Thus the kingdom is present.

(2) The kingdom is God's reign over all his realms, and this is without beginning and end. His rule over Israel and over the church are manifestations on earth and occur within a time frame, but neither exhausts the reign of God, for his reign is in heaven as well as on earth.

(3) The kingdom is present wherever Jesus is present. He represents the kingdom of God in the present age. Where Jesus was, there

was the power of God; so, where the Spirit of Christ is, the power of God is at work.

(4) The kingdom of God is associated in the Gospels with breaking the power of evil. The kingdom was connected with the preaching and miracles of Jesus. It continues to be present where he is preached.

(5) The rule of God comes to persons when Jesus forgives their sins. He manifests his power in forgiveness (Mark 2:5-12). He gives new life, eternal life. When sins are forgiven, the power of Satan over that person's life is broken.

(6) Acceptance of the kingdom is obedient response to Jesus.

(7) The kingdom of God creates a people.

(8) Final victory of God's kingdom is certain. God's kingdom is an eternal kingdom. The present blessings are a pledge of the ultimate fulfillment of hope.

CHRIST (MESSIAH)

"You are the Messiah, the Son
of the living God."

(MATT. 16:16)

The kingly title of Jesus was associated with his being the Messiah, or the Christ, the Anointed of God (Mark 15:32), and his anointing was related to his role as the inaugurator of a new covenant. The designation of Jesus as the Christ (the Anointed One) points back to another significant theme in the Old Testament that was important for the early church, the Messiah and what has come to be called the messianic hope.

Meaning of Messiah

The Hebrew word rendered in English as *messiah* meant "anointed with olive oil." It was translated into Greek as *christos,* represented in English by Christ (see John 1:41).

In Old Testament times, specially chosen servants of God were marked out for their task by pouring olive oil on their heads. This act was used in the consecration of priests (Exod. 29:7; 30:22-33) and in the appointment of kings (1 Sam. 10:1; 16:1, 13). It set them apart for their work (Exod. 28:41) and gave to them a sacred character (cf. Lev. 8; 1 Sam. 24:6). Anointing continued to apply primarily to kings and priests (cf. Zech. 4:14, "two anointed ones," presumably from the context Joshua the high priest [Zech. 3:8] and Zerubbabel the governor [Zech. 4:6-7]). There is at least one instance of the anointing of a prophet (1 Kings 19:16), but otherwise the anointing of prophets (Ps. 105:15, in this case the patriarchs) was metaphorical, describing the giving of the Holy Spirit to them (Isa. 61:1). Another clearly metaphorical application of the idea of anointing is the description of the Persian king Cyrus as the Lord's anointed (Isa. 45:1).

The metaphorical uses of anointing bring out the significance of the idea. Anointing marked someone out as the chosen of the Lord. In the references given in the preceding paragraph, anointing indicated the one whom God had chosen to be king or to perform the office of priest. The act showed that the person was an object of the Lord's favor and was chosen for a particular task. Luke gives the significance of being "the Messiah" by joining with it the supplementary title "the Elect One" or "the Chosen One" (Luke 23:35). The meaning that this ceremony had for the Hebrew people is indicated in Psalm 133:1-2 about the high priesthood: The joy of living together in unity is likened to "the precious oil on the head, running down upon the beard, on the beard of Aaron, running down over the collar of his robes." The next comparison is to the "dew of Hermon, which falls on the mountains of Zion" (Ps. 133:3). Both are signs of the Lord's blessing (Ps. 133:3). The thought of oil running down the face and the back of the neck may give a modern person a tingling feeling but hardly from the sense of the divine presence, yet for the ancient Hebrews this suggested the abundant outpouring of God's blessings, for olive oil was a precious as well as useful commodity. To receive this sign of God's favor indicated one was specially chosen by him.

In the Old Testament prophets, there are many passages about God bringing deliverance and blessings to his people in the future. Frequently there is a human leader involved as the agent or representative of God in accomplishing his purposes. Several different designations of this deliverer or leader are given (two of these are discussed below), but it is notable that there is no clear case where Messiah is the term chosen.[41] The combination of Israel's future hope with the category of Messiah is as much as anything a result of the Christian adoption of

41. There are passages where "anointed ones" appear in passages concerning the future hope — Isa. 61:1-5; Dan. 9:25-26 — but these seem not to have the later technical meaning.

the title Messiah for Jesus so that the whole Old Testament expectation of "a good time coming" has been called the messianic hope.

The Old Testament hopes and its terms for persons involved in bringing them about continued to be expressed in postbiblical Judaism. Messiah was only one of several labels used to characterize the future deliverer.[42] There are texts that speak of a Davidic king, "the anointed of the Lord." This association of "the Messiah" with the "Son of David" and with the "king" is reflected in the New Testament (Luke 20:41; 23:2). In other texts, the anointed priest takes precedence, or the two anointed figures may stand side by side. Some people expected the appearance of an eschatological prophet. Other works speak of a supernatural figure, one like a "Son of Man," who arises at the end of the age. In yet others, God himself might be described as acting directly, without reference to any human mediator or agent. All these figures have come to be subsumed under the category of the messianic hope, because Christians accepted Jesus as the fulfillment of them all: Son of David, king, priest, prophet, Son of Man, and God acting directly (in his person). He filled these and many other categories, as Christians used most of the available categories to describe the overwhelming significance of one who seemed to defy categorization.[43] For Christians, the designation Messiah "receives its content not through a previously-fixed conception of messiahship but rather from the person and work of Jesus Christ."[44] We shall

42. E. Ferguson, *New Testament Backgrounds*, 2nd ed. (Grand Rapids: Eerdmans, 1993), pp. 517-519, where references and bibliography are given. Cf. Nils Dahl, "Sources of Christological Language," in *Jesus the Christ: Historical Origins of Christological Doctrine* (Minneapolis: Fortress, 1991), pp. 113-136.

43. Among the important studies of the larger subject of Christology are the following: Oscar Cullmann, *The Christology of the New Testament* (Philadelphia: Westminster, 1959); F. Hahn, *The Titles of Jesus in Christology* (New York: World, 1969); G. N. Stanton, *Jesus of Nazareth in New Testament Preaching* (Cambridge: University Press, 1974); Martin Hengel, *The Son of God: The Origin of Christology and the History of Jewish-Hellenistic Religion* (Philadelphia: Fortress, 1976); C. F. D. Moule, *The Origin of Christology* (Cambridge: University Press, 1977); J. D. G. Dunn, *Christology in the Making* (Philadelphia: Westminster, 1980); Ben Witherington, III, *The Christology of Jesus* (Minneapolis: Fortress, 1990). N. T. Wright, *The Climax of the Covenant: Christ and the Law in Pauline Theology* (Minneapolis: Fortress, 1991) considers the effect of Pauline Christology on the covenant and law.

44. Nils Dahl, "The Messiahship of Jesus in Paul," reprinted in *Jesus the Christ: The Historical Origins of Christological Doctrine* (Minneapolis: Fortress, 1991), p. 17. At the same time, the events involving Jesus were read by Christians in the light of the promises and texts in the scriptures.

proceed to discuss Jesus in terms of Messiah and some related terms that carry special implications for the creation of a community.

Jesus as Messiah[45]

In the Jewish expectation, the center of attention was the blessings of the coming age. The emphasis was on the "age to come" itself, what has come to be called the "messianic age." The Messiah, when he was mentioned, was to be part of the "furniture" of this new age. For Christians, on the other hand, the important feature was the Messiah himself. The coming of the Messiah brought the new age.

A turning point in the ministry of Jesus came when his disciples confessed him as Messiah (Matt. 16:13-23; Mark 8:27-33; Luke 9:18-22). In Matthew 11:4-6 Jesus in replying to John the Baptist applied one of the passages about an anointed one (Isa. 61:1-3) to the description of his ministry. John had already pointed to him as the one who would baptize with the Holy Spirit (Matt. 3:11; Mark 1:7-8). A messianic function was to give the Holy Spirit, the power and sign of the new age. In Peter's Pentecost sermon, the bestowal of the Holy Spirit is added to the resurrection as evidence that Jesus was "Lord and Messiah" (Acts 2:32-33, 36). Jesus also brought the forgiveness of sins expected in the messianic age. As Son of Man he claimed "authority on earth to forgive sins" and in demonstration of that authority performed a miracle of healing (Mark 2:1-12).

The anointing of Jesus was not with the oil that consecrated priests and kings but with the Holy Spirit. "God anointed Jesus of Nazareth with the Holy Spirit and with power; . . . he went about doing good and healing all who were oppressed by the devil, for God was with him" (Acts 10:38). Even so Luke's use of Isaiah 61:1-3 as the passage with which Jesus launched his ministry indicates Jesus as anointed with the Holy Spirit (Luke 4:16-19). Matthew likewise applied Isaiah's prediction (Isa. 42:1) of the Spirit given to the Lord's Servant to Jesus' ministry (Matt. 12:18-21).

45. Oscar Cullmann, *The Christology of the New Testament* (Philadelphia: Westminster, 1959), pp. 111-136; Ferdinand Hahn, *The Titles of Jesus in Christology* (New York: World, 1969), pp. 136-239; C. F. D. Moule, *The Origin of Christology* (Cambridge: University Press, 1977), pp. 35-46; Hartmut Gese, *Essays on Biblical Theology* (Minneapolis: Augsburg, 1981), pp. 141-166; P. E. Satterwaite et al., eds., *The Lord's Anointed: Interpretation of Old Testament Messianic Texts* (Grand Rapids: Baker, 1995).

Apart from the time of the confession by Peter at Caesarea Philippi, Jesus acknowledged the title Messiah only at his trial. To the high priest's question, "Are you the Messiah, the Son of the Blessed One?" Jesus replied, "I am" (Mark 14:61-62). This was not his preferred self-designation, for he immediately shifted to talk about the Son of Man (Mark 14:62). As will be shown in the next section, the reason for this reticence apparently was that Messiah was understood by most people in a sense different from Jesus' understanding of his mission.

In view of the infrequency of the term Messiah in the ministry of Jesus, it is remarkable that this became such a common title in early Christian faith and preaching. This may have been due to the title being very much in the mind of first-century Jews, but for Christians likely much more significance attached to the fact that Jesus was crucified as a messianic pretender (Mark 15:12-14, 26; see above on Jesus' kingship). What was a reproach by his enemies his disciples proudly proclaimed as the truth (Acts 2:36; 3:18, 20). Jesus, they said, was God's chosen messenger and representative. And they set about, following the lead of Jesus himself (Luke 24:46), to find scriptural proof for the different kind of messiahship manifested by Jesus (Acts 17:2-4).[46] Christians took over the Jewish title "Messiah," but understood his function differently from the common Jewish expectation of the first century. In the Gentile, Greek-speaking church, the significance of the Hebrew title "Anointed" was soon lost, and "Christ" became no longer a title but part of his proper name (e.g., Rom. 1:4, 6; 1 Pet. 1:3).

Suffering Servant and Son of Man

The Christian content in the container bearing the label "Messiah" was supplied by other figures in the Old Testament, notably that of the Suffering Servant of Isaiah 40–55 and the Son of Man of Daniel 7.[47]

46. Nils Dahl, "The Crucified Messiah and the Endangered Promises," in *Jesus the Christ: Historical Origins of Christological Doctrine* (Minneapolis: Fortress, 1991), pp. 65-79, defends the Christian claim that the crucified and vindicated Messiah was "according to the scriptures" by pointing to the "plot" in scripture of God's endangered but reaffirmed promises.

47. T. W. Manson, *The Servant Messiah* (Cambridge: University Press, 1953); Oscar Cullmann, *The Christology of the New Testament* (Philadelphia: Westminster, 1959), pp. 51-82, 137-192; Ferdinand Hahn, *The Titles of Jesus in Christology* (New York: World, 1969), pp. 15-67; C. F. D. Moule, *The Origin of Christology* (Cambridge: University Press, 1977), pp. 11-22; James D. G. Dunn, *Christology in the Making*

These two figures were fused into the Christian description of the Messiah. The Servant provided the image of suffering (Isa. 53), and the Son of Man the image both of identification with humanity and of glorification after oppression (Dan. 7:11-14).

The reports in Acts of the faith of the earliest church identify Jesus as Messiah *and* as Servant *(pais)* of the Lord. In Acts 3, Peter proclaims Jesus as Messiah (Acts 3:20). His declaration that "God fulfilled what he had foretold through all the prophets, that his Messiah would suffer" (Acts 3:18) is explained by the identification made at the beginning and end of Peter's sermon of Jesus with the "servant of God," who was rejected and delivered over to Pilate but glorified by God (Acts 3:13) and raised up by God (Acts 3:26). The prayer recorded in Acts 4 calls Jesus the servant *(pais)* of the Lord two times. This designation is prepared for by reference to David as the Lord's servant (Acts 4:25) and the quotation from Psalm 2:1-2 referring to the Lord's Messiah (Acts 4:25-26). The prayer proceeds by explaining that the Psalm referred to the conspiracy of the rulers and peoples "against your holy servant Jesus, whom you anointed" (Acts 4:27). The prayer concludes with a petition for God to perform "signs and wonders . . . through your holy servant Jesus" (Acts 4:30). These passages make clear the early Christian identification of Messiah and Servant and hence the interpretation of the Messiah in terms of the "servant of the Lord" of the prophets, notably Isaiah.

The designation of "servant" is applied to the Lord's "anointed," the Davidic king, in Psalm 89:38-39 and to the "Branch" of David in Zechariah 3:8. This usage may have facilitated a messianic reading of the Servant passages in Isaiah. If, as most commentators conclude, there is an allusion to Isaiah 42:1 ("in whom my soul delights") at the baptism of Jesus (Matt. 3:17; Mark 1:11; Luke 3:22), then Jesus at his baptism accepted the role of servant at the same time he was anointed with the Holy Spirit. Matthew quotes Isaiah 42:1-4 about the Lord's servant, his chosen and beloved, on whom he poured out his Spirit, as fulfilled in Jesus' ministry of healing (Matt. 21:15-21). This passage about the servant as the one on whom the Spirit was poured out may have been one of the bridges making the connection between anointing (with the Spirit instead of oil) and thereby of the Messiah with the servant, so that what was said of the servant could be understood as applying to the Messiah.

(Philadelphia: Westminster, 1980), pp. 65-97; Marinus De Jonge, *Jesus, The Servant-Messiah* (New Haven: Yale, 1991); W. H. Bellinger Jr. and W. R. Farmer, eds., *Jesus and the Suffering Servant* (Harrisburg: Trinity Press International, 1998).

Luke reports that Jesus took as programmatic for his ministry another passage from Isaiah, one not speaking of the servant but very much in the spirit of the servant songs, Isaiah 61:1-2 (Luke 4:18).[48]

Jesus' preferred self-designation according to the Gospels was Son of Man. Whereas the term "Messiah" always appears on the lips of others, the title "Son of Man" appears in the Gospels only on Jesus' lips, and outside the Gospels only by his followers with reference to him (Acts 7:56; cf. Rev. 7:13). The basis for the use of this title and its precise significance in reference to Jesus are very much disputed,[49] but the most likely origin of his usage seems to be Daniel 7,[50] a passage that ties together "kingdom" and "one like a Son of Man." At the trial of Jesus, according to the Synoptic Gospels, Jesus acknowledged the title Messiah in response to the high priest's question, but immediately spoke of the Son of Man, quoting Daniel 7:13 expanded from Psalm 110:1 (Matt. 26:63-64; Mark 14:61-62; Luke 22:68-70).

The texts in which Jesus speaks of the Son of Man, where not a simple circumlocution for "I," cluster around the Son of Man's coming in glory and his suffering. Those texts that speak of the Son of Man's glory (e.g., Matt. 25:31; Mark 8:38; 13:26-27; 14:62) accord with the picture of Daniel 7. In addition, Jesus repeatedly spoke of the necessity of the Son of Man to suffer (Mark 8:31; 10:33; Luke 17:24-25), and he declared that this was written (Mark 9:12; 14:21, 49). A possible explanation for Jesus' statements is that he interpreted the Son of Man of Daniel as the Servant of the Lord of Isaiah.[51] It is also possible that the suffering of the Son of Man could be deduced from the oppression of the people under foreign rulers in the context of Daniel 7.[52] Perhaps facilitating an interpretation of the Son of Man as suffering was the use of the term in the Old Testament to describe the mortality of human beings (Job 25:6; Ps. 144:3-4). The dual nature of human beings (son of man) in their

48. F. F. Bruce, *New Testament Development of Old Testament Themes* (Grand Rapids: Eerdmans, 1968), pp. 84-85.

49. See G. R. Beasley-Murray, *Jesus and the Kingdom of God* (Grand Rapids: Eerdmans, 1986), pp. 219-312 and literature cited in his notes.

50. From different perspectives, this is the conclusion, among others, of R. H. Fuller, *The Mission and Achievement of Jesus* (London: SCM, 1954), pp. 98-104; Ben Witherington, III, *The Christology of Jesus* (Minneapolis: Fortress, 1990), pp. 238-248.

51. F. F. Bruce, *New Testament Development of Old Testament Themes* (Grand Rapids: Eerdmans, 1968), pp 29-30.

52. Marinus De Jonge, *Jesus, The Servant-Messiah* (New Haven: Yale, 1991), pp. 50-54 and studies cited by him.

lowliness and their exaltation set forth in Psalm 8 is applied to Jesus in Hebrews 2:5-9. Even the humanity is exalted, and Paul quotes Psalm 8:6 in reference to death being made subject to Christ (1 Cor. 15:27).

The New Testament usage of the images of Servant of the Lord and Son of Man for Jesus is problematic from the standpoint of the Old Testament texts, for a good case can be made that in each instance these figures have a collective sense in their original context, being simply ideal figures that personify the people.[53]

The Servant of Isaiah 40–55[54] in some passages seems clearly to be the nation: "O Jacob my servant, Israel whom I have chosen" (Isa. 44:1). In some cases, it is argued that the Servant is a righteous remnant within the nation. In yet other passages, the Servant is clearly distinguished from the nation as a whole, to whom he ministers, and seems to be presented as an individual (Isa. 49:5-6; 53:4-6, 8, 11-12).

My inclination, wherever possible, is to take a "both . . . and" position rather than to say "either . . . or." In this case, such an approach is facilitated by the Hebrew view of "corporate [or collective] personality,"[55] or "inclusive personality,"[56] or more neutrally stated, "the principle of representation."[57] What is described by these expressions is a view in which a group was seen as deriving from a concrete individual

53. Accepted, for instance, by T. W. Manson, *The Teaching of Jesus,* 2nd ed. (Cambridge: University Press, 1935), p. 227; and for Dan. 7 by C. F. D. Moule, *The Origin of Christology* (Cambridge: University Press, 1977), pp. 20-22.

54. H. H. Rowley, *The Servant of the Lord and Other Essays on the Old Testament* (London: Lutterworth, 1952), pp. 1-88; C. R. North, *The Suffering Servant in Deutero-Isaiah,* 2nd ed. (Oxford: University Press, 1956); W. Zimmerli and J. Jeremias, "*Pais, Pais Theou,*" *Theological Dictionary of the New Testament,* ed. G. Friedrich, tr. G. W. Bromiley (Grand Rapids: Eerdmans, 1967), 5.654-717.

55. Jean de Fraine, *Adam and the Family of Man* (Staten Island: Alba, 1965), gives a balanced discussion of the whole concept, which I follow in the subsequent sentences; his pp. 182-211 discuss the Servant of Yahweh and the Son of Man; H. Wheeler Robinson, "The Hebrew Concept of Corporate Personality," *Werden und Wesen des Alten Testaments* (Göttingen, 1936), pp. 49ff.; A. R. Johnson, *The One and the Many in the Israelite Conception of God* (Cardiff: University of Wales, 1942), pp. 1ff.; J. Pedersen, *Israel, its Life and Culture* (London: Oxford University Press, 1926), p. 475. For a criticism of the notion, see J. W. Rogerson, "The Hebrew Conception of Corporate Personality: A Re-Examination," *Journal of Theological Studies* n.s. 21 (1970): 1-16. P. L. Stepp, *The Believer's Participation in the Death of Christ* (Lewiston: Mellen, 1996), advocates "corporate identification." See also J. S. Kaminsky, *Corporate Responsibility in the Hebrew Bible* (Sheffield: Sheffield Academic Press, 1995).

56. Ernest Best, *One Body in Christ* (London: SPCK, 1955), chap. 11.

57. Oscar Cullmann, *Christ and Time* (Philadelphia: Westminster, 1950), p. 115.

(an ancestor or ruler) or as summed up concretely in one individual. From both viewpoints, there was an emphasis on the unity of the group. The community is entirely in each individual, and the individual finds selfhood in the community. Thus the group could be personified, not just abstractly but concretely, in a given individual. Conversely, the group could be thought of as functioning through an individual member who so completely represented it that he became identical with it.

As applied to the Servant Songs of Isaiah, this concept of corporate personality suggests that the prophet speaks not of the nation (or a part of it) personified as if an individual nor of an individual by himself but of a chosen individual who influenced the group and represented the group to such an extent that the group found embodiment in him. Corporate personality means that there is a continual shifting between the individual and the collective point of view.[58] Israel manifests herself in the Servant, and the Servant is the representative of Israel.

The Hebrew word *ebed* ("servant") is applied to the patriarchs (Exod. 32:13), Moses (Exod. 14:31), the prophets (Amos 3:7), kings (2 Chron. 32:16), especially David (2 Sam. 7:5 and frequently), and to the future Davidic king (Ezek. 34:23-24; 37:24; Zech. 3:8). The position of kings in the ancient world made them particularly apt individuals to stand for a whole people. If the Servant in Isaiah was understood as the king,[59] embodying the nation yet distinguishable from it, then there was an immediate basis for the New Testament's identification of the Messiah with the Servant. The Servant of Isaiah 53 suffered for the sins of the people (Isa. 53:4-6, 10-12), and this passage became the basis of the New Testament theology of atonement.[60] It is also notable that the Servant was associated with a covenant (Isa. 42:6-7; 49:8-9; cf. Matt. 26:28).

If the people was represented by the Servant, and the Servant personified the people, then we do not have to choose between the

58. H. H. Rowley, *The Servant of the Lord and Other Essays on the Old Testament* (London: Lutterworth, 1952), pp. 1-60, speaks of an oscillation between the nation and a future representative. On pp. 61-88 he suggests that Jesus himself brought together the suffering servant and Davidic Messiah.

59. Jean de Fraine, *Adam and the Family of Man* (Staten Island: Alba, 1965), p. 200; F. F. Bruce, *New Testament Development of Old Testament Themes* (Grand Rapids: Eerdmans, 1968), p. 89.

60. Barnabas Lindars, *New Testament Apologetic: The Doctrinal Significance of the Quotations* (Philadelphia: Westminster, 1961), p. 77; Peter Stuhlmacher, "Vicariously Giving His Life for Many, Mark 10:45 (Matt. 20:28)," *Reconciliation, Law, and Righteousness: Essays in Biblical Theology* (Philadelphia: Fortress, 1966), pp. 16-29, calls attention to other passages in Isaiah as well, especially Isa. 43:3-4.

corporate and individual interpretations of the Servant: some passages develop one aspect, some another. Moreover, we have an important basis for the relation of the Messiah and his people and thus for the understanding of the church in the New Testament.

A similar problem of interpretation is posed by, and a similar solution may be proposed for, Daniel 7. The four beasts of the beginning of this chapter represent governments (cf. vs. 12) that prevailed over God's holy people (vs. 21). The one like a Son of Man, a human being in other words (but more than a human being? — vs. 13), accordingly would be a term standing for God's people. And this seems to be confirmed by the way what is said in verses 13-14 ("to him was given dominion and glory and kingship, that all people, nations, and languages should serve him. His dominion is an everlasting dominion that shall not pass away, and his kingship is one that shall never be destroyed") is interpreted in verse 18 ("But the holy ones of the Most High shall receive the kingdom and possess the kingdom forever"; cf. vs. 22). Almost identical things as are said about the one like a Son of Man are said about the people in verse 27 ("The kingship and dominion and the greatness of the kingdoms under the whole heaven shall be given to the people of the holy ones of the Most High; their kingdom shall be an everlasting kingdom, and all dominions shall serve and obey them").

On the other hand, the interpretation of the Son of Man as an individual has in its favor the use of the language of a royal investiture in verses 13-14 and the way the words "king" and "kingdom" are used interchangeably in Daniel. The beasts with whom the Son of Man is contrasted would have been kings, not peoples. Moreover, the image of the Son of Man referred to an individual in later Jewish apocalyptic literature (2 Esdras 13 and 1 Enoch 37–71).[61]

Once more, the choice between the individual and collective interpretations is probably unnecessary. The people would surely have had a leader, that is, the Son of Man; and if the Son of Man is treated as truly an individual, he would surely have a community of followers.[62] Instead of being a corporate symbol, the Son of Man is the

61. G. R. Beasley-Murray, "The Interpretation of Daniel 7," *Catholic Biblical Quarterly* 45 (1983): 44-58, gives a different set of reasons for the interpretation of the one like a human being as an individual representative of the saints and refutes the interpretation of the "holy ones" in this chapter as angels and of the one like a human being as Michael.

62. F. F. Bruce, *New Testament Development of Old Testament Themes* (Grand Rapids: Eerdmans, 1968), p. 26.

individualization, the embodiment, the representative of the people. As such, he can be identified with the people. That the Son of Man exercised kingship (Dan. 7:13-14), that is, was a king, brings the interpretation into line with what was said above about the Servant of the Lord. This function of ruling facilitated the merging of the Son of Man with the title of Messiah in the New Testament.[63] It also has wider ramifications. These coincide with the interpretation of the figure as bearing a corporate identity, an individual who represents and embodies a collective whole. The terminology "Son of Man" suggests one who stands not only for the "saints" of the text but also for humanity. He is the representative human being. Humanity at the beginning was made to rule over the rest of creation (Gen. 1:27-28). In the same way, the "human being" of Daniel 7 rules. Humanity's dominion over creation finds its fulfillment in the "kingdom of the Son of Man."[64] The "one like a human being" in Daniel 7 combines the images of the people and of the rightful ruler of creation. Jesus is presented in the New Testament as the perfect representative of humanity, specifically as the second Adam (1 Cor. 15:45), who brings a dominion of life instead of a dominion of death (Rom. 5:12, 14, 15, 17).

The New Testament affirmation is that Jesus as an individual gives concrete expression to these Old Testament representations of the people. He was the embodiment of the true Israelite, so that what was said of the nation of Israel was applied by Christians to him (cf. the use of Hos. 11:1 in Matt. 2:15). Jesus was seen as synthesizing three figures out of the Old Testament heritage: Messiah (Son of David), Son of Man, and Servant of the Lord. All three carry with them an association with a people. The Messiah rules over a people; the Son of Man embodies the saints of the Most High who are given the kingship; and the Servant of the Lord suffers for the people and embodies their role of serving the Lord. Hence, we are prepared for the New Testament's presentation of Jesus as promising to found a new community.

63. Hartmut Gese, *Essays on Biblical Theology* (Minneapolis: Augsburg, 1981), pp. 152-160, argues that since the Son of Man in Dan. 7 was installed in the office of king, this title represented a transformation in the expectation of the Davidic Messiah.

64. Jürgen Moltmann, *The Church in the Power of the Spirit* (New York: Harper & Row, 1977), pp. 100-101.

Matthew 16:13-23

Matthew connects the confession of Jesus' messiahship by Peter with Jesus' promise to build a church. Although the authenticity and setting of Matthew 16:13-23 have been much discussed in modern scholarship,[65] our concern here is with the exegesis of the passage and what it tells us about the connection between the Messiah and a people.[66] Four questions pertinent to our interest need to be answered.

(1) What Is the Rock?

A prominent interpretation, especially in Roman Catholicism, is that Peter himself is the rock. The linguistic basis of this interpretation is that Jesus was presumably speaking Aramaic and in Aramaic there is no difference between the name Cephas (*kepha* = *Petros*, Greek for Peter[67]) and rock (*kepha*). In support of this interpretation may be cited Ephesians 2:20-21 and Revelation 21:4, where the twelve apostles are the foundation of the church. Peter was clearly the leader and often the spokesman for the twelve (e.g., Matt. 10:2; 15:15; 19:27). Peter was the first of the twelve to receive an appearance of the resurrected Jesus (1 Cor. 15:5; Luke 14:34). This was important for the beginning of the

65. On Peter in general and Matt. 16 in particular, see Oscar Cullmann, *Peter: Disciple, Apostle, Martyr*, 2nd ed. (Philadelphia: Westminster, 1962); Raymond E. Brown, Karl P. Donfried, and John Reumann, *Peter in the New Testament* (Minneapolis: Augsburg, 1973); Chrys C. Caragounis, *Peter and the Rock* (Berlin: Walter De Gruyter, 1990). Although the argument that Peter is the rock in Matt. 16:18 has been widely accepted even in Protestant circles as a result of the arguments presented by Cullmann, I find the alternative position argued by Caragounis more persuasive. The historicity and originality of the setting at Caesarea Philippi are defended by Ben F. Meyer, *The Aims of Jesus* (London: SCM, 1979), pp. 185-197, who, however, argues that "rock" as name of a man is intelligible only in the context of a bedrock on which to build (but that does not explain Matthew's use of two different forms of the word, nor does it seem to fit the character of Peter.)

66. R. Newton Flew, *Jesus and His Church: A Study of the Idea of the Ecclesia in the New Testament* (London: Epworth, 1956), demonstrates by the convergence of themes in all strata of the New Testament how the idea of a community is inherent in the ministry of Jesus even apart from Matt. 16:18. So also Ben F. Meyer, *The Church in Three Tenses* (Garden City: Doubleday, 1971), pp. 30-53 and idem, *The Aims of Jesus* (London: SCM, 1979), esp. p. 192, for equivalents of *ekklesia* in Jesus' teaching and his conclusions summarized on p. 221 in reference to "Jesus' self-understanding as messianic builder of the house of God."

67. So John 1:42.

church. The resurrection faith, which took root first among some of the women who followed Jesus (Matt. 28:1-8; John 20:1-18), was planted, among the twelve, first in Peter. He became the little stone around which other stones were gathered in the building up of the new community founded on faith in the resurrection (cf. 1 Pet. 2:5). He was the spokesman in preaching the first gospel sermon in Acts 2, so the beginning of the church was closely connected with Peter. Moreover, he was the one who brought the gospel first in an official way to Gentiles (Acts 10–11). It would clearly be consistent with the rest of the New Testament to say that there was a sense in which the church was built upon Peter and that this imagery is consistent with the prominent role that Peter played in the early days of Christianity. It may be observed, as many Roman Catholic scholars acknowledge, that this function of Peter in the beginning of the church did not make him a "pope," nor do the words of Matthew 16 make any provision for successors. In fact, this place of Peter as "foundation" was an unrepeatable activity.

Nevertheless, I am not persuaded that this interpretation is what Matthew 16 is talking about. The reason for my hesitation is not the fact that Paul declares, "No one can lay any foundation other than the one that has been laid; that foundation is Jesus Christ" (1 Cor. 3:11). This statement is not necessarily a contradiction to Peter being the rock, for if the imagery of a foundation in another sense could be applied to the apostles (Eph. 2:20), there is no problem in it also being applied to Peter.

The difficulties of applying the rock to Peter come in the text of Matthew 16 itself. (1) The wording does not naturally lend itself to this interpretation. On the surface level there is the change from the second person of direct address ("You are Peter") to the third person of indirect address ("on this rock"). If the author of Matthew had wanted to say that Jesus intended to build the church on Peter, there were certainly less ambiguous ways of doing it. (2) The Greek text of Matthew and some strands of the Syriac tradition (pertinent here because Syriac is a later form of Aramaic) make a distinction between the words for Peter and the rock. They seem to understand a different referent for Jesus' words. (3) Aramaic perhaps could have made a distinction, as Syriac did, either by different words or by the distinction between masculine and feminine (preserved in Greek by different endings). (4) At any rate, if Jesus used the same word with the same sense in both cases, the wordplay is lost. There is no wordplay if the same word is used twice with the same meaning. A play on words requires similarities of sound, different meanings of the same word (possible here if Jesus used the same word, once for Peter and once for another "rock"), or different words with the same idea (again possible here if Jesus used two different expressions represented by different but similar words in Greek). The differences in Greek and some Syriac texts indicate that a wordplay was intended here. (5) Nowhere else in the New Testament or earliest Christian texts is Peter understood as the foundation stone of the church. Where Matthew uses rock elsewhere in a symbolic sense, the reference is to the teachings of Jesus (Matt. 7:24).[68]

The theme of Matthew 16:13-23 is the Messiahship of Jesus and what this entails. The context is concerned with the person of Jesus rather than Peter. To understand the rock as the fact or truth of Jesus' Messiahship best fits the context. The passage as a whole is not talking primarily about Peter. The rock is the faith confessed by Peter, not Peter confessing the faith. Matthew has set the declaration about building the church in a larger context, and that must be taken into account in understanding what he meant for his readers to understand by the words of Jesus. That context, as will be brought out in answering the questions taken up below, has to do with Jesus' death and resurrection and their significance for his Messiahship.

This context of the death and resurrection of Jesus makes relevant some other passages for the understanding of the rock in Matthew 16:18. The use of the "stone" imagery elsewhere in the New Testament supports the interpretation of the rock as a reference to the Messiah crucified and resurrected.[69] The appropriateness of extending the study from rock *(petra)* to stone *(lithos)* is encouraged by the interchange of these words in Isaiah 8:14, one of the texts cited as a testimony to Jesus.

Matthew puts on the lips of Jesus one of the stone testimonies as

68. See Chrys C. Caragounis, *Peter and the Rock* (Berlin: Walter De Gruyter, 1990), pp. 44-57, 88-113.

69. Barnabas Lindars, *New Testament Apologetic: The Doctrinal Significance of the Quotations* (Philadelphia: Westminster, 1961), pp. 169-181, sees these stone testimonies as relevant to Matt. 16 but takes the stone as first of all belief in Christ, then afterward a symbol of Christ and his church. He calls attention to the allusion to Isa. 8:14 in Matt. 16:23 and decides Peter is both the "stone of stumbling" and the "precious cornerstone" (not foundation). This allusion connects the stone passages to the context in Matthew, but for the reasons already given I do not find it sufficient to make the identification of the rock of Matt. 16:18 with Peter. Cf. C. H. Dodd, *According to the Scriptures* (New York: Scribner's, 1953), passim. Stone imagery is also treated in Lloyd Gaston, *No Stone on Another: The Significance of the Fall of Jerusalem in the Synoptic Gospels* (Leiden: Brill, 1970).

an application of the parable of the wicked tenants: "The stone that the builders rejected has become the cornerstone" (Matt. 21:42; Mark 12:10-11; Luke 20:17, quoting Ps. 118:22).[70] In the context of Matthew, the rejected stone is the son of the landowner killed by the tenants in order to obtain the inheritance for themselves. The application of the parable draws on Daniel 2:34-35 (cf. Dan. 2:44-45) and Isaiah 8:14-15, "The one who falls on this stone will be broken to pieces; and it will crush anyone on whom it falls" (Matt. 21:44; Luke 20:18).

The application of Psalm 118:22 to Jesus, "whom you crucified, whom God raised from the dead" (Acts 4:10), could be made more explicit after the events, as seen in the preaching of Peter: "This Jesus is 'the stone that was rejected by you, the builders; it has become the cornerstone'" (Acts 4:11). The addition of the word "you" to the quotation makes pointed the interpretation of the "builders" as the Jewish leaders who were responsible for the death of Jesus. God reversed their judgment in raising Jesus, making the rejected stone the cornerstone.

Paul combines two stone passages from Isaiah (Isa. 8:14-15 and 28:16): The Jews who sought righteousness by works rather than on the basis of faith "stumbled over the stumbling stone, as it is written, 'See, I am laying in Zion a stone that will make people stumble, a rock that will make them fall, and whoever believes in him will not be put to shame'" (Rom. 9:33). The use of Isaiah 8:14-15 is notable, for in its original context the stone/rock is God himself.[71] According to 1 Corinthians 1:23 the "stumbling block" (a different word, "scandal") for the Jews was that the Messiah was crucified. That Paul by referring in Romans 9 to the stone laid in Zion has in mind particularly the resurrection of Jesus is brought out in his subsequent statement about believing "in your heart that God raised him from the dead," supported by repeating the quotation of the last clause of Isaiah 28:16, "No one who believes in him will be put to shame" (Rom. 10:9, 11). This association may be facilitated by the continuation of the passage in Isaiah 28, which in verse 18 declares, "Then your covenant with death will be

70. In the Old Testament context the rejected stone was perhaps Israel, rejected by the nations but chosen by God; if so, this is one of numerous Old Testament images that were collective in original meaning but individualized in reference to Jesus.

71. That Heb. 2:13 quotes verse 18 from the context of Isa. 8 as part of the discussion of the solidarity of Christ with his people shows how the imagery of a stone easily moved from the individual to the group (cf. 1 Pet. 2:4-5).

annulled, and your agreement with Sheol will not stand" (cf. Matt. 16:18, "the gates of Hades" = Sheol).

All of this comes together in the chain of "stone" passages cited in 1 Peter 2, appropriate from the one whose name means "rock." Jesus is the "living stone," the "chosen and precious" stone in God's sight (1 Pet. 2:4). We are reminded that "chosen" is one of the designations of the Messiah (Luke 23:35). In support of this description, Peter cites Isaiah 28:16: "See, I am laying in Zion a stone, a cornerstone chosen and precious; and whoever believes in him will not be put to shame" (1 Pet. 2:6). Jesus is precious to believers, but to unbelievers, those who rejected Jesus, there apply the words of Psalm 118:22, "The stone that the builders rejected has become the very head of the corner" (1 Pet. 2:7), and Isaiah 8:14, "A stone that makes them stumble, and a rock that makes them fall" (1 Pet. 2:8). The author then comments, "They stumble because they disobey the word."

These stone passages from the Old Testament are tied together by a complex of ideas associated with the experience of Jesus. He was rejected by the Jewish leaders. Many of the people stumbled and were offended at him because he did not conform to their expectations of the Messiah. Consequently, he was put to death. However, God had a different evaluation: God raised Jesus from the dead, making him the cornerstone of a new spiritual building. When one reads Matthew 16:13-23 with this association of ideas in mind, the rock imagery becomes particularly appropriate for what Jesus says about building his church and about his being killed and being raised.[72]

Whatever interpretation of the "rock" in Matthew 16:18 is found persuasive, whether Peter or the Messiahship, the decision on this question should not obscure the most important declarations made in the verse, namely that Jesus is the builder and the church is his. The church belongs to him, whatever functions others may have in it. The church is Messiah's people, not Peter's people. This fits what the passage is about, the Messiah and his work.

---

72. The association of stone or rock and foundation with a temple (Eph. 2:20-22; 1 Pet. 2:4-5), and the association of temple in turn with Jesus' body (John 2:19-22), raises the possibility of a relation between the words "I will build my church" and the words quoted against Jesus at his trial, "I will build another" temple (Mark 14:58). See Ernst Lohmeyer, *Lord of the Temple* (Richmond: John Knox, 1962), p. 67; Ben F. Meyer, *The Aims of Jesus* (London: SCM, 1979), p. 192, suggests that *ekklesia* in Matt. 16:18 expresses literally what the temple symbol symbolizes in the expectation that the Messiah would build the eschatological temple.

The use of the verb "to build" in reference to the church (a people) may be due to the association of the church with the new spiritual temple (see pp. 125ff.), and in any case is in accord with the Old Testament imagery of building in connection with God's people (Jer. 24:6; 33:7). A rock or stone is connected in Daniel 2:34-35, 44-45 with a community, God's people, and the reference to a "rock" in Matthew 16:18 is the main reason for thinking of the imagery of a physical building. Otherwise, the usage of "build a house" in the Greek of Deuteronomy 25:9 for producing children means that "build my church" would have no necessary connection with a building and might be imagery for building a people.

(2) What Does "The Gates of Hades Will Not Prevail" Mean?

The "gates of Hades" was a Semitic expression for the entrance to the realm of the dead, and, since the gates were the strongest part of a city's fortifications, referred to as the "power of death" (cf. Job 38:17; Ps. 9:13; 107:18; Isa. 38:10). That meaning makes unlikely, if it does not rule out altogether, any interpretation in terms of a conflict with the devil or the forces of evil, except indirectly since they may be seen as the ultimate cause of death. The crucial question has to do with the meaning of "it." As a feminine pronoun, it can refer to either of the feminine nouns in the context, the church or the rock, or to some idea in the context. Among the proposed meanings are the following: (1) The church will never fall into error. (2) The church will never cease to exist. (3) There will be a resurrection of the faithful. (4) Death will not prevail against Jesus' Messiahship; hence, he will rise from the dead. (5) Death will not prevail against the founding of the church. The first three suggested interpretations refer the "it" to the church, reasonable since "church" is the noun that immediately precedes. Yet all three of these proposals seem to be intrusions into the context, especially the first, and to direct attention more to the church than to the Messiah and what he does. The fourth interpretation refers the "it" back to the rock, understood as the truth confessed by Peter. This interpretation is in keeping with the theme of the passage, yet it seems to go against a point to be made below, namely that submitting to death was included in the work of the Messiah. In response to this objection it might be contended that the "powers of death" are distinct from death itself. Nevertheless, I offer a cautious preference for the fifth interpretation, even though it is not the interpretation that grammatically first suggests itself.[73] The idea expressed in the phrase "I will build my church," that is, what the Messiah will do, is what the powers of death will not prevent. Again, the important thing said, it should be pointed out, is unaffected by the interpretation adopted: Not even the gates of Hades are stronger than Jesus the Messiah.

(3) What Are the "Keys of the Kingdom of Heaven"?

The passage moves from a building, to gates, to keys. A popular image has Peter as the doorkeeper of heaven, deciding admission through the pearly gates to each person at death. This understanding of Peter goes back to an early medieval interpretation that identified Peter with a figure in Germanic mythology who was the porter of heaven. Despite the hold that this image of Peter has in the popular mind, it may quickly be dismissed from careful exegesis.

A more serious proposal is the claim that Peter was given authority over the kingdom of heaven. This accords with the general exaltation of Peter that many have found in this passage. If one is not so impressed that the purpose of the passage is to exalt the privileges of Peter, then one may look more closely at what the imagery of the keys means in biblical language. Certainly one entrusted with keys is a person in whom another has confidence, and the responsibilities that go along with having the keys may give a measure of authority, but that is secondary to the primary significance of possessing the keys and the imagery that goes along with them.

It is often observed that the background of the New Testament usage is provided by Isaiah 22:22: "I will place on [Eliakim's] shoulder the key of the house of David; he shall open, and no one shall shut; he shall shut, and no one shall open." Eliakim was certainly given an important position. The text itself, however, spells out what his function was: to open and shut. That is what one does with keys; they unlock and lock. Any authority conferred was secondary to the function that was involved in the use of keys. The reference to David gave this text an importance in messianic thought.

---

73. Colin Brown, "The Gates of Hell: An Alternative Approach," *SBL Seminar Papers 1987* (Atlanta: Scholars Press, 1987), pp. 357-367, takes the "it" as the church but otherwise approximates my interpretation by seeing the passage as a prediction of the passion and vindication with allusion to the "gates" of Ps. 118:20 and rejected stone of 118:22 (also in Matt. 21:42). See also Jack Lewis, "'The Gates of Hell Shall Not Avail against It' (Matt. 16:18)," *Journal of the Evangelical Theological Society* 38 (1995): 349-367.

Jesus drew on the imagery of keys in a nonmessianic, scribal context having to do with the interpretation of the law: "Woe to you lawyers! For you have taken away the key of knowledge; you did not enter yourselves, and you hindered those who were entering" (Luke 11:52). The key here gives access to knowledge and conduct based on it. Once more the use of the imagery is explained in terms of entering or not entering. The Matthaean parallel to this saying does not use the word "keys," but the other similarities in language may indicate that it is pertinent for what Matthew understood the significance of the keys in 16:19 to be. "But woe to you, scribes and Pharisees, hypocrites! For you lock people out of the kingdom of heaven. For you do not go in yourselves, and when others are going in, you stop them" (Matt. 23:13).

The closest approximation to Isaiah 22:22 occurs in Revelation. On the basis of his resurrection from the dead, "one like the Son of Man" declares, "I have the keys of Death and of Hades" (Rev. 1:18). That certainly involves authority over death and Hades, but that is not the specific point of reference in the terminology of having the keys. The detailed meaning is filled out by Revelation 3:7: "These are the words of the holy one, the true one, who has the key of David, who opens and no one will shut, who shuts and no one opens." Jesus Christ, the Son of Man, by reason of his resurrection now controls the way out of Hades, the grave (Rev. 1:18). Similarly, when he opens the door of opportunity, no one is able to shut it (Rev. 3:8).

The one with the keys opens and shuts doors; he permits or prohibits one from entering. In other words, keys have to do with access, entering or not entering into some thing or some place.

That understanding now gives us the "key of knowledge" to open the meaning of Matthew 16:19. Jesus' delegation of the keys to Peter is related to "binding and loosing." A modern interpretation suggests interpreting Matthew 16:19 in terms of exorcism, "to bind Satan and to release believers,"[74] but this has not won much favor. More likely interpretations refer to rabbinic literature,[75] where this phrase could mean to "prohibit or permit" certain actions according to the interpretation of the law (cf. Luke 11:52 above). In a related rabbinic usage the

74. Richard Hiers, " 'Binding' and 'Loosing': The Matthean Authorizations," *Journal of Biblical Literature* 104 (1985): 233-250.

75. Herman L. Strack and Paul Billerbeck, *Kommentar zum Neuen Testament aus Talmud und Midrasch,* Vol. 1, *Das Evangelium nach Matthäus,* 3rd ed. (Munich: C. H. Beck, 1961), pp. 738-741.

language could also mean to bind or forgive sins (cf. Matt. 18:18). The preceding discussion on the keys, as well as the parallel in Matthew 18:18, favors this last interpretation here. Peter was to declare the terms of admission to the kingdom of heaven, that is, give access to the rule of God over people's lives, which meant the forgiveness of sins. Such an understanding corresponds to the function Peter performed in the beginning of the church. He preached what people must do to obtain forgiveness of sins or to be saved, both Jews (Acts 2:37-40) and Gentiles (Acts 10:43; 11:18).[76]

The phrases "will be bound in heaven" or "will be loosed in heaven" have been much discussed. Is the future perfect tense here simply a periphrastic future (as in the NRSV translation quoted), or should it be taken literally, "will have been bound" and "will have been loosed in heaven"? Either way, the intention is surely to say that Peter is to act according to heaven's instructions.

(4) What Does It Mean to Be the Messiah?

To say that Jesus was the Messiah was one thing; to understand what that meant was something else. As a result of divine revelation, Peter had received the insight that Jesus was the "Messiah, the Son of God" (Matt. 16:17), but Jesus "sternly ordered the disciples not to tell anyone that he was the Messiah" (Matt. 16:20). Why? It seems that most people had different understandings from Jesus about what it meant to be the Messiah and different expectations of him (cf. John 6:15). It was not safe to proclaim that he was the Messiah until Jesus' understanding of what this involved was made clear. He had to redefine the word for his disciples before they could openly proclaim their newly acquired faith. So, "From that time on, Jesus began to show his disciples that he must go to Jerusalem and undergo great suffering . . . and be killed, and on the third day be raised" (Matt. 16:21). The strong negative reaction of Peter to this message (Matt. 16:22-23) shows how valid was Jesus' concern to put the right definition on Messiahship and how difficult it was to accomplish this with even his closest followers. For Jesus, to be the Messiah meant that he must suffer, die, and be raised from the dead.

76. The interpretation here agrees in its main points with that of G. R. Beasley-Murray, *Jesus and the Kingdom of God* (Grand Rapids: Eerdmans, 1986), pp. 181-185 but was arrived at independently.

And only after the fact did the disciples realize what all this meant (cf. Luke 24:44-46).

This unit of our study has dealt with much controverted problems of interpretation. Regardless of the exegetical decisions made on these questions, the difficulties in the text should not be allowed to obscure those items about which there is no doubt. Indeed, the central points of Matthew 16:13-23 are clear: (1) Jesus is the Messiah, that is, the Anointed One, with a royal position over a covenant community. (2) Immediately on the confession of his Messiahship is the promise of the church. We may say that the existence of the church is implied in the confession that he was the Messiah. (3) The church is the Messiah's. (4) The authority of the apostles (in this case Peter) is delegated. (5) Messiahship means suffering.

The death and resurrection of the Messiah prepares for the next unit of this study, the community of the Messiah. The Messiah comes forth from the people (cf. Rev. 12:1-6), and the Messiah is the beginning of a people. Even leaving out of consideration those passages in the Old Testament with a (primary) reference to the nation (Israel) that are interpreted in the New Testament of an individual (Jesus), we can say that the very concept of a Messiah makes sense only in the context of a people. An anointed, chosen representative of God is a leader of the people. He has a mission to a people. His death was for a people, and his resurrection provided the basis for the gathering of a new community.

COMMUNITY

> *"In days to come the mountain of the LORD's house shall be established as the highest of the mountains . . . ; all the nations shall stream to it. Many peoples shall come and say, 'Come, let us go up to the mountain of the LORD, to the house of the God of Jacob; that he may teach us his ways and that we may walk in his paths.' For out of Zion shall go forth instruction, and the word of the LORD from Jerusalem."*
>
> (ISA. 2:2-3)

Precedents from the Old Testament

God created a people from the descendants of Jacob in fulfillment of his promises to Abraham and Isaac. Some of the theological aspects of this "people of God" will be treated in the next chapter.[77] For now, we take note of the importance of the church's appropriation of the concept of being God's people, of being truly the Israel of God, in giving it a sense of historical identity, a strong sense of solidarity, and a sense of ethical responsibility.[78]

It is significant for the understanding of the church that God's purpose was to call a people and that he dealt with individuals in relation to a people and individuals came to him as members of the chosen people. His concern certainly was with individuals, but they were treated as part of a group and their development as individuals was related to their being part of a community. This social dimension of God's purposes and actions will be evident in subsequent chapters.

Although God had a people in the Old Testament, the frequent failures of that people led the prophets to proclaim future hopes. This section will speak of some of those expectations that are pertinent for the New Testament message about the community of Christ.

The prophets anticipated that the king from David's line would restore the fortunes of the nation (Jer. 23:5-6; Amos 9:11, 14; Mic. 5:2-4). An important part of the prophetic hope, in keeping with God's goal of unity, was the reuniting of God's people. Jeremiah declared in the words of God, "I will restore the fortunes of Judah and the fortunes of Israel, and rebuild them as they were at first. I will cleanse them from all the guilt of their sin against me, and I will forgive all the guilt of their sin and rebellion against me" (Jer. 33:7-8). Ezekiel expressed this hope by the prophetic symbolism of binding together two sticks, one for Judah and one for Joseph, so that God might make of them one nation ruled by one king with the result that they would be his people and he would dwell among them (Ezek. 37:15-28).

God's concern was not limited to Israel and Judah. The prophets anticipated a time when the non-Israelites would worship the Lord. "To him shall bow down, each in its place, all the coasts and islands of the nations" (Zeph. 2:11). In a passage significant for the early church's mission to the Gentiles (Luke 2:32; Acts 13:47), God addresses the Ser-

---

77. Paul D. Hanson, *The People Called: The Growth of Community in the Bible* (San Francisco: Harper & Row, 1986), traces the development of the notion of community through the various strata of biblical literature in terms of three themes — righteousness, compassion, and worship.

78. J. Robert Nelson, *The Realm of Redemption: Studies in the Doctrine of the Nature of the Church in Contemporary Protestant Theology* (Greenwich, Conn.: Seabury, 1951), pp. 18-19.

vant: "It is too light a thing that you should be my servant to raise up
the tribes of Jacob and to restore the survivors of Israel; I will give you
as a light to the nations, that my salvation may reach to the end of the
earth" (Isa. 49:5-6). The passage continues with a reference to the Servant as a "covenant to the people" (Isa. 49:8), a phrase that is parallel
with his being "a light to the nations" in 42:6. This concern in the
prophets with the nations continues the theme of God's call of Abraham
and covenant with him in order to bless all peoples (Gen. 12:3). There
would be a gathering together not only of God's restored people but
of the nations as well, to whom Israel would be witnesses on behalf of
the Lord.

> I will bring your offspring from the east, and from the west I will
> gather you; I will say to the north, "Give them up," and to the south,
> "Do not withhold; bring my sons from far away and my daughters
> from the end of the earth — everyone who is called by my name,"
> . . . Let all the nations gather together and let the peoples assemble. . . .
> Let them bring their witnesses to justify them and let them hear and
> say, "It is true." You are my witnesses, says the LORD, and my servant
> whom I have chosen, . . . my chosen people, the people whom I
> formed for myself so that they might declare my praise. . . . I am He
> who blots out your transgressions for my own sake, and I will not
> remember your sins. (Isa. 43:5-6, 9-10, 21, 25)

The second half of Isaiah is full of such predictions. "And the foreigners
who join themselves to the LORD, to minister to him, to love the name
of the LORD, and to be his servants. . . . Thus says the Lord GOD, who
gathers the outcasts of Israel, I will gather others to them besides those
already gathered" (Isa. 56:6, 8). "Nations shall come to your light, and
kings to the brightness of your dawn. Lift up your eyes and look
around; they all gather together, they come to you; your sons shall come
from far away, and your daughters shall be carried on their nurses'
arms" (Isa. 60:3-4). These passages in the Greek translation use for
"gather" the same word as is used for the assembling of the church (on
earth — Heb. 10:25; eschatologically — 2 Thess. 2:1). Revelation 7 sees
the redeemed as coming from "every tribe of the people of Israel" (Rev.
7:4-8) and "from every nation, from all tribes and peoples and languages" (Rev. 7:9).

God's plan was for the community of the age to come to be
composed of Jews and of Gentiles (cf. Eph. 2:11-17). The Jews as the

people of God since the time of Moses formed the root and trunk of God's spiritual tree. According to Paul's analogy of the olive tree in Romans 11:17-24, the Gentiles are branches from a wild olive tree grafted contrary to normal practice into the cultivated olive tree (Israel). This is the basis for the application of the language of the people of God (pp. 73ff.) to the church.[79] Since the Jewish people formed the root and gives support to the branches, there is no place for Gentile believers to have pride or express anti-Jewish attitudes (Rom. 11:20-21).

Many of the Old Testament themes about the age to come find classic expression in the prophetic oracle found in Isaiah 2:2-4 and Micah 4:1-3. Although not expressly quoted in the New Testament (it influences the wording of the quotation from Joel in Acts 2:17 and may be alluded to in Rev. 15:4), this text was very important in the early church's self understanding.[80]

> In days to come the mountain of the LORD's house shall be established as the highest of the mountains, and shall be raised above the hills; all the nations shall stream to it. Many peoples shall come and say, "Come, let us go up to the mountain of the LORD, to the house of the God of Jacob; that he may teach us his ways and that we may walk in his paths." For out of Zion shall go forth instruction, and the word of the LORD from Jerusalem. He shall judge between the nations, and shall arbitrate for many peoples; they shall beat their swords into plowshares, and their spears into pruning hooks; nation shall not lift up sword against nation, neither shall they learn war any more. (Isa. 2:2-3 = Mic. 4:1-2)

This passage was understood in the early church as a reference to the new covenant brought by Jesus Christ and the going forth of the apostles from Jerusalem to proclaim the word of God that brought peace to all peoples who accepted it.

79. Markus Barth, *The People of God* (Sheffield: Journal for the Study of the New Testament, 1983).

80. Everett Ferguson, "The Covenant Idea in the Second Century," in W. Eugene March, ed., *Texts and Testaments: Critical Essays on the Bible and Early Church Fathers* (San Antonio: Trinity University, 1980), pp. 156-157; Robert L. Wilken, "*In novissimis diebus:* Biblical Promises, Jewish Hopes and Early Christian Exegesis," *Journal of Early Christian Studies* 1 (1993): 1-19.

Prerequisites for the Church

The Israel of the Old Testament had grown from the twelve patriarchs, the sons of Jacob (Gen. 35:9-26). Jesus' calling of twelve disciples (Matt. 10:2-4; Mark 3:14; Luke 6:13) as a symbolic prophetic action made clear allusion to his mission to all Israel (Matt. 10:5-6; 15:24) and implied the founding of a new Israel when the former Israel rejected him (Matt. 19:28). Indeed, there was implicit in many of Jesus' teachings and actions, such as the giving of an authoritative interpretation of the law (Matt. 5–7), the formation of a community.[81] However, before the promise of Matthew 16:18 could be fulfilled, certain things had to happen. According to the New Testament presentation of the church, certain necessities had to be met.

(1) The crucifixion was necessary for Jesus to be the foundation of the church. "For no one can lay any foundation other than the one that has been laid; that foundation is Jesus Christ" (1 Cor. 3:11). Upon the confession that he was the Christ (Matt. 16:16), Jesus promised to build his church (Matt. 16:18) and then proceeded to explain what the Messiah must do: he must die (Matt. 16:20-21; cf. Luke 24:46). In order to be the Messiah, Jesus had to do the work of the Messiah. His death made him the foundation of a forgiven people.[82] The use of the "stone" testimonia from the Old Testament for the death and resurrection of Jesus (Rom. 9:32-33; Acts 4:11; Matt. 21:42; 1 Pet. 2:4-8) connects those events with the imagery of the foundation of a building ("cornerstone"). Jesus was the stone of stumbling, but God made that stone rejected by the builders (rulers) the foundation stone. Even if this stone is understood as capstone or keystone (cf. Eph. 2:20) instead of cornerstone, either way Jesus is the essential climax of God's purposes. He is the one to whom all others of God's people must be joined. If the argument above to the effect that those passages have some bearing on the "rock" of Matthew 16:18 is correct, then the direct connection of Jesus' death with the building of the church is reinforced. In case the building imagery does not emphasize sufficiently the closeness and the living relationship between Jesus and his people, then we should remember

---

81. R. Newton Flew, *Jesus and His Church* (London: Epworth, 1956), pp. 35-88.

82. Rudolf Pesch, *Das Abendmahl und Jesu Todesverständnis* (Freiburg: Herder, 1978), pp. 112, 114, 121, affirms that Jesus' understanding of the meaning of his death as atoning was constitutive of the church and without it the post-Easter history of his disciples is unintelligible.

the Old Testament conception of corporate personality, the living identity of the Messiah with his people, so that what he does intimately involves them. To maintain the building metaphor, his people are "stones" as he is "the living Stone" (1 Pet. 2:4).

The Old Testament spoke of God acquiring a congregation, redeemed to be his heritage (Ps. 74:2). This people he obtained so that they might declare his praise (Isa. 43:21). The prophets voiced the hope of a fully forgiven people (Jer. 31:31-34). The new covenant of forgiveness of sins required the shedding of Jesus' blood (Matt. 26:28; Heb. 9:16-17, 22). In his death, there is forgiveness of sins (Eph. 1:7). The church is a forgiven people, obtained (same word in Greek as Isa. 43:21; cf. Ps. 74:2) by God "with the blood of his own Son" (Acts 20:28). The church as a forgiven people derives from the saving event of Christ.

(2) The resurrection was necessary for Jesus to be head over the church. The resurrection "made him both Lord and Messiah" (Acts 2:36). At the resurrection and ascension, Jesus was exalted above all other authority and dominion and made "head over all things for the church" (Eph. 1:20-22). The resurrection was the actual as well as the theological ground of the beginning of the church, for the fellowship of Jesus' disciples broken by the crucifixion (Matt. 26:56; Mark 14:50) was reconstituted by the resurrection (Matt. 28:16-17; Mark 16:6-7; John 20:19). Following Isaiah's words about God laying a precious cornerstone in Zion (Isa. 28:16), he says, "Then your covenant with death will be annulled, and your agreement with Sheol will not stand" (Isa. 28:18). Although not expressly quoted in the New Testament, these words may have been in mind when the preceding stone passage was interpreted of the resurrection.[83]

The church will be those resurrected to eternal life. This occurs because of union with Christ. He is the firstfruits of the resurrection (1 Cor. 15:23), the firstborn from the dead (Col. 1:18). Hence, his people are "the church of the firstborn ones who are enrolled in heaven" (Heb. 12:23). Jesus is the leader of those who will be resurrected. The glorified Jesus signalled his exaltation by giving the Holy Spirit as a down payment of the future redemption (Eph. 1:14).

(3) The Holy Spirit had to be given as the life of the new community. The giving of God's Spirit was part of the Old Testament hope (Ezek. 36:27). Although the Spirit was active in the Old Testament and

---

83. See C. H. Dodd, *According to the Scriptures* (New York: Charles Scribner's Sons, 1953), for quotations as a pointer to a whole context.

in the ministry of Jesus (see further pp. 104-107), there was a sense in which the Spirit as a distinctive gift living within God's people did not come until after the resurrection of Jesus.

> [Jesus] cried out, "Let anyone who is thirsty come to me, and let the one who believes in me drink. As the scripture has said, 'Out of the believer's heart shall flow rivers of living water.'" Now he said this about the Spirit, which believers in him were to receive; for as yet there was no Spirit [or, the Spirit had not been given], because Jesus was not yet glorified. (John 7:38-39)

The call to "drink" echoes Isaiah 55:1 (cf. 12:3 and 49:10 for the imagery). What is quoted as "scripture" does not occur in these exact words. They may be a composite and interpretative quotation based on Zechariah 14:8 and Ezekiel 47:1-12. The sequence of interpretation may have been that Zion = Jesus = believers, or Zion = God's people = the church. Important for our purposes here, based on the association of the Spirit with living water,[84] is John's observation that the fullness of the presence of the Spirit as a living reality within believers had to await the glorification of Jesus. Similarly, for Paul there is a close connection between the resurrection of Christ and the Holy Spirit, both of which are designated "firstfruits" (1 Cor. 15:23; Rom. 8:23).[85] As we have noted above, the gift of the Holy Spirit is related to the forgiveness of sins (the new covenant in the death of Jesus) and was poured out by the resurrected Jesus. The messianic gift (the indwelling Holy Spirit) could be given only after the completion of the messianic work.

(4) There had to be a commission to give the church a mission. There had to be a message for the church to proclaim. This gave the church a purpose. The resurrected Jesus gave the "great commission" to his disciples to preach the gospel (Mark 16:15-16) of forgiveness of sins (Luke 24:47) and make disciples of all nations (Matt. 28:19). Paul understood the task of the proclaimers of the message about Christ (Rom. 10:13-17) in terms of Isaiah 52:7 — "How beautiful upon the

---

84. See above for Ezekiel's association of purification by water and the giving of a new spirit and p. 107 for the Spirit's association with life.

85. Oscar Cullmann, *Christ and Time* (Philadelphia: Westminster, 1950), p. 136. Barnabas Lindars, *New Testament Apologetic: The Doctrinal Significance of the Old Testament Quotations* (Philadelphia: Westminster, 1961), p. 253, notes the importance of Ps. 68:18, "You ascended . . . and receiving gifts from people" (read as in Eph. 4:8 as "gave gifts") for combining the ideas of ascension and the gift of the Spirit.

mountains are the feet of the messenger who announces peace, who brings good news [gospel], who announces salvation, who says to Zion, 'Your God reigns.'" The gospel that brings salvation centers on the facts of Jesus' death, burial, and resurrection (1 Cor. 15:1-4); only when these events had occurred was there the gospel in the full sense to be preached. The resurrected Jesus possesses "all authority" (Matt. 28:18), and on that basis he commissioned the gathering of disciples in the name of the Father, Son, and Holy Spirit (Matt. 28:19) and promised his continuing presence among his people (Matt. 28:20). The Isaiah quotation relates the preaching of the gospel of salvation to God's reign. The proclamation of Jesus as Messiah and of his forgiveness and blessings called a church into existence. Jesus had limited his mission to the Jews. The bringing in of Gentiles was an eschatological event. Only with the completion of the messianic work was there a proclamation to the nations. The power of the Holy Spirit was necessary to equip the disciples for this task (Luke 24:47-49). "But you will receive power when the Holy Spirit has come upon you; and you will be my witnesses in Jerusalem, in all Judea and Samaria, and to the ends of the earth" (Acts 1:8).

Pentecost as the Beginning

It is impressive to see the connections between the Old Testament expectations and the events recorded in Acts 2. Moreover, there are interesting connections between Matthew 16 and Acts 2. Jesus promised to build the church on his Messiahship (Matt. 16:18). Messiahship meant his death and resurrection (Matt. 16:21). Acts 2 proclaims Jesus as "Lord and Messiah" (Acts 2:36) on the basis of the death and resurrection.

According to Acts 11:15, the events of Acts 2 marked "the beginning." The beginning of what? Several items occur for the first time in Acts 2. These together mark the occasion as the beginning of a new age, the gathering of a new community, the beginning of the church.

(1) The beginning of the age of the Holy Spirit. The coming of the Holy Spirit is what Peter particularly had in mind in Acts 11:15 when he designated the events of Acts 2 as "the beginning." "The Holy Spirit fell upon them just as it had upon us at the beginning" (Acts 11:15). He referred to the coming of the Holy Spirit on the household of Cornelius, the Gentile centurion (Acts 10:44-46). He proceeded to recall "the word

of the Lord, how he had said, 'John baptized with water, but you will
be baptized with the Holy Spirit'" (Acts 11:16). These words from the
resurrected Jesus are recorded by Luke in Acts 1:5. At the close of his
first volume, Luke included in the commission of Jesus the promise, "I
am sending upon you what my Father promised; so stay here in the
city until you have been clothed with power from on high" (Luke 24:49).
He commences his second volume with further reference to the coming
of the Holy Spirit: "You will receive power when the Holy Spirit has
come upon you; and you will be my witnesses in Jerusalem, in all Judea
and Samaria, and to the ends of the earth" (Acts 1:8). The reader notes
three ideas associated with the coming of the Holy Spirit in these verses:
the Spirit is a promise from God (see the words of the prophets cited
under *Covenant* above; cf. Gal. 3:14; Eph. 1:13); the Spirit brings power
(cf. what is said under *Kingdom* above); and after receiving the Spirit
the disciples were to be witnesses (see below and pp. 163-164 on the
Spirit producing faith through the preached word).

Acts 1:5 and 11:16 identify the particular event of Acts 2 and the
like experience in Acts 10 as a "baptism in the Holy Spirit." The description of the event in Acts 2 speaks of a "sound like the rush of a
violent wind" that "filled the entire house where they were sitting"
(Acts 2:2), so they were indeed in a sense immersed in the Spirit.
"Tongues, as of fire," rested on each one (Acts 2:3), and "All of them
were filled with the Holy Spirit and began to speak in other languages,
as the Spirit gave them ability" (Acts 2:4). The disciples were thus filled
with power, and with Peter as a spokesman they gave their witness to
Jesus and his resurrection.

Peter's message refers to the Holy Spirit at the beginning, middle,
and end. In his introduction Peter quoted Joel 2:28-32, "In the last days
it will be, God declares, that I will pour out my Spirit upon all flesh"
(Acts 2:17-21) as fulfilled in what had happened (Acts 2:16). The promise
had been fulfilled. The age of the Spirit had begun. In the middle of the
sermon, Peter declared that this coming of the Spirit was the action of
the resurrected Messiah: "Being therefore exalted at the right hand of
God, and having received from the Father the promise of the Holy Spirit,
he [Jesus] has poured out this that you both see and hear" (Acts 2:33).
At the conclusion of his sermon, Peter promised to those who repented
and were baptized in the name of Jesus that they would "receive the gift
of the Holy Spirit" (Acts 2:38), that is, the Holy Spirit as a gift, because
"the promise is for you, for your children, and for all who are far away,
everyone whom the Lord our God calls to him" (Acts 2:39).

More will be said in the next chapter about the Spirit in the life of the church, but here it may be noted that the Spirit is promised to all who accept Christ. The baptism (immersion) in the Holy Spirit is spoken of as occurring only in Acts 2 and 10. The Holy Spirit as a gift is promised to all (more on this will be found on pp. 186ff. and 204 as part of the blessings of salvation). There are different manifestations of the activity of the Spirit, but the same Spirit (1 Cor. 12:4) is present in all the Messiah's people.

(2) The beginning of the public proclamation of Jesus as Christ. The climax of Peter's sermon in Acts 2 is the declaration: "Therefore let the entire house of Israel know with certainty that God has made him both Lord and Messiah, this Jesus whom you crucified" (Acts 2:36).[86] After the resurrection, Jesus explained that according to the scriptures, "The Messiah is to suffer and to rise from the dead on the third day," and that his disciples were "witnesses of these things" (Luke 24:46, 48). And when the Spirit came upon them they were to give their witness in Jerusalem and to the ends of the earth (Acts 1:8). Thus Peter confirmed the message of the disciples to the crowd on Pentecost: "This Jesus God raised up, and of that all of us are witnesses" (Acts 2:32). They were witnesses already in the sense that they had seen the Lord, both before and after his resurrection.[87] Now for the first time the disciples were witnesses in the sense of giving testimony,[88] telling what they had seen. During his ministry, Jesus would not allow his followers to proclaim their faith that he was the Messiah (Mark 8:29-30; 9:9). Jesus had to perform the messianic work involved in his death and resurrection before this truth could be openly proclaimed. Now the wraps were taken off.

(3) The beginning of the preaching of the gospel. The gospel had been preached beforehand in promise to Abraham (Gal. 3:8). Jesus had preached the gospel of the kingdom in preparation (Mark 1:14-15). Now for the first time it was preached in fullness as an accomplished fact. Paul outlines the facts of the gospel as the death, burial, and resurrection of Christ (1 Cor. 15:1-5). This is Peter's message in Acts 2. Only after

86. Barnabas Lindars, *New Testament Apologetic: The Doctrinal Significance of the Old Testament Quotations* (Philadelphia: Westminster, 1961), p. 46, notes that the conclusion is drawn from two Old Testament passages used in the sermon, "Lord" from Ps. 110 and "Messiah" from Ps. 16.

87. Luke uses the word in the sense of eyewitness.

88. This is the meaning normally in John.

these events had occurred could the good news of what God had done through Jesus be announced.

(4) The beginning of the offer of forgiveness in Jesus' name. God had forgiven sins in the Old Testament (e.g., Lev. 4–5; 16; Ps. 78:38). Jesus during his ministry had offered forgiveness directly while on earth; he had that power (Mark 2:1-12). In the Johannine account, the resurrected Jesus gave the Holy Spirit to the disciples and with it the authority to forgive sins: "He breathed on them and said to them, 'Receive the Holy Spirit. If you forgive the sins of any, they are forgiven them; if you retain the sins of any, they are retained'" (John 20:22-23). Luke's account of the coming of the Spirit is more spectacular (Acts 2:4, 14). Whether we have two different events with no connection to one another, two different accounts of the same experience, or John speaking symbolically of what was to happen, in both authors there is a connection between receiving the Spirit from Christ and offering forgiveness. Luke had included in his account of Jesus' commission to his disciples the words that "repentance and forgiveness of sins" were "to be proclaimed in his name to all nations, beginning from Jerusalem" (Luke 24:46). The call to repentance and forgiveness was included in the message on Pentecost. The forgiveness was announced "in the name of Jesus Christ" (Acts 2:38). Although spoken by the apostles and not personally by Jesus, the word of forgiveness is no less sure, for it is spoken "in his name."

(5) The beginning of the new covenant. According to the message of the prophets, the content of the new covenant, as discussed above, was forgiveness of sins (Jer. 31:34) and God's Spirit in the heart (Ezek. 36:27). These two elements are brought together in the promise of Acts 2:38 — "so that your sins may be forgiven; and you will receive the gift of the Holy Spirit." The content of the new covenant relationship of God with humanity was now available. According to the Hellenistic understanding of *diathēkē* as a will, the death of the testator must precede its taking effect (Heb. 9:16-17). It was only after the shedding of Jesus' blood that the new covenant was inaugurated (Heb. 9:15-22). To extend the analogy, the will had to be probated, and Peter's message in Acts 2 in effect was the reading of the will.

(6) The beginning of the gathering of a church. In the Matthaean version of the Great Commission, Jesus commanded the eleven "to make disciples of all nations, baptizing them in the name of the Father and of the Son and of the Holy Spirit, and teaching them to obey everything that I have commanded you" (Matt. 28:19). In Acts 2, there

is this same sequence of making disciples, baptizing, and continued instruction. "Those who welcomed his [Peter's] message were baptized" (Acts 2:41), and "They devoted themselves to the apostles' teaching" (Acts 2:42). "On that day about three thousand were added to the number of disciples" (Acts 2:41), and "All who believed were together and had all things in common" (Acts 2:44). According to the usage in Acts, the church is the disciples (note Acts 11:26 for "church" and "disciples" as equivalent, and compare the same statement made about the disciples in Acts 6:1, 7 as about the church in Acts 9:31).

(7) The beginning of corporate worship and life. Jesus and his disciples had already shared a common life together (cf. Luke 8:3; John 13:29 for incidental details of the sort generally missing from the Gospel records). What is noteworthy is that this common life continued without the personal presence of Jesus, although in the altered form necessary for a constantly growing community no longer confined to one place and one period of time. Those who were baptized on Pentecost "devoted themselves to the apostles' teaching and fellowship, to the breaking of bread and the prayers" (Acts 2:42; see Chap. 4). The following verses may be seen as elaborating on this description. They had "all things in common" (Acts 2:44), selling their possessions in order to provide for those in need (Acts 2:45). "Day by day, as they spent much time together in the temple, they broke bread at home and ate their food with glad and generous hearts, praising God and having the goodwill of all the people" (Acts 2:46).

People of the End Time

Peter began his sermon in Acts 2:17 with a quotation from Joel 2:28. In place of the Greek translation's "after these things" (which correctly renders the Hebrew), Acts substitutes "In the last days," likely borrowed from Isaiah 2:2 (= Mic. 4:1). The Hebrew behind this translation, and often the Greek phrase in the New Testament, means simply "in the future," without any eschatological or messianic reference.[89] In spite of this normal usage, it may be that the change in wording in Acts 2:17 was intended to bring out an eschatological application of Joel 2:28 to the new age of the Spirit that began at Pentecost. Early Christians

---

89. John T. Willis, "The Expression *be'acharith hayyamin* in the Old Testament," *Restoration Quarterly* 22 (1979): 54-71.

expressed the conviction that they were living in the "last days," and therefore that the church was the eschatological community.

This was so because of God's new revelation of himself through his Son. "Long ago God spoke to our ancestors in many and various ways by the prophets, but in these last days he has spoken to us by a Son, whom he appointed heir of all things" (Heb. 1:1-2). There is no more perfect or complete revelation than through his own Son, who is "the reflection of God's glory and the exact imprint of God's very being" (Heb. 1:3). The Christ is the ultimate authority (cf. Matt. 28:18). He is God's last and perfect word to humanity. "He was destined before the foundation of the world, but was revealed at the end of the ages for your sake" (1 Pet. 1:20). Hence, those who are Christ's people are those "on whom the ends of the ages have come" (1 Cor. 10:11).

The phrase "last days" does not necessarily indicate the nearness of the end, even if many early Christians likely believed that the time was short (1 Cor. 7:29; cf. Phil. 4:4). The emphasis is not on the word "days," which simply indicates an indefinite period of time, but on the word "last." The reference is to God's final act on behalf of humanity (Heb. 10:26-27). "Days" is no more to be taken literally than "hour" is in John's declaration "It is the last hour!" (1 John 2:18). "The duration of the last days does not affect their character as the last days."[90] The phrase describes the last dispensation. The revelation brought by Christ and the gathering of his people is something more than just another stage in God's dealings with human beings.

The covenant brought by Christ is permanent (2 Cor. 3:11). It has made all previous dealings of God with people obsolete (Heb. 8:13) and is the "eternal covenant" (Heb. 13:20) promised by the prophets (Isa. 61:8; Jer. 32:40; 50:5; Ezek. 16:60; 37:26). This covenant is the covenant of the "last days." The people in this covenant have come under the

---

90. F. F. Bruce, *New Testament Development of Old Testament Themes* (Grand Rapids: Eerdmans, 1968), p. 38. Cf. Oscar Cullmann, *Christ and Time* (Philadelphia: Westminster, 1950), p. 142 — "Where the certainty rules that the decisive battle has been fought through to victory, then only in the circle of understandable human curiosity is it still of importance to know whether the 'Victory Day' comes tomorrow or later. Theologically, that is, for salvation, this latter question has no further significance." See also G. B. Caird, "Eschatology and Politics: Some Misconceptions," in J. R. McKay and J. F. Miller, *Biblical Studies: Essays in Honor of William Barclay* (Philadelphia: Westminster, 1976), pp. 72-86, esp. p. 82 — The End time was a period of indefinite duration; once the End time began, that did not imply the End itself was immediate.

eternal kingship of the Son of Man (Dan. 7:14; Luke 1:33), in which they will share through eternity (Dan. 7:27; 2 Tim. 2:12; 2 Pet. 1:11). As a result of what Christ did, there is "an eternal gospel to proclaim to those who live on the earth — to every nation and tribe and language and people" (Rev. 14:6). Everyone who believes on the Son of Man = Son of God has "eternal life" (John 3:15-16, 36). To those who obey him he gives "eternal salvation" (Heb. 5:9; cf. "eternal redemption," 9:12, and "eternal inheritance," 9:15) from the eternal fire (Matt. 18:8; 25:41, 46; Jude 7). In him there is salvation "with eternal glory" (2 Tim. 2:10; cf. 1 Pet. 5:10).

The church is the eschatological community, the remnant gathered by God to be saved in the overthrow of the world, the people of the End time. They are enjoying the eschatological blessings of the forgiveness of sins and the gift of the Holy Spirit in the present, but they await the coming again of the Son of God and entrance into the future completion of God's purposes. This dual dimension of present and future, already and not yet, influences other aspects of the church to be considered in subsequent chapters. That perspective influences even those descriptions of the nature of church other than those related to history and eschatology. Throughout biblical history, God was gathering and educating a people for his own possession. The church is now the eschatological people of God. The nature of this new covenant people, who have come under the kingship of God and have received the blessings of the crucified and resurrected Christ, will be examined in the next chapter. The descriptions of this community to which we now turn show elements of continuity appropriate to the history of God's dealings with humanity of which this community is a part and elements of discontinuity with the past appropriate to the eschatological age which it shares and experiences.

2. *The Church and Her Lord: The Nature of the Church*

"The churches of God in Christ Jesus."   (1 THESS. 2:14)

AS AFFIRMED in the first chapter, the Messiah has a people. God's covenant is made with a chosen people, and his kingdom rules over a faithful and obedient people. This chapter will seek to expand on the meaning of the covenant people in Christ. It will consider first those descriptions that emphasize the community or corporate aspect of the people of God in Christ. Then it will take up some images of the church drawn from the natural or physical world, and finally it will study the Greek word *ekklēsia,* translated "church."

Of first importance, it must be noted that the characterizations of the church in the scriptures bring it into relation to the deity: some to God the Father (people of God, family of God), some to Jesus Christ (body of Christ, vine, sheep), some to the Holy Spirit (community filled with the Holy Spirit, temple in which God dwells through the Holy Spirit). Furthermore, all the principal descriptions of the nature of the church give prominence to Jesus as Lord over the church.[1] These descriptions of the essential reality of the church will provide the

---

1. For the title "Lord" see Oscar Cullmann, *The Christology of the New Testament* (Philadelphia: Westminster, 1959), pp. 195-237; Ferdinand Hahn, *The Titles of Jesus in Christology* (New York: World, 1969), pp. 68-135; C. F. D. Moule, *The Origin of Christology* (Cambridge: University Press, 1977), pp. 35-46.

perspective from which topics in subsequent chapters will be set forth.[2]

THE CENTRALITY OF CHRIST

"All the churches of Christ greet you."   (ROM. 16:16)

The descriptions of the nature of the church to be taken up below stress Christ's unique preeminence. If the church is the people of God, it is the people of God *in Christ.* If the church is the community of the Holy Spirit, the Holy Spirit is the gift of the resurrected Christ. The figures of speech that relate the church directly to Christ give him the preeminence. He is the whole body, or where distinguished from the body, he is its head. In the family of God, he is the "elder brother," the Son over the household. He is the husband of the church, his bride. He is the vine and the rightful heir and representative of the owner of the vineyard. He is the shepherd of the sheep and the gate into the sheepfold. He is the cornerstone of the new spiritual temple in which God dwells by the Spirit. The church is the assembly of God's people gathered in Christ's name. To invoke a category derived from Old Testament studies, the "collective personality" of the church is supplied by Christ.[3]

I observed repeatedly in my study for this book that designations of God in the Old Testament are applied in the New Testament to Christ (e.g., Lord, husband, shepherd), and in a similar way the images for Israel in the Old Testament are also applied to Christ (e.g., Son, beloved, servant). These titles and descriptions of Christ reflect his double place in the New Testament: the manifestation and revelation of God, and the origin and leader of the people of God.

Jesus, although the one who revealed God in the fullest way, was nonetheless fully identified with humanity. In his incarnation, he took on flesh and blood and assumed the full human condition (John 1:1-18;

---

2. For a comprehensive listing, see Paul S. Minear, *Images of the Church in the New Testament* (Philadelphia: Westminster, 1960). A critical, contemporary evaluation of the use of imagery or metaphor to describe the church is provided by H. Rikhof, *The Concept of Church: A Methodological Inquiry into the Use of Metaphor in Ecclesiology* (London: Sheed & Ward, 1981). Avery Dulles, *Models of the Church* (Garden City: Doubleday, 1987), discusses models employed in contemporary discussions of ecclesiology.

3. Jean de Fraine, *Adam and the Family of Man* (Staten Island: Alba, 1965), p. 247.

Heb. 2:10-18). He identified with humanity in his baptism, although he had no sins of his own (Matt. 3:14-15). In his ministry he was a "man of the people" (cf. Matt. 12), so that "the common people heard him gladly" (Mark 12:37 KJV). On the cross, he identified with the "worst" of humanity, as he was crucified with criminals. The extended arms on the cross are the welcoming arms of invitation, as he invites humanity to identify with him.

THE PEOPLE OF GOD

"You are God's own people." (1 PET. 2:9-10)

Peoplehood

We begin with a characterization of the church that emphasizes its continuity with the Old Testament and thus with the biblical history of salvation. "People of God"[4] aptly summarizes the description of Israel in the Old Testament (e.g., Deut. 32:9; cf. Heb. 11:25), so much so that in the New Testament "the people" without qualification can refer to Israel (2 Pet. 2:1). The combined expression "I am your God" and "You are my people" (Deut. 26:17-18; 29:12-13; Jer. 7:23; 11:4; 24:7; 31:33; Hos. 2:23) served as something of a covenant formula to describe the intimate relationship between God and his chosen people.[5] The Old Testament idea was still strong at the beginning of the Christian era, as seen in the birth narratives in Luke. The angel told Zechariah that his son John would "make ready a people prepared for the Lord" (Luke 1:17). The prophecy of Zechariah himself combined many themes encountered in

4. Nils A. Dahl, *Das Volk Gottes* (Oslo, 1941); more popularly, Dahl, "The People of God," *Ecumenical Review* 9 (1956): 154-161; Hans Küng, *The Church* (London: Burns & Oates, 1968), pp. 114-132; Daniel J. Harrington, *God's People in Christ: New Testament Perspectives on the Church and Judaism* (Philadelphia: Fortress, 1980); A. M. Stibbs, *God's Church: A Study of the Biblical Doctrine of the People of God* (Chicago: Inter-Varsity Fellowship, 1959); N. T. Wright, *The New Testament and the People of God* (Minneapolis: Fortress, 1992); Wolfgang Kraus, *Das Volk Gottes: Zur Grundlegung der Ekklesiologie bei Paulus* (Tübingen: J. C. B. Mohr, 1995). Without studying the label "people of God" specifically, Gerhard Lohfink, *Jesus and Community* (London: SPCK, 1985), stresses the continuity between Israel and the community gathered by Jesus.

5. John T. Willis, "'I Am Your God' and 'You Are My People' in Hosea and Jeremiah," *Restoration Quarterly* 36 (1994): 291-303.

this study: a people of God (Luke 1:68), who raises up a savior in the
house of David (Luke 1:69), remembers his holy covenant identified
with his oath to Abraham (Luke 1:72-73), grants forgiveness of sins
(Luke 1:77), and gives light to those in darkness (Luke 1:79). The language of "people of God" both provided the background for the concept of the church and served to describe a particular aspect of it.

To be the people of God carried the promise that he would live
among them (Lev. 26:11-12; Ezek. 37:27). Those passages that combine
the idea of being God's people with his living among them are applied
to present Christian living (2 Cor. 6:16–7:1; John 14:23) and are given
an eschatological fulfillment in the "new Jerusalem" (Rev. 21:3).[6] The
description "people of God" defined the character of the people and
identified who was their God.

"People" serves in the New Testament to emphasize Christians
as drawn from Gentiles as well as Jews (Acts 15:14), with the result that
in some passages (while keeping overtones of the inclusion of Gentiles)
it simply refers to the church (Acts 18:10). First Peter 2:9-10, appropri-
ating the covenant language of Exodus 19:5-6 supplemented by Hosea
2:23 and Isaiah 43:20-21, claims the full title "people of God" for Christians:

> You are a chosen race, a royal priesthood, a holy nation, God's own
> people, in order that you may proclaim the mighty acts of him who
> called you out of darkness into his marvelous light. Once you were
> not a people, but now you are God's people: once you had not
> received mercy, but now you have received mercy.

The idea of "people" permeates the passage. In English, the word
"people" is used for an aggregate of individuals: "How many people
are here?" Or, it applies to human beings as such: "People will be
people." In the Bible, "people" customarily means a single corporate
whole, a nation or a race viewed as a collective entity. In this sense,
someone may truly speak of "one people." We approximate this meaning when we speak of "the American people" or "the German people."
"People" most often in the Bible refers to God's people, Israel, although
the word may be used of other "peoples."

The word in Greek for "people" is *laos*, from which English derives

6. God's dwelling among his people will be expanded further under the topics
of Community of the Holy Spirit and Temple.

the word "laity." The word "laity" has been debased in modern speech from the noble conception of *laos* in the Bible. In modern usage we contrast the laity with the professionals (as in law or medicine) and particularly in religious language with the clergy or priesthood. Not so the Bible. In the Bible the *laos* is the whole people, not a part (not even the largest part). And in reference to Israel and the church, this is a chosen people, a people with a special status and dignity because of the relationship with God. The people is a priesthood (1 Pet. 2:9), not contrasted with it. Indeed, the people (all Christians) is also the clergy (Acts 26:18; Col. 1:12). The English word "clergy" derives from the Greek *klēros*, meaning a lot, a portion, a possession, or something assigned. According to 1 Peter 5:3, the spiritual shepherds are not to lord it over "their charges" (*klērōn*), that is, the people allotted or assigned to their care. By a curious (in view of modern usage) but not unusual semantic development, those who had a "charge" or "assignment," a *klēros*, became themselves the *klēros* or "clergy."[7]

The most important thing said about this people in 1 Peter 2:10 is that it is God's. One may compare Titus 2:14, "In order that he might purify for himself a people of his own," "of his own" in the sense of being "special," using the same word as the Greek translation of Exodus 19:5.[8] The defining characteristic of this people is that it is the "people of God." That is their peculiar, distinguishing feature: the divine possession.[9] The accent falls on God's creative activity, his choosing, his saving work, his possession (1 Pet. 2:9). He is the one who made it a people (1 Pet. 2:10) and not just a collection of individuals or a group organized around a false or lesser principle.[10] There is much concern today about what gives a person identity. For the church, identity comes from belonging to God.

Paul underscores that the church called from Jews and Gentiles is indeed a divine society by applying the words of Hosea 2:23 and 1:10 to it:

7. Hans Küng, *The Church* (London: Burns & Oates, 1968), p. 385.

8. Also Deut. 7:6; 14:2; 26:18.

9. "This sense of being God's possession constitutes its identity, its vocation, and its vision." Paul D. Hanson, *A People Called* (San Francisco: Harper & Row, 1986), p. 517.

10. "There is no life that is not in community, and no community not lived in praise of God." T. S. Eliot, "Choruses from 'The Rock,'" *The Complete Poems and Plays, 1909-1950* (New York: Harcourt, Brace, 1952), p. 101.

[God has made] known the riches of his glory for the objects of mercy, which he has prepared beforehand for glory — including us whom he has called, not from the Jews only but also from the Gentiles. As indeed he says in Hosea,

" 'Those who were not my people [Hebrew: "No kin of mine"] I will call my people,' and her who was not beloved [Hebrew: "one for whom no natural affection or compassion is felt"] I will call 'beloved.' "

"And in the very place where it was said to them, 'You are not my people,' there they shall be called children of the living God." (Rom. 9:23-26)

What is involved in being "not a people" is indicated in Deuteronomy 32:21, "So I will make them [Israel] jealous with what is no people, provoke them with a foolish nation." A pagan nation is not truly a "people" in the full biblical sense, because it is not chosen by God, follows the ways of idolatry and immorality ("foolish"), and so has a false center of unity. Paul makes the contrast for Gentiles outside of Christ and in Christ: "Remember that you were at that time without Christ, being aliens from the commonwealth of Israel, and strangers to the covenants of promise, having no hope and without God in the world" (Eph. 2:12). The love of God has now reached out to all "peoples" and changed that: "So then you are no longer strangers and aliens, but you are citizens with the saints and also members of the household of God" (Eph. 2:19). In accord with a number of Old Testament passages (Gen. 49:10; Num. 24:17-18; Isa. 2:2: Amos 9:11-12), the New Testament extended the "people of God" expressly to Gentiles, with the distinctive understanding that this was apart from keeping the whole law of Moses.

To return to 1 Peter 2:10, which also quotes Hosea 2:23, the parallelism of Hebrew poetry indicates that to be made a people is to obtain mercy. To feel a sense of oneness and community requires God's mercy. The reverse is also true — to obtain mercy is to be made a people. Only by God's calling and grace can individuals form a true community. That is a biblical message much needed in a fractured society of lonely and alienated individuals. We find our identity as persons only in community.

The church is then not simply the *bearer* of the message of reconciliation, in the way a newspaper or a telephone company can bear any message with which it is entrusted. Nor is the church simply the *result* of a message, as an alumni association is the product of a school or the crowd in the theater is the product of the reputation of the film. That men are called together to a new social wholeness is itself the work of God which gives meaning to history, from which both personal conversion (whereby individuals are called into this meaning) and missionary instrumentalities are derived.[11]

The church as product and bearer of the message of reconciliation is discussed elsewhere. Here we note, as Yoder emphasizes, that the church is even more intimately related to God's redemptive purposes. God's work, his "mercy," is to gather a people, not just to save individuals but to create a community. Indeed, on an adequate understanding of human nature, "saving individuals" requires the "social wholeness" of a reconciled community.

Other Biblical Terminology for the People of God

Many of the Old Testament descriptions for Israel are taken over by the New Testament in reference to the new people of God. This fact emphasizes the continuity in the history of salvation, but it also shows a newness, in that a new people is so designated. Even richer blessings are said to be theirs.

(1) *Israel of God.* "Israel" was applied to the nation particularly in its religious aspect (e.g., Pss. 98:3; 121:4), even when it failed to live up to its calling (Pss. 130:7-8; 131:3). Paul affirmed the perspective that physical descent was not sufficient for being a part of God's people: "For not all Israelites truly belong to Israel" (Rom. 9:6-8; cf. Matt. 3:9-10), so he could speak of "Israel after the flesh" (1 Cor. 10:18). Philippians 3:3 comes close to expressing the idea of a "spiritual Israel": "We are the circumcision, who worship in the Spirit of God and boast in Christ Jesus and have no confidence in the flesh." The only explicit use of the phrase "Israel of God" in the New Testament occurs in Galatians 6:16, but whether this refers to the church as Israel, refers to the old Israel, or includes the church as part of Israel is not evident.[12]

11. John Howard Yoder, "A People in the World: Theological Interpretation," in James Leo Garrett, Jr., *The Concept of the Believers' Church* (Scottdale, Penn.: Herald, 1969), p. 258.

12. Walter C. Kaiser, Jr., "Israel as the People of God," in Paul Basden and David S. Dockery, eds., *The People of God: Essays on the Believers' Church* (Nashville: Broadman, 1991), pp. 100-102.

(2) *Royal priesthood.* Israel at the inauguration of the covenant in Exodus 19:6 was designated a "priestly kingdom" (NRSV). This is part of the terminology applied to Christians in 1 Peter 2:9 (cf. 1 Pet. 2:5, "holy priesthood") and in Revelation 1:6. The implications of this description will be elaborated in subsequent chapters.

(3) *Holy nation.* This again is part of the privileged description of Israel in Exodus 19:6 appropriated in 1 Peter 2:9. Holiness, too, will get fuller study later.

(4) *Righteous remnant.* Out of the larger nation of Israel only a few were righteous, only a few were what the whole was meant to be. This became painfully evident in times of national apostasy and rebellion. Although only a remnant survived God's punishments on the people, that remnant became the object of God's favor. Paul quotes Isaiah 10:20-23 and 1:9 in Romans 9:27-28 to show that the small number of Jews who accepted Jesus as the Messiah had a precedent in the earlier history when God kept a faithful remnant out of the whole nation (cf. Rom. 11:1-5, "a remnant chosen by grace"). In the progressive narrowing down of God's people, the remnant was reduced to one man — Jesus, *the Righteous One* (Acts 3:14). Even his disciples fled at the end. In his death and resurrection, the people of God died and rose again, and so there was laid the foundation of a new people of God. Those incorporated into Christ form this new people.

(5) *Covenant people.* According to Romans 9:4, among the privileges of the Israelites was possession of the covenants. Since the theme of covenant and Christians' possession of a new covenant has already been discussed, it need only be noted here, in preparation for the next section, that God's original calling of a people in Abraham finds fulfillment in Christ (Gal. 3:6-29; Rom. 4:13-16; Luke 1:54-55, 72-73; Acts 3:25-26).

Election

The covenant was made with a particular people. God's people is a *chosen race* (1 Pet. 2:9), that is, a chosen group and not chosen individuals. The people of God is an elect people, a chosen people (1 Pet. 1:1 — "elect" and "chosen" are alternative English translations of the same word). For the connection between "people" and "election," note the parallelism in Psalm 105:43, "So he brought his people out with joy, his chosen ones with singing." God chose a people for his own possession

(1 Pet. 2:9); note the connection of election and possession in Psalm 135:4: "For the LORD has chosen Jacob for himself, Israel as his own possession." The idea of Israel, or the church, as a "chosen people" is often offensive, and the doctrine of election has been the subject of much theological controversy through the centuries. Hence, it is important to explore as carefully as we can the biblical doctrine of election.[13]

God's Choice of a People

Most of the references in the Bible to God's election have to do with the choice of a group, corporate election.[14] God chose Abraham, and all who are in him, that is, his descendants. The call of Abraham is first expressed in Genesis 12:1-2, and already the call includes the promise that from him will come a "great nation." The Hebrew word "know" is used in Genesis 18:18-19 for God choosing him and making of him a "mighty nation"; God knew him in a special and intimate way, revealing himself to Abraham and making Abraham and his family a recipient of promises and an instrument of blessing. The choice of Abraham by God continued to be a frequent theme in the Bible. For example, "Because God loved your ancestors, he chose their descendants after them" (Deut. 4:37). "You are the LORD, the God who chose . . . Abraham; and you . . . made with him a covenant to give to his descendants the land" (Neh. 9:7-8). The choice of Abraham included in its provisions his descendants (Isa. 51:2).

God likewise chose Jacob (or Israel) and all in him. The promises to Abraham were repeated to his son Isaac (Gen. 26:24) and his grandson Jacob (Gen. 28:13-14), in each case including the offspring in the blessing. Deuteronomy 7:6 uses the language of election for the people descended from Israel (Jacob): "For you are a people holy to the LORD your God; the LORD your God has chosen you out of all the peoples on earth to be his people, his treasured possession." This election was not

---

13. Especially helpful are H. H. Rowley, *The Biblical Doctrine of Election* (London: Lutterworth, 1950), and William W. Klein, *The New Chosen People: A Corporate View of Election* (Grand Rapids: Zondervan, 1990); note also T. C. Vriezen, *Die Erwählung Israels nach dem Alten Testament* (Zurich, 1953); Seock-Tae Sohn, *The Divine Election of Israel* (Grand Rapids: Eerdmans, 1991); and Christoph Barth, *God with Us: A Theological Introduction to the Old Testament* (Grand Rapids: Eerdmans, 1991), pp. 38-55, who correlates the themes of election, revelation, covenant, and promises.

14. For God's election of a community, not individuals, cf. Hans Küng, *The Church* (London: Burns & Oates, 1968), p. 143.

because of Israel's virtues but an expression of the Lord's love (Deut. 7:8). Choice by God made the people holy, consecrated, or set apart for God, because they became his special possession (cf. Deut. 14:2; Ps. 135:4). Once again, we note that choice of the patriarchs included their descendants (Deut. 10:15; cf. Acts 13:17). Israel was the "chosen people" not because of any merit or virtue of their own but by reason of God's love for and covenant with the patriarchs (Deut. 7:7-11; cf. 9:4-5).

God chose the tribe descended from Levi for the priesthood. "God has chosen Levi out of all your tribes, to stand and minister in the name of the LORD, him and his sons for all time" (Deut. 18:5). Notice the wording of the reminder of this choice in 1 Samuel 2:27-28a, 30. The promise to Levi was a promise to his family. The covenant with Levi held firm, but this did not guarantee that all the Levites would be faithful to their task (Mal. 2:4-9).

God chose David and his descendants for the kingship. This choice involved a rejection of Saul and his family (1 Sam. 13:14). The Lord's promise spoken by the prophet Nathan to David became filled with messianic overtones:

> When your days are fulfilled and you lie down with your ancestors, I will raise up your offspring after you, who shall come forth from your body, and I will establish his kingdom. . . . I will not take my steadfast love from him, as I took it from Saul, whom I put away from before you. Your house and your kingdom shall be made sure forever before me; your throne shall be established forever. (2 Sam. 7:12, 15-16)

An important echo of this election of the family of David is found in Psalm 132:11-12:

> The LORD swore to David a sure oath from which he will not turn back: "One of the sons of your body I will set on your throne. If your sons keep my covenant and my decrees that I shall teach them, their sons also, forevermore, shall sit on your throne."

The choice of David's lineage for the kingship did not prevent individual descendants of his from being rejected from the kingship nor indeed the complete cessation of a human representative in the office after the fall of Judah to the Babylonians. Election was not, therefore, incompatible with the condition, "If your sons keep my covenant and my decrees."

In these cases — Abraham, Jacob, Levi, David — the choice of an individual was the choice of a group, the descendants of the person chosen. The recognition of this divine choice is expressed in the New Testament: "The God of this people Israel chose our ancestors and made the people great during their stay in the land of Egypt" (Acts 13:17).

God's Choice of Christ

Particularly important for the understanding of the nature of the church is God's choice of Christ. Here, too, the election of an individual included a group, the people who belong to him.

The choice of a group in the Old Testament did not guarantee the inclusion of all individuals in that group in the blessings for which they were chosen. There was a progressive narrowing down of God's choice.[15] Not all the children of Abraham were chosen, only Isaac (Gen. 21:12; Rom. 9:7). Of Isaac's twin sons, Jacob was chosen (Gen. 25:23 and Mal. 1:2-3, quoted in Rom. 9:11-13). The words "I have loved Jacob, but I have hated Esau" seem particularly arbitrary and harsh unless one understands Hebrew usage. "To love" is "to choose"; "to hate" is not to choose. These words are not about emotions but are acts of will. Love is elective. Love in biblical language involves choice. Even out of the descendants of Jacob, God chose a remnant (Rom. 11:5, literally, "a remnant according to the election of grace," making a comparison to the times of Elijah in 1 Kings 19:10, 14, 17). Paul's argument in Romans 9:6-29 shows that God has always dealt with people on the basis of promise or call, not flesh or works.[16]

Christ is the "Chosen One" of God. God's choice within Israel finally focused on the One Person. One of the titles given to Jesus as the Messiah was God's "Chosen One." As such, he was acknowledged by the voice from heaven on the mount of transfiguration (Luke 9:35), and by this title the leaders of the Jewish people at the crucifixion defined the significance of Messiah (Luke 23:35).

Jesus is presented in the New Testament as the "seed," the offspring or descendant, of Abraham (Matt. 1:1; Gal. 3:16). He is the true

15. Oscar Cullmann describes an hourglass, speaking of a narrowing down to and expansion from Christ: creation, humanity, Israel, the remnant, *Christ*, the twelve, the church, humanity, the new creation — *Christ and Time* (Philadelphia: Westminster, 1950), pp. 115-116, summarized on p. 178.

16. Daniel J. Harrington, *God's People in Christ: New Testament Perspectives on the Church and Judaism* (Philadelphia: Fortress, 1980), p. 60.

Israel. Matthew 2:15 quotes Hosea 11:1 as referring to Jesus. The prophet's words referred to Israel, the son of God called from Egypt. Matthew could apply the text to Jesus as the embodiment of the nation. What happened to Israel in its calling and election was applicable to Jesus. What was true of Israel in the ideal sense was true of Jesus. In a similar way, Matthew 12:18-21 quotes Isaiah 42:1-4 as fulfilled in Jesus. In some of the "Servant Songs" of Isaiah (see p. 43) the servant is a group, either the nation of Israel or the faithful remnant within the nation (Isa. 41:8-9; 44:1). Matthew can individualize these statements, because Jesus fulfills what was intended by God for the people.

Similarly, Jesus is the son of David (Matt. 1:1; 21:9). His resurrection is presented as the fulfillment of the promise that a descendant of David would occupy his throne (Acts 2:30-31; 13:33, with reference to Ps. 2).[17]

Jesus Christ is God's Chosen One. He is the fulfillment of God's choice of Abraham, Jacob, and David.

God's Choice of Christians

All who are in Christ are included in his election. God chose Abraham (and all in him); God chose Jacob (and all in him); God chose David (and his descendants); God chose Christ (and all in him). Just as all who were "in" Abraham, Israel, or David were included in their election, so it is with Christ. The election of Christ entails the election of those in Christ. The plan of God for Christians is spoken of in the same way as for Christ: foreknown (1 Pet. 1:20; Rom. 8:29), predestined (Acts 4:28; Eph. 1:5: Rom. 8:29-30), and loved before the foundation of the world (John 17:24; Eph. 1:4). God continues to choose a category, a group — believers in Christ. Christians are in Christ as Jews are in Abraham and humanity is in Adam (cf. Eph. 1:10).[18]

17. Jesus was not a Levite, so his priesthood rests on something else — Heb. 7:14-15.

18. Jean de Fraine, *Adam and the Family of Man* (Staten Island: Alba, 1965), p. 249; Ernest Best, *One Body in Christ* (London: SPCK, 1955), chap. 2 on "Adam and Christ." Stig Hanson, *The Unity of the Church in the New Testament: Colossians and Ephesians* (Uppsala: Almquist & Wiksells, 1946), pp. 69-70, describes an "Adam collectivity," an "Abraham collectivity," and a "Christ collectivity." For the church as the "corporate 'body' of the resurrected Christ" and the contrast of the "corporate communities 'in Adam' and 'in Christ,' " see E. Earle Ellis, *Pauline Theology: Ministry and Society* (Grand Rapids: Eerdmans, 1989), pp. 8-17.

Paul wrote to the church of the Thessalonians, "For we know, brothers and sisters beloved by God, that he has chosen you" (1 Thess. 1:4), and then stated the reason for the confidence, "because our message of the gospel came to you not in word only, but also in power and in the Holy Spirit and with full conviction" (1 Thess. 1:5). As in most cases, the emphasis is on the chosenness of the people, not the act of choosing. In a subsequent passage Paul speaks in similar terms:

> We must always give thanks to God for you, brothers and sisters beloved by the Lord, because God chose you as the first fruits for salvation through sanctification by the Spirit and through belief in the truth. For this purpose he called you through our proclamation of the good news. (2 Thess. 2:13-14)

The means of salvation are the Spirit's sanctification and human faith. Election is connected with the gospel in the former passage, with faith in the latter. The faith is the result of the proclamation of the gospel, and both center in Christ. First Peter incorporates similar ideas. The address of the book is to those "who have been chosen according to the foreknowledge of God the Father in sanctification by the Spirit" with the goal of "obedience and sprinkling with the blood of Jesus Christ" (1 Pet. 1:2). They were a "chosen race" (1 Pet. 2:9) and are further defined as "you who believe" (1 Pet. 2:6-7).

Election of Christians is expressly stated to be in Christ:

> [God] chose us in Christ before the foundation of the world. . . . He destined us for adoption as his children through Jesus Christ. . . . In Christ we have also obtained an inheritance, having been destined according to the purpose of him who accomplishes all things according to his counsel and will. . . . In him you also, when you had heard the word of truth, the gospel of your salvation, and had believed in him, were marked with the seal of the promised Holy Spirit." (Eph. 1:4, 5, 11, 13)

The chapter as a whole is anchored in the historical events of Christ's death and resurrection. The same elements found in 1 and 2 Thessalonians and 1 Peter are brought together here: God's choice and predestination, the Holy Spirit, the proclamation of the gospel (the word of truth), and belief. The emphasis is that God's election occurred "in Christ." Those who are "in Christ" through hearing the word of truth, believing in Christ, and being sealed with the Holy Spirit are those who are "holy and blameless" children of God, according to God's love and good pleasure.

The same principles apply to the Johannine teaching. No one comes to Christ unless drawn by God's influence (John 6:44). The manner of that drawing is explained as hearing and learning from the Father (John 6:45; see further in the next chapter on the word of God producing faith). Christ chooses us before we choose him (John 15:16). No one, not even the devil, is able to snatch his followers from him (John 10:28-29), but they are able voluntarily to turn away from him (John 6:70; 13:18).

Christians are elect because they have been called by God and because of an act of his mercy. The church of God was "obtained with the blood of his own Son" (Acts 20:28).[19] The word "obtained" or "acquired" recalls the Greek of Isaiah 43:21, "The people whom I formed for myself so that they might declare my praise."

In Christ, Christians share the election of Abraham. As Christ is the unique "seed" or "offspring" of Abraham (Gal. 3:16), so those who are in Christ become the offspring or children of Abraham: "If you belong to Christ, then you are Abraham's offspring, heirs according to the promise" (Gal. 3:29). As spiritual children of Abraham through Christ, Christians share his election and blessings.[20] They become children of Israel, so that the same corporate or group terms are applied to them (1 Pet. 2:4-5, 9). All this is because of sharing Christ's election. As he is "the Elect One" or "the Chosen One" (see above), Christians are called "the elect ones" (1 Pet. 1:1-2). They share Abraham's and Israel's election by reason of sharing Christ's election. Just as Abraham's and Israel's election was corporate and included their descendants, so God in choosing Christ chose all those who are in him. One was in Abraham by natural birth; one is in Christ by a spiritual birth (Gal. 3:27).

It is not said in scripture that God has chosen Christians individu-

19. Waldemar Schmeichel, "Does Luke Make a Soteriological Statement in Acts 20:28?" *Society of Biblical Literature Seminar Papers 1982* (Chico, Calif.: Scholars Press, 1982), pp. 501-514, correctly translates, "church of God which he obtained for himself by the blood of the one who is his own," but surely the NRSV is correct in identifying God's "own" as his Son and not, as Schmeichel suggests, Paul.

20. It is notable how often "children of Abraham" are contrasted with bondage: to infirmity (Luke 13:11, 16), to sin (John 8:33-36), to elemental spirits of the world (Gal. 3:29–4:9), to the law (Gal. 4:21-31), to the devil and death (Heb. 2:14-16). John Dunnill, *Covenant and Sacrifice in the Letter to the Hebrews* (Cambridge: University Press, 1992), pp. 204-205.

ally.[21] He has chosen those in Christ; he has not chosen who will be in Christ. God elects a community, and the community he chooses now are those in Christ. A person may reject Christ and refuse the election. Israel at Sinai could have refused to be God's people. In some ways, it may be hard to imagine their doing so, yet in a few days they were worshipping the golden calf. Those once chosen may fall away (Rom. 9:6). For example, the Levites were chosen for the priesthood, but individual Levites could be disqualified (Lev. 10:1-2; 1 Sam. 2:27-36); the dynasty of David was forever, but individual descendants could be punished and rejected from the kingship (2 Sam. 7:16; Ps. 89:4, 28-45).

God's Choice of Individuals

Although most of the language of election in the Bible has to do with group election, God in special circumstances chose individuals for a specific task. Thus Moses, who was called to lead Israel out of Egyptian bondage (Exod. 3:1-12), is described as God's "chosen one" (Ps. 106:23). Jesus chose the twelve (John 6:70) to be representatives of Israel. Similarly, the resurrected Lord called and set apart Paul to be an apostle (1 Cor. 1:1; Gal. 1:15). These were chosen for ministry, a service, not for salvation.

Individuals chosen for a task could refuse. Moses argued with God, but then he complied with his call (Exod. 3:13–4:17). King Jeroboam I is a prime example: chosen as king over Israel (1 Kings 11:26-40) but later leading the people into sin and rejected (1 Kings 12:26–13:10). Judas fell away from his apostleship (Acts 1:17, 20). Paul could have said "No" to the risen Lord, although it is hard to imagine his doing so (1 Cor. 9:16).

Election to salvation, in contrast to the election of individuals for a ministry, is "in Christ" (Eph. 1:4).

Calling

"Calling" has already occurred several times in our discussion. No effort is made here to give a complete treatment of the New Testament

---

21. The common understanding of individual election was popularized in western Christian thought by the church father Augustine (d. 430) and became current in Protestantism through the influence of Martin Luther and John Calvin in the Reformation of the sixteenth century.

usage of the word (see more on p. 162 on *The Preaching of the Cross*), but some clarification must be made of the relation of calling and election.

The words for "call" *(kaleō)*, "calling" *(klēsis)*, and "called" *(klētos)* have the same root as the word "church" *(ekklēsia)*; the words for "elect" or "chosen" *(eklegomai, eklektos)* are different. God chooses, but human beings must assent. Human beings can reject the call of God (Isa. 50:2). Here is where there is a difference between calling and election. "Many are called, but few are chosen" (Matt. 22:14). This statement reflects the difference in the standpoint of the one issuing the call (as in Jesus' case) from that of the one answering the call. The one giving the call is acutely aware that not all respond favorably. The one who answers the call, on the other hand, does not think of others who do not respond, and for himself the call is a choice. Morally speaking, election by God comes as something that one cannot refuse. Theoretically, one may be conscious that there is a capacity to refuse, but morally speaking, "necessity is laid upon me" (1 Cor. 9:16). God's call is a choice by him (1 Cor. 1:1-2). Hence, Paul often makes no distinction between the calling and being chosen, and indeed the two are closely related. In both 1 Corinthians 1:26-27 and 2 Thessalonians 2:13-14 call and choice are paralleled with each other as different ways of saying essentially the same thing. Likewise in 2 Peter 1:10 calling and election are equivalent. Compare Revelation 17:14, "Called, chosen, and faithful." The distinctive feature of the New Testament usage is that God's call extends to Gentiles as well as Jews (Rom. 1:5-6; 9:24).[22]

Predestination

Predestination is the theological doctrine designed to explain why some people respond favorably in faith to the call of the gospel and some do not, a question the Bible does not answer. This theological doctrine is different from the biblical doctrine of election. The Greek verb sometimes translated "predestine" or "destine" *(proorizō)* might be better rendered "foreordain." The literal meaning is "to mark off the boundaries in advance." It comes from the word that gives us in English "horizon." The horizon sets the boundaries. The simple verb "to ordain" or "to appoint" is used principally by Luke and by him primarily for God's plans (Luke 22:22; Acts 2:23; 10:42; 17:26, 31). The emphasis

---

22. See further on the calling through the gospel in Chap. 3, pp. 161-163.

is not on how or who but on what God has ordained or appointed. Paul uses the word of Jesus being designated Son of God by the resurrection (Rom. 1:4).

The compound verb "foreordain" occurs six times in the New Testament, all but once by Paul. God decreed before the ages his wisdom revealed in Christ (1 Cor. 2:7). Otherwise, Paul speaks of the "who" that are foreordained. *Proorizō* occurs in Ephesians 1:5 and 11, in connection with election, to refer to Christians, who receive through Christ the privileges of adoption and inheritance. The concern here is with the group (Christians) appointed to receive these blessings. The idea may be compared to setting up in advance the entrance requirements for membership in an organization or the qualifications for a certain position. Even before the foundation of the world, God chose and ordained those in Christ for an exalted status. Paul's other two usages of *proorizō* occur in the next passage to be considered.[23]

Romans 8:28-30

All the key words of our subject occur in this context. Verse 33 refers to "the elect"; they are the ones being talked about. The plurals in the passage should be given their full force. The corporate body of believers is being talked about. Notice the ways in which they are described.

"Those who love God." This phrase echoes Deuteronomy 7:9 (cf. Deut. 6:5 and the quotation in 1 Cor. 2:9) and is an expression for the corporate people of God. Paul repeatedly shifts the emphasis from human beings back to God (cf. Gal. 4:9), and so the priority is with God's love (1 Cor. 8:3). It is his love that evokes the human love toward him. For those who respond to God's initiative with love toward him, God works in all things for (eschatological) good. Those who love God are equivalent to the called (cf. Rom. 1:7, where the called are beloved and saints). The calling is according to God's purpose. Several passages connect the Christian calling with God's purpose (Eph. 1:9; 3:11; 2 Tim. 1:9), and these connect his purpose (salvation) with Christ.

"Whom he foreknew." These are the same as those who love God and are called. "Know" in biblical language means to have a relation-

---

23. Paul J. Achtemeier, *Romans,* Interpretation: A Bible Commentary for Teaching and Preaching (Atlanta: John Knox, 1985), pp. 143-148, is helpful for distinguishing predestination from predeterminism and bringing out the hope that comes from the assurance that the future is in God's hands.

ship with someone (cf. Rom. 11:2 for "foreknew" in reference to Israel).
The *pro-* ("before") gives a strengthened form of the verb and asserts
the priority of God's initiative (cf. Rom. 5:5-8). God determined to have
a relationship with these. There is nothing necessarily pretemporal
stated here: God's historical initiative was in the death of Christ. Foreknowledge is connected with God's foreordination or determination
(Acts 2:23), so it is not merely an intellectual knowledge. The items in
the list are equivalent, and the emphasis is on God's plans for a people.
If a distinction in meaning is to be made, it should be noted that
foreknowledge precedes foreordination.

"Foreordained." As in Ephesians 1, the foreordination is related
to Christ. A future is realized in the present. God marked out this
destiny for his people, and that destiny is to be conformed to Christ.
To be conformed to the image of Christ is to put on a new self that is
restored to the divine image in which we were created (Col. 3:10), an
image that Christ bears (2 Cor. 4:4). The content and purpose of the
divine design is for people to become like Christ. For Christ as the
"Firstborn among many brothers" compare Hebrews 2:10-12. The language continues to speak of a group, this time with the imagery of a
family likeness.

"Called." Verse 30 has the verb form of the noun in verse 28, where
"called" is used, as it frequently is in the New Testament, as virtually
a technical term for Christians. "Called" in secular Greek commonly
meant "invited," but could mean "named," and it is sometimes difficult
to determine which is preferable in a given passage, unless one remembers the express connection on occasion between the call and the proclamation of the gospel (as 2 Thess. 2:13-14). As is common in Paul's
usage, the idea here is not just the invitation but the effective calling
through the preaching of the gospel.

"Justified." The justified are those declared righteous. Justification is always connected in Romans with faith. Compare verse 33,
where the "elect" are justified, even as here the "called" are the
"justified."[24]

"Glorified." Although there is an apparent temporal sequence in
the order of items, that is not the main idea. All the verbs are aorists;
the presence of "glorified" indicates that all should be seen as timeless
aorists.

---

24. Justification is studied further in Chap. 3, pp. 156-158.

Summary on Election

(1) *God elects.* The initiative in salvation is with God. Election is an expression of his love and mercy.

(2) *God elects a community.* God chooses individuals in order to choose a people as his own. The corporate nature of election emphasizes the importance of the church.

(3) *God now elects in Christ.* Election is related to Christ. The elect people are those in Christ, hence the absolute importance of being in Christ. Christians receive their election from Christ's election.

(4) *Election is for service.* Election does not say that the people involved are better than others, nor should it give them a sense of superiority (Deut. 7:7). Election rather is a call to service (Gen. 12:1-3). "You are a chosen race . . . in order that you may proclaim the mighty acts of him who called you" (1 Pet. 2:9). Election is for obedience and purification, "chosen . . . to be obedient to Jesus Christ and to be sprinkled with his blood" (1 Pet. 1:2). Thus will be achieved the purpose of God for those called "to be conformed to the image of his Son" (Rom. 8:29). This involves a call to suffering, as Christ suffered (1 Pet. 2:21; cf. 1:11). In the words of 2 Timothy 2:10, "Therefore I endure everything for the sake of the elect, so that they may also obtain the salvation that is in Christ Jesus, with eternal glory" (cf. Col. 1:24).[25] Election is more a matter of service and suffering than of status, although it does carry with it distinct privileges.

(5) *Election means separation and consecration.*[26] God, as a holy God, separated Israel from the other peoples to be his own and so expected them to make distinctions between clean and unclean (Lev. 20:24-26). God's presence made them holy and demanded holiness. Similarly, the New Testament connects the theme of election with holiness (1 Thess. 1:4 and 4:1-8; 1 Pet. 1:1-2, 15-16).

(6) *Election has a conditional element.* The election of those in Christ is unconditional, but whether one stays in Christ is conditional. One's

---

25. "Suffering is not the regrettable cost of holding positions which merit salvation; it is participation in the victory of Christ over the powers of this age. If one sees the cross of the Christian, as the New Testament does, as the reflection of and participation in the character of the saving work of Christ, then one does not seek it, but when it comes neither does one consider it simply as a matter of having been providentially chosen for a hard time." 2 Tim. 2:10 shows that election does not guarantee salvation.

26. T. J. Deidun, *New Covenant Morality in Paul* (Rome: Biblical Institute Press, 1981), pp. 16-17.

position in the chosen people can be lost. "Be all the more eager to confirm your call and election, for if you do this, you will never stumble" (2 Pet. 1:10). One may compare the history of the Israelites as God's chosen people. They remained the chosen nation, but many individuals lost their privileges. A person can fall away from or reject the status of being elect (Gal. 5:4, "you have fallen away from grace"; Heb. 3:12, "brothers and sisters . . . may . . . turn away from the living God"; Heb. 6:4, "those who have shared in the Holy Spirit . . . and then have fallen away").

(7) *Election is an assurance.* Romans 8:28-30, like the whole chapter, is a consolation and encouragement to Christians. The conclusion drawn from the affirmations about God's foreknowledge and predestination declares, "What then are we to say about these things? If God is for us, who is against us?" (Rom. 8:31). We may be weak and suffering, rejected and persecuted (Rom. 8:35-36), but "in all these things we are more than conquerors" (Rom. 8:37), because nothing "will be able to separate us from the love of God in Christ Jesus our Lord" (Rom. 8:39).

Implications of Being the People of God

(1) The church must be separated from the conduct characteristic of the world. Since you are God's people (2 Cor. 6:16), therefore you must live as God's people (2 Cor. 6:17) in order truly to be God's people (2 Cor. 6:18).[27]

(2) To be the people of God gives a sense of importance and purpose to life. On the other hand, the basis of that choice — the free grace of God in Christ — removes any basis for pride and contributes to a humble acknowledgment of dependence on God.

(3) The church can never be merely a free association of like-minded religious individuals.[28] It is not a democracy. It is always dependent on and defined by the free choice and call of God. The church has corporate peoplehood. Any people (if it really is a people) has its own character. The church is a people whose character is determined by the call and choice of God and by the Christ in whom it is called.

27. Hans Küng, *The Church* (London: Burns & Oates, 1968), p. 122.
28. Hans Küng, *The Church* (London: Burns & Oates, 1968), p. 126.

Persons sometimes try to make a congregation into their own image. Instead they need to be fashioned into the image of Christ.

(4) There are false (and potentially sinful) principles of unity around which people organize themselves. Persons find their sense of identity from citizenship in a nation, being of the same race, sharing a certain occupation or economic status, adhering to a particular political doctrine, participating in a certain social class, sharing the same level of educational attainment. The church is intended to transcend all of these bases of unity. True peoplehood is to be found in God through Jesus Christ (Gal. 3:28; Col. 3:11).

> The political novelty which God brings into the world is a community of those who serve instead of ruling, who suffer instead of inflicting suffering, whose fellowship crosses social lines instead of reinforcing them. This new Christian community in which the walls are broken down not by human idealism or democratic legalism but by the work of Christ is not only a vehicle of the gospel or fruit of the gospel; it is good news. It is not merely the agent of mission or the constituency of a mission agency. This is the mission.[29]

THE BODY OF CHRIST

"You are the body of Christ." (1 COR. 12:27)

The church is the people of God in Christ Jesus. It is the people of God because of now being in Christ. "The being of the people of God is grounded only in its God, and the being of the Christian community only in Jesus Christ as its Lord."[30] There was a "people of God" from the call of Abraham; there is a "body of Christ" only after the resurrection. The Christian knows God in Jesus Christ; he or she comes to God through Christ. The church arises through encounter with Christ; it begins with the experience of salvation in Christ (see Chap. 3).

29. John Howard Yoder, "A People in the World: Theological Interpretation," in James Leo Garrett, Jr., *The Concept of the Believers' Church* (Scottdale, Penn.: Herald, 1969), p. 274.

30. Karl Barth, *Church Dogmatics* IV.3 (Edinburgh: T. & T. Clark, 1962), p. 753.

"In Christ" and "With Christ"

Paul often uses the expression "in Christ" (and "in him" or "in whom," referring to Christ). The phrase can carry various nuances of meaning in different contexts,[31] and some of these are of special importance for the theme of the church in her relationship with Christ. "In Christ" sometimes carries the idea of incorporative union: "There is therefore now no condemnation for those who are in [union with] Christ Jesus" (Rom. 8:1); "So if anyone is in Christ [united to Christ], there is a new creation" (2 Cor. 5:17). "So that in him [incorporated into the person of Christ] we might become the righteousness of God" (2 Cor. 5:21). Or the thought may be the mode by which something is true: "For all of you are one [by being] in Christ Jesus" (Gal. 3:28). The locative idea may be present in the description of "the churches of Judea that are in Christ" (or, we could translate, "the churches of Christ that are in Judea" — Gal. 1:22). Or, sphere of reference may be the thought there, as it is in the description of individuals in Romans 16:7, "They were in Christ [were Christians] before I was." These examples show an intimate relation with Christ that goes beyond an ordinary association with him and suggests the theme of incorporation into him. Thus in some passages "in Christ" becomes virtually the same as "in the church."[32]

Death does not break this relationship of being in Christ ("the dead who are in Christ" — 1 Thess. 4:16). Paul describes the condition of "those who have died in Christ" (1 Cor. 15:18) as being "with Christ" (Phil. 1:23) or "with the Lord" (1 Thess. 4:17; 5:10; 2 Cor. 5:8). This state of being with Christ is the result of sharing in his experience: dying with him, rising with him, and being glorified with him (Rom. 6:3-4; 8:17).[33]

---

31. Ernest Best, *One Body in Christ* (London: SPCK, 1955), chap. 1 on "In Christ" and chap. 3 on "With Christ"; M. J. Harris, "Prepositions and Theology in the Greek New Testament," in Colin Brown, ed., *The New International Dictionary of New Testament Theology,* Vol. 3 (Grand Rapids: Zondervan, 1978), p. 1192.

32. Rudolf Bultmann, *Theology of the New Testament* (New York: Scribner's, 1951), Vol. 1, p. 311.

33. Robert C. Tannehill, *Dying and Rising with Christ: A Study in Pauline Theology* (Berlin: A. Töpelmann, 1967), studies the "with Christ" expressions. He finds two major groups of texts: passages about dying with Christ as a decisive past event, and those about dying with Christ as a present experience, especially in suffering (p. 6). Note his introductory words, "If the believer dies and rises with Christ, as Paul claims, Christ's death and resurrection are not merely events which produce benefits for the believer, but also are events in which the believer himself partakes" (p. 1).

The death and resurrection of Christ forms the basis, so that participation in Christ's death and resurrection determines the new life, gives it structure, and enables those who die with Christ to rise with him at his coming.[34]

The identification of his people with Christ comes to expression in many places in the New Testament (see p. 120 on Heb. 2). So close is that identification that what is done to Christ's people is done to him (Matt. 25:35-45), to persecute them is to persecute him (Acts 9:4-5), and to sin against them is to sin against Christ (1 Cor. 8:12). Even as Old Testament passages about the people are applied in the New Testament to Christ (pp. 46, 82), so a passage about the Davidic king (the Messiah) is extended to the church of the Messiah (Acts 4:25-29): the action of the authorities against Jesus continued in the threats against his disciples. The act of "baptism into Christ" (Rom. 6:3; Gal. 3:27) provides a basis for the identification of those baptized with the body of Christ (1 Cor. 12:13), so much so that the church can be identified with Christ (1 Cor. 1:13). This idea of a close relationship, indeed a union, of Christians with Christ is best known from the description of the church as the body of Christ.

Passages Using the Imagery of the Body of Christ

There has been much discussion of the origin and significance of the phrase "the body of Christ."[35] I find the most likely background to be the Old Testament and Jewish idea described as "corporate personality" or "extended personality"[36] (see pp. 43-44 and the discussion of cor-

34. Ibid., pp. 40-41, 75, 130.

35. L. S. Thornton, *The Common Life in the Body of Christ*, 3rd ed. (London: Dacre, 1950), Part II; John A. T. Robinson, *The Body: A Study in Pauline Theology* (London: SCM, 1952), pp. 49-72; Ernest Best, *One Body in Christ* (London: SPCK, 1955); Claude Welch, *The Reality of the Church* (New York: Scribner's, 1958), chap. 5; Eduard Schweizer, *The Church as the Body of Christ* (Richmond: John Knox, 1964); C. F. D. Moule, *The Origin of Christology* (Cambridge: University Press, 1977), pp. 47-96 on the "Corporate Christ"; E. Käsemann, "The Theological Problem Presented by the Motif of the Body of Christ," *Perspectives on Paul* (Philadelphia: Fortress, 1971), pp. 102-121; P. Bonnard, "L'église, corps de Christ," in *Anamnesis: Recherches sur le Nouveau Testament* (Geneva, 1980), pp. 145-158; Gosnell L. O. R. Yorke, *The Church as the Body of Christ in the Pauline Corpus: A Reexamination* (Lanham, Md.: University Press of America, 1991).

36. See p. 43, nn. 55-57 and on God's choice of Christians (p. 81, n. 18) for

porate election, pp. 79-81, 82, for the relevance of this idea for the figure of the body of Christ). If the adoption of the terminology of body for the concept was suggested to Paul by Greek usage (and this, too, is likely), the content was still supplied by Jewish ways of thinking, and Paul's use of the language of body fits the Old Testament ideas of a group derived from and finding their identity in one person. As Israel was both the forefather of the people and the whole people itself and Adam was both a person and humanity, so Jesus included all of his believers in himself.[37]

In this way of thinking, the "body of Christ" is more than simply a figure of speech or image, but expresses a real relationship. It is a "root metaphor," that is, it describes the basic character and nature of the church. The body finds its wholeness in Christ, and Christ has his fullness in his people. Members of the body are all interrelated. On the other hand, the "body of Christ" as a way of expressing "corporate personality" does not describe an ontological reality nor does it confer on the church an organic union with Christ. Although the body can never be separated from Christ, it often acts in ways that do not correspond to what the "body of Christ" ought to do: witness the Corinthian church, the first church to whom Paul invokes the "body" language. Their conduct hardly accords with what would be expected if the "mystical body of Christ" is considered in some sense as identical with Christ himself. The church, according to Paul's language, must never be separated from Christ; nor must it ever be confused with Christ.

Body of Christ in Romans and 1 Corinthians

Paul initially — in 1 Corinthians 12 and Romans 12 — approached the body imagery in order to deal with the plurality of individual members who together are part of a corporate whole. Even here I think Paul did not start with the Hellenistic idea of many parts yet

---

bibliography relating this idea to the figure of the body of Christ. Even if one rejects "corporate personality" as the background to Paul's language, there is certainly a strong corporate use of body language by Paul — John Ziesler, *Pauline Christianity*, rev. ed. (Oxford: University Press, 1990), pp. 49-65, who suggests that the corporate language conveys the thought of living under Christ's power and authority (p. 65).

37. Eduard Schweizer, *The Church as the Body of Christ* (Richmond: John Knox, 1964), p. 53.

having a likeness to an organism but with the Hebraic idea of one (Christ) who is the basis of the many. The picture of a body permits him to start with oneness, for unity is his concern. In Romans 12:6-8, he addresses individual believers on the following basis: "For as in one body we have many members, and not all the members have the same function, so we, who are many, are one body in Christ, and individually we are members one of another" (Rom. 12:4-5). Here Paul uses the human body succinctly to illustrate unity out of plurality, diversity of function, and the mutual bonds tying one to another.

In writing to the Corinthians, Paul affirmed that the bodies of Christians are "members of Christ" (1 Cor. 6:15). This makes inconsistent the taking of the body and using it for sexual immorality (1 Cor. 6:16). In a comparable way to the sexual union making a man and woman "one flesh," so being joined to Christ makes a person "one spirit with him" (1 Cor. 6:17).

The same themes as are found in Romans 12 are more fully developed in the lesson on unity later in the letter to Corinth (1 Cor. 12:12-27). Here Paul elaborates on what it means to be united to Christ as he expresses concern for the community as a whole: "For just as the body is one and has many members, and all the members of the body, though many, are one body, so it is with Christ" (1 Cor. 12:12). Once more, Paul starts with the human body, a unity but made up of diverse members. But instead of saying, as in Romans 12:5, that Christians are one body "in Christ," here he says that "Christ" is like the body. Christ is the whole; we are the parts. Unity is once more presented first. The body is one. This oneness includes diversity. Each member of the body has a different function, each function is necessary, and each part needs the other. Since the body "does not consist of one member but of many" (1 Cor. 12:14), no member should feel inferior (1 Cor. 12:15-19). Yet these "many members" are "one body" (1 Cor. 12:20), so there is no excuse for being conceited (1 Cor. 12:21-24). Rather, instead of dissension there should be mutual care for one another (1 Cor. 12:25-26). It should be noted that as the illustration is developed in this passage, the head is not Christ but simply another member of the body (1 Cor. 12:21). This accords with the initial affirmation that Christ is like a body — he is compared to the whole body, not to a part of it. The passage is summarized in a similar statement: "Now you are the body of Christ and individually members of it" (1 Cor. 12:27).

The Head and the Body in Colossians

Like Romans and 1 Corinthians, Colossians and Ephesians identify the church with the body of Christ (only now expressly saying "church" and not merely "we" or "you"), but unlike them these later writings call Christ the "head" of the body. Even in this regard, as we shall see, there is a different application of the language of "head." The same imagery may be used to teach different lessons as needed on different occasions.

When we read "head," we tend to think of the physiological function and anatomical importance of a body's head. Or, we think in figurative terms of a loose relationship, as when we speak of a "head of state" or "head of a business." Neither approach sets us on the right track for understanding Colossians and Ephesians. In Jewish corporate personality, the head stood for the whole. That provides the link between the language of 1 Corinthians and that of Colossians. "Head" also has other meanings that seem to provide the specific content of what is said in Colossians and Ephesians.

Colossians repeats the theme of unity, referring to the "one body" (Col. 3:15) in which the Christian calling occurs. This is presumably the church, in view of the theme of mutual harmony and peace as well as the other passages now to be mentioned, but it may be noted that reconciliation occurs by reason of Christ's fleshly body (Col. 1:22). The theme of mutual care is given a special application in Paul's statement that his sufferings complete "what is lacking in Christ's afflictions for the sake of his body, that is, the church" (Col. 1:24).

The distinctive emphasis of Colossians is set forth in the hymn in chapter 1:15-20, which functions in the letter to proclaim the superiority of Christ over the cosmic powers. Concerning his status it is said: "He is the head of the body, the church; he is the beginning, the firstborn from the dead, so that he might come to have first place in everything" (Col. 1:18). In Hebrew and in Greek, one meaning of the words for "head" was "beginning, origin, or source." (English has a similar usage in the expression "head waters" of a river.) That meaning seems to be the idea in Colossians 1.[38] All things were created in Christ (Col. 1:15-17). He is the "firstborn" in relation to creation; from him derived all of creation. Moreover, he is the beginning point of redemption, "the firstborn from the dead." Other persons who are delivered from death

---

38. C. F. Burney, "Christ the ARXH of Creation," *Journal of Theological Studies* 27 (1925): 160-177.

derive from him and his resurrection (cf. 1 Cor. 15:20, "firstfruits"). Christ is the head of the church, as he is the head of creation, in the sense of being its "source." He is the vital principle from whom the church derives its existence and meaning, and this is so by reason of his resurrection. This interpretation of the head gains support from the other reference to the church as a body in Colossians: "Not holding fast to the head, from whom the whole body, nourished and held together by its ligaments and sinews, grows with a growth that is from God" (2:19). Growth of the body derives from its head, the source here of sustenance as well as of life.

The church has its point of origin in Christ. It takes its rise from the saving work of Christ. The crucifixion made him the foundation of the church (pp. 60-61). His death was an act of grace which brought salvation and created a saved people. The resurrection, which is the topic of Colossians 1:18, made him the beginning point of a new people, those who share his victory over death. Wherever God acts for salvation of human beings, there is the church (see further pp. 135-137). The saving act of Christ constituted the church and continues to be constitutive of the nature of the church.

The remaining use of the word "head" in the letter (Col. 2:10) may contain the idea of preeminence or authority, and that is the meaning of headship in Ephesians.

The Head and the Body in Ephesians

Colossians emphasizes the preeminence of Christ, Ephesians the importance of the church. Even with the exalted view of the church in Ephesians, the superiority of Christ in this book is even greater. One meaning of the word "head" was first in rank, leader, chief, main part. And that meaning coincides with what is said in Ephesians about Christ as head of the church.

The statements in Ephesians about the church as the body of Christ repeat some of the same ideas found in Colossians and 1 Corinthians. There is "one body" (Eph. 4:4).[39] Whereas 1 Corinthians

---

39. Koshi Usami, *Somatic Comprehension of Unity: The Church in Ephesus* (Rome: Biblical Institute Press, 1983), studies Ephesians more from the standpoint of unity than of the body. A better treatment of the theme of unity is given by Stig Hanson, *The Unity of the Church in the New Testament: Colossians and Ephesians* (Uppsala: Almquist & Wiksells, 1946), pp. 121-161.

addresses the problem of dissension within the congregation, Ephesians deals with the unity of Jews and Gentiles. In the one body occurs the reconciliation of Jews and Gentiles to God (Eph. 2:16); therefore, "the Gentiles have become fellow heirs, members of the same body, and sharers in the promise in Christ Jesus" (Eph. 3:6). Christ saves the body (Eph. 5:23). Christ's loving care demonstrates that "we [the church — vs. 29] are members of his body" (Eph. 5:30). The church grows as the whole body works properly (Eph. 4:16); only now Christ as the head not only is the source (as in Colossians) of growth but also is the goal of the growth (Eph. 4:15). The purpose of ministry is "body building" (Eph. 4:12).

The statements about the headship of Christ point to his superiority, his leadership in relation to the church. "Christ is the head of the church" (Eph. 5:23), and his treatment of the church is the model of leadership for husbands in relation to wives (Eph. 5:23-30). As head of the church, he is the standard toward which the body grows (Eph. 4:15-16). The distinctive passage in Ephesians about Christ as head of the body exalts his authority in all things:

> God put his power to work in Christ when he raised him from the dead and seated him at his right hand in the heavenly places, far above all rule and authority and power and dominion, and above every name that is named, not only in this age but also in the age to come. And he has put all things under his feet and has made him the head over all things for the church, which is his body, the fullness of him who fills all in all. (Eph. 1:20-23)

Christ is the principle of authority for the church (Ephesians) because he is its creative source (its beginning point and origin — Colossians). A corollary of his position is the church's dependence and subordination. Interpreters are divided whether "fullness" has the active sense that the body is that which fills or completes Christ by being the mode of his working in the world or has the passive sense that the body is filled by the all-sufficient Christ. The latter may be preferred, but the two ideas are interrelated. The church as being filled with the divine fullness is the means through which that fullness is manifested to the world. Either interpretation gives tremendous importance to the church and emphasizes the closeness of its relationship to Christ, and neither interpretation must be seen as detracting from Christ's position as "head."

These passages about the church as the body of Christ indicate that the church is more than the sum of its human parts. The church has a prior reality in Christ, and that is the spiritual, heavenly dimension of its being. Christ exists before the church, and the church comes to existence through incorporation into him. The church exists as Jesus Christ exists, but he does not exist only as the church exists.[40] As an earthly entity, the church is the people; but it is a people with a divine origin in the call of God, a supernatural basis in the redemptive work of Christ, and a spiritual life from the Holy Spirit (see pp. 103ff.).

Titles Shared by Christ and His Body

Those whom Christ saves he calls his brothers and sisters (Heb. 2:11 — see further pp. 119-121, on the family of God). They become his people. Incorporation into Christ makes his people what he is. To be in Christ, to be the body of Christ, means to share his blessings and his status. Christ is the whole, yet he is in each of the parts: "Christ is all and in all" (Col. 3:11). What this involves may be seen in the following verse, where three of the messianic titles of Jesus are also ascribed to his people: "As God's chosen ones, holy, and beloved" (Col. 3:12).[41] These descriptions apply to members of the church because of their identification with Christ.

Chosen

As developed in the preceding unit, Christ is God's "Chosen One," or the "Elect One" (Luke 23:35; 1 Pet. 2:4). This was the significance of being the Messiah. "Chosen" was a designation of Israel as the servant of the Lord (Isa. 42:1) and was applied to angels (1 Tim. 5:21). In the plural, the word is used for Christians (Rom. 8:33; Titus 1:1; 1 Pet. 1:1-2; Rev. 17:14) and as a singular adjective only for Christians in a collective sense (1 Pet. 2:9). This pattern of using the singular for Christ and the plural for his people

---

40. Karl Barth, *Church Dogmatics* IV.3 (Edinburgh: T. & T. Clark, 1962), pp. 754-755.

41. The Prayer of Azariah in the Greek additions to Daniel has in parallelism "Abraham your beloved, . . . Isaac your servant, and Israel your holy one" (Dan. 3:35). The use of "servant" instead of Paul's "chosen" in parallel with "beloved" and "holy" is interesting in view of what is said below about the titles of Jesus and in the preceding chapter about Jesus as the "servant."

has only one exception in the New Testament, for Rufus (Rom. 16:13), and there the word may carry the connotation of "the choice or excellent" Christian rather than the theological meaning of God's election.

Holy

As "elect" and "chosen" translate one Greek word that can be used as an adjective or a noun, so the same is true for "holy" and "saint." "The Holy One" (the "Saint") is one of the messianic titles (cf. Acts 3:14; 4:27). In John 6:69, it is the equivalent of Peter's confession of Jesus as the "Christ" in Matthew 16:16, and in Mark 1:24 it is the title by which the evil spirit acknowledged Jesus. "Holy One" is a designation of God in the Hebrew scriptures (Isa. 1:4 and frequently in Isaiah; Hos. 11:9). "Holy ones" in the plural is a common description of Christians in the New Testament (Rom. 1:7; 16:15; 1 Cor. 1:2; 2 Cor. 1:1; Eph. 5:3). It was a designation of angels in Judaism (Ps. 89:5, 7 and in the Qumran literature; cf. 1 Thess. 3:13; 2 Thess. 1:10: Col. 1:12; Jude 14). The particular background of New Testament usage appears to be Daniel 7:13-14, 18, 21, 25, 27, where the "Son of Man" and the "saints of the Most High" appear in close association (as discussed on pp. 42-43, 45-46). The "holy ones," or "saints," according to the Jewish background was a designation for the community. Unlike later Christian usage, which can speak of "Saint Paul," "Saint Peter," etc., "saint" does not appear in the New Testament in the singular as a title or as an individual designation.[42]

Beloved

"Beloved" is a designation of Jesus that occurs in connection with his title as "Son of God" (at his baptism and transfiguration — Matt. 3:17 and 17:5 with parallels; cf. also Luke 20:13; 2 Pet. 1:17). It had the same significance as "Chosen One," and these are alternative readings in manuscripts of Luke 9:35. Although in reference to Jesus the adjectival form *agapētos* is more common, the equivalent participial form *agapemenos* is used (Eph. 1:6),[43] as it was for Israel in the Greek Old Testament

---

42. Phil 4:21-22 is not really an exception, for each individual is part of the holy community. Cf. Gerhard Delling, *Worship in the New Testament* (London: Darton, Longman and Todd, 1962), p. 20 n. 2, " 'The saints' [in the salutations of the epistles] . . . stands for the Church as a social entity and not for an aggregation of individuals."

43. The two words occur together in Isa. 5:1-2.

(e.g., Deut. 33:26). "Beloved" (in both singular and plural) occurs most often in the New Testament in the language of Christians for one another, but in reference to Christians as God's "beloved ones" it is always in the plural with reference to the group, whether in the adjectival form (Rom. 1:7; Eph. 5:1) or the participial form (Rom. 9:25-26; Col. 3:12; 1 Thess. 1:4; 2 Thess. 2:13).

The related and important shared title of "Son" or "Child" will be discussed below in connection with the family imagery applied to the church (pp. 116-119).

Importance of These Shared Titles

These common titles indicate that Christ's people share his messianic dignity. The church is the messianic people. The church as Christ's body becomes attached to him, incorporated into him. Thereby they become what he is — elect, holy, and beloved. What is said of him is true of his people. But these things are not true of the people's own nature; they are true only in a derivative sense, only through incorporation into Christ. Therefore, these things are true only collectively, not individually. The church is an elect race, a holy nation, a beloved people (cf. 1 Pet. 2:9). This status is a result of grace and comes about through union with Christ.

To summarize the significance of these terms for understanding the nature of the church: (1) they emphasize the collective concept of the church — these things are true of the people, not as individuals but as part of the group; (2) they emphasize the relation to Christ — they are true only in union with him as the source of the status; and, (3) following from this fact, they show the derivative nature of the church's status — it is the result of God's grace in Christ.

The Name "Christian"

The name by which the people of Christ have come to be commonly called — "Christians" — occurs only three times in the New Testament (Acts 11:26; 26:28; 1 Pet. 4:16).[44] The term is a Latin loanword constructed according to a common pattern from a proper noun plus the ending -ianus (Greek, -ianos), meaning a follower or adherent of the

---

44. E. J. Bickerman, "The Name of Christians," *Harvard Theological Review* 42 (1949): 109-124; H. B. Mattingly, "The Origin of the Name Christiani," *Journal of Theological Studies* n.s. 9 (1958): 26-37.

person named. The same word formation occurs in the New Testament for the "Herodians," members of the party of Herod, or supporters of Herod. The *Christiani*, therefore, are the "party of Christ," the followers or adherents of the Christ. The normal Greek construction, "those of Christ," is common (1 Cor. 1:12; 15:23; Gal. 5:24). The word "Christian" occurs primarily in contexts having to do with legal relations with outsiders, and seems to be especially a term, if not given by outsiders, used by them to distinguish the followers of Jesus from others. They were "Messiah's people," the followers of the Christ they were always talking about. The means by which the name "Christian" came into use in Acts 11:26 — whether given by pagans (not likely by Jews) or chosen by Christians (whether through Paul and Barnabas or others) — is disputed, but Luke's use of the verb often used for a divine oracle *(chrēmatizo)* may indicate that he wanted to suggest that, whoever first employed the name, its use carried divine approval or authorization.

Christians not only wear the name of Christ, they also share his anointing. Since Christ means "the Anointed One," identification with Christ includes identification with his anointing by God with the Holy Spirit (2 Cor. 1:21-22; 1 John 2:20, 27). Before turning to what this association with the Holy Spirit means for the nature of the church, we will draw together some implications of the church's being the body of Christ.

Implications of Being the Body of Christ

(1) The church is where Christ is, where he is preached and confessed, where he is working and obeyed. Christ is the creating and sustaining force of the church.

(2) The reverse side of this is that Christ is present in the church. Such is the closeness of solidarity of Christ with his people that they are assured of his presence in their corporate life.

(3) Christ is greater than the church. He is not confined to the church; he is not necessarily where a "church" is. Christ is the only indispensable "part"; indeed, he is the whole.

(4) Christ is the central reality of the church. The church is made up of those who take their life from him. Christ's people find meaning and existence from him.

(5) There is no salvation outside of Christ (Acts 4:12; Eph. 5:23).

(6) The church is a people, nothing more or less, but a particular

kind of people — the saved or redeemed people, the people of God in Christ.

(7) The church develops in obedience to Christ (Eph. 4:15). It is always subordinate to him, in "all things" (Eph. 1:22f.).

(8) There is only one body (Rom. 12:4-5; 1 Cor. 12). This means that within the body there is to be unity and no discord (1 Cor. 12:25), and there is to be sympathetic interest and mutual care (1 Cor. 12:26). Nearly all the references to the church as a body have the theme of unity.

(9) Christ's presence in the world is represented by his people. The church continues the ministry of Christ in the world (see Chap. 5). The different functions in the body represent a diversity contributing to unity (1 Cor. 12:28-30). Each member has a contribution to make to the growth of the whole (Eph. 4:16).

(10) The church is important (Eph. 1:23; 2:16; 5:23), as important as one's body is to oneself. The imagery emphasizes the social solidarity and priority of the group. Even as one cannot understand the human body by starting with the individual parts, so one cannot understand the church by starting with the individual Christians.[45] This imagery coincides with the other descriptions of the church in calling attention to its "corporate" nature.

THE COMMUNITY OF THE HOLY SPIRIT

"The communion of the Holy Spirit." (2 COR. 13:13)

The phrase "communion [fellowship] of the Holy Spirit" (2 Cor. 13:13; cf. Phil. 2:1) would ordinarily mean "participation in the Holy Spirit."[46] Even if not the grammatical sense intended, we may appropriately think of a fellowship established by the Holy Spirit. There is a theological sense in which the Holy Spirit creates a community, for the common participation in the Holy Spirit brings people together in community.[47]

45. Eduard Schweizer, *The Church as the Body of Christ* (Richmond: John Knox, 1964), p. 63.

46. See the discussion on pp. 364-373 and the bibliography in the notes there.

47. For 2 Cor. 13:13 having the sense "the community which arose through the common participation in the Holy Spirit," see Josef Hainz, *Koinonia: "Kirche" als Gemeinschaft bei Paulus* (Regensburg: Friedrich Pustet, 1982), pp. 47ff.; cf. George Panikulam, *Koinonia in the New Testament: A Dynamic Expression of Christian Life* (Rome: Biblical Institute Press, 1979), pp. 58-73.

The church is a fellowship created by the Spirit, and it is that because all share in the Spirit as the gift of Christ to his people. The church is a Spirit-filled community.[48] The common life of the body of Christ is the life of his Spirit.

Various experiences or common interests or shared principles may create human communities.[49] The roots are ultimately in impersonal objects. Where there is a personal interest, the tie is no stronger than the human spirit. The bond indeed may be a strong one, so that even if the members do not get along with one another as individuals, they still stay together because of something they have in common. The church, however, is a community, a fellowship, through the divine Spirit. Hence, in its very essence it is a divine creation, not a human product.

The Old Testament Expectation

Chapter 1 noted how the prophetic promise of a new covenant was bound up with the working of God's Spirit in creating a new heart and new spirit in his people (Isa. 59:20-21; Ezek. 36:25-27). The Old Testament included an expectation of a new order of things in an age of the Holy Spirit (Joel 2:28-32; Isa. 32:15).

In the New Testament, there is a strong sense of fulfillment. The age of the Holy Spirit (which is the age of the Messiah) had arrived, and the promises of the prophets were now realized. "In order that in Christ Jesus the blessings of Abraham might come to the Gentiles, so that we might receive the promise of the Spirit through faith" (Gal. 3:14; cf. Eph. 1:13, "the promised Holy Spirit"). The "newness" of the new covenant is particularly in the gift of the indwelling Holy Spirit.

God's glory *(kabod)* tabernacled among his people at the tent of meeting constructed in the wilderness (Exod. 40:34-38). The Holy Spirit was certainly present and active in the Old Testament.[50] What then was

---

48. Hans Küng, *The Church* (London: Burns & Oates, 1968), pp. 162-179, on "The Church of the Spirit"; C. Norman Kraus, *The Community of the Spirit: How the Church Is in the World,* rev. ed. (Scottdale, Penn.: Herald, 1993).

49. William G. MacDonald, "A People in Community: Theological Interpretation," in James Leo Garrett, Jr., *The Concept of the Believers' Church* (Scottdale, Penn.: Herald, 1969), pp. 145-147.

50. D. A. Tappeiner, "Holy Spirit," in G. W. Bromiley, ed., *International Standard Bible Encyclopedia,* rev. ed. (Grand Rapids: Eerdmans, 1982), 2.730-732 and bibliography, p. 742; Eduard Schweizer, *The Holy Spirit* (Philadelphia: Fortress, 1980), pp. 10-28.

different under the new covenant? At the risk of being overly precise, we may make two distinctions. First, in the Old Testament, there were Spirit-filled leaders but no Spirit-filled community. The Spirit came to certain leaders and selected individuals but not to all, but the Holy Spirit is promised to all in the Christian age (Acts 2:38-39). When Joshua became upset that Eldad and Medad were prophesying in the camp of Israel, Moses replied, "Are you jealous for my sake? Would that all the LORD's people were prophets, and the LORD would put his Spirit on them!" (Num. 11:26-29). What Moses wished for and Joel predicted (Joel 2:28-29) was declared fulfilled in Acts 2:16ff.: God poured forth his Spirit on "all flesh." Perhaps we can go further and make a second distinction. When the Spirit came to individuals under the old covenant, the visitation was temporary. The typical expression was that the Spirit "came upon" someone (Num. 24:2; Judg. 11:29; 14:6; 1 Sam. 10:10; Mic. 3:8). In contrast, the promise of the new covenant was for the abiding possession of the Spirit dwelling in the people and empowering them to live according to God's way (Rom. 8; see further p. 108).

The Holy Spirit in the Ministry of Jesus

The new age of the Holy Spirit was heralded in the ministry of Jesus.[51] The Holy Spirit was active throughout the life and work of Jesus, and he fully possessed the Holy Spirit. As the Messiah sent by God, Jesus "speaks the words of God, for he [God] gives the Spirit without measure" (John 3:34).

The Spirit in the Life and Work of Jesus

(1) The birth of Jesus was accomplished by the Holy Spirit (Matt. 1:18, 20).

(2) The Holy Spirit came on Jesus at his baptism (Matt. 3:16).

(3) The Holy Spirit launched Jesus' ministry (Luke 4:1, 14) and set the character of that ministry (Luke 4:18, quoting Isa. 61:1).

(4) Jesus' miracles, especially his control over evil spirits, were performed by the Holy Spirit (Matt. 12:28).

(5) The resurrection was by the Holy Spirit (Rom. 1:4; 8:11).

51. Raniero Cantalamessa, *The Holy Spirit in the Life of Jesus: The Mystery of Christ's Baptism* (Collegeville, Minn.: Liturgical, 1994).

(6) Jesus gives the Holy Spirit. As fully possessing the Spirit, Jesus as the Messiah is able to give the Spirit. John the Baptist baptized with water, but Jesus baptizes with the Holy Spirit (Mark 1:8). Since the Spirit is primarily the gift of the messianic age, only when Jesus completed his messianic work in the death and resurrection was the Spirit bestowed on others. During his ministry, Jesus gave his disciples power (Mark 6:7) but not the inner presence of the Spirit. By the resurrection, he became a life-giving Spirit (1 Cor. 15:45; John 7:38-39). In his capacity as Messiah, Jesus bestowed the Spirit on his disciples (John 20:22; Acts 2:33).

The Relation of Christ and the Spirit

Since Christ gives the Spirit, the Spirit remains secondary to Christ. The Spirit is dependent and derivative in his ministry and work. Note the descriptions of the Spirit: "Spirit of Christ" (Rom. 8:9), "Spirit of Jesus Christ" (Phil. 1:19), "Spirit of his [God's] Son" (Gal. 4:6). Particularly important for understanding the mission of the Holy Spirit is the following promise of Jesus:

> When the Spirit of truth comes, he will guide you into all the truth; for he will not speak on his own, but will speak whatever he hears, and he will declare to you the things that are to come. He will glorify me, because he will take what is mine and declare it to you. All that the Father has is mine. For this reason I said that he will take what is mine and declare it to you. (John 16:13-15)

The Spirit has nothing to reveal and nothing to say but what Jesus taught. The purpose of the Holy Spirit is to glorify Christ, not to glorify himself, not to glorify a messenger, not to glorify an experience. Everything the Spirit has is received from Christ. The identification of Christ and the Spirit becomes complete in 2 Corinthians 3:17, "The Lord is the Spirit."[52]

From the beginning, the church has had trouble from those claiming to act and speak from the Holy Spirit and so has had need to "test

---

52. John Ziesler, *Pauline Christianity*, rev. ed. (Oxford: University Press, 1990), pp. 46-48, has a good treatment of the relationship between Christ and the Spirit in Paul. More questionable is his suggestion that "Lord" in 2 Cor. 3:17 is a reference to the "LORD" in Exod. 34:34, the passage to which Paul makes allusion in the context. See also Gerald F. Hawthorne, *The Presence and the Power* (Dallas: Word, 1991).

the spirits" (1 John 4:1). That passage proceeds to offer an important criterion for testing the spirits: they are to be evaluated by conformity to the apostolic message. "Whoever . . . listens to us" knows "the spirit of truth" (1 John 4:6; see further p. 308, on prophets). The "word of God" (Eph. 6:17) is the Spirit's instrument in convicting the world of "sin, righteousness, and judgment" (John 16:8) and in testifying to Jesus. The description of the ministry of the Holy Spirit in John 16:13-15 provides a foundational test for determining whether something is indeed from the Spirit of Christ. The activity of the Spirit must always accord with the ministry, personality, and purposes of Christ. If a spirit is indeed the Spirit of Christ, it will always work in harmony with the ministry of Christ. We know the life and teachings of Jesus fully from the Gospels and the writings of his apostles. This may not answer all problems that arise, but Christ himself does give an objective criterion for testing the spirits.

The Holy Spirit in the Church

The Spirit is the life of the church. If the church is the body of Christ, the Spirit of Christ is the life of the body. Just as a body without the spirit is dead, so without the Holy Spirit there would be no church, no community at all. Possession of the Spirit indicates membership in the people of God, and participation in the Spirit is the basis of the corporate life. The Spirit gives life and sustains life to the body. The very words for Spirit in Hebrew *(ruach)* and Greek *(pneuma)* mean "wind" or "breath." No wonder then that there is an association in the scriptures of the Spirit with life (John 6:63; 1 Pet. 3:18; 1 Cor. 15:45).

The church, however, was not first a body into which God poured the Spirit as the living content. No, it was the coming of the Spirit that created the church,[53] as seen in the preceding chapter (p. 63; cf. Acts 2 and 11:15). As Jesus was born of the Holy Spirit, so was the church.

The Spirit is not like a contractor who builds a house and leaves it for new owners. Indeed, unless the Holy Spirit takes up residence and fills the vacuum left when sin is forgiven and evil driven out, other evil spirits will fill a person's life (Luke 11:24-26). So with the church.

---

53. "The Spirit is not what animates an already existing church, but the Spirit makes the church to be" — John D. Zizioulas, *Being as Communion: Studies in Personhood and the Church* (London: Darton, Longman and Todd, 1985), p. 132.

The Spirit continues to give life to the church, and that life is the life of Christ. The church is the community of the Spirit.

As the Spirit descended on Jesus at his baptism (Luke 3:21), filled him, and led him (Luke 4:1), so his experience is reproduced in a lesser degree in his church. The Spirit comes in baptism (Acts 2:38) and rests on his people (1 Pet. 4:14), fills them (Eph. 5:18), and leads them (Rom. 8:14). "As Jesus received the Spirit of God, so we received from Jesus what he received."[54]

The Indwelling of the Holy Spirit

Whereas Paul typically speaks of believers as "in Christ" (see p. 92), he speaks of the Spirit as in us.[55] This indwelling of the Holy Spirit is both individual and corporate. Paul instructed the Corinthians about the indwelling of the Spirit in the community — "Do you not know that you [plural] are God's temple and that God's Spirit dwells in you [plural]?" (1 Cor. 3:16) — and about the indwelling of the Spirit in the individual bodies of Christians — "Do you not know that your [plural] body [singular] is a temple of the Holy Spirit within you, which you have from God?" (1 Cor. 6:19). The plural "you" in 3:16 may be used distributively of individuals or may be a reference to the collective whole. "You are in the Spirit, since the Spirit of God dwells in you. Anyone who does not have the Spirit of Christ does not belong to him. . . . If the Spirit of him who raised Jesus from the dead dwells in you, he who raised Christ from the dead will give life to your mortal bodies also through his Spirit that dwells in you" (Rom. 8:9-11). "And because you are children, God has sent the Spirit of his Son into our [or your] hearts" (Gal. 4:6). "Guard the good treasure entrusted to you, with the help of the Holy Spirit living in us" (2 Tim. 1:14). The Holy Spirit is in the community because he is in the individual members, but it is also true that the Spirit is in the church and one receives the Spirit through connection with the Spirit-filled community. All Christians have the Spirit, and individuals have the Spirit only in the life of the community. We turn now to enumerate some of the works of the Spirit in the corporate activities of the church.

54. L. S. Thornton, *The Common Life in the Body of Christ*, 3rd ed. (London: Dacre, 1950), p. 137.

55. C. F. D. Moule, *The Phenomenon of the New Testament* (Naperville, Ill.: Allenson, 1967), p. 26.

The Spirit in the Life of the Church

The Spirit is present in and energizes many activities in the church.

(1) *Baptism.* "For in the one Spirit we were all baptized into one body" (1 Cor. 12:13). "He saved us . . . through the water of rebirth and renewal by the Holy Spirit" (Titus 3:5). The Holy Spirit is at work in baptism. He imparts the new life of Christ and becomes the bond uniting Christ with Christians and Christians with one another (see further pp. 186-188).

(2) *Sanctification.* "You were washed, you were sanctified, you were justified in the name of the Lord Jesus Christ and in the Spirit of our God" (1 Cor. 6:11). As "Holy" Spirit, his work is to make holy, to sanctify (2 Thess. 2:13; 1 Pet. 1:2). That begins in baptism and is carried forward in the Christian life.

(3) *Christian growth.* The Spirit produces the fruit of holiness (Gal. 5:22-23). In the natural world, growth is often slow and imperceptible, and it requires the presence of certain conditions. So it is in the spiritual realm: growth is often unspectacular and requires the right growing conditions, but it is the result of the influence of God's Spirit responded to in faith amidst the circumstances of life.

(4) *Love.* The Holy Spirit brings God's love to human hearts (Rom. 5:5; Gal. 5:22). The Spirit is the Spirit of God (Rom. 8:9), and God is love (1 John 4:16), so the close association between the Spirit and love is to be expected. Love is the highest and greatest of God's gifts (1 Cor. 13:13). Where the Spirit is, there is love.

(5) *Joy.* The Holy Spirit inspires joy in those who receive the word of the gospel (1 Thess. 1:6).

(6) *Morality.* The indwelling Holy Spirit serves as the basis of Christian moral conduct (1 Cor. 6:9-20; see further p. 356).

(7) *Serving God.* All Christian service to God is done in the Spirit and is made possible by the new life of the Spirit (Rom. 7:6).

(8) *Worship.* Christian worship is now performed "in the Spirit" (John 4:23-24; Phil. 3:3) and is the offering of "spiritual sacrifices" (1 Pet. 2:5; see pp. 222-225). Specific acts of corporate worship are offered "in the Spirit" or "with the spirit" (1 Cor. 14:15).

(9) *Prayer.* Prayer is offered "in the Spirit" (Eph. 6:18; Jude 20). The presence of the Spirit within makes possible the address to God as "Abba, Father" (Gal. 4:6). "The Spirit intercedes" when "we do not know how to pray as we ought" (Rom. 8:26).

(10) *Preaching.* The Holy Spirit is active in the preaching of the

gospel (1 Thess. 1:5). He inspired the prophets (1 Pet. 1:11),[56] and the word of God is his sword in the warfare with evil (Eph. 6:17; cf. Rev. 1:16).

(11) *Leadership and ministry.* The Holy Spirit qualifies and calls persons for leadership and ministry in the church (Acts 20:28; 1 Cor. 12:4, 28; see pp. 291ff.).

(12) *Guarding the truth.* The indwelling Holy Spirit makes possible the defense and safekeeping of the apostolic teachings deposited in the church (2 Tim. 1:14).

(13) *Enduring suffering.* It is by the Holy Spirit that Christians are able to meet persecution and suffering (1 Pet. 4:14).

(14) *Creating unity.* The Spirit creates reconciliation and unity (Eph. 2:14-18, 21-22; 4:3-4) and this out of diversity (1 Cor. 12). The Spirit is the principle of unity in the church (see further pp. 401-402).

(15) *Spiritual power.* The above points may be summed up in the thought that the Holy Spirit of God is the source of spiritual strength for living the Christian life (Eph. 3:16). All these things represent but the first fruits of the Spirit (Rom. 8:23), for the power of the Spirit will result ultimately in resurrection (Rom. 8:11).

We have emphasized what the Spirit does and so what participation in the Spirit means. The Spirit is God's gift and assistance to his people in becoming what he wants them to be. In Chapter 6, we will look at the fellowship itself, or community created by this participation in the Spirit. Sharing in the Holy Spirit, who is the Spirit of Christ, creates the Christian fellowship.

Charismata

Modern Pentecostal and Charismatic movements have called attention to the *charismata* ("grace gifts"). Except for 1 Peter 4:10, the word occurs only in the Pauline writings, and his usage is rather different from what modern usage might lead one to expect. Any free gift of God can be termed a *charisma* (singular). Paul uses the plural *(charismata)* for the privileges associated with God's call of Israel (Rom. 11:29) and the singular for the salvation from death and eternal life in Christ Jesus (Rom. 5:15-16; 6:23). A physical deliverance from death can be called a *charisma* (2 Cor. 1:7), as can the power of living celibate (1 Cor. 7:7).

56. For the argument that these are Christian prophets, see Duane Warden, "The Prophets of 1 Peter 1:10-12," *Restoration Quarterly* 31 (1989): 1-12.

Paul through his personal presence was able to mediate a spiritual gift for the strengthening of others (Rom. 1:11). As here, there are several passages where the nature of the *charisma* is left indeterminate. Timothy's gift (1 Tim. 4:14; 2 Tim. 1:6) may have been something miraculous (see below), but may have been his function as an evangelist recognized by the church (see pp. 311, 330). The question is worth raising because the lists of gifts in Romans 12:6 and 1 Peter 4:10-11 include rather "ordinary" human abilities as being themselves special benefits from God to be used for the good of his people.

These verses leave only 1 Corinthians 12 for separate comment. Paul had already indicated in 1 Corinthians 1:7 the rich diversity of gifts in the Corinthian church, and the usage of 1 Corinthians 7:7 shows that he is not thinking exclusively or even primarily of "supernatural" manifestations (whatever evaluation the Corinthians themselves may have put on things). Only in 1 Corinthians 12:4-11 are the *charismata* brought into relation to the Spirit, and here the Spirit is the instrument of God and Christ (1 Cor. 12:28-30). The gifts are to be used for the common good (1 Cor. 12:7; see p. 295). The greater gifts (1 Cor. 12:31) are those that build up the community (1 Cor. 14; see p. 245). The "more excellent way" (1 Cor. 12:31) involves the abiding qualities of faith, hope, and love (1 Cor. 13:13), not the temporary gifts (1 Cor. 13:8-12; see further below).

Miraculous Manifestations

The list of activities of the Spirit in the church given on pages 109-110 represents what the Spirit does for all believers. The central thrust of New Testament teaching about the work of the Holy Spirit clearly has these spiritual qualities and activities in view. When Paul speaks of the Holy Spirit apart from problems associated with claims to possess the Spirit, he gives prominence to the ethical role of the Spirit.[57] Human attention, however, tends to focus on the more spectacular ecstatic and miraculous manifestations of the presence of the Spirit.

It is easy to gain the impression that the Bible is a book of miracles. A closer examination reveals that miracles came only at particular times in biblical history. The miracles cluster at significant moments of rev-

57. T. J. Deidun, *New Covenant Morality in Paul* (Rome: Biblical Institute Press, 1981), pp. 53-58.

elation and crisis in the history of God's saving deeds. The time of the Exodus and the subsequent wilderness wandering and conquest of Canaan, when Israel was delivered and shaped into a nation and the law of Moses was revealed, was one period when "signs and wonders" abounded. Another cluster of mighty deeds occurs in connection with the crisis for Israel presented by the challenge of Canaanite Baal worship during the time of the prophets Elijah and Elisha. And, of course, the greatest number of miracles are associated with the brief public ministry of Jesus and the early years of the church.

Recognition of the occasions of miraculous activity points to the purpose miracles served in the divine economy. They did not call attention to themselves but pointed to God's saving activity and his word of revelation. That purpose is clearly stated in a passage that places God's word of salvation in the ministry of Christ in relation to Israel's history:

> Therefore we must pay greater attention to what we have heard, so that we do not drift away from it. For if the message declared through angels was valid, and every transgression or disobedience received a just penalty, how can we escape if we neglect so great a salvation? It was declared at first through the Lord, and it was attested to us by those who heard him, while God added his testimony by signs and wonders and various miracles, and by gifts of the Holy Spirit, distributed according to his will. (Heb. 2:1-4)

"Signs and wonders" repeats the standard description of God's acts in connection with the Exodus (e.g., Ps. 135:9).[58] They along with the miracles and distributions of the Holy Spirit served in the new age of salvation as God's personal testimony, attesting the messenger (Acts 2:22) and the message (Mark 16:20; Acts 14:3).[59]

The miraculous gifts of the Holy Spirit functioned to confirm the word of salvation spoken by the Lord and his apostles. It was not promised that they would endure, as faith, hope, and love would (1 Cor. 13:8-13). The Spirit is still at work doing the things listed in the preceding section. These are the important and permanent works of the Spirit on behalf of God's people in Christ.

58. Jürgen Moltmann, *The Church in the Power of the Spirit* (New York: Harper & Row, 1977), p. 39.

59. For the association of miracles ("power") with the preached word note Rom. 15:19; 1 Cor. 2:4; 1 Thess. 1:5.

Implications of Being the
Community of the Holy Spirit[60]

(1) The church as the community of the Spirit exists wherever there are two or more believers gathered around the Lord Jesus. Where the Lord is, there is his Spirit (cf. 2 Cor. 3:17).

(2) The church as the community of the Spirit practices spiritual unity. We are united because we possess the same Spirit (1 Cor. 12:13). Legal, political, or institutional unions are ineffective without the unity of the Spirit.

(3) The church as the community of the Spirit preserves individuality while denying both individualism and collectivism. Individualism that has its roots in selfishness is destroyed; individualism rooted in possession of particular gifts and graces (1 Cor. 12) is developed as long as these are used for the common good. Much of modern individualism does not distinguish self-consciousness from the Holy Spirit, and collectivism absolutizes the group at the expense of both the individual and the Holy Spirit. Under the guidance of the Spirit, the individual develops for the service of the whole.

(4) The church as the community of the Spirit recognizes the equality of believers, since they all possess one and the same Spirit (1 Cor. 12:13). The diversity of function in the body does not exalt one part above others.

(5) The church as the community of the Spirit is the foundation for Christian ethics and discipline (1 Cor. 6:1-20; Gal. 6:1).

(6) The church as the community of the Spirit has but One Teacher (Matt. 23:10). The churches must hear what Jesus, through the Spirit, says to them (Rev. 2–3). Christ is the source of revelation and truth (John 14:26; 16:13-15). The spiritually minded will recognize his teachings (1 Cor. 2:12-16; 14:37). All human "teachers" must appeal for verification of their message to the same Spirit who resides in those taught (1 John 2:27).

(7) The church as the community of the Spirit must test the many spirits at large in the world (1 John 4:1). Not every claimed manifestation of the Spirit is the work of the Holy Spirit of God.

(8) The church as the community of the Spirit does not deny the

---

60. This section is adapted from William G. MacDonald, "A People in Community: Theological Interpretation," in James Leo Garrett, Jr., *The Concept of the Believers' Church* (Scottdale, Penn.: Herald, 1969), pp. 162-164.

material aspects of life but puts the priority on spiritual things (John 6:63).

THE FAMILY OF GOD

*"The household of God,
which is the church of the living God."*   (1 TIM. 3:15)

We turn now to explore the nature of the church in terms of certain human experiences — the family, agricultural activities, and construction work. These, as the first three descriptions, also relate, respectively, to God, Christ, and the Holy Spirit.

Various Uses of Family Imagery

"House" referred not only to the dwelling place but also to the dwellers in the building, the "household" or "family." This usage for the church is found not only in the text verse cited above but also in 1 Peter 4:17, where the "household of God" is "us," and Hebrews 3:2-6, where Moses is contrasted as a faithful servant in God's house with Jesus as the Son over God's house, "whose house are we" who hold firm our hope.[61] Indeed, "household" appears to be the primary imagery for the church in Hebrews.[62] The members of this household (Eph. 2:19) share a common faith (Gal. 6:10).

According to this family imagery for the church, God is the Father over his house; indeed, he is the source and pattern of human fatherhood (Eph. 3:14-15). Although there is a sense in which he is "Father of all" (Eph. 4:6; cf. Acts 17:28), the usual biblical language speaks of him as Father in relation to his spiritual children (John 1:12-13; 1 John 2:29; 3:9; 4:7; 5:1, 4, 18). For them there is access to him as Father in prayer (Matt. 6:6-9; Rom. 8:15). To them he gives his love (1 John 3:1), his fatherly provision (Matt. 7:7-11), and his fatherly discipline (Heb. 12:4-11).

---

61. *Oikos* could be used for the temple, a community, or the created world, and Heb. 3:2-5 may draw on these varied meanings before making the application to God's people in verse 6 — Harold W. Attridge, *The Epistle to the Hebrews* (Philadelphia: Fortress, 1989), pp. 108-111. Cf. Halvor Moxnes, ed., *Constructing Early Christian Families* (London: Routledge, 1997).

62. John Dunnill, *Covenant and Sacrifice in the Letter to the Hebrews* (Cambridge: University Press, 1992), pp. 34-36.

In the description of the church as a household, the overseers of the church function as stewards (Titus 1:7; 1 Tim. 3:5; see p. 323), administering its affairs on behalf of the Father, who is head of the household.

Another use of family imagery is to describe the relationship of God with his people as that of husband and wife. This imagery occurs frequently in the prophets for God and Israel (e.g., Jer. 2:2; Ezek. 16:8-14; Hos. 2:1–3:1). The Old Testament often spoke of Jerusalem as "virgin daughter Zion" (2 Kings 19:21; Isa. 23:12; 37:22; Lam. 2:13). The bridal imagery is appropriated in the New Testament as a description of Christ as the bridegroom and the church as his bride.[63] The thought is anticipated in the analogy used by John the Baptist (John 3:29) and Jesus himself (Mark 2:19) concerning Jesus as the bridegroom. This teaching is most extensively developed in Ephesians 5:22-33, where the loving care and leadership of Christ is matched by his people's response of submission and desire to please him. Reference is made to the nuptial bath and the wedding vows (Eph. 5:26) in order to bring out the purity of the church (Eph. 5:27). The relation of Christ and the church is presented as the model for human marriage. The bridal imagery is employed elsewhere to stress the church's purity (2 Cor. 11:2) and her sense of expectation in preparation for the eschatological consummation of union with Christ (Rev. 19:7-8; 21:2, 9). The nuptial imagery expresses the lordship of Christ over the church, a lordship based on and expressed in love.

A different use of the family imagery is Paul's reference to himself as a "father" to his converts (1 Cor. 4:15), whom he cared for like a father (1 Thess. 2:11; like a nurse in 2:7) and whom he described as his children (1 Tim. 1:2; Titus 1:4). This is descriptive language. Jesus forbade the use of "Father" as an official designation or honorary title for human beings (as also that of "Rabbi" or "Teacher" — Matt. 23:8-9).[64]

For those who must give up their earthly family in order to follow Jesus or to proclaim the gospel, he makes the promise that in this life they will receive a hundredfold — "brothers and sisters, mothers and children" (Mark 10:29-30). These are the "brothers and sisters" in the family of God by reason of possession of the same Spirit of God (Rom. 8:14-16; Gal. 4:5-7).

63. Claude Chavasse, *The Bride of Christ: An Inquiry into the Nuptial Element in Early Christianity* (London: Faber and Faber, 1940); Richard A. Batey, *New Testament Nuptial Imagery* (Leiden: E. J. Brill, 1971).

64. Gerhard Lohfink, *Jesus and Community* (London: SPCK, 1985), pp. 45-48.

Christ as Son and Christians as Children

In the language of Hebrews 3:6 referred to above, Christ is the Son over his Father's house. Although the actual phrase "Son of God" does not occur in the Old Testament, the idea of sonship in relation to God is applied to Israel (Exod. 4:22-23; Deut. 14:1; Hos. 11:1), angels (Job 1:6; Ps. 29:1), and the king (Ps. 2:6-9). All three meanings occur in the New Testament, with the first and third being especially significant. Jesus as the embodiment of Israel (Matt. 2:15) and as the royal Messiah (Matt. 16:16; Mark 14:61; Luke 1:32) was preeminently "Son of God."[65] The association of the title "Son of God" with "Christ" (Matt. 16:16; 26:63; Luke 4:41; John 11:27; 2 Cor. 1:19; cf. the equivalent term for Christ in Luke 9:35 and the variant readings in John 1:34), although this is not true of all uses of the title "Son of God" in the New Testament, is perhaps due to "son of God" being a royal status in the Old Testament (Pss. 2:6-9; 89:3-4, 26-27; 1 Chron. 17:13; 22:10; cf. the equivalence of "Son of God" and "King of Israel" in John 1:49). This designation is one of the important titles that Jesus shared with his people. (1) Sometimes the imagery used is that of adoption: although Jesus is Son of God by nature, Christians are children of God by adoption (Gal. 4:4-6).[66] (2) Sometimes the imagery is that of becoming children of God by a spiritual new birth (John 1:12-13; cf. 3:3-5). (3) Or again, to follow the imagery of the body of Christ explored above, through incorporation into Christ his people become what he is, in this case "sons of God" or "children of God" (Gal. 3:26-27).

With reference to divine sonship, the Johannine literature uses the

---

65. Brendan Byrne, 'Sons of God' — 'Seed of Abraham' (Rome: Biblical Institute Press, 1979). Oscar Cullmann, The Christology of the New Testament (Philadelphia: Westminster, 1959), pp. 273-275, questions its use in Judaism for the Messiah. For the title see also Ferdinand Hahn, The Titles of Jesus in Christology (New York: World, 1969), pp. 299-346; James D. G. Dunn, Christology in the Making (Philadelphia: Westminster, 1980), pp. 12-64.

66. Brendan Byrne, 'Sons of God' — 'Seed of Abraham' (Rome: Biblical Institute Press, 1979), pp. 215-216, concludes that huiothesia in Paul has to do with status rather than an initiating act and so can be better translated "sonship" than "adoption," and thus corresponds to my third category. James M. Scott, Adoption as Sons of God: An Exegetical Investigation into the Background of Huiothesia in the Pauline Corpus (Tübingen: Mohr, 1992), defends the translation "adoption" (the normal Greek and Roman meaning) and argues, against those who have denied this meaning, that Jewish society did have a comparable concept if not with the same legal understanding as Greeks and Romans.

word "Son" only for Jesus. Unlike Paul, who sometimes uses "sons" for Christians (as Gal. 3:26), 1 John confines the language of "Son" to Christ and uses a different word, "children," for Christians. The same limitation of "Son" occurs in the Gospel of John.[67]

The language of sonship is applied to Jesus especially in connection with his obedience to the Father and acceptance of the suffering that this entailed. Satan recognized Christ as Son of God in the temptations (Matt. 4:3, 6) when he sought to divert Jesus from the mission he assumed at his baptism (Matt. 3:15-17). Peter's confession that Jesus was Son of God was followed by the teaching of the necessity of his suffering (Matt. 16:16, 21). The centurion's confession that Jesus was God's Son comes at the cross (Matt. 27:54; Mark 15:39). There seems to be more than an allusion to Jesus himself as Son in the parable of the wicked tenants, who killed the landowner's son (Matt. 21:33-41). Jesus' address to God as "Abba," Father, is preserved in the account of his prayer of submission in Gethsemane (Mark 14:36). Whereas for the Gospel writers, Jesus must suffer because he is Son, for the author of Hebrews, who starts with his exalted status, the obedient suffering is in spite of the sonship: "Although he was a Son, he learned obedience through what he suffered" (Heb. 5:9).

As in Matthew 16:17 the sonship was a matter of special revelation, so in other passages it reflected a unique closeness of Jesus with the Father so that he was able to reveal him (Matt. 11:25-27; cf. John 14:8-10). It was considered remarkable when there was something about the Father's plans that the Son did not know (Matt. 24:36; Mark 13:32).

Jesus was declared "Son of God" at his birth, a birth accomplished by the Holy Spirit (Luke 1:35). His sonship was declared again at his baptism, when the Spirit came on him (Luke 3:21-22). Moreover, the title "Son of God" is especially associated with Jesus' resurrection and exaltation (Mark 14:61-62; Acts 13:33-34; 1 Thess. 1:10), perhaps under the influence of 2 Samuel 7:12-14.[68] He was designated "Son of God" by the resurrection through the Spirit (Rom. 1:4). The association of all

67. John 12:36 is not really an exception, for "sons of light" is a Semitic expression that uses "sons of" to refer to a group who share a certain characteristic and is not the normal Greek usage.

68. Marinus De Jonge, *Jesus, The Servant-Messiah* (New Haven: Yale, 1991), p. 73. This text may also be important for the association of the resurrection with Jesus' kingship — see pp. 25, 27. Note, too, that Ps. 2:7, quoted at the baptism in the Synoptic accounts, is applied to the resurrection in Acts 13:33 (cf. Heb. 5:5; 1:5).

three of these moments with the Holy Spirit connects the title "Son of God" with the anointing that made him Messiah (Acts 10:38).

Jesus' people become children of God by the Holy Spirit, whether one thinks in the imagery of a natural birth ("born of the Spirit," John 3:3-9) or of an adoption ("the Spirit that makes us sons," Rom. 8:15 [NEB]). This sonship is accomplished by faith and declared at baptism, when the Spirit is received (Gal. 3:26-27; 4:6). The designation of Christians as children of God is not associated in the New Testament with natural birth,[69] but baptism is a new birth (John 3:5), so the association of Jesus' sonship with his birth and his baptism is combined in the case of Christians with their baptismal new birth. Baptism is also a resurrection (Col. 2:12). Moreover, at the resurrection, Christians receive a status more literally of "sons of God." This was one of the designations of angels in the Old Testament (Job 1:6; Ps. 29:1); to be known as "sons of God," therefore, is an indication of the exalted status of those who are in Christ. In explaining life in the resurrection, Jesus says that those resurrected "are like angels and are children of God, being children of the resurrection" (Luke 20:34-36). Just as the baptismal new birth is accomplished by the Holy Spirit, so the resurrection will be by the Holy Spirit (Rom. 8:11; cf. 8:23 where the resurrection is likened to an adoption).[70] Thus the experience of Christians parallels that of Christ.

Paul uses the same verb "sent forth" *(exapostellō)* to describe God's sending of his Son (Gal. 4:4) and his sending of the Spirit (Gal. 4:6). God sent his Son so that we might become sons and sent the Spirit to the sons to make the sonship effectual.[71]

Paul's argument in Romans 9:6-29 shows that several terms prominent in our study — the "called," "seed," "people," and "sons" — are essentially equivalent.[72] By sharing in Jesus' life and status, Christians are privileged to address God in the same way as Jesus did, as "Abba, Father" (Mark 14:36; Rom. 8:15; Gal. 4:6).

Sons are heirs. Thus in the parable of the wicked tenants the son of the landowner is designated the heir, and the tenants kill him in

---

69. The subject of infant baptism is discussed on pp. 195-201.

70. Brendan Byrne, *'Sons of God' — 'Seed of Abraham'* (Rome: Biblical Institute Press, 1979), p. 99, takes "spirit of adoption [sonship]," contrary to the NRSV, as "the Holy Spirit that goes with or pledges sonship."

71. L. S. Thornton, *The Common Life in the Body of Christ*, 3rd ed. (London: Dacre, 1950), pp. 115-121.

72. Brendan Byrne, *'Sons of God' — 'Seed of Abraham'* (Rome: Biblical Institute Press, 1979), pp. 130-138.

order to obtain the inheritance (Mark 12:6-7). An inheritance to be received is a normal corollary of the language of sonship or children. The children of God are "heirs of God and joint heirs with Christ" (Rom. 8:15-17). The child of God is an heir of God (Gal. 4:5-7). This is because of identification with God's Son himself (1 Cor. 1:9). Christians possess the inheritance because of their incorporation into Christ.

Brothers and Sisters of Christ

Jesus declared that his true family was not his mother and brothers according to the flesh, but "whoever does the will of my Father in heaven is my brother and sister and mother" (Matt. 12:46-50). This is an important declaration concerning his spiritual family and an important description of what characterizes that family. Human children have the nature of their parents and tend to imitate them. The same is true of the spiritual family. "To do the will of the Father in heaven" is to express his nature (1 John 2:29; 3:2, 9; 5:1-2, 18) and to imitate his love (Eph. 5:1-2).

"The brothers" (the plural includes "sisters") became a common designation for the Christian community. The nonliteral use of the term for fellow members of a religious community was already well established by New Testament times, both among Jews (cf. Ps. 22:22, where in the Greek translation "brothers" and "church" appear in parallelism) and other peoples. The term identified a sense of family solidarity among those not related by blood. I count thirty occurrences in Acts alone for "brothers" as a designation for Christian believers acting in their corporate capacity, making this Luke's favorite designation for the church. The letter cited in Acts 15:23 epitomizes the broadened Christian usage, for "brothers" is used not only for the community of Jewish believers in Jerusalem but is applied also to the communities of Gentile origin in the region of Antioch. Even leaving aside references to individual persons in the singular as a spiritual brother, the religious use of "brothers" in the plural for the new spiritual family of God surfaces in all the remaining books of the New Testament except Titus, 1 Peter (which has "brotherhood — 2:17; 5:9), and 2 John. Paul, in his heaviest concentration of the terminology, refers to brothers in 1 Thessalonians nineteen times.[73] The

73. K. Schäfer, *Gemeinde as "Bruderschaft": Ein Beitrag zum Kirchenverständnis des Paulus* (New York: Peter Lang, 1989).

usage is in all an impressive testimony to the prevalent sense of closeness and unity in the early church.

The solidarity of Christ with his people is the theme of Hebrews 2:5-18.[74] He became like us in every respect (Heb. 2:17) so that we might become like him. He took on our nature of flesh and blood (Heb. 2:14) and underwent our suffering (Heb. 2:10, 18). Through his suffering and death, he destroyed the power of death (Heb. 2:14-15), made atonement for the sins of the people (Heb. 2:17), and is qualified to help those who experience temptation (Heb. 2:18). This was his grace to human beings. Through his humanity, he calls his people his brethren. The sanctifier and the sanctified have the same Father (Heb. 2:11). Therefore, he identifies his people as of the same family, his brothers and sisters (Heb. 2:11). As "God is not ashamed to be called their God" (Heb. 11:16, and thus they are "the people of God"), so "Jesus is not ashamed to call them brothers and sisters" (the family of God, or people of Christ). The author quotes Isaiah and the Psalms as the words of Jesus. The people of Christ are the children whom God has given to him (Heb. 2:13 = Isa. 8:18). Especially noteworthy for the topic of this book is the identification of the brothers and sisters with the church assembled in praise of God (Heb. 2:12 = Ps. 22:22). Jesus praises God "in the church." He proclaims the name of God to his brothers and sisters.

One of the designations applied both to Christ and to his people is "firstborn," a description related to several of the themes emerging from this section of our study. Christ in his status as "Son of God" had the rank of firstborn in relation to all of God's creation (Col. 1:15; Heb. 1:6). The title "firstborn" is applied to him especially in relation to the resurrection, "the firstborn from the dead" (Col. 1:18; Rev. 1:5; cf. the imagery of firstfruits in 1 Cor. 15:20). "Firstborn" was a designation of Israel as the people of God (Exod. 4:22; cf. in a different sense Heb. 11:28) and of the Davidic king (Ps. 89:27). God's predestining activity in Christ was so that "he might be the firstborn among many brothers" who were conformed to his image (Rom. 8:29). Thus his people are called the "firstborn ones" (Heb. 12:23), sharing in the rights of inheritance (cf. Heb. 12:16) that belong to the Firstborn One (Heb. 1:6).[75] The thought here may be that they are "firstborn" as sharing in his resur-

---

74. Geoffrey W. Grogan, "Christ and His People: An Exegetical and Theological Study of Hebrews 2:5-18," *Vox Evangelica* 6 (1969): 54-71.

75. Harold W. Attridge, *The Epistle to the Hebrews* (Philadelphia: Fortress, 1989), p. 375.

rection, a suggestion strengthened not only by the description "enrolled in heaven" but also by their association with the angels.

AGRICULTURAL IMAGES

"You are God's field."   (1 COR. 3:9)

The Vine and the Vineyard

The thoughts of solidarity and union between Christ and his people, which the author of Hebrews expresses in the language of sharing the same flesh and blood, and which Paul expresses under the image of the body, the Gospel of John expresses under the imagery of the vine (John 15:1-11). Psalm 80:8-18 compares Israel to a vine planted by God and describes her history in terms of what happened to a vine. Thus we have another example of the New Testament applying to Jesus what refers to the nation in the Old Testament. Jesus identifies himself as the vine (John 15:1, 5), the whole vine. As Jesus is the body with many members in 1 Corinthians 12:12, 27, so here he is the vine with many branches (John 15:2, 5). "Branches" perhaps says too much; we might better translate "twigs." Jesus is the whole; his disciples are part of him. He exists without his disciples, but his disciples cannot exist apart from him (John 15:2, 4-6). All the twigs together do not make a vine; only as joined to Christ and receiving nourishment from him will they bear fruit. Christ includes within himself the church, but the church is not Christ. Viewed from its divine element, the wholeness of the church is in Christ apart from its human members. From this perspective it would be correct to say that the church is greater than the sum of its parts.

In the Old Testament "the house of Israel" was described as the Lord's vineyard (Isa. 5:1-7; cf. also 27:2-6).[76] Jesus drew on this background in three of his parables: the laborers in the vineyard (Matt. 20:1-16), the two sons (Matt. 21:28-32), and the rejected tenants (Matt.

---

76. Willy Rordorf, "La vigne et le vin dans la tradition juive et chrétienne," *Université de Neuchâtel, Annales 1969-1970,* pp. 131-146, reprinted in idem, *Liturgie, foi, et vie des premiers chrétiens: études patristiques* (Paris: Beauchesne, 1986), pp. 493-508; John Willis, "The Genre of Isaiah 5:1-7," *Journal of Biblical Literature* 96 (1977): 337-362.

21:33-46). The first teaches the sovereign generosity of God, the second the importance of doing the father's will, and the last concludes with God giving his vineyard to a new people who will produce the desired fruits. The church is not expressly identified with the vineyard, but the parables point toward it. The parable of the laborers refers to the calling of the sinners in Israel who came late to the service of God, and perhaps by extension to the calling of the Gentiles. The parable of the two sons makes the point that the "tax collectors and prostitutes," who first refused the righteousness of God, repented and entered the kingdom of God ahead of the rulers of the people. The calling of the Gentiles seems expressly intended by the form the parable of the rejected tenants receives in Matthew. The leaders of the Jewish people were unfaithful in their responsibilities and so were to be replaced. The church of the Gentiles is anticipated in verse 43: the kingdom will be taken away and given "to a nation [ethnei] that produces the fruits of the kingdom." All three parables as applied to the church have in common with the imagery of the vine the necessity of producing the fruits of righteousness that God as the landlord and husbandman desires. They add the element of faithful work and obedience in the service of God.

The Sheep and the Sheepfold

The Gospel of John also makes use of the imagery of a shepherd and his sheep to describe the relations of Christ with his people (John 10:1-18).[77] As God owns the vineyard in which Jesus is the vine (John 15:1), so God owns the sheep for whom Jesus is the shepherd (cf. John 10:15, 17). Besides the imagery for a people and their leader, the sheep theme is used in a ministerial context (see pp. 318-319, 321) and in a redemptive sense.

God's people in Old Testament times were called sheep: "We are the people of [God's] pasture, and the sheep of his hand" (Ps. 95:7); "We are his people, and the sheep of his pasture" (Ps. 100:3; cf. Ezek.

---

77. For Christ as the "Shepherd King" and the shepherd/flock imagery in general, see F. F. Bruce, *New Testament Development of Old Testament Themes* (Grand Rapids: Eerdmans, 1968), pp. 100-114; also Barnabas Lindars, *New Testament Apologetic: The Doctrinal Significance of the Quotations* (Philadelphia: Westminster, 1961), pp. 127-132.

34:31). The description of people as sheep is not at all complimentary, but the point is not to describe human nature but to affirm something about God. As a shepherd cares for his sheep, so God cares for his people (Ps. 23; 78:52; 80:1; Isa. 40:10-11). There is a need for leadership so that "the congregation of the LORD may not be like sheep without a shepherd" (Num. 27:17). The leaders of God's people are described as shepherds (Ezek. 34; Zech. 11). In contrast to those frequently wicked rulers, Jesus came as a ruler who would truly shepherd the people (Matt. 2:6, quoting Mic. 5:2-4) and seek the lost sheep (Matt. 18:12-14; Luke 15:3-7). Shepherd is one of the many functions of God in the Old Testament applied to Jesus in the New Testament.

The portrayal of Jesus as a "Lamb" has to do primarily with his sacrificial work (John 1:29; Rev. 5:12), but the prominence of this figure in Revelation may have something to do with his embodiment of the people as sheep (cf. Rev. 14:1).[78] According to the Johannine paradox, the Lamb will shepherd the redeemed (Rev. 7:17). The Lamb and shepherd descriptions unite in Jesus' death, for he is "the Lamb that was slaughtered" (Rev. 13:8) and the "good shepherd" who "lays down his life for the sheep" (John 10:11; cf. Heb. 13:20).

John 10:1-18 identifies Jesus in several roles related to sheep in addition to that of the good shepherd who gives his life for the sheep. The passage begins with a parable (John 10:1-6) and continues with a meditation on the parable, directing attention to Jesus as the "door" or "gate" to the sheepfold (John 10:7-10) and as the shepherd (John 10:11-18).[79] Jesus is the gate into the sheepfold through whom one must enter for protection and go out for pasture (John 10:7-10). Only through Jesus is there entrance into the safety and security of the sheepfold. Moreover, he is the shepherd who leads and knows the sheep and whose voice they know (John 10:2-5, 27). Only in following Jesus is spiritual nourishment to be found. Knowing the shepherd is particularly important because of the propensity of sheep to go astray (Isa. 53:6; 1 Pet. 2:25). The theme of unity is also connected with the imagery, for there is to be "one flock, one shepherd" (John 10:16-18), apparently with allusion to the bringing of Gentiles into the one fold. By following Jesus the sheep are gathered into one flock.

78. The imagery of God's people as sheep continued in Jewish apocalyptic literature — e.g., *1 Enoch* 90.

79. Shifting references within the passage have caused interpreters problems. Some suggested solutions and an acceptance of the integrity of the passage may be found in G. R. Beasley-Murray, *John*, Word Biblical Commentary 36 (Waco: Word, 1987), pp. 162-172.

The imagery of disciples as sheep emphasizes the indispensable role of Jesus as the shepherd. "Sheep without a shepherd" is a description of helplessness and lostness (Matt. 9:35; 10:6; 15:24). And so, in reference to his approaching death, Jesus applied the language of Zechariah 13:7-9, "I will strike the shepherd, and the sheep will be scattered" (Matt. 26:31; Mark 14:27) to himself and his disciples. Jesus seeks the lost sheep (Luke 15:3-7; cf. 19:10) and characterizes his disciples as the "little flock" (Luke 12:32).

AN ARCHITECTURAL IMAGE

"You are . . . God's building."   (1 COR. 3:9)

A Building

Paul sometimes combined agricultural and architectural metaphors (1 Cor. 3:9; Eph. 3:17; Col. 2:7), as well as combining the metaphors of a body and a building (Eph. 4:16). This combination has Old Testament precedents (as in Jer. 1:10; 24:6).

Unlike modern English usage, the word "church" in the Bible does not refer to a building but to a people. The church, however, is compared to a building. Construction imagery is applied in various ways in the New Testament.

In developing the image of the church as a building, Paul compares his work as a missionary apostle to that of a "skilled master builder" who laid the foundation on which other preachers had built (1 Cor. 3:10; cf. Rom. 15:20). The unique foundation of this spiritual building is Jesus Christ (1 Cor. 3:11; cf. 2 Tim. 2:19). The different materials in the construction represent the converts as indicative of the quality of work of the laborers (1 Cor. 3:12; cf. 2 Tim. 2:20-21); the actual church has a mixed composition like the different materials in a house. The time of testing will reveal the quality of the construction and so serves as a warning to the builders (1 Cor. 3:13-15). Paul frequently used the family of words meaning "building" ("edify") to describe activities connected with the church.[80]

In the Gospels, Jesus promised, as we studied in Chapter 1, to

80. See the word study on pp. 286-288.

"build" his church (Matt. 16:18). The words of Psalm 118:22 are applied to Jesus himself as the cornerstone (or keystone) of the people of God (Matt. 21:42 and parallels; Acts 4:11; 1 Pet. 2:7); so also Isaiah 28:16 (1 Pet. 2:6; cf. Eph. 2:20). That the imagery of the foundation can be applied to Jesus (1 Cor. 3:11), the apostles (Rev. 21:14), and the apostles and prophets (Eph. 2:20) is a reminder that illustrations can be used in different contexts to teach different lessons without being contradictory. Individual Christians are the stones built on Jesus, the living stone (1 Pet. 2:4-5), to make a spiritual house.

The Temple

The building to which the church is most often compared is the temple.[81] This is probably the reference in the "spiritual house" in 1 Peter 2:4-5. The main emphasis in verses 4-10 is on election as the holy people of God,[82] but the references to Jesus as "a living stone," to Christians as "living stones," and to "a holy priesthood" offering "spiritual sacrifices" suggest not just any building but specifically the temple. Hence, the "spiritual house"[83] may be taken as the house in which the divine Spirit lives (cf. the texts on p. 108), that is, a temple.[84]

81. Ernst Lohmeyer, *Lord of the Temple: A Study of the Relation Between Cult and Gospel* (Richmond: John Knox, 1962); C. F. D. Moule, "Sanctuary and Sacrifice in the Church of the New Testament," *Journal of Theological Studies* n.s. 1 (1950): 29-41; Alan Cole, *The New Temple: A Study in the Origins of the Catechetical 'Form' of the Church in the New Testament* (London: Tyndale, 1950); Bertil Gärtner, *The Temple and the Community in Qumran and the New Testament* (Cambridge: University Press, 1965); R. J. McKelvey, *The New Temple: The Church in the New Testament* (Oxford: University Press, 1969); I. Howard Marshall, "Church and Temple in the New Testament," *Tyndale Bulletin* 40 (1989): 203-222.

82. Demonstrated by J. H. Elliott, *The Elect and the Holy: An Exegetical Examination of 1 Peter 2:4-10* (Leiden: E. J. Brill, 1966).

83. One of the specialized uses of "house" was for a temple, the home of the deity (cf. in reference to the temple in Jerusalem Matt. 21:13; 23:38 and parallels). Hence, "house" in Hebrews, although primarily referring to a household or people (Heb. 3:2-6), may keep the overtones of the temple when it is associated with priesthood (Heb. 10:21). (See the discussion of the Hebrews passages above on pp. 114, 120.)

84. *Pace* J. H. Elliott, *The Elect and the Holy* (Leiden: E. J. Brill, 1966), pp. 149-166, who argues that *oikos* means "household" (as in 1 Pet. 4:17) and "that spiritual house" is equivalent to "royal house" in 1 Pet. 2:9. But would not the idea that the community is both royal and priestly (v. 9) lead to the equation of royal house and

Christ is the cornerstone (v. 6), to which the other stones are joined. As a community, Christians are not only a building but a body of functioning priests within the temple. Their sacrifices are "acceptable to God through Jesus Christ."

The ancient pagan world built temples to house the cult statue; the significance of temples was that they were the house of the deity. Similarly, in Israel, the tabernacle (Exod. 40:34) and then the temple (1 Kings 8:10-13, 20) were the "house of God," with the significant difference that there was no statue representing the deity. The tabernacle symbolized the presence of God among his people and was the place where he met his people in revelation and atonement (Exod. 29:42-43; 33:7-14; Lev. 16; Deut. 12:5-7). The temple succeeded to this function as the symbol of God's presence among the people for forgiveness and blessing (e.g., 1 Kings 6:12-13; 8:10-13, 29-53; 9:3; Ps. 132:13-18). The temple as the house of the deity is reflected in the wording of Matthew 23:21. The temple was the center of worship (see further pp. 218-220). The tabernacling of God among his people at the central sanctuary is comparable to the way that in his Spirit he lives in the church. In the period of time preceding the life of Jesus, it seems that among some Jews there emerged the thought that the community was a temple (notably at Qumran).[85]

The thought of Christ's body as a temple is the theological basis for the description of the church as a temple. The Gospel of John presents Jesus as the new temple.[86] The interpretation of the temple as the body of Jesus in John 2:19-22 may be an example of Johannine double meaning: the physical body as the tabernacle of God (cf. John

---

temple? *Oikos* refers not infrequently in Jewish and Christian literature (as well as pagan) to "house (of God)," temple. R. J. McKelvey, *The New Temple: The Church in the New Testament* (Oxford: University Press, 1969), pp. 125-131, accepts *oikos* in 1 Pet. 2:5 as "temple," but judges that it is termed "spiritual" because it is built of consecrated persons who make their self-oblation here rather than because it is where the Spirit is active.

85. Bertil Gärtner, *The Temple and the Community in Qumran and the New Testament* (Cambridge: Cambridge University Press, 1965), chap. 3; but see W. W. Grasham, "The Priestly Synagogue: A Re-examination of the Cult at Qumran" (Ph.D. thesis, Aberdeen, 1985), summarized by I. Howard Marshall, "Church and Temple in the New Testament," *Tyndale Bulletin* 40 (1989): 215-217. It seems likely that to whatever extent the Qumran community thought of themselves as a temple, this was an interim arrangement until the arrival of the eschatological temple.

86. R. J. McKelvey, *The New Temple: The Church in the New Testament* (Oxford: University Press, 1969), pp. 75-82.

1:14, "tabernacled among us") and the church as the new temple[87] (for God and Christ's dwelling in believers, cf. John 14:23). (If this secondary interpretation may be reading too much of the Pauline conception of the body into the statement, it is at least clear that Paul used both body [1 Cor. 12:27] and temple [1 Cor. 3:16] for the church.)

The words of Jesus quoted in John 2:19-22 are likely behind the accusations made at Jesus' trial (Mark 14:57-58; cf. 15:29). The testimony is characterized as "false," probably because it misunderstood (by taking literally) what Jesus meant.[88] The words "I will build another [temple] not made with hands" (Mark 14:58) parallel the promise of Jesus "I will build my church" (Matt. 16:18). The case presented in Chapter 1 for the "rock" of Matthew 16:18 being the Messiahship of Jesus would be applicable here, if there is the further allusion to the rock on which the temple was built.[89] The declaration of Jesus in Matthew 12:6, "that which is greater than the temple is here," may be personal ("someone") or a reference to the presence of God (the *shekinah* in Jewish thought), which made the temple holy and so was greater than the temple. If the latter, there is a claim that God dwells in Jesus more than in the temple.[90] Moreover, if Jesus in Romans 3:25 is to be understood as the "mercy seat," the place of atonement, rather than "means of expiation" (see p. 151), then the connection with the temple becomes especially significant, for the Christian receives forgiveness in Christ instead of at the Holy of Holies in the Jerusalem temple. These associations of Jesus and God's presence with the temple find expression in the statement of Revelation 21:22 that there is no temple in the new Jerusalem, because God and the Lamb are its temple.

87. Alan Cole, *The New Temple* (London: Tyndale, 1950), p. 28.

88. R. J. McKelvey, *The New Temple: The Church in the New Testament* (Oxford: University Press, 1969), pp. 67-72. See also the references in n. 81 and the comments in Chap. 4 at n. 8. Donald Juel, *Messiah and Temple* (Missoula: Scholars Press, 1977), argues that even if Jesus never said what he is charged with saying, Mark intends it to be understood as true at a deeper level. See also Ben F. Meyer, *The Aims of Jesus* (London: SCM, n.d.), pp. 180-185, 201-202.

89. Ben F. Meyer, *The Aims of Jesus* (London: SCM, 1979), p. 185, for the "rock" of Matt. 16:18 as the cosmic rock that was the site of the temple and the lid of the underworld.

90. Bertil Gärtner, *The Temple and the Community in Qumran and the New Testament* (Cambridge: University Press, 1965), pp. 115-116. Ernst Lohmeyer, *Lord of the Temple* (Richmond: John Knox, 1962), p. 84, notes that in the ministry of Jesus there was something greater than the temple (so than the priest), the prophet (Jonah), and the king (Solomon) — Matt. 12:6, 41-42.

The imagery of the temple is frequently applied to the church. First Corinthians 3:16-17 refers to the local church as the temple of God. God's Spirit dwells in the community, and that makes it holy. The temple still had the same significance as elsewhere in the ancient world — the home of the deity — only now that home was a people and not a building. Consequently, one must not act in a way disruptive or destructive of God's holy community. These verses follow on Paul's use of the building imagery to describe his apostolic work of founding the community and his warning for others to take care how they build on the foundation of Christ that he had laid (1 Cor. 3:10-15). The Jewish emphasis on one temple would have given to this comparison of the church to a temple a further emphasis on oneness, the unity of the church so much needed at Corinth. The application of temple language to the individual Christian in 1 Corinthians 6:19-20 may be derived from and an application of the idea of the community as a temple. The indwelling of the Spirit in the body is the basis for an appeal against sexual immorality. The consequences of the presence of God among his people for their conduct is the point also of 2 Corinthians 6:17–7:1. This passage repeats the idea of the community as the temple, and the Old Testament quotations stress that the church is now the dwelling place of God.[91] The holiness resulting from this relationship requires separation from idolatry and all defilement.

The climactic statement on the church as the temple of God is Ephesians 2:19-22. Once more the emphasis is on the people — "citizens" and "members of the household." Only now the church is viewed as universal, not local. The unity is that of races, Jews and Gentiles. (In his cleansing of the Jerusalem temple, Jesus referred to the prophecy of the eschatological temple as "a house of prayer for all peoples" [Isa. 56:7; Mark 11:17].) The "access" (Eph. 2:18) to the temple (and its worship of God) denied Gentiles (Eph. 2:14) is made available by the Spirit. The verb form of the noun translated "access," "to bring" or "to approach," is used in the Old Testament for presenting animals for sacrifice (e.g., Lev. 16:1ff.; 23:8ff.) and for appearing at the temple before God (e.g., Ezek. 44:13, 15). This time a doctrinal rather than a moral teaching is drawn from the imagery. The description of a temple is elaborated: the apostles and prophets form the foundation, and Christ is the foun-

---

91. I. Howard Marshall, "Church and Temple in the New Testament," *Tyndale Bulletin* 40 (1989): 217-218, observes that God is omnipresent in the world and dwells with the individual, but the church is where he meets with his people as a people.

dation stone (or capstone).[92] Christ provides the unity, and in him the structure grows to completion. The temple itself is "in the Lord," even as it is a dwelling place "in [or by] the Spirit" (cf. 1 Cor. 3:16). The temple continues to mean the home of God. The mode of his presence is by the Holy Spirit.

God meets people in forgiveness in the church. The tabernacle and then the temple was the place of the sin offerings and where the people received forgiveness (Lev. 4-5; 16). Although the author of Hebrews applies the atonement effected by Christ to the heavenly sanctuary (Heb. 9), the benefits of that atonement are applied in the earthly community described as a temple (Eph. 2:13-22). The church, as will be developed in the next chapter, is the community of the saved, the people who receive, proclaim, and live by the reconciliation effected by Christ.

The passages on the church as a temple emphasize that it is God's. The church as a temple is connected with the presence of God (2 Cor. 6:16-18), of Christ (Matt. 18:20), and of the Holy Spirit (1 Cor. 3:16). God dwells there, and that makes it holy. Christ is the cornerstone of this new temple. The indwelling of the Holy Spirit (see p. 108) has moral and doctrinal consequences about conduct and unity. Individuals in the church are "living stones" in whom the divine presence dwells and so must conduct themselves accordingly. The church as the temple is where believers experience the presence of God.

THE MEANING OF *EKKLĒSIA*

> *"When you come together as a church."*   (1 COR. 11:18)

The English word "church" derives from the Greek adjective "the Lord's" *(kyriakos)*.[93] It apparently entered northern European languages from the Goths, who heard this Greek word applied to church buildings ("the Lord's [house]") and appropriated the word into their language. Thus we have in Germany *Kirche* and in Scotland "Kirk." Hence, the

---

92. R. J. McKelvey, *The New Temple: The Church in the New Testament* (Oxford: University Press, 1969), pp. 114, 195-204, defends the traditional rendering "cornerstone" against the translation "capstone" argued for in several publications by J. Jeremias. J. H. Elliott, *The Elect and the Holy* (Leiden: E. J. Brill, 1966), p. 24, concurs.

93. The *k* sound became *ch,* and the vowels were run together.

use of the word "church" for a building is proper in English, but this is not true for the Greek word it translates.

The Greek word translated "church" is *ekklēsia*. Its basic meaning was "assembly,"[94] referring to what was done and not where it was done. The popular etymology deriving the word from "called out" (*ek + kaleō*) is not supported by the actual usage of the word. The emphasis was on the concrete act of assembly, not a separation from others.[95] The New Testament reflects the important stages in the history of the word's usage as well as the distinctive Christian content given to the word.

Ekklēsia was used of any assembly, but its primary use in classical Greek was for the assemblies of the citizens of a Greek city. In the direct democracy of the Greek city-states, many decisions that in modern representative democracies are made by elected legislative and judicial bodies were made in meetings of all the citizens, who comprised only a small percentage of the inhabitants of a city. The secular Greek usage is employed by Luke in his account of the riot at Ephesus in Acts 19. The mob gathered in the theatre is called an *ekklēsia* (Acts 19:32, 40). The city clerk contrasted that irregular gathering with the "regular assembly," the lawful, duly called meeting of the citizens (Acts 19:39).

The Jews adopted this Greek word to describe the assemblies of Israel, including those at some of the great moments of salvation history (Deut. 9:10; 23:2-4, 9; 31:30; Josh. 8:35; 1 Kings 8:14; 1 Chron. 28:8; Neh. 8:2). The people are sometimes called the "assembly of the LORD" (Deut. 23:1-4; 1 Chron. 29:20), "assembly of God" (Neh. 13:1), "assembly of the people of the LORD" (Judg. 20:2), "assembly of the people" (Ps. 107:32), or "assembly of the holy ones" (Ps. 149:1). *Ekklēsia* was used exclusively to translate the etymologically equivalent Hebrew word *qahal*, but was not the only word used to render that Hebrew root. Another word used to translate *qahal* was *synagogē*, most often used to translate the Hebrew word for "congregation," *'edhah*. In the separate development of Judaism and Christianity *synagogē* became the Jewish

---

94. G. Johnston, *The Doctrine of the Church in the New Testament* (Cambridge: University Press, 1943); J. Y. Campbell, "The Origin and Meaning of the Christian Use of the Word EKKLESIA," *Journal of Theological Studies* 49 (1948): 130-142; Roy Bowen Ward, "Ekklesia: A Word Study," *Restoration Quarterly* 2 (1958): 164-179; K. L. Schmidt, *"Ekklēsia,"* *Theological Dictionary of the New Testament*, ed. G. Kittel, tr. G. W. Bromiley (Grand Rapids: Eerdmans, 1965), 3.501-536; J. W. Roberts, "The Meaning of Ekklesia in the New Testament," *Restoration Quarterly* 15 (1972): 27-36.

95. The theological point about the separation of the church from the world is a biblical teaching — John 15:19; 17:16; 2 Cor. 6:16–7:1.

word and *ekklēsia* the Christian word for the gathered people, but in an early Jewish Christian context both words could be used without difference of meaning (James 2:2 and 5:14). It is disputed whether the references to the assemblies of Israel gave to *ekklēsia* the connotation of "people of God" in Jewish usage. An actual assembly seems all that can be certainly inferred from the usage, even in later Jewish writings.[96] So it would seem that the word did not have a technical sense for the "people of God," and the most that can be said is that it may have acquired this connotation through association. Nonetheless, *ekklēsia* was a noble word from its political use in Greek civic life, and this made appropriate its adoption by Jews for their religious assemblies. The Jewish usage of *ekklēsia* is reflected by Luke in his reference in Stephen's speech to Moses "in the congregation [assembly] in the wilderness" (Acts 7:38).

Paul on occasion used *ekklēsia* in its concrete sense of an actual assembly to refer to the meetings of Christians. This usage is particularly clear in his references to the assemblies of Christians at Corinth — "when you come together as a church" (1 Cor. 11:18); "in church I would rather speak five words with my mind" (1 Cor. 14:19); "women should be silent in the churches" (1 Cor. 14:34; cf. 14:35). At other times, he refers to those people who assemble, whether the whole church, as at Corinth (1 Cor. 14:23), or a smaller group, as in a house church (Rom. 16:5; Philem. 2).[97] From this, it was natural to use *ekklēsia* for the people, whether assembled or not. The great majority of instances of the word are in reference to a local church, hence the use of the plural for churches in a given region (1 Cor. 16:1, 9; Gal. 1:2, 22; Acts 15:41; 16:4-5). The use of the word for the people who customarily assemble but whether assembled or not shows that it had become a technical term. Connotations from the Jewish background in reference to God's people prepared for this usage if it did not already anticipate it.

---

96. E.g., Sirach 21:17; 23:24; 31:11; 44:15; 50:20.

97. John D. Zizioulas, *Being as Communion: Studies in Personhood and the Church* (London: Darton, Longman and Todd, 1985), p. 249, contrary to most interpreters, takes the phrase "church in your house" as referring not to a family-centered gathering but the assembly of all the faithful of a city who met as the guests of a particular house, so that there was only one such "household church" in each city at the time. Josef Hainz, *Ekklesia: Strukturen paulinischer Gemeinde-Theologie und Gemeinde-Ordnung* (Regensburg: Friedrich Pustet, 1972), p. 346, argues the opposite: Paul distinguishes the meetings of house churches from meetings of the whole church.

Less frequently, *ekklēsia* is used in a universal sense for all believers (Matt. 16:18; Eph. 1:22; Col. 1:18). This universal sense is in keeping with the Old Testament usage, which most often referred to meetings of the whole nation of Israel. Whether the local or universal sense came first is in some respects a false alternative. Although Paul's usage for the local assemblies occurs first in our surviving literature, the Jerusalem church presumably referred to itself as *ekklēsia,* so from the beginning the first local church was itself the universal church.[98] The idea of assembly is not lost even in the extension of the word to the universal people of God, for in the background is the eschatological assembly of all the saved, which is described by different but kindred expressions (2 Thess. 2:1; Matt. 24:31); and perhaps the eschatological gathering is intended once by *ekklēsia* itself (Heb. 12:23).[99] There will be a time when the universal church is in assembly, when the Lord comes again. That eschatological "Day" gives urgency to the earthly meetings together of Christians (Heb. 10:25), which exemplify and anticipate the final gathering.

Since the word "assembly" in itself says nothing about the nature of the assembly, often descriptive phrases are added to the word in order to characterize the Christian assembly. These phrases do not give names to the church in an official sense but are descriptions of the nature of the church. Sometimes the qualifying phrases refer to the Christians who compose the church. This may be a geographical designation: "the church of the Thessalonians," then further identified as "in God the Father and the Lord Jesus Christ" (1 Thess. 1:1; 2 Thess. 1:1). Or the geographical location may be in the secondary position: "the church of God that is in Corinth" (1 Cor. 1:2; 2 Cor. 1:1); "the churches of God in Judea" (1 Thess. 2:14).[100] Or the description may have to do with the nature of the people who make up the assembly: "all the churches of the Gentiles" (Rom. 16:4); "the assembly of the firstborn ones who are enrolled in heaven" (Heb. 10:23).

---

98. Josef Hainz, *Ekklesia: Strukturen paulinischer Gemeinde-Theologie und Gemeinde-Ordnung* (Regensburg: Friedrich Pustet, 1972), pp. 227-249, delineates differences between Paul's usage and that of the first community at Jerusalem.

99. Harold W. Attridge, *The Epistle to the Hebrews* (Philadelphia: Fortress, 1989), p. 375, shows that the "assembly of the firstborn" is not of angels (v. 22) but of human beings, the faithful, who are enrolled in the heavenly registry, but it is indeterminate whether the assembly is still on earth or is the anticipated heavenly gathering. For the author of Hebrews, the two are seemingly collapsed into one.

100. For other geographical designations, see Acts 8:1; 9:31; 11:22; Rom. 16:1; 1 Cor. 16:1, 19; 2 Cor. 8:1; Gal. 1:2; Col. 4:16; Rev. 1:4; 2:1, 8, 12, 18; 3:1, 7, 14.

More often the qualifying phrase used with *ekklēsia* relates the church to God or to Christ: "the church of God" (1 Cor. 10:32; 11:22; 15:9; Gal. 1:13; 1 Tim. 3:5, 15); "churches of God" (1 Cor. 11:16; 2 Thess. 1:4); "churches of Christ" (Rom. 16:16); "churches in Christ" (Gal. 1:22). The character of the Christian assembly is defined by its relation to the deity.

The designation *ekklēsia* calls attention to the importance of meeting together for the nature of the church, and this feature will be studied further in Chapter 4. By way of anticipation, it may be affirmed now that the church, by definition, is an assembly. It is the people who meet together on a regular basis. The word *ekklēsia* identifies the people of God as assembled. When it comes together, the church exemplifies that it is indeed the church, an assembly (1 Cor. 11:18). There are to be times when in a given locality "the whole church comes together" (1 Cor. 14:23).

The meeting of the church occurs in the name of Jesus Christ. The church meets because it is called together in Christ. The church derives its being and essence from Christ. This is so because God has acted definitively for human salvation in his death and resurrection. The Old Testament expectations centered on covenant, kingdom, and Messiah (Chap. 1) involved a forgiven people who receive the Holy Spirit. That way of describing the nature of the church, that is, as the community of saved people, will be the subject of the next chapter.

3. The Church and Her Savior: Salvation and Church Membership

"Christ is the head of the church,
the body of which he is the Savior."　　　　　　(EPH. 5:23)

THE question of the membership or composition of the church is answered by the study of the nature of the church in the preceding chapter: the church is the people of God, the body of Christ, the community of the Holy Spirit; that is, it is a people characterized by its relation to the deity. One becomes a part of the church by being in the people of God, being incorporated into the body of Christ, and receiving the Holy Spirit. Thus membership in the church is part of a broad doctrinal perspective. If, as studied in the preceding chapter, the nature of the church is that of Christ, then becoming a part of Christ, identification with his people, incorporation into him, answers the question of church membership. This chapter directs attention to what is involved in how one is brought into this relationship.

The same idea may be expressed as "being saved." In this chapter, we approach the subject of the membership of the church in relation to the doctrine of salvation. Another way of describing the nature of the church, in addition to the images studied in the preceding chapter, is to say that the church is those persons who are saved from their sins.

The church, therefore, may be defined as the community of the saved. In other words, soteriology determines ecclesiology.[1]

This manner of describing the church brings us once more to the centrality of Christ for understanding the church, for his very mission, as recorded by Luke, was "to seek out and to save the lost" (Luke 19:10). The church is the product of the saving purposes of God as expressed in Jesus Christ. God obtained the church "with the blood of his own Son" (Acts 20:28; cf. for the idea Ps. 74:2). As a result, "There is salvation in no one else" (Acts 4:12). Christ is said to be the Savior of the church, his body (Eph. 5:23). Christ saves the church.[2]

Those who are saved from their sins are added by God to the number of his people (Acts 2:47). Some manuscripts of Acts 2:47, followed in the Authorized Version, read "the Lord added to the church" those being saved. The textual evidence is decisive that the word "church" was not in the original text, but "church" was a correct interpretive scribal addition to explain the meaning of the Greek phrase translated in the NRSV "to their number."[3] The Lord daily made additions of those being saved, and he gathered them into one community.

A negative way of saying the same thing about the church is suggested by 1 Peter 4:17-18. There the church is contrasted with those who are lost. The "household of God," the church, the "righteous," are saved, but no hope is given to those "who do not obey the gospel of God." To turn the statement around, those who obey the gospel of God make up the household of God.

Such passages suggest the right way to describe the relationship between the church and salvation. The church does not save (Christ is the Savior), but neither does it have no connection with salvation. The church is the people who are saved. Some depend on the church to save them. Others make only the most minimal connection between salvation and church membership, saying that one is saved by one means and becomes a church member in another way. Both positions

---

1. Anton Houtepen, *People of God: A Plea for the Church* (London: SCM, 1984), chap. 4.

2. For the title "Savior" applied to Christ, see Oscar Cullmann, *The Christology of the New Testament* (Philadelphia: Westminster, 1959), pp. 238-245.

3. Everett Ferguson, " 'When You Come Together': *Epi To Auto* in Early Christian Literature," *Restoration Quarterly* 16 (1973): 202-208, shows the frequency with which this Greek phrase, meaning "in the same place" or "together" or even "in community," was used for the church and its assemblies.

misunderstand the biblical teaching. God places the saved in the church, which is his people. The church is the community of the saved.

This manner of speaking raises another question: why do people need saving? There is thus a prior subject that requires consideration: the doctrine of sin. Hence, we are led to an examination of the human condition.

HUMAN NEED

> *"All have sinned and fall short*
> *of the glory of God."* (ROM. 3:23)

The declarations in scripture of universal human sinfulness (Rom. 3:9-18, quoting Pss. 141:1-3 and 53:1-3; cf. Rom. 3:23) are confirmed by individual consciences. This situation provides the place to begin in describing the human condition and a point of contact for the preaching of the gospel.

The Nature of Human Beings

The New Testament meaning of sin can be seen only from the Old Testament background. The fullest and profoundest discussion of human nature in the Bible is found in Genesis 1–3.[4] There is here disclosed the paradox of human nature: greatness and wretchedness, majesty and misery. According to Genesis 1:26-27 mankind, male and female, is made in the image of God and appointed lord of creation. This is the greatness of human beings. According to Genesis 2:7, the first man was made from the dust of the earth with all the weakness of clay and, as the story unfolds, subject to temptation, sin, sickness, and death. This is the wretchedness of the human condition. For all the greatness, human life is derivative, dependent on the Creator for everything. And so, there is revealed the paradox of dominion and dependence.

---

4. A different approach but making some of the same theological points is Gianfranco Ravasi, "Ueberschattet vom Baum der Erkenntnis: Hermeneutische Anmerkungen zu Genesis 2–3," *Internationale katholische Zeitschrift: Communio* 20 (1991): 294-304; English condensation, "Hermeneutical Comments on Gn 2–3," *Theology Digest* 39 (1992): 241-247.

Of all the competing worldviews, only the biblical doctrines of creation and fall account for the dual nature of humanity: aspirations, ideals, and moments of greatness; yet falling short, filled with frustrations and failures.

Theologians debate whether the fall is historical or symbolic. It is both. It is the story of the first human couple; it is also the story of every man and every woman. Four great realities of human nature are found in the narrative of Genesis 3.

Temptation

The first great reality of human nature revealed in Genesis 3 is the experience of temptation. Temptation came to Eve through three avenues: She "saw that the tree was good for food, and that it was a delight to the eyes, and that the tree was to be desired to make one wise" (Gen. 3:6). Scripture elsewhere has other threefold expressions of temptation to sin. There is likely no conscious allusion to this passage, but the description of what is involved in the sinful world in 1 John 2:16 offers a rough parallel: "the desire of the flesh, the desire of the eyes, the pride of life." Another threefold expression of influence to sin comes in the temptations of Jesus. Unlike Matthew's order, which leads to a messianic climax (Matt. 4:1-11), Luke's order offers a closer parallel to the order of Genesis 3: turning the stones to bread (desire of the flesh), seeing all the kingdoms of the world over which to exercise authority (delight to the eyes), throwing himself down from the pinnacle of the temple (tempting God by claiming a special or godlike position) (Luke 4:3-12). Each of these three sets of three temptations has differences, so as not to be strictly parallel, yet there are similarities. All three groups of three types of temptation relate to pleasures, possessions, and the prestige of the world.

Behind all the avenues through which temptation comes to a person lies a basic temptation, made clear in Genesis 3:1-5. That is the temptation to deny our creaturely status and to rebel against God. The human inclination is to desire the creation and deny the creator (Rom. 1:25). Humans desire to live life on their own terms. The serpent promised Eve, "You will be like God" (Gen. 3:5). That is the fundamental temptation: we want to be our own god. The exalted position of human beings in the creation perhaps makes them especially susceptible to this desire to play God.

There has been much speculation about what kind of tree was the "tree of the knowledge of good and evil" (Gen. 2:17). It may have been a special tree, but it does not matter from a horticultural standpoint. Any tree would have done. The good is to do what God says; evil is not to do what God says. Any act of disobedience brings this experiential knowledge. "To know good and evil" elsewhere in the Old Testament indicates "to determine or to decide good and evil." And this in the biblical understanding is a divine prerogative.[5] Human beings, however, want to decide for themselves what is good and evil, what is right and wrong. Only God can make that determination. We want to take the place of God. That is the basic temptation. It was the downfall of Eve and Adam; it is our downfall.

The reality of temptation reveals another reality — the freedom of the will. Without freedom to choose, there would be no temptation. The basic biblical perspective maintains human responsibility to resist sin and its influence (cf. the words of the New Testament on resisting the devil — Eph. 6:11-13, 16; James 4:7; 1 Pet. 5:9). The fact is, however, that human beings do not master the sin that lurks at the door (Gen. 4:7) and instead yield to temptation.

Sin

The second great reality of human nature manifested in Genesis 3 is the experience of sin. The experience of Eve and Adam is everyone's experience. All have sinned. "Just as sin came into the world through one man, and death came through sin, and so death spread to all because all have sinned" (Rom. 5:12). Every man is his own Adam, and every woman is her own Eve.

Basic to human sinfulness is the failure to acknowledge God as God. When Paul in Romans 1 described the sinfulness of the world apart from God, he stressed the failure to honor God and give thanks for his gifts (Rom. 1:21, 28). What is involved in sin according to the biblical descriptions may be summed up as disobedience. In the words of 1 John 3:4, "Every one who commits sin is guilty of lawlessness; sin is lawlessness," or in another translation, "transgression." Sin is to disobey the law or commands of God. Even as Adam and Eve were

5. W. Malcolm Clark, "A Legal Background to the Yahwist's Use of 'Good and Evil' in Genesis 2-3," *Journal of Biblical Literature* 88 (1969): 266-278.

told not to eat of the fruit of the tree in the middle of the garden but did so, in the same way any disobedience of the commands of God constitutes sin.

As the presence of temptation demonstrates free will, so the practice of sin awakens conscience. Conscience is the feeling of inward pain for doing what one has been taught is wrong. There came this knowledge of good and evil to Adam and Eve. Conscience is often defined as an inner guide to conduct, but it is this only in a secondary sense. It is first of all a monitor that reproves past actions, and as a consequence of this may serve to give guidance in future moral choices. Conscience is informed by teaching and past experience. For that reason, one person's conscience may judge differently from another's, and the moral code in one culture may differ from that in another culture. Thus conscience is not so much an active initiator in moral matters as a moral capacity. Although the moral codes may differ, the capacity to feel guilt and to make moral judgments is common to all persons. The conscience as a latent capacity is awakened by transgression.

After Adam and Eve disobeyed the divine command, they saw themselves as naked and tried to hide from God (Gen. 3:7-11). We still react in the same way. Our response may be more sophisticated, but our excuses are still fig leaves. In essence we too try to run away and hide from accountability. Yet "before God no creature is hidden, but all are naked and laid bare to the eyes of the one to whom we must render an account" (Heb. 4:13).

When Adam and Eve were found, they did as all human beings do, they tried to escape responsibility by blaming someone else. The man blamed "the woman whom you gave to be with me" (Gen. 4:12), and the woman blamed "the serpent [who] tricked me" (Gen. 4:13). "The Devil made me do it."

Here there is demonstrated the universal human dilemma — capable of the good and knowing better, but not living up to it. Here is the twofold nature of human beings: the image and the dust.

Punishment

As a consequence of sin, there follows the third reality of human nature described in Genesis 3, the experience of punishment (the eviction from the garden). Punishment for sin is inescapable.

The punishment on the woman is stated in Genesis 3:16, "I will greatly increase your pangs in childbearing." We should be clear that the punishment is not the childbearing itself. The command to "be fruitful and multiply, and fill the earth" (Gen. 1:28) was part of the original order of creation that God pronounced good (Gen. 1:31). Marriage and parenthood were divinely instituted as part of the goodness of creation. The punishment on the woman had to do with the circumstances of childbearing, not the childbearing itself: "in pain you shall bring forth children." In spite of the pains of childbearing, the woman's natural desire would be for her husband, and he was given the leading role in the marriage relationship (Gen. 3:16). This subordinate position in the family and later in the people of God, although not a denial of woman's abilities, natural or spiritual, was not to be reversed until the heavenly reversal of the human condition (Luke 20:34-36).

Similarly, the punishment on the man (Gen. 3:17-19) was not work itself, but the circumstances accompanying the work. In the garden before the fall, Adam had the responsibility to till and keep the garden (Gen. 2:15). Work, although we often pretend not to think so, is good for a person. It is the means whereby we define ourselves as persons and is therefore a privilege.[6] After the fall, the work involves "toil" and produces "sweat," and the soil brings forth thorns and thistles as well as plants good for food.

Pain is in the world as a result of sin. It is not part of the original order of creation. In addition to these distinctive punishments on woman and man, there was the common punishment of expulsion from the garden and the tree of life (Gen. 3:22-24).

The ultimate punishment for sin was death: "You are dust, and to dust you shall return" (Gen. 3:19). God had warned that if Adam ate of the fruit of the tree in the middle of the garden he would die (Gen. 2:17), and Eve knew this (Gen. 3:3). Although spiritual death, separation from God, was involved, the elaboration of the punishment (the return to dust) indicates the specific connotation of physical death. The "big lie" of the serpent was to deny this consequence of sin and to appeal to human pride (Gen. 3:4). Human beings go to great lengths to avoid, if not deny, this unpleasant prospect, but we are born to die. This is the great fact of human nature with which all must live. "It is appointed for mortals to die once, and after that the judgment" (Heb. 9:27).

In spite of the consequences of the first transgression, the image

---

6. The first question asked in getting acquainted with a person is, "What do you do?" One defines who a person is in terms of the work done.

of God in which male and female were created (Gen. 1:26-27), whatever content is given to this, remained after the fall (Gen. 9:6).[7] Adam and Eve were cut off from the tree that was the source of life; that tree of life, however, is again accessible in the heavenly Jerusalem (Rev. 22:2).

Redemption

If the story ended here, the prospects for humanity would be bleak indeed. Happily for human beings, there is more to the story. Another great reality of human nature is the hope of redemption. When God placed his curse upon the serpent (Gen. 3:14), he also made a promise: the offspring of the woman "will strike your head, and you will strike his heel" (Gen. 3:15). Christians have often seen this as the first messianic prophecy. That claims too much. As far as the text goes, it is simply a statement of the superiority of humanity over snakes. The conflict of humanity and animals is one aspect of fallen creation that will be overcome in the eschatological age, when animals are at peace and "a little child shall lead them" (Isa. 11:6-10). Although the snake would strike at the heel, that heel of the offspring of woman, humankind, would strike the head of the serpent. From the standpoint of the coming of Christ, it is possible to see a fullness of meaning and a specific reference not apparent in the original text of Genesis, as perhaps reflected in Romans 16:20. Since Christ has come, we know how humanity would prevail over the embodiment of evil. Humanity triumphs over temptation, sin, and punishment through one man, the offspring of woman. Although bruised by the strikes of Satan, Christ crushed the head of the foe.

Human beings triumph over evil through the new Adam, the perfect Man. " 'The first man Adam became a living being'; the last Adam became a life-giving spirit" (1 Cor. 15:45).

> For if the many died through the one man's trespass, much more surely have the grace of God and the free gift in the grace of the one man, Jesus Christ, abounded for the many. . . . If, because of the one man's trespass, death exercised dominion through that one, much more surely will those who receive the abundance of grace and the

7. The context of Gen. 1:26-27 relates the image of God to the human responsibility to rule the created order; in Gen. 9:6 the image of God serves to stress the dignity of human beings as related to God and therefore to be respected. John T. Willis, "The Dignity and Suffering of Humankind according to the Hebrew Bible," *Stone-Campbell Journal* 1 (1998): 231-241.

free gift of righteousness exercise dominion in life through the one man, Jesus Christ. (Rom. 5:15, 17)

Jesus Christ is the real, true man — what a human being was meant to be. He is the typical, representative person, the leader of the new humanity conformed to the Creator's plan.

Further Theological Reflections on Sin[8]

Alternative Views of Sin

Two opposite views have been maintained about the relation of humanity to sin: depraved in all his being versus inherently good. In spite of isolated texts that might be cited, neither view presents the overall biblical teaching. An alternative theological position will be set forth in the following sections, but in a preliminary way I record my agreement with Pierre Bonnard on the following five points: (1) The New Testament speaks of sin only to affirm it is overcome by the new work of God in Christ. (2) Sin in the Bible is disobedience, enmity against God, doubt of his love, hatred of human beings. (3) The whole person sins and not a part. (4) The New Testament does not explain the origin of sin, and sin is not essential to human nature. (5) The New Testament awaited the day when sin will be definitively annihilated, but for now sin has lost its power to separate from the love of God.[9]

The common Greek word for "sin" is *hamartia*. It means a fault, a failure, an error in judgment. The verb form, *hamartano*, means literally "to miss the mark," "to fail in one's purpose." This may be more or less serious depending on the mark missed or the matter in which one fails. The Bible pours a much stronger content into the word. Since sin is against God, and it is the divine standard that is missed, sin becomes exceedingly serious. There is often in the Old Testament usage the

8. Sin is discussed in the works on biblical theology. My discussion is much influenced by a series of church bulletin articles written by Ralph V. Graham for the Collingswood, N.J., Church of Christ between 1961 and 1963. For the human predicament of being under the divine displeasure and in a condition of personal alienation in relation to sin, the flesh, the law, and death, see R. P. Martin, *Reconciliation: A Study of Paul's Theology* (Atlanta: John Knox, 1981), pp. 48-70.

9. Pierre Bonnard, "Cinq remarques bibliques sur le péche," in *Anamnesis: Recherches sur le Nouveau Testament* (Geneva, 1980), pp. 61-70.

element of willful, stubborn rebellion or neglect. Because of God's special relationship with his people, sin is a violation of a relationship, a breach of contract.[10]

There is a weakness and perversity in the human will, yet human beings are capable of choosing the right. When left to their own devices, however, they choose the wrong.

How Is Sin Possible?

God is good; he is not evil. He is not the author of evil, nor can he be tempted by evil (cf. James 1:13). He does not want sin in the world, and he does not directly produce it. Nevertheless, God maintains the conditions which make sin possible, and he has a purpose which appears to make it inevitable. In biblical language, when God sends or allows the influences that result in sin, he can be said to cause it (cf. Exod. 7:3 and 8:32; 1 Sam. 16:14). Humans were made in the likeness of God and for fellowship with him. Yet they are dependent beings, in creation and in moment-by-moment existence. The proper relationship to God is that of acknowledging dependence upon and responsibility to him in humble and grateful trust. Yet the image of God, the position of dominion over creation, and the purpose of fellowship with God tempt human beings to want to be like God, and so they do the very things that contradict their relationship with God.

Virtue, character, and selfhood are a matter of choosing and discriminating between values. There can be no freedom of choice where there are no alternatives. Without an alternative, a person could not know or demonstrate a preference for God or dedication to him. One could not know whether love for God was supreme or not. To continue under these conditions would leave a person no more than a machine or like a patient under hypnosis controlled by the will of another. Without real choice, human nature would lack personality and maturity; a person would be like a baby neither knowing self nor individuality or distinctness from the environment.

Human freedom includes freedom to reject God as well as freedom to choose God, or it is not freedom at all. The possibility of sin, then, is in the human freedom to turn away from God and from the responsibility to acknowledge dependence on God.

10. Wayne A. Meeks, *The Origins of Christian Morality* (New Haven: Yale, 1993), p. 122.

Why Is Sin Universal?

The Bible (Rom. 3:23; 5:12) and experience testify that sin is universal. Christian theology has related this universality of sin to the doctrine of original sin. Although often reinterpreted, it refers historically to the teaching popularized by Augustine (5th century) that humanity shares the guilt of Adam's transgression. This results from everyone inheriting a nature that is polluted. The transmission of sin occurs in the same way as the transmission of human nature, sexual generation. An alternative explanation current in Puritan theology is that Adam was the "federal head" of the human race; in that capacity he involved all his descendants in his transgression. Both of these views are theological explanations; neither has a direct biblical base, even if derived from selected texts.[11] As far as express biblical texts go, the fall altered the human condition; it did not alter human nature. Human beings no longer live in Paradise and now struggle in surroundings where the influence of sin is great. Their nature is weakened by the generations who have sinned. On the other hand, the universality of sin cannot be simply blamed on human finiteness, ignorance, and environment.

The story of the first parents is also the story of everyone's temptations and fall. Why everyone chooses to love self rather than God is left unexplained in scripture. It remains a fact. Perhaps statistical probability enters in here. Given enough choices, a person is sure to make a number of wrong choices. And the probability increases with the influences of history, circumstances, and associates upon an individual. The effects of a weakened human nature inclining us to sin are intensified by the examples of sin about us.

What Is Sin Not?

There are many inadequate ideas about sin that circulate in popular culture, even in the churches.

(1) Sin is not a hangover from medieval superstition about an easily angered God or from a dour Puritan disposition. This view may

---

11. Any "kind of inherited sinfulness or inherited guilt is alien to the New Testament" — Anton Houtepen, *People of God: A Plea for the Church* (London: SCM, 1984), p. 64.

take a secular form that denies there is such a thing as sin, or a religious form that seeks to avoid "guilt trips" by not taking sin seriously.

(2) Sins are not restrictive mores or petty vices. This statement is not meant to say that customs may not have moral implications nor that "little sins" are not really sins. It rather means that much, much more is involved.

(3) Sins are not simply "wrong acts," as if by prohibiting the deeds, sin is removed. Nor is sin "wrong motives" alone. Motives are central, but one may do wrong with the best of intentions and with a clear conscience (witness Saul of Tarsus — Acts 23:1; 26:9-11; cf. 1 Tim. 1:13).

(4) Sin is not the violation of arbitrary laws based on false inter- pretations of scripture that someone might try to bind on the conscience of another.

(5) Sin is not acceptance of persons with whose ideas one does not agree or whose practices are not condoned.

Sin is much more serious than these things and involves the very center of one's being and life.

What Does Sin Involve?

There are certain characteristics or elements involved in sin that show its seriousness.

(1) *Rebellion against God.* Sin is a decision that humans have the right to determine what is good and evil (Gen. 3:22). It puts the self in the driver's seat and refuses to recognize God as God. The attitude of Jesus was the opposite, for he refused Satan's enticement to push God out of the picture and take over for himself (Matt. 4:1-10).

(2) *Ingratitude.* Sin involves a failure to acknowledge God as cre- ator of everything and the giver of every good gift (Rom. 1:21, 25, 28; James 1:17). It is a failure to respond lovingly to God's love. A basic sin is an ungrateful heart. This often is associated with forgetfulness (one may compare the forgetfulness and ingratitude rebuked in Pss. 78:7-8, 11, 35; 106:7, 13, 21, 47).

(3) *Self-love, or self-absorption.* Sin is the turning away from love for God to love for self as the highest good. Notice its company in 2 Timothy 3:2. The problem is inordinate self-love. There is a proper amount of self-love. Self-acceptance is essential to the acceptance of others, and in Jesus' teaching love for self is assumed as the measure of neighbor-love (Matt. 22:39). Self-respect is necessary for spiritual

growth. Two opposites to be avoided are self-satisfaction that one is perfect and the feeling that one is helpless to do better. The proper balance is maintained by loving self for the sake of God.

(4) *Pride.* Someone has observed that the English word "sin" has "I" at the center. Pride is often used in a weaker or even favorable sense (as "taking pride" in a worthwhile endeavor), but earlier Christian moralists were right in seeing it as a root sin. As a sin, pride refers to excessive self-regard, a presumed self-sufficiency (James 4:6 and 1 Pet. 5:5, quoting Prov. 3:34). Hence, it denies one's creaturely limitation. It represents the delusion that one can save the self. The pride of power imagines itself the complete master of its own existence and seeks the mastery of others. In the same way, intellectual, moral, or spiritual pride imagines its own conceptions to be free of self-interest and arrogates to itself divine authority.

(5) *A perverse will.* Not the wrong acts, but the perversion that exists at the center of the self constitutes the essence of sin. This is what requires the transformation of the inner being (Rom. 12:2). The root of sinful deeds is found in lusts, desires, and motives. The perverse will opposes God's will whether by hostility or indifference. It may oppose God even when doing good things. A stubborn will deviates from the essential destiny given to human beings. A will turned away from God frustrates objectivity, corrupts the reason, destroys the sense of justice, depreciates others, and resents criticism. Such a will produces anarchy in human life.

(6) *Alienation, or turning away, from God.* Sin involves separation (Isa. 59:2) and estrangement — from God, from one's true being, and consequently from reality and other persons. The alienation comes from the difference between what one is and what God expects. It represents the desire for independence from God and the distrust of his goodness. One becomes a stranger to God because of making self the center.

(7) *Unbelief.* Romans 14:23, "Whatever does not proceed from faith is sin," refers in context to confidence that something is right and not to the full biblical sense of faith, but the statement is also true in a broader sense. Sin is any activity apart from faith, and unbelief will result in sinful conduct.[12] Unbelief precedes egoism, sensuality, and godlessness. Distrust prevents fellowship with God. Disobedience is the consequence.

---

12. Leander Keck, *Paul and his Letters* (Philadelphia: Fortress, 1979), p. 93, on Rom. 14:23 — Sin is not acting out of the "freedom of living by sheer trust in God."

nexistence. Sin is often associated in scripture with death ; Rom. 6:16). As long as a person is becoming what he or she d by creation to be, there is a participation in true being and a person acts so as to frustrate this potentiality, there is a participation in non-being. True self-realization is to fulfill one's potentiality in God. He is the true being and the true existence.

Birth and Consequences of Sin

James 1:14-15 lays out the sequence of temptation, sin, and punishment according to the imagery of conception, birth, and death. "One is tempted by one's own desire, being lured and enticed by it; then, when that desire has conceived, it gives birth to sin, and that sin, when it is fully grown, gives birth to death." Desire plus opportunity equals temptation. Consent to the temptation produces the deed. Or, the temptation may be thought of as arousing the wrong desire, leading to the consent of the will and the doing of the deed.

The end result of sin is death. Physical death began with Adam and Eve; in every case, sin produces spiritual death. "For the wages of sin is death" (Rom. 6:23), but graciously that verse continues, "but the free gift of God is eternal life in Christ Jesus our Lord." One earns and deserves death for sins; life is a free gift. And it comes from God through Christ. "My pessimism about man is exceeded only by my optimism about God."

GOD'S ACTION

"For God so loved the world that he gave his only Son,
so that everyone who believes in him may not perish
but may have eternal life."   (JOHN 3:16)

In view of the biblical doctrine about human nature and sin, the only way human beings can be saved is for God in his grace to take the initiative. The message throughout the Bible is of God as a gracious God who forgives sins. The oft-repeated confessional formula of Israel was this:

"The LORD, the LORD, a God merciful and gracious, slow to anger, and abounding in steadfast love and faithfulness, keeping steadfast love for the thousandth generation, forgiving iniquity and transgression and sin, yet by no means clearing the guilty." (Exod. 34:6-7; cf. Num. 14:18; Neh. 9:17; Ps. 103:8; Joel 2:13; Jon. 4:2)

In expression of this nature, he gave himself freely in Jesus Christ for human forgiveness. The only way humans can receive God's grace is to believe this good news and trust him. As the preceding section was a theological reflection on the nature of sin, this section turns to the theological topic of the atonement.[13]

The etymology of the English word "atonement" is not certain, but one explanation is that it is derived from "at-one-ment," that is, the condition of being at one, the making one of those estranged. Through Christian history thinkers have advanced various theories of the atonement — the ransom, satisfaction, and moral-exemplary having been the most prominent. The Bible, however, does not present a "theory of the atonement." In many of its teachings, the Bible reveals a fact or declares a truth, but does not offer an explanation of why or how this is so. The saving significance of the death and resurrection of Jesus is one of these subjects. The Bible does not offer a systematic explanation of how the atonement works or why God accepts the death of Jesus as providing forgiveness of sins. The writers of the New Testament do describe the meaning of what God has done in terms familiar to the people of the time. They employ various images drawn from familiar experiences to convey a truth. These images describe or illustrate a reality, but they do not actually explain how the reality works. We now turn to the religious, relational, commercial, forensic, and military language employed to describe the significance of the death of Jesus.

---

13. James Denney, *The Death of Christ* (New Hork: Hodder & Stoughton, n.d.); Leon Morris, *The Apostolic Preaching of the Cross* (Grand Rapids: Eerdmans, 1956); Vincent Taylor, *The Atonement in New Testament Teaching*, 3rd ed. (London: Epworth, 1958); Morna D. Hooker, "Interchange in Christ," *Journal of Theological Studies* n.s. 22 (1971): 349-361; idem, "Interchange and Atonement," *Bulletin of the John Rylands Library* 60 (1978): 462-481; Martin Hengel, *The Atonement* (Philadelphia: Fortress, 1981); Leon Morris, *The Atonement: Its Meaning and Significance* (Downers Grove, Ill.: InterVarsity, 1983); Paul S. Fiddes, *Past Event and Present Salvation: The Christian Idea of Atonement* (Louisville: Westminster/John Knox, 1989); Anthony J. Tambasco, *A Theology of Atonement and Paul's Vision of Christianity* (Collegeville, Minn.: Liturgical Press, 1991); H. D. McDonald, *The New Testament Concept of the Atonement: The Gospel of the Calvary Event* (Grand Rapids: Baker, 1994).

Different Descriptions of the Atonement

Sacrifice — The Language of Worship

An important description of the death of Jesus is provided by the terminology of sacrifice.[14] Sacrifice was the universal language of religion in the ancient world. Although there were sacrifices of grain, fruit, incense, and liquids, many sacrifices involved the killing of an animal. Hence, it is no wonder that this imagery of sacrifice is applied to the significance of Jesus' death on the cross.

The language of sacrifice is not as common as might be expected in describing the death of Jesus, but it is frequent enough to show that this familiar imagery was readily used to interpret the significance of what happened on the cross. "Christ loved us and gave himself up for us, a fragrant offering and sacrifice to God" (Eph. 5:2). An extended discussion of the death of Jesus under the imagery of the Old Testament sacrificial system is provided in Hebrews 7:1–10:10.

A special case of sacrificial language is provided by the *hilaskomai* word group.[15] There has been dispute whether to translate as "propitiate," which in English has a person as the object, or "expiate," which in English refers to a thing. Since both words are no longer common in English, recent translations avoid the debate by choosing "atone" or "make atonement" as the rendering. *Hilaskomai* in classical Greek meant "to placate" or "to appease" an angry person or deity. In the Old Testament, this word group was used to translate, among other Hebrew words, those from the *kipper* family. The Hebrew word means either "to cover" or "to wipe away," and then with reference to sin "to make atonement" or "to ransom."[16] It is the word in *Yom Kippur,* the Day of Atonement.

14. Vincent Taylor, *Jesus and His Sacrifice* (London: Macmillan, 1937); B. B. Warfield, "Christ Our Sacrifice," *Biblical Foundations* (London: Tyndale, 1958), pp. 163-198; Frances Young, *Sacrifice and the Death of Christ* (London: SPCK, 1975), pp. 64-81; Robert J. Daly, *The Origins of the Christian Doctrine of Sacrifice* (Philadelphia: Fortress, 1978); B. D. Chilton, *The Temple of Jesus: His Sacrificial Program Within a Cultural History of Sacrifice* (University Park: Penn State Press, 1992); Roger T. Beckwith and Martin J. Selman, eds., *Sacrifice in the Bible* (Grand Rapids: Baker, 1995).

15. C. H. Dodd, *The Bible and the Greeks* (London: Hodder & Stoughton, 1935), pp. 82-95; Leon Morris, *The Apostolic Preaching of the Cross,* 2nd ed. (Grand Rapids: Eerdmans, 1956), pp. 125-185; D. Hill, *Greek Words and Hebrew Meanings* (Cambridge: University Press, 1967), pp. 23-48; Kenneth Grayston, "Hilaskesthai and Related Words in LXX," *New Testament Studies* 27 (1981): 640-656.

16. L. Koehler and W. Baumgartner, eds., *Lexicon in Veteris Testamenti Libros* (Grand Rapids: Eerdmans, 1958), pp. 451-453, give these definitions: verb — cover

In New Testament usage, the *hilaskomai* family of words always has sin as its object. "So that he might be a merciful and faithful high priest in the service of God, to make a sacrifice of atonement for the sins of the people" (Heb. 2:17). The biblical (Hebrew) idea, without this word, is expressed in Hebrews 9:26, "He has appeared once for all at the end of the age to remove sin by the sacrifice of himself." The noun *hilasmos* occurs with the same meaning of the removal of sin: "He is the expiation [atoning sacrifice] for our sins" (1 John 2:2); "In this is love, not that we loved God but that he loved us, and sent his Son to be the expiation [atoning sacrifice] for our sins" (1 John 4:10). One may compare the noun *hilastērion*, used in the Greek Old Testament and Hebrews 9:5 for the mercyseat over the ark of the covenant. The same word is used in Romans 3:25, "God put forward Christ as a sacrifice of atonement by his blood." The passage may be comparing Christ specifically to the mercyseat, or the meaning may be more generally that Christ is the place or means of atonement.[17]

The translation of *hilaskomai* as "expiate" rather than "propitiate" does not question God's wrath, only whether the wrath of God is the object of this word group. Its presence in the background of thought is another matter. Actually, the debate over whether *hilaskomai* has a personal or impersonal reference in the Bible and whether the elements of God's wrath and punishment are included in the word has obscured the main difference between the New Testament and pagan thought. In the New Testament, instead of a sacrifice offered by human beings to God, this word group refers to a sacrifice made by God himself (Rom. 3:25: 1 John 4:10). Some passages use the expected language of a sacrifice offered to God (Eph. 5:2), but the New Testament usage of *hilastērion*

(but noting that the Akkadian root means "to wipe off"), make amends, make atonement, exempt from punishment; noun — ransom. R. L. Harris et al., *Theological Wordbook of the Old Testament* (Chicago: Moody, 1980), Vol. 1, pp. 452-453, derive the verb from the noun "ransom," rejecting the etymological association with the Arabic "cover," and define the verb as "make atonement," "make reconciliation," "purge." H. Gese, "The Atonement," *Essays on Biblical Theology* (Minneapolis: Augsburg, 1981), pp. 93-94, emphasizes the idea of substitution in the Hebrew word.

17. Leon Morris, "The Meaning of *Hilasterion* in Romans III.25," *New Testament Studies* 2 (1956): 33-43, concludes that the reference is not to the mercy seat nor the day of atonement, but to the removal of the wrath of God. James D. G. Dunn, *Romans 1–8* (Dallas: Word, 1988), pp. 171-172, combines the ideas of propitiation and expiation. See also Daniel P. Bailey, "Jesus as the Mercy Seat: The Semantics and Theology of Paul's Use of *Hilasterion* in Romans 3:25," *Tyndale Bulletin* 51 (2000): 155-158.

and *hilasmos* stands the pagan Greek idea on its head. God is not appeased or propitiated. He himself acts to remove the sin that separates human beings from him. Instead of humans offering the sacrifice, God himself expiates or makes atonement for sins. God performs the sacrifice. The divine action for human salvation completely reverses the usual understanding of religion and worship.

Reconciliation — The Language of Personal Relations

"To reconcile" meant originally "to exchange" and then "to change from enmity to friendship, to make friends again."[18] The idea of reconciliation is not part of the usual religious language in the Septuagint or Hellenistic Greek. It derives from personal relationships, especially secular diplomatic terminology. The word is exclusively Pauline in the New Testament. Paul describes salvation as humanity being brought into a state of friendship with God. Where there was enmity, there is now peace.

All the important elements in the imagery of reconciliation applied to the human relationship to God are found in 2 Corinthians 5:18-20:

> All this [the new creation] is from God, who reconciled us to himself through Christ, and has given us the ministry of reconciliation; that is, in Christ God was reconciling the world to himself, not counting their trespasses against them, and entrusting the message of reconciliation to us. So we are ambassadors for Christ, since God is making his appeal through us; we entreat you on behalf of Christ, be reconciled to God. For our sake he made him to be sin who knew no sin, so that in him we might become the righteousness of God.

The subject of the action, the one doing the reconciling, is God himself. God does not need to be reconciled to us; we need to be reconciled to God. Since our sins against God have estranged us from God, God must take the initiative to restore the relationship. "All this is from God."

18. J. A. Fitzmyer, "Reconciliation in Pauline Theology," *To Advance the Gospel: New Testament Studies* (New York: Crossroad, 1981); R. P. Martin, *Reconciliation: A Study of Paul's Theology* (Atlanta: John Knox, 1981); P. Stuhlmacher, *Reconciliation, Law and Righteousness* (Philadelphia: Fortress, 1986); Cilliers Breytenbach, *Versöhnung: Eine Studie zur paulinischen Soteriologie* (Neukirchen-Vluyn: Neukirchener, 1989).

The object of the reconciliation is we human beings. "For if while we were enemies, we were reconciled to God through the death of his Son, much more surely, having been reconciled, we will be saved by his life" (Rom. 5:10).

In human relationships, there is often the need for a mediator to effect reconciliation; it may be in employer-employee disputes, in business dealings, in legal conflicts, or in personal disagreements. The mediator between God and humanity is Jesus Christ (1 Tim. 2:5-6). God effected the reconciliation in Christ. "Through Christ we have now received reconciliation" (Rom. 5:11). The circumstance in which Christ mediated this reconciliation was his death on the cross. He "died for the ungodly" (Rom. 5:6), so God did not count the trespasses of human beings against them (2 Cor. 5:19).

The theme of Jesus' ministry was "peace" (Acts 10:34-36). That peace was primarily between God and humanity (Rom. 5:1), but the context in Acts 10 would have had relations between Jews and Gentiles near the surface if not the primary point. That theme of peace between Jews and Gentiles becomes explicit in Ephesians 2:14-15, 17.[19] The reconciliation of both Jews and Gentiles to God occurs in the one body of the church (Eph. 2:16). Reconciliation with God is the basis for reconciliation among human beings. The bringing of Jews and Gentiles into one body overcame the major religio-cultural barrier of the ancient world. No modern animosity offers a greater barrier to peace and unity.

Reconciliation transforms human conduct in the present. In Christ, we become the righteousness of God. For the practical consequences of reconciliation in conduct, note Colossians 1:20-22:

> Through him God was pleased to reconcile to himself all things, whether on earth or in heaven, by making peace through the blood of the cross. And you who were once estranged and hostile in mind, doing evil deeds, he has now reconciled in his fleshly body through death, so as to present you holy and blameless and irreproachable before him.

19. Peter Stuhlmacher, "Jesus as Reconciler: Reflections on the Problem of Portraying Jesus Within the Framework of a Biblical Theology of the New Testament" and "'He is our Peace' (Eph. 2:14): On the Exegesis and Significance of Ephesians 2:14-18," *Reconciliation, Law, & Righteousness: Essays in Biblical Theology* (Philadelphia: Fortress, 1986), pp. 1-15, 182-200.

Enemies, or those who think themselves enemies, do hateful things to each other. Friends do good things for each other. Human estrangement from God results in bad conduct; being brought back to a state of friendship with God results in good conduct.

The reconciliation begun with the death of Jesus on the cross is not completed. What was inaugurated in Christ must continue until the final resurrection (cf. Rom. 11:15). Hence, there is now a ministry of reconciliation (2 Cor. 5:18), conducted by the ambassadors of God who bring the message of reconciliation (2 Cor. 5:19) to those who are entangled in sin.

Redemption — The Language of the Marketplace

What God did through the death of Christ is also described in commercial language.[20] The language of purchase is explicit in 1 Corinthians 6:19-20, "Do you not know . . . that you are not your own? For you were bought with a price." On the basis that a buyer owns what he purchases, Paul concludes that we are not free to use our bodies in any way we want but must use them to glorify God. Paul likely has the slave market particularly in mind (cf. 1 Cor. 7:23). Other passages use the same ordinary word for a commercial purchase *(agorazō)* to describe God's ownership of his people (2 Pet. 2:1; Rev. 14:3-4), specifying the blood of Christ as the price of the purchase (Rev. 5:9). Without the special aspect of a purchase, the notion of acquiring or possessing is present in Acts 20:28, "the church that he obtained with blood."

The word "redeem" literally means "to buy back," and the Greek noun for redemption *(apolytrosis)*, which was used for buying back a slave or a captive, is used for the "redemption from transgressions" (Heb. 9:15) "that is in Christ Jesus" (Rom. 3:24; cf. 1 Cor. 1:30). Redemption too, as was true of an ordinary purchase, is connected with the blood of Christ (Eph. 1:7). This redemption may be viewed as the present forgiveness of sins (Col. 1:14) or the future redemption of the body (Rom. 8:23; cf. Eph. 1:14; 4:30).

---

20. B. B. Warfield, "The New Testament Terminology of Redemption," *Biblical Foundations* (London: Tyndale, 1929), pp. 199-245; S. Lyonnet and L. Sabourin, *Sin, Redemption, and Sacrifice* (Rome: Biblical Institute, 1970): I. H. Marshall, "The Development of the Concept of Redemption in the New Testament," *Reconciliation and Hope*, ed. R. Banks (Grand Rapids: Eerdmans, 1974), pp. 153-169.

The "ransom" family of words *(lytron, lytroō)* was especially used for buying back those who were captives, whether by armies, pirates, or brigands. The emphasis in the Greek Old Testament and the New Testament is more on the resultant deliverance and freedom than on the price paid. Usage of the verb in the New Testament includes 1 Peter 1:18f, where the ransom price is the blood of Christ, and Titus 2:14, where the emphasis is on deliverance from iniquity to a life of good deeds. The noun is used by Jesus in Matthew 20:28 and Mark 10:45, "The Son of Man came not to be served but to serve, and to give his life a ransom for many" (cf. 1 Tim. 2:5-6). The verbal echoes of Isaiah 43:3-4 (cf. also 45:14-17; 49:3; 52:13–53:12) suggest that Jesus took on the substitutionary suffering of Israel as God's servant by giving his life as a ransom for all.[21]

The emphasis in the language of ransom on the result of being set free points up the difficulty with some expressions of the "ransom theory" of the atonement. The New Testament use of the imagery is designed to make one point: the fact of deliverance. As with the imagery about the nature of the church, one must be careful not to extend the analogy beyond what the New Testament does. The biblical authors declare the fact or truth of the atonement under the imagery of a ransom. They do not go further to explain how this worked. That is what the ransom theory in some of its expressions sought to do. If God paid a price for human redemption, it was asked, to whom did he make the payment? It must have been the devil. If so, what is the claim of the devil over human life, and is it a just claim? And so the speculation goes. One finds it hard to give biblical answers to unbiblical questions. It is better to leave this description where the other imagery is, as a use of language familiar to the people of the time to reveal the significance of what God did in Christ. To make any of these descriptions into a theory, or to extend them beyond the biblical usage, is, at best, to say more than can be confirmed, and, at worst, to say something the Bible does not say. Once more, let it be noted, God is the one who does the ransoming.

---

21. Peter Stuhlmacher, "Vicariously Giving His Life for Many, Mark 10:45 (Matt. 20:28)," *Reconciliation, Law, and Righteousness: Essays in Biblical Theology* (Philadelphia: Fortress, 1986), pp. 23-24, pointing out that *lytron* corresponds to the Hebrew *kopher*, which means a substitution or ransom. The article as a whole (pp. 16-29) argues that Mark 10:45 is authentic.

Justification — The Language of the Law Court

The average person in the Greek world had much more direct experience with the law courts than does the average person today. This was because any person (but usually a trained orator) and not a professional lawyer could argue cases, and many more disputes were settled in the public assemblies of citizens than is true today. Justification was a legal or forensic term, meaning to be declared righteous. English usage prefers "righteousness" for the noun and "justify" for the verb in translating words from the same root in Greek.

The language of justification in the Old Testament has a juridical and forensic (declaratory) sense. It refers especially to proper conduct within the covenant relationship. In the secular context, to be justified was to be approved by the king. The New Testament continues the same idea. When the concept is placed in the religious sphere, God is the King who has pronounced a verdict that entirely alters the condition of the person before him. God has pronounced the verdict of "not guilty" upon the sinner, or better, "guilty but pardoned," so that the sentence of punishment is not executed. There is in both testaments recognition of human righteousness in the broad sense of conduct approved by God, but our primary interest here is in the righteousness of God, that is God's activity in justifying (declaring righteous) or vindicating his servants.[22]

Paul is the author who makes the greatest use of the language of justification, and for him the verdict of God is declared in the unique fact of Christ crucified and risen (Rom. 4:25). The human condition, as outlined above, is essentially defined by the divine condemnation for sin. Notice the collection of judicial terms in Romans 5:18: "Just as one man's trespass led to condemnation for all, so one man's act of righteousness leads to justification [acquittal — RSV] and life for all." God's justifying activity (the "righteousness of God") is revealed in the gospel (Rom. 1:17).

Justification is received (accepted) by (through) faith. The believer relies on the work of God accomplished in Christ and renounces all

---

22. Markus Barth, *Justification* (Grand Rapids, 1971); Nils Dahl, "The Doctrine of Justification," *Studies in Paul* (Minneapolis: Augsburg, 1977), pp. 95-120; E. Käsemann, "The Righteousness of God in Paul," *New Testament Questions of Today* (Philadelphia: Fortress, 1969), pp. 169-182; M. A. Seifri, *Justification by Faith: The Origin and Development of a Central Pauline Theme* (Leiden: Brill, 1992); James D. G. Dunn and Alan M. Suggate, *The Justice of God: A Fresh Look at the Old Doctrine of Justification by Faith* (Grand Rapids: Eerdmans, 1995).

claims to a righteousness of his own. He is justified by faith, because the reliance is now on the sole righteousness of God.

The meaning of the phrase "the faith of Christ" (Rom. 3:22, 26; Gal. 2:16; 3:22; Eph. 3:12: Phil. 3:9) is disputed.[23] Is the reference to our faith in Christ, or to Christ's faith in God? Or is the phrase equivalent to "the gospel of Christ," "the truth of Christ," "the mystery of Christ," and other expressions for the system or plan of salvation? The decision in individual passages does not greatly affect the overall understanding of New Testament teaching. There is no doubt that Christ's faithfulness in carrying out the plan of God was the means through which God justifies the ungodly (Rom. 3:21-26; 1 Cor. 1:30; 2 Cor. 5:21). Even if all the passages speaking of "the faith of Christ" refer to Christ's faith, there are many passages remaining where righteousness is connected with human faith (Rom. 4:11, 13; 9:30; 10:6, 10; Gal. 5:5).

Paul often associates justification with faith. A succinct statement is Philippians 3:9: "That I may be found in Christ, not having a righteousness of my own that comes from the law but one that comes through faith in Christ [or through the faithfulness of Christ], the righteousness from God based on faith." Paul's emphasis on justification by faith occurs primarily in Romans and Galatians, that is, in a context defending the reception of the Gentiles into the church without requiring them to submit to circumcision and other requirements of the law of Moses.[24] Justification by faith (whether Christ's faith in service to God or human faith in receiving God's grace) is contrasted with the law as a system or principle of justification. Justification by faith, in the sense of human faith, is not absolutized in the way it often has been in Protestant theology. Rather it is a way of universalizing the gospel, for the response of faith is open to all, Gentiles as well as Jews. The law of

23. George Howard, "On the Faith of Christ," *Harvard Theological Review* 60 (1967): 459-465; idem, "The Faith of Christ," *Expository Times* 85 (1973-74): 212-214; A. T. Hultgren, "The *Pistis Christou* Formulation in Paul," *Novum Testamentum* 22 (1980): 248-263; R. B. Hays, *The Faith of Jesus Christ: An Investigation of the Narrative Structure of Galatians 3:1-4–4:11* (Chico, Calif.: Scholars Press, 1983); Morna Hooker, "Pistis Christou," *New Testament Studies* 35 (1989): 321-342.

24. E. P. Sanders, *Paul, the Law, and the Jewish People* (Philadelphia: Fortress, 1983), p. 10 and passim, esp. pp. 46-47, 113-114, makes the distinction for Paul between how one gets "in" (by faith and not by works of law) and how one who is already "in" behaves (he keeps the law of God). The law is not an entrance requirement, but the law (with certain exceptions) should be fulfilled. Cf. James D. G. Dunn, *The Theology of Paul's Letter to the Galatians* (Cambridge: University Press, 1993), esp. pp. 76-85.

Moses was given to the Jews, and one was born into relation with it or in effect had to become a Jew to share in the relationship. There had to be another principle of justification, available to all, in the new age that welcomed Gentiles. A spiritual principle of justification was required — the faith principle, not the flesh principle. Understanding justification in terms of its Old Testament background of God's faithfulness to the covenant in claiming a people for himself brings this image into relation with the community idea (see pp. 2-14 on the covenant).

The debate between Protestant and medieval theology concerning whether God imputes or infuses righteousness into the believer may similarly be an exaggerated difference. The juridical background of the language of justification supports the forensic or declaratory meaning of the terms. But that is not the whole story. The righteousness "imputed" is a real righteousness. The person to whom God for Jesus' sake no longer imputes sins is "righteous" before God, and that is all that matters. A "pardoned sinner" is really pardoned and therefore truly "righteous."

The person thus pardoned can and must lead a truly new and righteous life. "Having been set free from sin, you have become slaves of righteousness" (Rom. 6:18). Justification by God releases the spiritual energy that makes possible living a justified life. The person who has been justified by God then pursues righteousness (1 Tim. 6:11; 2 Tim. 2:22). Righteous living includes (and this meaning reflects a Hebrew and Jewish usage) the doing of charitable deeds (Matt. 6:1-2; 2 Cor. 9:9). Human righteous conduct is the consequence of God's justifying activity in Christ.

The emphasis in the use of judicial imagery, as in the others employed in the New Testament, is on what God does.

Victory — The Language of Warfare

God's action in Christ is described in the military imagery of a victory won over the forces of evil that hold humanity in their power. "He disarmed the rulers and authorities and made a public example of them, triumphing over them in it [the cross; or in him, Christ]" (Col. 2:15). The verb translated "triumphing over" means primarily "to lead in a triumphal procession," referring to the practice of Roman armies to celebrate a triumph after defeating an enemy. The same verb occurs in 2 Corinthians 2:14, where Paul describes God as leading us in triumphal procession, or perhaps "causes us to triumph." The language of "rulers and authorities," or "principalities and powers," is applied to intermediary spiritual beings who oppose the purposes of God and seek to rule over humanity. In a world that was very conscious of the presence of intermediary spiritual powers influencing human life, the Christian gospel's promise of deliverance from them and transfer into Christ's benevolent realm (Col. 1:13) had a powerful appeal.[25] Jesus showed his victory over the forces of evil in his ministry (Matt. 12:22-32; Mark 1:23-27; Luke 10:17-19), so ultimate victory is assured to his people (Rev. 12:7-8, 17; 19:19-20).

The military imagery is often used in reference to the Christian life, either for the armor to be worn in the conflict (1 Thess. 5:8; Eph. 6:10-17) or as an illustration of the necessary attitudes and conduct (2 Cor. 10:3-5; 2 Tim. 2:3-4).

Military victory overcomes the evil powers, justification overcomes law and guilt, redemption overcomes slavery to sin, reconciliation overcomes hostility and chaos, and sacrifice overcomes the need for appeasement. Whether one thinks in terms of the temple, personal contacts, the marketplace, the law court, or the battlefield, God is at work. Each image of the atonement emphasizes what God did: he makes the atoning sacrifice, he reconciles, he redeems, he justifies, he wins the victory. In all aspects God is triumphant.

Further Theological Reflections on the Atonement

Importance of the Blood

All the New Testament descriptions of the atonement center in Christ, and specifically in the cross. Often the blood is mentioned. The shedding of blood is obviously associated with sacrifice (Rom. 3:25; Heb. 9:12-14). The blood of Christ is mentioned also in connection with ransom or redemption (Eph. 1:7; Heb. 9:12), reconciliation (Col. 1:20), and justification (Rom. 5:9). The New Testament teaching about salvation is closely tied in with a blood atonement. The author of Hebrews explicitly connects the blood of Jesus with the shedding of blood that inaugurated the old covenant and continued to be central to its ceremonies: "Indeed, under the law almost everything is purified with blood,

25. G. B. Caird, *Principalities and Powers: A Study in Pauline Theology* (Oxford: Oxford University Press, 1956); Everett Ferguson, *Demonology of the Early Christian World* (New York: Mellen, 1984), pp. 1-32, 143-176; Clinton E. Arnold, *Powers of Darkness: Principalities and Powers in Paul's Letters* (Downers Grove: InterVarsity, 1992).

and without the shedding of blood there is no forgiveness of sins" (Heb. 9:22).[26] This teaching is often offensive to modern sensibilities, but given the practices and understandings of the ancient world, and especially the biblical teaching that "life is in the blood" (Lev. 17:11), nothing else would be expected in the interpretation of the shedding of the blood of Jesus on the cross.[27] A profound truth is expressed by the blood atonement. "There is no substitute for blood."

Inadequate Views of the Atonement

An exaggeration of the importance of the blood has led to the suggestion that one drop of Jesus' blood would have been sufficient for universal atonement. This may have some theoretical justification as paying honor to the blood of Christ, but could also be seen as questioning the divine wisdom, because so much more, both in quantity of blood and in suffering, was involved in Jesus' death. Theological speculation seems never content to leave matters where the biblical texts leave them.

A common theological position holds to limited atonement, that Christ's death was only for the elect. It is true that the benefits of Christ's death are applied only to the elect, but to say that he died only for the elect goes against too many explicit statements of scripture. "Just as one man's trespass led to condemnation for all, so one man's act of righteousness leads to justification and life for all" (Rom. 5:18). God "desires everyone to be saved and to come to the knowledge of the truth" (1 Tim. 2:4). Christ is a "ransom for all" (1 Tim. 2:6). "We have our hope set on the living God, who is the Savior of all people, especially of those who believe" (1 Tim. 4:10). Christ "is the atoning sacrifice for our sins, and not for ours only but also for the sins of the whole world" (1 John 2:2). The death and resurrection of Jesus made salvation available to all.[28] The appropriation of that salvation will be developed below.

An opposite view to that of limited atonement makes salvation

26. John Dunnill, *Covenant and Sacrifice in the Letter to the Hebrews* (Cambridge: University Press, 1992), gives a sociological and anthropological interpretation of the language of sacrifice in Hebrews; on blood, see esp. pp. 231-234.

27. On the necessity of the death of the animal and with it the shedding of blood in the Old Testament ritual of atonement, see Hartmut Gese, *Essays on Biblical Theology* (Minneapolis: Augsburg, 1981), pp. 93-116.

28. Terry L. Miethe, "The Universal Power of the Atonement," in Clark H. Pinnock, ed., *The Grace of God, The Will of Man* (Grand Rapids: Zondervan, 1989), pp. 71-96.

even for the elect uncertain. Some see the death of Christ as providing only a "chance" at salvation. The terminology is poorly chosen even for the view intended, for what is meant is the opportunity. A lottery rewards a few of those who enter; that is a chance. But God says, "Everyone who calls upon the name of the Lord will be saved" (Acts 2:21, quoting Joel 2:32). Christ died not to give a chance, but to give a certainty of salvation. "He has appeared once for all at the end of the age to remove sin by the sacrifice of himself. . . . So Christ, having been offered once to bear the sins of many, will appear a second time, not to deal with sin, but to save those who are eagerly waiting for him" (Heb. 9:26-28). That promise gives confidence to human life in the face of death and judgment. There are opposite temptations: complacently to presume on divine forgiveness, or to despair before the divine demands. Both attitudes misunderstand the gospel message.

Another inadequate view of the atonement applies the death on the cross only to those who live on this side of the cross. The benefits extend both ways. It is true that under the Mosaic law there was a reminder of sins each year (Heb. 10:3), but there was a real forgiveness promised to people at that time (cf. such passages as Lev. 4–5; 16; 1 Kings 8:30-39, 50). The Christian may affirm that this forgiveness was granted in anticipation of the perfect sacrifice of atonement by Jesus Christ, but in the experience of the people there was no less assurance of forgiveness, because it was based on the promise of God. That assurance is made even stronger for people today by reason of the death and resurrection of Jesus.

The Preaching of the Cross

The preaching of the gospel provides the connection between the once for all action of God at the cross and the continuing human appropriation of salvation. The crucifixion and resurrection of Jesus were God's action, God's initiative. His initiative took place in history, at the cross and in the commission to preach the cross. There is a parallel here with the story of Israel. God's act at the Exodus created a people by their common experience of deliverance. This people still had to be organized and given a distinctive way of life. That took place through the giving of the law at Sinai. There was both a victory and a proclamation. In a comparable way, Calvary had to be followed by Pentecost. The victory accomplished in the Christ-event must be communicated. The God who acts in a personal way for human salvation requires a response from the people.

The word "gospel" means "good news." Paul summarizes "as of first importance" what he received and handed on: "that Christ died for our sins . . . that he was buried, and that he was raised on the third day," and all of this was "in accordance with the scriptures" (1 Cor. 15:3-5). Those facts he said were the gospel that he preached, that converts received and stood upon, and by which they were saved (1 Cor. 15:1-2). They were the fulfillment of what God had "promised beforehand through his prophets in the holy scriptures" (Rom. 1:1-4). The gospel writers ground this proclamation to which Paul refers in a command by the resurrected Christ (Matt. 28:18-20; Mark 16:15-16; Luke 24:47-49). This "great commission" comes at the close and climax of the Gospels. It is set in the heart of the redemptive acts: after the death and resurrection of Jesus and before his ascension and the descent of the Holy Spirit. Its fulfillment began with the events in Acts 2. First Corinthians 15:1-5 ties the preaching of the gospel to the subject of the atonement. Preaching the good news about Jesus is preaching what accomplishes the atonement.

The prominence of the theme of "calling" in the New Testament (see also p. 86) derives from the importance of preaching and teaching the message from God about Christ. The words for "call" or "calling" could refer to "name, designation," but in the New Testament, especially Paul, they refer to "invitation, summons." Even as God's grace called Paul to be an apostle (Rom. 1:1; 1 Cor. 1:1; Gal. 1:15), so God called people to himself (1 Thess. 2:12) through the gospel (2 Thess. 2:14), with the result that "the called" becomes a description of Christians (Rom. 1:6-7; 1 Cor. 1:2, 24). The calling is to hope (Eph. 1:18; 4:4; cf. Phil. 3:14; 1 Tim. 6:12; Heb. 3:1; 1 Pet. 5:10), and as a holy calling (2 Tim. 1:9) it requires appropriate living (Eph. 4:1; 1 Thess. 4:7; see Chap. 6). God issues his call or invitation through his word.

The preaching of the gospel of Jesus dead, buried, and raised provides the transition from the divine to the human sides of salvation. The preaching of the gospel calls forth the human response, but even this human side of salvation is God-initiated. God instituted not only the salvation but also the proclamation of the salvation. The preaching is commissioned by God through Christ. This was Paul's understanding of his ministry; he was divinely commissioned, so that he felt under obligation to preach (Gal. 1:11-12, 15-16; 1 Cor. 9:16-17). God "gave us birth by the word of truth" (James 1:18). So, preaching is a part of God's plan of salvation. It must be carried out by human beings, but under a divine commission. Preaching is God's planned way to unite his re-demptive action in Christ and human reception of that redemption.

Both medieval sacramentalism and modern revivalism's doctrine of the direct operation of the Holy Spirit tended to blur the distinctive place of preaching in God's plan. Among modern theologians, Karl Barth has called attention again to the theological significance of the preached word.

HUMAN RESPONSE

> *"The proclamation of Jesus Christ . . .*
> *to bring about the obedience of faith."* (ROM. 16:25-26)

Faith

Importance

The proclamation of God's grace calls forth a response from human beings. The basic human response to God's saving action in Christ may be expressed by and is summed up in the word "faith." The fundamental importance of faith is set forth in several passages. "Without faith it is impossible to please God" (Heb. 11:6); "we are justified by faith" (Rom. 5:1); "in Christ Jesus you are all children of God through faith" (Gal. 3:26); "by grace you have been saved through faith" (Eph. 2:8).

The characteristics of biblical, saving faith may now be discussed.

Produced by the Preaching of the Gospel of Christ

How does a person come to believe? One explanation, derived from the church father Augustine and passed on to Protestants by Martin Luther and John Calvin, is that God predestines those who will be saved and gives to them faith. The direct opposite of this teaching is the secular view that faith is an arbitrary attitude arising from a person's own irrational, perhaps superstitious, decision. The biblical explanation falls between these extremes.

Saving faith comes by hearing the word about Christ. The word of God is associated with power (e.g., Heb. 1:3). The power of God that works for salvation is identified with the "gospel" (Rom. 1:16) and more specifically with the "word of the cross" (1 Cor. 1:18). The word of God has power to save, but it must be implanted in the human heart (James 1:21). The "heard word" saves. Paul explains how faith is produced: "So faith comes from hearing what is told, and hearing through the message about Christ" (Rom. 10:17, Williams). Paul contrasts the law of Moses with preaching the cross of Christ as the source of the gift of the Holy Spirit: "It was before your eyes that Jesus Christ was publicly exhibited as crucified! . . . Did you receive the Spirit by doing the works of the law or by believing what you heard?" (Gal. 3:1-2; cf. 3:5)." Since the message is Christ, accepting the message means believing in him.

The scriptures ascribe the divine begetting to the instrumentality of the divine word (James 1:18; 1 Pet. 1:23-25; 1 John 3:9; cf. John 1:12-13). One should note how often the Bible connects the word or speaking with believing. A striking phraseology is found in Acts 14:1, "Paul and Barnabas . . . spoke in such a way that a great number of both Jews and Greeks became believers." Faith is the response to the proclaiming of the Christian message (John 17:20; Rom. 10:14-15; 16:25-26; 1 Cor. 15:11). Receiving the message and searching the scriptures "whether these things were so" resulted ("therefore") in believing (Acts 17:11-12). The consistent order of conversion is summarized in Acts 18:8, "Many of the Corinthians who heard Paul became believers and were baptized."

Since faith comes from hearing the word, there is a sense in which one may say that faith is given by God. The verse usually cited to support this idea does not say so: "For by grace you have been saved through faith, and this is not your own doing; it is the gift of God" (Eph. 2:8). "This," which is neuter in Greek, grammatically cannot refer to faith, which is feminine, but must refer to the idea of salvation as the gift of God. Nevertheless, faith is not human generated. An individual does not produce faith in him/herself or in another person. Only the word that sets forth the mighty, loving, salvific action of God can do this. God's loving action has always, throughout biblical history, launched faith. Faith is not faith in faith, but faith in God's action (Heb. 11:6). Since God supplies the content of faith and the means by which it is created, he is the one who gives faith. He may, furthermore, give the influences that make for receptivity and so prepare for faith (Acts 16:14). On the other hand, God does not directly create the response. He does not give faith to some and withhold it from others. Since the word that produces faith is God's word, God is the ultimate source of faith. The preached word produces faith.

The Elements of Faith

The nature of the saving faith produced by the word of God may be seen from the example of Abraham as presented in Romans 4. Paul argues against the necessity of Gentile believers submitting to circumcision and the law of Moses by appealing to the case of Abraham. "Abraham believed God and it was reckoned to him as righteousness" (Rom. 4:3, quoting Gen. 15:6). Abraham is an example of what it means to believe so as to be accounted or declared right, or just, by God, to be forgiven not by works but as God's gift (Rom. 4:4-8). This happened before Abraham received circumcision (Rom. 4:9-12) and so demonstrates the principle on which God accepts people (Rom. 4:13-15) and assures that the promises to Abraham are available to Gentiles as well as to his fleshly descendants, that is, to all who share his faith (Rom. 4:16-25, and see pp. 3-4 on the covenant with Abraham).

The nature of Abraham's faith is especially evident in Romans 4:17-25. For the purposes of this exposition, we will work backwards through the passage. Verse 25 is what Christ did for us — he was handed over to death and raised. Verses 23-24 state the benefit for us — we are reckoned as righteous. Verse 22 declares the basis — faith. Verses 19-21 are the key to the nature of faith. It is trust in the promises of God — "being fully convinced that God was able to do what he had promised." Verse 18 states the promise to Abraham. Verse 17 affirms the nature of the God who made the promises. Abraham believed in the same God, the God with the same nature, in whom Christians believe: a God "who gives life to the dead and calls into existence the things that do not exist" (vs. 17), the God "who raised Jesus our Lord from the dead" (vs. 24). Faith in that kind of God means being fully persuaded that he will do what he has said he will do.

An analysis of faith shows that it involves the intellect, the emotions, and the will. It encompasses the assent of the intellect, the trust of the emotions, and the obedience of the will. All three elements are in the story of Abraham in Genesis 12:1-9. Abraham assented to the call of God, trusted God's promise to make of him a great nation, and obeyed God by departing from all that was familiar in order to go to a country yet to be shown to him. The essential element is the middle term, but trust presupposes the acceptance of something as true and results in acting upon it. These three elements of biblical faith require some elaboration.

Assent   Faith involves the acceptance of a truth, an intellectual assent. "Faith comes by hearing." Information is given, or a proposition is stated. God must first speak. His word is the basis of faith; it is accepted or rejected. Hebrews 11:6 thus is not an arbitrary statement. The only way to receive a revelation is by faith; the only way to know God's will is to believe what he says.

Some statements are so compelling that one is branded as stupid for not accepting them: For example, "There is a city named Moscow." Other statements call for a decision: For example, "There is a God." Religious statements belong in this latter category, for religion deals with the unseen, where the evidence cannot be overwhelming to the senses. Faith is a conviction concerning "things not seen" (Heb. 11:1). Moreover, religion involves ultimate concerns; it is about issues on which one has to take a stand. A person cannot be neutral about ultimate concerns. To attempt to avoid the question of God is to make a decision about God. The evidence for God is not satisfied by giving passive assent in the same way one may acknowledge "there is a Moscow" without it having any practical consequences (unless one decides to go there). Not to accept that two plus two equals four may cause some inconveniences but hardly is of ultimate significance.

These statements illustrate that we believe a lot of things in the sense of intellectual acceptance, but this by itself is quite different from saving faith. Out of all the things to which we give mental assent, there are some of these in which we place our trust.

Trust   Faith involves not only mental consent but also trust. It requires surrender and commitment.

Trust means confidence, taking someone at his/her word. "I trust that person" means "I have confidence in what he does; I believe he'll do what he says." Trust is the act in which one may rely on the faithfulness, the trustworthiness of another; that his promise holds and what he asks he asks of necessity. Even as human assent answers to the truthfulness of God, so trust rests on the trustworthiness of God. He is faithful (Rom. 3:3-4), and he expects this in return. Faith in God involves the element of faithfulness. Such is the special force of "faith" in the examples cited in Hebrews 11; in the context of Hebrews, these heroes of faith are commended for their faithfulness, trusting God and doing what he commands.

Romans 4:21 has already been cited as describing this central aspect of faith — being fully convinced that God will do what he says.

In this light, Ephesians 2:8 becomes more meaningful. Salvation is a gift. The only way to receive a gift is in faith, in grateful acceptance. One takes the gift. Again, we find that faith is not an arbitrary condition imposed by God, but expresses the only way to take what God offers. Salvation is "through faith." It is the channel of accepting salvation. Salvation in this passage is not "because of faith," as if it were a meritorious condition which we perform. It is a gift we receive in the only way any gift is received.

Trust is where biblical faith goes beyond mental consent. It is being fully convinced, laying hold of something. There follows an emotional security and persuasion from this commitment to what God gives.

Karl Barth has explained faith as trust in this way: "Faith is holding, in spite of all that contradicts it, once for all, exclusively and entirely to God's promise and guidance."[29] This description of faith may be illustrated from Abraham. The characteristics given by Barth are rearranged in my exposition according to the order they are manifested in the story of Abraham. Three episodes in his career done "by faith" according to Hebrews 11:8-12, 17-18 (the call to leave his homeland, the promise of a son, and the sacrifice of Isaac) correspond to the three points in Barth's characterization of faith.

Trusting God is a complete commitment — "exclusively and entirely." In Genesis 12:1-9, Abraham answered God's call to forsake fatherland, friends, and family. Trust in God excludes any other objects of loyalty. It requires a total loyalty that excludes other loyalties. There is no more trusting the self — justifying, excusing, and attempting to save oneself. One depends on God for all of that. In God alone is there faithfulness.

Trusting God is done "in spite of all that contradicts." Abraham certainly could see much to contradict his faith — his own age and the barrenness of Sarah's womb (Rom. 4:19). He was seventy-five at the time of his call in Genesis 12 and ninety-nine when God promised him numerous offspring in Genesis 17. Nevertheless, in spite of his incredulity, Abraham accepted God's promise. On that basis he was led to a higher reality that was truer and more trustworthy than human reason and human experience.

Moreover, this trust is a "once for all" act. Faith is not an opinion

29. Karl Barth, *Dogmatics in Outline* (New York: Philosophical Library, 1949), pp. 15-21.

replaceable by another. It is an ultimate choice. Faith defines a final relationship. It demands faithfulness (Rev. 2:10). The faithfulness of God is matched by a person's once-for-all surrender. Abraham demonstrated this characteristic of trust in the story of the sacrifice of Isaac in Genesis 22. Once Abraham had started following God, he had to follow all the way. However hard it was to comprehend intellectually or to accept emotionally, Abraham acquiesced in the divine command. He had already made the crucial decision long before, "once for all," to do what God required of him.

A human being may express this kind of trust in another than God — for example, in a non-Christian religion or a secular philosophy. Committed Communists trusted their ideology exclusively and entirely, in spite of all that contradicted it (and much did, so much so that in most countries the system of government based on it collapsed), and once for all. Hence, in order to distinguish saving faith from other kinds of faith, we must add another element to the description of faith. Abraham in Genesis 22 reveals what that element is.

Obedience   Faith involves obedience. Whom does one obey? The answer to this question determines the real object of faith. Abraham's assent and trust led him to obey God's voice (Gen. 22:18). One of the meanings of faith is faithfulness; the book of Hebrews brings out this aspect of faith (Heb. 3:1-14; 10:22-23, 39; 11:1–12:2). Faithfulness requires obedience.

Faith and obedience are often combined in the Bible. Paul spoke of "the obedience of faith" at both the beginning and ending of Romans (Rom. 1:5; 16:26).[30] The phrase refers to the obedience that accompanies faith or "faithful obedience." From the biblical perspective, faith and obedience are equivalent. There was no faith that was not obedient, and the Hebrew word for "faith" *(emuna)* included trust and obedience. The antithetical parallelism of John 3:36 is instructive: "Whoever believes in the Son has eternal life; whoever disobeys the Son will not see life." The opposite of belief is expressed not as unbelief but as disobedience. The opposite of disobedience is belief. One may also compare the equiv-

---

30. Don B. Garlington, *"The Obedience of Faith": A Pauline Phrase in Historical Context* (Tübingen: J. C. B. Mohr, 1991), argues that although the phrase "obedience of faith" is a Pauline coinage the concept was common in Judaism and the point of contention between Paul and his Jewish opponents was not faith versus legalism but the application of faith's obedience to "all the Gentiles for the sake of his name" (Rom. 1:5).

alence of disobedience and unbelief in Hebrews 3:18-19. In other words, faith means obedience.

Human beings as creatures must obey God. Some of God's gifts are unconditional (Matt. 5:45), but some are conditional. A good illustration of a conditional promise is the healing of Naaman in 2 Kings 5. He was commanded by Elisha to wash in the Jordan River seven times, and only after he did so was he cured of his leprosy. The power to heal was not in the waters of the Jordan, but in God; yet Naaman remained unhealed until he complied with the conditions for the healing. If God attaches a condition to a promise, faith in the promise includes fulfilling the condition.

Hebrews 11:30 provides a further illustration of how faith and obedience are tied together in relation to a conditional promise. "By faith" the walls of Jericho fell down according to the promise of God (Josh. 6), but only "after they had been encircled for seven days." Joshua was not an early physicist who figured out that the people by marching in step would set up the rhythmic sound waves that would cause the walls to collapse (note the way an army breaks ranks in crossing a bridge lest they cause it to collapse). The walls fell down not by human effort but by the power of God according to his promise. On the other hand, Joshua was not like some modern religionists. He did not conclude that since his army could not break down the walls and since God had promised to deliver the city to them, there was nothing for them to do. If they had sat down to await the fall of the city, their bones would have bleached on the Jericho plain. Faith was the reason the walls fell down; the time at which they fell down was after God's condition was met. The fall of Jericho was no less the act of God and no less by faith because the Israelites complied with the divine command to march around the walls for seven days.

Relation of Faith to Its Expressions

Faith and Baptism   The perspective developed on a conditional promise and illustrated from Naaman and the fall of Jericho may help to explain the relation of the New Testament teaching on faith and on baptism. Faith saves, but when? At the point of believing, or when the divine condition attached to the promise is met?

Baptism is an act of faith, not a work in the sense of Romans 4. Its place in the human response to God's action in Christ will be elaborated further below, but for now we note that as a condition attached to God's promise of salvation it is not opposed to faith. "Repent, and be baptized every one of you in the name of Jesus Christ so that your sins may be forgiven" (Acts 2:38). "For in Christ Jesus you are all children of God through faith. As many of you were baptized into Christ have clothed yourselves with Christ" (Gal. 3:26-27). *Faith* is the *reason why* a person is a child of God; *baptism* is the *time at which* one is incorporated into Christ and so becomes a child of God.

Baptism is not a work, either in the sense of merit or of Christian works (as discussed below). One cannot define work in such a way as to include baptism and exclude faith. There is a sense in which faith itself is a work: "They said to him, 'What must we do to perform the works of God?' Jesus answered them, 'This is the work of God, that you believe in him whom he has sent'" (John 6:28-29). Some have tried to make the work in verse 29 something that God does, but the question of verse 28 that is being answered makes it clear that the work is something human beings do. So, if "work" is taken to mean something done by human beings, then faith no less than baptism is a "work." If "work" is defined as something meritorious, then baptism no more than faith is a work. If works are understood as good deeds done because of salvation (see below), then baptism is not a work, because it is the means of receiving the salvation promised to believers. Both faith and baptism are conditions of receiving salvation: "The one who believes and is baptized will be saved" (Mark 16:16, long ending).

The teaching of baptism for the remission of sins (see pp. 183-186) is not a contradiction to justification by faith. Indeed, baptism for the remission of sins is an expression of justification by faith. Baptism is an act of faith, dependent on the promise of God and a submission to him as the appointed way of claiming the promise. The death and resurrection of Christ are the basis of salvation on the divine side. Faith is the basis of salvation on the human side. Baptism represents the "when," not the "how" (God's action), nor the "why" (faith) of salvation. It is the appointed time at which that salvation offered to faith is applied and becomes effective in the person's life.

Faith and Works   Human good works do not save but are the result of salvation. "For we are what he has made us, created in Christ Jesus for good works, which God prepared beforehand to be our way of life" (Eph. 2:10). Good works do not save, but saved people work. Some of those good works will be categorized in Chapter 6.

Romans 3:28 and James 2:24 have sometimes been thought to be in contradiction; their proper interpretation will focus the issue of faith and works. Paul says, "for we hold that a person is justified by faith apart from works prescribed by the law." James says, "You see that a person is justified by works and not by faith alone." If those two statements are placed side by side, it is hard to imagine a more express contradiction.

Paul	James
Justified	Justified
By faith	By works
Apart from works	Not by faith alone

An examination of the context of these two passages, however, reveals that none of the key terms is being used in the same sense. Neither faith, works, nor justification means the same thing in the context of Paul's and James's statements.

Paul in Romans 3:21–4:25 is using "faith" as the principle of justification in contrast to the Law of Moses as the principle of acceptance by God. He is discussing the basis of the human relationship to God, the basis on which one becomes part of the covenant people of God. Faith is contrasted to physical birth and circumcision as the means of becoming children of Abraham. The faith that he is describing is defined in Romans 4:21. Abraham was "fully convinced that God was able to do what he had promised" and acted on that trust in obedience to God's commands (see p. 168). James, on the other hand, has the act of believing in mind, or more specifically, according to the analysis above, the giving of mental assent to a proposition. What he means by faith is clear from 2:19, "Even the demons believe — and shudder." The demons know God exists, but they do not act accordingly. There is a great difference between this kind of believing and the trusting faith Paul is talking about in Romans.

The works under discussion are also different. Paul specifies the works he means as "works prescribed by the law" (Rom. 3:28), that is, the Law of Moses given to the Jews that included circumcision. It may be proper to extend the principle of Paul's argument to encompass any works that are made a basis of justification and an attitude of "law-keeping" as the principle of salvation, but this extended application still does not exclude baptism as an act of faith by which one enters into the relationship with God (Rom. 6:1-11) nor the necessity of doing good works after one becomes a Christian (Rom. 12–13). James 2, in contrast, does refer to the good works of the Christian life. He defines in verses 15-17 the works he is talking about: clothing the naked and feeding the hungry. And that for the "brother or sister." James clearly refers to those already Christians. He is not talking about works done in order to become Christians. Verse 17, "So faith by itself, if it has no works, is dead," may have a wider application (even as Paul's point about law may be extended to cover other "laws") to include a principle that God requires an active, working faith, but in this context the reference is not to works by which one becomes a Christian but works done after and because one is a Christian.

The justification talked about is different in the two authors. Paul's whole discussion shows that he is talking about God's activity in declaring a people righteous, in bringing a people into relationship with him.[31] James, on the other hand, has to do with righteous conduct that is approved by God, ultimately at the last judgment. Therefore, placed in their own contexts, the statements of Paul and James, which appear so contradictory, are not contradictory at all. Even where they use the same illustration from Abraham, they are talking about two different subjects.

Paul in other contexts, where he speaks of Christian activities, uses "work" in a favorable way.[32] These passages affirm that faith results in good works. "Remembering before our God and Father your work of faith and labor of love and steadfastness of hope in our Lord Jesus Christ" (1 Thess. 1:3). The interior conviction of the heart is manifested in the exterior concrete activity. Therefore, Paul can declare in Galatians, where he has a strong polemic against binding the ceremonial aspects of the law of Moses, that "The only thing that counts is faith working [active] through love" (Gal. 5:6).

Philippians 2:12-13 offers another way to express the relation of faith and works: "Work out your own salvation with fear and trembling; for it is God who is at work in you, enabling you both to will and to work for his good pleasure." The word translated "work out" can mean "accomplish, achieve"; the thought here is not to produce or bring about one's own salvation but to bring salvation to fulfillment or accomplish-

31. See n. 24.

32. See E. P. Sanders, *Paul, the Law, and the Jewish People* (Philadelphia: Fortress, 1983), esp. chap. 3, and Morna Hooker's review of his earlier work on *Paul and Palestinian Judaism* in her "Paul and 'Covenantal Nomism,'" *Paul and Paulinism: Essays in Honour of C. K. Barrett*, ed. M. D. Hooker and S. G. Wilson (London: SCM, 1982), pp. 47-56.

ment, to make it actual or effective. To play on the English translations, one does not work for salvation but works out from the salvation initiated or effected by God; one works out what God works in.

Concluding Observations   Faith is no more meritorious than works. It is the acceptance of a gracious gift. The importance of accepting a great gift does not detract from the significance of the gift, unless one glories in the acceptance. The Christian glorifies the cross (Gal. 6:14), not the acceptance of the cross (i.e., our faith and obedience to it). Faith means reliance on the word of God. Some forms of the doctrine of salvation by "faith only" end in the very thing the doctrine was meant to oppose, namely trusting in what one does (in this case in one's faith), which is the same as trusting in oneself. When someone abandons the objective guarantee of God's word (when the conditions are met, the promise is assured), there is substituted a subjective assurance. The question, "Do I have saving faith?" still comes. "I feel" is not a biblical answer. Believing that I believe is not enough. We are saved by faith, because of faith, and through faith, but the object of that faith must be the promises of God. A Christian does not trust his/her faith for salvation; the trust is in God.

A person can be assured of salvation. There is nothing more certain than the promises of God. He is trustworthy and faithful. Trust in him is being fully convinced. "Do I have the right kind of faith?" "Do I have enough faith?" God has given an objective assurance in the condition of water baptism. Human nature seems to require some outward bodily action to express trust and commitment: raising the hand, coming down the aisle, kneeling, or something else. God has given the objective, outward expression of faith in Christ — baptism in the name of Christ. If one has enough faith to be baptized, one has faith enough to be saved. If one's faith is in Christ as Savior, one will follow him in baptism. It is trusting God and his word to be baptized.

A Confessed Faith

Faith demands an expression. How does one express a trusting obedient faith? If faith involves the mind, emotions, and will, the expression of it will involve the whole self. Faith is confessed by word and act.

There may be many occasions when one is called upon to confess faith in Jesus in addition to the initial acknowledgment of him. The confession made at the time of conversion, as is evident from the association with salvation and justification, is the theme of Romans 10:9-10: "If you confess with your lips that Jesus is Lord and believe in your heart that God raised him from the dead, you will be saved. For one believes with the heart and so is justified, and one confesses with the mouth and so is saved." The wording indicates that this is a formal, public confession, a "calling upon the name of the Lord" made in response to hearing the message about Christ (Rom. 10:13-17). The faith in the heart finds expression in the confession with the mouth. And the confession on the lips corresponds to the faith in the heart. That belief is a conviction that God raised him from the dead. To say that "Jesus is Lord" is to declare that God raised Jesus from the dead. The victory over death made him Lord of life and death, Lord of the dead and the living (Rom. 14:9). Confession that Jesus is Lord is a confession of faith in the resurrection.

According to Acts 2:36, Peter preached that the crucified Jesus has been made by God "both Lord and Christ [Messiah]." That same Peter confessed his faith in Jesus with the words, "You are the Christ [Messiah], the Son of the living God" (Matt. 16:16). The confession that Jesus is the Christ is also a confession in the resurrection. Following Peter's confession, Jesus explained what it meant to be the Messiah: he "must undergo great suffering . . . and be killed, and on the third day be raised" (Matt. 16:21). The confession that Jesus is the Messiah is a confession that he did the work of the Messiah — to die and to be resurrected. As the Messiah, he is God's chosen ruler. He is Son of God, "declared to be Son of God with power . . . by resurrection from the dead" (Rom. 1:4).

The confessions that Jesus is Lord, that Jesus is the Christ, and that Jesus is the Son of God thus all have an identical content. They express a faith that God raised him from the dead. Why the different wording? It seems likely that the confession that Jesus is the Messiah was at home in a Jewish setting, and the confession that Jesus is Lord was at home in a Gentile setting. In both cases, the object of the confession (Jesus) and the content (the resurrection) were the same.

The confession that "Jesus is Lord and Christ" is made by act as well as by word. The action of baptism is a confession of faith in the resurrection. "When you were buried with him in baptism, you were also raised with him through faith in the power of God, who raised him from the dead" (Col. 2:12). The act of baptism displays the burial and the resurrection of Jesus. One submits to immersion only if he or she has faith in the resurrection. One goes down into the water believing in the working or activity of God. Baptism acknowledges Jesus as Lord of one's life and king of the universe. God was at work in the death and resurrection of Jesus. Response to God's action is to put trust in what he did and confess it. As God raised Jesus, so he raises the baptized believer to a new life (Rom. 6:4). Baptism is a confession that Jesus is Lord, Christ, and Son of God. Submitting to baptism is identical to the faith that is confessed.

The story of Abraham once more offers an analogy. "By faith Abraham, when put to the test, offered up Isaac. . . . He considered the fact that God is able even to raise someone from the dead — and figuratively speaking, he did receive him back" (Heb. 11:17-19; cf. Rom. 4:17 and the discussion on p. 165 on the content of Abraham's faith). Faith in the God who raises the dead, specifically Jesus Christ, is the heart of the Christian faith. That is the faith that is confessed by word and deed when one becomes a Christian. That is the faith by which one becomes identified with Christ and so a part of his spiritual body, his people, who wear his name.

Repentance

Importance

The human response to the preaching of the gospel of God's action in Christ is also described by the word *repentance*. The importance of repentance is emphasized in many texts. It was the theme of the preaching of John the Baptist (Matt. 3:1-2), of Jesus (Matt. 4:17; Luke 13:3), of the apostles during the ministry of Jesus (Mark 6:12), and at his command after his resurrection (Luke 24:47), a command addressed to both Jews (Acts 3:19) and Gentiles (Acts 11:18). "God . . . commands all people everywhere to repent" (Acts 17:30).

Meaning

Repentance, as it pertains to human relations with God, may be defined as that change of mind or heart, produced by godly grief, which leads to a reformation of life. The fundamental idea is that of turning, or returning; in the religious sense, a returning to one's due obedience to God. The Hebrew background gives to the Greek word *metanoia* (change of mind) the specific idea of (re)turning to God (cf. Mal. 3:7). Repentance involves a fundamental reorientation of the whole personality. There is definitely a moral aspect to this change, but in New Testament preaching there was also a strongly eschatological notion — a turning to God with a view to the coming age of the kingdom and to divine judgment.

Godly Grief   Godly grief or sorrow produces repentance.

The passage that gives the fullest discussion of repentance in the New Testament is 2 Corinthians 7:8-10. The context is not conversion repentance but repentance by those who are already Christians. The passage concerns their conduct, but presumably the same word meanings and principles discussed here apply to conversion. There is a difference between "to regret" *(metamelomai)* and "to be sorry or to grieve" *(lupeo)*. *Regret* is a weaker word for a change of attitude, wishing one had not done something. *Sorrow* goes deeper and suggests distress, grief, inward pain. It moves one to do something about mistakes made. Paul could wish he had not sent his letter that caused the Corinthians grief, but he no longer regretted it (vs. 8), because their grief led to repentance (vs. 9).

Paul further distinguishes godly grief and worldly grief (vs. 10). We may elaborate on the distinction. They are produced by different influences. Worldly sorrow may be caused by the frowns of others, by punishment experienced, or by failure in what is undertaken. Godly sorrow, in contrast, is caused by respect for God and his violated law. The conviction of sinfulness brings a change in understanding so as to respect God's law. The people on Pentecost, "when they heard this [that they had crucified the Christ], were cut to the heart and said to Peter and to the other apostles, 'Brothers, what should we do?' Peter said to them, 'Repent, and be baptized' " (Acts 2:37-38). Repentance is not the conviction of sin but what one resolves to do about it. Godly sorrow may also arise out of consideration of God's goodness ("Do you not realize that God's kindness is meant to lead you to repentance" — Rom. 2:4). Godly and worldly grief also have different ends. As Paul says, "Worldly grief produces death" (vs. 10). An extreme example is Judas. In regret and sorrow for his betrayal of Jesus, he took his life (Matt. 27:3-5). Worldly sorrow does not always lead to suicide, but it does lead to spiritual death. Godly grief, however, "produces a repentance that leads to salvation and brings no regret" (vs. 10).

Reformation of Life   Even as godly grief leads to repentance, so repentance results in a reformation of life. So close is the association that "repent" is sometimes translated "reform," but properly the change of life is the result of the repentance. Jesus spoke of repenting seven times a day (Luke 17:3-4); a reformation would take longer than this. In Matthew 3:8, John the Baptist told his hearers to "Bear fruit worthy of repentance." Paul described his preaching as declaring to the Gentiles that they should "repent and turn to God and do deeds consistent with repentance" (Acts 26:20). A person has not experienced genuine repentance unless a change in life is produced. Repentance demands making past wrongs right. Where necessary and possible, this would require restitution of what was wrongly acquired (so Zacchaeus, in Luke 19:1-10, who goes beyond Lev. 6:1-7, but cf. Exod. 22:1). The Golden Rule (Matt. 7:12) demands restitution, for we would want those who wronged us to correct the situation. The turning to God finds expression in the good deeds of a reformed life. The proof of repentance is seen in a changed life.

Change of Will What comes between godly grief and a reformation of life? The inward change that results from godly grief and issues in a reformation of life is what constitutes repentance in the strict sense. Repentance is a change of will in regard to sin. It is the resolve to quit doing evil and start doing right. This may be expressed as a change of "mind" or of "heart," but perhaps the strength of the idea is best captured by the word "will." The idea is expressed in some of the nonconversion uses of repentance, as when God "repented" of his plan to destroy Nineveh when the people turned from their evil ways (Jon. 3:10) or when Esau failed to find a change of mind in his father Isaac concerning the birthright (Heb. 12:17).

Repentance may be used in a comprehensive sense to include the sorrow, the resolve to do better, and the amendment of one's conduct. Faith, too, as we saw, often has the broad sense of one's response to God as well as the narrower meaning of the trust in God which is at the heart of that response. Similarly, repentance may have the meaning of this total turning to God. In a narrower sense, it is the act of will at the center of this change.

If repentance is a change of will in regard to sin and God, how can it be said that God gives repentance (Acts 11:18)? Likely the idea in this verse is that God gave a place for repentance. There is another sense in which it can be said that God gives repentance, even as he gives faith. God's word by his Spirit brings the conviction of sin (John 16:8; Acts 2:37) that leads to faith and repentance. He gives the motives (Rom. 2:4) and the opportunities (2 Pet. 3:9) for repentance.

Relation to Conversion

Another word used to represent the change involved in becoming a Christian is *epistrephō*, "to turn," a word that refers to the physical act of turning but also means "to change" the mind or the course of action, so that in the moral or religious sense it may be translated "to convert."[33] The noun form is used for "the conversion of the Gentiles" (Acts 15:3). Most passages where the verb refers to a spiritual turning refer to Gentiles' coming to God: Acts 11:21, "A great number became believers and turned to the Lord"; Acts 14:15, "You should turn from these worthless things [idolatry] to the living God"; Acts 15:19, "Those Gentiles who are turning to God"; Acts 26:18, "To turn from darkness to light and from the power of Satan to God, so that they may receive forgiveness of sins and a place among those who are sanctified by faith in me"; and 1 Thessalonians 1:9, "How you turned to God from idols, to serve a living and true God." These passages indicate that the word was a general term for conversion, but particularly emphasizing the actions involved and where used with faith something subsequent to it. Sometimes *epistrephō* is used with the word "repent" (Acts 3:19; 26:20). If a distinction is to be observed, "repent" refers more to the inward turning and "convert" to the outward acts of turning.

The literal meaning of turning suggests an illustration of the place of repentance in conversion. A person is walking in one direction, stops (the conviction of sin; godly sorrow), decides to turn around (repentance), turns around (conversion), and walks in the opposite direction (reformation of life). Of course, an individual's experience may not lend itself to analysis in such a precise fashion. There is involved a change in understanding, in feeling, in will, and in actions.

There has been some discussion of the relation of faith to repentance in conversion. Which comes first? It was noted above that in Acts 11:21 believing precedes "turning," but repentance precedes "turning" in Acts 3:19. In the two passages where faith and repentance are mentioned together, repentance precedes faith: "Repent and believe in the gospel" (Mark 1:15) and "I testified to both Jews and Greeks about repentance toward God and faith toward our Lord Jesus" (Acts 20:21). Faith and repentance have different objects in these two cases: repen-

33. Ronald D. Witherup, *Conversion in the New Testament* (Collegeville, Minn.: Liturgical, 1994).

tance as the turning from sin to God and faith in Jesus or the gospel. It seems unlikely that in any of these passages the sequence is significant. Some would argue theologically and insist on the priority of faith as the root of all human response to God. Belief in God, Christ, and his word leads to a change in understanding, the sorrow for sin and desire to do better. Probably we should not think in terms of sequence at all but in terms of describing a total response to God according to different perspectives. That response will entail both faith and repentance. In different cases one will precede the other, or they may come together in a way that cannot be differentiated.

Baptism

Baptism is an expression of repentance and faith, and is itself a confession.[34]

Importance

Baptism is prominent in the New Testament as a positive ordinance of the gospel. The immediate predecessor of Christian baptism was the baptism administered by John the Baptist. John's baptism differed from Jewish ritual baths in being administered by him (hence his title "the Baptizer" — Mark 1:4, 5, 8) rather than being self-administered and in being a one-time eschatological act for the forgiveness of sins (Matt. 3:6-7; Mark 1:4), and differed from proselyte baptism (if it was practiced this early) by being administered to Israel. Christian baptism differed from John's baptism in being associated with faith in Jesus Christ and so administered in his name (Acts 19:4-5; cf. Mark 1:7) and in promising the Holy Spirit as well as forgiveness of sins (Acts 19:2-3; cf. Mark 1:8).

In further distinction from the baptism administered by John the

---

34. See especially G. R. Beasley-Murray, *Baptism in the New Testament* (Grand Rapids: Eerdmans, 1973), who gives a thorough discussion of the passages mentioned in this section along with references to the scholarly literature. For other treatments see W. F. Flemington, *The New Testament Doctrine of Baptism* (London: SPCK, 1948); O. Cullmann, *Baptism in the New Testament* (London: SCM, 1950); J. Ysebaert, *Greek Baptismal Terminology* (Nijmegen: Dekker & Van de Vegt, 1962); A. George et al., *Baptism in the New Testament: A Symposium* (London: Geoffrey Chapman, 1964); O. S. Brooks, *The Drama of Decision: Baptism in the New Testament* (Peabody: Hendrickson, 1987).

Baptist, from the religious purifications among the Jews (including those of the Qumran community and proselyte baptism), and from the use of water for purification in pagan religions, Christian baptism is based on the baptism of Jesus and the command of the resurrected Jesus.

Christ's baptism is the foundation of Christian baptism. Several features connected with baptism to be discussed below are evident in Jesus' baptism by John the Baptizer. The usual association with forgiveness of sins (in John's baptism Mark 1:4; Luke 3:3) is implied in John's reluctance to baptize Jesus (Matt. 3:13-14), in response to which Jesus answered, "It is proper for us in this way to fulfill all righteousness" (Matt. 3:15). Explicit in the text is the association of Jesus' baptism with sonship and the gift of the Holy Spirit. At the baptism of Jesus, the Spirit came upon him and God acknowledged him as his Son (Matt. 3:16-17; Mark 1:10-11; Luke 3:21-23). Then he was empowered to begin his ministry. Only when the Spirit came in Acts 2 did the disciples begin preaching the gospel. So for Christians, at baptism they are acknowledged as children of God (Gal. 3:26-27) and receive the Spirit (Gal. 4:5-7) and then begin a life of service. At his baptism, Jesus launched his messianic ministry and accepted the way of the cross. Even as Jesus identified himself with humanity at his baptism, so at baptism his followers identify themselves with him, his ministry, and his cross. One is baptized because Christ was, with all that means.

After the cross and resurrection Jesus gave a command to his disciples that included the administration of baptism: "All authority in heaven and on earth has been given to me. Go therefore and make disciples of all nations, baptizing them in the name of the Father and of the Son and of the Holy Spirit, and teaching them to obey everything that I have commanded you" (Matt. 28:18-20). His followers perform baptism as part of making more disciples for the Lord.

Meaning

Baptism is associated with many key ideas involved in conversion.

Confession of Faith   Faith is confessed at the time one becomes a Christian, as discussed on pp. 174-175, both with the lips and by the act of water baptism. Those "who received the word" about Jesus were baptized (Acts 2:41). Baptism is a "calling on the name" of the Lord (Acts 22:16; see further on this phrase on p. 211). The reference is likely to the confession of faith made at the baptism (cf. the Western text of Acts 8:37 and the use of Joel 2:32 in Acts 2:21 and Rom. 10:13). Such may be indicated by the description of baptism as "in the name of" Jesus Christ (see references below).[35] The association with faith in Jesus as the Christ was a distinguishing mark of Christian baptism (Acts 19:4-5). Hebrews 10:22-23 associates confession with the washing with water.[36]

Baptism is a pledge of allegiance, an oath of loyalty to Christ. This may be the meaning of 1 Peter 3:21, the translation of which is not generally agreed upon. The word for "answer" or "pledge" may reflect contractual language for the agreement which one consented to.[37] If that is the sense here, the baptismal confession represents the pact, the covenant into which one enters with God. Whether the statement refers to a pledge that proceeds from a good conscience or is a pledge to maintain a good conscience is not easy to determine. Either way, there is an indication of the commitment associated with baptism.

At baptism not only does the candidate call on the name of God, but God's name is called on him. The words of Matthew 28:19 about baptism "into the name of the Father and of the Son and of the Holy Spirit" have since early days been used as a formula pronounced by the administrator of baptism. The same phrase "into the name of" occurs in Acts 8:16 with reference to "the Lord Jesus" and in Acts 19:5-6 to "Jesus Christ." Paul's rebuke of the Corinthians for identifying with party leaders, "Or were you baptized into the name of Paul?" (1 Cor. 1:13, 15), implies a connection between baptism and the name worn. After baptism into Christ one wears the name of Christ. One now lives a Christian life because of becoming a Christian at baptism.

Three prepositional phrases in Greek are rendered in English "in the name of." There is some basis in contemporary usage for distinguishing the significance of each, but the meanings often shaded off into one another. *Eis to onoma* (Matt. 28:19; Acts 8:16; 19:5; 1 Cor. 1:13)

---

35. Joseph Crehan, *Early Christian Baptism and the Creed* (London: Burns Oates & Washbourne, 1950), chapter I.

36. Hence, the confession in Heb. 4:14 is likely the baptismal confession also. Hebrews 5:11–6:3 reflects instruction given in connection with baptism. See p. 185 for more on Heb. 10.

37. G. C. Richards, "I Pet. iii 21," *Journal of Theological Studies* 32 (1931): 77 defines the word as meaning "promise elicited by a formal question," and translates, "a pledge proceeding from a clear conscience"; cf. also E. G. Selwyn, *The First Epistle of St. Peter* (London: Macmillan, 1949), pp. 205-206.

was used in legal and commercial contexts for "to the account of" or "into the possession" of someone and in Jewish circles was equivalent to a rabbinic phrase for "with respect to" or "with regard to" someone, but there are places where it seems indistinguishable from the next phrase. *En tō onomati* (Acts 10:48) often has the idea of "with the mention of the name," "naming or calling on the name" of someone, especially out of regard for the person or as an act of worship, but sometimes it seems to mean "to act in the person of or as representing" someone. Consequently, it can carry the idea of "by the authority of" and so shade into the meaning of the next phrase. *Epi tō onoma* (Acts 2:38) was used in the Septuagint for calling on someone's name or for mentioning someone's name, especially in order to invoke his authority ("by the authority of"), and this fits most of the occurrences in Luke.

Act of Repentance   Baptism is a result of repentance and an expression of that repentance. The baptism administered by John the Baptist was a "repentance baptism" (Mark 1:4; Luke 3:3; Acts 19:4). The people confessed their sins (Matt. 3:6; Mark 1:5), and John gave specific instructions about what repentance required (Luke 3:7-14). That association between repentance and baptism continued in Christian baptism. The people on Pentecost "were cut to the heart" and wanted to know what they should do about their sinful condition (Acts 2:37). Peter told them to "Repent, and be baptized every one of you in the name of Jesus Christ" (Acts 2:38).

Baptism is involved in the turning associated with repentance. Acts 3:19 offers a parallel to Acts 2:38. Four terms are in both verses: two are the same, and the other two in suggestive parallelism:

Acts 2:38	Acts 3:19
Repent	Repent
Be baptized	Turn to God
Sins forgiven	Sins wiped out
Gift of the Holy Spirit	Times of refreshing

The identity of the first and third items suggests a certain equivalence between the second and fourth items. According to the illustration offered on page 178 above, repentance is the decision to turn, and baptism is the turning around. Repentance is the inward turning, and baptism is the outward turning, which is followed by the new life of walking in the opposite direction. Baptism is the act that expresses the rejection of sin and the turning to follow God.

If the human element is in the forefront when baptism is thought of as a confession of faith and an act of repentance, more important are the things God does in baptism. To these aspects of baptism we now turn.

Forgiveness of Sins   The walking in God's way that follows on repentance and baptism is made possible because baptism brings forgiveness of sins. Or better stated, baptism is the appointed time at which God pronounces forgiveness. Faith takes away the love of sin, repentance takes away the practice of sin, and baptism takes away the guilt of sin. The association of washing in water with purity made it natural to associate the immersion bath with the washing away of sins.

Acts 2:38 states the purpose of repentance and baptism: "Repent, and be baptized every one of you in the name of Jesus Christ so that your sins may be forgiven." The Greek construction is a regular way of expressing an object or goal: "for," "unto," or "in order to obtain" forgiveness of sins. Some have doubted this purpose of baptism and have tried to translate differently, but the grammar will not permit it. Exactly the same construction and wording occurs in Matthew 26:28, "This is my blood of the covenant, which is poured out for many for the forgiveness of sins." No one would suggest that Jesus' blood was poured out "because of the forgiveness of sins." He did not die because sins were already forgiven, nor was his blood poured out as a symbol of the forgiveness of sins. There is no doubt that the blood was shed "in order to effect the forgiveness of sins." The same translation must be given to Acts 2:38. This is not to suggest that theologically the water of baptism is equivalent to the blood of the cross, but the wording requires the same grammatical meaning, the same object or goal. The blood provides forgiveness by the divine action; baptism appropriates that forgiveness for the penitent believer.

This teaching of forgiveness of sins in baptism is expressed in other verses by the imagery of washing or cleansing. "And now why do you delay? Get up, be baptized, and have your sins washed away, calling on his name" (Acts 22:16). Baptism washes away sins, but not the water itself, for the act is accompanied by the confession of faith, "calling on the name" of the Lord. And this faith is engendered by the preaching of the word (Rom. 10:13). The power of forgiveness is not in the water or in the act. The power is in God and the blood of Christ; it is received because one calls on the name of the Lord, and it is received in baptism. The act is an appropriate expression for what God does. "God gives all to faith; God gives all in baptism."[38]

"And baptism . . . now saves you — not as a removal of dirt from the body, but as an appeal to God for a good conscience [*or* a pledge to God from a good conscience], through the resurrection of Jesus Christ" (1 Pet. 3:21). Peter clearly distinguishes the baptismal washing from an ordinary bath and a ceremonial cleansing. The difference is made, on the part of the individual, by the verbal commitment and the association with a good conscience, and, on the part of the divine action, by the effect of the resurrection of Jesus Christ. There is no magical power in the water nor merit in the act itself, for the value comes not from the water but from the intention with which the act is performed. The statement is not to be absolutized, but when placed in the total context of the gospel, it remains true, "Baptism saves."

Another verse using the imagery of cleansing or washing in connection with baptism is Ephesians 5:26 — Christ loved the church "in order to make her holy by cleansing her with the washing of water by the word." The imagery is that of the nuptial bath by the bride (cf. Ezek. 16:8-12). The purifying is by water and by word. The "word" may be the candidate's confession of faith, the baptismal formula by the baptizer, the preached gospel, or the promise of God. The analogy of the wedding ceremony plus New Testament and early Christian practice favors the confession accompanying baptism.[39]

Paul brings together washing, being sanctified, and being justified on the basis of the name of Christ and the Spirit of God in 1 Corinthians 6:11. It may be overly schematic, but the three verbs can be related to the three divine names invoked in baptism: baptism is in the name of Christ (Acts 10:48; cf. 1 Cor. 1:13); the Spirit sanctifies (Rom. 15:16; 2 Thess. 2:13; but related to God in 1 Thess. 5:23 and Christ in 1 Cor. 1:2); and God justifies (Rom. 8:33). Regardless, the washing of baptism involves being sanctified or set apart as God's holy people and receiving the justification that comes through faith.

---

38. G. R. Beasley-Murray, *Baptism in the New Testament* (Grand Rapids: Eerdmans, 1973), p. 273, "God's gracious giving to faith belongs to the context of baptism, even as God's gracious giving in baptism is to faith."

39. B. F. Westcott, *Saint Paul's Epistle to the Ephesians* (London: Macmillan, 1906), pp. 84-85; E. Ferguson, "Baptismal Motifs in the Ancient Church," *Restoration Quarterly* 7 (1963): 203, reprinted in *Studies in Early Christianity,* Vol. XI, *Conversion, Catechumenate, and Baptism in the Early Church,* ed. E. Ferguson (New York: Garland, 1993), p. 353.

Similarly, Hebrews 10:19-23 brings together "the blood of Jesus," "full assurance of faith," baptism, and "the confession of our hope." Baptism is referred to in the phrase "our bodies washed with pure water." The heart is "sprinkled clean [i.e., purified, the inner sanctification] from an evil conscience [the consciousness of sins and an evil attitude]" at the same time the body receives the outward washing.[40] Such is related to "the confession of our hope." Since baptism is "in the name of Jesus," and is a "calling on the name of the Lord" (Acts 22:16), it must be a baptism at which one confesses faith. As an act of penitent faith, it obtains the washing away or forgiveness of sins, which is to be sanctified and justified.

According to these passages, baptism is a washing, cleansing, or purifying. Such descriptions pick up the prophetic promises about the new age. Ezekiel 36:22-31 associates a new heart with the Spirit, repentance, and cleansing with water (sprinkling water in vs. 25 follows Old Testament ritual purifications and does not describe the mode of a Christian's cleansing, for which see pp. 201-203). The real basis of cleansing is the blood of Jesus (1 John 1:7). Nevertheless, just as in some Old Testament cleansings there was the application of blood and water (Lev. 14:4-7 and cf. 51-52) followed by a bath (vss. 8-9), so in a Christian's cleansing there is the combination of the blood and water (cf. Heb. 10:22). The close relation of the cross to baptism is further indicated by 1 Corinthians 1:13.[41] There must be an objective necessity about baptism, or the New Testament writers could not speak of baptism in the way they do.

Water itself does not touch sins, but washing in water perfectly symbolizes what takes place when the command on which forgiveness is conditioned is obeyed. The act corresponds to the cleansing that is promised when it is obeyed (1 Pet. 3:21). In the same way, baptism perfectly symbolizes the death and resurrection discussed on pages 189-191.

The perspective outlined here makes problematic the designation of baptism as a sacrament. On the broadest definition of a sacrament, "the outward sign of an inward grace," baptism may be considered a sacrament, but it does not fit the ways in which the parts of this defi-

40. N. A. Dahl, "A New and Living Way: The Approach to God according to Hebrews 10:19-25," *Interpretation* 5 (1951): 407-408.
41. R. Pesch, *Das Abendmahl und Jesu Todesverständnis* (Freiburg: Herder, 1978), pp. 115-122, shows the link between the atonement and baptism. Jesus understood his death as atoning, bringing the forgiveness of sins; baptism, too, was for the forgiveness of sins, "in the name of Jesus."

nition are usually related. Roman Catholics have traditionally emphasized the inward grace, so much so that the benefits are applied in the
rite if no resistance is offered (hence, an infant receives forgiveness of
original sin in baptism). In medieval theology this teaching concerning
the sacraments was expressed by the Latin phrase *ex opere operato*,
meaning that the work (the sacrament) and its benefits were accomplished from the doing of the work itself and were not dependent on
the person performing the work. The phrase has come to stand for the
objective efficacy of religious acts, and although faith was presupposed,
it was not necessarily personal faith (in the case of infant baptism the
faith was that of the church and/or the parents). Protestants, on the
other hand, have emphasized the sign aspect, so baptism is a sign of
God's forgiveness that is given to a faith that has already happened (in
the case of adult baptism) or will happen (in the case of infant baptism)
and does not require the sign for it to happen (hence, the baptism is
actually unnecessary). Against these ideas, the New Testament teaches
that baptism has real value but draws that value only from the command of God and from an active faith. It is both necessary to the
accomplishment of forgiveness under ordinary circumstances and the
symbol of what is accomplished.

This book has consciously avoided a separate category of "sacraments" in its organization of the material. Such a category is a later
theological construct for which there is no explicit New Testament
authorization. Moreover, it seems preferable to treat the actions sometimes called sacraments in the living context of their place in the church
rather than to pull them out of that context and put them in a separate
category.

Some have felt that this teaching about the relation of baptism to
the forgiveness of sins makes it a "work" and so contradicts the teaching
of salvation as a gift received by faith. It is hoped that the larger
treatment of biblical teaching in this chapter will alleviate that concern.
For now it may be noted that the person being baptized is passive in
baptism. Nothing could more accurately express complete submission
and receptiveness of grace than this act. Especially is this true for
immersion (see pp. 201-203), where the person yields to submersion
under the water.

Gift of the Holy Spirit   Continuing with Acts 2:38, we learn that the
person who repents and is baptized in Jesus' name for the forgiveness
of sins is promised, "and you will receive the gift of the Holy Spirit."

The promise is made to the penitent who is baptized. The gift is not a gift given by the Holy Spirit but the Holy Spirit himself as a gift (also Acts 10:45, "The gift of the Holy Spirit had been poured out even on the Gentiles"; cf. Acts 5:32, "The Holy Spirit whom God has given those who obey him"; contrast Acts 8:20).

According to Acts 2:38, baptism precedes the bestowal of the Holy Spirit. One may compare Galatians 4:6, "And because you are children, God has sent the Spirit of his Son into our hearts, crying 'Abba! Father!'" God did not send the Spirit in order to make people his children, but because they were adopted as his children he placed the sign of sonship in them, the Spirit enabling them to address him intimately as "Father" (cf. Rom. 8:15-17).

There was a special case where the Spirit preceded baptism in the conversion of the household of Cornelius in Acts 10:44-48. The Spirit came on them while Peter was preaching, so Peter said, "'Can anyone withhold the water for baptizing these people who have received the Holy Spirit just as we have?' So he ordered them to be baptized in the name of Jesus Christ" (Acts 10:47-48). Quite clearly the coming of the Holy Spirit was a sign that God accepted Gentiles, and that therefore they should receive the water baptism that incorporated them into the people of God in Christ. That was the use made of the episode in Acts 11:1-18, especially verses 15-18. This special case was to prove that God accepted the Gentiles.

The normal order was for the Spirit to be given after and as a result of baptism. In Acts 19:1-6 those who had received John's baptism and had never heard of the Holy Spirit were baptized again, this time in the name of the Lord Jesus, so that they might receive the Holy Spirit. The gift of the Holy Spirit, as well as the association with the name of Jesus and confession of him, is a distinguishing characteristic of Christian baptism.

Another instance in Acts where the coming of the Spirit is separated in time from baptism is the conversion of the Samaritans in Acts 8:14-17. In each case where there is a separation of the coming of the Spirit from baptism, there is a special occasion marking the spread of the gospel to a new group about which there might be some doubt or some special problem — Samaritans (Acts 8), Gentiles (Acts 10-11), disciples of John (Acts 19). That Luke intends his first account, his showcase narrative (Acts 2), to represent normal practice finds some confirmation in Paul's words: "You were washed, you were sanctified, you were justified in the name of the Lord Jesus Christ and in the Spirit of

God" (1 Cor. 6:11). This passage brings together the washing (baptism) with the name of Christ and the Holy Spirit.[42] Other passages associating the Spirit with baptism will be discussed below in relation to the new birth and entrance into the church. The bestowing of the Holy Spirit is one of the things God does in baptism.

New Birth Baptism as a new birth is one way of describing what God does at baptism. He forgives sins and gives the Holy Spirit. Another way of expressing these gifts is to say that God imparts new life at baptism.

The key passage here is John 3:3-5: "Very truly, I tell you, no one can see the kingdom of God without being born from above [or born anew]. . . . No one can enter the kingdom of God without being born of water and Spirit." The new birth described here is one birth of two components, not two births. The two parts of this one birth are water and Spirit. A lot is said about "born again Christians"; actually there is no other kind of Christian. The way one becomes a Christian is to be born again. Those who use this phrase usually mean by it a subjective, emotional conversion experience. I would not want to take away from the importance of experience, but the Bible by rebirth refers to an objective change, an objective act which changes a person's status and relationship. There are two elements of the new birth, despite the efforts of some to dehydrate the rebirth.

The new birth is accomplished by God. "By his great mercy he has given us a new birth into a living hope through the resurrection of Jesus Christ" (1 Pet. 1:3). The agency of the new birth is the word of God. God initiates the new birth through the preaching of the gospel: "You have been born anew, not of perishable but of imperishable seed, through the living and enduring word of God. . . . That word is the good news that was announced to you" (1 Pet. 1:23-25).

A parallel verse to John 3:5, but using a different word with a different conceptual background, is Titus 3:5: "God saved us, not because of any works of righteousness that we had done, but according to his mercy, through the water [washing] of rebirth [regeneration] and renewal by the Holy Spirit." The word rendered "rebirth" in the NRSV is *palingenesia*. This word was used in philosophical literature for the

---

42. The aorist tenses for the anointing, sealing, and giving of the Spirit in 2 Cor. 1:22 indicate a definite occasion, probably the baptismal bestowal of the Holy Spirit.

regeneration of the world, hence for a new age (cf. Matt. 19:28 for the word in an apocalyptic sense). The concept of a renewed world seems more likely as the background of Titus 3:5 than the idea of rebirth based on the imagery of physical birth. The bath, then, is related to the new world, the new age. It is accompanied by a renewing that is accomplished by the Holy Spirit.[43] One preposition, "through," governs both phrases, "bath of the new age and renewal of the Holy Spirit." These two phrases follow an *a-b-b-a* pattern. The new age and the renewal are related respectively to the water and the Spirit. Titus 3:6 may be a generalizing statement about the role of the Holy Spirit or may be a reference to the separate act of giving the Holy Spirit to indwell the convert. Although there is a continuity between what the Spirit does in baptism and his indwelling, conceptually these are different functions. The similarity with John 3:5 is that once more the newness involves two elements, water and Spirit.

Reference to the water precedes the Spirit in both John 3:5 and Titus 3:5. It seems likely that these verses speak not of something the Spirit does before baptism but what the Spirit does in baptism. The Spirit imparts the new spiritual life. This is something objective. The renewing by the Holy Spirit is what God does, not what a person feels. The Spirit gives a new heart and new spirit (Ezek. 36:26), so that one becomes a new creature (2 Cor. 5:17) who lives a new life (Col. 3:8-11). In view of this, translators of John 3:3 and 5 might have done better, in spite of the reference to the mother's womb in verse 4, to render "begotten" rather than "born." The Spirit recreates and renews life in connection with baptism, but more than that he also takes up residence in the one baptized (see discussion on p. 108). This further activity of the Spirit may be included in Titus 3:6, "This Spirit he poured out on us richly through Jesus Christ our Savior."

Death and Resurrection What is expressed in Johannine language as new birth or birth from above is expressed by Paul as a death and the resurrection of a transformed life. Colossians 2:12 was noticed above

---

43. James D. G. Dunn, *Baptism in the Holy Spirit* (Philadelphia: Westminster, 1970), pp. 165-170, construes the passage differently: the washing is of regeneration and renewal, and both are effected by the Holy Spirit. Even if the passage is read this way, it does not follow that the washing is figurative for the regeneration and renewal; *loutron* would have been chosen because of the washing involved in baptism, although it is readily granted that the spiritual significance is the important teaching of the passage.

on baptism as confession of faith. Paul's most extended discussion is in Romans 6.

> Do you not know that all of us who have been baptized into Christ Jesus were baptized into his death? Therefore we have been buried with him by baptism into death, so that, just as Christ was raised from the dead by the glory of the Father, so we too might walk in newness of life.
>
> For if we have been united with him in a death like his, we will certainly be united with him in a resurrection like his. We know that our old self was crucified with him so that the body of sin might be destroyed, and we might no longer be enslaved to sin. . . . So you also must consider yourselves dead to sin and alive to God in Christ Jesus. (Rom. 6:3-11)

This passage and 1 Peter 3:18-22 both connect baptism and its saving effects with the resurrection of Christ. As Christ died, was buried, and was raised, so baptism expresses death to sin, the burial of the old self, and resurrection to a new life.[44] There is both a negative and a positive aspect — a cancelling of the old and the initiation of the new. The old self that was a slave to sin is crucified and buried. God who raised Jesus raises the one baptized to a new life. This is the working of God in baptism.

As the Spirit was active in the new birth, so the Spirit is active in the resurrection to a new life. Although the Spirit is not mentioned in Romans 6, the Spirit is closely associated with the resurrection in Romans 8, and the language picks up the themes of Romans 6.

> If the Spirit of him who raised Jesus from the dead dwells in you, he who raised Christ from the dead will give life to your mortal bodies also through his Spirit that dwells in you. So then, brothers and sisters, we are debtors, not to the flesh, to live according to the flesh

---

44. James D. G. Dunn, *Baptism in the Holy Spirit* (Philadelphia: Westminster, 1970), p. 143, makes much of Paul not explicitly linking baptism with the idea of resurrection, but this is demanding too much literalness. What else are we to make of the connection, "Just as Christ was raised . . . , so we too walk in newness of life" (Rom. 6:4) and the contrast of dead and alive "in Christ" (Rom. 6:11) if not an association of the baptismal experience with resurrection? The mention of the resurrection of the convert is explicit in Col. 2:12, and even if *en hō* refers to Christ and not to baptism (Dunn, p. 155), baptism is still the occasion at which one is raised with Christ through faith. On the passage as a whole, see P. L. Stepp, *The Believer's Participation in the Death of Christ: "Corporate Identification" and a Study of Romans 6:1-14* (Lewiston: Mellen, 1996).

— for if you live according to the flesh, you will die; but if by the Spirit you put to death the deeds of the body, you will live. (Rom. 8:11-13)

What happened to Christ historically happens to others spiritually, and that in turn anticipates what will happen really at the end of time. The convert participates in Christ's death, burial, and resurrection. There is a sharing in his experience. That makes baptism a richly meaningful act. More is involved than an imitation or repetition of what Christ did; what he did becomes operative in the life of the believer. Here is the link in the doctrine of the atonement between Christ and a human being. How can what Christ did affect a person today? Objectively, there is God's acceptance. Subjectively, there is human appropriation.

Baptism may be described as an act of dynamic symbolism, a symbol that partakes of the reality symbolized. Just as the prophets of the Old Testament often conveyed their message by acts as well as by words (Isa. 20; Jer. 27–28; Ezek. 4), so baptism may be understood as a prophetic sign or symbol. The prophetic messages were conditional on the response of the people, and the symbolic actions partook of the reality proclaimed, for they, too, were the word of the Lord. Baptism began with John as an eschatological sign of cleansing; it was given deeper symbolism in Christianity by the death and resurrection of Christ. Anything but immersion destroys the symbolism of the act.

Baptism is a link between the atonement (see pp. 183-186 on forgiveness of sins) and Christian living. The purpose of Paul's reference to baptism in Romans 6 is to show the inconsistency of a life of sin in one who understands the meaning of baptism. Romans 6 does not say it is impossible for a baptized person to sin, but that it is inconsistent to do so. To practice sin is to deny the reality of conversion (Rom. 6:11, 12, 14; Col. 2:20; 3:5, 12). As a death to sin and a resurrection to a new life, baptism says something very important about the life to be lived after baptism. Since baptism means sin is crucified and buried and a new life is raised, this indicates the kind of life to be lived — righteous and not sinful. We are to be dead to sin but alive in and for God.

Membership in the Church Baptism places one in the church. "For in [or by] the one Spirit we were all baptized into one body . . . and we were all made to drink of one Spirit" (1 Cor. 12:13). This again is God's doing, to incorporate a person in the body of Christ. Baptism is not just an individual transaction. It is not just an act of personal salvation. It is a community or social act. One is now made a part of God's people. The Spirit places the person in the one body. Having the one Spirit is the means of sharing in the one body.

"Baptize in" is normally followed by the element in which the baptism occurs, and such is Paul's usage in 1 Corinthians 10:2. Hence, some have argued that water baptism is not in view in 1 Corinthians 12:13 and that Paul is using baptismal imagery to refer to being submerged in the Spirit.[45] This is possible but seems unlikely, since Paul

---

45. James D. G. Dunn, *Baptism in the Holy Spirit* (Philadelphia: Westminster, 1970), pp. 127-131, offers the following arguments:

(1) The six other usages of "baptism in the Holy Spirit" have the Spirit as the element (Matt. 3:11; Mark 1:8; Luke 3:16; John 1:33; Acts 1:5; 11:16). The numbers are not so impressive, for the passages report only two sayings in a nearly set phrase (always "Holy Spirit") and none is in Paul. When Paul uses the preposition *en* with Spirit, it is normally instrumental ("by") — in 1 Corinthians alone note 6:11; 12:3 (twice), 9 (twice); 14:16 (textually uncertain).

(2) "Baptize" does not itself specify water. However, since the overwhelming use in early Christian literature is to water baptism, the presumption favors such a reference unless the context makes clear that there is another reference. The subsequent statement about "made to drink" the Spirit, or alternatively "watered, irrigated" with the Spirit, refers to a separate event from the baptism by (or in) the Spirit but is most likely suggested by the presence of water in the baptism.

(3) Paul draws a metaphor from the rite, and this metaphorical usage occurs in Gal. 3:27; 1 Cor. 6:11; Rom. 6:3; and Col. 2:12; Eph. 5:26 (pp. 109-113, 120-123, 139-146, 153-157, 162-165). The common usage, on the other hand, once again places the burden of proof on one who contends for a metaphorical meaning. The imagery of "clothing" in Gal. 3:27 does not make "baptize" a metaphor; the construction refers to a concrete act ("as many of you as were baptized") as the basis ("for") of the metaphor of clothing, introduced in order to explain how being "in Christ" makes one "seed of Abraham." In the discussion of conversion-initiation in Galatians (pp. 106-115) Dunn rather arbitrarily allows only "receive the Spirit" as not metaphorical. The "washing" is indeed a "spiritual cleansing" in 1 Cor. 6:11, but the reason such a word is chosen is to allude to the baptism in water. Rom. 6:4, Dunn grants, refers to water baptism, so there seems no reason to take verse 3 as metaphorical. In Col. 2:12 the metaphor is "burial"; and it takes place "in baptism." The "washing" of Eph. 5:26 is probably an allusion to the bridal bath, but what would lead Paul to make the analogy if not water baptism? As Dunn allows throughout, baptism is part of the process of conversion-initiation (e.g., pp. 78, 91, 227-228), so why take the references to

in every other use of "baptized" in 1 Corinthians has water baptism in mind (1:13-17 [five times]; 10:2; even the enigmatic 15:29). Therefore, I prefer to take "in the one Spirit" to be instrumental: "by means of the one Spirit" a person is baptized into the one body. Such is the use of the phrase "in one Spirit" in verse 9 and in the important baptismal text in 1 Corinthians 6:11, where the repetition of the aorist tense ("you were washed, you were sanctified, you were justified") indicates the reference to the same event. The washing was accomplished "in [by] the name of the Lord Jesus Christ and in [by] the Spirit of our God." The Spirit is the agent of the effects of baptism.

If the locative sense (the Spirit as the element) should nonetheless be preferred in 1 Corinthians 12:13, there may still be a reference to water baptism. The typology of 1 Corinthians 10:2, "in the cloud and the sea," may suggest a simultaneous immersion in the Spirit and the water, to which allusion is made in 1 Corinthians 12:13. If so, the baptism in water is also a baptism in the Spirit. To be dipped in the baptismal water is to be dipped in the Spirit.[46]

---

baptism in such a context as metaphorical and not the references to "confession," for instance, as also metaphorical?

(4) In order to support the metaphorical interpretation Dunn claims that "to be baptized into" someone or something (metaphorical) is not the same as "to be baptized into the name" (the water rite) (p. 171). Since "name" in the ancient world stood for the person, this seems to be a quite artificial distinction. To be baptized into the name of Christ is the same as to be baptized into Christ.

(5) In New Testament teaching external rites are not to be confused with inner realities (p. 146; cf. pp. 15, 137). This is certainly true, but the Bible throughout expects an external expression of the inner realities. Dunn allows water baptism as the occasion for confession of faith, commitment, and the gift of the Spirit (e.g., pp. 17, 151). This way of putting the relationship would seem to remove most of the objections voiced against taking Paul's references to baptism as indicating the actual immersion in water.

If the "one baptism" of Eph. 4:5 is water baptism, as Dunn says, where does that leave Spirit baptism? Dunn, as many other scholars, is guilty of an ahistorical reading of the New Testament without reference to the practices and literature of the church in the early centuries. Only a few Gnostics (Tertullian, *On Baptism*) tried to dehydrate the New Testament references to baptism. Relevant to 1 Cor. 12:13 is the association of water baptism and baptism with or by the Holy Spirit (Justin Martyr, *Dialogue with Trypho* 18-19; 29.1; 43.2)

46. L. S. Thornton, *The Common Life in the Body of Christ*, 3rd ed. (London: Dacre, 1950), pp. 87-94.

The New Testament places no significance on the person who performs the baptism. The emphasis is always on the person's response of faith and the divine action. Paul in 1 Corinthians 1:13-17 does not depreciate baptism itself but its human administrator. The preaching of the gospel that results in baptism is much more important than the person who assists the believer in being baptized. Paul, as modern missionaries, recognized the potential for party loyalties from attachment to a prominent preacher or church leader. John 4:1-2, although dealing with the ministry of Jesus, is relevant here. Jesus was making and baptizing more disciples than John, yet Jesus was not himself doing the baptizing. His disciples were doing that. What was done by his disciples was done by Jesus. The person doing the baptizing was not the important matter; what was important was the fact that it was done and the purpose that motivated it.

Even if the Spirit is not the instrumental means of the incorporation into the body of Christ in 1 Corinthians 12:13, the verse still teaches that the end result is becoming one body. In that one body "we were all made to drink of one Spirit," for the body of Christ is where the Spirit is. "We were all baptized" and "We all drank of one Spirit" are grammatically parallel, so we have another passage where baptism and the Spirit are brought together as twin aspects of becoming a Christian. This verse adds the thought that this experience adds one to the body.

The same thought of incorporation into the church is expressed elsewhere by Paul as being baptized into Christ (see Rom. 6:3 discussed on p. 190). In Galatians 3:27, being baptized "into Christ" is described as being clothed with Christ. And being in Christ puts one in the people of God (Gal. 3:28-29). Since Christ is the body (1 Cor. 12:12), to be baptized into Christ is to be baptized into the body, that is, into the church as the people of God. Both Galatians 3:28 and 1 Corinthians 12:13 make incorporation into Christ independent of racial, social, and sexual distinctions.

Baptism serves as the act of initiation into the church. Any group or organization has to have some act which marks off its members from others, however informal this may be. This is especially true in the realm of religion. Not only does the church need something to identify its members, but people need something they can look back on and say, "At that time I became a Christian, a member of the church." God has designated something as the decisive act that only the truly converted will do. Baptism is the line between the church and the world.

Membership in the church is more a result than a purpose of

baptism. One is baptized not so much in order to join the church as to accept Christ and receive his salvation. Part of what is involved in that is incorporation into the people of Christ. God adds the person to the church, the community of the saved. The church is created by God. With membership go both privileges and responsibilities. Baptism carries responsibilities to the church as well as bringing the privileges of belonging to the community of believers. The relationship of baptism to the church is a reminder that conversion and salvation is not only an individual act but is also a corporate act. Salvation places a person in a saved community.

Concluding Observations   Baptism provides an objective assurance of having received God's promised salvation in Christ. That may lead to the subtle temptation to trust in baptism for salvation instead of trusting in God, his act in Christ, and his word of promise.

Similarly, there are other things that can become misplaced objects of trust. One person may trust his or her faith as a guarantee of salvation. Another person may trust in some experience as the assurance of salvation. Yet another may depend on doctrinal correctness for salvation. As valuable and desirable as these things, or other things that may become the basis of assurance, may be, they must not become the objects of trust. There often seems to be a temptation to rely on something else rather than to trust in God's grace in Christ. Truly to trust in God includes responding to him in the appointed way.

Subjects of Baptism

Penitent Believers

What has been said about the meaning of baptism identifies the proper subjects of baptism. Baptism is an act of faith and repentance. It is a faith confessed in action and an expression of the turning involved in repentance. It brings a forgiveness of sins to those convicted in their heart. It is not a work by those already saved. Hence, the proper persons to receive baptism are penitent believers, or believing penitents. Only to such can baptism have the full meaning outlined above.

Infant Baptism   The theology of baptism presented in the New Testament would seem to rule out infant baptism, in spite of its long history in Catholic and Protestant churches. Against the practice are the following facts. (1) There is no mention of the baptism of infants in the

New Testament. (2) Every account of baptism in the New Testament shows it to be response by believers (cf. Acts 18:8 as representative). (3) The evidence of church history places the beginning of infant baptism at the end of the second century.[47]

Various efforts have been made to hurdle the historical and theological barriers to infant baptism. Four arguments will be briefly examined.

Evidence in the New Testament for infant baptism is claimed from the examples of household baptism. It is argued that the term for "house" or "household" *(oikos)* includes infants. It is true that this word would include children if they were present, but the term does not require that they were present or say anything about the age of any children who might be in the household. Infants are not necessarily included, and there are things said in the accounts of household conversion that exclude them. The angel told Cornelius that Peter would bring a message by which his "entire household will be saved" (Acts 11:14). Besides the implication of this statement of hearing and understanding the message, "all his household" is described as fearing God (Acts 10:2). Lydia "and her household" were baptized (Acts 16:15). No details are given, but since Lydia was head of her own business and household and nothing is said about a husband, it seems the household was her slaves and business associates and the presence of infants highly unlikely. The jailor at Philippi "and his household" were promised salvation if he believed (Acts 16:31), so "They spoke the word of the Lord to him and to all who were in his house" (Acts 16:32). "He and his entire family were baptized" (Acts 16:33), and "he and his entire household rejoiced" (Acts 16:34). Any children in this household were able to hear the word of the Lord and rejoice at their baptism. At Corinth "Crispus . . . became a believer in the Lord, together with all his house-

---

47. The efforts of Joachim Jeremias, *Infant Baptism in the First Four Centuries* (London: SCM, 1960) and *The Origins of Infant Baptism* (Naperville, Ill.: Allenson, 1963), to find infant baptism in apostolic times were thoroughly answered as far as historical evidence is concerned by Kurt Aland, *Did the Early Church Baptize Infants?* (Westminster: Philadelphia, 1963), *Die Stellung der Kinder in den frühen christlichen Gemeinden — und ihre Taufe* (Munich, 1967), and *Taufe und Kindertaufe* (Gütersloh, 1971). A plausible setting for the origin of infant baptism is suggested by Everett Ferguson, "Inscriptions and the Origin of Infant Baptism," *Journal of Theological Studies* n.s. 30 (1979): 37-46; from another perspective see D. F. Wright, "The Origins of Infant Baptism — Child Believers' Baptism?" *Scottish Journal of Theology* 40 (1987): 1-23. A collection of the sources may be found in Everett Ferguson, *Early Christians Speak* (Abilene: ACU Press, 1987), pp. 55-65.

hold" (Acts 18:8). His household included only those old enough to become believers. Paul baptized "the household of Stephanas" (1 Cor. 1:16), and "they were the first converts in Achaia, and they have devoted themselves to the service of the saints" (1 Cor. 16:15).

Another approach is to blend the old and new covenants and to argue that as in Israel one was born into covenant relationship with God and received circumcision as the sign of being in the Abrahamic covenant (Gen. 17:11; cf. Rom. 4:11), so now one is born into the people of God and receives baptism as the seal of salvation. The problem with this argument is that the New Testament did not give baptism the place of circumcision.[48] Christian circumcision is the work of the Spirit within the heart (Rom. 2:28-29; Phil. 3:3; contrast Eph. 2:11), and the gift of the Holy Spirit, not baptism, is identified as the seal of the covenant (2 Cor. 1:21-22; Eph. 1:13-14; 4:30). The gift of the Holy Spirit continued in early Christian thought to be spoken of as spiritual circumcision, and the association of circumcision with baptism was a secondary development because baptism was the time at which the Spirit was bestowed.[49] The one passage in the New Testament where there appears to be an association of circumcision with baptism is Colossians 2:11-12. The "circumcision of Christ" refers to the death of Christ, followed by his burial and resurrection. That is the spiritual circumcision, "made without hands," in which one participates through union with Christ. The body of flesh is stripped off, as was Christ's, and one is buried and raised in baptism. The baptism is not itself the spiritual circumcision, for baptism is administered by human hands. The most that can be said is that baptism is associated with the time or occasion of a person's participation in the circumcision of Christ, because baptism is a burial and resurrection. The real correspondence is between the physical act of the old covenant and its spiritual counterpart in the circumcision of the heart (cf. Deut. 30:6; Jer. 4:4) in the new covenant (an activity of the Holy Spirit). The argument from circumcising infants under the old covenant to baptizing infants now is a theological construct without direct warrant in the New Testament texts.

Another support for infant baptism has been found in Jewish proselyte baptism. Any children in the family that converted to Judaism

---

48. James D. G. Dunn, *Unity and Diversity in the New Testament*, 2nd ed. (London: SCM, 1990), pp. 159-160.

49. Everett Ferguson, "Spiritual Circumcision in Early Christianity," *Scottish Journal of Theology* 41 (1989): 485-497.

received the purification bath along with their parents. The difficulty with this argument is the uncertain date of proselyte baptism. The requirement of immersion for proselytes is not certainly attested until the late first century.[50] Even if we could be sure that it was earlier, it seems not to have been comparable to Christian baptism, and it is not clear what if any influence therefore it would have had on the Christian rite. Even if the maximum possibilities are allowed for the parallel between the two rites, there is an important difference. Children who were received into Judaism with their parents could renounce their place in Judaism without being considered apostates, a concession not granted to children born after the conversion nor to subsequent generations. This indicates that children of the first generation of converts were considered somewhat anomalous and entitled to make a choice for themselves whether to follow their parents into the Jewish faith.[51]

For Catholics and many Protestants, the principal theological justification for infant baptism is found in the doctrine of original sin. Kurt Aland has associated the rise of infant baptism in the late second century with the development of a doctrine of infant stain associated with birth.[52] But the historical sequence seems to be the reverse. Infant baptism arose first on other grounds, and the idea that infants needed purification developed (at least in part) as a consequence of the practice. From the idea of an infant stain there developed the doctrine of original sin. Although this doctrine was widely held in Africa at Augustine's time, it is instructive to note that in his debate with Pelagians he argues from infant baptism (which Pelagius accepted) to original sin (which Pelagius did not accept). Original sin was not the basis of the practice, but the practice was the basis of the doctrine (since everyone agreed that one purpose of baptism was forgiveness of sins). If the doctrine of original sin in the sense of inherited guilt (not attested in the early history of Christianity) is found wanting in biblical support (as argued in the section on sin, p. 145), then this theological support for infant baptism also falls.

50. J. J. Collins, "A Symbol of Otherness: Circumcision and Salvation in the First Century," *To See Ourselves as Others See Us,* ed. J. Neusner and E. S. Frerichs (Chico, Calif.: Scholars Press, 1985), p. 171.

51. Pat E. Harrell, "Jewish Proselyte Baptism," *Restoration Quarterly* 1 (1957): 159-165, with reference to b. Kethuboth 11a.

52. See references in n. 47; cf. nn. 11 and 28.

Condition of the Child   The theology of the child is little developed in churches that practice believers' baptism.[53] Yet the status of the child is urgently in need of clarification as a foundation for religious education and as an explanation of the relation of the young person to the Christian community.

Sometimes there has been a tendency to come out where the old revivalism did: one must be lost in order to be saved, so the child is painted as a little sinner. Perhaps related is the tendency to baptize at a younger and younger age. Or, little or no attention may be given to the child.

One line of approach is from the doctrine of creation. God pronounced his creation good (Gen. 1:31). The doctrine of inherited guilt from Adam was rejected above as lacking biblical support. Children would then be born innocent.

The New Testament gives positive assessments of children. According to Matthew 18:1-4 a person must become like a child in order to enter the kingdom of heaven, and according to Matthew 19:13-15 the kingdom of heaven belongs to such as the little children. These statements would imply that children are under the rule of God; otherwise, it would hardly make sense to say that others must become like children to enter the kingdom. These passages are not baptismal texts but are important declarations of the condition of children in God's sight.

The child of a Christian grows up in holiness. Paul argues against a believer divorcing an unbelieving mate on the grounds that the believer sanctifies the unbeliever, a conclusion justified by this consideration: "Otherwise, your children would be unclean, but as it is, they are holy" (1 Cor. 7:14). The background of Paul's argument is Jewish ideas of ritual purity or impurity. Salvation is not under consideration: Paul does not assume that an unbeliever is saved because the spouse is a believer (vs. 16). The question is the legitimacy of the marriage relationship so that it is proper to remain in the marriage. A corollary is the condition of the children; are they in a state of purity as it relates to the Christian community? Paul indicates that the answer is "Yes." Nothing is said here about baptism; the state of holiness comes from the believing parent not from baptism and no impurity requires the cleansing of baptism. If all children are born innocent, then the child

---

53. But see Gideon Yoder, *Evangelism and Ministry to Children* (Scottdale, Penn.: Herald, 1959); Marlin Jeschke, *Believer's Baptism for Children of the Church* (Scottdale, Penn.: Herald, 1983).

of a Christian parent has an added advantage, for that child grows up (even if incompletely) under Christian influence and in some contact with the Christian community.

The child of a Christian home is in some kind of relation to the Lord — "Children, obey your parents in the Lord. . . . And, fathers, do not provoke your children to anger, but bring them up in the discipline and instruction of the Lord" (Eph. 6:1-4). The child of Christian parents sustains a special relation to the Lord that the child of non-Christians would not.

There must be some way in which the religious experience of the child is not denied and treated as non-Christian but the real meaning of believer's baptism maintained. If the child is in a positive relationship to the kingdom of God and to the church, as the above texts indicate, then it is proper to teach the child to pray, to study the Bible, and to practice Christian morality. The child is to be taught to know the Lord.

What then does baptism mean for the child who has grown up in a Christian home? It must still retain the positive significance that it has for the adult convert from the world, but it would not have the same sense of a radical break with the past. It would mark a break with sin, in anticipation and resolve, if not in extent of experience. The baptism of a child of Christian parents should be seen in continuity with the childhood religious experience. Now is the time of deliberate choice and expression of personal faith (not still the faith of the parents). We may note the connection of baptism and confession of faith in the New Testament. At this time, one makes a profession of faith as his or her own. The young person assumes church responsibilities,[54] and the church assumes some responsibilities for the person's conduct beyond those responsibilities belonging to the immediate family. Baptism is the person's acceptance of Christ and of responsibility for public involvement in the life of the church. Those who observe infant baptism have something comparable in confirmation, a practice without biblical precedent. This practice shows the necessity for such a public declaration of one's place in the church. When the biblical practice (believer's baptism) is changed, a substitute for it must be found. Those who perform infant baptism but take personal faith seriously have to give to something else (i.e., confirmation) the value baptism has in the New Testament.

54. One may compare the Jewish *bar mitzvah*, when the child becomes a "son of the commandment" with responsibility to assume the duties of the law.

At what time does baptism become appropriate? When can a decision for a life of faith be responsibly made? How long is a child in a state of "holiness"? How long does the blood of Christ and the faith of the parents cover the person before a public acceptance of the blood and a personal acknowledgment of the faith is made? When does one assume responsibility for the self? When is there a real understanding and not just knowing the right words to say? The Bible does not give an age. The person must face the consciousness of sin (which to some degree may come quite early) and the necessity of assuming responsibility for actions (that may be very much later).

If a child is in some relation to the church, a service of infant blessing, on the order of Matthew 19:13-15, is in order. It is always proper to pray God's blessings on children and ask for his guidance for parents in rearing their children. At the same time parents can commit themselves to their task, and the church can commit itself to the spiritual nurture of its families.

Action of Baptism

The baptism commanded by Jesus in the making of disciples is an immersion in water. The topic formerly was warmly debated, but in these days there is general scholarly agreement. Several lines of evidence converge in support of the baptismal action as a dipping.

The etymology of the word *baptizō* (from *baptō*) as "to dip, plunge, immerse, wash completely" is little disputed. The contention that by New Testament times the word had come to be used to mean "to purify ceremonially" without reference to the manner of the application of the water is a conjecture without basis in the texts. The meaning "dip, immerse, submerge" is continued in a secular sense among authors of New Testament times. For instance, Josephus uses *baptizō* for a person drowning[55] and for a ship sinking (his most frequent usage),[56] both very thorough submergings.

Jewish practice in New Testament times for ritual washing was a complete immersion of the body.[57] This was true in Pharisaic prescrip-

---

55. *War* 1.437; *Antiquities* 15.55.

56. *War* 2.556; 3.368; 3.525, 527; *Antiquities* 9.212; cf. *War* 3.423 and *Life* 15 for waves overwhelming a ship but not sinking it.

57. I. Abrahams, " 'How Did the Jews Baptize?' " *Journal of Theological Studies* 12 (1911): 609-612.

tions that became normative for Judaism and in sects like the Qumran community. The evidence of literary texts has been confirmed by the discovery in Israel of a large number of *mikwaoth* (immersion baths) from the first century.[58] Doubts about the feasibility of immersing 3,000 persons on Pentecost (Acts 2), for instance, have been completely dispelled by the large number of immersion pools found on the temple mount to accommodate the needs of priests and throngs of worshippers to be in a state of purity as they approached the temple.

The New Testament descriptions of baptism imply a full bath. John chose his place for baptizing because of the abundance of water (John 3:23). Jesus came up from the water after his baptism (Matt. 3:16). It was unnecessary for him to have been in the water if it was only poured or sprinkled on him. Later church practice in this regard led artists to the strange fantasy of Jesus standing waist deep in water while John poured water on his head (such pictures do not occur until medieval western times). Philip's baptizing of the Ethiopian treasurer required them both to get out of the chariot, go down into the water, and to come up out of the water (Acts 8:38-39), foolishly unnecessary unless a dipping was performed.

The symbolism of burial and resurrection (Rom. 6:3-4; Col. 2:12) is meaningful for an immersion but difficult to visualize for some other action. That symbolism is applied practically in such subsequent statements as "your life is hidden with Christ in God" (Col. 3:3).

The evidence of early church history is conclusive on early Christian practice.[59] Two exceptions appear in the sources. The *Didache* 7 allows pouring water three times on the head if there is not sufficient water for an immersion. Sickbed baptism could be administered by applying water on the body if it was dangerous to take the person to a place for a full immersion (Cyprian, *Epistle* 69 [75].12). Both circumstances were considered exceptional, and it was a long time before

---

58. Ehud Netzer, "Ancient Ritual Baths *(Miqvaot)* in Jericho," *The Jerusalem Cathedra* 2, ed. L. I. Levine (Detroit: Wayne State, 1982), pp. 106-119; Bryant G. Wood, "To Dip or Sprinkle? The Qumran Cisterns in Perspective," *Bulletin of the American Schools of Oriental Research* 256 (1984): 45-60; Wm. S. LaSor, "Discovering What Jewish Miqva'ot Can Tell Us About Christian Baptism," *Biblical Archaeology Review* 13 (Jan.-Feb., 1987): 52-59; E. P. Sanders, *Jewish Law from Jesus to the Mishnah* (Philadelphia: Trinity Press International, 1990), pp. 214-227.

59. Some of the evidence is collected in Everett Ferguson, *Early Christians Speak* (Abilene: ACU Press, 1987), pp. 33-54.

something other than immersion became common (and that western branch of the church).

GOD'S GIFTS

> *"His divine power has given us everything needed*
> *for life and godliness, through the knowledge of him*
> *who called us by his own glory and goodness."*   (2 PET. 1:3)

Enough has been included in the previous discussion about what God does that only a summary and reaffirmation of some points already made are required at this point.

Three Tenses of Salvation

God's gifts may be summarized in terms of three great promises of the gospel: forgiveness of sins, gift of the Holy Spirit, and eternal life. These promises apply salvation to the past, present, and future of the human condition. The Christian receives from God salvation from past sins, a present life of salvation, and the hope of future salvation.

The forgiveness of sins is promised in Acts 2:38 to penitent believers who are baptized. God's forgiveness removes the barrier between himself and his creatures. It changes the human condition from a state of guilt and alienation to a state of being justified and reconciled. The forgiveness of sins in Acts 2:38 is equivalent to the salvation in 2:40 — Peter "exhorted them saying, 'Save yourselves from this corrupt generation.'" What has been developed in this chapter explains how this verse is to be understood. Salvation is not ultimately in human beings, but in accepting God's gifts and meeting his conditions there is a part human beings have in their salvation; in this case repenting and being baptized for the forgiveness of sins is the means of saving themselves.

It may be thought that at baptism all past sins are forgiven, and then persons have to do the rest for themselves. Not so. Forgiveness applies not only to past sins. The conditions that brought forgiveness at baptism — God's grace in the blood of Christ received in faith and repentance — continue to bring forgiveness after baptism. Baptism continues to be effective in washing away sins (Acts 22:16), if the conditions that made baptism something more than a washing in water (1 Pet. 3:21) continue to obtain, namely faith in the crucified and resurrected Christ and a penitent attitude before God. Conversely, if one loses faith and a penitent attitude, baptism loses its saving significance. The continuing benefit of baptism leads to the consideration of the present gift of God.

God gives help in living out one's salvation (Phil. 2:12) in the Christian way of life. The Holy Spirit provides the link between baptism and the Christian life. The Holy Spirit not only sanctifies (1 Cor. 6:11; 1 Pet. 1:2) but also gives new life in baptism (John 3:5) and takes up residence in the one converted (Acts 2:38; 5:30; Rom 8:9; 1 Cor. 6:19). The Holy Spirit provides the continuing present benefits of God's one-time action in the cross and the one-time commitment in baptism (there is "one baptism" — Eph. 4:5). He is the power of the Christian life. God not only gives "gifts," but he also gives himself, his very own Spirit. It is the Spirit of Christ that makes the church the body of Christ (1 Cor. 12:13). People often want to objectify or psychologize the presence of the Spirit and so to identify the coming of the Spirit with some feeling. This is not true of the baptismal gift of the Spirit in the New Testament. Hence, some want to rationalize the presence of the Spirit and try to explain how the Spirit comes to dwell in persons (usually through the words of scripture). The proper perspective is to view the gift of the Holy Spirit in the same way as the forgiveness of sins. Both rest on the promises of God, and God cannot lie. We may not be able to explain how God forgives sins or how the Spirit dwells in us, and we may not be able to point to some experience as a personal guarantee. Just as we trust in God for the forgiveness of sins, so we trust in him that the Spirit dwells in us.

The third great promise of the gospel is eternal life (John 3:15-16, 36; Rom. 6:22-23). Eternal life is sometimes spoken of as a present possession, especially in the Johannine writings (John 5:24; 6:47; 17:3); sometimes as a future hope (Matt. 19:29; Rom. 2:7; Titus 1:2). Eternal life is a quality of life, life that comes from the realm of eternity and is characterized by eternity. Its present possession does not mean that it cannot be lost (Gal. 5:4; Heb. 10:26, 36-39). The future life will be in continuity with the present life of grace (1 Thess. 5:4-9). Those who do not have eternal life now will not receive it in the future. The full realization of eternal life belongs to the world to come. Then those who obey Christ will enjoy "eternal salvation" (Heb. 5:9).

Salvation and the Church

Properly understood, "to be in the church is to be in Christ, and to be in Christ is to be in the church."[60] One is not "in Christ" because of being "in the church," but one is "in the church" because of being "in Christ." Membership in the church is not a matter of separate choice by the one joined to Christ (as if one could belong to Christ and not belong to his people). To be saved is to be in Christ, and to be a Christian is to be a member of the church. God by the same action that saves places the person in the redeemed community. Nor is the church in the Bible an invisible body. It is always treated in the New Testament as a visible community of people, identifiable and distinct from the surrounding world. The church is part of God's redemptive plan. Not only is a visible fellowship part of God's saving action, but it is also the context in which the salvation is lived out and the new life actualized. Moreover, the church is the means of communicating the saving gospel.

Paul as a missionary did not simply make converts; he planted and built churches. Perhaps this was connected with the Jewish heritage from which he worked and from which influence many of his converts came, but it is important to note that he left behind communities, not isolated believers. Mission work is more than converting individuals; it is establishing churches. And so we turn to the activities of the churches that result from salvation.

---

60. Claude Welch, *The Reality of the Church* (New York: Scribner's, 1958), p. 165.

4. The Church and Her High Priest: Worship and Assembly

*"Since we have a great priest over the
house of God, let us approach with a
true heart in full assurance of faith."*　　(HEB. 10:21-22)

JESUS set the pattern for his people in rejecting any object of worship other than God: "Worship the Lord your God, and serve only him" (Matt. 4:10, quoting Deut. 6:13; 10:20). He taught the proper manner of worshipping God: "in spirit and truth" (John 4:24). He became himself the way of coming to God (John 14:6).

Having examined in previous chapters the nature of the church and the salvation that produces its membership, our study proceeds to consider how the salvation in Christ expresses itself, in other words, the activities of the church. These activities will be discussed in three chapters. They are schematized according to their reference to God — worship; their reference to other human beings — work and ministry; and their reference to the individual — life and fellowship. Any such scheme is inadequate, for, as will be seen, there is much overlapping, whatever the primary thrust. In this chapter, worship will be seen to have a significant horizontal relationship with other worshipers as well as a vertical relationship with God as the object of worship. The work and ministry of the church (Chap. 5) is a service to God directed both to fellow believers and to unbelievers. The new life in Christ in its ethical dimension (Chap. 6) is social as well as personal, including fellowship with other believers and a witness to non-believers. For the present, we examine worship as one of the responses to God's saving activity in Christ.

WORD MEANINGS

"The God who made the world and everything
in it . . . is (not) served by human hands,
as though he needed anything."   (ACTS 17:24)

The English Word

"Worship" is derived from two parts: "worth" (worthy) and "ship" (condition or quality). Worship says that the object is worthy, and to worship God is to ascribe worth to him. This one English word has to do duty for several words in Greek.

The Greek Words

The most common word for worship was *proskyneō* ("to kiss the hand toward," "to do obeisance," "to prostrate oneself"). It had the most specific content of the words for worship: to bow or fall down before an object of veneration. Since it could be done before a human being of higher rank from whom a benefit was desired, its frequent occurrences in the Gospels in reference to Jesus do not necessarily indicate acceptance of his divinity or messianic status by those who approached him in this way (more ambiguous in Matt. 8:2 and 9:18 than in 28:9, 17; note the mocking use in Mark 15:19). From the specific act came a general usage for "worship" or "acts of reverence" (John 12:20; Rev. 14:7). It could be directed toward human beings (Acts 10:25, in this case rejected), the idols of paganism (Acts 7:43), the devil or his agents (Matt. 4:9; Rev. 13:4), angels (Rev. 22:8, but rejected), or the true God (Rev. 7:11). Only in 1 Corinthians 14:25 is the term used in reference to a church meeting, and here it is done by an "outsider."

The English word "liturgy" is derived from the Greek *leitourgia* (verb *leitourgeō*),[1] a word referring to public service (cf. Rom. 13:6), but

---

1. N. Lewis, "*Leitourgia* and Related Terms," *Greek, Roman, and Byzantine Studies* 3 (1960): 175-184 and 6 (1965): 227-230.

used in Jewish and Christian literature of the early Christian era predominantly for religious service (see p. 224 on Rom. 15:16). The broader sense of noncultic service may be illustrated by 2 Corinthians 9:12 and Romans 15:27, the contribution for the needs of the saints, but even here there may be a metaphorical use of the sacrificial meaning (as in Phil. 2:17; cf. 2:30). The common use of the word in the New Testament, reflecting the Greek Old Testament, is for the Jewish temple service (Luke 1:23; Heb. 9:21; 10:11), and thus it is used also for Jesus' priestly ministry (Heb. 8:2, 6). Paul uses this family of words for his preaching ministry (Rom. 15:16), and this fact, along with usage in early extracanonical Christian literature,[2] may give the meaning of "preaching," or specifically "prophesying," for the only usage of the word in the New Testament in the context of a Christian meeting, Acts 13:2.

Another common word for worship in the Greek world was *latreuō* ("to perform religious service," "to carry out cultic duties"; noun *latreia*). It is used in the New Testament for pagan worship (Acts 7:42; Rom. 1:25), but properly belongs to God alone (Matt. 4:10). The word most often designates Jewish worship (Acts 7:7; 26:7; Rom. 9:4; Heb. 8:5; 9:1, 6, 9; 10:2; 13:10). That worship included fasting and prayers in Luke 2:37. A metaphorical use of the word occurs in John 16:2. Paul used the word to describe his service to God in Romans 1:9 (another instance of his use of cultic language for his service to the gospel; cf. 1 Tim. 1:3; Acts 24:14; 27:23). Christian worship is contrasted to Jewish in Philippians 3:3 (connected with the Spirit and with Jesus) and Hebrews 13:10 (referring to the sacrifice of Jesus). Christian worship is described by this word in Hebrews 9:14 and 12:28, as is the heavenly worship in Revelation 7:15 and 22:3. *Latreia* for Christians is no longer the temple sacrifices but the rational offering of their bodies as living sacrifices in doing the will of God (Rom. 12:1-2).

Thrēskeia was another word for "religious service" or "cult," the external expressions of worship. It refers to Judaism in Acts 26:5 and the worship of angels in Colossians 2:18.[3] Its only application to Christianity in the New Testament occurs in James 1:26-27, where true reli-

---

2. *Didache* 15.1 and *1 Clement* 8.1 of prophets.
3. Fred O. Francis, "Humility and Angelic Worship in Col 2:18," *Studia Theologica* 16 (1962): 109-134, takes the genitive case in "worship of angels" as subjective so that the persons described consider themselves to be exalted to participate in the heavenly worship of God by the angels. This departure from the usual interpretation of the phrase as referring to worship directed to angels is rejected by Eduard Lohse, *Colossians and Philemon* (Philadelphia: Fortress, 1971), pp. 117-119.

gion is defined in terms of good deeds and conduct. In contrast to "worthless religion," which does not control the tongue, "pure and undefiled religion" is care for widows and orphans and keeping oneself unstained by the world.

Sebomai and cognates meant "to worship" in the sense of show reverence or respect for one. It was used for the worship of the pagan deity Artemis (Acts 19:27; cf. Rom. 1:25 for worshipping the creature rather than the Creator). Matthew 15:9 and Mark 7:7 (quoting Isa. 29:13) use the word for vain worship of God. The participle is used for Gentiles who reverenced the God of the Jews (several times in Acts — e.g., 13:43, 50; 17:4, 17). The only express reference to Christian worship is Acts 18:13, where the Jews charged Paul with teaching "people to worship God in ways . . . contrary to the law."

Eusebeia — a general word for religion, piety, or devotion — could also refer to worship. In Greco-Roman literature, it almost always refers to cultic activities involving paying proper reverence or adoration. With reference to deity it meant the attitude of dutiful ritual observance and obligation. With reference to human beings (especially the duty to parents) it meant the attitude of respect and loyalty to another person. But, in every case, it referred not just to the attitude (as often do the English words "devotion," "piety," and "godliness") but also the activity by which the attitude was expressed. The verb is used in the common Greek senses of worship of the pagan gods in Acts 17:23 and of discharging obligations to members of one's family in 1 Timothy 5:4. The adjective refers to devout God-fearers in Acts 10:2, 7. Most occurrences of the word group are in the Pastoral Epistles and 2 Peter, those books in the New Testament that most reflect Hellenistic terminology and attitudes. The occurrences of *eusebeia* in reference to Christian godliness for the most part do not specify a content of what was included in the designation. The reference to false teachers' "outward form of godliness" (2 Tim. 3:5) is in keeping with the word's association with proper ceremonies (an appearance contradicted by their bad conduct — vss. 2-4, 6). Where the context does suggest a content for the Christian use of the word, it has to do not with dutiful observances but with the good conduct of the proper Christian lifestyle: "the quiet life" (1 Tim. 2:2), the imagery of (moral) "exercise" (1 Tim. 4:7), and the association with "righteousness, faith, love, endurance, gentleness" (1 Tim. 6:11). Similarly, the placing of "godliness" between endurance and brotherly love in 2 Peter 1:6-7 shows an understanding of Christian *eusebeia* as moral and ethical conduct, made explicit in 3:11, "holy manner of living and godliness."

A pattern emerges from the New Testament use of the Greek vocabulary for worship. These words for worship derive from the ritual actions of the Greco-Roman world, especially the temple service, both pagan and Jewish. Notice, however, what Christianity has done to these words. Instead of referring to ritual or ceremonial activities, the language of cult is applied to the Christian life, especially its moral conduct and good deeds. As will be developed more below, since the one sacrifice of Christ has been offered once and for all (Heb. 7:27; 9:12; 10:10), all the ancient cultic language, permeated with the language of sacrifice, was in early Christian usage "spiritualized" and shifted to the horizon of the Christian's moral life. Cultic terminology is used metaphorically in the New Testament; hence, a cultic or priestly understanding of Christian worship is out of the question.[4]

Not only do the words for worship in the ancient world not refer in their Christian context to ritual or cultic acts, but rarely do they occur even in regard to the Christian assembly. Exceptions are 1 Corinthians 14:25 (and here not to the activity of Christians in the assembly) and probably Acts 13:2 (prophesying, according to the interpretation advanced above). Consequently, any distinction in principle between assembly for worship and service in the world is ruled out, as is any distinction between priests and laity (see further pp. 220-226). In this regard, we may perhaps assign a symbolic significance to the usage of the English word *services* for both religious meetings and benefits rendered to people. It is appropriate that the same English word expresses service to the world and services in honor of God.

There is a phrase in the Old Testament for worship that, in its Greek translation, was taken over in the New Testament to express Christian worship: "to call upon *(epikaleō)* the name of the Lord." This is a set phrase in the Old Testament for the general practice, in whatever outward form throughout human history, of calling upon God in worship (e.g., Gen. 4:26; 12:8; Deut. 4:7; 2 Chron. 6:33; Pss. 99:6; 105:1; 116:17). There was the expectation that Gentiles, too, would call on the Lord (Isa. 55:5-6, Greek; Zeph. 3:9). In this regard, Joel 2:32, "Everyone who calls on the name of the LORD shall be saved," became very important, expressly quoted in significant texts twice in the New Testament (Acts 2:21; Rom. 10:12-14). To call upon the name of the Lord

---

4. Ferdinand Hahn, *The Worship of the Early Church* (Philadelphia: Fortress, 1973), pp. 35-38, 61-62; C. F. D. Moule, "Sanctuary and Sacrifice in the Church of the New Testament," *Journal of Theological Studies* n.s. 1 (1950): 29-41.

might refer to prayer, but often has the special connotation of confession. Especially appropriate to these contexts that speak of salvation is the usage in reference to baptism (cf. pp. 180-181, 183 on Acts 22:16). "The Lord" in the Old Testament was God, and the New Testament refers to calling upon the Father (1 Pet. 1:17). The word "to call upon" in the sense of worship in the New Testament, however, perhaps by way of the application of the title "Lord," most often is addressed to Christ (Acts 7:59; 9:14, 20-21; 22:16; 2 Tim. 2:22). "To call upon the name of our Lord Jesus Christ" is virtually a definition of Christians in 1 Corinthians 1:2 (see further p. 234).

Those who call upon the name of the Lord are those who have first been called by God through his word (pp. 161-163). The other side of calling on the name of the Lord is to have his name called upon one. This, too, was Old Testament usage (Deut. 28:10; 2 Chron. 7:14; Isa. 43:7). The idea was that people over whom the name of the Lord was called enjoyed his protection and blessing. The extension of this prospect to the Gentiles (Amos 9:12) was quoted in the New Testament (Acts 15:17). The concept remained alive among Jewish Christians (James 2:7). Those who call on the name of the Lord have his name called over them (cf. p. 181). The worship of God and Christ involves a reciprocal relationship.

THEOLOGICAL FOUNDATIONS OF WORSHIP

"God is spirit, and those who worship him
must worship in spirit and truth."   (JOHN 4:24)

The meaning of Christian worship may be best seen in the light of its theological bases. These doctrinal points are part of the total biblical revelation, but the special features of Christian faith give certain distinctive emphases to the church's worship.[5]

---

5. Ralph P. Martin, "Patterns of Worship in New Testament Churches," *Journal for the Study of the New Testament* 37 (1989): 59-85, finds among the elements that gave coherence to worship in the New Testament (1) the centrality of Christ, who brought and embodied the revelation of God as Father and in whose name the worship of God occurred, (2) the awareness of the Holy Spirit, and (3) concern for others.

The Nature of God

The nature of God determines how he is served. This is true of pagan religions as well. If God were a God of nature, he would be served by naturalistic rites, such as those intended to promote the fertility of nature. If God were a philosophical principle, the highest human activity would take the form of meditation. Similarly, the qualities of the biblical God govern the way he is worshiped.[6] The biblical definitions of God are accompanied by statements of the proper response to him. This is notably true of the three Johannine descriptions of God.

(1) "God is spirit, and those who worship him must worship in spirit and truth" (John 4:24). In view of the context, to worship in spirit here means worship that is not tied to a place; it is what takes place in the spiritual realm. The phrase "in spirit" can refer to the human spirit (Rom. 1:9; 2:29) or to the Spirit of God (Rom. 8:9; Eph. 2:18; 6:18; Phil. 3:3). Such passages express a contrast with the flesh and things pertaining to the flesh as the basis of the relationship with God or the means of worshipping him. "In truth" refers to "reality," as opposed to what is false or what is not permanent (John 3:21; 4:23; 8:44; 18:37; 1 John 1:6; 2:21), or to "sincerity" or "genuineness" in contrast to pretense or mere words (1 John 3:18, "in reality," is possible here too; 2 John 1; 3 John 1; cf. Phil. 1:18). The adjective "true" in John 4:23 suggests the "real" or "genuine" worshipers. "Truth" in John is related to Jesus (John 1:14; 14:6), the Spirit (John 14:17; 1 John 5:6), and the word of God (John 17:17).

(2) "God is light. . . . [W]e walk in the light as he himself is in the light" (1 John 1:5, 7). Light and darkness in this context contrast righteousness and sin. Since God is light, his people are in the light too. As there is no darkness in God, his people must not walk in darkness. "Walk" in Biblical language refers to conduct, way of life. People in the light have been cleansed from sin by the blood of Jesus, and so must walk in righteousness and brotherly love (as spelled out in the remainder of 1 John).

(3) "God is love. . . . He loved us and sent his Son to be the atoning sacrifice for our sins. Beloved, since God loved us so much, we also ought to love one another" (1 John 4:8-11). God showed his love in

6. Nils Dahl, "The Neglected Factor in New Testament Theology," *Jesus Christ: The Historical Origins of Christological Doctrine* (Minneapolis: Fortress, 1991), pp. 153-163.

sending his Son, so that we might have life in him (cf. John 3:16). The resultant behavior by those who have received the love of God is to love their fellow human beings, defined in very practical ways in 1 John, helping with the goods of this world those who are in need, even laying down one's life for another (1 John 3:11-18).

(4) Alongside the declaration of God's nature as love must be placed the affirmation in other passages of his holiness: "As he who called you is holy, be holy yourselves in all your conduct; for it is written, 'You shall be holy, for I am holy'" (1 Pet. 1:15-16). The quotation is from Leviticus 19:2 (cf. 11:44f.; 20:7). Holiness in the Old Testament often emphasizes cultic purity (ceremonial cleanness) as well as moral purity. Although the contrast has been exaggerated, as if the Old Testament neglects the moral dimension, it seems fair to say that the New Testament differs in emphasizing exclusively moral and spiritual holiness. God's people are to share his nature — his love and his holiness. And once more the response to God is expressed in terms of the total conduct of life. What 1 John described as light is here expressed by holiness, and the holy conduct of a holy people is a pervasive theme through 1 Peter (cf. 2:5, 9).

(5) The holiness of God prepares one to consider his awe-inspiring presence that can break forth in wrath. The worship of God is related to his awesome presence: "We offer to God an acceptable worship with reverence and awe; for indeed our God is a consuming fire" (Heb. 12:28-29). The author of Hebrews had earlier contrasted Israel assembled at Sinai (Heb. 12:18-21) with Christians assembled in the presence of God, describing their present status in heavenly terms (Heb. 12:22-24). If the former scene was fearful, the blessings of their present condition should warn Christians not to reject the voice of the Lord (Heb. 12:25-26). The God who shook the earth at Sinai will take away all that is temporal, leaving only his eternal kingdom. The God who made such a fearful revelation at Sinai is the same God to be worshiped now. In gratitude for receiving the unshakable kingdom, his people will remain faithful in every way, not turning their backs on the new revelation in Jesus but practicing Christian love (Heb. 13:1ff.).

(6) Christians "worship the living God" (Heb. 9:14; cf. 3:12). The designation "living God" often occurs in contrast with the lifeless idols of paganism (Jer. 10:10 in the context of the chapter; Acts 14:15; 1 Thess. 1:9). In Hebrews 9, the designation highlights the contrast between the necessity for repeated external purifications by the blood of dead animals and the once-for-all purification of the conscience by the blood of

Jesus, who by offering himself "through the eternal Spirit" obtained an "eternal redemption" (vv. 6-14). The whole passage is in a context of contrast between the worship of Israel in an earthly sanctuary and Christ's high-priestly ministry in the heavenly "tabernacle." His eternal sacrifice is in keeping with the nature of God as "living." Similarly, God's worshipers are purified from "dead works," a designation of moral wrongs in Hebrews 6:1. As the "only God" (1 Tim. 1:17; John 17:3), he only is to be worshiped (Matt. 4:10).

The Atoning Work of Jesus

Jesus' promise of forgiveness of sins abrogates the atoning system of the earthly temple. This is the message of Hebrews 7–10, which describes his once-for-all sacrifice in the heavenly temple (Heb. 9:11-12) and to which frequent reference will be made in connection with other points. Jesus during his ministry provoked criticism because he offered forgiveness directly, instead of through the priestly temple sacrifices ordained by God in the law of Moses (see Mark 2:1-12 and parallels). He instituted a new covenant in his blood "poured out for many for the forgiveness of sins" (Matt. 26:28).[7] According to Hebrews, the blood of Jesus establishes a new covenant (Heb. 10:29;12:24; 13:20), sanctifies a new people (Heb. 9:14; 10:29; 13:12), and opens a new way of approach or worship to God (Heb. 10:19-20; cf. 9:12), so an earthly temple with continual sacrifices can no longer be of consequence.

Jesus, acting as Lord of the temple, cleansed it (Mark 11:15-17 and parallels). The original contexts of Jesus' quotations, "a den of robbers" (Jer. 7:11) and "a house of prayer for all nations" (Isa. 56:7), show a correlation between the destruction of the temple and the incorporation of the Gentiles into God's people. Jesus explicitly predicted the temple's destruction (Mark 13:2 and parallels). Since the temple served for other sacrifices than those for forgiveness (the daily burnt offering, thank offerings, peace offerings), this destruction had implications beyond the system of atonement. Jesus' eternal ministry, and thus all Christian

7. "The many" may allude to Isa. 53:12 and mean "for the nations" — so Ernst Lohmeyer, *Lord of the Temple* (Richmond: John Knox, 1962), p. 40. For the atonement theme in Jesus' words at the last supper see Joachim Jeremias, *The Eucharistic Words of Jesus* (New York: Scribner's, 1966), pp. 222-237; Ben Meyer, "The Expiation Motif in the Eucharistic Words: A Key to the History of Jesus," *Gregorianum* 69 (1988): 461-487.

worship, now centers on a perfect sanctuary, not made with hands, in heaven (Heb. 9:11, 24). Since "the Most High does not dwell in houses made with human hands" (Acts 7:48; cf. Isa. 66:1), Jesus promised to destroy the Jerusalem temple and replace it with another "not made with hands" (Mark 14:58).[8] That phrase would have been understood by his hearers as the eschatological temple, but after the resurrection his followers gained a new perspective (cf. John 2:21 for his body as the temple). The presence of the risen Lord now replaced the presence of God in the temple.

Moreover, Jesus during his earthly ministry repudiated the rules of purity as understood by the Pharisees. His teaching on what truly defiles — evil actions coming from evil thoughts rather than eating with unwashed hands, that is, what comes forth from the person, not what enters into him or her (Matt. 15:1-20; Mark 7:1-23) — had among its implications, as Mark notes, the abolition of the food laws of Judaism (Mark 7:19). His teaching on the Sabbath observance (Matt. 12:1-8; Mark 2:23-28; Luke 6:1-5) placed human need above legal interpretations of the law and his own presence as superior to the law. In Matthew's account, reference is made to the fact that in the law itself temple work had precedence over the Sabbath law.

The relation of Jesus to the temple, sacrifices, and priesthood will be elaborated in the next section. (The centrality of Jesus to the activities in the assembly of the church will be developed later in this chapter.) Enough has been said here to show that in Jesus any theological basis for a sacrificial or cultic worship centered in an earthly temple has been removed. "Since we have confidence to enter the [heavenly] sanctuary by the blood of Jesus, by the new and living way that he opened for us . . . , and since we have a great priest over the house [temple = people] of God, let us approach with a true heart in full assurance of faith" (Heb. 10:19-22). This passage draws on Old Testament imagery to stress the importance of the Christian's privileges in approaching God, and it leads into a statement of the Christian assembly (Heb. 10:25), thus relating what is done in the assembly of the church to the worship in the heavenly sanctuary.[9]

8. The accusation against Jesus is based on his teaching; Mark describes it as false testimony because it was misunderstood in a literal way and so garbled by the witnesses. See Alan Cole, *The New Temple* (London: Tyndale, 1950); also Chap. 2, n. 81 and the next section below on The New Temple in his Body.

9. N. A. Dahl, "A New and Living Way: The Approach to God According to Hebrews 10:19-25," *Interpretation* 5 (1951): 401-412.

Christian worship is distinguished from all other, because it is done with reference to Jesus Christ: "Whatever you do, in word or deed, do everything in the name of the Lord Jesus, giving thanks to God the Father through him" (Col. 3:17).

The Access to God through the Holy Spirit

Christ has made direct access to God in the heavenly sanctuary possible. That access is also related to the Holy Spirit. "For through [Christ Jesus] both [Jew and Gentile] have access in one Spirit to the Father" (Eph. 2:18). The Holy Spirit provides a life that in some measure already participates in the future life (Eph. 1:13-14; Heb. 6:4). The Holy Spirit, furthermore, maintains the connection and communication between human beings and God. We have noted the possibility that John 4:23-24 refers to the Holy Spirit in describing the true worship that God seeks. There is a strong relationship between the Spirit and truth in the Gospel of John (John 14:17; 15:26). He guides the disciples into "all the truth" (John 16:13). The Spirit is the medium of the revelation of truth in Jesus. Paul also speaks of this role of the Spirit in revelation (1 Cor. 2:10, 13; Eph. 3:5). The Spirit not only establishes the communication between God and human beings through his role in revelation, but he also mediates the human response to God. Paul is the writer who refers most to this function of the Spirit — Romans 8:26; Galatians 4:6; Ephesians 5:18-21; 6:18; Philippians 3:3. The activity of the Spirit in the worship of the church, especially prayer, is noted in Chapter 2 in the discussion of the church as the community of the Holy Spirit (p. 109).

The Result of Salvation

With the coming of salvation in Christ and the rule of God in human hearts persons are bound directly to God's will and can serve him in gratitude. The worship, as well as the message and faith of Christians, is concerned with God's saving acts. Since the doctrine of salvation is explicated in Chapter 3, we may be content here merely to refer to this great truth. God's saving work in Christ enables his people to approach him with boldness, freedom of speech (*parrhēsia*). This word referred to outspoken, frank, or open speech, and so to confidence. It was used in the Gospel of John for Christ's preaching, in Acts for the preaching of the gospel, and in Paul for his apostolic activity (probably even in Eph. 3:12, where the context suggests that the boldness pertains to proclaiming the mystery rather than to freedom of speech in approaching God). Especially pertinent for this section of our study is its use in Hebrews for the security of the Christian's faith that not only must be held on to (Heb. 3:6; 10:35) but that also gives the right of free approach to God (Heb. 4:16; 10:19). In 1 John also it refers to assurance before God, both at the judgment (1 John 2:28; 4:17) and in prayer now (1 John 3:21f.; 5:14).[10] Worship to God is one of the results of salvation in Christ and the gift of the Holy Spirit. Worship is response.

THE NEW TEMPLE IN HIS BODY

> "'Destroy this temple, and in three days
> I will raise it up.' . . . He was speaking
> of the temple of his body."
>
> (JOHN 2:19, 21)

The Church as a Temple[11]

The ancient world did not view a temple primarily as a meeting place for worshipers but as the house (or home) of the deity, for the cult statue was kept there. Worship to the ancient world meant temple with its accompanying statue, altar for the sacrifice of animals and other food products, and priesthood. This was no less true of Judaism, with the exception that there was no statue representing God (a cloud symbolized the coming of God's presence to the tabernacle — Exod. 40:34-38). The temple in Jerusalem formed the center of the Jewish nation, and its cult was the symbol of her relationship with God. Religious life centered around the festivals, and the priesthood had a privileged position in the national life. During the Exile and Second Temple period, alternative understandings found a place in Jewish thought so that, for some, the temple became less important, and in Rabbinic Judaism reli-

---

10. W. C. Van Unnik, "The Christian's Freedom of Speech," *Bulletin of the John Rylands Library* 44 (1962): 466-488.

11. See the discussion of the church as a temple and the bibliography in Chap. 2, n. 81. There the concern is what the temple imagery says about the nature of the church. It was noted above that Christ replaced the old temple worship. The subject now is the new worship accomplished in the church as a new temple.

gious activities such as prayer and study of the law were understood as acceptable sacrifices.

Christianity carried these tendencies to reinterpret worship further, so that it represented a radical break with what the ancient world understood by religion. Picking up on prophetic declarations, early Christians affirmed over against Jews dedicated to the temple that "The Most High does not dwell in houses made with human hands" (Acts 7:48), followed by a quotation from Isaiah 66:1-2 (cf. also 1 Kings 8:27), and over against the popular religion of pagans that "The God who made the world and everything in it . . . does not live in shrines made by human hands, nor is he served by human hands" (Acts 17:24-25).

The new interpretation by Christians is especially evident in the book of Hebrews, but is not confined to it. Hebrews uses cultic language in order to preach the common Christian message about salvation in Christ.[12] The language of the ceremonies in the tabernacle and temple was applied to the redemptive work of Christ (Heb. 9:11-14) and the life of salvation on the basis of him (Heb. 10:19-25). Cleansed by the blood of Jesus (Heb. 10:14, 19), Christians can enter the true, heavenly sanctuary, where Jesus ministers as high priest (Heb. 8:1-2; 9:11, 24). Christianity rejected worship restricted to a particular holy place (John 4:21-24) or to holy days and seasons (Col. 2:16; cf. Rom. 14:5-6 for days as indifferent), spoke only of the believing community as priestly with no provision made for a special priesthood chosen from it (1 Pet. 2:5, 9), and reinterpreted the language of sacrifice for the life dedicated to God (Rom. 12:1). The temple was the community. The New Testament put no emphasis on the place of worship — house, synagogue, or temple — because wherever the community gathered was the place of worship.[13]

There are hints, especially in the Johannine writings, associating Jesus with the tabernacle or temple as the dwelling place of God. This theme is announced in the prologue to the Fourth Gospel, where Jesus is said to have "tabernacled among us" and to have manifested the "glory" of God's presence that once dwelled in the temple (John 1:14; cf. 2:19-22; Rev. 21:22). Through Jesus, God comes to dwell in those who

---

12. John Dunnill, *Covenant and Sacrifice in the Letter to the Hebrews* (Cambridge: University Press, 1992), p. 261, where he concludes that to find in Hebrews warrant for a Christian expiatory cultus and a separate priesthood is to contravene the argument of the letter.

13. J. J. von Allmen, *Worship: Its Theology and Practice* (London: Lutterworth, 1965), pp. 242-243.

keep his word (John 14:23). Thus the community and not a physical structure became the temple, for God lived in the people not in a building (1 Cor. 3:16; 2 Cor. 6:16; Eph. 2:19-22). The idea of Jesus (and then the church) as a temple opened the way for an alternative system of religion.

Even more fully and more explicitly than the connection of Jesus with the temple is the connection made between Jesus and priesthood and sacrifice. The Epistle to the Hebrews presents Jesus as the officiating priest (Heb. 4:16–5:10; 7:1–8:6), the atoning sacrifice (Heb. 9:1–10:18), and the altar (Heb. 13:10). Thus the essential elements of the Old Testament worship — temple, priesthood, and sacrifice — were seen as fulfilled in Jesus. Through relationship with him, the church constitutes a reinterpretation of all the institutional aspects of worship in the ancient world.

The temple was the place of worship and of meeting between God and his people in the Old Testament. Jesus not only destroyed the temple but also became himself the new temple. Although the application of temple language to worship is not prominent in the New Testament (1 Pet. 2:4-5 being one place where the association is made), it would be in the mind of readers of the New Testament from the associations of temples in pagan and Jewish thought. However, it should be noted that it is only the theological concept of the temple that is important in the New Testament understanding of the church and worship; the actual ritual of the temple is not evident in distinctively Christian meetings (early Jewish Christians of course did frequent the temple — e.g., Acts 3:1; 21:20ff.).[14] The new understanding of worship in the New Testament is closely connected with the idea of church.

Priest and Priesthood

Apart from references to Jewish and pagan priests, the New Testament uses the word for "priest" seldom. Most occurrences are in Hebrews in connection with the priesthood of Christ.[15] The author early enunciates his high-priestly Christology: Christ is a "merciful and faithful high

14. I. Howard Marshall, "Church and Temple in the New Testament," *Tyndale Bulletin* 40 (1989): 222. The book of Revelation does describe the heavenly worship in terms drawn from the temple liturgy, but it is problematic the extent to which this corresponds to Christian congregational worship.

15. Oscar Cullmann, *The Christology of the New Testament* (Philadelphia: Westminster, 1959), pp. 83-107.

priest" (Heb. 2:17), who is able "to sympathize with our weaknesses" (Heb. 4:14-15). God appointed him high priest (Heb. 3:1; 5:5), not in the Levitical order, but in the order of Melchizedek (Heb. 5:6-10). Chapter 7 develops the superiority of Jesus' priesthood in its similarities to that of Melchizedek[16] over that of the Levites: (1) permanency based on indestructible life, so not requiring continual replacement because of death; (2) higher authority, as giving blessing to Abraham and receiving tithes from him; (3) appointment by an oath of promise, not by a legal requirement concerning physical descent; (4) a perfect sacrifice sufficient once for all, not repeated day after day. The conclusion drawn, perhaps in answer to pagan or Jewish reproaches of Christians' not having the normal priestly apparatus of cult, is that "we have such a high priest" (Heb. 8:1; cf. 7:26). Christ, therefore, is indeed "a great priest over the house of God" (Heb. 10:21), evidently the family or people of God, according to the usage in Hebrews (note esp. Heb. 3:5-6, "we are his house"), but in view of the imagery of Hebrews the connotation of temple is not to be ruled out (a building may be indicated in Heb. 3:3-4). After developing the themes of sanctuary (Heb. 8) and sacrifice (Heb. 9–10), the author in the conclusion alludes to the priestly theme by means of an analogy between Jesus' sacrifice and the activities of the Jewish high priest on the day of atonement (Heb. 13:8, 10-12, 20).

The words for priests and priesthood are applied to Christians only in 1 Peter and Revelation. In every case, the usage is collective; the community of Christians, not the individual Christian, is priestly.[17] This is particularly evident in 1 Peter 2:5, 9, where the word is *hierateuma*, "a body of functioning priests," used in parallel to "spiritual house," "elect race," "holy nation," and "people for God's possession."[18] The source of these designations is Exodus 19:6, where the reference is to the whole

16. The word "resembling" (Heb. 7:3) indicates that Melchizedek's priesthood is like that of the Son of God, not the other way around.

17. Hans Küng, *The Church* (London: Burns & Oates, 1968), pp. 363-379. Cf. James Leo Garrett, Jr., "The Biblical Doctrine of the Priesthood of the People of God," in H. L. Drumwright and Curtis Vaughan, eds., *New Testament Studies: Essays in Honor of Ray Summers* (Waco: Markham Press Fund, 1975), pp. 137-149. For a somewhat different perspective, Thomas F. Torrance, *Royal Priesthood*, new ed. (Edinburgh: T. & T. Clark, 1993).

18. See J. H. Elliott, *The Elect and the Holy* (Leiden: E. J. Brill, 1966), pp. 64-70 and passim; cf. E. G. Selwyn, *The First Epistle of St. Peter* (London: Macmillan, 1947), pp. 281-298. Against Elliott's interpretation of "royal" as a noun for "royal residence" (pp. 149-154), J. Ysebaert, *Die Amtsterminologie im Neuen Testament und in der Alten Kirche* (Breda: Eureia, 1994), pp. 199-200, defends the adjectival usage, "royal priesthood."

nation of Israel. Revelation employs the word for "priests" (Rev. 1:6; 5:10, also with clear reference to Exod. 19:6; and 20:6, in parallel to 5:10), but always in the plural and with reference to the collective body of believers.

Those books that speak of the priesthood of Christians (1 Peter and Revelation) do not speak of Christ as a priest, and the book that develops the priesthood of Christ (Hebrews) does not speak expressly of the priesthood of Christians. Moreover, the usual terminology in Hebrews is "high priest" (not "priest") when referring to Christ.[19] Nevertheless, priest may be considered another of the titles shared in common between Christ and Christians (pp. 99-101).[20] First Peter 2:4-5 by linking the Stone and stones implies the identification of believers with their Lord, and Revelation 1:6 says Christ "made us . . . priests."

The "priesthood of all believers" has been an important concept in Protestantism. For Martin Luther, it meant the duty of every Christian to hear the confession of fellow Christians, speak the word of forgiveness to them, and to sacrifice the self to God.[21] It came to mean for various Protestant bodies the right of all Christians to approach God without a mediator, to interpret the scriptures for themselves, or to preside at worship activities. All of these applications are inferences that have nothing to do with the explicit biblical texts. The references to Christians as priests, drawn as they are from Exodus 19:6, refer to the *status* of Christians, not their function. The church is a priestly people. For activities associated with this circle of ideas we must turn to the language of sacrifice.

Sacrifices of the Christian Priest

"Every high priest [is] chosen . . . to offer gifts and sacrifices for sin" (Heb. 5:1). Jesus has performed that atoning function, as the author of

---

19. J. H. Elliott, *The Elect and the Holy* (Leiden: E. J. Brill, 1966), pp. 169-174, on the differences between 1 Peter and other New Testament statements on priesthood.

20. John M. Scholer, *Proleptic Priests: Priesthood in the Epistle to the Hebrews* (Sheffield: JSOT Press, 1991), argues that, according to Hebrews, because Christians are Christ's "brothers" (Heb. 2:10-18), they implicitly share a priestly status; moreover, their activities are described in ways analogous to the Septuagint description of the Levitical priesthood. See also N. A. Dahl, "A New and Living Way: The Approach to God According to Hebrews 10:19-25," *Interpretation* 5 (1951): 406-407.

21. Paul Althaus, *The Theology of Martin Luther* (Philadelphia: Fortress, 1966), p. 314.

Hebrews argues. The sacrifice of atonement by Jesus was discussed in the preceding chapter. There were other kinds of sacrifice in addition to sin offerings, and the language of sacrifice is employed in the New Testament for various activities by Christians. "We have an altar" (Heb. 13:10), but unlike what was known in the pagan and Jewish worlds. The church as a priestly people offers "spiritual" sacrifice.[22]

(1) Hebrews 13:15 describes praise and thanksgiving as sacrifices: "Through Jesus, then, let us continually offer a sacrifice of praise to God, that is, the fruit of lips that confess his name." Christian praise is offered to God through the mediation of Christ, who according to the context sanctifies "the people by his own blood" (Heb. 13:12). The sacrifice of praise is offered by "us," the people together. Employing language from Psalm 50:14, 23 and Hosea 14:2, the author speaks of the "sacrifice of praise" and the "fruit of lips"[23] instead of the fruit of crops or offspring of animals. Similarly, Hebrews 12:28 says, "Let us give thanks, by which we offer worship well pleasing to God." A sacrificial context is given for prayer in Revelation 8:3-5.

(2) Hebrews 13:16 includes acts of benevolence as sacrifices: "Do not neglect to do good and to share what you have, for such sacrifices are well pleasing to God." Material sacrifice is now not what is burned on the altar but what is used to help those in need. Matthew twice puts on the lips of Jesus the quotation of Hosea 6:6, "I desire mercy and not sacrifice" (Matt. 9:13; 12:7). The prophet declared God's desire for mercy in addition to, or more than, but not instead of sacrifice. The Christian application of the prophecy put acts of mercy ("doing good and sharing") in the place of the sacrifices on the literal altar. "Well pleasing" is the same word used in Hebrews 12:28 and 13:21.

(3) Philippians 4:18 employs sacrificial language for another use of financial resources, support for preaching of the gospel: "I have received from Epaphroditus the gifts you sent, a fragrant offering, a sacrifice acceptable and well pleasing to God." The Philipppian church had sent money to assist Paul in his needs. We meet the word "well pleasing" again, but also expressions used in the Old Testament for sacrifices received by God: "fragrant offering" (Gen. 8:21; Exod. 29:18;

22. Cf. for a different arrangement and lacking the point about a holy life (except as implied by Rom. 12:1), Alan Richardson, *An Introduction to the Theology of the New Testament* (London: SCM, 1958), pp. 299-301; on the theme in general, Francis M. Young, *Sacrifice and the Death of Christ* (London: SPCK, 1975), esp. pp. 47-64.

23. Also found at Qumran — 1QS ix.4; x.6.

Ezek. 20:40-41, a prophecy about the age to come) and "acceptable" (Isa. 56:7, another eschatological reference; cf. *Sirach* 35:6).

(4) Paul in Philippians 2:17 adopted an image from sacrificial ritual to describe his own self-giving in the work of preaching, perhaps even an allusion to the prospect of his martyrdom: "I am being poured out as a libation over the sacrifice and the service of your faith." The pouring out of a drink offering often accompanied other sacrifices (e.g., Exod. 29:40; 37:16; Num. 28:7, 24; 2 Kings 16:13). Paul likened to such an act (cf. 2 Tim. 4:6) the pouring out of his life in accompaniment of the offering of the Philippians' faith. Since the person making the drink offering was the one offering the sacrifice, I prefer to take the "sacrifice and service" as referring to the faith of the Philippians being presented by Paul to God (sacrifice as the victim) rather than the Philippians offering the sacrifice (as the act), whether of their faith or something offered by their faith.[24]

In Romans 15:16, Paul more clearly expresses that the apostolic ministry of bringing the gospel to the Gentiles is itself the work of a priest. He likens himself to a priest presiding over the offering up of the Gentiles to God: "Grace [was] given me by God to be a servant of Christ Jesus to the Gentiles in the priestly service of the gospel of God, so that the offering of the Gentiles may be acceptable, sanctified by the Holy Spirit." Five terms here are drawn from the sacrificial activity of priests. "Servant" *(leitourgos)* is from the family of words found in Philippians 2:17, used in Greek for public service and in the Greek Old Testament for the sacrificial work of priests and Levites (e.g., Exod. 28:43; 30:20; Num. 4:3ff.; and esp. Isa. 61:6). "Priestly service" *(hierourgeō)* is literally "do the work of a priest." "Offering" *(prosphora)* is the common word for gifts brought for sacrifice; it is used here for the Gentile converts brought as an offering to God. "Acceptable" *(euprosdektos)* is a strengthened form of the word used in Philippians 4:18 and is used elsewhere for sacrifices that are pleasing (1 Pet. 2:5; and for another form of Christian ministry in Rom. 15:31). "Sanctified" *(hagiazō)*, among other things, referred to the consecration of things and persons for ritual purposes (e.g., Exod. 29:44; Lev. 8:11-12; Ezek. 37:28;

---

24. Contra J. B. Lightfoot, *Saint Paul's Epistle to the Philippians* (London: Macmillan, 1913), p. 119; I-Jin Loh and Eugene A. Nida, *A Translator's Handbook on Paul's Letter to the Philippians* (Stuttgart: United Bible Societies, 1977), pp. 73-75; Ralph P. Martin, *Philippians,* New Century Bible Commentary (Grand Rapids: Eerdmans, 1980), pp. 106-108.

48:11); here the Gentiles, previously unclean, have been purified by the Holy Spirit so that they are acceptable to God.

(5) 1 Peter 2:5 does not specify the content of the "spiritual sacrifices" offered by the Church as a "holy priesthood," but the context suggests that the holy life, the Christian moral and ethical conduct, is in mind.[25] Such is spiritual because it is made possible through the power of the Holy Spirit (see pp. 356-357). This passage is connected with the preceding point because the Christian manner of life includes making known the "mighty acts of God" (1 Pet. 2:9, 11-12). The stress in 1 Peter on manner of life (1 Pet. 1:15, 17, 18; 2:12; 3:1, 2, 16) and doing good (1 Pet. 2:14, 15, 20; 3:6, 17; 4:19) further connects 1 Peter 2:5 with the next passage to be discussed.

(6) Romans 12:1 in its language of offering the body (the person or self) constitutes the high point of the Christian conception of sacrifice: "Present your bodies as a living sacrifice, holy and well pleasing to God, which is the worship proceeding from your spiritual nature." The verb "present" had a technical meaning in the Greek world for the bringing of sacrifice. The Christian presents not a dead body of an irrational animal killed and then burned on the altar but himself or herself, thus a "living" and "rational" sacrifice. The adjective "holy" reminds us of the verb "sanctified" in Romans 15:16. "Well pleasing" is the same word (*euarestos*) encountered above in Hebrew 13:16 and Philippians 4:18. "Worship" (*latreia*; verb form used also in Heb. 12:28) will be discussed below. *Logikē*, usually rendered "rational," "reasonable," or sometimes "spiritual" (note the parallel expression in Rom. 1:9), I have paraphrased because any of these forms used to modify worship is subject to misunderstanding. The phrase was used in the literature of the time to refer to worship that proceeded from the highest part of human nature, the reasoning faculties, to what belonged to the realm of words and thoughts (*logos*) and was immaterial.[26] As verse two proceeds to explain, the living sacrifice of one's body according to the reason involves separation from a life conformed to the world's standards and the transforming of the mind so as to approve the will of God.

It is noteworthy, in view of the future Christian development, that the New Testament does not use the language of sacrifice in connection

---

25. J. H. Elliott, *The Called and the Holy* (Leiden: E. J. Brill, 1966), pp. 174-185.
26. C. F. D. Moule, "Sanctuary and Sacrifice in the Church of the New Testament," *Journal of Theological Studies* n.s. 1 (1950): 34.

with the eucharist.[27] This absence corresponds to the absence of any priestly terminology for the leaders in worship and at the eucharist. More will be said about this below on the Lord's supper (pp. 254-255) and in the next chapter on ministry (pp. 282, 299).

ATTITUDES TOWARD WORSHIP AND IN WORSHIP

"The true worshipers will worship the Father
in spirit and truth, for the Father seeks such as
these to worship him."   (JOHN 4:23)

Worship and Assembly

Modern usage applies the word "worship" to the assembly of believers gathered for corporate acts of devotion. As the passages about spiritual sacrifice and the word studies above show, the New Testament usage of the words for worship is much broader, including the Christian moral life and acts of service on behalf of people.[28] The common meaning of worship today represents a narrowing down of the New Testament meaning of worship. It selects one aspect of worship and applies the word exclusively (or almost so) to that aspect. Worship properly understood, however, covers the Christian life as well as the Christian assembly, all acts of service and devotion to God. This does not make the assembly less important but serves to make Christian existence in all its expressions sacred. It would be better to speak of "assembly" or some such word to describe the congregational gatherings of Christians. Worship to God occurs in the church meetings, but not exclusively there. The assembly is communal worship in contrast to private worship. After this section on attitudes, therefore, the subsequent discussion in this chapter will be developed under the rubric of the assembly, and an effort will be made to correlate the Godward and the manward dimensions of the assembly. The limitation of the concept of worship

27. See my "Spiritual Sacrifice in Early Christianity and its Environment," *Aufstieg und Niedergang der Römischen Welt*, II.23.1, ed. H. Temporini and W. Haase (Berlin: De Gruyter, 1980), pp. 1151-1189.

28. My viewpoint is similar to, but was developed before reading, I. Howard Marshall, "How Far Did the Early Christians *Worship* God?" *Churchman* 99 (1985): 216-229.

to activities at formally stated times and places is one common misunderstanding of worship. There are others.

Misunderstandings of Worship

Certain erroneous concepts of worship are prevalent, even (or perhaps especially) among religious people.

(1) *The external or mechanical interpretation.* Worship may be understood as formal religious exercises. Many think of worship as items to be performed in order to fulfill a duty. This is a carryover from the cultic or temple understanding of worship shown above to have been abrogated by Christ. On the external or rote interpretation, acts of worship have a benefit from the doing, the going through the motions. By doing certain things people improve their heavenly credit rating. Romans 2:1-11 is helpful in showing that God does not owe us anything for being religious as such. God's people ought to do the things that he requires, and there are times when the routine is valuable for itself, even if the heart and feelings are not fully in the things done. The concern here is with the reason behind these things, why we do them. What is the attitude toward their doing? Is it the mere fulfilling of an obligation, the rote performance of certain acts, or is it the response to a gracious God? As John 4:23-24 says, worship must be done spiritually and truly, sincerely and genuinely. Many biblical passages teach against the mere ritual interpretation of life and show God's concern with the heart as the basis of outward actions. This is true not only of the New Testament (Matt. 5:17-48) but was also the burden of the message of the Old Testament prophets (Isa. 1:10-17; Jer. 7:1-15; Hos. 6:6; Amos 5:24; Mic. 6:6-8). The worship of the New Testament is not simply the substitution of a new set of religious exercises for those of ancient Israel.

(2) *The individualistic interpretation.* This understanding of worship sees it only as private religious devotions, even if these are done in the corporate setting of the assembled church. In the assembly, the people do individual religious exercises together. The emphasis is on meditation. If the individual's function in the first interpretation is simply to be present or to perform certain activities, the function here is primarily to meditate. As a consequence of this view, some would say that they can worship as well at the lake as in church. That view understands worship as an individual or private activity. A person can meditate, pray, and think about spiritual things as well or perhaps better some-

where else than in church; and these things should be done. But there are some things that can be done only in assembly. The church is a group, and the assembly is a corporate activity (Heb. 10:24-25). Here there is expressed the concern for "one another" (cf. Col. 3:16). The Lord's supper is to be compared not to eating alone in a restaurant full of people but to a community or family meal, where the being together is as important as the eating (1 Cor. 10:17; 11:33). This is why there is an emphasis on mutual reconciliation in the New Testament teaching (Matt. 5:23-24). Corporate worship has the advantage over individual worship that a symphony orchestra has over a soloist. The assembly is different from other aspects of the religious life, because there is opportunity to express the fact that the people are "church." Here may be fulfilled the mutual responsibilities of encouragement, service, and love. The emphasis in the group gathering is on others rather than on self.

(3) *The emotional uplift interpretation.* This understanding of worship causes people to come to church for what makes them feel good. They come for what they can get out of it. "We act as if God existed to meet our needs, when, the truth is, we do not even know what our real needs are until God reveals Himself to us and we discover our true selves."[29] Worship is secularized when the focus shifts to the enhancement of the worshipers. Even very religious people equate praise for God with emotional exuberance rather than with the objective recital of God's qualities and deeds. Making worship "useful" destroys it, because this introduces an ulterior motive for praise. As a result of this misunderstanding, planners of worship think in terms of the emotional impact of what is said and done. And if one fails to feel better the comment is heard, "I didn't get anything out of church today, so I don't think I'll come back." These people come for a sense of uplift. As will be developed more fully below, the proper goal of the assembly is edification of the body (1 Cor. 14:26), and this involves instruction and understanding, the recital of God's acts in word and ceremony, and therefore intelligible speech and action, not emotional or aesthetic satisfaction (1 Cor. 14:2-3, 5, 19, 31).

(4) *The performance interpretation.* Closely related to the expectation of emotional uplift from worship is the association of worship with

29. Wayne E. Ward, "The Worship of the Church," in Paul Basden and David S. Dockery, eds., *The People of God: Essays on the Believers' Church* (Nashville: Broadman, 1991), p. 67.

entertainment. On this misunderstanding, instead of being participants, those who are present are observers of what the leaders do. And those who have a more visible role are more performers than leaders in the activities. The assembly is no more an occasion to show off one's gifts than it is to seek self-edification. The goal should be what contributes to spiritual maturity in Christ (Col. 1:28), and this requires the involvement of all who are present.

These misunderstandings, like most misunderstandings, have an element of truth in them and grow out of aspects in the assembly: the members should be present, they should meditate, they will be blessed spiritually by being present, and everything should be done as well as the participants are capable. The fuller truth is that the assembly is to be spiritual, corporate, instructive, and directed toward God. It should be an occasion that raises the consciousness of God and focuses attention on others.

Proper Attitudes

Passages cited above in connection with the theological bases of worship have indicated some of the proper attitudes with which God is to be served: "spirit and truth" (John 4:23-24); "reverence and awe" (Heb. 12:28); "full assurance of faith" (Heb. 10:22). At this point, we will note some further attitudes associated with fundamental Christian doctrines. We will relate these to the doctrines of God, Christ, and the Holy Spirit, because it is notable how many expressions in the New Testament related to worship are stated in what may be called "trinitarian" terms (Matt. 28:19; 2 Cor. 13:13; Gal. 4:6; Eph. 2:18; Heb. 9:14).[30]

(1) The basic human attitude before God is the sense of dependence and humility. This follows from the truth that God is Creator. All that humans have and are comes from God. The Bible repeatedly affirms that the One God is the Creator (Acts 14:15; 1 Cor. 8:6). As the Maker of the world and everything in it, he has *need* of nothing, not even worship (Acts 17:24-25). The origin of sin was in the human desire to be a god (Gen. 3:5-6). Hence, the Bible treats very seriously idolatry,

---

30. See also John 14:16-17, 26; 15:26; 1 Cor. 12:4-6; 2 Cor. 1:21; Gal. 3:11-14; Eph. 3:14-17; Titus 3:4-6; Heb. 10:29; 1 Pet. 1:2.

the worship of anything other than God (note the extension of the meaning of idolatry in Eph. 5:5 and Col. 3:5).

Before the Creator of all things, the creature can only be humble and recognize his or her dependent condition. Everything comes from God. We can only give God that which is his own. All life for believers is lived in this attitude toward God. They approach him in the assembly of the church, as the gathered people of God, in the consciousness that he is Creator and in the realization that only in humble dependence on him can they live and serve. It will be seen below that the nature of things established in creation is appealed to in order to support certain regulations in the church.

(2) Because of their salvation in Christ, Christians come to God in thanksgiving and joy. Sin has separated the creature, made good (Gen. 1:31), from the Creator (Isa. 59:2). A basic human sin is lack of gratitude to God, even for his gifts of creation (Rom. 1:21). The atonement in Christ cancels sin and brings human beings back into fellowship with God. In answer to the question, "Who will rescue me from this body of death?" Paul exclaims, "Thanks be to God through Jesus Christ our Lord!" (Rom. 7:24-25). God's *grace* in Christ produces *thanksgiving*, and appropriately these two words are etymologically related in Greek, even as the two ideas are theologically related. "Grace, as it extends to more and more people, [increases] thanksgiving to the glory of God" (2 Cor. 4:15)." "As you therefore have received Christ Jesus the Lord, continue to live your lives in him . . . abounding in thanksgiving" (Col. 2:6-7). The Christian stance in life is thanksgiving to God in Jesus Christ "always for all things" (Eph. 5:20; cf. 1 Thess. 5:18). Hence, thankfulness is an acceptable worship offered to God (Heb. 12:28). Thanksgiving is also part of the heavenly worship (Rev. 4:9; 7:12; 11:17).

Joy is an attitude closely related to thanksgiving (Col. 1:11). It is a quality consistent with reverence (Matt. 28:8). Salvation is an occasion of joy (Luke 10:20). The announcement of the birth of Jesus involved not only the usual joy of a human birth but was good news for all the people of a Savior (Luke 2:10). The presence of Jesus brought rejoicing (Luke 13:17; 19:6, 37; John 8:56; 20:20). The joy of receiving the message of salvation in him (Acts 8:39; 13:48; cf. 11:23; cf. Matt. 13:20, 44) corresponds to the joy in heaven over the repentance of the sinner (Luke 15:7, 10). There is "joy and peace in believing" (Rom. 15:13; cf. Phil. 1:25). Philippians is noted for its insistence that Christians "Rejoice in the Lord" (3:1; 4:4), but 1 Thessalonians also says, "Rejoice always"

(1 Thess. 5:16). Such an attitude is possible, even in sufferings, because the Christian is sharing in the experience of Christ that leads to glory (1 Pet. 4:13). Rejoicing is an anticipation of the eschatological union with Christ (Rev. 19:7; cf. Matt. 25:21, 23). Joy provides a transition to the next point, for it is often stated to be a product of the Holy Spirit (Acts 13:52: Rom. 14:17; Gal. 5:22; 1 Thess. 1:6) and is associated with hope (Rom. 12:12).

(3) From the Holy Spirit comes expectation and hope as characteristics of the Christian attitude. Biblical hope, unlike the modern use of the word, is not a wishing for or wanting something. There is a basis for expectation that the object of hope will be realized. Hope is desire plus expectation. One of the sources of Christian hope is the possession of the Holy Spirit. "May the God of hope fill you with all joy and peace in believing, so that you may abound in hope by the power of the Holy Spirit" (Rom. 15:13). "For through the Spirit, by faith, we eagerly wait for the hope of righteousness" (Gal. 5:5). The Holy Spirit is given to the believer as a seal of belonging to God and as a guarantee of God's eschatological blessings (Rom. 8:23; 2 Cor. 1:21-22; 5:5; Eph. 1:13-14). Thus the gift of the Spirit provides the secure basis for hope. Hope is closely connected in the New Testament with the quality expressed by the English words (translating *hypomonē*) endurance, steadfastness, or perseverance (Rom. 8:25; 15:4; 1 Thess. 1:3; cf. Tit. 2:2). The thought of endurance is expressed without use of the word in Hebrews 6:11 and 10:23. The latter reference is in a passage bringing together ideas from worship and the assembly. The assembly of the church is related to heavenly worship (as will be seen below) and so gives expression to hope.

THE IMPORTANCE OF THE ASSEMBLY

"Do not neglect to meet together."   (HEB. 10:25)

Passages about Coming Together

Some mistakenly conclude that understanding worship as including all of the Christian life minimizes the importance of the assemblies of the church. Not so. The New Testament has a rich doctrine of the Christian assembly and shows that the coming together of believers is important.[31] Faith may be private or individual in the sense that someone cannot believe for another, but faith has a community expression and involves a group. If one can sustain one's faith without the support of common worship, then it is not the Christian faith that is held.

The sheer number of passages in the New Testament about Christians coming together is impressive. The frequency of these statements shows the importance of the assembly to early Christians. We group the passages according to the Greek terms "come together" (*sunerchomai*), "gather together" (*synagō*), "assemble" (*synathroizō*), and "the same place" (*epi to auto*).

"Come together" is used in Acts of the crowd gathered on Pentecost (Acts 2:6), of the gathering at Cornelius's house (Acts 10:27), and of the women gathered for prayer outside Philippi (Acts 16:13). It is the word used in 1 Corinthians 11 and 14 for the assemblies of the church (1 Cor. 11:17, 33-34; 14:26). The coming together is specified as "in church" ("in assembly") in 1 Corinthians 11:18, as "in the same place" in 1 Corinthians 11:20; and all three expressions are combined in 1 Corinthians 14:23: "if the whole church comes together in one place."

"Gather together" ("to congregate," verb form of synagogue) is used of the gatherings of Christians to pray (Acts 4:31), to teach ("gathered together in church" — Acts 11:26), to hear a missionary report (Acts 14:27), to decide a disputed issue (Acts 15:6, 30), to eat the Lord's supper (Acts 20:7-8), and to decide a case of discipline (1 Cor. 5:4; cf. its use in Matt. 18:20). The equivalent compound form of the verb and noun (*episynagō, episynagogē*) is used in the admonition against deserting church meetings in Hebrews 10:25 and in the description of the gathering together of the elect at the end of the age (2 Thess. 2:1; Matt. 24:31; and Mark 13:27).

"To assemble" or "gather into a group," fairly common in classical Greek, is rare in the New Testament, but it is used in Acts 12:12 for a prayer meeting.

The phrase *epi to auto* can mean "together," but it can also mean "in the same place," and when it occurs in connection with the verbs "to come together" or "gather together" must mean the latter (1 Cor. 11:18; 14:23). It seems to have acquired on occasion in early Christian literature almost a technical sense of "in the assembly," "in the church meeting." This may be the sense of Acts 2:44 (cf. 2:1, where the phrase

---

31. Ervin Bishop, "The Assembly," *Restoration Quarterly* 18 (1975): 219-228.

must mean "in one place," since "together" is redundant) and consequently also in Acts 2:47.[32]

The cumulative impression of these passages is to demonstrate how often the early Christians were together in meetings and consequently the importance of these meetings for them. Christianity was not a private religious experience.

The Assembly and Worship

The comprehensive use of the language of worship in the New Testament developed above certainly includes (indeed especially so) the meetings together of Christians for religious purposes. In the light of this broader understanding of worship, the assembly is part of ministering to others. In community there is strength. Individual weaknesses are overcome through the encouragement of others. People need one another. And the meetings of the church provide the opportunity for learning of needs, planning to meet them, and acting together. Forsaking the assembly is not a sin against an institution, but against the brothers and sisters to whom we owe mutual edification and fellowship (Heb. 10:25).[33]

The assembly of Christians is part of their total service to God. More than that, as the remainder of the chapter will unfold, it holds a central place in that service. Even if one puts emphasis on those passages noted above where worship is defined in terms of service to others, the assembly as the time of meeting together for mutual encouragement is worship. Yet this would be a minimal view, for such service to others is in the context of worship to God; and there must be times when attention is focused primarily on God and divine things.

The church in assembly not only provides encouragement to its members but also approaches God (Heb. 10:19-25). Only in relation to the transcendent do temporal things appear in the right perspective. In the Psalms, the assembly of God's people was the place for praise to him and the place where his awesome presence was felt. Hebrews 2:12 quotes from Psalm 22:22, "I will tell of your name to my brothers and

32. Everett Ferguson, " 'When You Come Together': *Epi to auto* in Early Christian Literature," *Restoration Quarterly* 16 (1973): 202-208; see above, p. 136.

33. N. A. Dahl, "A New and Living Way: The Approach to God According to Hebrews 10:19-25," *Interpretation* 5 (1951): 411-412.

sisters; in the midst of the congregation I will praise you." The next verse continues, "You who fear the LORD, praise him! All you offspring of Jacob, glorify him; stand in awe of him, all you offspring of Israel!" (Ps. 22:23). Hebrews 12:23-28 similarly connects the "assembly of the firstborn who are enrolled in heaven" with offering "to God an acceptable worship with reverence and awe."

As discussed on pages 211-212, "to call upon the name of the Lord" was the general phrase in the Old Testament for worship to God, a worship that acknowledged him in confession and prayer. This phrase is used to characterize Christians in 1 Corinthians 1:2, "those who in every place call on the name of our Lord Jesus Christ." Paul by these words reminds the *"ekklēsia* of God" at Corinth that they are not alone.[34] The phrase "in every place" (in Christian usage based on Mal. 1:11) seems to have had a special reference "to every place of meeting," and not the general adverbial sense of "everywhere" (cf. 1 Thess. 1:8; 1 Tim. 2:8; less obviously 2 Cor. 2:14).[35] In the Christian meetings, Christ is worshipped by calling on his name.

Moreover, proclamation and worship have a common content — God's acts of grace. The proclamation and confession of God's wonderful deeds (1 Pet. 2:9; Heb. 10:23; 13:15) looks back to his historical acts of grace in Christ and forward to the accomplishment of his will when Christ comes again. This recital both praises God for his salvation and declares to human beings that salvation.

The assembly, therefore, is related to the work of the church that will be discussed in the next chapter — proclaiming God's word, strengthening believers, and ministering to their needs. The assembly exemplifies worship as the whole Christian life. It epitomizes the church's worship and service to God.

The Assembly in Relation to the Doctrine of the Church

The assembly exemplifies the doctrine of the church. As discussed on

34. By uniting the church at Corinth with Christians at other places he anticipates the emphasis later in the letter that their practices must conform to those of other churches. "Every place" is equivalent to "all the assemblies" in 1 Cor. 4:17; 7:17; 11:16; 14:33.

35. Everett Ferguson, *"Topos* in 1 Timothy 2:8," *Restoration Quarterly* 33 (1991): 65-73.

pages 129-133, the word "church" means assembly. To be a church, it must meet. In order not to be a collective designation for individuals with certain characteristics, the church must manifest that it is a body by being together. A family is not a family if it is never together or at least bound in memory of past gatherings and hope of future reunions. The church may survive where there is a poor program of religious education, little evangelism, virtually no benevolence; but it will not survive where it does not meet.

In assembly, the church becomes itself.[36] It becomes conscious of itself, confesses itself to be a distinctive entity, shows itself to be what it is — a community (a people) gathered by the grace of God, dependent on him, and honoring him. The assembly allows the church to emerge in its true nature: a redeemed community. The word "church" occurs in the Greek Old Testament especially for the assemblies at the great moments in salvation history (p. 130). Similarly for the church, through the encounter with the Lord it learns what it means to be truly a saved people. As redeemed, it is separated from the world, and the assembly in God's presence makes the church aware of its rupture from the world. In the experience of reconciliation with God, the people know reconciliation also with one another and express this by being together in unity. As a community, the church has a life of its own. It is a people called together by God (and not by human choice). The assembly is the community's celebration of its life, its faith and its fellowship. The church is a people, and a people must manifest itself as such by assembling. The assembly reinforces the need for solidarity and community in order to sustain the life of faith.

The Assembly in Relation to Other Doctrines

Certain specific doctrines are represented in the assembly. The church has been termed "a community of memory and hope." The assembly remembers the atonement in the joint participation of the Lord's supper. More than this, by the very togetherness of the act of coming together there is shown salvation and unity. Redemption is not solely individual but has to do with a people. Justification has brought us together at the foot of the cross. The body nature of the church is manifested in the

36. J. J. von Allmen, *Worship: Its Theology and Practice* (London: Lutterworth, 1965), pp. 42-43.

meeting. Such acts as the kiss of peace express reconciliation and peace.[37] The oneness in the assembly is meant to show reconciled relationships within the body of Christ.

The church as a community of hope is also exemplified in the assembly. The eschatological importance of the assembly is seen in several ways.[38] As discussed previously, the same word *(episynagō)* is used for the meetings of the church now (Heb. 10:25) as is used for the gathering together of the elect at the Lord's second coming (Matt. 24:31; Mark 13:27; 2 Thess. 2:1). The meeting together symbolizes the eschatological assembly of God's people. The assembly looks forward to the day of Jesus' coming again. At the meeting there is encouragement to faithfulness while directing attention to the day of judgment (Heb. 10:25-31).

Between the two advents of Jesus, the atonement and the eschaton, the assembly of the church exemplifies and sustains the continuing fellowship and unity of God's people. The activities in the assembly, as will be seen below, proclaim God's saving acts, look forward to the second advent and the heavenly victory of God's people, and express and encourage fellowship and unity. Other doctrinal points will be made in connection with the individual activities in the assembly.

THE DAY OF ASSEMBLY

*"On the first day of the week, when we met
to break bread."*   (ACTS 20:7)

The connection of the assembly with the events of salvation and with eschatology points to one particular day as especially associated with the assembly, that is, the Lord's day, the day of the resurrection.[39] The

---

37. E. Kreider, "Let the Faithful Greet Each Other: The Kiss of Peace," *Conrad Grebel Review* 5 (1987): 39-41.

38. For the eschatological context of worship see D. E. Aune, *The Cultic Setting of Realized Eschatology in Early Christianity* (Leiden: Brill, 1972).

39. From the abundant literature I prefer the viewpoints of Paul Cotton, *From Sabbath to Sunday* (Bethlehem, PA: Times Publishing, 1933); Willy Rordorf, *Sunday* (Philadelphia: Westminster, 1968); and especially D. A. Carson, ed., *From Sabbath to Lord's Day* (Grand Rapids: Zondervan, 1982). For other viewpoints see Samuele Bacchiocchi, *From Sabbath to Sunday: A Historical Investigation of the Rise of Sunday Observance in Early Christianity* (Rome: Pontifical Gregorian University Press, 1977),

church as a people must manifest itself by assembling together. It may meet at many times for various purposes, as the list given above of passages referring to the meetings of the early church shows, but at the minimum it will meet on Sunday because of the participation of the assembly in the events of Easter and Pentecost that called it into existence.[40]

Terminology

Early Christian literature used four terms to refer to the same day of the week. The "first day of the week" was the Jewish designation. The phrase refers to the first day between the Sabbaths (Sabbath used in the sense of "week," since the Sabbath defined the week for Jews), and accords with the custom of numbering the first five days in the week leading up to the day of Preparation (Friday) and the Sabbath (the seventh day, Saturday). Modern Greek follows the Jewish method of designating the days of the week except for the substitution of "Lord's day" for "first day." The "first day of the week" is the most common name for this day in the New Testament, and it continued in usage in the early church in writings addressed to Jews or reflecting a Jewish milieu.

Another designation reflecting the custom of numbering the days of the week was "eighth day." The terminology probably originated in a Hellenized Jewish-Christian context where there was a desire to "trump" the Jewish usage that made the Sabbath the climax of the week. It lent itself also to a typological interpretation of "eighth day" in the Old Testament. It is doubtful that the reference to "eight days" in John 20:26 influenced the usage, but it is possible that the passage reflects the same background that led to the adoption of this description. More likely, the passage simply reflects the ancient practice of inclusive numbering according to which the second "first day of the week" would be

---

and Roger T. Beckwith and Wilfrid Stott, *This Is the Day: The Biblical Doctrine of the Christian Sunday* (Greenwood, SC: Attic Press, 1978), both examined in my "Sabbath: Saturday or Sunday? A Review Article," *Restoration Quarterly* 23 (1980): 172-181. Unjustly neglected is the old work by C. Callewaert, "La synaxe eucharistique à Jérusalem, Berceau du dimanche," *Ephemerides Theologicae Lovanienses* 15 (1938): 34-74.

40. J. J. von Allmen, *Worship: Its Theology and Practice* (London: Lutterworth, 1965), p. 221.

the "eighth day." The special reason for the adoption of the terminology of "eighth day," however, seems to have been a Hellenistic context where the number eight was a symbol for the heavenly world and the age to come, a symbolism adopted in Jewish apocalyptic writings. Eschatological symbolism made "eighth day" particularly appropriate for the day of the resurrection. As a somewhat more learned, if not esoteric, term this name had a limited currency.

The pagan designation was "day of the Sun" (or "Sunday"), the terminology followed in the Germanic languages of northern Europe and in English. It follows the practice of identifying days of the week with heavenly bodies, which in turn were identified with pagan deities. This terminology is missing from the New Testament but appears in second-century writings addressed to pagans.

The distinctively Christian name for this day was "Lord's day." It appears in the New Testament only in Revelation 1:10, but "Lord's day" was the name that came to prevail in Christian usage. It is preserved not only in modern Greek but in the Romance languages of southern Europe. "Lord's day" seemed peculiarly appropriate as the designation for the day on which Jesus arose from the dead.

The Jews began their day at sunset, so the "first day" began for them at what would be in modern American terminology Saturday evening. Romans began the day at midnight, and Greeks often at sunrise. This difference in reckoning the beginning and ending of a day results in different interpretations of when the gathering in Acts 20:7 occurred (our Saturday night or Sunday night?). From the indications of time given, I rather think Greek usage was being followed by Luke, and the gathering occurred on Sunday night. The determination of this point does not affect the theological significance of "the first day of the week." Whatever method of time reckoning is observed in a given culture would apply to Christian practice. In a Jewish context, Saturday evening would be on the "Lord's day"; in a Roman, Greek, or modern American context the "Lord's day" would begin at a later time.

New Testament Passages

The Gospel writers do not generally give much attention to chronological matters. In view of this, it is notable that the four unanimously record the day of the week on which Jesus arose from the dead — the first day of the week (Matt. 28:1-10; Mark 16:1-8; Luke 24:1, 13, 21, 46;

John 20:1-19). Thus on the first day of the week he was declared to be the Son of God (Rom. 1:4). The resurrection made him Lord of both the dead and the living (Rom. 14:9), the one who will be "judge of the living and the dead" (Acts 10:41-42; 17:31).

Moreover, Jesus met with his disciples after the resurrection on the first day of the week. John makes a particular point of this occurring not only on the day of the resurrection but also one week later — John 20:1, 19, 26.

It seems likely that the events in Acts 2 (the coming of the Holy Spirit, the "birthday of the church," the first gospel sermon, the conversion of 3,000, and the beginning of Christian worship and corporate life) occurred on the first day of the week. Pentecost (Acts 2:1) came on the first day of the week, according to one method of reckoning the time references in Leviticus 23:15-16. The Pharisees, to the contrary, interpreted the "sabbath" of that passage as being "Passover," with the result that Pentecost could come on any day of the week, even as Passover did. Most modern commentators, following Josephus, assume that the reckoning of the Pharisees was observed at the temple and is reflected in Acts.[41] The Sadducees, however, reckoned the "sabbath" as the Sabbath of Passover week, with the result that Pentecost, fifty days after the day following the Sabbath (on the inclusive method of counting again) always fell on a first day of the week. Luke's language has been much discussed, but it is possible that even if the temple was following the Pharisees' calendar, Luke was following the Sadducees. Again, the presence of the time reference indicates that this fact had some special significance for Luke.

The early church assembled to partake of the Lord's supper on the first day of the week (Acts 20:7). There were daily meetings of Christians in the early days, and it has been widely held on the basis of Acts 2:46 that there was daily communion. If so, this is the only evidence in the early centuries for the practice. It is not certain that the "breaking of bread" here is a reference to communion (cf. the usage for beginning an ordinary meal in Acts 27:33-36); nor is the construction unambiguous that "daily" modifies "breaking bread" as well as "being

---

41. See the evidence collected in Kirsopp Lake and Henry J. Cadbury, *The Acts of the Apostles*, Vol. 4 of *The Beginnings of Christianity*, ed. F. J. Foakes-Jackson and Kirsopp Lake, Part I (London: Macmillan, 1933), pp. 16-17. This, however, was before the discovery of the Dead Sea Scrolls gave evidence of the greater prominence of competing calendars in first-century Judaism.

together in the temple." Whatever is made of Acts 2:46, weekly communion early established itself as the norm throughout the Christian world. There were assemblies especially for the purpose of taking the Lord's supper (1 Cor. 11:20, 24, 25-26, 33).

There is evidence of weekly Christian meetings also in 1 Corinthians 16:1-2. Paul's instructions concerning the collection have often been taken as referring to a private activity, principally on the basis of the phrase "by himself," which can mean "at home" or "privately," but can also mean "in his own judgment" (Rom. 12:16; 1 Cor. 3:19; 2 Cor. 1:17), referring to the decision of each person how much to give (cf. 2 Cor. 9:7). Several considerations argue in favor of a public contribution to a church treasury. (1) A common day on which this was to be done, the first day of the week (and note that the instructions were given not only to Corinth but also to the churches of Galatia — 1 Cor. 16:1), points to a corporate activity, not private (when no particular day would matter). The specification of a particular weekly day makes sense only if it was a special day that offered some occasion or opportunity for the activity. (2) This is strengthened not only by the other evidence of Christian meetings on the first day but also by the Jewish practice of the weekly collection of alms in the synagogue and distribution to the poor.[42] (3) The word "collection" (*logeia*) seems to refer only to public collections by groups, including religious groups, not a private activity. (4) The reference in 2 Corinthians 8:6 to "complete" the collection would make no sense if it was private; the statement implies there were group funds that fell short. (5) Moreover, a private storing up would require collections when Paul came, the very thing he does not want. (6) The church was to choose its messengers to carry its funds to Jerusalem, a fact that emphasizes that this was an organized church activity. The whole passage refers to a congregational collection and disbursement of funds.[43]

On the Lord's day (Rev. 1:10), the Lord, who is "the living one" (Rev. 1:18), is present among the lampstands that symbolize the churches (Rev. 1:13, 20). The New Testament is silent about Christians meeting as a church on the Sabbath day. No doubt most Jews who became Christians continued to observe the Sabbath day (Acts 21:20-21). Paul and other Jewish Christians attended the synagogue and used the opportu-

---

42. Emil Schürer, *The History of the Jewish People in the Age of Jesus Christ*, rev. and ed. G. Vermes, F. Millar, M. Black, Vol. II (Edinburgh: T. & T. Clark, 1979), p. 437.

43. E. Earle Ellis, *Pauline Theology: Ministry and Society* (Grand Rapids: Eerdmans, 1989), pp. 94f.

nity it afforded to preach Jesus (Acts 13:14-16; 17:1-2, 10; 18:4; cf. 6:9). There is no evidence, however, of purely Gentile converts keeping the Sabbath (the different customs are probably reflected in Rom. 14:5-6), nor of Christians having their distinctive meetings (for the Lord's supper) on the Sabbath. Actually the Sabbath and Lord's day are two different kinds of days. The former was in the Old Testament a day of rest, a day on which by the first century Jews in addition had come to have their meetings; the latter was a day of meeting, which came in later Christian practice to be a day of rest. There was no incompatibility in Jewish believers observing both days, each in its distinctive way, the Sabbath as a day of rest and the Lord's day as a day of meeting. From that perspective it is incorrect to speak of the one day "replacing" the other. For Gentile Christians, however, the Sabbath had no significance, and they adopted the Lord's day as their one special religious day.

Testimony of History

The uniform testimony of early church history confirms that the assemblies of the church were on Sunday. Many early Christian texts speak of the custom of meeting on the first day of the week to take the Lord's supper.[44] These Christian sources regularly connect this day and Christian meetings with the resurrection of Jesus. They stress the joyfulness of the day for Christians.

Doctrinal Considerations

The connection of the first day of the week with the resurrection of Jesus expressed in both the New Testament and other early Christian texts gives the day its doctrinal significance. Even as the Sabbath day was chosen for a doctrinal purpose for the Jews, so the Lord's day gave a doctrinal purpose to the day of meeting.

The first day of the week is the day of Jesus' resurrection and the

---

44. The texts from the second century are collected and interpreted in my *Early Christians Speak*, 3rd ed. (Abilene: ACU Press, 1999), pp. 67-79. More extensive collections are found in W. Rordorf, *Sabbat et dimanche dans l'Eglise ancienne* (Neuchâtel: Delachaux and Niestlé, 1972) and Thomas K. Carroll and Thomas Halton, *Liturgical Practice in the Fathers* (Wilmington: Michael Glazier, 1988), pp. 17-76.

day when he met with his disciples. It is, therefore, the Christian's day of deliverance from sin and the power of death (Rom. 5:10, 17, 21; 8:11). Christians meet, moreover, on this day because they are particularly conscious on the day of the resurrection of Christ's presence in their midst (cf. Luke 24:13-35). If the Pentecost of Acts 2 was also a first day of the week, then there is the added significance of this day as the birthday of the church and the celebration of the presence of the Spirit in the church. By way of the resurrection, the first day is further connected with the eschatological coming of Jesus; the resurrected Jesus will come again in glory (Acts 1:11; 1 Cor. 11:26).

The Sabbath had special religious meaning for the Jews. It commemorated the Exodus from Egypt according to Deuteronomy 5:12-15. It is true that Exodus 20:8-11 gives as the reason for the remembrance of the seventh day the rest by God from creation on the seventh day. The religious and political life of many peoples furnishes examples of commemorating something on a day chosen for another reason (e.g., celebrating the birthday of Jesus on December 25 to replace a pagan holiday, and in modern America the observance of certain national holidays like President's day and Columbus day on a Monday so as to give a long weekend). In the same way, the day to commemorate the national deliverance of Israel from bondage was placed on the seventh day because of the rest from creation. The Sabbath was given to Jews alone (cf. Ps. 147:19-20 for the Law as a whole), and such was the Jewish understanding in the first century.[45] The day had significance only to them. Christians had a different day of deliverance.

It is perhaps significant that the adjective "Lord's" (*kyriakos, -ē*) occurs only twice in the New Testament — in reference to the Lord's supper (1 Cor. 11:20) and to the Lord's day (Rev. 1:10).[46] Both are peculiarly the Lord's, and both belong together, united to each other by the resurrection. The day, as the day of the resurrection, is the day for taking

45. Although some Hellenistic Jewish authors did make universal claims for the Sabbath as part of their apologetic for Judaism, other Jews understood the Sabbath as an ordinance for Israel alone — references in Roger T. Beckwith and Wilfrid Stott, *This is the Day* (Greenwood, SC: Attic, 1978), pp. 8-11, 17-19. Cf. also Harold H. P. Dressler, "The Sabbath in the Old Testament," and C. Rowland, "A Summary of Sabbath Observance in Judaism at the Beginning of the Christian Era," in D. A. Carson, *From Sabbath to Lord's Day* (Grand Rapids: Zondervan, 1982), pp. 34, 44-55.

46. Willy Rordorf, *Sunday* (Philadelphia: Westminster, 1968), p. 303, gives the dictum: "No Lord's Supper without Sunday, no Sunday without the Lord's Supper."

the supper; and the supper, in remembrance of the event of salvation, gives significance to the day.

PURPOSES OF THE ASSEMBLY

"Whatever you do, in word or deed, do everything
in the name of the Lord Jesus, giving thanks
to God the Father through him."

(COL. 3:17)

Distinctiveness of the Assembly

The assembly of the church is a distinctive expression of the church. Not everything acceptable in other contexts has a place in the church meeting. Paul in 1 Corinthians indicates that there are times when "the whole church comes together" (1 Cor. 14:23), "when you come together as a church" [or "in church"] (1 Cor. 11:18; cf. 11:20). Special considerations apply for these occasions. Paul makes a distinction between behavior that is appropriate elsewhere and what can be done in the assembly, between outside activities and assembly activities. Thus, he distinguishes eating to satisfy hunger "at home" and coming together "to eat the Lord's supper" (1 Cor. 11:20, 22, 33-34). Again, although he claimed to speak in tongues more than all the Corinthians (1 Cor. 14:18) and says he would like for all of them to be able to speak in tongues (1 Cor. 14:5), he yet declares, "in church I would rather speak five words with my mind, in order to instruct others also, than ten thousand words in a tongue" (1 Cor. 14:19). Furthermore, he does not impose permanent silence on women, only "in the churches [assemblies] women should be silent" (1 Cor. 14:34). Paul does not support the idea that if something is right or good at other times it may be done in church.

The examples cited from 1 Corinthians show that appropriateness in the assembly is not a question of gifts. Speaking in tongues was a gift of the Spirit (1 Cor. 12:10-11), but this fact did not give the speaker in tongues the right to speak in church. Other purposes and standards apply there. If an interpreter was present, then one could exercise the gift in the assembly (1 Cor. 14:27); otherwise, the speaker in tongues was to be silent (1 Cor. 14:28) and limit his use of the gift to private occasions (1 Cor. 14:2). The distinctiveness of the assembly may be seen in its special objectives.

Specific Purposes

Glorify God

The goal of the Christian is to glorify God in all that is said and done (1 Cor. 10:31), and this is especially so when the church is together.[47] "To God be the glory in the church and in Christ Jesus to all generations, forever and ever" (Eph. 3:21). The verse is not limited to the meetings of the church, but giving God glory "in the church" certainly includes doing so when the church is in assembly. God's plan for human salvation is for the praise of his glory (Eph. 1:6, 12, 14). Many things are mentioned as bringing glory to God: confessing Jesus as Lord (Phil. 2:11); bearing spiritual fruit (John 15:8); keeping the body pure (1 Cor. 6:20); extending the grace of the gospel to others (2 Cor. 4:15; Gal. 1:24); generosity in giving (2 Cor. 9:11-13); harmony in the church (Rom. 15:5-7); righteousness (Phil. 1:11). Christians give glory to God "through Jesus Christ" (1 Pet. 4:11). They especially do so when they meet together.

Glorifying God in the assembly means that the assembly will reflect the character of God. Thus Paul corrects abuses in the assemblies of the Corinthian church by reminding the Corinthian Christians that "God is a God of peace" (1 Cor. 14:33), so "all things should be done decently and in order" (1 Cor. 14:40). This word was especially pertinent for the Corinthians' meetings, but other attributes of God, as mentioned above, will also regulate activities in the assembly so that this purpose of honoring God may be carried out. Thus the assembly will reflect the doctrine of creation and God's created order. Specifically, human sexual distinctions based on creation will continue to be observed (1 Cor. 11:3-16; 14:34-36 — see further pp. 341-344).

Exemplify the Church

The word for "church" in Greek is "assembly." The assembly is meant to exemplify what the church is. The assemblies of the church are a time for distinctively Christian activities. Christians will seek to glorify God in all their lives, and the church will manifest itself and its presence in other ways, but when it comes together "as a church" it will especially express its nature and its concerns. Paul reminded the Corinthians that

---

47. G. Wainwright, *Doxology: The Praise of God in Worship, Doctrine and Life* (New York: Oxford University Press, 1980).

what he taught them he taught in all the churches (1 Cor. 4:17; 7:17; 11:16). He invokes this principle specifically in regard to the assembly in 1 Corinthians 14:33, "As in all the churches of the saints." This common practice of the churches does not mean uniformity in every respect but does indicate sufficient commonality to reflect a common identity. The congregational meeting will shape the character of the people, and in so doing this purpose shades into the next one to be mentioned.

Edify Christians [48]

God is glorified and the church is exemplified when the community is edified. The most extensive discussion in the New Testament of the assembly is 1 Corinthians 14.[49] In this chapter, Paul sets forth edification as the goal of the Christian assembly: "When you come together, . . . let all things be done for edification [building up]" (1 Cor. 14:26). Everything done in the assembly should contribute to edification, or building up the members. Paul's directions were aimed at correcting certain abuses in the assemblies at Corinth, so we cannot expect a complete discussion. What is said gives important principles that are normative for the church and can be applied to other situations. Specifically, Paul attempted to exclude uninterpreted tongues from the meetings, and he did so by insisting that the verbal activities must edify. A fuller treatment of the theme of edification will be found on pages 286-288. For the present, note will be taken of the emphasis on edification in 1 Corinthians 14, where the context is the church assembly. Some form of "edify" or "build up" occurs seven times in the chapter (vss. 3, 4 [twice], 5, 12, 17, 26). These verses show that edification requires instruction — teaching and learning; it requires speech that is intelligible. Even speech addressed to God must be understandable and edifying to others in the assembly (1 Cor. 14:16-17). The church meetings are designed for the spiritual improvement of the members.

---

48. G. Bornkamm, "On the Understanding of Worship," in *Early Christian Experience* (London: SCM, 1969), pp. 161-169; Ervin Bishop, "The Assembly," *Restoration Quarterly* 18 (1975): 219-228.

49. Among the commentaries, note especially H. Conzelmann, *1 Corinthians* (Philadelphia: Fortress, 1975), pp. 232-247; G. Fee, *The First Epistle to the Corinthians* (Grand Rapids: Eerdmans, 1987), pp. 652-713. In addition, see Ralph P. Martin, *The Spirit and the Congregation: Studies in 1 Corinthians 12–15* (Grand Rapids: Eerdmans, 1984), pp. 57-88.

Express and Promote Fellowship

The assembly promotes the community or "body" life of the church. The sense of being one people and acting with one accord results from the whole congregation being frequently together. The first disciples in Jerusalem "devoted themselves to the apostles' teaching and fellowship, to the breaking of bread and the prayers" (Acts 2:42). The word for "together," or "with one accord" *(homothymadon)*, a favorite with Luke, describes the early Christians: They "spent much time together in the temple" (Acts 2:46; cf. 4:24; 5:12; 15:25); "So that together you may with one voice glorify God" (Rom. 15:6). The meeting together was a time for "encouraging one another" (Heb. 10:25), an opportunity lost when neglecting to meet together.

Properly Impress Outsiders

Paul in 1 Corinthians 14:23-25 assumes the presence of non-Christians at the meetings of the church in Corinth and uses their likely reactions as an argument in favor of prophecy over speaking in tongues. It is consistent with the other purposes for there to be meetings aimed especially at outsiders. The attitudes and reactions of nonbelievers will not be determinative of the Christian assembly, so these considerations are secondary to other purposes, but this factor should be noted. Seen in relation to the other purposes of the assembly, the impression on outsiders will be supportive of the other goals.

Commemorate and Proclaim Salvation

The remembrance and declaration of God's saving activity in Christ glorifies God, shows what the church is all about, edifies believers, unites Christians in the faith, and calls unbelievers to faith. The Lord's supper especially serves this purpose. Such is evident from 1 Corinthians 10:14-17 and 11:17-34, for in celebrating the Lord's supper the church remembers and reenacts the salvation in Christ. All the activities in the assembly discussed below serve this purpose.

Criteria for Activities in the Assembly

The above stated purposes provide criteria for what is done in the assembly.

(1) *That which accords with the will of God.* God has placed in the assembly those activities that will fulfill its purposes, and he has left out those that do not contribute to its purposes. To glorify God means to seek his will in all things. For the Christian age this means relating everything to the "name of Jesus Christ."

(2) *That which reflects the character of God.* Paul, in order to correct the disorders in the assemblies of Christians at Corinth, invoked the character of God as a standard to govern how the meetings were conducted. "God is not a God of disorder but of peace" (1 Cor. 14:33); therefore, "let all things be done decently and in order" (1 Cor. 14:40). Peace and good order were the aspects of God that the Corinthian church needed. Other aspects of the nature of God may call for emphasis in other situations.

(3) *That which is spiritual.* The nature of God and of the church dictates that the assembly of the church not cater to the fleshly or carnal, the ritual or cultic (John 4:21, 23-24; Phil. 3:3; Col. 2:16-23; 1 Pet. 2:5). By the same token, the true worshiper does not seek experiences, emotions, or sentiment for their own sake. That which is spiritual may make one feel good or give a feeling of uplift, but these things are by-products of seeking God and the welfare of fellow believers. Those who seek an individual emotional experience in the assembly place themselves in the camp of the immature Corinthians whom Paul corrected in 1 Corinthians 14 rather than in the camp of Paul himself.

(4) *That which is edifying.* According to 1 Corinthians 14, as noted above, that which is edifying is understandable, instructive, and contributes to spiritual improvement. In the assembly one seeks not to please the self but to benefit the community. The "greater gifts" are those that edify the church (1 Cor. 12:31; 13:13; 14:5).

ACTIVITIES IN THE ASSEMBLY

*"They devoted themselves to the apostles'
teaching and fellowship, to the breaking
of bread and the prayers."*   (ACTS 2:42)

Some activities mentioned as occurring when Christians met together will be discussed in other contexts in this book: selecting leaders (pp. 310-318), exercising discipline, and solving problems (pp. 377-386). The concern here is with those activities that were a regular part of the weekly meetings of the church, even though all except the Lord's supper were also individual activities not limited to the assembly. All these activities are brought into special relation to Jesus Christ. Jesus' meetings with his disciples after the resurrection in Luke 24 centered on two activities in which Jesus was made known — the breaking of bread (vv. 13-35, esp. 31 and 35) and interpretation of the scriptures (36-53; cf. 32) — and the liturgy of the table and the liturgy of the word have remained two foci of Christian meetings.[50]

The New Testament does not provide evidence for an "order of worship."[51] Acts 2:42 is often taken as reflecting such an order,[52] but probably the most that can be said is that it is a listing of some of the corporate activities of Christians. The same goes for 1 Corinthians 14, the fullest discussion of a Christian meeting in the New Testament but lacking any concrete expression of the order in which the items occurred.[53] We cannot take the book of Revelation as representing earthly worship, any more than it reflects the earthly organization of the church.[54] The imagery is drawn from the temple, not the Christian congregations. The lack of later evidence of any continuity makes it highly unlikely that Revelation reflects an actual practice; if it did, surely the influence of Revelation itself would have ensured continuity of the practice. The elements of the structure of a service are there (as in Acts 2:42 and 1 Corinthians 11 and 14), but neither the specific arrangements of the service nor the actual wording of hymns and prayers. This absence of a New Testament "order of worship" gives only a relative unimpor-

---

50. J. J. von Allmen, *Worship: Its Theology and Practice* (London: Lutterworth, 1965), pp. 22-23, however, becomes too speculative in seeing these events and the very plan of the Synoptic Gospels as corresponding to the order of worship. For other texts combining the table and teaching see Acts 1:4; 2:42, 46; 5:42; 10:41f.; 20:7-11; cf. John 21:9-23.

51. G. J. Cuming, "The New Testament Foundation for Common Prayer," *Studia Liturgica* 10 (1974): 88-105, puts together an order of service from liturgical elements mentioned in the New Testament, but is rather arbitrary (as concerns the contents of the New Testament) in the arrangement. If Paul's epistles reflected what became later liturgical order, why does he discuss the Lord's supper in 1 Corinthians 11?

52. E.g., J. Jeremias, *The Eucharistic Words of Jesus* (New York: Scribner's, 1966), pp. 118-119.

53. Eduard Schweizer, *Church Order in the New Testament* (London: SCM, 1961), p. 223, suggests that 1 Cor. 11 and 12–14 reflect an order of the Lord's supper followed by the service of the word, but the order in which items are taken up in 1 Corinthians may be dictated by other considerations.

54. G. Bornkamm, "Presbys, etc.," *Theological Dictionary of the New Testament*, ed. G. Friedrich, tr. G. W. Bromiley (Grand Rapids: Eerdmans, 1968), 6.668-669.

tance to liturgical forms, because the congregational meetings must take some form. The "order" may not be important, but what is in the order of service, what gives "form" to it, is important as expressing the nature of the church, the relationship of its members to God and one another, and the spirit of worship and service. The forms will be those that best express what the church is and its purposes in assembling.[55] Since there is no "order of worship" in the New Testament, we arrange the activities in the assembly for organizational purposes: the Lord's supper first as a central act of the assembly, and the other focus — the word — last as a reprise of the preceding chapter where the word was central to conversion and in order to make a connection with the following chapter on the ministry and organization of the church.

Lord's Supper[56]

Both theologically and sociologically, the Lord's supper was the central act of the weekly assemblies of the early church. There were meetings

55. J. J. von Allmen, *Worship: Its Theology and Practice* (London: Lutterworth, 1965), pp. 80-86. His list of components is, as in Acts 2:42, the word of God, the Lord's supper, prayers, and Christian fellowship — pp. 129-183.

56. In addition to items in the bibliography for this chapter on worship in general, add the following: Y. Brilioth, *Eucharistic Faith and Practice Evangelical and Catholic* (London: SPCK, 1930), chaps. 1–2; A. J. B. Higgins, *The Lord's Supper in the New Testament* (London: SCM, 1952); Oscar Cullmann and F. J. Leenhardt, *Essays on the Lord's Supper* (Richmond: John Knox, 1958); Ernst Käsemann, "The Pauline Doctrine of the Lord's Supper," *Essays on New Testament Themes* (SBT; Naperville, IL: Alec R. Allenson, 1964), pp. 108-135; J. Delorme, *The Eucharist in the New Testament* (Baltimore: Helicon, 1964); J. Jeremias, *The Eucharistic Words of Jesus* (New York: Scribner's, 1966); Scott McCormick, Jr., *The Lord's Supper: A Biblical Interpretation* (Philadelphia: Westminster, 1966); E. Schweizer, *The Lord's Supper according to the New Testament* (Philadelphia: Fortress, 1967); G. Bornkamm, "Lord's Supper and Church in Paul," *Early Christian Experience* (London: SCM, 1969), pp. 123-160; P. Benoit et al., eds., *The Breaking of Bread, Concilium* 40 (New York: Paulist, 1969); Eric C. Rust, "The Theology of the Lord's Supper," *Review and Expositor* 66 (1969): 35-44; Willi Marxsen, *The Lord's Supper as a Christological Problem* (Facet; Philadelphia: Fortress, 1970); I. Howard Marshall, *Last Supper and Lord's Supper* (Grand Rapids: Eerdmans, 1980); Xavier Léon-Dufour, *Sharing the Eucharistic Bread: The Witness of the New Testament* (New York: Paulist, 1987); Jon L. Berquist, *Ancient Wine, New Wineskins: The Lord's Supper in Old Testament Perspective* (St. Louis: Chalice, 1991); Bruce Chilton, *A Feast of Meanings: Eucharistic Theologies from Jesus through Johannine Circles* (Leiden: Brill, 1994); Eugene LaVerdiere, *The Eucharist in the New Testament and the Early Church* (Collegeville: Liturgical, 1996); Eleanor Kreider, *Communion Shapes Character* (Scottdale: Herald, 1997).

to take the Lord's supper (1 Cor. 11:20-21, 33), and these occurred on the first day of the week (Acts 20:7). The Lord's supper is expressive of the central realities of the Christian faith and of what the church is all about.

The New Testament uses the word "body" in reference to Jesus in four senses: (1) the physical body of his incarnation (Heb. 10:5; Luke 23:52); (2) the glorified body of his resurrection (Phil. 3:21); (3) the spiritual body of his church (Col. 1:18; Eph. 1:23); and (4) the bread of the Lord's supper (Matt. 26:26). Each of these usages has a bearing on the nature of the church. The Son of God became flesh and blood (John 1:14; 19:34; Heb. 2:14) so that by his death and resurrection he might redeem a new people of God (Col. 1:18-20; Phil. 2:5-10; Acts 20:28). These people will some day share the likeness of his glorification (Phil. 3:21; 1 Cor. 15:44; 1 John 3:2). Paul unites concepts (3) and (4) when he declares that by partaking of the one bread Christians become the one body of Christ (1 Cor. 10:16-17). But first the Spirit at baptism must incorporate them into the body of Christ (1 Cor. 12:13). Receiving spiritual nourishment from the Lord (John 6:35-40, 47-58, 63), they are transformed into his glory (2 Cor. 3:18).[57]

Aspects of the Lord's Supper

Ideas associated with the Lord's supper are expressed by the terminology used in the New Testament and in Christian history to refer to this activity. A consideration of several terms will point to the aspects relevant to the doctrine of the church. Each aspect has a special reference to Christ.

(1) *Thanksgiving or eucharist.* The prayer for the bread and cup was the great moment of the church's thanksgiving for the salvation brought by the death and resurrection of Jesus. Eucharist was the most common term in the early church for the breaking of bread in the assembly. Although the noun *eucharistia* is not used in the New Testament to refer to the act, the verb *eucharisteō*, "give thanks," is used in all four of the institution narratives (Matt. 26:27; Mark 14:23; Luke 22:17, 19; 1 Cor. 11:24; in parallel with *eulogeō*, "bless," in Matt. 26:26 and Mark 14:22; cf. 1 Cor. 10:16). The basis of thanksgiving is the salvation that brought

---

57. This paragraph is taken from my study booklet *The New Testament Church* (Abilene: ACU Press, 1968), p. 60. The subsequent points are based on ibid., pp. 60-64.

the church into existence. The act of thanksgiving calls attention to what the congregation gives to God.

(2) *Lord's supper.* The Lord's supper has been the most common term in Protestant churches. Its usage in 1 Corinthians 11:20 refers to the context of a meal which was the occasion for the disorders in the church at Corinth (a meal — the Last Supper — was the setting in the Gospels for the institution of this special act). Related to the meal idea is Luke's common phrase "the breaking of bread" (Acts 2:42, 46; 20:7, 11; 27:35), studied further below (as is the relation of a common meal to the remembrance of the death of Jesus). The term "Lord's supper" is a reminder that this is an activity that is peculiarly the Lord's. It is his supper (1 Cor. 11:20), in contrast to one's own supper (1 Cor. 11:21), and "his table" (1 Cor. 10:21). He sets a table for his people, invites them to it, and presides at the gathering. The eating and drinking are done in his honor. Jesus' giving of the bread and wine to his disciples was a symbol of the gift of salvation to them and their reception of it. He provides the spiritual nourishment for his people (cf. the symbolic language of John 6 about the bread from heaven — vss. 31-38, 48-58, 63). Failure to partake properly of this spiritual nourishment leaves one weak and sickly (1 Cor. 11:30). The language of Lord's supper calls attention to what God gives to his people.

(3) *Communion or koinonia.*[58] Another common term for the Lord's supper translates the Greek *koinonia,* fellowship or communion (1 Cor. 10:16-17). The passage in 1 Corinthians 10:14-21 points out that eating at idol temples established a communion with demons. Likewise eating of the sacrificial offerings in Judaism made the participants partners of the altar. Sacrifices in paganism and Judaism were often followed by sharing in a meal from part of the sacrificial animal and other products. When Christians eat the bread and drink the cup, they are sharing in Christ's sacrifice and its benefits. They are participating in Christ's body and blood, that is, they are identifying with his life and death.

The Lord promised to be with his disciples always (Matt. 28:20). The Lord's supper is a pledge of that continuing presence. In the bread and wine there are presented tokens of his body and blood. These are a pledge of continuing fellowship with him.

One of the earliest names for the communion was "breaking bread" (Acts 2:42; 20:7). Breaking bread calls attention to the fellowship

58. James D. G. Dunn, *Unity and Diversity in the New Testament,* 2nd ed. (London: SCM, 1990), p. 165.

aspect of the Lord's supper as a sharing of food together. The meaning of this act is discussed below as one of the special problems connected with the Lord's supper calling for explanation to modern believers.

Table fellowship in the biblical world was full of rich associations of closeness and sharing. The communion with the risen Christ establishes a communion with fellow believers. There is a unity through allegiance to a common Lord. The common bread expresses the unity of the redeemed community (1 Cor. 10:17). Communion shows one's participation in the church, for the church is the body of Christ (1 Cor. 12:12). Eating of the "one loaf" identifies the participants as "one body" in Christ (1 Cor. 10:17). It is only in the one body that the benefits of Christ's death are received (cf. Eph. 2:16). The fellowship aspect of the Lord's supper thus is very important for the understanding of the church. Taking the one loaf exemplifies the one body (the church). The supper for which thanks is given establishes a communion or fellowship among believers, and it maintains and sustains unity with Christ until he comes again. The language of communion or fellowship calls attention to the mutual sharing, with the Lord and with one another, that characterizes the church.

(4) *Memorial or anamnēsis.*[59] The present experience of communion with Christ and fellow believers is based on a past event. Paul's record of Jesus' words of institution contains the command, "Do this in remembrance of me" (1 Cor. 11:24, 26). An alternative translation would be "Do this memorial [*anamnēsis*] of me." The aspect of commemoration is made clearer by reference to Jewish practices. Jesus' words, "This is my body," may be related to the words of Exodus 12:11, "It is the Passover of the Lord." When the Jews celebrated the Passover memorial (*mnēmosynon* — Exod. 12:14), there was more than the recalling of a past event. Each Jew who celebrated the Passover became himself a participant in the Exodus event. The Mishnah enjoined, "In every generation a man must so regard himself as if he came forth himself out of Egypt" (Pesaḥim 10.5). The deliverance from bondage became his own experience. Thus, instead of simply calling the past to mind, the past was brought into the present and its benefits made operative.

---

59. N. Dahl, "Anamnesis," *Studia Theologica* 1 (1947): 69-95; reprinted in English without complete annotation as "Anamnesis: Memory and Commemoration in Early Christianity," in *Jesus in the Memory of the Early Church* (Minneapolis: Augsburg, 1976), pp. 11-29; Xavier Léon-Dufour, *Sharing the Eucharistic Bread: The Witness of the New Testament* (New York: Paulist, 1987), pp. 102-116.

Paul further says that performing this memorial of Jesus "proclaims his death" (1 Cor. 11:26). In the Lord's supper there is a showing forth, a reenactment.[60] Here another Old Testament concept will be helpful in appreciating the significance of what Jesus did at the Last Supper. In breaking the bread and pouring out the wine, Jesus performed an act of prophetic symbolism. The prophets delivered the "word of the Lord" by actions as well as words, by signs as well as voice (cf. Isa. 20:2-6; Jer. 28:2-10; Ezek. 4–5). The action portrayed and shared in the reality being enacted. In the same way, Jesus' actions at the Last Supper enacted the giving of himself soon to occur. Jesus' flesh was broken and given for humanity (John 19:34; 20:25-28; 1 Cor. 11:24), and his blood was poured out for the remission of sins (Matt. 26:28). By repeating the actions of Jesus in breaking the bread and distributing the cup, believers participate in what he did; by the symbolism, they bring those past events into the present and make them living reality. The language of memorial calls attention to the fact that, although this is a human act, the important consideration is what God does for his people.

(5) *Anticipation of the messianic banquet.*[61] The proclaiming of the Lord's death in the memorial is "until he comes" (1 Cor. 11:26). There is a future, eschatological reference in the sharing of the bread and wine. The Lord's supper not only brings the past into the present and creates a present fellowship, but it also proclaims a future event. In a sense it brings the future into the present. Indeed, the predominant note in the early Christian observance was not sorrowful remembrance as at a funeral but joyful expectation. The crucified Christ is also a living Lord, and the present fellowship is a guarantee and anticipation of a fuller fellowship yet to be enjoyed.

The Jewish eschatological hope was sometimes set forth in terms of God providing a banquet for his people (Isa. 25:6; Matt. 8:11; Luke 13:29). This provides part of the background for the banquet parables recorded by Luke (Luke 14:1-24) and may be behind the reference to the "marriage supper of the Lamb" (Rev. 19:9). Jesus at the Last Supper spoke of eating and drinking in the kingdom of God (Matt. 26:29; Luke 22:16, 18; cf. 22:27-30). The church's repeating of Jesus' symbolic acts is

---

60. Bonnie Bowman Thurston, " 'Do This': A Study on the Institution of the Lord's Supper," *Restoration Quarterly* 30 (1988): 207-217.

61. Geoffrey Wainwright, *Eucharist and Eschatology* (New York: Oxford University Press, 1981).

done with the same eschatological reference, sharing a foretaste of the blessings of the end time. The church is set between the center (the cross) and the consummation (the coming again) of history. The Lord's supper holds those two foci together. The language of the messianic banquet calls attention to the future hope that goes with the past event.

(6) *Covenant meal.* All four institution narratives speak of a "new covenant" in reference to the blood of Jesus.[62] The sacrifice of Christ brought a new covenant based on forgiveness of sins (Heb. 8:6–9:26). The wording of Matthew 26:28 makes explicit that the covenant is associated with forgiveness. To drink from the cup is to share in this covenant of blood. The old covenant was inaugurated by sacrifice, the sprinkling of the blood of the covenant (for the phrase, cf. Zech. 9:11), and the eating of a covenant meal (Exod. 24:3-11). For Christians, the eating of the bread and drinking from the cup is an act of renewing covenant allegiance to the Lord. This is a relationship that excludes all other religious loyalties (1 Cor. 10:21). The church is the people of the new covenant, who have a new meal as its expression. The covenant language marks the participants as being especially the Lord's, and calls attention to the meal as being for those alone who share the covenant.

(7) *Sacrifice.* The sacrificial character of the eucharist has been much debated. Jesus' words at the Last Supper (Matt. 26:28 and parallels) combine an allusion to an atoning sacrifice ("for many" and "poured out" — Isa. 53:12) and a covenant sacrifice ("blood of the covenant" — Ex. 24:8) as constituting a new covenant ("forgiveness of sins" — Jer. 31:31), and so he referred to his coming death as both an atoning and a covenant sacrifice. The bread represented himself ("body") as a sacrifice, and blood suggested death and sacrifice. On the other hand, sacrificial language is notably absent from New Testament texts that speak explicitly of the Lord's supper. The closest approximation is the comparison to Jewish and pagan sacrifices in 1 Corinthians 10:16-21, but the point of comparison is not the sacrifice at the altar but the meal that follows the sacrifice.[63] Nevertheless, all agree that prayer and thanksgiving are acceptable sacrifices under the new covenant, so it is appropriate to speak of a "thank offering" with reference to the eucharist.[64]

---

62. For the text of Luke 22 see below, p. 258.

63. I. Howard Marshall, *Last Supper and Lord's Supper* (Grand Rapids: Eerdmans, 1980), p. 122.

64. W. Rordorf, "Le sacrifice eucharistique," *Theologische Zeitschrift* 25 (1969): 335-353.

Christ has made his sacrifice once for all (Heb. 10:10); the representation of that sacrifice in the acts of the eucharist are declarations to human beings, not to God. The church is a living continuation of the once-for-all sacrifice of Christ. At the table it makes its sacrifice of thanksgiving for the atoning sacrifice of Christ. The church lives in the humiliation of the cross and by the power of the resurrection. The Lord's supper brings the church once more to these realities and reminds it that the resurrection is an assurance of the power of the sacrificial life. The church not only shares in the benefits of Christ's sacrifice, but it also offers its own self-sacrifice to God. The language of sacrifice can be abused in connection with the eucharist, but it calls attention to what is central in this act.

(8) *Sacrament or mystery.* What the Latin church and its heirs have called "sacraments," the Greek church has called "mysteries." Both words lack specific biblical warrant in reference to the eucharist. The wide variety of meanings given to "sacrament" plus the theological baggage associated with the concept that has been accumulated through the centuries make this a difficult concept to apply. Nevertheless, it seems that the terminology is here to stay, so much so that some refer to the eucharist as "the sacrament." The most generally accepted definition of a sacrament is "a visible sign of an invisible reality." Some put the emphasis on the sign aspect; others, on what is considered the reality signified. According to this broad definition, the eucharist may be considered a sacrament, but so may many other things not usually considered sacraments. With reference to the actions of Jesus at the Last Supper, I consider the interpretation in terms of prophetic symbolism, or enacted parable, suggested above more helpful. In the church's continuation of his words and actions, there are promises and gifts of God associated with the doing of these,[65] such as spiritual nourishment and renewal. The biblical concepts developed above are more accurate ways of describing the meaning of the communion in New Testament churches.

"Sacrament" entered theological vocabulary as the Latin translation of the Greek word *mystērion,* "mystery." This Greek word is used by Paul to refer to God's plan to save humanity through the death and

---

65. A. D. Nock describes baptism and the eucharist by the Latin *dona data* ("gifts given") — "Hellenistic Mysteries and Christian Sacraments," *Mnemosyne,* ser. 4, vol. 5 (1952): 177-213; reprinted in *Essays on Religion and the Ancient World,* ed. Zeph Stewart (Oxford: Clarendon, 1972), Vol. 2, pp. 791-820, esp. pp. 803-811.

resurrection of Christ, a purpose once hidden but now made known through the preaching of the gospel (1 Cor. 2:1; Eph. 1:9; 3:3-4, 9; Col. 1:26-27; 2:2). The connection of the eucharist with Christ may perhaps give some warrant for calling it a mystery, but in theological usage it has not kept the Pauline sense of a revealed secret. Nevertheless, the word "mystery" in its modern usage may still be a useful reminder of the limits of human knowledge. We do not fully understand how God works in blessing his servants, and we must not rationalize everything. The concept of mystery may preserve our sense of wonder and reverence before things divine. Still this is not such a central concept as to make this a more suitable word than the biblical terms for the eucharist. This terminology does call attention to what is beyond human experience and understanding in God's dealings with people.

Attitudes in Taking the Lord's Supper

The believer comes to the Lord's supper with the concepts developed above in mind. In addition, certain spiritual exercises are appropriate at this time.

(1) *Self-examination.* "Examine yourselves, and only then eat of the bread and drink of the cup" (1 Cor. 11:28). In their context, these words are probably related to mutual relations (see point 3 below) but may be given a wider application. Paul speaks of eating and drinking "in an unworthy *manner*" (1 Cor. 11:27). This is very different from being worthy of taking the supper. No one is worthy of God's grace; that's why it is grace. No one is worthy of what God has done in Christ, and likewise no one is worthy of the Lord's supper or any other spiritual activity. One comes to the table because of being spiritually needy. That realization assures a worthy manner of partaking, of receiving the continuing fellowship and blessing of the Lord.

(2) *Confession.* The self-examination will lead to a confession of sins. Thinking on the events of the passion of Jesus will bring vividly to mind why Jesus had to go to the cross. The reminder of the salvation accomplished through his death and resurrection will call forth confession.

(3) *Reconciliation.* The Lord's supper is a community act, not a private communion. Hence, one will make every effort to come to the communion in harmony with the brothers and sisters of the community. There will be loving thoughts and prayers for those with whom one is united in this shared experience.

(4) *Rededication.* The celebration of the covenant leads to a renewed dedication to the Lord. Loyalty to him excludes associations with all that is sinful (1 Cor. 10:21).

(5) *Joy.* Reliving the events of redemption and experiencing the anticipation of the end time brings eschatological joy. The "glad and generous hearts" of Acts 2:46 may not be limited to the breaking of bread in church but certainly includes it.

Special Problems connected with the Lord's Supper

Some problems in New Testament references about the Lord's supper, although important in their own right, are not so important for the doctrinal study of the church and so may be treated more cursorily here than required in other contexts; other problems have a significant bearing on the interpretation of the activity and its relation to the church.

(1) *The Last Supper and Passover.* The problem here is interpreting the chronological references in the Gospels. The Synoptic Gospels seem to say that the Last Supper was a Passover (Luke 22:7, 11-15 appears to be explicit; cf. Matt. 26:17-19; Mark 14:12-16), but the language of John seems to say that Jesus was crucified on the day before the evening when the Passover meal was eaten (John 18:28, 39; 19:14, 31). Other than accepting that there is a contradiction in the sources, three types of solutions have been proposed. (a) Accept the implied Synoptic chronology and reinterpret John so that "eating the Passover" refers to the whole week of unleavened bread and the day of Preparation refers to the day of Preparation (Friday) of Passover week, not of Passover itself.[66] (b) Accept the implied Johannine chronology and reinterpret the Synoptics so that Jesus' disciples made preparations for the Passover meal but the Last Supper was a night or two earlier and the events of the betrayal and arrest prevented it actually being observed (Jesus desired to eat it with the disciples — Luke 22:15-16 — but was not able to do so).[67] (c) Reconcile the discrepancy by saying Jesus and his disciples were following a different calendar from that followed by the temple authorities. The discovery of the calendar differences between

66. Barry D. Smith, "The Chronology of the Last Supper," *Westminster Theological Journal* 53 (1991): 29-45.

67. This view once enjoyed greater scholarly support than it seems to enjoy now — F. W. Farrar, *The Gospel According to St. Luke* (Cambridge: University Press, 1886), pp. 377-379; A. Plummer, *The Gospel According to S. John* (Cambridge: University Press, 1892), pp. 379-380.

the Qumran community and the Jerusalem priesthood has increased acceptance of this explanation.[68]

The Last Supper probably was the Passover meal for Jesus and his disciples.[69] Even if it was not a Passover, because of the season of the year Passover themes dominated the atmosphere. Hence, it is appropriate to interpret the Last Supper and the subsequent death of Jesus in terms of the Passover, that is, as a new covenant meal based on a new act of deliverance (cf. John 19:36; 1 Cor. 5:7).[70]

(2) *The correct text of Luke 22.* A small group of manuscripts representing the "Western" text omits verses 19b-20. Since the general tendency of this family of witnesses is to expansion of the text, the places where it is shorter than other manuscripts receive special consideration. The long text, however, has such strong textual support that most textual critics now accept it as original.[71] This longer text raises a question because it includes two sayings about a cup, one before and one after the bread. This may be a fuller account of the events, because at a Passover meal there were actually four times when the cup was served. The shorter text's omission of the second reference to a cup does not seem to be evidence that some churches observed a reversed order of cup first and then bread.

(3) *The breaking of bread.*[72] When Jesus took bread, gave thanks, and broke it (Matt. 26:26; Mark 14:22; Luke 22:19), he did what any Jew presiding at a meal would do to begin the meal (cf. the feeding miracles of Jesus — Matt. 14:19; 15:36; Mark 6:41; 8:6; Luke 9:16 — also Luke

68. A. Jaubert, *The Date of the Last Supper* (New York, 1965), suggests that Jesus and his disciples followed the Essene calendar instead of the temple calendar; I. Howard Marshall, *Last Supper and Lord's Supper* (Grand Rapids: Eerdmans, 1980), pp. 71-75, explains the difference as between the Pharisees (Synoptics) and Sadducees (John).

69. J. Jeremias, *The Eucharistic Words of Jesus* (New York: Scribner's, 1966), pp. 15-88, gives a strong argument that the Last Supper was a Passover meal, but Xavier Léon-Dufour, *Sharing the Eucharistic Bread: The Witness of the New Testament* (New York: Paulist, 1987), pp. 306-308, finds none of his arguments probative.

70. Joseph M. Stallings, *Rediscovering Passover: A Complete Guide for Christians* (San Jose: Resource Publications, 1989).

71. J. Jeremias, *The Eucharistic Words of Jesus* (New York: Scribner's, 1966), 139-159, has given a thorough study, concluding that the longer text of Luke 22 is original (but I do not agree with his explanation that the shorter text arose from an effort to protect the eucharist from profanation — p. 158).

72. C. F. D. Moule, *Worship in the New Testament* (Richmond: John Knox, 1961), pp. 18-28; Xavier Léon-Dufour, *Sharing the Eucharistic Bread: The Witness of the New Testament* (New York: Paulist, 1987), pp. 21-45.

24:30; Acts 27:35). Jesus did not do something different. He did familiar actions but endowed them with a new meaning. He made the common gesture into a parabolic action. What was new was identifying the bread with his body and the cup with the new covenant in his blood. The breaking of bread continued to be a term for beginning a meal (it did not mean "to take a meal"), as in ordinary Jewish meals (Acts 2:46; 20:11; 27:35), so each reference in the New Testament must be examined to determine if a eucharistic reference is intended.[73] In the second century, the breaking of bread assumed technical significance among Christians, and of course for the early disciples after the Last Supper the familiar table blessings could never be without a reminder of the Lord.

(4) *The prayer of thanksgiving or blessing.* The words of blessing gave special significance to the bread and fruit of the vine. Sharing in the bread and wine was a sharing in the blessing pronounced over them.

The words for thanksgiving *(eucharistia)* and blessing *(eulogia)* are used interchangeably in reference to the prayer accompanying the breaking of bread and offering of the cup: "Blessing" over the bread and "thanksgiving" over the cup in Matthew 26:26-27 and Mark 14:22-23; "thanksgiving" over the bread and no separate verb specified for the cup in Luke 22:19 and 1 Corinthians 11:24 (but note the "cup of blessing" in 1 Cor. 10:16). The typical structure of Jewish prayer begins, "Blessed art Thou, O Lord, Our God, . . . who. . . ." The word "blessing" (to speak well of) is characteristic of Jewish prayer. In Judaism one blesses God for his qualities and his deeds.[74] This is the same as "to give thanks" to God for his favors and gifts, and although *eucharistia* has no equivalent in the Hebrew Bible, the thanksgiving formula was current in Judaism in New Testament times, especially at Qumran.[75] Both words continued in Christian use, but "to give thanks" became the characteristic Christian word for prayer at the Lord's supper (hence called eucharist). The New Testament represents a combination of the two prayer formulas. The same interchange, in a passage showing they are used synonymously, occurs in 1 Corinthians 14:16-17.

In Jesus' words "This is my body" (Matt. 26:26; Mark 14:22; Luke 22:19; 1 Cor. 11:24) and "This is my blood" (Matt. 26:28; Mark 14:24),

73. That "to break bread" of itself meant an ordinary meal for Luke would seem to be contradicted by his usage of "to eat bread" (Luke 14:1, 15) for this meaning.

74. On *berakh* see C. F. D. Moule, *Worship in the New Testament* (Richmond: John Knox, 1961), p. 41.

75. J. M. Robinson, "Die Hodajot-Formel in Gebet und Hymnus des Früh-christentums," *Apophoreta* (Berlin: Töpelmann, 1964).

according to Jewish usage, the body refers to his person (the Aramaic word for body also meant "self" or "ego"; in the Old Testament cf. such passages as Pss. 16:9; 63:1 for the whole body), and the blood to his soul or life (Lev. 17:11; "blood" at the Last Supper stands for "soul" in Isa. 53:12).[76] These words have been a storm center of controversy. What did Jesus mean? Is there a change in the substance of the elements? Does "is" mean "represents"? In the continuing celebration of the eucharist by Jesus' disciples, what does the prayer of consecration do? An approach to these problems is afforded by the Jewish understanding of prayer in relation to ordinary food.[77] Against those who "forbid marriage and demand abstinence from foods," 1 Timothy 4:4-5 states: "For everything created by God is good, and nothing is to be rejected, provided it is received with thanksgiving; for it is sanctified by God's word and by prayer." The word of God has declared marriage good and the food of the earth good (Gen. 1:28-31; 2:16-17; 9:3-4). Prayer sanctifies, or sets aside, these good things for a particular use. Prayer sanctifies marital relations, and thanksgiving for food sanctifies it for use in nourishment of the body. In a similar way, Jesus' words at the Last Supper declared a different significance for the bread and wine, and the prayer over the bread and cup in the church set these apart for a different purpose. The bread and fruit of the vine, although the same as might be eaten at table for nourishment or refreshment at other times, are no longer ordinary bread and juice of the grape. Their significance is different. They stand for the body and blood of Jesus. There is now a change in relation, not of the material or substance itself. Another illustration is provided by meats offered in sacrifice to idols, discussed in 1 Corinthians 8 and 10. Although idols are nothing (1 Cor. 8:4) and so food offered to an idol is really no different, for those accustomed to idol worship it is different (1 Cor. 8:7). Hence, a Christian cannot participate in idolatrous feasts (1 Cor. 10:19-21; cf. 2 Cor. 6:16), but meat once sacrificed now sold in the public market or served in a private meal at a friend's house may be eaten, provided it is not made a religious test (1 Cor. 10:25-30). It may be the same meat. The difference is in the circumstances and purposes of the eating: an act of idolatrous worship or an ordinary meal for the nourishment of the body. The same principle applies to the elements of

76. Xavier Léon-Dufour, *Sharing the Eucharistic Bread: The Witness of the New Testament* (New York: Paulist, 1987), pp. 119, 142.

77. C. F. D. Moule, *Worship in the New Testament* (Richmond: John Knox, 1961), pp. 26-27, 41-43.

the Lord's supper. What is the intention? Is one eating bread and drinking fruit of the vine, or is one making a memorial of the death of Jesus Christ? The change in the purpose and relation of the elements is effected by the prayer, which expresses the intention in the use of the elements.[78]

(5) *The setting of a common meal.* The "Lord's supper" was instituted at a meal. Jesus gave special significance to ceremonies associated with the beginning and ending of the meal: breaking bread and blessing a cup.[79] Note the specification "after supper" (Luke 22:20; 1 Cor. 11:25). At least since Paul's correction of the abuses at Corinth (1 Cor. 11:17-34), the memorial of the death of Jesus has been separated spatially and temporally from the ordinary meal in Christian usage. From the beginning of the church, indeed, the words and actions associated with the bread and cup had a special meaning distinct from the meal. This situation is reflected in Matthew and Mark, where there is no interest in the meal except for what pertained to continuing church practice. They narrate only the parts of the last supper significant for Christian practice (e.g., the singing of a hymn) and thus show the taking of the bread and wine as a distinct act.

The meal itself had a separate development in Christian history as the love-feast (or agape — Jude 12). The love-feast developed in early Christian history as a meal for fellowship and charity for the poor.[80] Eating together in a church context has continued in Christian history to have religious significance through various expressions.

Prayer[81]

Prayer is a constant element in the individual Christian's religious life (Rom. 12:12; 1 Thess. 5:17), but the concern in this section, in keeping

---

78. Cf. C. F. D. Moule, *Worship in the New Testament* (Richmond: John Knox, 1961), pp. 35-37.

79. At the Passover it is not absolutely clear which of the last three servings of the cup was the "cup of blessing," probably the third, taken after the eating of the lamb.

80. For the earliest texts describing the love feast, see Everett Ferguson, *Early Christians Speak*, 3rd ed. (Abilene: ACU, 1999), pp. 129-136.

81. A. Hamman, *La Prière*, Vol. I, *Le Nouveau Testament* (Tournai: Desclée, 1959); George Buttrick, *Prayer* (New York: Abingdon, 1942); Fred L. Fisher, *Prayer in the New Testament* (Philadelphia: Westminster, 1964); A. L. Ash, *Prayer* (Austin: Sweet, 1967); D. Coggan, *Prayers of the New Testament* (London: Hodder and Stoughton, 1974); Patrick D. Miller, *They Cried Unto the Lord: The Form and Theology of Biblical Prayer* (Minneapolis: Fortress, 1994); Oscar Cullmann, *Prayer in the New Testament* (London: SCM, 1995).

with the subject of the church, is corporate prayer. (The contrast between congregational and individual prayer is evident in Paul's words about speaking in tongues — 1 Cor. 14:2, 16, 28.) Similarly, no effort is made at a complete theology of prayer; only some aspects that seem particularly appropriate for the overall thrust of this book are included.

The New Testament offers several indications of prayer in a congregational setting (e.g., Acts 4:23-31; 12:12; 1 Cor. 14:14-15, which is discussing the assembly; so also 1 Tim. 2:1-2). Many features of private prayer and congregational prayer are the same, but the group setting gives a distinctive color to the prayers. The leader of the prayer is not speaking his private prayers in a public setting, and the people are not overhearing someone else's prayers. The leader is speaking for the people to God; as their representative he is voicing their corporate concerns. The people themselves are praying while their spokesman is leading their thoughts and giving expression to their praise and petitions. To speak on behalf of the people to God is a solemn responsibility requiring careful thought and preparation.

Under the general heading of prayer are included specialized forms of address to God: doxologies (words of praise), confessions of faith, and acclamations. Examples of doxologies in the New Testament include 1 Timothy 1:17; 6:16; 1 Peter 4:11; Revelation 5:13.[82] Paul often used words of praise to punctuate his doctrinal discussions (Rom. 1:25; 9:5) or to conclude them (Rom 11:36; Eph. 3:20f.). Doxologies often conclude the main contents of New Testament letters (Phil. 4:20; 2 Tim. 4:18; Heb. 13:21; 1 Pet. 5:11) or the letters themselves (Rom. 16:25-27; 2 Pet. 3:18; Jude 24-25). All these expressions of praise probably reflect the actual language included in prayers or independent exclamations in church.

Confessions of faith may have had a place in the regular services of the church, as well as in connection with baptism and the Lord's supper.[83] The Old Testament confession that "God is one" (cf. Deut.

---

82. G. Delling, *Worship in the New Testament* (London: Darton, Longman and Todd, 1962), pp. 61-69, distinguishes "doxology" ("to him be the glory . . .") and eulogy ("praised [blessed] is . . .").

83. G. Delling, *Worship in the New Testament* (London: Darton, Longman and Todd, 1962), pp. 77-82; Ralph Martin, *Worship in the Early Church* (Grand Rapids: Eerdmans, 1964), pp. 53-65; O. Cullmann, *The Earliest Christian Confessions* (London: Lutterworth, 1949); V. H. Neufeld, *The Earliest Christian Confessions* (Leiden: E. J. Brill, 1963); J. N. D. Kelly, *Early Christian Creeds*, 2nd ed. (London: Longmans, 1960), pp. 6-29.

6:4) is repeated in the New Testament (Rom. 3:30: 1 Cor. 8:4; Gal. 3:20; 1 Tim. 2:5). References to confession of Jesus are numerous (e.g., 1 Cor. 12:3; Phil. 2:11; 1 John 2:22; 4:15). Fuller statements are also found (1 Cor. 15:3-5; Rom. 1:3-4; 8:34; 2 Tim. 2:8). Other confessional statements combine faith in God and Christ (1 Cor. 8:6; Rom. 4:24; 1 Tim. 2:5f.; 1 Pet. 1:21). The combination of God and Christ is especially notable in the greetings of New Testament letters (1 Cor. 1:3; Gal. 1:3; Eph. 1:2; Phil. 1:2; 2 Thess. 1:2; 1 Tim. 1:2; 2 Pet. 1:2; 2 John 1, 3). Trinitarian statements (see p. 229) are less often explicitly confessional (but see 1 Cor. 6:11; 2 Cor. 13:13; 1 Pet. 1:2; Heb. 10:29). Hymnic passages in the New Testament take the form of confessions of faith in Christ (see on Singing pp. 269-270).

Acclamations were often Hebrew or Aramaic words and phrases borrowed in Greek: *Hallelujah* ("Praise the Lord" — Rev. 19:1-6), *Hosanna* ("Save now" — Matt. 21:9, 15; Mark 11:9-10; John 12:13); *Maranatha* ("Our Lord, come" — 1 Cor. 16:22); and *Amen* ("May it be so"). The last has become so much a part of prayer language even today as to deserve special treatment.

The corporate nature of prayer is brought out by the word "Amen."[84] This Hebrew word, very frequent in the Old Testament, was an affirmation of truth and came to be a term of ratification used especially in prayer. Amen was the congregational unison acclamation at the close of a prayer in the Jewish synagogues and in the early church (cf. "Amen" as a response in Rev. 5:14). Paul refers to the practice in 1 Corinthians 14:16 (cf. also 2 Cor. 1:20), where his argument is that the assembled people cannot respond with "Amen" (and the implied "It is true") if they do not understand what has been spoken in the prayer. This practice of the congregational "Amen" at the close of the prayer shows the words spoken by one person to be a corporate act, the expression of the whole people.

The Distinctiveness of Christian Prayer

Christian prayer has much continuity with its Old Testament and Jewish antecedents. The distinctiveness of Christian prayer is that it is

---

84. C. F. D. Moule, *Worship in the New Testament* (Richmond: John Knox, 1961), pp. 72-75; G. Delling, *Worship in the New Testament* (London: Darton, Longman and Todd, 1962), pp. 71-74.

done with reference to Jesus Christ.[85] The Gospel of John connects prayer with the name of Jesus (John 14:13-14; 15:16; 16:24, 26). To pray "in his name" is to pray with respect to him, according to his nature and teachings, indeed as an act of worship to him — invoking his name. "In the name of Christ" is not a formula to be repeated but describes the nature of Christian prayer: to ask while mentioning his name. Prayer "in the name of Christ" presupposes faithfulness to his mission and submission to his will.

The Christian comes to God on the basis of the relationship established by Jesus Christ and through his mediation (1 Tim. 2:5, a statement applicable to everything done in the assembly).

Christian prayer is rooted in the example and teaching of Jesus. Especially does the Gospel of Luke call attention to the prayer life of Jesus: he prayed at his baptism (Luke 3:21); before the choosing of the Twelve (Luke 6:12); before the confession of his messiahship (Luke 9:18); at the transfiguration (Luke 9:29); in the garden (Luke 22:39-46); on the cross (Luke 23:34, 46). These and other times of prayer (Luke 4:42-43; 5:16; 22:31-32) were part of a pattern that prompted his disciples to ask him to teach them how to pray, resulting in the giving of the model prayer (Luke 11:1-2). Moreover, Jesus taught many parables about prayer (Luke 11:5-13; 18:1-14).

As incorporated into Christ and sharing his Sonship (Gal. 3:26), Christians may address God in the same way Jesus did, as Father (*Abba* — Mark 14:36).[86] The preservation of the Aramaic word *Abba*, the family word for father, in the prayer language of the early church (Rom. 8:15; Gal. 4:6) shows the importance of this concept for the early disciples. Important expressions are not translated when a religion goes from one language to another, but the word in the original language is taken over in the new language. This is especially so in regard to worship (cf. the acclamations above and the borrowing of the Greek word *baptisma* in other languages). The same intimate and open approach to God enjoyed by Jesus characterizes the approach of his disciples to God. Jesus himself taught his disciples to address God in this way (Luke 11:2). The community dimension of this relationship is present in Matthew's wording, "Our Father" (Matt. 6:9).

---

85. G. Delling, *Worship in the New Testament* (London: Darton, Longman and Todd, 1962), pp. 116-120.

86. "Father" without the Aramaic word in Jesus' prayers — Matt. 11:25-26; John 11:41; 12:27; 17:1.

The one time in the Gospels that Jesus' address to God as *Abba* is preserved (Mark 14:36) is in his struggle in the Garden when he resolves, "Not what I will, but what you will." The intimacy of prayer to God as Father does not obscure God's sovereignty over human life. To call him Father does not mean easy familiarity. The goal of prayer to God as Father, as it was for Jesus, is submission to the will of God. Prayer is not a way of getting human will done in heaven, but of getting God's will done on earth (Matt. 6:10).

Both Romans 8:15 and Galatians 4:6 connect the address to God as *"Abba,* Father" with possession of the Spirit. The Holy Spirit makes possible the same approach to God as Father that Jesus had. Jesus' eschatological gift of the Holy Spirit to his people brings about this closeness to God and open access to his presence. The Holy Spirit aids the prayers of Christians, making intercession according to the will of God (Rom. 8:26-27).

Christians may approach the throne of grace with boldness (Heb. 4:16). A royal throne is normally associated with majesty. In Christ the Christian knows the throne of God the King as a seat of graciousness. This is true because Jesus Christ, the Son of God, is the high priest over the house of God (temple and people — Heb. 4:14-15; 10:21). Christian prayer is an expression of confidence in the relationship with God because of Christ and the gift of the Spirit.

Prayer in the New Testament Church

Luke continues the interest in prayer shown in his Gospel by noting the occasions of prayer in the early church: in the regular meetings of the disciples (Acts 1:14; 2:42; perhaps 6:4); when choosing and appointing leaders (Acts 1:24; 6:6; 13:3; 14:23); during times of persecution (Acts 4:24-31; 12:5, 12; 16:25); in receiving new converts (Acts 8:15); when seeking forgiveness of postbaptismal sin (Acts 8:22-24); by those who sought salvation (Acts 9:11; 10:4, 30-31) and who were instruments of bringing the message (Acts 10:9); in obtaining healing (Acts 9:40; 28:8); and at times of farewell (Acts 20:36; 21:5).

The richest source of information about prayer in the New Testament is the letters of Paul, which contain many prayers. Whether Paul's epistles, especially his prayers, reflect liturgical elements, the contents of the prayers indicate his doctrinal concerns for the churches. Without being exhaustive, we note that Paul gives thanks to God for his grace (1 Cor. 1:4; cf. 2 Cor. 4:15), consolations (2 Cor. 1:3-5), and indescribable gift (2 Cor. 9:15); for deliverance from death (Rom. 7:25); for food (1 Cor. 10:30); for all things (Eph. 5:20; cf. 1 Thess. 5:18). He gives thanks for his churches — for their faith (Rom. 1:8); their faith, love, and hope (Col. 1:4-5, 12; 1 Thess. 1:2-3; 2 Thess. 1:3; Philem. 4); their reception of the gospel (1 Thess. 2:13; 2 Thess. 2:13); their participation in the sharing of the gospel (Phil. 1:3-5); and their generosity in giving (2 Cor. 9:11-12). Paul prayed that his churches might have joy and peace (Rom. 15:13; 2 Thess. 3:16), that their love might increase (Phil. 1:9; 1 Thess. 3:12), that they might be filled with spiritual understanding (Eph. 1:17; Col. 1:9) and spiritual strength (Eph. 3:16; 2 Thess. 2:17), that they might be sanctified (1 Thess. 5:23), and that God would direct their hearts to love and steadfastness (2 Thess. 3:5). Paul's missionary work was a special concern of prayer (Rom. 10:1; Col. 4:3; 2 Thess. 3:1).

The references to fasting by disciples are most often in connection with prayer (Matt. 6:5-18; Luke 2:37; Acts 13:3; 14:23). Fasting was an accompaniment to prayer (cf. the addition of "fasting" in some manuscripts at Mark 9:29 and 1 Cor. 7:5; and the substitution of fasting for praying in some manuscripts of Acts 10:30) and served to intensify prayer. It appears to have been normally a voluntary act by individuals rather than a congregational act,[87] allowed in the period between the comings of Jesus rather than commanded (Matt. 9:14-15).

References to the posture in prayer tend to be rather incidental, indicating that other aspects of prayer were more important than the physical position. Postures referred to include standing (Mark 11:25; Luke 22:46; John 11:41; 17:1; 1 Tim. 2:8), kneeling (Luke 22:41; Acts 7:60; 9:40; 20:36; 21:5; Eph. 3:14), and prostration (Rev. 5:14; 7:11; 11:16; 19:4).[88]

Parts of Prayer

The components of prayer may be expressed in various ways. The following outline adopts a popular acronym on the word ACTS.[89] These parts of prayer roughly correspond, although not in the same order, to

87. Gerhard Delling, *Worship in the New Testament* (London: Darton, Longman, and Todd, 1962), pp. 109-110, perhaps claims too much that fasting was not a congregational activity (Acts 13:2-3; 14:23 may involve more than the leaders).

88. Gerhard Delling, *Worship in the New Testament* (London: Darton, Longman and Todd, 1962), pp. 104-107.

89. Ralph P. Martin, *The Worship of God* (Grand Rapids: Eerdmans, 1982), pp. 36-37 makes the same classification, except he uses intercession instead of supplication.

the elements in Jesus' model prayer for his disciples (the Lord's prayer — Matt. 6:9-13;[90] cf. also 1 Tim. 2:1 on types of prayers). Every prayer would not have to include all these elements. Some prayers might well concentrate on one element. Keeping the various types of prayer in mind will preserve a sense of balance in the contents of typical congregational prayer.

(1) Adoration. Prayer is an expression of praise. The opening three petitions of the model prayer may be understood as expressions of praise and adoration to God, the heavenly Father. In the language of the Psalter, praise of God is both descriptive (God is) and narrative (God does). Similarly in Christian prayer, God may be praised for who he is (2 Cor. 1:3) and for what he has done (Acts 4:24-26; Eph. 1:3ff.).

(2) Confession. Confession includes a double usage: confession of faith and confession of sin. They are related. The confession of who God is and of faith in him makes one aware of difference from God and so of sinfulness. Likewise, the confession of sin opens the way to forgiveness and greater faith. The model prayer begins with a confession of who God is and concludes with petitions for forgiveness and deliverance from the power of the evil one.

(3) Thanksgiving. Thanksgiving is a specification and personalizing of praise. In this particular form, this element is lacking from the model prayer. Thanksgiving, on the other hand, is a characteristic of Paul's prayers (see below and cf. Phil. 4:6; Col. 2:7; 4:2; 1 Tim. 2:1). Part of the formula with which he opens his letters is a thanksgiving period in which he establishes his ties with the recipients and anticipates the concerns of the body of the letter to follow.[91] Paul, the apostle to the Gentiles, may have been an important figure in making the phraseology "I give thanks to God" the characteristic statement in Christian prayer, rather than the form "Blessed be the God who . . ." (see the discussion of "thanksgiving" and "blessing" under the Lord's supper, p. 259).

(4) Supplication. This refers to the petitions made to God. We thank him for his gifts and make our requests known to him (Phil. 4:6). The petitions of the model prayer concentrate on spiritual concerns and

90. G. Delling, *Worship in the New Testament* (London: Darton, Longman and Todd, 1962), pp. 120-122, interprets the Lord's prayer as a congregational prayer. "Our Father" stresses the communal nature of the prayer in Matthew 6:9.

91. Paul Schubert, *Form and Function of the Pauline Thanksgivings* (Berlin, 1939); Peter T. O'Brien, *Introductory Thanksgivings in the Letters of Paul* (Leiden: E. J. Brill, 1977).

needs: the kingdom and will of God, deliverance from temptation and sin. The model prayer, however, does not neglect physical needs — the basic necessity of "daily food." Included in supplications will be petitions for the welfare of others, intercessions (1 Tim. 2:1).[92] This dimension especially keeps to the forefront the community dimension of prayer.

Singing[93]

Singing was closely related to prayer in ancient times (cf. 1 Cor. 14:15; James 5:13) and so belongs to the daily religious life as well as to the assembly. The same elements of prayer noted above are applicable to singing. The distinctiveness of Christian song is that it, like prayer, is done "in the name of our Lord Jesus Christ" (Eph. 5:19; cf. Col. 3:16-17), that is, with reference to him and in worship of him. Although Ephesians 5:19 and Colossians 3:16, which provide rich sources for the discussion of early Christian singing, have as their literary context the Christian life in a larger sense, the statements are drawn from practices in church.[94] The practice of the assembly is to influence the entire Christian life. Other texts make clear the presence of song as a congregational activity (Matt. 26:30; 1 Cor. 14:15, 26).

92. G. P. Wiles, *Paul's Intercessory Prayers* (London: Cambridge University Press, 1974).

93. Lucien Deiss, *Hymnes et prières des premiers siècles* (Paris: Fleurus, 1963), Part I; Gottfried Schille, *Frühchristliche Hymnen* (Berlin, 1965); Reinhard Deichgräber, *Gotteshymnus und Christushymnus in der frühen Christenheit: Untersuchungen zu Form, Sprache, und Stil der frühchristlichen Hymnen* (Göttingen, 1967); G. Delling, *Worship in the New Testament* (London: Darton, Longman and Todd, 1962), pp. 82-91; G. Delling, "Hymnos et al.," *Theological Dictionary of the New Testament*, Vol. 8 (Grand Rapids: Eerdmans, 1972), pp. 489-503; Martin Hengel, "Hymns and Christology," *Between Jesus and Paul* (Philadelphia: Fortress, 1983), pp. 78-96.

94. As in 1 Cor. 14, the assembly is the literary setting but something from outside the assembly is used to reinforce the teaching (vv. 7-11), so in Eph. 5 and Col. 3, although the literary setting is the Christian life, something from the assembly (singing) is used to reinforce the point. I have hereby consciously made a minimal claim for these verses. Many commentaries see evidence from the context that these texts refer to the assembly; e.g., Eduard Lohse, *Colossians and Philemon* (Philadelphia: Fortress, 1971), pp. 149-153; Rudolf Schnackenburg, *Ephesians: A Commentary* (Edinburgh: T. & T. Clark, 1991), pp. 237-238.

A Note on Terminology

Ephesians 5:19 and Colossians 3:16 refer to "psalms, hymns, and spiritual songs." Since these words have different etymological backgrounds — Psalms of the Old Testament, formal praise, and general song — efforts have been made to identify different types of songs from these words. These efforts, however, are misguided. Usage in the Septuagint and other Greek Jewish writings near New Testament times show that the terms were used interchangeably.[95] No precise distinctions can be made between the words. The combination had its precedent in these contemporary sources, and the full manner of expression was intended to give comprehensiveness to the statement.

A Theology of Singing [96]

The biblical passages about singing offer a rich doctrinal content to this activity.

(1) Song is a way of *preaching* Christ. Christ is both the ground and the content of Christian song. Christians sing about Christ. If they sing about God, it is especially what God has done through Christ; if about the Holy Spirit, it is the Holy Spirit as the gift of Christ; if about instruction to one another, it is the life in Christ. The early Christian hymns that have been identified in the New Testament (e.g., Phil. 2:6-11; 1 Tim. 3:16) have Christ as their content.[97] The characteristic feature of the earliest Christian hymns is that they were songs of praise to Christ. He is the standard for the content of songs in the assembly that meets in his name.

(2) Song is a *confession of faith* made by the lips. Hebrews 13:15

95. H. Schlier, *"Ado,"* and G. Delling, *"Hymnos et al.,"* Theological Dictionary of the New Testament (Grand Rapids: Eerdmans, 1964 and 1972), Vol. 1, p. 164 and Vol. 8, p. 499; A. A. R. Bastiaesen, *"Psalmi, hymni,* and *cantica* in Early Jewish-Christian Tradition," *Studia Patristica* 21 (1989): 15-26.

96. Oskar Söhngen, "Theologische Grundlagen der Kirchenmusik," *Leiturgia* IV (Kassel, 1961), pp. 2-15.

97. A. M. Hunter, *Paul and his Predecessors* (Philadelphia: Westminster, 1961), chap. 4; Jack T. Sanders, *The New Testament Christological Hymns; Their Historical Religious Background* (Cambridge: Cambridge University Press, 1971); Ralph P. Martin, *Carmen Christi: Philippians ii.5-11 in Recent Interpretation and in the Setting of Early Christian Worship* (Cambridge: Cambridge University Press, 1967); Martin Hengel, "Hymns and Christology," *Between Jesus and Paul* (Philadelphia: Fortress, 1983), pp. 78-96.

employs a word *(homologeō)* that can be translated "confess," "acknowl-edge," or "praise," and that is often brought into connection with the word "sing" in the Psalms (e.g., Ps. 18:49, quoted in Rom. 15:9; 138:1). Singing is a way of acknowledging God — praising him and confessing faith in him. This is done by praising and expressing gratitude. Song is to be with thankfulness (Eph. 5:19-20; Col. 3:16). Thanksgiving ac-knowledges God as the source of blessings.

(3) Song expresses the *indwelling Spirit* and *word of Christ*. The preceding points about the spiritual nature of Christian song and the confession of faith that is made "through him" (Christ) leads to this description. Ephesians 5:18-19 associates singing with being filled with the Spirit; Colossians 3:16 parallels singing with the teaching and ad-monishing that express the indwelling word of Christ. Singing is the result of being filled with the Holy Spirit and of possessing the word of Christ. The Spirit and the word belong together, and vocal praise is a consequence of their presence. The singing, therefore, will be spiritual in nature and will accord with the word of Christ. The knowledge of salvation in Christ, the acceptance of God's grace, and the receiving of the Holy Spirit as the firstfruits of redemption — these lead to song.

(4) Song as praise is a *spiritual sacrifice* (Heb. 13:15). The Old Testa-ment had presented thanksgiving as accompanying sacrifice (Ps. 26:6), the equivalent of sacrifice (Jon. 2:9; Ps. 141:2), and a substitute for sacrifice (Ps. 50:14, 23). The New Testament connects singing with the Spirit (1 Cor. 14:15) and speaks of "spiritual songs" (Eph. 5:19; Col. 3:16). The singing of the church is a spiritual activity. It is one of the offerings that replaces for Christians the sacrifices of the Mosaic law; it is a sacrifice which is *continually* available.

(5) In song there is sharing in *heavenly, eschatological* praise. The heavenly beings are constantly singing praise to God — Revelation 4:8, 10-11; 5:8-12; 14:2-3; 15:2-3.[98] The church by its song joins this heavenly chorus. The barriers between earth and heaven, time and eternity, are temporarily lowered. Christian song is a heavenly activity, an anticipa-tion of the activities of the end time.

(6) Song is for *mutual edification*. The singing in the assembly is not only directed to God in praise but also is directed to one another

---

98. The hymns in Revelation, however, are not actual congregational hymns: "Though containing many traditional elements, they are not derived from early Christian liturgy but are literary creations of the author" — David Aune, *The New Testament in its Literary Environment* (Philadelphia: Westminster, 1987), p. 243.

for teaching and admonition. Ephesians 5:19, in addition to "singing and making melody to the Lord," refers to "speaking to one another" ("singing among yourselves" — NRSV). 1 Corinthians 14:26 enjoins that the psalms in the assembly, as everything else there, is to be for communal edification. Since edification requires understanding of what is said (1 Cor. 14:9, 16-17, 19), melody is secondary to the words (cf. 1 Cor. 14:15 for singing "with the mind"). The melody must support and deepen the message and not obscure it. Teaching occurs through song (cf. Col. 3:16, where "teaching and admonishing" may be distinct from the "singing," but are closely parallel to it).[99] This purpose of edification provides another criterion to which songs in the assembly are to conform. The praise, confession, and proclamation through song contribute to community edification.

(7) Song exemplifies the *unity of the church*. "So that together you may with one voice glorify the God and Father of our Lord Jesus Christ" (Rom. 15:6). Singing together symbolizes and expresses the unity of the church. The harmony in which all participate is a beautiful and specific way of showing that the members of the one body are united to the Lord and to one another. Singing not only expresses unity but also helps to effect unity. It has a unifying function in giving a sense of common identity and creating solidarity. The corporate or body life of the church finds expression in the blending of voices in song.

(8) Song involves the *whole person*. The passages already cited emphasize wholeness: spirit and mind (1 Cor. 14:15); words with the heart (Eph. 5:19; Col. 3:16) and the lips (Heb. 13:15). There is an Old Testament background for linking the lips and the soul in passages like Psalm 71:23. Singing engages the mind, heart, and the organs of speech; the intellect, the emotions, and the physical self are involved. The tongue is the instrument on which God is praised, and this is done from the heart, and intelligibly.

(9) Song expresses *deep religious emotion*. "Are any cheerful? They should sing songs of praise" (James 5:13). The musical aspects add to the emotional impact of what is expressed in song, and this is so for

---

99. The "psalms, hymns, and spiritual songs" may be construed with the "singing," making the "teaching and admonishing" a separate expression of the indwelling word of Christ (so the NRSV); or "the psalms, hymns, and spiritual songs" may be construed with the "teaching and admonishing," thus taking the "singing with grace in your hearts" as a supplementary description. The parallel in Eph. 5:19 favors the latter interpretation, and it is argued for by Martin Hengel, *Between Jesus and Paul* (Philadelphia: Fortress, 1983), p. 79.

corporate as well as individual singing. Nevertheless, singing in church is not for the sake of the beauty of the music. The quality of the music is to enhance all the doctrinal elements mentioned, not to call attention to itself.

Instrumental Music [100]

Musical instruments occur in the New Testament as part of everyday life (Matt. 9:23; 11:17; Rev. 18:22) and as illustrations (1 Cor. 13:1; 14:7-8),[101] but they are never mentioned as part of the assemblies of the church or accompanying Christian religious music. Their only appearance in a worship context is in the book of Revelation, where, drawing on the imagery of the temple, the voices of the heavenly singers are compared to stringed instruments (Rev. 14:2-3); the instruments symbolize singing (cf. Rev. 15:2-3) in the same way that incense does prayer (Rev. 5:8-9). The testimony of early Christian literature is expressly to the absence of instruments from the church for approximately the first thousand years of Christian history.[102]

The doctrinal aspects of music listed above are applicable to vocal music. Although instrumental music could be seen as satisfying some of these doctrinal points, it does not meet the criteria of edifying, instructive, spiritual, and rational worship. The voice is much more a matter of the self than any other gift of praise, and it brings an understandable content to the participants.

The arguments advanced in support of instrumental music fail to carry the case:

(1) It was used in the Old Testament. There it was an accompaniment of the sacrificial cultus (e.g., 1 Chron. 23:5; 2 Chron. 29:20-36), the abolition of which would have eliminated its accompaniments. The presence of something in Old Testament worship would legitimate many things in the church that no Christian group would want to practice.

---

100. Everett Ferguson, *A Cappella Music in the Public Worship of the Church* (Abilene: ACU Press, 1988); Jimmy Jividen, *Worship in Song* (Fort Worth: Star: 1987); Jack P. Lewis, "New Testament Authority for Music in Worship," *The Instrumental Music Issue* (Nashville: Gospel Advocate, 1987), pp. 14-59; Rubel Shelly, *Sing His Praise: A Case for A Cappella Music as Worship Today* (Nashville: 20th Century Christian, 1987).

101. W. S. Smith, *Musical Aspects of the New Testament* (Amsterdam, 1962).

102. J. W. McKinnon, "The Church Fathers and Musical Instruments" (Dissertation, Columbia University, 1965).

(2) It is included in the words "psalm" and "make melody" (*psallō*). This is true of one stage in the history of the usage of these words but not of late Jewish and of Christian usage, where a vocal expression is all that can be affirmed (so clearly in 1 Cor. 14:15; James 5:13).[103] Actual word usage and context determine word meanings in given passages, not etymology. If an instrument were included in the meaning of the words, then it would seem that an instrument is required, but few are willing to go so far as to say that one must be used. As an alternative, "make melody" (*psallō*) in Ephesians 5:19 might be taken as a generic command covering any type of music, but this is untrue to actual Christian usage of the word in the early centuries.

(3) Its absence in the early church was a cultural matter, due to the associations of instrumental music with idolatry and immorality. The cultural explanation is an assertion lacking in proof. It is true that instruments were associated with idolatry and immorality, but this cannot be said of Jewish temple music. Moreover, these associations applied to vocal music as well, and singing was not rejected in the early church. Religious instrumental music was available to the early Christians if they had wanted to employ it.

(4) It is an aid to singing. It certainly may serve this use. However, this contention contradicts argument (1), for playing instruments was an act of worship in the Old Testament (Psalm 150 and many of the Psalms where praise or worship is done with an instrument). This argument not only makes the weakest case for the use of instruments, but the assertion also is often untrue, for in practice instruments (and the same is true for special choruses) frequently discourage or even replace congregational singing.

Giving[104]

The readiness to give is a constant feature of the individual Christian life (Rom. 12:13; James 2:14-17). Giving is also done corporately through

---

103. See my *A Cappella Music*, pp. 1-27, the lexica, and especially H. Schlier, "*Ado*," and G. Delling, "*Hymnos et al.*," *Theological Dictionary of the New Testament*, ed. G. Kittel and G. Friedrich (Grand Rapids: Eerdmans, 1964, 1972), Vol. 1, p. 164 and Vol. 8, p. 499.

104. Jouette M. Bassler, *God and Mammon: Asking for Money in the New Testament* (Nashville: Abingdon, 1991).

the church (Acts 4:34-35; 11:29-30). This activity finds specific expression in the Christian meeting. It has been argued above (p. 240) that 1 Corinthians 16:1-3 indicates the collection of a contribution at the weekly assembly. This passage is talking about church giving to meet church needs. Paul's instructions indicate that giving is to be periodic ("on the first day of every week"), personal ("each one of you"), planned ("whatever one may prosper"), preventive ("so that contributions need not be taken when I come"), and purposeful ("to take your gift to Jerusalem").

Giving in church, like the other activities already discussed, is related to Christ. Jesus provides the motive and the example for Christian giving. "For you know the grace of our Lord Jesus Christ, that though he was rich, yet for your sakes he became poor, so that by his poverty you might become rich" (2 Cor. 8:9). Giving to the church advances all aspects of the work of the church, to be discussed in the next chapter — evangelistic, educational, and eleemosynary.

Although many passages in the Bible speak about giving, the most extended discussion occurs in 2 Corinthians 8–9, where Paul urges the Corinthians to complete what they had promised to give for the relief of believers in Judea (Rom. 15:25-28; 1 Cor. 16:1-4; 2 Cor. 8:1-6, 10-11).[105] It is notable that Paul does not appeal to economic necessity, humanitarian feelings, or simply charitable motives, but describes giving as a spiritual activity related to fundamental Christian doctrines. We select for comment some of the terms that Paul uses in 2 Corinthians 8–9 to describe giving, three of which occur in 8:4 — grace, fellowship, and ministry.

(1) Giving is a *grace (charis)*. Christian giving is rooted in Christ's act of giving (2 Cor. 8:9). The doctrinal basis for all Christian giving is what Christ did. It is the nature of God to give (John 3:16), so to give is to share in a divine activity. The Macedonian Christians had responded in the same spirit of their Lord (2 Cor. 8:1-4). To give is a grace, a favor, a privilege — a manifestation of the grace of God. Paul now urges the Corinthian Christians to participate in this grace (2 Cor. 8:6). They, too, should abound in this grace of giving (2 Cor. 8:7). Paul was organizing the work of grace, and the churches were cooperating (2 Cor. 8:19), so God's grace was being shown through a human undertaking. What makes this work possible is God's giving (2 Cor. 9:8). Giving is a

---

105. For the larger context, see Keith Nickle, *The Collection: A Study in Paul's Strategy* (London: SCM, 1966); a more popular treatment of 2 Corinthians 8–9 in Ralph P. Martin, *The Worship of God* (Grand Rapids: Eerdmans, 1982), pp. 73-79.

sign that God's grace is present in one's life (2 Cor. 9:14). God's grace comes to his people so that they might show grace to others. This leads to grace, in the form of thanksgiving, being returned to God (2 Cor. 9:15; *charis* here means "thanks"). 2 Corinthians 9:15 catches up all the thoughts of chapters 8–9 in a grand climax. Giving begins in God, flows through people, and returns to God in thanksgiving.

(2) Giving is an act of *fellowship* (*koinōnia*, to have or take a part). Fellowship appears to have been Paul's favorite word for contributing (cf. Rom. 12:13; Phil. 4:15). He encourages the Corinthians by reference to the Macedonians' sharing (2 Cor. 8:4) and to the anticipated generosity of their own sharing with the saints in their need and with all others (2 Cor. 9:13; see p. 369). Monetary contributions to the work of the Lord is a sharing, a participation in that work. The historical context of 2 Corinthians 8–9 made the contribution of the Gentile churches for the Jewish believers an important expression of Christian unity. This fellowship aspect of giving calls attention to the church as the context of Christian giving (cf. Acts 2:42-45; 4:32).

(3) Giving is a ministry, a service (*diakonia*). The Macedonians' giving was a sharing in a ministry (2 Cor. 8:4). Giving is service performed for the saints (2 Cor. 9:1). The relief of the saints not only satisfied their physical needs but also was a spiritual service (2 Cor. 9:12). Paul saw the contribution from the Gentile churches for the Jewish Christians as uniting Jew and Gentile in Christ, so he describes it in the highest spiritual terms. It would lead the Jews to give thanks to God and help them appreciate their Gentile brothers. This ministry of financial giving is a way of glorifying God (2 Cor. 9:13) by those who give, and it causes others to glorify him (cf. Matt. 5:16). All Christians have a ministry, and giving is a way of serving others. Paul's language sanctifies all proper use of money as service to God.

(4) Giving is a priestly service (*leitourgia*). Paul combines the most general word for "service" (*diakonia*) and the noblest in 2 Corinthians 9:12, "the service of this priestly ministry." *Leitourgia,* as discussed on pages 208-209, was a word for priestly service and sacrificial worship in the Old Testament. The New Testament does not have animal sacrifice and a sacrificing priesthood but applies the word to other activities. Paul uses it in the same context both for his preaching (Rom. 15:16) and for giving (Rom. 15:27, also discussing the contribution for the Judean Christians: "if the Gentiles had fellowship in the Jews' spiritual blessings, they ought in material things to render priestly service to the Jews").

(5) Giving is a *blessing (eulogia)*. The promised contribution was a "gift," a "bounty," a "blessing" (2 Cor. 9:5). Paul expected it as a "willing gift," not as an exaction or something coveted. It was something deliberately done for the good of another, for "God loves a cheerful giver" (2 Cor. 9:7). Giving is a benefit conferred on another. "He who sows blessings will reap blessings" (a literal rendering of 2 Cor. 9:6). Giving is done by those who have been blessed by God (2 Cor. 9:9-10). One can never outgive God. The word "blessing" refers to speaking well, and we usually associate blessing with words; but it includes acts. Giving is bestowing a blessing, and deeds speak louder than words (cf. James 2:15f.).

(6) Giving is a *test* or *proof (dokimē)*. The giving by the Macedonian Christians passed the test (2 Cor. 8:2). The test was now applied to the Corinthian Christians (2 Cor. 9:13). Their giving was a proof of obedience, and a means of confessing the gospel of Christ. Since the gospel is the story of giving, indeed is a giving, a person's giving is a proof of the response to it.

These points show the high spiritual level Paul assigned to giving. He sought to motivate by appealing to the fundamental principle of Christian faith. Giving is related to the foundation of the gospel and is an expression of the appropriation of the very nature of the gospel. These principles apply to all giving, not just to the giving of money, which is the subject of 2 Corinthians 8–9. The basic response to the gospel and foundation of all giving is first to give the self to the Lord (2 Cor. 8:5).

The weekly giving to the church is both a measure and exemplification of the believer's daily stewardship of God's blessings. The language of stewardship refers to the practice in the ancient world of giving to a trusted slave or employee the administration of the owner's property or business (in Greek *oikonomia*, "management of the household" — Luke 12:42; 16:13; metaphorical for various other functions — Rom. 16:23; 1 Cor. 4:1; Gal. 4:2; Tit. 1:7). The biblical theme of stewardship derives from the premise that God creates all and so owns all (Gen. 1:1; Deut. 10:14; Ps. 24:1). His claims as creator are enhanced by his redemptive activity, his saving plan itself referred to as a "stewardship" or "administration" (Eph. 1:3-5, 9-10; 3:9). Hence, human beings are accountable to God for their use of what he has placed at their disposal (Gen. 1:26-30). As he has given generously (Matt. 6:25-34; 7:7-11; James 1:5, 17), so those who have received from him are to give generously (Matt. 10:8; Rom. 12:8; 2 Cor. 9:8-11). This stewardship applies to all

God's gifts (cf. 1 Pet. 4:10; 1 Cor. 4:7), including material possessions (Matt. 6:19-24; Acts 20:35; 1 Tim. 6:17-18). Giving to the church supports those in need (Acts 4:34-37; 11:28-30) and the preaching and teaching of God's word (1 Cor. 9:3-14; Phil. 4:15-16). It is expected of stewards that they will be faithful (1 Cor. 4:2) and prudent (Luke 12:42, 48), because they will have to give account of their stewardship (Luke 16:2).

Reading and Preaching the Bible

The saving word (cf. James 1:21) that connects the redemptive event to the present and to the future must be alive in the church. The preaching and teaching of the word of God are discussed in the preceding chapter as part of the plan of salvation and in the next chapter as part of the work of the church. It remains here, therefore, only to highlight this activity in the congregational assembly.[106] Delivering and receiving the word of the Lord are part of public service to God.

The content and goal of preaching and teaching are stated in Colossians 1:28: "It is Christ whom we proclaim, warning everyone and teaching everyone in all wisdom, so that we may present everyone mature in Christ." Since the coming of Jesus, the word of God centers in him. God speaks now through his Son (Heb. 1:1-2). Christians receive the Hebrew scriptures as the word of God, but those scriptures are now interpreted in the light of Jesus and the salvation that is through faith in him (2 Tim. 3:15). The pattern of interpreting the Old Testament in

---

106. Several studies have attempted to correlate parts of the New Testament to Jewish patterns of preaching: (1) to later rabbinic homilies: J. W. Bowker, "Speeches in Acts: A Study in Proem and Yellamedenu Form," *New Testament Studies* 14 (1967): 96-111; Wilhelm Wuellner, "Haggadic Homily Genre in I Corinthians 1–3," *Journal of Biblical Literature* 89 (1970): 199-204; this approach is criticized as anachronistic by Karl Paul Donfried, *The Setting of Second Clement in Early Christianity* (Leiden: Brill, 1974), pp. 19-48; or (2) to Hellenistic Jewish sermons: Peder Borgen, *Bread from Heaven* (Leiden: Brill, 1965); Lawrence Wills, "The Form of the Sermon in Hellenistic Judaism and Early Christianity," *Harvard Theological Review* 77 (1984): 277-299; the latter is criticized for incorrectly distinguishing its characteristics from classical rhetoric by C. Clifton Black, "The Rhetorical Form of the Hellenistic Jewish and Early Christian Sermon: A Response to Lawrence Wills," *Harvard Theological Review* 81 (1988): 1-18. For the formal analysis of early Christian exhortations and homilies see also James I. H. McDonald, *Kerygma and Didache: The Articulation and Structure of the Earliest Christian Message* (Cambridge: University Press, 1980), pp. 39-69.

relation to Christ goes back to Jesus himself (Luke 24:44-47), and so from the beginning the disciples placed the words of Jesus alongside the ancient scriptures (John 2:22).

In the assembly, the word of the Lord is dispensed. Scripture reading has to do with the nature of the church and its gathering together. The church is a people called by the word of God, and that word continues to call the people together in assembly. Timothy was instructed, "Give attention to the public reading of scripture, to exhorting, to teaching" (1 Tim. 4:13, NRSV). Reading the scriptures and bringing a lesson based on them was part of the synagogue service in Jesus' time (Luke 4:16-21). Presumably this continued in Christian congregations.[107] In addition to the Jewish scriptures, Christian writings were read. First attested in this regard are the letters of Paul (Col. 4:16; 1 Thess. 5:27); for the Gospels, Mark 13:14 may refer to such public reading; for Revelation, see 1:3; 22:18. The assembled people of God are gathered, among other reasons, to hear the word from God. The church is a people drawn by the word of God.

First Corinthians 14 discusses the verbal activities in the assembly in order to correct abuses in the meetings of the church. Hence, Paul gives most attention to prophesying and speaking in tongues. He exalts prophecy as a rational, understandable form of speech in order to eliminate uninterpreted tongues from the assembly (1 Cor. 14:1-5, 13-17, 26-31). Speaking in tongues is a private religious experience (1 Cor. 14:2, 4), so unless interpreted it is out of place in the assembly, but prophesying speaks "to other people for their upbuilding and encouragement and consolation" (1 Cor. 14:3 and cf. 5). "In church I would rather speak five words with my mind, in order to instruct others also, than ten thousand words in a tongue" (1 Cor. 14:19). Instruction is one of the principal goals of the assembly. The different modes of public speaking conveying this instruction might include "a teaching, a revelation, a tongue, or an interpretation" (1 Cor. 14:26). These same activities are referred to in 1 Corinthians 14:6. The tongues must be interpreted, so the communication will involve "revelation or knowledge or prophecy or teaching." The four words represent two pairs: revelation and prophecy, knowledge and teaching. These pairs refer to two principal forms of address to the church, that by prophets and that by teachers.

The biblical texts containing the revelation and knowledge of apostolic times must continue to be proclaimed and taught. The scrip-

---

107. Attested in the second century by Justin Martyr, *I Apology* 67.

tures must be interpreted and applied. Therefore, the basic form of preaching in the church today is the exposition of scripture. There are special needs that sometimes require topical sermons, and there are other occasions when other types of preaching are appropriate; but in the regular assembly of the church to hear the word of the Lord, the most appropriate form of preaching is expository. This requires that the preacher penetrate the text and then relate it to the spiritual needs of the hearers. The person who makes a faithful exposition and application of God's message is bringing "the word of God" to the people. He is truly God's spokesman and so has an awesome task. Even as the person who leads the congregation in prayer speaks for the people to God, the preacher of the word speaks for God to the people. Accordingly, the preacher must always remember that he is a servant of the word, not its master. The hearers have a responsibility too; note Jesus' admonition, "Let anyone with ears listen" (e.g., Matt. 11:15). Hearing with understanding makes one aware of being in the presence of the Lord and so is a worship experience.

A sermon preached in faith, based on scripture, praising God's deeds, and showing consequent obligations and consolations is indeed an act of worship. God is at work in the gospel (Rom. 1:16), and his word is living and active (Heb. 4:12). The church is a preaching church. It is a people that lives by the word of the Lord. Because the church is a people who have heard the word and continue to listen to it and seek to be guided by it, the church is a worshipping people.

Selected Bibliography on Worship

Delling, Gerhard. *Worship in the New Testament.* London: Darton, Longman and Todd, 1962.

Martin, Ralph P. *Worship in the Early Church.* Grand Rapids: Eerdmans, 1964.

Martin, Ralph P. *The Worship of God: Some Theological, Pastoral, and Practical Reflections.* Grand Rapids: Eerdmans, 1982.

Moule, C. F. D. *Worship in the New Testament.* Richmond: John Knox, 1961.

Schweizer, Eduard, "Worship in the New Testament," *Neotestamentica. German and English Essays 1951-1963* (Zwingli, 1963).

Torrance, James B. "The Place of Jesus Christ in Worship." *Church Service Society Annual* 40 (May 1970): 41-62. Reprint in Ray Anderson, ed., *Theological Foundations for Ministry*. Grand Rapids: Eerdmans, 1979. Pp. 348-369.

Von Allmen, J. J. *Worship: Its Theology and Practice*. London: Lutterworth, 1965.

Willis, Wendell. *Worship*. Austin: Sweet, 1973.

5. The Church and Her Bishop: The Continuing Ministry

> *"You have returned to the Shepherd
> and Bishop of your souls."*   (1 PET. 2:25)

EVEN as the English word "services" in the context of the church has a double reference to general Christian benefits extended to others and to the congregational assembly for worship to God, in a similar way the English word "ministry" is applied both to the general service of the church for others and to the role of leadership exercised in performing the work of the church. Both aspects of ministry will be considered in this chapter — the work of the church and the ministers who lead in its performance.

THE WORKER AND HIS WORKS

> *"We must work the works of him who
> sent me while it is day; night is coming
> when no one can work."*   (JOHN 9:4)

The redemptive work of Jesus (Chap. 3) is the source of the church and of its ministry. It must be referred to once more as the presupposition for what the church is all about. Not only Jesus' death and resurrection but also his total earthly ministry formed part of his mission of salvation. That provides the basis for the work and ministries of the church.

281

The Redemptive Work

Jesus' mission was redemptive. His atoning death was a unique and unrepeatable work for human salvation (Heb. 10:12, 14). Jesus' sacrificial death, therefore, was a ministry that the church cannot continue. The church can share in his sufferings and continue his afflictions (Col. 1:24); he did not exhaust all the sufferings that must be experienced by God's people, and these may be voluntarily accepted, as in Paul's case, for the sake of the church.[1] But Jesus' redemptive sufferings were complete and cannot be added to. The church, nonetheless, shares in Jesus' redemptive work; she, too, exists to seek and save the lost. God's goal is the salvation of all (1 Tim. 2:4), and the church participates in that. God works through her to bring the benefits of Jesus' atoning death to bear on lost human lives. This is accomplished through the church's proclaiming the message of the atonement, demonstrating redemption in its life, and working for the redemption of all people.

The Earthly Ministries of Jesus

In his earthly ministry leading up to the cross, Jesus made a proclamation of the kingdom of God and demonstrated its effects in the good he did for people. Two passages associated with Peter give such a twofold description of ministry. Acts 10:36-38 summarizes Jesus' ministry as "preaching peace"[2] and "doing good and healing all who were oppressed by the devil"; similarly, 1 Peter 4:11 summarizes the ministries of the church as speaking the words of God and serving (cf. Acts 6:2, 4).

Matthew gives a threefold instead of a twofold summary of the work of Jesus. As the "teaching Gospel" of the early church, arranged with the needs of teachers in mind,[3] the Gospel of Matthew adds teaching to preaching and healing and places it first in the list of Jesus' activities. Matthew twice summarizes Jesus' ministry in almost identical words. According to Matthew 4:23,

---

1. Colin Kruse, *New Testament Models for Ministry: Jesus and Paul* (Nashville: Thomas Nelson, 1983), pp. 145-151, suggests Col. 1:24 is to be understood against the background of the servant passages of Second Isaiah with the individual aspects (vicarious suffering) fulfilled in Christ and the corporate aspects (mission and other sufferings) fulfilled in Christ and his people

2. Peace is a theme in Luke (e.g., 1:79; 2:14; 10:5-6; 19:38; Acts 9:31).

3. Paul S. Minear, *Matthew: The Teacher's Gospel* (New York: Pilgrim, 1982).

> Jesus went throughout Galilee, teaching in their synagogues and proclaiming the good news of the kingdom and curing every disease and every sickness among the people.

Jesus' ministry was threefold: teaching, preaching, and healing.[4] This statement corresponds to the classification of his work as edification, evangelism, and benevolence (in a broad sense) to be elaborated below in the description of the work of the church.

Matthew 9:35 gives the same description of Jesus' work:

> Jesus went about all the cities and villages, teaching in their synagogues, and proclaiming the good news of the kingdom, and curing every disease and every sickness.

This latter passage continues with the information that the disciples were sent out as extensions of his ministry.

> When he saw the crowds, he had compassion for them, because they were harassed and helpless, like sheep without a shepherd. Then he said to his disciples, "The harvest is plentiful, but the laborers are few; therefore ask the Lord of the harvest to send out laborers into his harvest." (Matt. 9:36-38)

These words are preparatory to the mission discourse in Matthew 10. The text of the Gospel continues in chapter 10 with the naming of the twelve apostles and the commissioning of them to "go, proclaim the good news" and "cure the sick" (Matt. 10:7, 8). The disciples as sent forth under the "limited commission" (limited to the people of Israel — 10:5-6) thus shared in Jesus' ministry of preaching and healing. Teaching is not included in the commission in Matthew 10, for the disciples were still in the place of "students," and teaching is included in their commission only after they finished their apprenticeship with Jesus (Matt. 28:18-20). One of the incidental verbal links connecting 9:35-38 with chapter 10 is the reference to the people who were objects of the ministry as lost "sheep" in 9:36 and 10:6. The other Gospels from their own perspectives present Jesus' activity as a model for his disciples as they continue his ministry (Mark 1:17; 10:42-45; John 13:12-16). John 14–17 tells of the Holy Spirit as a power in the apostles to continue the ministry of the earthly Jesus. The function of the disciples in multiplying the presence of Jesus among the

---

4. The same threefold activity is to be found in Matt. 11:1-6.

people is precedent for understanding the church's ministry as an extension and continuation of the ministry of Jesus (see further below).

The Work of the Church

"For we are what he has made us, created in Christ Jesus for good works, which God prepared beforehand to be our way of life" (Eph. 2:10). The new creation in Christ Jesus results in the doing of good works, the same types of good works with which Jesus was concerned.

The church continues in principle the works Jesus did in his earthly ministry. The church is the body of Christ (see above, pp. 91-103). Christ does his work in the world now through the church, and the work of the church is to offer Christ to the world. When the church fails to do the work of Christ, it becomes the corpse instead of the body of Christ.

Matthew's threefold description of the earthly ministry of Jesus corresponds to the activities of the church. His order in listing Jesus' activities reflects the structure of the church: pastors and teachers, evangelists, and deacons. Changing that order to the historical or logical sequence in the church's mission, we note that even as Jesus' ministry was a preaching, teaching, and healing ministry, so he gave each of these tasks to his followers.

Evangelism[5]

Evangelism characterized Jesus' ministry. All three Synoptic Gospels summarize Jesus' ministry in terms of preaching the gospel (in addition to Matt. 4:23, see Mark 1:14-15 and Luke 4:14-21, all significant for their location at the head of the accounts of Jesus' ministry). Evangelism formed the content of the risen Jesus' last commands to his disciples in the "Great Commission" with which the Gospels conclude.

> Go therefore and make disciples of all nations, baptizing them in the name of the Father and of the Son and of the Holy Spirit. (Matt. 28:19)

> Go into all the world and proclaim the good news to the whole creation. The one who believes and is baptized will be saved; but the

5. Michael Green, *Evangelism in the Early Church* (Grand Rapids: Eerdmans, 1970).

one who does not believe will be condemned. (Mark 16:15-16, long ending)

Repentance and forgiveness of sins is to be proclaimed in his name to all nations, beginning from Jerusalem. (Luke 24:47)

As the Father has sent me, so I send you. . . . Receive the Holy Spirit. If you forgive the sins of any, they are forgiven them; if you retain the sins of any, they are retained. (John 20:21, 23)

Not only did Jesus engage in evangelism and command it of his followers, but the early church also was evangelistic. Acts 8:4 is typical: "Now those who were scattered went from place to place, proclaiming the word." The members of the communities who did not actually engage in evangelism assisted the missionaries and evangelists by prayer (2 Thess. 3:1; Col. 4:3f.), material help (Phil. 4:14-19), hospitality (3 John 8), and by being lights through their adhesion to the word (Phil. 2:15f.).[6]

The theological importance of the preached word for producing faith was discussed above in Chapter 3 (pp. 161-164). That discussion may be supplemented here by noting the impressive variety of words used for preaching to unbelievers. In Acts 8 alone the following words occur: "preach the gospel" (*euangelizomai*, "evangelize," Acts 8:4, 12, 25, 35, 40 [its frequency makes appropriate the designation of Philip as "evangelist" — Acts 21:8]); "proclaim" (*kēryssō*, "herald," Acts 8:5), "say" (*legō*, Acts 8:6), "speak" (*laleō*, Acts 8:25), and "testify" (*diamartyreō*, "bear witness," Acts 8:25). If one spreads the net elsewhere in Acts other words occur — for example: "announce" (*anangellō*), Acts 20:20, 27; *katangellō*, Acts 4:2; 13:5, 38; 15:36), "speak boldly" or "freely" (*parrēsiazomai*, Acts 9:27, 28; 14:3; 19:8), argue" (*dialegomai*, "dialogue" or "discuss," Acts 17:2, 17; 18:4, 19; 20:7, 9), "persuade" (*peithō*, Acts 19:8, 26; 28:23), "exhort" (*parakaleō*, "appeal to" or "encourage," Acts 2:40; more often addressed to believers — e.g., Acts 11:23; 14:22; 15:32; 16:40), "admonish" (*noutheteō*, "warn," Acts 20:31). This is not an exhaustive list of words or of references. The point is the emphasis in the text on the importance and frequency of speaking the word for the mission of the church and on the variety of forms this speaking might take.

As Jesus proclaimed the kingdom of God, so the church bears witness to the reign of God and calls people to repentance in view of

6. Jean Delorme, ed., *Le Ministère et les ministères selon le Nouveau Testament* (Paris: Seuil, 1974), pp. 297-298.

Christ's coming again. In a sense, the exalted Jesus continues to preach through the proclamation of the church (Eph. 2:17). Preaching, as was seen in Chapter 3,[7] is part of the redemptive task, and to this extent the church engages in the redemptive work of Christ. It does so even though suffering is entailed. The church is central in God's saving history. As an extension of Christ's saving mission, the church engages in evangelistic and missionary activity. By its nature it reaches out to embrace all whom God calls. Evangelism is the very lifeblood of the church. Where the church is not evangelistic, it dies. The true church must be a preaching church.

Edification

Edification (the building up in the faith) is a natural outgrowth from evangelism.[8] The persons converted by the missionary preaching and evangelistic work then had to be instructed how to live as members of the church. As has been noted, Matthew gives more explicit attention to this teaching content of Jesus' ministry than do the other Gospels. Thus, the Sermon on the Mount is presented as a block of teaching given to those who were already in some sense "disciples" (Matt. 5:1-2, perhaps in contrast to the "crowds," but see Matt. 7:28 for the crowds also hearing the teaching). Not only did Jesus spend time proclaiming God's kingdom to the people, but he also spent time with the inner circle of disciples, instructing them in the mysteries of the kingdom. Following the teaching in parables addressed to "the whole crowd," Jesus, again according to Matthew, explained to the "disciples" the "secrets of the kingdom of heaven" (Matt. 13:2, 10-11).[9] Jesus knew that there was a need for those who responded to the call of the kingdom to be instructed more fully in what this involved. Matthew's version of the Great Commission follows the command to baptize with the instruction, "teaching them to obey everything that I have commanded

---

7. See the treatment of the Great Commission and preaching in the redemptive activity of God for the theological significance of the preached word, pp. 161-164.

8. The distinction between evangelism and edification as *kerygma* (proclamation) and *didachē* (teaching), conceptually valid as activities, does not correspond to the usage of these words in detail and is not exemplified in distinctive structural forms — James I. H. McDonald, *Kerygma and Didache: The Articulation and Structure of the Earliest Christian Message* (Cambridge: University Press, 1990), pp. 1-7.

9. The distinction between teaching to the crowd and teaching to the disciples is even more pronounced in Mark — 4:1-12; 7:17-23; 9:28-29; 10:10-12, 23-31.

you" (Matt. 28:20). In view of the example and command of Jesus, it is no surprise that the early church gave much attention to the spiritual nurturing and maturing of converts (Eph. 4:11-16; 2 Pet. 1:1-10).

If we were to follow the imagery of the church as a body, the work of teaching new converts would be expressed by the language of spiritual growth or health (Col. 2:19; Eph. 4:16).[10] Besides the numerical growth of the church ("the word of the Lord grew" — Acts 6:7; 12:24; 19:20; cf. 1 Cor. 3:6, 7; Col. 1:6), the New Testament speaks of growth in faith (2 Cor. 10:15), in righteousness (2 Cor. 9:10 — here clearly benevolent works), in the knowledge of God (Col. 1:10), in grace and knowledge (2 Pet. 3:18), and more comprehensively "into salvation" (1 Pet. 2:2) or "into Christ" (Eph. 4:15; cf. 4:13). Ephesians mixes the imagery of a body and of a building, speaking of "grow[ing] into a holy temple" (Eph. 2:21) and "building up [the body] in love" (Eph. 4:16).

The Pauline letters often describe the work of teaching or instruction by the word "edification," using the imagery of constructing a building.[11] Edification means primarily the "act of building" but also the finished "building." "To edify" means "to build, to construct, to build up." The words are used in this literal sense in the New Testament, but our interest now is in the metaphorical sense, a spiritual building up. The basis for this metaphorical sense is the comparison of the church to a building (1 Cor. 3:9-12), specifically a temple (1 Cor. 3:16f.; 1 Pet. 2:5; Eph. 2:20-22).[12]

What according to Paul is involved in edification? His fullest exposition of the subject is found in 1 Corinthians 14.[13] This chapter addresses the problem at Corinth of speaking in tongues, a gift that became an expression of pride and selfish individualism. From Paul's corrections we learn negatively some things edification is not: it is not a feeling of uplift or what makes one feel good; it is not a matter of

---

10. This is done by Karl Barth, *Church Dogmatics*, IV/2 (Edinburgh: T. & T. Clark, 1958), pp. 641-676, quoted in Ray S. Anderson, ed., *Theological Foundations for Ministry* (Grand Rapids: Eerdmans, 1979), pp. 258-301.

11. P. Bonnard, *Jesus-Christ edifiant son Eglise: Le concept d'edification dans le Noveau Testament* (Neuchâtel: Delachaux & Niestlé, 1948); O. Michel, "*Oikodomeo, et al.*," *Theological Dictionary of the New Testament*, ed. G. Friedrich, tr. G. W. Bromiley (Grand Rapids: Eerdmans, 1967), 5.136-148; Ingrid Kitzberger, *Bau der Gemeinde: Das paulinische Wortfeld Oikodome/(Ep)oikodomein* (Würzburg: Echter, 1986).

12. See discussion of this image for the church on pp. 125-129 and for its worship on pp. 218-220.

13. See the treatment of this passage on p. 245.

emotion, private experience, or sentiment; it is not what benefits, makes to feel good, or pleases the individual. Although Paul granted that the tongue-speaker edified himself, he disparaged this practice (1 Cor. 14:4, 19). In contrast, Paul's emphasis on edification in the assembly gives priority to the good or benefit of the group (1 Cor. 14:2-5). Edification requires the mind, instruction, and understanding (1 Cor. 14:16-19). If no one understands, no edification takes place. The assembly of the church should be directed toward the benefit of others, and at its heart is intelligible speech that gives instruction, encouragement, and consolation.

What is the importance of edification? Edification is the stated purpose or goal of many activities in the church, and these statements demonstrate its importance. Indeed, it is the members' goal for the church itself (1 Cor. 14:12), and as seen in the last paragraph it is held up as the purpose of the assembly of the church (1 Cor. 14:26). Edification, furthermore, is the goal of ministry in the church (2 Cor. 10:8; 13:10; Eph. 4:11-12), but this responsibility is not the concern of the leadership exclusively, for every member contributes to growth in edification (Eph. 4:16). Therefore, edification is a goal also of personal relations (1 Cor. 10:23-24; Rom. 15:2; 1 Thess. 5:11). For this to be achieved, a person's speech must aim at what is edifying (Eph. 4:29; 2 Cor. 12:19).

What produces edification? Faith is the beginning (Jude 20). Love accomplishes edification (1 Cor. 8:1); this is what distinguishes biblical edification from purely academic, scholarly knowledge and from secular learning. Peace promotes edification — in personal relations (Rom. 14:19) and in the absence of persecution (Acts 9:31). Good examples are edifying, even as bad examples may encourage one in doing wrong (1 Cor. 8:10). The word of God produces edification (Acts 20:32).

Eleemosynary (Benevolent) Work[14]

Eleemosynary work (deeds of mercy) also characterized the ministry of Jesus. Another summary of Jesus' activities, besides those noted above, emphasizes the benevolent and merciful nature of his deeds of power: "The blind receive their sight, the lame walk, the lepers are cleansed, the deaf hear, the dead are raised, and the poor have good

14. C. E. B. Cranfield, "Diakonia in the New Testament," in *Service in Christ*, ed. James I. McCord and T. H. L. Parker (Grand Rapids: Eerdmans, 1966), pp. 37-48; cf. Hans Küng, *The Church* (London: Burns & Oates, 1968), pp. 391-393.

news brought to them" (Matt. 11:4-5). The Gospel texts often note that Jesus' merciful deeds were motivated by compassion for human need (Matt. 14:14; 15:32 [= Mark 8:2]; 20:34; Luke 7:13). Jesus instructed his followers to be similarly concerned about meeting human needs, declaring that judgment would be determined by such conduct and teaching that he was to be seen in each needy person: the hungry, the thirsty, the stranger, the naked, the sick, and the prisoner (Matt. 25:31-46).[15] With such vivid teaching and example of conduct from Jesus before it, the early church readily responded to physical needs (Acts 4:34; 11:29-30).

New Testament teaching is abundant on the benevolent requirements of the Christian life, from Paul in Romans 12:13 to James in 1:27; 2:15-16.[16] Love required expression in practical assistance (1 John 3:16-18; 4:7-11, 19-21). Although recognizing a first responsibility to fellow believers (Gal. 6:10), Christians extended loving service to non-Christians as well (Matt. 5:43-48; 1 Thess. 3:12; Rom. 12:14, 20).

Christians may lack the miraculous power demonstrated by Jesus and the apostles, but they will nonetheless be concerned with healing — caring for the sick (Matt. 25:36) and providing the medical and spiritual help that they can (James 5:14-15). Their charitable work will be undertaken in the meekness and humility of Christ, indeed seeing Christ in those to whom they minister (Matt. 25:40, 45).

However useful the above classification may be for understanding the work of the church, any classification is somewhat artificial, and these words in themselves do not exhaust even the threefold work of the church. Moreover, there is often overlapping, so no sharp distinction between the activities should be maintained. An act of charity may be the most evangelistic thing that can be done in a given situation; for some persons in the grip of sinful conditions, telling the message about Jesus may be the most benevolent thing to be done for them. Repeating the gospel story may be instructive and edifying to believers flagging in their zeal, and instruction in Christian ethics may have an evangelistic appeal to outsiders looking for a higher standard of moral life.

The important point is that Jesus continues his work through the church. The work of the church is not "busy work" or an arbitrary agenda to distinguish its members from other people. Ministry in the church corresponds to the work. There are special workers to take the

15. On seeing Jesus in others, cf. Heb. 13:2.
16. See further in Chap. 6 on the Christian life, e.g., pp. 361-362.

lead in the performance of the works which are essential to being a church of Christ. The ministries exercised in the church are the ministries exercised by Jesus. And these are expressions of the divine mission for humanity: redemption, spiritual growth, and care for needs.

THE GIVER AND THE GIFTS

"But each of us was given grace according to the
measure of Christ's gift. Therefore it is said, 'When he
ascended on high . . . he gave gifts to his people.' . . .
The gifts he gave were that some would be apostles,
some prophets, some evangelists, some pastors
and teachers."   (EPH. 4:7-11)

Resurrection and Ministry

Even during his earthly ministry, Jesus called his disciples to share his ministry (Matt. 10). He trained his followers for their work and sent them out for limited periods of time with a mission limited to Israel (Matt. 10:5-6; cf. Mark 6:7-13; Luke 9:1-6; 10:1-12). That mission, as seen above, was an extension of Jesus' own ministry. Ministry in the church, however, is primarily the gift of the resurrected Christ.[17] The theological grounding of the ministry of the church is not only in the earthly work of Jesus that his followers are called to imitate and to share but also in the commission given and gifts bestowed by the resurrected Jesus. After the resurrection, Jesus commissioned the disciples to continue his ministry and sent the Holy Spirit to equip them. All four Gospels and Acts combine a commission saying with one of the resurrection appearances (Matt. 28:18-20; Mark 16:15f., long ending; Luke 24:46-49; John 20:21-23; Acts 1:8). The resurrection, for the original apostles and for Paul, was bound up with a command and commission from Christ to work for him and under his direction. When the personal presence of Jesus was to be removed, he authorized his followers to continue his ministry, no longer limited to Israel but now on a worldwide basis.

The resurrected Jesus declared:

17. T. W. Manson, *The Servant-Messiah* (Cambridge: Cambridge University Press, 1953), pp. 95ff.

"All authority in heaven and on earth has been given to me. Go therefore and make disciples of all nations, baptizing them in the name of the Father and of the Son and of the Holy Spirit, and teaching them to obey everything that I have commanded you. And remember, I am with you always, to the end of the age." (Matt. 28:18-20)

The commission to make converts and to instruct in all the teachings of Jesus rested on a direct authorization of the resurrected Lord who speaks with all authority. Since this was a post-resurrection commission, Luke specifically connected it with the continuing presence and power of the Spirit of Jesus:

"But you will receive power when the Holy Spirit has come upon you; and you will be my witnesses in Jerusalem, in all Judea and Samaria, and to the ends of the earth." (Acts 1:8; cf. Luke 24:46-49)

The Spirit enabled the apostles to continue the ministry of Jesus in the world — to speak for him and to act with his authority.

Not only did the Twelve and others receive their commission from the resurrected Christ, but also Paul understood in the same way his apostolic call to preach the gospel to the Gentiles. The commission was a gift of grace, bestowed by the risen Christ, and empowered by the working of the Holy Spirit.

When God, who had set me apart before I was born and called me through his grace, was pleased to reveal his Son to me, so that I might proclaim him among the Gentiles. (Gal. 1:15-16)

[After referring to the resurrection of "Jesus Christ our Lord," Paul says,] through whom we have received grace and apostleship to bring about the obedience of faith among all the Gentiles. (Rom. 1:4-5)

Because of the grace given me by God to be a minister of Christ Jesus to the Gentiles. . . . [W]hat Christ has accomplished through me . . . by the power of the Spirit of God. (Rom. 15:15-19)

It is notable for the connection between the resurrection of Christ and his continuing ministry through his disciples that Paul speaks of Christ working through him. In addition to his historical, personal connection with the Twelve, Jesus through his Spirit works directly and not mediately with those called to ministry. Luke's accounts of the call of Paul make similar points about his being commissioned by the risen Christ to go to the Gentiles. Note especially Acts 26:14-18:

"I am Jesus, whom you are persecuting. But get up and stand on your feet; for I have appeared to you for this purpose, to appoint you to serve and testify to the things in which you have seen me. . . . I am sending [*apostellō*] you [to the Gentiles]."

Ministry was a gift of grace and required the working of the Holy Spirit to qualify and empower its performance. This was true not just for apostleship, but for all functions of ministry. Jesus not only called ministers to continue his work, but he also equipped them with the necessary gifts to enable them to do the assigned tasks.

Gifts, Service, and Leadership[18]

Ephesians 4:7-11 states that "each of us was given grace," and includes among the gifts of the ascended Christ to his church various ministers in addition to the apostles: prophets, evangelists, pastors, and teachers. The New Testament presents a close correlation between gifts of God's grace given to each of his people, the use of these gifts in service to one another, and leadership as a result of the service performed.[19] Every ministry in the church is based on a grace-gift, and every minister of the church in the exercise of his/her ministry is a gift of Christ to the whole.

Gifts

The principal passages on gifts, in addition to Ephesians 4, are found in Romans 12; 1 Corinthians 12; and 1 Peter 4.

We have gifts that differ according to the grace given to us: prophecy, in proportion to faith; ministry, in ministering; the teacher, in teach-

18. See E. Earle Ellis, *Pauline Theology: Ministry and Society* (Grand Rapids: Eerdmans, 1989), pp. 26-30, 35-50, for ministry as an activity of the Holy Spirit.
19. I have discussed the interrelationship of these points in "Authority and Tenure of Elders," *Restoration Quarterly* 18 (1975): 142-150. Cf. these statements: "*Charismata* are those gifts or events whose source is God's grace, whose purpose is a concrete service and whose nature is a manifestation of the power of the Holy Spirit" — Ray S. Anderson, ed., *Theological Foundations of Ministry* (Grand Rapids: Eerdmans, 1979), p. 448; "There is no charisma that is not a diakonia, and no diakonia that is not a charisma" — Josef Hainz, *Ekklesia: Strukturen paulinischer Gemeinde-Theologie und Gemeinde-Ordnung* (Regensburg: Friedrich Pustet, 1972), p. 316.

ing; the exhorter, in exhortation; the giver, in generosity; the leader, in diligence; the compassionate, in cheerfulness. (Rom. 12:6-8)

Now there are varieties of gifts, but the same Spirit; and there are varieties of services, but the same Lord; and there are varieties of activities, but it is the same God who activates all of them in everyone. To each is given the manifestation of the Spirit for the common good. To one is given through the Spirit the utterance of wisdom, and to another the utterance of knowledge according to the same Spirit, to another gifts of healing by the one Spirit, to another the working of miracles, to another prophecy, to another the discernment of spirits, to another various kinds of tongues, to another the interpretation of tongues. All these are activated by one and the same Spirit, who allots to each one individually just as the Spirit chooses. . . .

And God has appointed in the church first apostles, second prophets, third teachers; then deeds of power, then gifts of healing, forms of assistance, forms of leadership, various kinds of tongues. (1 Cor. 12:4-11, 28)

Like good stewards of the manifold grace of God, serve one another with whatever gift each of you has received. Whoever speaks must do so as one speaking the very words of God; whoever serves must do so with the strength that God supplies, so that God may be glorified in all things through Jesus Christ. (1 Pet. 4:10-11)

These passages stress the variety of gifts bestowed by God through his grace on human beings. Every Christian has a "gift" and possesses the "Spirit" (see pp. 107-110). In this sense, all believers are equal and of the same spiritual rank. But this equality allows for the diversity of "gifts."[20] These gifts include powers that we would today regard as supernatural — prophecy, healing, working miracles. The *charismata* (on the word itself, see pp. 110-111) include, no less than these, other gifts that we associate with natural abilities — teaching, exhorting, having money to give in benevolence, showing compassion, etc. Even in these natural talents, a certain "gift" is involved, for some

20. Cf. Karl Barth, *Church Dogmatics*, IV/2 (Edinburgh: T. & T. Clark, 1958), pp. 690-695, on the necessity for all Christians to serve, but not in the same function: The church "is not a collective where the individual is of no importance. . . . In the life of the Christian community each individual has his own necessary place, and the service of each individual is indispensable to that of the whole." Quoted in Ray S. Anderson, *Theological Foundations for Ministry* (Grand Rapids: Eerdmans, 1979), p. 711.

persons possess greater ability than others and do these things with greater ease and effectiveness. Permanent as well as temporary gifts are no less from God and the result of the working of his Spirit. God is the source of abilities, of whatever kind.

Different kinds of ministries are rooted not only in the ministries of Jesus and the works which he gives to the church to do but also in the gifts bestowed on individuals for the good of the church. Both *charisma* and office (properly understood as recognized function) are present in the New Testament and belong together in the church.[21] Both immediate Spirit-inspired activities and structures for continuing community life existed side-by-side in New Testament congregations. Gifts are given to enable persons to continue the work begun by Christ in the world. These ministries are not self-chosen but are dependent on the use of abilities and the recognition of these by others.

Paul, who has the most to say of any New Testament writer on the subject of gifts, quickly moves the subject of spiritual gifts in 1 Corinthians 12 from exclusively the Spirit (1 Cor. 12:1-3) to include Christ and God (1 Cor. 12:4-6) and from the individual to emphasize the welfare of the whole body (1 Cor. 12:7, 12-26). The variety of gifts originates in unity (1 Cor. 12:4-11), and all gifts are to contribute to unity (1 Cor. 12:12-26). Paul further offers standards for the use of gifts. (1) The gifts must confess Jesus (1 Cor. 12:3), and their use must accord with his nature (1 Cor. 12:12, 27; Eph. 4:13-16; cf. John 16:12-15, discussed on pp. 106-107). (2) The gifts must be exercised in love (1 Cor. 13). (3) Accordingly, the gifts must produce a community benefit (1 Cor. 14; see pp. 286-288 on edification).

The fundamental biblical viewpoint on gifts of all kinds is expressed in 1 Corinthians 4:7, "What do you have that you did not receive? And if you received it, why do you boast as if it were not a gift?" No amount of practice, training, or effort will make one a concert pianist who does not have the gift of music, a star track performer who does not have the gift of athletic ability, or a great writer who does not have the gift of words. The other side of this is true also: No amount of ability will make a person outstanding in an endeavor who does not use, develop, and work at it. The Spirit works in the believer

---

21. Kevin Giles, *Patterns of Ministry among the First Christians* (Melbourne: Collins Dove, 1989), p. 14, who proceeds to observe that the episodic, "charismatic" interpretations of ministry by some scholars is closer to the concept of Paul's opponents at Corinth than to that of the apostle himself.

to develop talents and gifts for the upbuilding of the body. Gifts must be used.

Service

"It is not the gift itself that is important, but its use."[22] For Paul "the test of a genuine *charisma* lies not in the fact that something supernatural occurs but in the use which is made of it."[23] The gifts are not given for selfish enjoyment but for ministry to others. All the passages about gifts, either explicitly or implicitly, say that they are to be employed for service to others. All gifts in believers are in effect "body gifts." First Corinthians 12:7 states the basic principle, "To each is given the manifestation of the Spirit for the common good." This common good refers specifically to the welfare of the church. "The gifts he gave were . . . to equip the saints for the work of ministry, for building up the body of Christ" (Eph. 4:11-12). Since the abilities are not a person's own, but are gifts, the user is in the position of a steward with a steward's responsibilities for their usage: "Like good stewards . . . serve one another with whatever gift each of you has received" (1 Pet. 4:10). Romans 12:6-8 does not expressly state that the gifts are to be used, but the wording implies this, and many translations supply the thought (RSV, NIV, REB). Gifts make possible service, and the different kinds of service depend on the different gifts.

Leadership

According to the New Testament perspective, leadership is based on service. The biblical teaching anticipated long ago the modern discovery by the business world of "servant-leadership."[24] Jesus had stated the principle clearly to his followers and invoked his own practice as their model:

> A dispute also arose among them as to which one of them was to be regarded as the greatest. But he said to them, "The kings of the Gentiles lord it over them; and those in authority over them are called benefactors. But not so with you: rather the greatest among you must

22. Jürgen Moltmann, *The Church in the Power of the Spirit* (New York: Harper, 1977), p. 297.
23. Ernst Käsemann, "Ministry and Community in the New Testament," *Essays on New Testament Themes* (Naperville, Ill.: Alec R. Allenson, 1964), p. 17.
24. Robert K. Greenleaf, *Servant Leadership* (Mahwah, N.J.: Paulist, 1977).

become like the youngest, and the leader like one who serves. For who is greater, the one who is at the table or the one who serves? Is it not the one at the table? But I am among you as one who serves." (Luke 22:24-27; cf. Matt. 20:25-28; Mark 10:42-45)

Authority among the followers of Jesus is the moral authority of those who show the most interest in and do the most in the way of loving service for others.

Several passages speak to the matter of leadership resulting from service rendered. Paul addressed the Thessalonians in these words: "We appeal to you, brothers and sisters, to respect those who labor among you, and have charge of you in the Lord and admonish you; esteem them very highly in love because of their work" (1 Thess. 5:12-13). Why esteem them? Because of their office? No. "Because of their work." He invoked the same principle in writing to the Corinthians: "You know that members of the household of Stephanas were the first converts in Achaia, and they have devoted themselves to the service of the saints; I urge you to submit to such people, and to everyone who works and toils with them" (1 Cor. 16:15-16). They should be subject or put themselves at the service of what kind of people? To those who "have devoted themselves to the service of the saints," "to those who work and labor."[25] Hebrews has one of the strongest passages about obedience to leaders in the New Testament, but it still grounds the obedience in the response to work performed: "Obey your leaders and submit to them, for they are keeping watch over your souls and will give an account" (Heb. 13:17). Why obey them? Because of the office they hold? Because of authority given them? No, but because of the service they perform: "For they are keeping watch over your souls."

This perspective on leadership coincides with the way the word for servant (*diakonos*) is used for virtually every category of persons in the church (see the listing on pp. 299 and 334).[26] If the word "office" is

---

25. Cf. Paul's use of "fellow workers" for those engaged in or assisting missionary activity and the continuing nurture of churches — Rom. 16:3, 9, 21; Phil. 2:25; 4:3; Col. 4:11: 1 Thess. 3:2; Philem. 1, 24.

26. "It is not without significance that the technical term for functions in the Church which necessarily involve some measure of leadership [*diakonia*] has from the first been a word which signifies not pre-eminence or power but simply humble service, and, further, that it is the same word that was used of Christ's own service of men and also of the service owed by every Christian to God, to Christ, to his fellows" — C. E. B. Cranfield, "Diakonia in the New Testament," in *Service in Christ*, ed. James I.

to be used in the church, it is not to be thought of as "official" in the sense of governmental or military officials but as referring to a function: "whoever aspires to the episcopate desires a good work" (1 Tim. 3:1); the evangelist has a "work" to do (2 Tim. 4:5). The designated or recognized workers in the church have a task, a ministry, a service to perform, not a title or official position.

Who are the natural leaders in a congregation? Those who do the work, those active in serving others, those taking the lead in doing what needs to be done. From this principle the specific "offices" or recognized functions in the church arise. The kind of service determines the position of leadership. The gift of preaching exercised in the right spirit brings one to leadership in evangelism. The gift of teaching and pastoral care exercised in the spiritual nurture and care of others brings one to leadership in edification. The gift of meeting needs in a caring and humble way brings one to leadership in benevolence.[27]

To summarize, gifts lead to service, and service results in leadership. Every function in the church is a gift of grace. God gives the ability and with it the opportunity and responsibility to use it for the good of the community. Three things are prerequisites for leadership in a congregation of Christ's people: (1) the necessary gifts (abilities or qualifications) for doing the work; (2) the use of these gifts in service to others in such a way as to show that one can and will do the work; and (3) recognition or acknowledgment of the leadership and thus a willingness to follow by the people among whom the work is to be done. All three are necessary. To have the requisite ability and to be active do not of themselves give a person a particular position in a congregation. There must also be the recognition of leadership by the voluntary act of following. One has to have the recognition of the church as well as the gifts and doing the work to be a bishop, evangelist, or deacon in the church. (See pp. 310-318 on the meaning of ordination.)

From these principles it follows that the leaders of a congregation perform an enabling ministry. Leaders are that: leaders. They do not do the work for others. They show others how and help others to do it. They

McCord and T. H. L. Parker (Grand Rapids: Eerdmans, 1966), p. 38. "Humble service" perhaps says too much; see the discussion of word usage under "Deacon" on pp. 333-334.

27. Hans Küng's classification of Paul's lists of charisms (gifts) as those of preaching, service, and leadership (*The Church* [London: Burns & Oates, 1968], p. 184) corresponds to the classification of the work of the church given above and of the ministries of the church based on its work developed below.

provide the ideas, the example, the "know-how" of knowledge and experience. This point conforms to Ephesians 4:11-16. The gifts of apostles, prophets, evangelists, pastors, and teachers were "to equip the saints for the work of ministry, for building up the body of Christ, until all of us come to the unity of the faith and of the knowledge of the Son of God, to maturity, to the measure of the full stature of Christ" (Eph. 4:12-13). The ministers are given to the church to perform a helping or equipping ministry. Ministry has as its goal helping others to grow in Christ Jesus.

THE MINISTER AND THE MINISTERS

> *"As the Father has sent me, so I send you."*   (JOHN 20:21)

Jesus Christ is *the minister* of the church.[28] He is the one universal and comprehensive minister of his church, exercising the one essential ministry of the church. All ministry in the church derives from him. The work of the church is to continue Jesus' work among human beings. The various ministers of the church derive their ministry from him by continuing certain aspects of his all-sufficient ministry.[29] As Jesus was a preacher, so there are preachers in the church; as Jesus was a teacher, so there are pastors and teachers in the church; as Jesus was a doer of good, so there are recognized servants in the church. They are privileged to be called to share in his work on behalf of his people. The

---

28. "Jesus Christ . . . is himself *the* apostle, prophet, teacher, evangelist, pastor and deacon" — Hans Küng, *The Church* (London: Burns & Oates, 1968), p. 395.

29. "Behind the forms of ministry which they humanly exercise there stands the ministry which is that of Jesus Himself. It is Jesus who speaks when the word of the Gospel is truly preached. It is Jesus who is proffered and who blesses when the sacraments are rightly administered. It is Jesus who heals or helps when practical assistance is extended to the needy. It is Jesus who bears and endures when persecution or hardship is imposed and accepted. It is Jesus who rules when spiritual discipline is exercised." G. W. Bromiley, *Christian Ministry* (Grand Rapids: Eerdmans, 1959), pp. 16-17. Cf. T. W. Manson, *The Church's Ministry* (Philadelphia: Westminster, 1948), pp. 12-33, esp. pp. 22 and 107 for the life of the church continuing the messianic ministry of Jesus rather than being an extension of the incarnation; pp. 23-24 for Jesus' ministry as the one essential ministry. W. D. Davies, "Light on the Ministry from the New Testament," *Christian Origins and Judaism* (Philadelphia: Westminster, 1962), pp. 231-245, offers essentially my perspective on ministry as continuing the ministry of Christ, except that he discusses only preaching and teaching.

distribution of the various functions of Christ among a variety of functionaries shows that no one person can assume the whole of his work. Nevertheless, Christ provides for a continuation of ministry among his people. He remains the pattern and standard for these various ministries.

Jesus' disciples did not function as rabbis, making their own disciples and setting up a chain of tradition, but brought others into personal discipleship to Jesus (Matt. 11:28-30; 23:8; 28:18f.; John 8:31; cf. 1 Cor. 1:12f.).[30] Since Christ is the Bishop and Shepherd, the Preacher, the Teacher, and the Deacon of the church, his disciples remain related to him directly and not through the intermediaries who share these aspects of his ministry.

Because of the all-sufficiency of Christ's priestly ministry (Heb. 7-10), no provision is made in the New Testament for a continuation of his priestly functions, and no minister of the church is called a priest.[31] No functionary in the church continues Christ's high-priestly and atoning role, no more so than his kingly role. As in the Old Testament, the whole people are priestly and royal (1 Pet. 2:5, 9 and Rev. 1:6, following Exod. 19:6), but unlike the Old Testament, there is no special priestly class among the New Testament people.

Even as Jesus characterized himself as a servant or minister (Luke 22:27; Mark. 10:45), so the servant family of words (*diakon-*) became the comprehensive description for all types of ministry in the church. *Diakonia* (usually translated "ministry" or "service") is used in the book of Acts alone in the following ways: for the apostleship of the Twelve (1:17, 25), the daily distribution of food to widows (Acts 6:1), preaching (Acts 6:4), relief for victims of famine (11:29; 12:25), and Paul's apostolic ministry (20:24; 21:19).[32]

Classification of Ministries

There are various ways that the ministries of the church may be classified so as to bring out their relationship to Christ, the church, and its work.

30. K. Rengstorf, *"Mathetes," Theological Dictionary of the New Testament,* ed. G. Kittel, tr. G. W. Bromiley (Grand Rapids: Eerdmans, 19967), Vol. 4, pp. 415-459, esp. pp. 434-440, 444-455.
31. See further pp. 220-226 on priestly language in the New Testament.
32. See further above on service, p. 295, and below on deacons, pp. 333ff.

From the Standpoint of the Mission of the Church

The workers in the church correspond to the work of the church. The church continues Jesus' proclaiming, teaching, and benevolent ministries. Jesus' "great commission" to his disciples following his resurrection gave the work of the church to be "Make disciples of all nations, . . . teaching them to obey everything that I have commanded you" (Matt. 28:19-20). To paraphrase, this is to evangelize them and nurture them in the faith, including the practice of Jesus' teachings concerning ethics and benevolence. Looked at from the standpoint of the nature of the work of the church, there are verbal, pastoral, and diaconal ministries in the church.

First Peter 4:11 summarizes the ministries of the church in two groups: "whoever speaks" and "whoever serves," the speaking ministries and the serving ministries. Similarly, Acts 6:2 and 4 speaks of the ministry of tables (administering relief, benevolence) and the ministry of the word and prayer (the speaking roles of preaching/teaching and worship), and Paul uses *diakonia* ("ministry") for both his apostolic ministry of the word (Rom. 11:13; 2 Cor. 5:18) and his relief efforts for the poor in Judea (Rom. 15:25, 31; 2 Cor. 8:4; 9:1, 12).[33] The verbal ministries include evangelizing the unconverted and teaching the converted. The teaching work of the church is both verbal and pastoral. It overlaps with but does not exhaust the pastoral care and direction of believers. The diaconal ministries according to this classification include all the serving activities described by *diakonia* in the New Testament other than the ministry of the word itself.

From the Standpoint of Office

If one turns from the standpoint of the church to the standpoint of its representative functionaries, the same result obtains. The ministries of the church when examined in terms of office or function show little difference from the classification in terms of the mission or work of the church. Thus there are ministries of evangelism, of edification, and of

---

33. Josef Hainz, *Ekklesia: Strukturen paulinischer Gemeinde-Theologie und Gemeinde-Ordnung* (Regensburg: Friedrich Pustet, 1972), p. 181, suggests that in Rom. 12:6-8 prophecy (the word) and ministry (service) are lead concepts for the items that follow, but "ministry" could be of the word, according to John N. Collins, *Diakonia: Re-Interpreting the Ancient Sources* (Oxford: University Press, 1990), pp. 232f.; similarly, he considers the ministry of 1 Pet. 4:11 indeterminate (p. 232).

benevolence. These correspond to the functionaries known as evangelists (proclaimers), pastors (those who give spiritual nurture), and deacons (those who serve other needs). These will be discussed below.

From the Standpoint of Their Commission

The functionaries who fulfill the work of the church ultimately receive their commission to serve from the Lord. This authorization, however, comes in different ways, according to the nature of the function and the circumstances under which it is performed. The commission may come directly from the Lord, mediately from the church, or spontaneously from the situation. There were temporary ("extraordinary") ministers, who were personally commissioned by Jesus and/or endowed with supernatural gifts by the Spirit (apostles, prophets, inspired teachers, and workers of miracles); appointed ("ordained") ministers, who were recognized by the church to serve as its leaders in evangelism, pastoral care, and other forms of service (evangelists, pastors, and deacons); and "ordinary" ministers (that is, all Christians), who by reason of opportunity, need, or circumstance may according to their ability tell their neighbor about Jesus, deal with a spiritual problem, or meet a need.

Temporary/Occasional Functionaries

Apostles [34]

The word *apostolos* means "one sent" and refers especially to one sent on a mission and possessing the authority conferred by the sender.

---

34. J. B. Lightfoot, "The Name and Office of Apostle," *St. Paul's Epistle to the Galatians*, 2nd ed. (London: Macmillan, 1866), pp. 92-101; H. Vogelstein, "The Development of the Apostolate in Judaism and its Transposition in Christianity," *Hebrew Union College Annual* 2 (1925): 99-123; T. W. Manson, *The Church's Ministry* (Philadelphia: Westminster, 1948), pp. 34-56; K. H. Rengstorf, "*Apostolos,*" *Theological Dictionary of the New Testament,* ed. G. Kittel, tr. G. W. Bromiley (Grand Rapids: Eerdmans, 1964), Vol. 1, pp. 407-447; Hans Küng, *The Church* (London: Burns & Oates, 1968), pp. 344-359; W. Schmithals, *The Office of Apostle in the Early Church* (Nashville: Abingdon, 1969); R. Schnackenburg, "Apostles Before and During Paul's Time," in *Apostolic History and the Gospel,* ed. W. Ward Gasque and Ralph P. Martin (Grand Rapids: Eerdmans, 1970), pp. 287-303.

Although the background to the New Testament usage has been sought in the redeemer figure of Gnosticism or the *shaliach* of rabbinic Judaism, there is a lack of evidence concerning both for the period prior to or contemporary with the New Testament. It seems most likely that both the New Testament "apostle" and the rabbinic *shaliach* are derived from a common Jewish concept of "sending," best represented in the Old Testament accounts of the call and commissioning of prophets.[35]

Christ himself served as the pattern for the New Testament apostolate. "Consider Jesus, the apostle and high priest of our confession" (Heb. 3:1). Jesus was God's representative or ambassador to the human race.[36] The Gospel of John correlates God's sending of Jesus with Jesus' sending of his disciples. Jesus prayed to the Father, "As you have sent me into the world, so I have sent them into the world" (John 17:18); and after his resurrection, he declared to the disciples, "As the Father has sent me, so I send you" (John 20:21).[37] Those sent by Christ were to be received as Christ himself (John 13:20; Matt. 10:40). Jesus was the perfect apostle, the embodiment of the apostolic office. The sending of others in the early church derived from his own sending by the Father.

The word "apostle" is applied to various types of messengers in the New Testament. The translation "delegate" would cover most of these usages. The mission and authority of those sent depended on who did the sending and what task was assigned.[38]

(1) On the lowest level are the "messengers of the churches" (2 Cor. 8:23) commissioned by the Gentile churches to carry a monetary gift to the Jewish churches. They were chosen by the churches for a specific task, as was Epaphroditus by the church at Philippi (Phil. 2:25).

35. Francis H. Agnew, "The Origin of the NT Apostle Concept: A Review of Research," *JBL* 105 (1986): 75-96.

36. Colin Kruse, *New Testament Models for Ministry: Jesus and Paul* (Nashville: Thomas Nelson, 1983), pp. 13-33. Cf. Louis Bouyer, *The Church of God, Body of Christ, and Temple of the Spirit* (Chicago: Franciscan Herald Press, 1982), pp. 314-316: The apostolate of the apostles has its model and source in the mission of the Son from the Father with the difference that Christ accomplished redemption and the apostle applied that redemption to human beings.

37. Although the latter passage shifts from *apostellō* for the sending of Jesus to *pempō* for the sending of the disciples, there does not seem to be a significance in the change, for the two verbs are used synonymously by John — C. K. Barrett, *The Gospel According to John* (London: SPCK, 1965), p. 473.

38. Josef Hainz, *Ekklesia: Strukturen paulinischer Gemeinde-Theologie und Gemeinde-Ordnumg* (Regensburg: Friedrich Pustet, 1972), pp. 152-53.

(2) In some passages "apostles" seems to carry a meaning equivalent to "missionaries" (a word in English derived from what is roughly the Latin equivalent of the Greek "apostle"). There is often uncertainty in the text whether these persons were sent out by churches with a broader commission to evangelize than the limited function of the "money messengers" in 2 Corinthians 8:23 or were sent out personally by the resurrected Jesus, with or without confirmation by the churches. There is some uncertainty also concerning which passages belong in this category. Fairly certain is Romans 16:7, "Andronicus and Junia, . . . they are prominent among the apostles" (since Junia is likely a woman's name, a husband and wife missionary team is probably indicated). The meaning of "missionary" appears to be the usage of Acts 14:4 and 14 where Barnabas and Paul are called "apostles," apparently with reference to their being sent out by the church at Antioch at the behest of the Holy Spirit in 13:1-3. Similarly, the linking of Paul and Barnabas in 1 Corinthians 9:6 suggests the meaning of missionaries for "the other apostles" of 9:5; and see 1 Corinthians 15:5-7 for apostles as a different, broader category than the Twelve. The persons sarcastically described by Paul as "super-apostles" and then as "false apostles" (2 Cor. 11:5, 13)[39] were Jewish-Christian missionaries who were upsetting the church at Corinth.[40] The plural "apostles" in 1 Thessalonians 2:7 may include Silas and Timothy as apostles (1 Thess. 1:1); likewise 1 Corinthians 4:9 and 9:5 may reflect the meaning "missionary." Whether Galatians 1:19 represents a broader use of "apostle" than the Twelve depends on the interpretation of the construction: Does the exception clause apply to the whole preceding statement (implying that James is an apostle) or only to the verb "saw" (placing James outside the group of apostles not seen)?[41]

39. Cf. Rev. 2:2, "those who claim to be apostles." There would be no doubt about the identity of the Twelve, so a category encompassing a larger number is indicated. These false apostles among the seven churches in Asia would probably not be the same as Paul's opponents in 2 Corinthians.

40. Dieter Georgi, *The Opponents of Paul in Second Corinthians* (Philadelphia: Fortress, 1986); Jerry L. Sumney, *Identifying Paul's Opponents: The Question of Method in 2 Corinthians* (Sheffield: JSNT, 1990).

41. Grammatically, both interpretations are possible. Linguists tend to favor the former interpretation: e.g., E. D. Burton, *The Epistle to the Galatians* (Edinburgh: T. & T. Clark, 1921), p. 60, and F. F. Bruce, *The Epistle to the Galatians* (Grand Rapids: Eerdmans, 1982), p. 101; but others point out that James was not usually regarded as an apostle: e.g., Hans Dieter Betz, *Galatians* (Philadelphia: Fortress, 1979), p. 78.

(3) There is a limited, technical use of "apostle" in the New Testament to refer to the Twelve and Paul, and it was this meaning that came to prevail in Christian terminology. The restricted sense is represented by the vision of the new Jerusalem in Revelation: "And the wall of the city has twelve foundations, and on them are the twelve names of the twelve apostles of the Lamb" (Rev. 21:14). Luke's account of the choosing of the Twelve makes the connection with the title "apostle": "[Jesus] called his disciples and chose twelve of them, whom he also named apostles" (Luke 6:13; Matt. 10:2; some mss. of Mark 3:14). The number twelve was probably selected because of its symbolic connections with the twelve tribes of Israel (cf. Luke 22:30; Matt. 19:28), and so is important for the understanding of Jesus' followers as the reconstituted people of God.[42]

During the personal ministry of Jesus, the preferred term for the Twelve was "disciples" (but not applied to them exclusively), for this was their relationship to Jesus. Mark 3:13-15 says that Jesus appointed the Twelve first so that they might be with him and second so that he might send them forth (verb form of the noun "apostle") to preach and to have authority to cast out demons. In connection with their preaching mission (Matt. 10:2, 5; Mark 3:14) and then especially after the resurrection (book of Acts) the term "apostle" came into greater currency, for at these times they served as Jesus' messengers and representatives.

The application of the title "apostle" to Paul was a matter of controversy in the early church. Although Paul sometimes used apostle to mean missionary (see above), his vigorous polemic, insisting on his personal call by the risen Lord to this position and function (Gal. 1–2; 2 Cor. 11-12), is itself an indication of a technical usage of the term from the earliest days of the church. No one could deny that Paul was an apostle in the sense of missionary. At most, one could deny that his calling came from the Lord, not just from the church (Gal. 1:1), but even on this point there is some indication that Jesus called some to be missionaries in addition to his calling of the Twelve (1 Cor. 15:5, 7; 2 Cor. 11:13). Nevertheless, Paul's argument and usage indicates something more than "missionary" was involved in the dispute, for he insists on his equality with Peter and the other "pillars" of the church (Gal. 2:7-9). In contrast to Peter (and the Twelve), Paul's apostleship (and others') was to Gentiles (Gal. 2:7-9). Galatians 1:17 suggests Paul's recognition

---

42. Note the association of the two ideas, the twelve tribes and the twelve apostles, in Rev. 21:12, 14. Cf. John P. Meier, "The Circle of the Twelve," *JBL* 116 (1997): 635-672.

of the Twelve as the first apostles of the church and also the use of the word "apostles" for some who were stationary in Jerusalem and hardly "missionary." It may be that Paul's activities gave the sense of "missionary" to apostles, who in the primary sense were "delegates," either of the Lord or of the churches.

For Paul the office of apostle included, in addition to the task of preaching and establishing churches (Rom. 11:13; 15:15-20; 1 Cor. 9:2), the right to financial support (1 Cor. 9:4-7; 2 Cor. 11:7-9), the power to perform miraculous signs (2 Cor. 12:12), and authority to command (1 Thess. 2:6). He especially connected the function of the apostle with having seen the risen Lord and having been commissioned by him (Rom. 1:5; 1 Cor. 9:1; 15:8; Gal. 1:1; 2:8). For him the apostolic task involved sharing in the humility and sufferings of Christ (2 Cor. 10–13).[43] In view of later developments it is notable that he says nothing about a right to confer ordination.

The qualifications and work of the "apostles of Christ" are closely interconnected. The betrayal and suicide by Judas occasioned the selection of a replacement in order to fill up the symbolic number of apostles to the Jews to twelve. Peter set forth the requisite qualifications:

> So one of the men who have accompanied us during all the time that the Lord Jesus went in and out among us, beginning from the baptism of John until the day when he was taken up from us — one of these must become a witness with us to his resurrection. (Acts 1:21-22)

Two names were put forward as meeting the qualifications. The taking of lots revealed the Lord's choice and so preserved the principle of the Lord himself choosing his apostles (Acts 1:23-26). To have seen the resurrected Christ was not sufficient by itself to make one an apostle: one had to be commissioned by Christ (cf. 1 Cor. 15:5-7). In addition to the point on which Paul laid emphasis, seeing the risen Christ, it was necessary for inclusion in the Twelve, as fulfilling the apostleship to Israel, to have been a part of the company associated with Jesus throughout his earthly ministry (which was directed to the Jewish people). This association with Jesus during his ministry, moreover, meant that they could verify the continuity between the earthly Jesus

---

43. John Howard Schütz, *Paul and the Anatomy of Apostolic Authority* (Cambridge: University Press, 1975). And note Scott J. Hafemann, *Suffering and Ministry in the Spirit: Paul's Defense of his Ministry in II Corinthians 2:14–3:3* (Grand Rapids: Eerdmans, 1990).

and the resurrected Christ. The Twelve were unique witnesses to the earthly life and resurrection of Jesus, and he called them to proclaim this (Matt. 28:16-20; Luke 24:46-48; Acts 1:2, 8; Rom. 1:1-5). Their qualifications to be apostles dictated their work, and their work was based on their unique qualifications. The centrality of the resurrection and the apostolic testimony to it explains why the "apostles" head the lists of functionaries in the church and God's gifts to it (1 Cor. 12:28; Eph. 4:11)

In the nature of the case, the apostles had an unrepeatable ministry. With their passing, no one else could give the testimony that they could. Their witness to the life, teachings, and resurrection of Jesus made them the foundation of the church (Eph. 2:20). In the reversed imagery of the apostles as laying the foundation (Rom. 15:20; 1 Cor. 3:10), they equally belong to the beginning of the church, for such a task is chronologically limited.[44] When a few years later the apostle James was killed (Acts 12:2), no successor for him was chosen, the reason being that James still held his office. Judas had renounced his apostleship and fallen away from his ministry (Acts 1:20, 25). Death in the case of James, by way of contrast, did not end his testimony to the resurrection; in fact, his death as a martyr to his faith only enhanced his witness to the resurrection. Hence, he continues to fill his apostolic function as the foundation on which the church exists. Paul's statement that Christ appeared to him "last of all" (1 Cor. 15:8) indicates that there would be no continuation of the office of apostle in the church. Paul viewed himself as an exception ("one untimely born" — 1 Cor. 15:8), for the Lord would not continue his appearances and commissioning of apostles. The authority of the apostles remains after their death in the authority of their testimony.[45]

The apostolate as a missionary task requires personal continuation in the church (see further on evangelists, pp. 329ff.); apostles as plenipotentiaries of Jesus have no successors in the church. The church today has the same "apostles of Christ" as the first-century church had, the Twelve and Paul. They are still the foundation of Christian faith and the basis for the life of the church. One could speak of successors to the apostles in their work as missionaries, but there can be no "apostolic succession" to their function as foundation of the church.

44. Oscar Cullmann, *Peter: Disciple, Apostle, Martyr* (Philadelphia: Westminster, 1962), pp. 220-224.

45. Jean Delorme, *Le Ministère et les ministères selon le Nouveau Testament* (Paris: Seuil, 1974), p. 345.

Prophets[46]

Prophets usually follow apostles in the Pauline listing (1 Cor. 12:28; Eph. 4:11). They were closely linked with the apostles in the foundation of the church (Eph. 2:20), because they shared with them in the revelation of divine truth (Eph. 3:5). Prophets in biblical language were spokespersons for God, receiving divine messages and communicating them to people. There were women prophets, as there had been in the Old Testament, in the early church (Acts 2:17-18; 21:9: 1 Cor. 11:5).

Jesus during his ministry was popularly regarded as a prophet, indeed as "the (eschatological) prophet" (Matt. 21:11, 46; Luke 24:19; John 6:14).[47] One interpretation in the early church of the significance of Jesus was that he was the prophet like Moses whom the people were to hear (Acts 3:22-23). Jesus Christ was himself, therefore, *the prophet* who revealed the will of God for the new dispensation. Prophets in the early church found in him the model and example for their ministry. They were extensions of his unique prophetic ministry.

In the book of Acts prophets appear in the role of predicting the future (Acts 11:27-28; 21:10-11). Because of the special problems at Corinth, Paul emphasized the instructive, edificatory work of prophets — speaking for "upbuilding, encouragement, and consolation" (1 Cor. 14:3-4; cf. Acts 15:32). But across the strands of New Testament literature the common idea uniting the functions of prophets is their association with revealing God's will (Eph. 3:5; 1 Pet. 1:10-12; 1 Cor. 14:6, pairing revelation and prophecy, and knowledge and teaching; cf. 14:26, "revelation" apparently referring to what was communicated by a prophet; 14:29-31; Acts 13:1-3, assuming that the Spirit spoke through the prophets). This included distinguishing true from false "revelations" (1 Cor. 14:37; cf. 1 John 2:20, 27; 4:1-6), revealing the secrets of the human heart

---

46. H. A. Guy, *New Testament Prophecy* (London: Epworth, 1947), chap. 3 on Jesus and chap. 4 on the first-century church; David Hill, *New Testament Prophecy* (Atlanta: John Knox, 1970); W. Grudem, *The Gift of Prophecy in 1 Corinthians* (Washington: University Press of America, 1981); D. E. Aune, *Prophecy in Early Christianity and the Ancient Mediterranean World* (Grand Rapids: Eerdmans, 1983); for the forms of prophetic speech in the New Testament, cf. James I. H. McDonald, *Kerygma and Didache: The Articulation and Structure of the Earliest Christian Message* (Cambridge: University Press, 1980), pp. 12-38.

47. Oscar Cullmann, *The Christology of the New Testament* (Philadelphia: Westminster, 1959), pp. 13-50; Ferdinand Hahn, *The Titles of Jesus in Christology* (New York: World, 1969), pp. 352-406.

(1 Cor. 14:23-25), identifying leaders for the church (1 Tim. 1:18; 4:14), and strengthening believers (Acts 15:32). Prophets revealed new truth, in distinction from teachers (to be discussed on pp. 327-329), who expounded the meaning and made the application of the revelation.[48]

Individual prophets received only partial revelation, so they only "knew in part" (1 Cor. 13:9, 12). Hence, they might need to have their message clarified, and their messages were subject to discernment by other gifted persons (1 Cor. 14:37f.). An individual prophet was not the judge of his own message; the community had to test the prophets, for there were false prophets (1 Cor. 14:29; 1 John 4:1).[49] Paul, therefore, submits the prophets to the necessity of discernment, including (1) judgment by the community (1 Thess. 5:19-22), (2) judgment by other prophets (1 Cor. 14:29), and (3) accord with apostolic teaching (1 Cor. 14:37f.).

The Johannine literature similarly offers objective criteria for testing the "spirits": (1) the teaching heard "from the beginning" of the gospel (1 John 2:24), including (2) the factual test of conformity to what was taught by the original proclaimers of the word ("whoever listens to us" — 1 John 4:6), (3) the doctrinal test of confession of Jesus as the divine Christ (1 John 4:1-6, 13-15), and (4) the moral test of practical expressions of brotherly love (1 John 4:7-12, 16-21). (See the treatment on pp. 106-107 of the work of the Holy Spirit as testifying to Jesus — John 16:12-15.)

The Once-for-Allness of Certain Functionaries

Paul in 1 Corinthians 12:28 refers to other occasional functions performed in the early days of the church — "deeds of power, gifts of healing, forms of assistance, forms of leadership, various kinds of tongues."

These and other unusual aspects of the working of the Holy Spirit in the early church were temporary. Paul in 1 Corinthians 13:8-13 contrasted the permanent, abiding qualities of faith, hope, and love with the temporary and passing phenomena of prophecies, speaking in

48. "The role of the prophet was to transmit new revelation to the church, that of the teacher to transmit old revelation to the church" — James D. G. Dunn, *Unity and Diversity in the New Testament* (London: SCM, 1990), p. 112.

49. E. Earle Ellis, *Pauline Theology: Ministry and Society* (Grand Rapids: Eerdmans, 1989), p. 39.

tongues, and revealed knowledge. He uses three illustrations: the difference between the partial and the complete, the difference between what is appropriate for the child and for the adult, and the difference between the dimness of what is seen in a metal mirror and the clarity of face-to-face perception. Prophecies, tongues, and knowledge are incomplete, belong to childhood, and are unclear; faith, hope, and love are complete, belong to maturity, and bring full personal knowledge.

The temporary nature of certain gifts was the recognition of the church itself in its early history. As noted above, very soon the term "apostle," except where preserving the broader meaning of "missionary," was limited in Christian usage to the Twelve and Paul. Although prophecy was not denied in principle, no prophets were accepted as authentic after the early second century, and the effort of the Montanist movement to revive prophecy was repudiated. Other gifts of the Spirit were foreign to the experience of the leadership of the church.

The provision within the New Testament (especially the Pastoral Epistles) for a settled ministry of persons with natural qualifications shows the expectation of a church existing without the continuous presence of charismatic leaders. The instructions concerning bishops and deacons in 1 Timothy and Titus anticipated the passing from the scene of prophets and teachers. Within the New Testament there coexisted the inspired, temporary ministers and the ordinary continuing ministers, as may be seen from Acts and the Pastoral Epistles.[50] The presence alongside the trilogy of "apostles, prophets, and teachers" mentioned in 1 Corinthians 12:28 of "evangelists and pastors" in Ephesians 4:11 reflects a similar situation.[51] In the Pastoral Epistles there is no anticipation of the continuing presence of divinely inspired prophets and teachers who would be available on a regular basis to speak the word of the Lord and interpret its meaning.

In the nature of the case these extraordinary manifestations of the Spirit belonged to the beginning of the church and not to its continuation. When the revelation was given and confirmed (Heb. 2:3-4) and the church was established, the special guidance of Spirit-inspired

50. The *Didache* may be compared as describing a transition situation, when itinerant apostles, prophets, and teachers might still appear, but provision is made for the appointment of resident bishops and deacons for the continuing ministry of the church.

51. E. Best, "Ministry in Ephesians," *Irish Biblical Studies* 15 (1993): 146-166, notes that in Ephesians the ministry of apostles and prophets was considered to have been fulfilled but evangelists, shepherds, and teachers had a continuing role.

functionaries was not needed and indeed could be detrimental to individual spiritual growth in discernment and maturity.

The extraordinary ministers belonging to the foundation period of the church have a continuing function through their testimony to the resurrected Christ and revelation of his message. They do not (and in some respects cannot) have personal successors; the church still has the same apostles and prophets as in the first century, for their words of testimony and revelation preserved in scripture form the foundation of the church's message and faith. Both the functions and the same functionaries are permanent in the church. This feature belongs to the once-for-allness of the original revelation (e.g., 1 Cor. 15:8; Eph. 1:9-10; 3:5-11). The case is different with the ordinary ministers. The functions remain in the church, but the persons filling these functions are new with each generation. Instead of an appointment by the Lord and special endowment with his Spirit, they receive appointment by the church.

Meaning of Ordination[52]

"Ordination" is being used here to refer to the whole process of appointment to ministry in the church, including both the selection and the installation to a given function.

The occasional/temporary ministers discussed above received a direct divine call and appointment. The Lord personally chose his apostles, and the Holy Spirit inspired prophets and endowed other functionaries with special gifts. The concern of this section is with those continuing/permanent ministers chosen by the Lord mediately through appointment by the church.

The divine choice was evident also in the selection of certain persons to fill responsibilities that did not require unique or supernatural qualifications. The Holy Spirit speaking through inspired prophets designated Paul and Barnabas for missionary work (Acts 13:1-3). Prophetic utterances pointed to Timothy as a fit person for the work of an

---

52. E. Lohse, *Die Ordination im Spätjudentum und im Neuen Testament* (Göttingen: Vandenhoeck & Ruprecht, 1951); Everett Ferguson, "Jewish and Christian Ordination," *Harvard Theological Review* 56 (1963): 13-19; idem, "Ordination in the Ancient Church (IV)," *Restoration Quarterly* 5 (1961): 130-146; M. Warkentin, *Ordination* (Grand Rapids: Eerdmans, 1982).

evangelist (1 Tim. 1:18; in view of that statement, 1 Tim. 4:14 should be translated, "Do not neglect the gift that is in you, which was given to you on account of prophecies [not 'through prophecy'] with the laying on of hands of the council of elders").[53] Such a Spirit-revealed choice is probably the meaning of Acts 20:28, "the Holy Spirit has made you bishops," although the joint actions of the Spirit and congregations in other places (e.g., Acts 6:1-6; 13:1-3; 15:22-28) leave open the possibility that men chosen in some other way but with the approval of the Holy Spirit could be described as placed in the church by the Holy Spirit.[54] In these cases where local churches were more directly involved in the ministry to be performed, the divine choice was recognized and endorsed by the church involved, as indicated for Paul and Barnabas at Antioch in Acts 13:1-3 and for Timothy in Lystra (Acts 16:1-3; 1 Tim. 4:14).

In addition to direct divine appointment and equipment, the New Testament church knew various other methods of selection to ministry. There might be selection by the founding missionaries and evangelists. Acts 14:23 may be taken in one of two ways: "[Paul and Barnabas] appointed [or *ordained*, according to the later Christian usage of the verb *cheirotoneō*] for them elders in every church by prayer with fasting and entrusted them to the Lord"; or "[Paul and Barnabas] selected [according to the earlier Hellenistic usage of the word] for them elders in every church and entrusted them to the Lord by prayer with fasting."[55] The

---

53. Cf. Revised English Bible; Kevin Giles, *Patterns of Ministry among the First Christians* (Melbourne: Collins Dove, 1989), pp. 184ff.

54. The church today may truly be said to have bishops made by the Holy Spirit when it appoints according to scriptural principles men on whom the Holy Spirit has bestowed the requisite qualifications. And F. F. Bruce takes this as the sense even for Acts 20:28 — *Commentary on the Book of Acts: The English Text* (Grand Rapids: Eerdmans, 1954), p. 416.

55. The noun form *cheirotonia* became the technical term in Greek Christian usage for "ordination." It meant in classical Greek election by show of hands. In Hellenistic times it became a general word for selection or appointment, however the choice was made. In spite of many statements in modern writers that it meant the laying on of hands, this was not the case. *Cheirothesia* was the word for this action. The fact that laying on of hands (see below) was employed in the ordination ceremony has nothing to do with the development of *cheirotonia* as the word for ordination; that is a development from the Hellenistic meaning of appointment. Everett Ferguson, "Ordination in the Ancient Church (IV)," *Restoration Quarterly* 5 (1961): 137-139, 143-144; idem, "Eusebius and Ordination," *Journal of Ecclesiastical History* 13 (1962): 142-144.

latter interpretation accords better with early Christian usage, but the former (without sacramental connotations) cannot be ruled out.

Quite common was the practice of the whole local church making a choice. This was the method employed in the selection of the seven servants in Acts 6:5. Similarly the churches chose (*cheirotoneō*, selected or appointed) a representative to accompany Paul in carrying relief to Judea (2 Cor. 8:19). The church in Jerusalem joined with the apostles and elders in choosing Judas Barsabbas and Silas to be sent as their representatives to Antioch (Acts 15:22). The congregation could function as well as Spirit-inspired prophets or founding missionaries as the organ of the divine choice of ministers. Wherever the initiative in the selection lay, whether with the Holy Spirit speaking through prophets, with missionary evangelists, or with the whole church, others affected in the decision concurred in the choice. Even where the choice was made or revealed by the Spirit, there was a human recognition (Acts 13:1-3; 1 Tim. 4:14); where there was congregational selection, the leadership gave approval (Acts 6:6). The principle of joint participation is well summarized by Acts 15:22, "the apostles and the elders with the consent of the whole church" (Acts 15:22). The designation of ministers involved the divine choice, the choice and/or approval by the community and by its leaders or other ministers, and the person's readiness to serve.

In contrast to the variety in methods of selection recorded in the New Testament, all accounts of installation in which details are given refer to prayer accompanied by the laying on of hands and/or fasting, both activities serving as a supplement to and reinforcement of prayer. This procedure occurs in the appointment of the Seven in Acts 6:6, the sending out of missionaries in Acts 13:3, the appointment of elders in Acts 14:23, and the recognition of an evangelist in 1 Timothy 4:14.[56] Leadership in the process of appointment might be taken by apostles and prophets (Acts 6:1-6; 13:1-3, the wording in both passages suggesting a close relationship with the church, on whose behalf they were acting), evangelists (Titus 1:5), or elders (1 Tim. 4:14).

The fullest account of appointment to church office in the New Testament occurs in Acts 6:1-6.[57] It is characteristic of Luke's method

---

56. John P. Meier, "*Presbyteros* in the Pastoral Epistles," *Catholic Biblical Quarterly* 35 (1973): 323-345, supports the meaning of *presbyteriou* as "college of presbyters," so the translation should not be "ordination to the presbyterate" (pp. 339-342). He further affirms that Timothy and Titus were not *episkopoi* (p. 345).

57. See my "Ordination According to Acts," *Acts: The Spreading Flame* (Searcy, AR: Harding University, 1989), pp. 376-377.

to give one full account of something and at other times make briefer summaries (sometimes including different details). The steps in the procedure followed in the selection and installation of the Seven may be outlined as follows:

(1) Recognition of a need: "the Hellenists complained against the Hebrews because their widows were being neglected in the daily distribution of food." The twelve apostles said to the whole company of the disciples, "It is not right that we should neglect the word of God in order to wait on tables" (Acts 6:1-2). The testimony to the resurrection of Jesus, "serving [the ministry of] the word" (v. 4), was something only the Twelve could do. "To serve tables" was a work others could do just as well. Selecting persons to take charge of that activity would bring more persons into the leadership of the church (probably from the Hellenists, up to this time not represented in the leadership), multiply the work that could be done, and make possible more efficient accomplishment of the work.

(2) Instructions on qualifications for persons to meet the need: "men of good standing, full of the Spirit and of wisdom" (Acts 6:3). Teaching preceded the selection. A certain type of person was needed according to the work to be done and the situation in the congregation.

(3) Examination of who had the requisite qualities: "From among yourselves look for seven men" (Acts 6:3). "The whole community of the disciples" (v. 2) looked at those in their number in order to consider the best persons. The method of considering or testing the men is not described, but the community itself would have already known the men and been in a position to determine who should assume the responsibilities.

(4) Selection by the congregation: "the whole community . . . chose" the seven men (Acts 6:5). How is not related: voice vote, show of hands, secret ballot, or some other method? The apostles had called the church together, pointed out the problem, and laid down the qualifications required, but the actual selection was made by the whole multitude of believers.

(5) Presentation of the persons chosen: "they had these men stand before the apostles" (Acts 6:6). The congregation gave a formal and public presentation of the men whom they had chosen. This constituted their official recognition that these men had their endorsement and approval to serve.

(6) Setting apart for the work: they "prayed and laid their hands on them" (Acts 6:6). The presumption is that the apostles did this, and

such a shift in the subject of sentences is not unusual in Luke's writing, but grammatically it is possible to take the "whole community" (v. 5) as still the subject. The difficulties of all the people actually laying on hands would indicate this was done by representatives, and the most likely to function in this way would be the Twelve. The ambiguity argues that no special significance attaches to apostles being the ones doing the laying on of hands. Rather, the emphasis rests on the fact that the men began their ministry with the authorization of the church and with its benediction and blessing, expressed in prayer to God.

The meaning of the laying on of hands in appointment to office in the church has been widely disputed and often misunderstood. A proper understanding of this gesture will clarify the meaning of the whole process of ordination.[58]

The laying on of hands, or leaning upon with the hands, was widely used in the Old Testament: especially by the offerer in presenting sacrificial animals (Leviticus, *passim*) but also by witnesses on a blasphemer to be stoned (Lev. 24:14; cf. Susannah 34), by the people in consecrating the Levites (Num. 8:10), and by Moses in appointing Joshua as his successor (Num. 27:15-23; Deut. 34:9).[59] This gesture has been interpreted as signifying the creation of a substitute or the transfer of something.[60] It became central in rabbinic ordination, which understandably has been often understood as the background to Christian practice, despite the absence of evidence for its use for this purpose prior to A.D. 70.[61] Another gesture, the gentle touching with the hands, was used in the Old Testament to accompany the pronouncing of a blessing (Gen. 48:14).

Which gesture and which meaning lay behind Christian practice? Several arguments make a strong case that touching as a sign of blessing was the Christian practice.

58. Everett Ferguson, "Laying on of Hands: Its Significance in Ordination," *Journal of Theological Studies*, n.s. 26 (1975): 1-12, which covers the evidence of the early church, as well as of the New Testament.

59. Everett Ferguson, "Ordination in the Ancient Church (I)," *Restoration Quarterly* 4 (1960): 125-127. For the use of the Old Testament texts in Acts, see my "Laying on of Hands in Acts 6:6 and 13:3," *Restoration Quarterly* 4 (1960): 250-252.

60. Hartmut Gese, *Essays on Biblical Theology* (Augsburg: Minneapolis, 1981), pp. 104-106, argues for the meaning identification (or substitution) rather than transference.

61. See the contrast I make between "Jewish and Christian Ordination," *Harvard Theological Review* 56 (1963): 13-19.

(1) Jesus used the laying on of hands in conferring a benediction. Note the blessing of the little children in Mark 10:13-16 (cf. Matt. 19:13; Luke 18:15). The practice of Jesus was surely the most important factor in determining Christian usage and meaning.

(2) Unlike rabbinic ordination, Christian ordination always associated the laying on of hands with prayer. Indeed, the prayer appears to have been the constant element, with the laying on of hands and/or fasting being present to support the time of prayer (cf. Acts 6:6; 13:3; 14:23). The prayer indicates the background of the usage to be Jewish blessings.

(3) The laying on of hands appeared in varied contexts in Christian usage; the New Testament mentions, in addition to the blessing of children and appointment to church office, healings (Mark 6:5; Acts 28:8) and imparting the Holy Spirit (Acts 8:14-19; 19:6). The one idea that unites these varied usages is the conferring of a blessing. The type of blessing might vary, and that was why the prayer was central. It specified verbally the kind of blessing intended by the outward gesture. The imparting of the Holy Spirit is sometimes taken to be the primary significance of the laying on of hands, particularly in ordination. However, it was only one of the kinds of blessing that might be signified by the gesture. It is not mentioned in the New Testament as the gift imparted in appointment to church office; indeed, where the facts are known, the persons receiving the laying on of hands already possessed the Spirit (Acts 6:3; 13:1-3). Even in the conferring of the Holy Spirit in Acts 8, prayer is mentioned (Acts 8:15). The laying on of hands appears to be a symbolic expression of identification with and personal specification of the object of the blessing, which was spelled out in the prayer.

(4) Early Christian art used the laying on of hands to depict scenes where a blessing was intended. Speaking must be suggested in art by some gesture, and the way artists showed a blessing was by portraying a laying on of hands. Especially striking are the representations of the feeding miracles in which the Bible says that Jesus "blessed" the bread and fish (i.e., said a prayer of thanksgiving), but says nothing about a gesture accompanying the words (e.g., Matt. 14:19). The scene is common in Christian art and is depicted by Jesus placing his hands on the bread and fish.

(5) When the church fathers in the fourth century came to interpret the significance of what was done in ordination, they interpreted the laying on of hands as a blessing and gave centrality in the ordination

to prayer.[62] The laying on of hands was an enacted prayer. Soon, since the prayer of ordination included a petition for the sending of the Spirit on the person being ordained and the laying on of hands was associated with imparting the Spirit in other contexts, the gift of the Spirit came to be associated with the accompanying gesture in ordination as well; but this was a secondary development.

(6) The conceptual background to Christian usage is indicated by ecclesiastical Syriac, a kindred language to Hebrew developed from biblical Aramaic. The technical vocabulary for ordination in Christian Syriac is built on the same root as the Hebrew word for laying on of hands in blessing, not from the root used for other kinds of imposition of hands.

These arguments indicate the significance of ordination to a work in the church. The prayer and laying on of hands as an induction into formal service of a congregation constituted the bestowal of a blessing. They were an expression of approval and authorization by the congregation to act in leadership on its behalf and a petition for the divine favor upon the person in carrying out the designated task. This meaning finds explicit statement in the text of the New Testament. Acts 14:23 indicates that the persons appointed by prayer and fasting were "commended to the Lord." Acts 14:26 reflects Luke's understanding of the significance of the prayer and laying on of hands in Acts 13:1-3. Paul and Barnabas "sailed back to Antioch, where they had been commended to the grace of God for the work that they had completed." This was the meaning of ordination in the New Testament church: giving commendation of a person before God and committing or entrusting that person to God for the ministry.

Appointment by prayer and the laying on of hands is a reminder that the Lord gives ministers to his church (see pp. 290ff. on ministry as a gift). God instituted the functions in the church, set the qualifications for ministry, and makes possible the attainment and performance of the various ministries. Ministry is not produced by the church, but is the result of the work of Christ and is dependent on God's blessings. Nevertheless, the church recognizes its ministers, and this recognition is essential to service among believers. Those appointed can rest assured that whom God chooses and calls to ministry he blesses.

To be set apart for an office is a recognition of a service already

---

62. Everett Ferguson, "Ordination in the Ancient Church (II)," *Restoration Quarterly* 5 (1961): 28-30 (especially).

being engaged in. Thus, it is a "recognition," not a "license" to power. The Holy Spirit has already given an empowerment to perform ministry.

The work of the church surveyed above was carried out by all the members: "those who were scattered" from Jerusalem "went from place to place, evangelizing" (Acts 8:4). All the Christians addressed in Hebrews were commanded "to exhort one another every day . . . so that none of you may be hardened by the deceitfulness of sin" (Heb. 3:13); all had the responsibility "to exercise the oversight so that no one fails to obtain the grace of God" (Heb. 12:15);[63] and God did not overlook their "work and the love showed for his sake in serving the saints" (Heb. 6:10). The ordained ministers — evangelists, bishops, and deacons, to be considered more extensively below — correspond to the works given to the whole church. Are these persons to do the work for everyone else? Surely not. The ordained pastors, preachers, and servants in a church are not its only pastors, preachers, and servants. Others engage in pastoral, evangelistic, and diaconal work. But if this is so and these works are to be done by everyone, why then does the church have special functionaries?

The specially appointed ministers personify and embody for the members the work of the whole church. These ordained ministers represent to the church the nature of her own vocation, and objectify her ministry before the world. The congregation appoints as bishops, evangelists, and deacons those perceived as gifted in these areas. They are role models of different types of ministry; they serve as examples to others in doing what is the work of the whole church, a work that in turn is the work of Christ. The church appoints men who will be leaders in shepherding, leaders in evangelizing, and leaders in serving. They do not do the work for others, but they lead and help the rest of the church in doing that which is the task of everyone. Ordination is the recognition and setting apart to ministry of those who will represent to others and exemplify what the church is all about. The essence of the life of the church is ministry (diakonia). Some who do this very well are acknowledged by the community of believers awarding the title to them. Ministers in whatever capacity are representatives of the whole who will lead the rest of the church in their Christian activities.[64]

---

63. Cf. the use of the word for oversight, in the sense particularly of care for physical needs, in Matt. 25:36, 43 and James 1:27.

64. John N. Collins, *Are All Christians Ministers?* (Collegeville, Minn.: Liturgical Press, 1992), makes the valid point that there were duly appointed believers to

It may be noted that the passages on selection and setting apart to ministry in the church make no connection between this and the right to celebrate sacraments. The common statement today in many different church bodies about "ministry of the word and sacraments" has no biblical authorization. Those who exercised a ministry of the word might receive ordination, but there is no New Testament connection between ordination and administration of the sacraments or leadership in worship.[65] Indeed, no special class or classes in the New Testament were given competence in administering baptism (note 1 Cor. 1:14), presiding at the Lord's supper, or leading in worship (in dealing with the disorders in 1 Cor. 11 and 14 Paul addresses no particular group in the church as responsible to correct matters).

The relationship of these principles as they relate to Christ, the church, and ministry may be represented by a diagram:

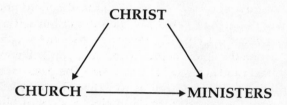

THE SHEPHERD AND THE SHEPHERDS

"Shepherd my sheep."   (JOHN 21:16)

Discussion of ordination leads to a consideration of those ministers appointed or recognized by the church. The New Testament provides for the continuation of ministers who will have a personal and living presence in the church. They, too, are God's gift to his people, for they are part of his provision for the ongoing life of his church. These functionaries correspond to the threefold work of the church outlined at the beginning of this chapter.

---

carry out special tasks of spiritual service for the development of the church but seems to be unduly restrictive of the word *diakonia* in applying it only to select persons set aside by the church to some office.

65. Michael Green, *Freed to Serve: Training and Equipping for Ministry* (London: Hodder & Stoughton, 1988), p. 29.

The Gospel of Matthew, as noted above, emphasizes the time that Jesus spent teaching his disciples. This spiritual nurture of the disciples was a pastoral ministry. All ministry derives from Jesus, and the shepherds in the church continue this aspect of the all-encompassing ministry of Jesus. Christ and his gifts are the standard of all ministry in the church. Even so, he is the model of the pastoral ministry in the church. Jesus remains the "Chief Shepherd" (1 Pet. 5:4) or "Great Shepherd" (Heb. 13:20). Other shepherds are "under shepherds," extending the shepherding ministry of Jesus and serving under his example and directions.

The resurrected Jesus, according to the Gospel of John, commissioned Peter to "shepherd my sheep" (John 21:16; cf. vss. 15 and 17, "feed"). It is appropriate, therefore, that 1 Peter makes extensive use of pastoral language, describing Christians as sheep and Jesus, the author, and the elders of the church as shepherds. "For you were going astray like sheep, but now you have returned to the shepherd and guardian [bishop] of your souls" (1 Pet. 2:25). Identifying himself as a "fellow elder" (or "shepherd," 1 Pet. 5:1), Peter promises the shepherds of the church that "when the chief shepherd appears, you will win the crown of glory that never fades away" (1 Pet. 5:4).[66] The pastoral language is applied to other apostles, as well as to Peter. The apostles as part of their founding of the church formed its first pastors or bishops (Acts 1:20). Paul presented himself, after Jesus, as a model for the elder-bishops of the church (Acts 20:17-35).

The function of shepherd or guardian was a definite office, or, better, "good work" (1 Tim. 3:1),[67] or place in the church.

Names

Three separate passages in the New Testament employ three distinct terms to describe the same group of functionaries in the church.

66. John H. Elliott, "Ministry and Church Order in the NT: A Tradition-Historical Analysis (1 Pt 5,1-5 & plls)," *Catholic Biblical Quarterly* 32 (1970): 367-391 would extend the discussion of elders in an official sense through verse 5, arguing that "younger" (cf. Lk. 22:25f.) refers to members of the community subordinate to the elders, having the sense specifically of "new converts" (pp. 379ff.). He further details the parallels of 1 Pet. 5:1-5 with John 21 (pp. 383f.).

67. The phrase indicates a "charitable deed," thus a benevolent act for the welfare of others — Kevin Giles, *Patterns of Ministry among the First Christians* (Melbourne: Collins Dove, 1989), p. 38; Jürgen Roloff, "Church Leadership according to the New Testament," *Theology Digest* 44 (1997): 139-147.

I exhort the elders among you to pastor the flock of God that is in your charge, exercising the oversight. (1 Pet. 5:1-2)

From Miletus [Paul] sent a message to Ephesus, asking the elders of the church to meet him. When they came to him, he said to them: . . . Keep watch over yourselves and over all the flock of which the Holy Spirit has made you overseers [bishops] to shepherd the church of God that he obtained with the blood of his own Son. (Acts 20:17, 28)

I left you behind in Crete for this reason, so that you should put in order what remained to be done, and should appoint elders in every town, as I directed you. . . . For a bishop, as God's steward, must be blameless. (Titus 1:5-7)

First Peter says that the elders' work is to pastor or shepherd the flock and be bishops ("exercising the oversight," although some manuscripts lack this phrase). Paul addressed the elders as bishops (guardians, overseers), whose work was to be a pastor or shepherd. The letter to Titus equates elders with bishops, who are also stewards. These terms all describe the same class of functionaries in the church. The same task may have many names, even as the same title could be used of various activities (as may be seen in the broad application of *diakonos*, "deacon," for many different functions — p. 334).

The relationship of the Greek terms and their various English translations may be set forth in chart form:

Greek	Transliteration	Latin	English
presbyteros	presbyter	senior	elder (older person)
episkopos	bishop	supervisor (superintendent)	overseer
poimen		pastor	shepherd (herder of sheep)
oikonomos			steward (warden of sty)

Jesus was called shepherd and bishop (1 Pet. 2:25) but not "elder," no doubt because that was a specific office in the Jewish society of his day which he did not fill. The absence of that term in reference to Jesus does not affect the general validity of the point that Jesus is "the bishop" of the church and that elders are extensions of his pastoral ministry.

The work of shepherds[68] in looking after sheep — protecting them, leading them to water and pasture, caring for their injuries, seeking them when lost — from early times had become widely used in the Near East to provide imagery to describe political and religious leaders. This metaphorical use is reflected in the Old Testament (Isa. 56:11; Jer. 23:4; 50:6; Nah. 3:18; Zech. 10:3). Ezekiel 34 provides the most extensive use of the imagery, and in its condemnation of the leaders of Israel offers a negative description of the conduct that should not characterize shepherds. By way of contrast, the Johannine Jesus presents himself as the "Good Shepherd," with a positive description of what a shepherd should be (John 10:2-16; cf. pp. 122-124 on this imagery for the church). Shepherds (or pastors, and equivalent to elders/bishops — Acts 20:28; 1 Pet. 5:1-2), especially in their teaching work, are among Christ's gifts to his church (Eph. 4:11).

The elders[69] in the early church derived their name and function, similarly, from Judaism, which had known this position from Old Testament times (Num. 11:16-24; Deut. 21:19-20; 1 Kings 21:8-11).[70] The Jewish elders mentioned in the Gospels were most often members of the Great Sanhedrin in Jerusalem (e.g., Mark. 11:27; 14:53), but there were elders in the local Jewish communities, and these, too, are mentioned in the New Testament (Luke 7:3). The Jewish elders were older men of experience and wisdom whose principal function was judicial — deciding disputed cases, interpreting the Law, and administering discipline. They also preserved the traditions of the people (Deut. 32:7) and served as examples. Elders in early Christian congregations continued to perform the same functions — overseeing the affairs of the

---

68. J. Jeremias, "Poimēn, etc.," Theological Dictionary of the New Testament, ed. G. Friedrich, tr. G. W. Bromiley (Grand Rapids: Eerdmans, 1968), Vol. 6, pp. 485-502.

69. G. Bornkamm, "Presbys, Presbyteros, etc.," Theological Dictionary of the New Testament, ed. G. Friedrich, tr. G. W. Bromiley (Grand Rapids: Eerdmans, 1968), Vol. 6, pp. 651-672; Alexander Strauch, Biblical Eldership: An Urgent Call to Restore Biblical Church Leadership (Littleton, Colo.: Lewis & Roth, 1988); A. R. Campbell, The Elders (Edinburgh: T. & T. Clark, 1994).

70. Hanaoch Reviv, The Elders in Ancient Israel: A Study of a Biblical Institution (Jerusalem: Magnes Press, 1989); for New Testament times, cf. James Tunstead Burtchaell, From Synagogue to Church: Public Services and Offices in the Earliest Christian Communities (Cambridge: University Press, 1992), pp. 228-233, and for the New Testament itself, pp. 292-299; Timothy M. Willis, The Elders of the City: A Study of the Elders-Laws in Deuteronomy (Atlanta: SBL, 2001).

community (Acts 11:30), deciding disputes (Acts 15:6, 22), and preserving the teachings (1 Tim. 5:17). Since elder was already a title or position in Judaism, when it was adopted by Christians, there was already a definite concept in mind. Although a young man obviously did not have the maturity required for the office, the position was not tied to age per se.

As in Jewish communities, elders (plural) always appear as a collegial group in Christian congregations (Acts 14:23; 21:18; 1 Tim. 4:14; James 5:14; cf. Phil. 1:1, "bishops and deacons").[71] A plural leadership has its own dynamics. A singular leadership is more efficient, so governments and armies want a single commander, and businesses and institutions want a single executive. But Jewish and Christian communities at the turn of the era followed a different pattern. Where the goal is not efficiency but spiritual growth, there a plural leadership offers the advantage of multiple mature examples and the opportunity for understanding and judgment drawn from collective experience.[72]

"Bishop"[73] was used in Hellenistic Greek for various kinds of managers, foremen, supervisors, and inspectors. It could refer to state officials with various civic functions, to supervisors at sanctuaries (but without cultic functions), to construction foremen, and in an educational context to tutors. It also could be used of a scout or watchman, and in that sense it was used of certain philosophers. In a religious sense it could be used of the gods, who exercised providence and watched over compacts. Although the distinction is not rigid, in general elders appear in the New Testament in contexts more Jewish (Acts 11:30: James 5:14) and bishops appear in contexts more Gentile (Phil. 1:1; 1 Tim. 3:1-2). Nevertheless, there was at Qumran a functionary similar to the Hellenistic bishop, the *mebaqqer*, an etymological equivalent in Hebrew of "overseer." His func-

---

71. Where the word occurs in the singular, it is in a nontechnical sense for an older person (1 Tim. 5:1), in a representative sense for a person as part of the group of elders (1 Tim. 5:19), or in a specialized sense as a title of honor (2 and 3 John). These are not exceptions to the rule that a plurality of elders presided over early Christian congregations.

72. Eric G. Jay, "From Presbyter-Bishops to Bishops and Presbyters," *The Second Century* 1 (1981): 125-162, traces the rise of the single bishop in Christian congregations.

73. In addition to the works in the selected bibliography see Jean Colson, *L'Evêque dans les communautés primitives,* Unam Sanctam 21 (Paris: Cerf, 1951); H. W. Beyer, *"Episkopos,"* Theological Dictionary of the New Testament, ed. G. Kittel, tr. G. W. Bromiley (Grand Rapids: Eerdmans, 1964), pp. 608-620.

tions included teaching and judging the members, handling the money of the community, assigning work, and examining new applicants for membership.[74] Whereas "elder" emphasized more the age, experience, and judiciousness of the leaders of Christian communities, "bishop" emphasized the more active side of their work in managing affairs, guarding the group, and directing activities. The word "bishop" suggests more a singular role than a plural role, so when one chief elder emerged in some churches at the beginning of the second century, it was natural that this was the term used for this person.

Steward was another common secular term in Hellenistic-Roman times, but it, too, represents an institution known in Old Testament times (Gen. 39:4f.; Isa. 22:15; 36:3). Its use for an elder/bishop in Titus 1:7 reflects the household imagery of the Pastoral Epistles.[75] A steward was a trusted slave or freedman charged with managing household or other affairs for the owner. The church is presented as the family or household of God the Father (1 Tim. 3:15); the stewards take care of its affairs for him. Since a steward took care of what was not his own but belonged to another, he was expected to be prudent (Luke 12:42) and above all faithful (1 Cor. 4:1-2), for he would have to give account to the owner (Luke 16:2; cf. Heb. 13:17). This title did not acquire the widespread currency in ecclesiastical usage that the other terms did.

Qualifications

Two clearly marked lists of qualifications of the bishop/elder are found in 1 Timothy 3:1-7 and Titus 1:5-9.[76] The contents are quite similar, but even the same ideas are often expressed in different wording. The purpose in both passages is to say, "This is the kind of man you want."

The specific items may be grouped in certain categories. Most have to do with character and habits or temperament. Other qualifications relate to experience ("not a recent convert" — 1 Tim. 3:6), reputa-

74. Bo Reicke, "The Constitution of the Primitive Church in the Light of Jewish Documents," in *The Scrolls and the New Testament,* ed. Krister Stendahl (New York: Harper, 1957), p. 154.

75. David C. Verner, *The Household of God: The Social World of the Pastoral Epistles* (Baltimore: Scholars Press, 1983), in spite of the book's title, fails to develop the structural implications of the household imagery in the letters.

76. A homiletic treatment in John MacArthur, *Church Leadership: 1 Timothy 3:1-13* (Chicago: Moody, 1989).

tion ("well thought of by outsiders" — 1 Tim. 3:7), intellect ("an apt teacher" — 1 Tim. 3:2), and domestic relations (1 Tim. 3:2, 4; Titus 1:6). The last seems to have been particularly important as the training and proving ground for responsibilities in the church: "For if someone does not know how to manage his own household, how can he take care of God's church?" (1 Tim. 3:5).

Two opposite tendencies, both incorrect, have been exhibited toward these lists of qualifications. One is to set the standards so high that virtually no one can meet them and so not appoint men to the work. The other is to minimize the requirements with the attitude of choosing the best available even if unqualified. Both approaches have the consequence of ignoring or setting aside the instructions and thus not taking seriously the biblical standards for congregational leadership.

Duties

The responsibilities of the Christian pastor/elder/bishop may be learned from the New Testament in three ways: from the names given to them, from their qualifications, and from the specific instructions given to them.

Each name given to the congregational leaders suggests something different, but each supplements and enriches the other. The title "elder" indicated the community leaders, the honored men, who by reason of experience and wisdom were recognized as examples. They preserved the traditions and way of life, they interpreted the law, they settled disputes, and they assigned discipline. The title "bishop" suggested a manager, administrator, or supervisor. Since it did not have the specific content that the word "elder" had, it had the flexibility to develop according to the developments within the church. The position of "steward," as someone who took care of the property of another, carries the idea of responsibility for seeing that jobs are done, for finances, and for general welfare. The term "shepherd" indicated a person with care for the well-being of others, responsibility to protect and provide for others. This imagery evokes the picture of a shepherd leading and the sheep following (cf. John 10:4).

The qualifications in 1 Timothy 3 and Titus 1 are not arbitrary but are related to the work to be done. Certain qualities are expressed because certain responsibilities must be met. Some of the items in the lists may serve as illustrations of the principle that there is a correlation between the qualifications stated and the duties to be performed. The overseer "must not be a recent convert" (1 Tim. 3:6), thus an experienced and proven leader, because in his position he had to know and understand the faith. He must be "well thought of by outsiders" (1 Tim. 3:7) because he represented the church to those on the outside. He must "manage his own household well" (1 Tim. 3:4) because he did for the church what a father did for his family (or in this case a steward for the Father). He must be "hospitable" (1 Tim. 3:2; Titus 1:8) because he hosted the church in his home for its meetings and received Christians from other places. He must make proper use of money (1 Tim. 3:3; Titus 1:7), not just as a matter of reputation, but because he took care of the funds and property of the community. He must be peaceful (1 Tim. 3:3; Titus 1:7f.) because he was a peacemaker, a judge in disputes among the members. He must be able to teach (1 Tim. 3:2) because he was responsible for teaching in the church.

The specific instructions given to the presbyter-bishops reinforce the picture drawn from the names and lists of qualifications. First Peter 5:2-3 tells the elders to "shepherd" and "be a bishop"; the new information in the passage is the manner in which this is to be done. It is spelled out both negatively and positively in three antitheses: "not under compulsion [not of necessity] but willingly, . . . not for gain but eagerly [readily]," not as lords but as examples. The phrase "as God would have you do it" (missing from some manuscripts) admirably sums up the manner in which the work of the elder is to be done. There is no sense of tension between the elders and those with a gift, whether of speaking or of serving, mentioned a few verses before (1 Pet. 4:10-11).

Acts 20:28 tells the elders/bishops "to shepherd the church," to "keep watch over yourselves and over all the flock." The whole address in Acts 20:18-35 is pertinent, the special concern of which is warning against false teachers. Hence the need for watchfulness and to "be alert" (vss. 30-31). The tasks of the shepherd are to guard against enemies of the sheep and provide them with nourishment. For the latter, note the association of pastors with teachers in Ephesians 4:11.

Titus 1:9 continues the concern with instruction in the face of false teachers. The elder-bishop's[77] work is both positive and negative: to exhort in the truth and to reprove its opponents. "He must have a firm

---

77. John P. Meier, "*Presbyteros* in the Pastoral Epistles," *Catholic Biblical Quarterly* 35 (1973): 323-345, supports the identification of presbyters and bishop in this passage (pp. 337-339).

grasp of the word that is trustworthy in accordance with the teaching so that he may be able both to preach [exhort] with sound doctrine and to refute those who contradict it."

First Timothy 5:17 speaks of "the elders who rule well." The word means literally those who "preside" or "stand in front of," and so refers to those who lead, those who manage or conduct affairs, and then those who care for and provide for (cf. 1 Thess. 5:12; Rom. 12:8; 1 Tim. 3:4). Although all elders were to be capable of teaching (1 Tim. 3:2), not all "labor[ed] in preaching and teaching," that is, gave much time and attention to it.[78]

Several of these instructions ("rule") and descriptions ("stewards") imply what we would call administrative responsibilities. This responsibility is consistent with what has been seen about the activities of all the members. The elder-bishops give organization to the members of the body who are gifted in various ways, not by the elders themselves but by God. The elders do not grant to persons roles or gifts. They work these people into the work of the body. Even as in a human body we try to employ all the "members" appropriate to a task, so also in the body of Christ.

Elders were also leaders in prayer: Any who are sick "should call for the elders of the church and have them pray over them" (James 5:14).[79]

Responsibilities of the Congregation

First Timothy 5:18 lays down the principle that it is proper to provide financial support for those elders who "labor," who devote their time to the work of leading and teaching the people.

Moreover, respect for elders requires that an accusation against one of them must be supported by the evidence of two or three witnesses (1 Tim. 5:19).[80]

---

78. Cf. Paul's use of "labor," not only for manual labor (1 Cor. 4:12; Eph. 4:28), but also for his apostolic work (1 Cor. 15:10; Gal. 4:11; Col. 1:29) and the work of local leaders in the church (1 Cor. 16:16; 1 Thess. 5:12). Cf. n. 25.

79. The anointing with oil was a medical treatment (cf. Isa. 1:6; Mark 6:13; Luke 10:34), so the instructions combine the use of medicine and prayer in treating the sick.

80. John P. Meier, "*Presbyteros* in the Pastoral Epistles," *Catholic Biblical Quarterly* 35 (1973): 323-345, argues that the pericope on elders covers 5:17-25 (pp. 325-337) and is chiastic in structure: a supporting argument is given by J. William Fuller, "Of Elders and Triads in 1 Timothy 5.19-25," *New Testament Studies* 29 (1983): 258-263.

Other instructions about responsibilities of the people to their spiritual leaders do not employ the words for elders/bishops/pastors, but the teaching presumably covers them as well. Thus 1 Thessalonians 5:12-13 commands the people to "respect" (know, recognize) their leaders and to "esteem them very highly in love." Hebrews 13:7, 17 says to "obey" (trust in, follow) and "submit" (yield) to the leaders while imitating their faith.

These instructions, of course, are to be understood in relation to the principles of servant-leadership presented above and Jesus' teachings about the attitudes of leaders (Luke 22:25-26). A people voluntarily submitting to those in whom they recognize the moral and spiritual leadership they want to follow is not the same as leaders insisting on being obeyed because of their position. The authority of elders/bishops is the moral authority that comes from their loving service, their example, and their spiritual knowledge and experience.

Teachers

The construction of the Greek of Ephesians 4:11 brings "pastors and teachers" into close relationship as one category distinct from the preceding groups. The discussion of the work of elders/bishops/pastors above has highlighted their teaching ministry. Teaching might be done also by apostles (2 Tim. 1:11), prophets (1 Cor. 14:3), preachers (1 Tim. 4:6, 11; 6:2), deacons (1 Tim. 3:9), and women (Titus 2:4).[81] Nevertheless, there were teachers in the early church who were neither elders nor any of these others, and to this class of functionaries attention is now turned.

Teachers shared with pastors the work of edifying believers. Some of these teachers apparently were specially inspired for this function (1 Cor. 12:28; cf. Acts 13:1 for the association of teachers with prophets), but inspiration was not essential to the teaching task (albeit performing

81. Robert C. Worley, *Preaching and Teaching in the Earliest Church* (Philadelphia: Westminster, 1967), although written to refute C. H. Dodd's distinction between *kerygma* and *didache* in the early church and despite many problems in execution of this goal, yet contains much useful material relevant to teaching. James I. H. McDonald, *Kerygma and Didache: The Articulation and Structure of the Earliest Christian Message* (Cambridge: University Press, 1980), pp. 101-124, also taking exception to Dodd, identifies *paradosis* (tradition) as providing the structure of teaching in the early church.

the very important purpose of protecting the accuracy of what was taught), and the concern here is with teachers in the continuing life of the church.

Teachers were especially associated with moral instruction and the practical application of the revelation. The content of early Christian teaching may be categorized as exposition of the Old Testament in the light of Christ, preservation and application of the teachings of Jesus, and instruction on how to live as a Christian.[82] Both doctrinal matters and elementary practical instruction were within the scope of the teaching ministry. Teachers thus contributed in an important way in the work of edification.

The activity of teaching occurs much more frequently in the early church than does the title "teacher." The great majority of the occurrences of the noun *didaskalos* (teacher) in the New Testament are in the Gospels and refer to Jesus, who is frequently addressed with this title (e.g., Matt. 8:19; Mark 4:38). Perhaps his warning that "you have one teacher" (Matt. 23:8) helped to reserve the title for Jesus alone. As Jesus is "the Prophet" and "the Shepherd" of the church, so he is "the Teacher." Nevertheless, as was true of other aspects of his ministry, others continued the function of teaching in the church, even if more often expressed in other words. He provided the model and example for future teachers.

The ability to teach is one of the gifts of the Spirit (Rom. 12:7). The activity of teaching and the principle of financial support for teachers are expressed in Galatians 6:6, "Those who are taught in the word must share in all good things with their teacher." There is a fellowship of teaching and learning; those who impart spiritual things should receive material support from those taught (cf. Rom. 15:27 in another context). The author of Hebrews expects Christians to become teachers of others: "For though by this time you ought to be teachers, you need someone to teach you again the basic elements of the oracles of God" (Heb. 5:12).

The fullest discussion of the teaching office in the church is found in the third chapter of James. Only superficially in contradiction to Hebrews 5:12, James warns, "Not many of you should become teachers . . . for you know that we who teach will be judged with greater strictness" (James 3:1). As Peter identified himself with the elders (1 Pet. 5:1), James identified himself with the teachers. His reminder of the serious-

---

82. Kevin Giles, *Patterns of Ministry among the First Christians* (Melbourne: Collins Dove, 1989), 118ff.

ness and importance of teaching is followed by the discussion of the use of the tongue (James 3:2-12). Teaching requires the use of the tongue, and the ease with which the tongue sins explains the strictness of the judgment on teachers and the caution against a hasty desire for the position of a teacher. If one could avoid sinning with the tongue, he or she would be a perfect person. The teacher, however, has no choice but to speak, and so accepts the greater risks and responsibilities of the use of the tongue. The last paragraph of the chapter (vss. 13-18) returns more directly to the function of the teacher. James talks about the wise person, picking up the theme of wisdom from the Old Testament. In addition to kings, priests, and prophets, Judaism had known the office of the wise (cf. Jer. 18:18). These were teachers, and they produced the wisdom literature of the Jews. In later Judaism the rabbis continued to be known as "the wise."[83] James contrasts the heavenly wisdom to be exemplified by the true teacher with earthly wisdom. His words are a challenging description of the qualifications and work of the Christian teacher.

THE PREACHER AND THE PREACHERS

"Do the work of an evangelist."   (2 TIM. 4:5)

One of the speaking ministries was that of the preacher, or evangelist. The Synoptic Gospels and Acts summarize Jesus' ministry in terms of the proclamation of the Gospel (Mark 1:14-15; Luke 4:18-19; Acts 10:36-37). Christ was a preacher, *the preacher.* Preachers or evangelists continue the evangelistic work of Christ and take the lead in personifying the evangelistic task of the church.

Even as the verb form "to teach" was more common, especially outside the Gospels, than the noun "teacher," so the verbal forms of "preaching the gospel" are much more common than the noun "evangelist," which occurs only three times in the New Testament. These occurrences, however, are significant, and indicate a distinct function or "office" in the church. Philip, one of the Seven in Acts 6, is called

---

83. U. Wilckens, *"Sophia, etc.,"* *Theological Dictionary of the New Testament,* ed. G. Friedrich, tr. G. W. Bromiley (Grand Rapids: Eerdmans, 1971), Vol. 7, pp. 505-506, notes that rabbinic literature used *sopher* for rabbis from earlier times and *hakam* for contemporaries.

"the evangelist" (Acts 21:8), appropriate in view of the account of his preaching ministry in Samaria and in the coastal cities of Judea (Acts 8). Ephesians 4:11 lists evangelists after apostles and prophets as among the gifts of the risen Christ to the church. Second Timothy 4:5 exhorts Timothy to "do the work of an evangelist." It is strange the extent to which commentators and others follow the postapostolic tradition in regarding Timothy as a bishop (never so called in the Bible) rather than the express biblical text itself in identifying Timothy as an evangelist.[84] Timothy is consistently distinguished in 1 and 2 Timothy from the bishops/elders, about whom instructions are given in the third person (1 Tim. 3 and 5), whereas Timothy is addressed directly in other terms: In addition to "evangelist," he is a "minister" (1 Tim. 4:6), the "Lord's servant" (2 Tim. 2:24), and a "man of God" (1 Tim. 6:11). Paul's co-workers, besides Timothy and Titus, may be described as evangelists or missionary apostles, although these words are not used of them (e.g., Col. 1:6-8; 4:7-8; Phil. 4:3).

Nevertheless, there is a connection between apostles and evangelists. Paul most often described his ministry in terms of preaching the gospel (e.g., "evangelize" in Rom. 1:15; 1 Cor. 1:17; Gal. 1:8; "proclaim" in 1 Cor. 1:23; Gal. 2:2; 1 Thess. 2:9; note especially the association of "preacher and apostle" in 1 Tim. 2:7; 2 Tim. 1:11). Evangelists lacked the personal commission of the Lord's apostles, but shared the missionary work of other apostles, although not limited to it.

Qualifications

The letters to Timothy and Titus give lists of qualities to be possessed by evangelists, although not as clearly demarcated as the lists about bishops and deacons (1 Tim. 3; Titus 1). Second Timothy 2:24-25, in wording similar to 1 Timothy 3, requires ability in teaching, kindness, patience, and gentleness: "The Lord's servant must not be quarrelsome but kindly to everyone, an apt teacher, patient, correcting opponents with gentleness." A long list of requirements is set forth in 1 Timothy 6:3-11. Verse 11 says that the conduct of verses 3-10 is to be avoided, but the "man of God" is to "pursue righteousness, godliness, faith, love,

---

84. Everett Ferguson, "The Ministry of the Word in the First Two Centuries," *Restoration Quarterly* 1 (1957): 21-31; idem, "Church Order in the Sub-Apostolic Period: A Survey of Interpretations," *Restoration Quarterly* 11 (1968): 225-248.

endurance, gentleness." Purity was required (1 Tim. 5:22); so, too, was exemplary behavior in "speech, conduct, love, faith, and purity" (1 Tim. 4:12). As a general summary, Timothy was expected to "pay close attention" to himself and to his teaching (1 Tim. 4:16; cf. other general statements in 2 Tim. 3:14-15; 4:1-5).

Work

The word "evangelist" means "one who preaches the gospel." The other terms used give other indications of the work done by these men. As a "servant of Christ Jesus" he is a minister of the word, putting the Lord's instructions before the brothers and sisters (1 Tim. 4:6). As "the Lord's slave" (2 Tim. 2:24) he follows the orders of the Lord and serves him. This is done by bringing his word to others. "Man of God" (1 Tim. 6:11) was a designation of the prophets (1 Kings 13:1-32). This description indicates again the person's belonging to God. The association with prophets indicates the task of bringing the message of God to the people, but there is no indication of that word being directly given to the evangelist as was true for prophets.

The accounts of the work of evangelists indicate various kinds of preaching and associated activities. The evangelist Philip labored to win new converts, as in his evangelizing Samaria (Acts 8:5-13) and the Ethiopian treasurer (Acts 8:26-39). This preaching ministry involved both traveling (Acts 8:40) and locating for a period of time (Acts 21:8 — Philip was still in Caesarea some twenty years after Acts 8:40).

Having made converts, or arriving at a place where there were believers with a deficient church life, the evangelists worked to organize churches. Titus was left in Crete "for this reason, so that you should put in order what remained to be done, and should appoint elders in every town" (Titus 1:5).

Contrary to common assumptions and to what might be expected from the etymology of "evangelist," the work of evangelists was not limited to making new converts or planting churches. Timothy and Titus, as evangelists, were to strengthen the faith of those already converted and refute false teaching in already well-established churches. "If you put these instructions before the brothers and sisters, you will be a good servant of Christ Jesus" (1 Tim. 4:6) — that would include the previous contents of the book: refutation of false teaching (1 Tim.

1:5-20), matters of worship (1 Tim. 2:1-15), church organization (1 Tim. 3:1-13), and warnings of apostasy (1 Tim. 4:1-5). Titus, likewise, was to "teach what is consistent with sound doctrine" (Titus 2:1), including instruction in Christian living to different age groups and social classes within the church (Titus 2:2-10). Important in this task of strengthening believers was the refutation of error. "I urge you . . . to remain in Ephesus so that you may instruct certain people not to teach any different doctrine" (1 Tim. 1:3 — and this in a church with elders). Titus was told to "rebuke [certain persons] sharply, so that they may become sound in the faith" (Titus 1:13). That teaching was an important part of the preaching ministry is shown by the frequent references in the Pastorals to teaching (1 Tim. 4:11, 13; 2 Tim. 2:24; 4:2; Titus 2:1). Evangelists were engaged in edification as well as in evangelizing.

Evangelists also had a responsibility to perpetuate the evangelistic work of the church by training others to carry on this task. Timothy was commanded, "What you have heard from me through many witnesses entrust to faithful people who will be able to teach others as well" (2 Tim. 2:2). This statement may have a broad reference to the transmission of Christian teaching in general, but more likely has in mind those who will continue Timothy's own ministry, that is, those able to teach in the capacity he exercised.

As a summary of the public work of evangelists, note may be taken of 1 Timothy 4:13: "Give attention to the public reading of scripture, to exhorting, to teaching." Preaching the word included not only proclaiming the message but also convincing, rebuking, and encouraging (2 Tim. 4:2).

These activities could be so demanding that provision was made for preachers to be supported in order for them to devote full time to their labors. "The Lord commanded that those who proclaim the gospel should get their living by the gospel" (1 Cor. 9:14). Paul used the same Old Testament text (Deut. 25:4) to justify financial support for apostles and evangelists (1 Cor. 9:9) as is used for elders (1 Tim. 5:18).

This information indicates that evangelists or preachers had a specific function intended to be permanent in the church. They had a definite "work" and "ministry" (2 Tim. 4:5) to perform. Provision was made for the continuation of persons to perform this task (2 Tim. 2:2). And, indeed, the evangelistic function exists in the very nature of the mission of the church. If the church is to continue the ministry of Jesus in the world, if it exists as God's agent for the salvation of human beings, then evangelizing is essential to the church, and so there must be those who exemplify this work and lead all the members in the performance of it.

THE SERVANT AND THE SERVANTS

"I am among you as one who serves."   (LUKE 22:27)

One category of spiritual gift was to serve (1 Pet. 4:11; Rom. 12:7). Jesus was described as the "servant of the circumcision" (Rom. 15:8), and he chose to describe his messianic work as "not to be served but to serve, and to give his life a ransom for many" (Mark 10:45). Jesus' career was preeminently a life of doing good (Acts 10:38). His work of bringing spiritual and physical healing to people is continued in the church, where it is represented especially by the deacons, the appointed servants to take the lead in this broad area of ministry.

Modern Christian usage employs the words for service (the *diakon*-family) both as a general word for all types of "ministry" and as a specialized word for the care of the poor, ill, and needy. The broad usage better corresponds to the ancient meaning, and the narrower usage is a specialized application of a particular development within Christian language.

The family of words from the root *diakon*- was applied in ancient Greek to intermediaries of various kinds, agents (especially where movement was involved), and so to couriers or those who deliver things for others.[85] The fairly frequent association with delivering messages, sometimes as a messenger of the gods,[86] corresponds to the New Testament use of the word group in connection with dispensing the word of God (e.g., in Paul's usage — Rom. 11:13; 1 Cor. 3:5; 2 Cor. 3:6; Eph. 3:7; Col. 1:25; cf. Acts 20:24; 21:19). Ancient usage also applied the *diakon*- words to performing deeds, where the mediation involved

---

85. Older works, such as H. W. Beyer, *"Diakoneo, etc.," Theological Dictionary of the New Testament*, ed. G. Kittel, tr. G. W. Bromiley (Grand Rapids: Eerdmans, 1964), Vol. 2, pp. 81-93 and J. M. Barnett, *The Diaconate: A Full and Equal Order* (New York: Seabury, 1981), pp. 13-42, must now be revised in the light of John N. Collins, *Diakonia: Re-Interpreting the Ancient Sources* (Oxford: University Press, 1990); for the definitions given, see his pp. 77-95; for New Testament passages, pp. 195-256.

86. John N. Collins, *Diakonia: Re-Interpreting the Ancient Sources* (Oxford: University Press, 1990), pp. 96-132; idem, *Are All Christians Ministers?* (Collegeville, Minn.: Liturgical, 1992).

doing something for someone who gave the instructions.[87] The New Testament, too, has passages that correspond to this usage of performing commissions for others, especially where travel is involved (e.g., Acts 11:29; 12:25; Rom. 15:31; 2 Cor. 8:19-20). This family of words could be used of waiters or those who attended persons at table or in household chores, a meaning sometimes reflected in the New Testament (John 2:5, 9; Luke 22:27; Acts 6:2), but the original meaning evidently was not "serve at table," for this was only one of many varied uses.[88] In several cases the task indicated by the word is left wholly undefined by the context (e.g., 2 Tim. 1:18; Heb. 6:10; Rev. 2:19).

The function of a *diakonos* according to the ancient sources, therefore, could be enormously varied. It was commonly of a subordinate nature but was not necessarily menial and did not reflect poorly on the person involved.[89] The New Testament continued the ancient pattern of using *diakonos* for many different types of persons performing many different types of service: Christ (Rom. 15:8), the apostles (Mark 9:45; 10:43), Paul's co-workers (who may be included in the next two categories — 1 Thess. 3:2; Col. 1:7; 4:7), missionaries (1 Cor. 3:5), evangelists (1 Tim. 4:6), all believers (John 12:26), civil magistrates (Rom. 13:4), messengers of Satan (2 Cor. 11:15), waiters (John 2:5, 9), and special functionaries in the church (Phil. 1:1). The difference between these is in the type of service rendered and for whom. It is the last group that is the subject of this section — the special servants of the church for whom Christian usage gave to the general word *diakonos* the specific, technical designation of "deacon." This specialized use of the word is actually quite rare in comparison to the total number of occurrences in the New Testament.

The deacons continue the serving ministry of Jesus. They have the special privilege of representing the distinctive aspect of the ministry of Jesus that was his preferred way of characterizing himself and his work — serving.

87. John N. Collins, *Diakonia: Re-Interpreting the Ancient Sources* (Oxford: University Press, 1990), pp. 133-149.

88. Roy A. Harrisville, "Ministry in the New Testament," in *Called and Ordained: Lutheran Perspectives on the Office of the Ministry,* ed. Todd Nichol and Marc Kolden (Minneapolis: Fortress, 1990), pp. 4-6; John N. Collins, *Diakonia: Re-Interpreting the Ancient Sources* (Oxford: University Press, 1990), pp. 150-168.

89. John N. Collins, *Diakonia: Re-Interpreting the Ancient Sources* (Oxford: University Press, 1990), pp. 141-146.

Qualifications

A clear indication of a special class of functionaries in the church is the presence of a list of qualifications by which they are distinguished from others. Such a list occurs in 1 Timothy 3:8-13. The list contains items similar to those in the list for bishops that precedes, but with a special concern with those qualities necessary for the special work of deacons (see below).

(1) Serious — sober-minded, men of sound mind with mature judgment; prudent, dignified, grave, and sincere.

(2) Not double-tongued — not two-faced, not spreaders of gossip, those who say what they mean and mean what they say.

(3) Not indulging in much wine — more than not drunken but also not impaired in any way by drink (or other habits).

(4) Not greedy for money — not covetous, not lovers of money, but instead generous.

(5) Holding fast to the mystery of the faith with a clear conscience — sound and strong in the faith with a good conscience.

(6) Tested — proved in experience and conduct, not new Christians and not untried in responsibilities.

(7) Blameless — of good report.

(8) Married only once — or husband of one wife, representing the purity and stability of one marriage.

(9) Managing children and households well — good leaders and good managers as proved in family and household affairs.

Work

Just as the *diakon-* word group could cover a quite varied field of service involving agency or mediation on behalf of another, so the work of deacons in the early church did not inherently involve the limitations sometimes imposed in the later history of the church. Nevertheless, there are a number of principles implied by the New Testament texts that suggest some distinctions applicable to the work of deacons.

The word "deacon" is more often paired with "bishop" than with elder (Phil. 1:1; 1 Tim. 3, although there are exceptions in early Christian literature). The natural counterpart of "elder" would be "younger" (1 Pet. 5:1, 5), but "overseer" and "servant" or "agent" go together. The name "deacon" suggests that these are assistants who serve under the supervision of the bishops/elders. All who are in positions of responsibility need trusted and capable subordinates.

Some distinguish between elders and deacons by assigning to the former spiritual affairs and to the latter temporal affairs. Support for this has been found in Acts 6, where the apostles instructed the church to choose seven men for the task of administering the daily distribution of food to widows so that they might devote themselves to prayer and preaching. The presence of the verb form "to serve" (or "to be a deacon") in verse 2 ("to wait on tables"), in view of the wide variety of ways this family of words is used in the New Testament (the related noun is used of the apostles' "serving the word" in vs. 4), lends little support to the idea that these men were the first deacons. What the passage does support is the principle of a differentiation of function in the ministry of the church. The apostles were not "too good" to do menial tasks; serving tables was not "beneath them"; nor was benevolent work less important than preaching. But it made no sense for the apostles to leave off doing what only they could do, witness to the ministry of Jesus, in order to spend time doing what many others could do as well or better than they, minister to widows who came from a segment of the community with which they were not well acquainted. A division of labor according to abilities and qualifications was more efficient.

On that basis, deacons have often been given primary responsibility for temporal affairs in the church. Thus, in early church history[90] the deacons ministered to the needy, visited the sick, administered church property, and assisted at worship. They were described as the "eyes" and "ears" of the bishop.

This distinction between temporal and spiritual can be overdrawn. Deacons were servants in every area of the church's life. Even as among the Seven, Stephen and Philip were soon found preaching

---

90. J. G. Davies, "Deacons, Deaconesses and the Minor Orders in the Patristic Period," *Journal of Ecclesiastical History* 14 (1963): 1-15, repr. in Everett Ferguson, ed., *Studies in Early Christianity*, Vol. 13: *Church, Ministry, and Organization in the Early Church Era* (New York: Garland, 1993), pp. 237-251; G. W. H. Lampe, "Diakonia in the Early Church," in *Service in Christ*, ed. J. I. McCord and J. H. L. Parker (Grand Rapids: Eerdmans, 1966), pp. 49-64; J. M. Barnett, *The Diaconate: A Full and Equal Order* (New York: Seabury, 1981), pp. 43-131; L. R. Hennessey, "*Diakonia* and *Diakonoi* in the Pre-Nicene Church," in *Diakonia: Studies in Honor of Robert T. Meyer*, ed. T. Halton and J. P. Williams (Washington: Catholic University of America, 1986), pp. 60-86.

and not just administering a benevolent program (Acts 6–8), deacons had opportunity to teach, if in more informal and private settings than the "pastors and teachers." Even as an overlap was observed (p. 289) between the different categories of the work of the church, so among the ministers of the church there is not an exclusive division of labor: deacons can speak the word of the Lord, evangelists do benevolent acts, and pastors may be engaged in both works as well. Nevertheless, it is appropriate that some persons be given leadership in the physical, benevolent, and related activities, so that others can devote their primary time to evangelistic and pastoral work.

The qualifications indicate men who were among the people, involved in their lives and knowing their needs and problems. Hence, they had to be persons of seriousness of purpose who were not tale-bearers. As administering the benevolent funds and other fiscal affairs of the church, they must be above reproach in their handling of money and goods. They must be good examples in their own family life and in their conduct, since for many they would represent the church. They must be proved in their own faith, for what they said would carry great weight with those among whom they worked.

We conclude that deacons are agents of the bishops and interme-diaries between them and the members of the congregation, and in this work they represent and mediate the servanthood of Jesus.

WOMEN SERVANTS[91]

> "Tell the older women . . .
> to teach what is good."
>
> (TITUS 2:3-5)

Women were prominent in serving Jesus during his ministry. Luke names some of the important women who accompanied Jesus and the Twelve in their itinerant ministry and who "provided for [ministered to] them out of their resources" (Luke 8:1-3). In the early history of the church, women were active in many ways: prophesying (Acts 2:17-18; 21:9; 1 Cor. 11:5), teaching (Acts 18:26; Titus 2:3-5), working for the

---

91. The recent literature on women in the Bible and early Christianity is enormous. For an entrée into some of the issues see E. Earle Ellis on "Paul and the Eschatological Woman," in *Pauline Theology: Ministry and Society* (Grand Rapids: Eerdmans, 1989), pp. 53-86.

church and to advance the gospel (Rom. 16:6, 12; Phil. 4:2-3), and serving in various capacities (Acts 9:36; 16:15, 40). Did women receive appointment or recognition for special ministries in the church? Two classes of women may have been recognized as having distinct ministries.[92]

Deaconesses[93]

Deaconesses or women deacons are known from early church history to have performed duties among females that were inappropriate for male deacons.[94] Were they present in the New Testament church? Two passages may indicate that they were, but both passages are ambiguous.

Romans 16:1-2 reads: "I commend to you our sister Phoebe, a deacon [servant, minister] of the church at Cenchreae, . . . for she has been a benefactor [patroness] of many and of myself as well." The interpretation turns on the significance of *diakonos* here. Since the word can be used for a specific office in the church (Phil. 1:1; 1 Tim. 3:8), that meaning cannot be ruled out. On the other hand, in view of the word's predominantly nontechnical usage in the New Testament, the probability is against a reference to a recognized office in the church here. Of more significance for Phoebe's status and influence is the description of her as *prostatis*, the feminine of a word for a leader, ruler, president, guardian, and in Greek and Roman society a patron. This indicates that Phoebe was a person of some wealth and social standing, and it is likely that she owned a home that provided a meeting place for the church and hospitality to Paul and other Christians. This would have given her considerable prominence even if not an officially recognized position in the church.

A somewhat stronger case can be made for 1 Timothy 3:11, which

---

92. C. H. Turner, "Ministries of Women in the Primitive Church: Widow, Deaconess and Virgin in the First Four Christian Centuries," in *Catholic and Apostolic*, ed. H. N. Bate (London: Mowbray, 1931), pp. 316-351; J. Daniélou, *The Ministry of Women in the Ancient Church* (Westminster: Faith, 1974); R. Gryson, *The Ministry of Women in the Early Church* (Collegeville: Liturgical, 1976); Everett Ferguson, "Women in the Post-Apostolic Church," in Carroll D. Osburn, ed., *Essays on Women in Earliest Christianity*, Vol. 1 (Joplin, Mo.: College Press, 1993), pp. 493-513.

93. A. G. Mortimort, *Deaconesses: An Historical Study* (San Francisco: Ignatius, 1986).

94. *Didascalia* 16.

interrupts the list of qualifications of deacons with the statement: "Women likewise must be serious, not slanderers, but temperate, faithful in all things." The ambiguity here derives from the fact that the Greek word *gynē* can mean woman or wife. The general meaning "women" would seem to be out of place in this context, but women servants in a nontechnical sense is perhaps not out of the question. The two major alternatives in interpretation are "wives of the deacons" (and perhaps of the bishops too) or "women deacons." Deacons were primarily male, but provision could have been made for female deacons here. The structure of the chapter might favor this: "Now a bishop must be . . ." (3:2); "Deacons likewise must be . . ." (3:8); "Women likewise must be . . ." (3:11). The seeming interruption of qualifications for deacons might not be that at all, for the matters that follow (vss. 12-13) are not specific qualities but have to do with family relationships and the general principle that good service has its rewards. On the other hand, *gynē* would be expected to mean "wife" when used in context with men without other specification. The requirements stated for women would not seem to pertain to any particular duties (yet the four items closely parallel the first three and fifth items in the qualifications of deacons), and the work of deacons (and bishops), who are here required to be married men, would certainly require that their wives have certain characteristics. On balance, the probability favors women deacons as the meaning of 1 Timothy 3:11, but this interpretation is far from certain.

No conclusive case can be made for deaconesses from these verses, nor can this position be ruled out. No biblical principle appears to prohibit the recognition of women in serving capacities in a church.

Widows[95]

The situation is different with widows. The New Testament makes provision for an order of widows, to be supported by the church while they perform certain tasks on its behalf. The relevant passage, 1 Timothy 5:3-16, requires some preliminary clarification.

The passage distinguishes the "real widow" (vss. 3, 5, 16) from widows in general. A widow was a woman bereaved, a wife who had lost her husband. She might have been left well-provided for, or have

---

95. Bonnie Thurston, *The Widows — A Women's Ministry in the Early Church* (Minneapolis: Fortress, 1989).

family who could provide for her financial needs (vss. 3, 16 — the NRSV without textual support adds the word "really" in the first part of the latter verse, obscuring the distinction between widows in general and those truly bereaved; "real" is in the Greek at the end of the verse to describe the widows who must be cared for by the church). The "younger widow" had the possibility of remarriage, and that was encouraged (vss. 11, 14). The "real widow," the widow genuinely or truly bereaved, in contrast, was "left alone"; she had no adequate means of support and her only hope was in God (v. 5). Such truly bereaved widows were legitimate objects of the church's charity (vss. 3, where "honor" includes financial support, and 16, the verses which bracket the passage). Their only and sufficient "qualification" for assistance was their need.

Another category of widows is introduced into the discussion in 5:9-13, the "widow put on the list," or "the enrolled widow."[96] To be put on the list identified particular widows not only to receive financial support (if needed) but more significantly also to serve the church in certain ways. An enumeration of definite qualifications, comparable to what is done in regard to bishops and deacons in chapter 3, is a clear indication of a distinct class beyond the "real widows." Applying the principle that qualifications were not arbitrary but were related to the work to be performed, we can gain a rather clear picture of the activities of the "order" of widows.

(1) "One who has brought up children" — so with the necessary experience to have orphans in the community placed in her care.

(2) "One who has shown hospitality, washed the saints' feet" — so she could be maintained in her own house to provide a guest house to receive traveling Christians, very necessary in an age without many adequate accommodations for travelers.

(3) "One who has helped the afflicted and devoted herself to doing good in every way" — so able to provide nursing care for the sick and needy.

(4) Not "gossips and busybodies" — but visiting younger women to teach and admonish them (cf. Titus 2:2-5).

Widows put on the list apparently took a "pledge" (v. 12) not to

96. Marcia Moore, "The 'Widows' in 1 Tim. 5:3-16," in Carroll Osburn, ed., *Essays on Women in Earliest Christianity* (Joplin, Mo.: College Press, 1993), pp. 321-366, states very well the case for distinct classes of widows being under consideration in the passage.

remarry and to give the remainder of their lives to the service of the church. The resulting arrangement provided for a matching of needs that had to be met (care for orphans, travelers, and the sick, and women to teach women) with persons capable of meeting those needs but themselves perhaps in need of assistance. Moreover, there were definite advantages in requiring work in return for support, so that the widows did not feel that they were simply "charity cases." In the postapostolic church there is reference to two classes of widows recognized by the church: those not able to take an active role, who devoted themselves to prayer, and those appointed for serving the needs of others.[97] These two classes correspond to the distinction between the "real widows" (1 Tim. 5:5) and the "enrolled widows" (1 Tim. 5:10-11).

Limitations on Women's Ministry

The qualifications of elder-bishops discussed above have in mind only men filling this responsibility (1 Tim. 3:2, 4-5; Titus 1:6). Leadership in the family or household was placed with the husband (1 Cor. 11:3; Col. 3:18; Eph. 5:21-33). As noted on pages 114-115, the church is described as a family or household (cf. 1 Tim. 3:15). Accordingly, leadership in the church, as the family of God, was given to those who were heads of households (1 Tim. 3:4-5).

Two passages, in addition, place specific limitations on women's activities in church and, therefore, call for fuller comment. Both have to do with the assembly of the church.

1 Corinthians 14:33b-35 reads:

> As in all the churches of the saints, women should be silent in the churches. For they are not permitted to speak, but should be subordinate, as the law also says. If there is anything they desire to know, let them ask their husbands at home. For it is shameful for a woman to speak in church.

The passage offers several difficulties. One is textual: a few manuscripts place verses 34-35 after verse 40. This is often taken as an evidence of interpolation,[98] but it may as easily be explained by a scribe either accidentally omitting the passage and restoring it out of place or pur-

---

97. *Apostolic Church Order* 5.

98. Gordon Fee, *The First Epistle to the Corinthians* (Grand Rapids: Eerdmans, 1987), pp. 699-708.

posefully rearranging the material.[99] There is no textual evidence for omission of the passage, so as a matter of canon, this is part of the biblical text, wherever placed.

The kind of speaking referred to and the extent of the silence enjoined have provoked several speculations. The simplest approach is to let the context decide, for both words, "speak" and "be silent," occur in the preceding verses (vss. 26-32). The speaking under consideration is the addressing of the congregation (in this instance by those with the gifts of prophecy and of speaking in tongues) or the speaking for the congregation (as in prayer — vss. 15-17); the silence is not absolute but the ceasing from such speech. Congregational speech (such as singing or saying the "Amen") would not be excluded. If some type of dis-orderly speech were all that was involved, Paul would have forbidden that and regulated the speech, as he does with the prophets and tongue speakers (vss. 27-32); instead, he forbids the women speaking altogether (in an authoritative way, as in prophesying and teaching, or in a rep-resentative way, as in praying). One type of speech is specified as forbidden: questioning. In this instance it would be questioning that disrupted the assembly or challenged the authority of the speaker (as in the discerning of the prophets), or the type of questioning used among the Jewish rabbis as a method of teaching.

The prohibition of women prophesying or giving authoritative teaching in the assembly would seem to contradict 1 Corinthians 11:2-16, where the women prayed and prophesied. It is not certain that these activities occurred in the assembly, for 1 Corinthians 11:17 seems to mark a transition from commendation to rebuke and to a new setting, "when you come together." The Corinthian church apparently was following Paul's customs (1 Cor. 11:2), but sought an explanation of them in view of criticism from some (1 Cor. 11:16). Paul regulated the manner in which the spiritual gifts could be exercised, without speaking here of the occasion. Praying and prophesying could be in a group or in "public" but not in an assembly of the church (cf. Acts 21:8-12). The ranking established at creation regulated the relations of male and female (1 Cor. 11:3, 7-12). A woman's wearing a veil was the cultural expression (1 Cor. 11:5-6, 13-15) of those relationships appropriate in that circumstance. The distinctive positions of male and female were

99. See the refutation of Fee's reasoning by Antoinette Clark Wire, "Prophecy and Women Prophets in Corinth," in *Gospel Origins and Christian Beginnings*, ed. James E. Goehring et al. (Sonoma: Polebridge, 1990), pp. 134-150.

not based on the culture but on what God instituted at creation; culture dictated how those distinctions were expressed in the given society. Thus 1 Corinthians 14:34 supports the subordinate position of women in the assembly from the law (Gen. 3:16 would seem to be the passage in mind, but Paul could also be observing the fact that all leadership in worship in Israel was in the hands of males). The prohibition of 1 Corinthians 14:33b-35, as reflecting relations established at creation, was not a local requirement because of disturbances at Corinth but was in accord with practice "in all the churches of the saints."

The context of the assembly is quite evident for the instructions in 1 Corinthians 14 (vss. 19, 23, 26). The assembly is not so evident as the setting for the instructions in 1 Timothy 2, but this interpretation seems correct. The instructions to women include the following words:

> I desire, then, that in every place the men should pray, lifting up holy hands without anger or argument. . . . Let a woman learn in silence with full submission. I permit no woman to teach or to have authority over a man; she is to keep silent. (vss. 8, 11-12)

The "every place" of 1 Timothy 2:8 is to be taken as "every meeting place," "every place of assembly,"[100] bringing this passage into parallel with 1 Corinthians 14:33b-34. The prayers of 1 Timothy 2:1-2 are the public prayers of the church. In the assemblies the men pray, "lifting up holy hands" (1 Tim. 2:8), the common posture of prayer at the time. The women were to appear in public dressed "modestly and decently" (1 Tim. 2:9-10). In the setting of the public assembly of the church the woman was not "to teach or to have authority over a man" (1 Tim. 2:11); in other settings the Pastoral Epistles enjoin teaching on certain women (Titus 2:4-5). Her "quiet" and submissive role (1 Tim. 2:11-12) coincides with 1 Corinthians 14. The basis, again, is the created relationship between man and woman (1 Tim. 2:13-14). The preservation of male and female distinctions gave to each a distinctive sphere that established his and her identity. Women by nature have a role that assures their identity, for men cannot fill it. That may explain why men are given a distinctive role; although it appears arbitrary, it marks a sphere for them, just as women have a sphere of their own. Men are assigned the leadership in the public affairs of the church, and women

---

100. Everett Ferguson, "*Topos* in 1 Timothy 2:8," *Restoration Quarterly* 33 (1991): 65-73.

the role of wife and mother, with the accompanying responsibilities for family nurture (1 Tim. 2:15).

These limitations apply only to the assembly of the church. It is not explicit in the text why a limitation would have been made in this area but not in others, but the theological reasons on which the limitation is grounded may permit some inferences as an explanation. The assembly exemplifies the church as the people of God and so reflects God's hierarchical order of creation. When the church comes before God in a special way, it appears according to the created relationships. Moreover, the assembly is to reflect the character of God (1 Cor. 14:33, 40 — in this case peace and order), and so God's created order. This carries no implication of inferiority for women nor of negative judgment on women's ability. Any given woman may be the spiritual or intellectual superior of any given man. The designated roles are signs pointing to something more fundamental: that God is God and human beings are his creatures who must respect his institutions.

AUTONOMY AND COOPERATION

"The flock of God that is in your charge'   (1 PET. 5:2)

As presented in the New Testament, each local church is *the church*, full and complete in itself. The *ekklēsiai* are not a splitting into parts of the universal *ekklēsia*, nor is the *ekklēsia* a sum of the *ekklēsiai*. Each church is the whole church in miniature, a manifestation of the whole in a given locality. Thus Paul can address "the church of God that is in Corinth" (1 Cor. 1:2), the local manifestation of the one church of God. Each eucharistic community was in full unity with the rest by virtue not of an external superimposed structure but of the whole Christ represented in each of them.[101] The problem of local and universal is

---

101. In this and the following sentence I borrow the wording of John D. Zizioulas, *Being as Communion: Studies in Personhood and the Church* (London: Darton, Longman and Todd, 1985), p. 157. Cf. also K. Schmidt, *"Ekklēsia," Theological Dictionary of the New Testament*, ed. G. Kittel, tr. G. W. Bromiley (Grand Rapids: Eerdmans, 1965), p. 506, "Each community represents the total community," and p. 534, "The individual congregation represents the whole body"; Josef Hainz, *Ekklesia: Strukturen paulinischer Gemeinde-Theologie und Gemeinde-Ordnung* (Regensburg: Friedrich Pustet, 1972), p. 239, "Every community is for Paul in the full sense a 'Church of God'" (cf. pp. 250-252).

resolved apart from any idea of the local church being incomplete or any scheme of one church over another but in the sense of a unity in identity.[102]

Local churches were the only medium through which early Christians carried on their religious work, whether in missions (Acts 13:1-3; 14:25-28), charity (Acts 11:28-30), or education (Heb. 10:24-25). Each community of believers was sufficient to do its work. No larger organizations, such as characterize so much of Christendom today, were put in place in apostolic times. When there were problems affecting more than one congregation, representatives of one church went to the church whence the problem arose to discuss the matter (Acts 15:1-2). The meeting in Acts 15 is often termed the first church council. It does establish the precedent of meetings between representatives of churches to discuss problems and plan a common course of action, but this ad hoc meeting set no precedent for continuing or permanent conciliar or synodal bodies. No continuing organization was created.

The apostles did exercise extracongregational supervision of the Christian bodies that emerged (cf. Acts 8:14; 11:19). The testimony of the apostles remains the foundation of the church, and they remain the ambassadors through whom the will of the Lord is known. It is noteworthy, however, that when they anticipated the removal of their personal presence, they did not appoint successors to continue the supervision of the churches but only local leaders who were "entrusted to the Lord" (Acts 14:23) and commended "to God and to the message of his grace" (Acts 20:32).

This independence by the local church is often called "congregational autonomy," that is, self-governing congregations. Autonomy is not a wholly satisfactory word. In regard to faith and practice the church is a monarchy, subject to its Lord. But in matters of opinion, expediency, and human judgment each church is an independent, self-governing unit, and in this sense autonomy is an appropriate word.

But autonomy is not isolation. The early churches practiced a fullness of fellowship, cooperation, mutual assistance, and communication. There was a sense of being one body under one Lord (Eph. 4:4-5). There were to be no dividing barriers between believers, whether racial (Eph. 2) or cultural (Rom. 14–15). Examples of local churches cooperating together may be seen in Acts 11:28-30; Romans 15:25-26; and 2 Corinthians 8:1-5. Such mutual cooperation is evident throughout the

---

102. See further on unity on pp. 399ff.

pages of the New Testament, but this was done without creating an organization higher than local churches.

FORM AND SPIRIT

> *"Do you not know that you [pl.] are God's temple*
> *and that God's Spirit dwells in you [pl.]? If anyone*
> *destroys God's temple, God will destroy that person.*
> *For God's temple is holy, and you [pl.] are that*
> *temple."*
>   (1 COR. 3:16F.)

Much of this chapter has necessarily dealt with matters of form. It has sought to spell out the apostolic form given to the church. This does not mean that form is as important as spirit. The Spirit must be active first. But spirit must take some outward form. Even as the Word became flesh, so the Spirit must express itself in some form. Spirit must be embodied in order to give a visible presence and to accomplish the Lord's work. Spirit and structure are not opposed to each other. The New Testament knows no invisible church. That is a later theological concept to explain anomalies between the biblical teaching and the realities of the church at given historical periods. It is a concept that should not be used to avoid the task of giving proper form to the spiritual realities of the church. There is a unity between spirit and form in the New Testament picture of the church.

Much of the Christian world considers matters of form indifferent or even optional. Debates over polity such as divided Anglo-Saxon Christianity in the seventeenth century are now outmoded in the present ecumenical climate. And we are not contending for a rigid form; the apostolic pattern allows for flexibility to meet changing needs and circumstances. There is, however, a form that best embodies the spirit, a form that inheres in the nature of the church and its work. The Qumran community was fervently apocalyptic yet very detailed in its organizational regulations. Its existence, therefore, calls into question two long-standing but false assumptions about the early church: an eschatological or apocalyptic community had no interest in structures or fixed patterns, and ecclesiastical office arose only when apocalyptic fervor waned.[103]

---

103. Daniel J. Harrington, *God's People in Christ: New Testament Perspectives on the Church and Judaism* (Philadelphia: Fortress, 1980), p. 37.

The church, too, was strongly eschatological in its faith (Chap. 1), but it had organizational structures from the beginning. These underwent changes and development even in apostolic times, but to say that forms are inimical to the spirit of early Christianity is to misapprehend the nature of the early Christian movement and the historical realities.

By connecting matters of organization and ministry to Christ and his earthly work, we have attempted to give priority to the spirit and at the same time show a unity of spirit and form. The organic nature of the church expresses itself in certain ministries. The organization of the church is not arbitrary, nor is it optional. The church has essential functions. Ministry expresses these functions, which are in turn to carry out the work of the Lord.

Selected Bibliography on Ministry and Organization

Anderson, Ray S., ed. *Theological Foundations for Ministry.* Grand Rapids: Eerdmans, 1979.

Bartlett, David L. *Ministry in the New Testament.* Minneapolis: Fortress, 1993.

Bromiley, G. W. *Christian Ministry.* Grand Rapids: Eerdmans, 1959.

Burtchaell, James Tunstead. *From Synagogue to Church: Public Services and Offices in the Earliest Christian Communities.* Cambridge: University Press, 1992.

Colson, Jean. *Les Fonctions ecclésiales: Aux deux premiers siècles.* Paris: Desclée de Brouwer, 1954.

Cooke, Bernard. *Ministry to Word and Sacraments: History and Theology.* Philadelphia: Fortress, 1976.

Delorme, Jean, ed. *Le Ministère et les ministères selon le Nouveau Testament.* Paris: Seuil, 1974.

Ellis, E. Earle. *Pauline Theology: Ministry and Society.* Grand Rapids: Eerdmans, 1989.

Giles, Kevin. *Patterns of Ministry among the First Christians.* Melbourne: Collins Dove, 1989.

Gore, Charles. *The Church and the Ministry.* New ed. rev. by C. H. Turner. London: Longmans, Green, 1919.

Harnack, Adolph. *The Constitution and Law of the Church in the First Two Centuries.* London: Norgate and Williams, 1910.

Hatch, Edwin. *The Organization of the Early Christian Churches.* London: Rivingtons, 1888.

Kruse, Colin. *New Testament Models for Ministry: Jesus and Paul.* Nashville: Thomas Nelson, 1983.

Lemaire, A. *Les Ministères aux origines de l'Église.* Paris: Cerf, 1971.

Lewis, Jack P. *Leadership Questions Confronting the Church.* Nashville: Christian Communications, 1985.

Lightfoot, J. B. "The Christian Ministry." *St. Paul's Epistle to the Philippians.* London: Macmillan, 1913. Pp. 181-269. Reprint introduction by P. E. Hughes. Wilton, Conn.: Morehouse, 1983.

Lindsay, T. M. *The Church and the Ministry in the Early Centuries.* London: Hodder and Stoughton, 1903.

Malherbe, Abraham J. *Paul and the Thessalonians: The Philosophic Tradition of Pastoral Care.* Philadelphia: Fortress, 1987.

Manson, T. W. *The Church's Ministry.* Philadelphia: Westminster, 1948.

Morris, Leon. *Ministers of God.* London: IVF, 1964.

O'Grady, John. *Disciples and Leaders.* Mahwah, NJ: Paulist, 1991.

Paul, Robert S. *Ministry.* Grand Rapids: Eerdmans, 1965.

Riesenfeld, Harald. "The Ministry in the New Testament." A. Fridrichsen, ed., *The Root of the Vine.* New York: Philosophical Library, 1953. Pp. 96-127.

Schweizer, Eduard. *Church Order in the New Testament.* London: SCM, 1961.

Streeter, B. H. *The Primitive Church.* New York: Macmillan, 1929.

Von Campenhausen, H. *Ecclesiastical Authority and Spiritual Power in the Church of the First Three Centuries.* London: Black, 1969.

Wehrli, Eugene S. *Gifted by their Spirit: Leadership Roles in the New Testament.* Cleveland: Pilgrim, 1992.

Ysebaert, J. *Die Amtsterminologie im Neuen Testament und in der Alten Kirche: Eine lexikographische Untersuchung.* Breda: Eureia, 1994.

6. The Church and Her Teacher: The New Way of Life

"You have heard that it was said. . . .
But I say to you. . . ."   (MATT. 5:21-22)

JESUS, among other things, was a teacher. This was the most common
title by which he was addressed in his personal ministry (see pp. 286,
328). He presented his teachings as the authoritative word of God (Mark
1:22). Over against the interpretations of the law current in his day, he
set his own, "I say to you . . ." (Matt. 5:21-48). The resurrected Jesus
delivered an authoritative way of life to be followed by his disciples,
instructing that those who had been baptized be taught "to obey everything that I have commanded you" (Matt. 28:20). He not only taught
by word of mouth, but he also as a teacher set an example by his own
conduct of how his disciples should live (e.g., Matt. 10:25; John 13:15).

It has been appropriately said that there are two sides to being a
Christian: believing and behaving. The early chapters of this book
considered aspects of believing. This chapter focuses on behaving (cf.
1 Tim. 3:15). The concern is not with a complete treatment but rather
some aspects of conduct that have particular relevance for understanding the church.

If the worship of the church reflects salvation as a response to God,
and if the work of the church reflects salvation as a mission to outsiders,
then life in the church and the church's fellowship express salvation
principally in the relations of Christians with one another. At the same
time, moreover, it maintains an important witness to those on the outside.

The salvation in Christ and membership in his church find expression in a new way of life. This chapter will examine some features of this new life in Christ Jesus: ethics, fellowship, discipline, Christian liberty, the church in relation to society, and unity. The new way of life has a theological basis that gives a distinctive character to why Christians live as they do. This way of life is expressed in and supported by the mutual fellowship of believers, a fellowship that allows liberty in most matters but a fellowship that must be withdrawn when conduct deliberately violates the basis of the fellowship. The goal of the way and life and its fellowship is the cultivation of the unity summed up in Christ that is God's goal for his creation (Eph. 1:10).

MORALITY AND COMMUNITY

"How one ought to behave in the . . . church
of the living God."   (1 TIM. 3:15)

The motifs and images of the church discussed earlier carry with them implications about behavior. A covenant people is bound by the stipulations of the covenant. The people of the kingdom live under the rule of God. The body of Christ acts under the directions of the head. The temple of the Holy Spirit is holy in word and deed. The family of God responds to the Father's love. The resultant conduct in its turn creates the sense of community: living by the covenant confirms covenant loyalty; submitting to the king makes visible the kingdom; acting as a body develops solidarity; exhibiting the family characteristics bonds the family together.

Christian conduct defines the character of the church. There is a reciprocal relationship: a common morality shapes the community, and the community shapes its members' morality. "Making morals means making community."[1]

Becoming a Christian was not merely an act of individual conversion (however personal it may have been): it was becoming a part of

---

1. Wayne A. Meeks, *The Origins of Christian Morality: The First Two Centuries* (New Haven: Yale, 1993), p. 5. Meeks here and elsewhere has emphasized the importance of the moral life for the social formation of community. My heading for this section is suggested by the title of his first chapter, and the section itself is based on his observations (viz., pp. 26, 36, 109, 179, 213-214).

the Christian community. The section below on the soteriological motivation for Christian ethics gives some indication of how frequently
the language of salvation and imagery associated with conversion occur
in passages giving instruction about Christian conduct. This moral
instruction, set in the context of group standards, reinforces the fact
that Christian conversion involved being incorporated into an alternative community that perceived itself (and was perceived by outsiders)
to have a distinctive lifestyle. The convert entered a primary reference
group (the church) different from what had been the person's primary
social group in the past: whether of family, city, club, philosophical
school, or religious association. This gave importance to inculcating not
only the story of the group but also the characteristic behavior that was
a consequence of this story.

When converts were told that those who do certain things "will
not inherit the kingdom of God" (1 Cor. 6:9-10; Gal. 5:21; Eph. 5:5), they
were being told something about the community they were joining.
Habitual practices create a sense of identity. We are who we are because
these are the things we do. And if these things are done in a group and
because of being in a group, the sense of belonging and distinctiveness
is strengthened. Certain kinds of conduct establish social boundaries.
And those social boundaries themselves significantly frame the moral
thinking of those within the group. Thus, the topic of the new way of
life in Christ is significant for an understanding of the New Testament
doctrine of the church. Christian morality is intimately wrapped up
with the Christian community.

THE NATURE OF CHRISTIAN ETHICS

> *"He bore our sins in his body on the cross, so that,*
> *free from sins, we might live for righteousness."*   (1 PET. 2:24)

General Principles

The Christian life flows from salvation in Christ and incorporation into
him (see further below under the Theological Foundations for Ethics).
The nature of the Christian life is governed by Christ and what he has
done for us. The disciple lives out salvation in daily life. "Work out
your own salvation with fear and trembling; for it is God who is at

work in you, enabling you both to will and to work for his good pleasure" (Phil. 2:12-13). As observed on pages 172-173, the command is not to "work for,"[2] but to "work out," or, as I would prefer, simply "to work" your salvation, and this is possible because God works within. The Christian life is both a gift and a task. "Task" is not used here in a "self-help" sense. Rather, our task is to become what we are in Christ (children of God, holy, justified, etc.).[3] We are "in Christ," so we live and treat one another accordingly. The church is the sphere or realm for actualizing the new creation, the new humanity, and it provides mutual help for this task.

An identifying mark of God's people is how they live. This was one of the main points in early Christian apologetics.[4] Jesus put the matter incisively in John 13:35: "By this everyone will know that you are my disciples, if you have love for one another." The point is probably not so much that conduct proves that one is a disciple as that conduct is a witness to Christ. The truth claims of Christianity are seriously damaged when Christians do not live as Christians. Ultimately, truth must be judged on other grounds, but an important indication of whether something is true is what results from its practice: "By their fruits you will know them" (Matt. 7:20) applies to ideas as well as to people. The failure of Christians to live up to their teachings is a serious matter but does not invalidate the faith they profess. The value of high standards is in part precisely that they are just beyond the grasp: this gives an ideal toward which to reach and by which to judge human endeavors.

Christian ethics are "Kingdom ethics," not universal ethics. They are ethical standards given to a redeemed people. This is especially true of the Sermon on the Mount, which is addressed neither to individuals nor to humanity as a whole but to the new Israel.[5] It would be good if

2. Although *katergazomai* can mean "work for" or "earn," it also means "accomplish" or "practice," and either of the latter is preferable in the context of biblical teaching.

3. T. J. Deidun, *New Covenant Morality in Paul* (Rome: Biblical Institute Press, 1981), p. 83, revises this statement to say that the Christian imperative is "let God be what he is."

4. See the collection of texts and discussion in Everett Ferguson, *Early Christians Speak* (Abilene: ACU Press, 1987), pp. 193-218.

5. Gerhard Lohfink, *Jesus and Community* (London: SPCK, 1985), p. 35; Ben Wiebe, *Messianic Ethics: Jesus' Proclamation of the Kingdom of God and the Church as Response* (Waterloo: Herald, 1992), pp. 122, 160-166.

all lived by the teachings of Jesus, but it is unrealistic to expect people who do not accept the Lordship of Jesus to adopt his teachings on their merits alone. The Golden Rule (Matt. 7:12), as nearly as any ethical principle, will stand the test of application to all circumstances. Yet even it cannot be absolutized in all circumstances and presupposes grace and conversion. For example, how will the drunkard understand "do unto others as you would have them do to you"? He will buy the other fellow a drink. That is not what Jesus meant. The redeemed heart is necessary for the application of even this teaching from Jesus. Christian ethics are for those who have come under the rule of God. The non-Christian is a sinner, not because he has not been baptized or because he does not keep Christian ethics, but because of the transgression of his own moral code and the rejection of the knowledge of God available to him (Rom. 1:18–2:29). Conversely, the motivations for Christian ethics are not "natural" or pragmatic but grow out of the Christian gospel. Christian moral teachings are for those who accept the rule of God in their lives.

Our concern in this section of the chapter will not be the specifics of Christian ethical conduct but rather the doctrinal reasons behind Christian conduct. In the process of citing passages that bring out these guiding principles many specifics of morality will be included, but the emphasis in our discussion will be on the bases of the conduct.

Theological Foundations for Ethics in the New Testament

Many moral people who are not Christians will act in the same way in a given situation that Christian teaching enjoins. Christian moral conduct may or may not be the same as what a non-Christian would do in the circumstances. Even where the conduct is the same, the Christian acts for different reasons. The Christian, as Christian, does not choose a given course of conduct because it will win the approval of others, because it will contribute to success (however defined in the given culture), because it will bring an earthly reward, or because it accords with moral teachings or ethical principles arrived at on natural presuppositions. For example, it may be true, as Benjamin Franklin said, that "Honesty is the best policy." What if it does not appear to be the best policy? The Christian is not honest because of "policy" considerations but because it is God's teaching for his life.

The point may be illustrated from motivations given to young people in matters of sexual morality. There was a time (and for many this is still the case) when the arguments against sexual relations outside marriage included such considerations as the following: there might be an unwanted baby; there is the danger of venereal disease; and what will the neighbors say? Those arguments do not carry much weight any more. Contraceptive measures can greatly reduce the possibilities of pregnancy. Medicines can cure or alleviate the symptoms of many sexually transmitted diseases. (The current scare from AIDS has brought a terrifying new danger that gives added force to this argument.) And in recent times there has been great likelihood that the neighbors themselves are indulging in such conduct, so the reproach of society no longer has whatever deterrent force it may have had. Such pragmatic considerations may have to be used in reasoning with non-Christians. Christians, however, do not govern their conduct on such bases. They have more important reasons for what they do. On the matter of sexual behavior, consider the arguments by Paul in 1 Corinthians 6:9-20 (on which, see pp. 356-357).

All the motivations for the moral teaching given by New Testament writers are religious and are rooted in fundamental Christian doctrines. These motivations for ethics are the same themes that we have found running throughout our study. Most of the bases for ethics will be found expressed in Ephesians, the New Testament book with the greatest attention given to the doctrine of the church.

Theology

Christian conduct is rooted in the will of God. Christ set the pattern, for he came into the world to do the will of God (cf. Matt. 26:39; John 6:38; Heb. 10:5-7, 9).[6]

Ethics for Christians is related to the kind of person God is. "You were taught . . . to clothe yourselves with the new self, created according to the likeness of God in true righteousness and holiness" (Eph. 4:24). "Therefore be imitators of God, as beloved children" (Eph. 5:1). It is natural for children to be both influenced by and to imitate the examples of their parents. Even so the children of God are expected to

6. Wayne A. Meeks, *The Origins of Christian Morality* (New Haven: Yale, 1993), pp. 150-173. "Most frequent of all [the expressions concerning the will of God] is the phrase 'to do the will of God'" (p. 152).

take on God's characteristics. Jesus taught, "Be perfect, therefore, as your heavenly Father is perfect" (Matt. 5:48 — for the meaning see p. 362 below). The children of God imitate him because they are obedient to him.

The operative principle for the Christian is: "This is the will of God" (1 Thess. 4:3). And, as that verse continues, the will of God is "(y)our sanctification." Paul introduces the ethical section of Romans with reference to "the will of God," which he defines as "good, acceptable, and perfect" (Rom. 12:2). Peter as well as Paul appeals to the will of God in an ethical context (1 Pet. 4:2) and sees this as entailing holiness. He repeats the Old Testament teaching: "Like obedient children, do not be conformed to the desires that you formerly had in ignorance. Instead, as he who called you is holy, be holy yourselves in all your conduct; for it is written, 'You shall be holy, for I am holy'" (1 Pet. 1:15-16, quoting Lev. 11:44-45; 19:2; 20:7). John promises that those "who do the will of God live forever" (1 John 2:17).

It is not only the holiness of God that serves as a basis for Christian moral teaching. Both Peter (1 Pet. 2:3) and Paul (Rom. 2:4) appeal to the goodness (grace) of God as a motive for conduct. As a specific illustration of the principle, God's giving motivates Christian charity (2 Cor. 9:7-8). Throughout the Bible God's people are expected to act in the way God has acted (cf. Deut. 10:17-19; 15:13-15; 24:17-22).

Several of these contexts associate the immoral behavior of pagans with ignorance of God (Eph. 4:18; 1 Thess. 4:5; 1 Pet. 1:14). Those who do not know God do not know his will and so do not do what he requires. Knowledge is used in these passages not so much to refer to information but in the biblical sense of the knowledge that comes from relationship. Paul blames Gentile immorality on a rejection of God and of what can be known about him (Rom. 1:18-32). Ignorance of God is cured not by information but by repentance.

Christology[7]

Even as Christians are called upon to imitate God as their Father, so

---

7. Hieronymus Cruz, *Christological Motives and Motivated Actions in Pauline Paraenesis* (New York: Peter Lang, 1990), develops the christological motivation for ethics much more extensively than my brief remarks do, and he concludes (pp. 438-441, 443) that Christ is the real motive in the Pauline paraenesis and that the christological basis is what makes an ethical requirement specifically Christian.

they are called to imitate the life of Christ. Ephesians 5:1 follows the command to be imitators of God with a reference to the example of Jesus: "And live in love, as Christ loved us and gave himself up for us" (Eph. 5:2).

Paul, furthermore, said, "Be imitators of me, as I am of Christ" (1 Cor. 11:1). He appealed to Christians to have the mind of the Christ who went to the cross as the warrant for the Christian attitude and treatment of others (Phil. 2:4-8). Peter applied the principle of imitating Christ to a willingness to experience suffering for the sake of Christ: "For to this you have been called, because Christ also suffered for you, leaving you an example, so that you should follow in his steps" (1 Pet. 2:21).

The real basis for the Christian life is the salvation given in Christ (see Chap. 3). A new life is received through being joined to Christ (Rom. 6:1-23). That experience involves a death to sin, so the practice of sin is inconsistent with the new condition. If a person is in Christ, that person will live Christ's kind of life. The new life in Christ is a sharing in God's plan and an imitation of Christ.

Pneumatology

Since the Holy Spirit is given to the baptized believer as the mark of the new age, the Christian lives life with reference to the Spirit. "Do not grieve the Holy Spirit of God, with which you were marked with a seal for the day of redemption" (Eph. 4:30).

The new life in Christ is given through the Holy Spirit and is lived in him. The Holy Spirit makes possible the living of the Christian life. He is the power behind Christian conduct. Christ provides the dynamic with the demand, the power with the pattern, of the new life.

Paul in Galatians 5:16-26 contrasts living according to the flesh, the natural person, with living according to the Spirit. The principle is that if we have life by the Spirit, we are to be guided in our behavior by the Spirit (Gal. 5:25). The works of the flesh (Gal. 5:19-21) are crucified (Gal. 5:24), and the Spirit produces the fruit of righteousness in one's life (Gal. 5:22-23).

The indwelling of the Spirit is the basis of Paul's argument against sexual immorality in 1 Corinthians 6:13-20. The body belongs to Christ and so must not be joined to a prostitute (vs. 15). Such conduct is to defile the Holy Spirit that dwells in the human body as in a holy temple (vss. 18-19). Such an argument would not be meaningful to a non-

Christian, but to the Christian who understands the meaning of Christian teaching, it constitutes a powerful appeal.

Soteriology

The experience of salvation in Christ is often made the basis of ethical injunctions. This is the principal thrust of Ephesians 4–5. Some verses make the connection between salvation and conduct quite explicit. After describing the condition of pagans, Paul exclaims, "That is not the way you learned Christ!" (Eph. 4:20). "You were taught to put away your former way of life, . . . and to be renewed in your minds, and to clothe yourselves with the new self" (Eph. 4:22-24). The experience of salvation governs the way one treats others: "Be kind to one another, tenderhearted, forgiving one another, as God in Christ has forgiven you" (Eph. 4:32). That sets a very high standard for personal relations: treat others the way God has treated you. Chapter 5 of Ephesians continues the theme. Positively, the teaching is "to live in love, as Christ loved us" (Eph. 5:2). Negatively, this means "Fornication and impurity of any kind, or greed, must not even be mentioned among you, as is proper among saints" (Eph. 5:3).

Colossians contains parallel ethical instruction, as so much else, to Ephesians. The standard for the "new self" is likeness to God. The ethical instruction arises out of the vision of the saved humanity, "renewed according to the image of the creator" (Col. 3:10). Picking up the baptismal language of Colossians 2:12, the author applies the consequences for life: "So if you have been raised with Christ, seek the things that are above, where Christ is" (Col. 3:1). "Put to death, therefore, whatever in you is earthly: fornication, impurity, passion, evil desire, and greed (which is idolatry)" (Col. 3:5). "These are the ways you also once followed, when you were living that life. But now you must remove all such things — anger, wrath, malice, slander, and abusive language from your mouth. Do not lie to one another, seeing you have stripped off the old self with its practices" (Col. 3:7-9). "As God's chosen ones, holy and beloved, clothe yourselves with compassion, kindness, humility, meekness, and patience" (Col. 3:12). Death and resurrection, and removing and putting on clothes, are baptismal imagery applied to the moral consequences of conversion. The believer renounces the old way of life and accepts the new way of life in Christ because of being redeemed: "You know that you were ransomed from the futile ways inherited from your ancestors, not with perishable things like silver or gold, but with the precious blood of Christ" (1 Pet. 1:18-19).

Eschatology

The Christian lives a certain way, furthermore, not only because of the past experience of salvation but also because of the future, the end time.[8] Life is directed toward a future that is in God's hands. The eschatological perspective is not prominent in Ephesians, but the ethical section does contain the warning, "Be sure of this, that no fornicator or impure person or one who is greedy (that is, an idolater), has any inheritance in the kingdom of Christ and of God" (Eph. 5:5).

Eschatology has usually been appealed to as a threat of judgment. Such is the application in 2 Peter 3:11-12: "Since all these things [the elements of the world — vs. 10] are to be dissolved in this way [in fire — vs. 10], what sort of persons ought you to be in leading lives of holiness and godliness, waiting for and hastening the coming of the day of God."

Eschatology functions on a different level in 1 Peter 4:7-8. Instead of being the negative motivation of fear of punishment, eschatology here regulates conduct in a positive way by setting the character of life: "The end of all things is near; therefore be serious and discipline yourselves for the sake of your prayers. Above all, maintain constant love for one another." Since the end is near, "therefore" a certain kind of conduct follows. Because Christians live in the last days, they live a life that pertains to the end time.

The characteristics of this "end time" kind of life are brought out more fully in 1 Thessalonians 4:13–5:11. The Thessalonian Christians were troubled by uncertainties concerning the Lord's second coming. Paul maintains the eschatological tension between imminence and indefiniteness by affirming the uncertainty of the date and the certainty of its occurrence. In the interim there is a definite kind of conduct that pertains to the end time. "For you yourselves know very well that the day of the Lord will come like a thief in the night. . . . But you, beloved, are not in darkness, for that day to surprise you like a thief; for you are

---

8. Philip LeMaster, *Discipleship for All Believers: Christian Ethics and the Kingdom of God* (Scottdale, Penn.: Herald, 1992), discusses how eschatology and ecclesiology shape ethics, taking the resurrection of Christ and the church as a foretaste of the new age as providing the proper context for discipleship.

all children of light and children of the day; we are not of the night or of darkness. . . . But since we belong to the day, let us be sober, and put on the breastplate of faith and love, and for a helmet the hope of salvation" (1 Thess. 5:2-9). Since the eschatological hope spoke of the "day of the Lord," Paul makes a play on the concepts of day (light) and night (darkness). Christians belong to the light, so the "day of the Lord" holds no fear for them. By the same token their conduct accords with light and not the darkness in which unbelievers live. There is a continuity between the Christian life and the second coming of Jesus. The Jesus who comes will be the same Jesus known as Savior now. The kind of life lived in faithfulness to Jesus has continuity with what will be experienced at the coming again of Jesus.

The eschatological perspective calls attention to the transience of life and puts emphasis on those things of enduring value. Those abiding or permanent qualities — e.g., faith, love, and hope (1 Thess. 5:8; 1 Cor. 13:13) — are cultivated by the Christian and remain significant whatever else happens. If the Lord returns soon or later, these virtues provide the way to live.

Ecclesiology

The church provides both a standard and a structure for the new life in Christ. Ephesians contains numerous passages in which one's relations with others in the church provide the motive and basis for proper conduct. The ethical section begins with an appeal to humility, gentleness, patience, forbearance, and unity based on there being "one body" (Eph. 4:1-4). The end of the fourth chapter commands moral conduct, but with a difference — the reasons given for the conduct are not what one usually hears. "So then, putting away falsehood, let all of us speak the truth to our neighbors" (Eph. 4:25). To tell the truth and not to lie is common moral teaching, but notice the basis given: "For we are members of one another." The statement follows from the comparison of the church to a body. A person is in serious trouble — mentally or morally — when s/he lies to her/himself. To lie to fellow members of the body of Christ is the ecclesiological equivalent of psychological schizophrenia. Christians do not lie because of their relationships with one another.

The prohibition of stealing comes next: "Thieves must give up stealing; rather let them labor and work honestly with their own hands" (Eph. 4:28). The injunction might sound common enough, but rather distinctively religious is the reason given: "So as to have something to share with the needy." The motivation is not just to avoid mistreating someone else, or even to provide for the needs of oneself and one's family. It is to have something to give to those in need, a characteristically Christian behavior. Concern for others again is at the forefront.

The next command returns to proper speech: "Let no evil talk come out of your mouths" (Eph. 4:29). The opposite kind of speech is described once more in characteristically Christian terms related to community life: "But only what is useful for building up, as there is need, so that your words may give grace to those who hear." One's speech is to bring benefit to the hearer. Instead of tearing the person down, whether by slander or by bad influence, the speech is to aim at edification. It is to bring grace, or a blessing (Col. 4:6; note the soteriological description of the same moral teaching in Col. 3:5-10).

The ecclesiological concern becomes dominant and even more explicit in Ephesians 5, where Christ and the church are presented as the standard for husband and wife relations (Eph. 5:22-33). This pervasive use of the imagery of the church as a basis for ethical conduct encourages Christians in all their behavior and in all aspects of life to consider how the church should (not only by its teachings but also by its very nature) provide guidance in moral decisions and also to think of what effect a given line of conduct will have on others, namely the church.

Paul uses the implications for the church in his admonitions to the Corinthians. "Do you not know that you are God's temple and that God's Spirit dwells in you? If anyone destroys God's temple, God will destroy that person. For God's temple is holy, and you are that temple" (1 Cor. 3:16-17). Such are the disastrous consequences of division in the church, against which Paul is writing in this context. The principle is broader. The church is the temple of God. Conduct affecting the church affects God and his Spirit.

Personal relations are elaborated in Philippians 2:1-5 according to the principle of seeking the welfare of others above self: "Do nothing from selfish ambition or conceit, but in humility regard others as better than yourselves. Let each of you look not to your own interests, but to the interests of others" (Phil. 2:3-4). The ethical life of Christians takes place not only in the context of society at large, but more particularly in a special social organism, the church. Concern for it and its members guides ethical decisions and conduct.

This concern for the church does not mean that Christians have no concern for the world. Their lives are also conducted with an eye on the world. As far as standards are involved, what the world thinks does not control Christian conduct. But Christians will be concerned about the reputation of the church in the world (1 Tim. 3:7) and will not tolerate a lower standard than the world (1 Cor. 5:1). The Thessalonian Christians were told to work to support themselves, "so that you may behave properly toward outsiders and be dependent on no one" (1 Thess. 4:12). "Conduct yourselves wisely toward outsiders, making the most of the time" (Col. 4:5). The world may not set the standards, but Christians live before the world and especially in matters of judgment must take into account the attitudes of outsiders.

The Primacy of Love

Ephesians may be taken as a starting point also for the discussion of love as central to Christian motivation. The phrase "in love" occurs with great frequency — referring to God's love (Eph. 1:4), Christians' love for one another (Eph. 4:2, 15, 16) in imitation of the divine love (Eph. 5:2), and perhaps both together (Eph. 3:17).

The command to love others[9] was not a new commandment with Jesus and the church. Jesus quoted the law of Moses in defining the greatest commandments as to love God and to love one's neighbor (Matt. 22:34-40, quoting Deut. 6:5 and Lev. 19:18). The Golden Rule (Matt. 7:12) has parallels in the Judaism of Jesus' day and in the teachings of other moral teachers.[10] Jesus and his teachings and example did bring a new definition, a new depth of meaning, to the command to love. "This is my commandment, that you love one another as I have loved you" (John 15:12). Jesus has become the standard for the Christian of what it means to love. The Christian's motives and actions will always be measured by this standard. The world and others may have their own definitions of love, but the Christian definition is provided by God's actions in Christ. Jesus' own conduct even went beyond his further statement of what is involved in love: "No one has greater love

---

9. Ceslaus Spicq, *Agape in the New Testament* (St. Louis: B. Herder, 1963); Victor P. Furnish, *The Love Command in the New Testament* (Nashville: Abingdon, 1972).

10. A. Dihle, *Die goldene Regel: eine Einführung in die Geschichte der antiken und frühchristlichen Vulgarethik* (Göttingen, 1962); W. D. Davies, *The Setting of the Sermon on the Mount* (Atlanta: Scholars Press, 1989).

than this, to lay down one's life for one's friends" (John 15:13). Even as Jesus taught his disciples to love their enemies (Matt. 5:43-44),[11] so he died for the salvation of his enemies (Rom. 5:6-10).

Jesus' command to love enemies (Matt. 5:44) is followed by an appeal to be children of God the Father, who set the example of sending sunshine and rain on the righteous and unrighteous (Matt. 5:45). The command to "be perfect as your heavenly Father is perfect" (Matt. 5:48) is to be understood in this context. It is not a command to be morally blameless, as desirable as that is, but rather a command to be complete, "perfect," in regard to love, that is to love all persons, as God does. This interpretation is confirmed by the Lukan parallel to this context: "Be merciful, just as your Father is merciful" (Luke 6:36).

These passages indicate for us the proper meaning of the biblical word "love." The English word "love" has to do duty for many meanings — sexual, familial, familiar, and charitable.[12] It is no wonder that there is confusion in the general populace, who will think in terms of sentiment if not romantic notions of love. Biblical love, on the other hand, has to do with the will and the accompanying actions. It is the settled goodwill toward another and the determination to act for that person's welfare.

> The ethic that is based entirely upon the commandment "Thou shalt love" is the supreme ethic because it never allows the practicer of it to be comfortable. The very essence of Christian love is that it is for ever restless and unappeased. A man's conscience may be appeased when, conceiving Christianity to be a list of rules, he can look back at the day's end and say "I have kept all the rules. I have done all the 'Thou shalt nots.'" A man's conscience can never be appeased when the very seat of it is in his heart and his spirit; when it does not "love" because he is good, but is good because he loves. His love can never be satisfied so long as he knows there is a single sorrow in the world, a single injustice which he has not been able or has not done his best to remove or to lessen.[13]

(See further pp. 392, 395 on Christian liberty.)

11. John Whittaker, "Christianity and Morality in the Roman Empire," *Vigiliae Christianae* 33 (1979): 209-225, argues this was not unique in the Greco-Roman world.

12. C. S. Lewis, *The Four Loves* (New York: Harcourt, Brace, 1960).

13. Ernest H. Jeffs, quoted in A. Gordon Nasby, ed., *Treasury of the Christian World* (New York: Harper, 1953), p. 209.

The Practice of Holiness

Holiness is also a concern in Ephesians, as in all the Bible. The letter is addressed to "the saints [holy ones] who are in Ephesus" (Eph. 1:1). The purpose of Christ's love for the church is "to make her holy" (Eph. 5:26). The phrase "holy and blameless" occurs twice, as Christ's goal for the church (Eph. 5:27) and as the purpose of God's election (Eph. 1:4). There is a conduct that is fitting for "saints" (Eph. 5:3), because in Christ there is a "new self, created according to the likeness of God in true righteousness and holiness [different word, *hosiotes*]" (Eph. 4:24).

The declaration that "God is love" (1 John 4:16) is balanced in the Bible by the affirmation that God is holy (Lev. 11:44-45; 1 Pet. 1:16). God is holy love. The biblical title of God "the Holy One (of Israel)" (e.g., Ps. 89:18; Isa. 1:4; 41:14), as observed on page 100, was appropriated for Jesus, "the Holy One (of God)" (Mark 1:24; John 6:69). Israel was set apart to be a "holy nation" (Exod. 19:6). His people in Christ are denominated "the holy ones" or "the saints" (Rom. 8:27; 2 Cor. 13:12). If Paul's phrase "called, saints" in his salutations (Rom. 1:7; 1 Cor. 1:2) is an adaptation of the phrase in the Septuagint for a "holy assembly" (Exod. 12:16; Lev. 23:2-4),[14] then there is an emphasis in the term "the saints" on Christians as forming a holy community and so on the social nature of their holiness (cf. 1 Pet. 2:9). "Holy" means "separated," "set apart," or "consecrated." Holiness has to do with setting boundaries and making distinctions: some things are acceptable to God, some things are not. When these boundaries are defined by God's standards of purity and sanctification, the holiness is neither impractical "other-worldliness" nor legalistic self-righteousness. The Old Testament emphasis on the holy God having a holy people (Lev. 19:2; 20:7, 26) distinct from the nations of the world by their conduct is continued in the New Testament (1 Pet. 1:15-16).

We may even speak of a New Testament "Holiness Code."[15] There is a difference from the Old Testament "Holiness Code" in that the usage of the vocabulary of holiness in the New Testament is not ritual but predominantly moral. Set apart as a possession for God, the church is to

---

14. L. Cerfaux, *The Church in the Theology of St. Paul* (New York: Herder & Herder, 1959), p. 118.

15. Philip Carrington, *The Primitive Christian Catechism* (Cambridge: University Press, 1940), followed by E. G. Selwyn, *The First Epistle of St. Peter* (London: Macmillan, 1947), pp. 363-466, esp. 369-375.

practice holy living, although the New Testament is realistic about human weakness and sinfulness.[16] The sanctification of the church is by God through his Spirit (1 Cor. 6:11; 1 Pet. 1:2). That separation from the world and setting apart to the service of God occurs through response to the call of the gospel (2 Thess. 2:13). Believers are holy by reason of their divine calling (1 Thess. 5:23-24; 2 Tim. 1:9; 2 Pet. 1:3; see pp. 86, 162). God's purpose is that his people then live a life appropriate to their holy status (Eph. 5:3). That means living a holy life according to God's will (1 Thess. 4:3-4). Human beings must cooperate with the Spirit of God and submit to the teachings of the word of God, but becoming holy does not result from human effort. The Spirit produces the fruit of righteousness in the obedient believer (Gal. 5:22-23; see p. 109).

FELLOWSHIP

> *"So that you may fellowship with us; and truly*
> *our fellowship is with the Father and with his*
> *Son Jesus Christ."*   (1 JOHN 1:3)

The support provided by fellowship with other Christians is necessary in order to live the kind of life discussed above. The new way of life brought by Jesus was first taught to the community of his disciples during his earthly ministry. Jesus gathered disciples around himself, and those disciples in association with the Lord shared a common life and so formed a fellowship. The church is a continuation of that fellowship of the first disciples gathered around their Lord. After the resurrection, the Lord was in heaven, but by the Holy Spirit the fellowship was continued. Faith as personal trust in Christ produces a fellowship with Christ that in turn forms a fellowship among those who share the same faith in him.

Various Expressions for Close Association

Paul often describes close association in the church by compounds with the preposition *syn*. Thus he spoke of himself and the Romans being mutually encouraged by each other's faith (Rom. 1:12) and asked them to join him in earnest prayer on behalf of his ministry to Jerusalem

16. Hans Küng, *The Church* (London: Burns & Oates, 1968), pp. 319-344.

(Rom. 15:30). He described the Philippians as contending along with him, in the manner of athletes competing side by side, in the cause of the gospel (Phil. 1:27; 4:3) and being fellow imitators of him (Phil. 3:17). Christians suffer together with Christ and will be glorified with him (Rom. 8:17; cf. 2 Tim. 2:11-12), even as they share one another's sufferings and joys (1 Cor. 12:26; Phil. 2:17). They are fellow heirs of Christ (Rom. 8:17; Eph. 3:16). Paul further described his co-workers as fellow prisoners (Rom. 16:7; Col. 4:10; Philem. 23), fellow slaves (Col. 1:7; 4:7), fellow workers (Rom. 16:3, 9, 21; Phil. 2:25; 4:3; Philem. 1), and fellow soldiers (Phil. 2:25; Philem. 2). Occurrences of "fellow participants" will be included in the discussion of koinōnia to follow.

I have chosen to give the major discussion of this corporate nature of the Christian life in terms of the Greek word koinōnia, "fellowship," and its cognates. The English word "fellowship" refers to the state or condition of being "fellows." The Greek word koinōnia (and its cognates) means to have in common.[17] It comes from the same root as koinē, "common," as in koinē Greek, that is, the common Greek of New Testament times. The word was applied in Greek thought to all types of activity — legal, social, civic, sexual, and religious — in which there was a common element that was shared in or that affected all the participants. The word could carry the dynamic idea of "to give a share" as well as the static concept "to have a share." In Pauline usage (and he uses the word group more than the rest of the New Testament combined), there is a strong communitarian sense, a community with someone is created by common participation in something. Among the English words used to express the meaning of the Greek word are joint

17. My discussion is closest to that of George Panikulam, Koinonia in the New Testament: A Dynamic Expression of Christian Life (Rome: Biblical Institute Press, 1979), with some insights from Josef Hainz, Koinonia: "Kirche" als Gemeinschaft bei Paulus (Regensburg: Friedrich Pustet, 1982). Cf. also J. Y. Campbell, "Koinonia and its Cognates in the New Testament," Journal of Biblical Literature 51 (1932): 352-380; F. Hauck, "Koinonos, etc.," Theological Dictionary of the New Testament, ed. G. Kittel, tr. G. W. Bromiley (Grand Rapids: Eerdmans, 1965), 3.797-809; Michael McDermott, "The Biblical Doctrine of Koinonia," Biblische Zeitschrift N.F. 19 (1975): 64-77. An Anglican contribution to the theology of the church built around the theme of fellowship is L. S. Thornton, The Common Life in the Body of Christ, 3rd ed. (London: Dacre, 1950). Written with Roman Catholic concerns but containing helpful biblical and theological insights is Jerome Hamer, The Church is a Communion (London: Geoffrey Chapman, 1964). A Greek Orthodox theology of the church working with the category of communion is John D. Zizioulas, Being as Communion: Studies in Personhood and the Church (London: Darton, Longman and Todd, 1985).

participation, communion, mutuality, sharing. The community dimension of the concept makes *koinōnia* a particularly important word for
the study of the doctrine of the church.

We will proceed by looking at most of the usages of the *koin-* word
group in the New Testament, classified somewhat arbitrarily according
to the theological bases of fellowship and the concrete expressions of
fellowship, and then considering some practical applications of the
concept.

Theological Foundations of Fellowship

(1) Christian fellowship is a fellowship with the Father. "And truly
our fellowship is with the Father and with his Son Jesus Christ" (1 John
1:3). It has a divine source in God's desire for a relationship with human
beings and in God's call through the gospel. This fellowship results in
sharing in the divine life. "He has given us . . . his precious and very
great promises so that through them you . . . may become participants
of the divine nature" (2 Pet. 1:4).

(2) Christian fellowship is distinctively a fellowship with Christ,
because the Father extends his fellowship through his Son. "God is
faithful; by him you were called into the fellowship of his Son, Jesus
Christ our Lord" (1 Cor. 1:9). The goal of God's call is fellowship with
his Son, and so response to the call is a participation with the very
person of Christ. Since Paul throughout 1 Corinthians is endeavoring
to develop a true community life among the divided Corinthians, there
is not far from his thought that communion with Christ is more than
an individual relationship with Christ. There is established a community on the basis of the relationship with Christ.

(3) The fellowship is also with the Holy Spirit. "The grace of the
Lord Jesus Christ, the love of God, and the fellowship of the Holy Spirit
be with all of you" (2 Cor. 13:13). Commentators are divided whether
the Holy Spirit here is an objective genitive (a sharing in the Holy Spirit)
or a subjective genitive (a community established by the Holy Spirit).
In favor of the subjective genitive is the presence of the two parallel
phrases in the doxology, in each of which the noun in the genitive case
does the acting: the grace is given by Jesus Christ and the love is given
by God. However, normal usage of *koinōnia* with the genitive means a
sharing or participation in the object identified in the genitive case (as
in 1 Cor. 1:9 above). This best fits a prayer of benediction, "May they

have a participation in the Holy Spirit," and would pick up the reference to the Holy Spirit at the beginning of the letter (2 Cor. 1:21f.; yet almost all references to the Spirit in 2 Corinthians refer to the community). It may be that grammarians are more precise than Paul intended. Is it possible that both meanings were in his mind, a community which arose through the common participation in the Holy Spirit?

The same construction occurs in Philippians 2:1, "If there is . . . any fellowship in the Spirit." Paul is here listing the bases of his appeal for unity among the Philippian Christians. Both an objective and subjective genitive may be in mind: since there is a sharing in the Spirit they form a community in the Spirit. On the basis of sharing in the Spirit, the Philippian Christians are to have mutual love and harmony.

The Epistle to the Hebrews, using instead of *koinōnos* the virtually synonymous *metochos,* speaks of being "partners [sharers] of Christ" (3:14) and "sharers [partners] of the Holy Spirit" (6:4).

(4) Christian fellowship is based on and comes about through the gospel message. God's call to fellowship is made known through the gospel. The message about Christ, inspired by the Holy Spirit, is itself a basis of fellowship. "We declare to you what we have seen and heard so that you also may have fellowship with us; and truly our fellowship is with the Father and with his Son Jesus Christ" (1 John 1:3). Fellowship with God and Christ is based on the apostolic proclamation of God's reaching out for fellowship in the incarnation. The eternal life that was with the Father was revealed to human witnesses. People are called into a fellowship. What is declared concerning the eternal life that became incarnate in Jesus Christ establishes a fellowship among proclaimers and believers of that message, a fellowship that has a divine basis and origin.

(5) Fellowship is based on a shared or common faith. This is the counterpart to the gospel: the message declared must be received in faith. Philemon 6, I suggest, should be translated "In order that your sharing in the faith may become effective in the recognition of all the good that is ours with reference to Christ."[18] The possessive "your" thus modifies the phrase "fellowship of faith," (= sharing or participation in the faith), and not solely the word "faith." Philemon loved the saints and had a share in their common faith in the Lord Jesus (vs. 5), and Paul wants Philemon's participation in the faith to find further

18. For the connection of "the good" with the gospel and salvation see Rom. 10:15; Phil. 1:5-6.

expression. The participation in the common faith produces a community where love is shared.

(6) The Lord's supper is appropriately called "communion" or "fellowship" (1 Cor. 10:16-22, where words from the *koin-* root occur four times and the related *metechō* twice). Paul in 1 Corinthians 10:16-17 makes concrete what is involved in the fellowship with the Son stated in 1:9. Fellowship with Christ means participation in his body and blood. Paul's argument is not that Christians take the Lord's supper because they are a community, but that they are a community because of participation in the body and blood of Christ. The "body of Christ" in 1 Corinthians 10:16 is the body on the cross; the "one body" of 1 Corinthians 10:17 is the church. Thus we include the Lord's supper here as part of the theological basis for fellowship and as a further elaboration of what is included in fellowship with Christ. However, we should note that the purpose of Paul's argument here is the implication this has for the Christian community. Fellowship with Christ creates a fellowship with others, and this community with Christ excludes competing communities. (Therefore, the Lord's supper could also be considered one of the expressions of fellowship discussed below.) Paul is not arguing from Jewish and pagan ideas about sacrificial meals to an understanding of the Lord's supper, but the reverse. The significance of the communion with Christ shows what was involved in Jewish and pagan rites. Union with Christ in the cup and bread excludes communion with demons in the meals associated with idolatry. There is in the background the Jewish thought that "breaking bread" created and expressed table fellowship. Similarly, sharing the Lord's supper creates and declares a closeness of relationship. But again we must note that it is from the fellowship with the Lord (vs. 16) that the fellowship with other believers proceeds (vs. 17). They take the supper because they are a community in the Lord. Paul in 1 Corinthians 11 considers the manner in which the Lord's supper is observed as an important expression of unity (see the last unit of this chapter). The Lord's supper thus reflects both the divine and human dimensions of fellowship and so may provide a transition to the expressions of fellowship, but first some summary observations on the points made thus far.

These theological points have implications for the expressions of fellowship to be explored below. Communion with one another is based on communion with God (1 John 1:6-7). The vertical relationship creates the horizontal. Thus Paul expresses concern for the "believers for whom Christ died" (1 Cor. 8:11; cf. Rom. 14:16). Fellowship is God-given, not self-chosen. A common fellowship with the Lord produces a fellowship of those who share it. Why is there a "church" in the first place? Because believers found one another at the foot of the cross. Christians are not together because they first liked each other and chose to be together (as in a human fraternity or sorority). They are together in Christ; therefore they choose to manifest the dynamics and consequences of that relationship in their lives together as fellow Christians. In a human family, one is born into it, and the members learn love for one another. The family tie is a given, and that is the origin and basis of love. Similarly, love is an expression of fellowship in the family of God, not the basis for the fellowship. Some of the ways in which fellowship based on God, the divine gifts, the divine call, and its acceptance are expressed will now be considered.

Expressions of Fellowship

(1) The contribution of material possessions for the needs of others is called *koinōnia*, fellowship; indeed, this is the most frequently occurring usage of this word in the New Testament. The church's response to grace and its praise to God according to 2 Corinthians 8–9 is expressed in giving (see p. 275). In reference to the contribution being gathered among the Gentile churches for the Christians in Judaea, Paul speaks in 8:4 of "sharing [*koinōnia*] in this ministry to the saints" and in 9:13 of "the generosity of your sharing [*koinōnia*] with them." Paul expressly calls the collection for the poor in Jerusalem a *koinōnia* in Romans 15:26, and in the next verse he explains that it is appropriate for the Gentiles to minister material things to the Jews because the Gentiles first shared in spiritual blessings from the Jews. *Koinōnia* well expresses the purpose of the collection among the churches Paul founded, a sense of fellowship and community among Gentile and Jewish believers. Giving is a concrete expression of sharing and enhances the sense of community. Thus Paul commands, "Contribute [*koinōneō*] to the needs of the saints" (Rom. 12:13). Note also Hebrews 13:16, "Do not neglect to do good and to share [contribute, *koinōneō*]."

(2) Cooperation in the advancement of the gospel is another expression of fellowship. The giving of material possessions may assist the preaching and teaching of the gospel, but this is only one form that assistance in the proclamation of the gospel may take. The *koinōnia* family of words is used often by Paul for joint participation in spreading the gospel. He declared his own purpose to "do all things on behalf of

the gospel, in order that I may be a fellow participant [with other Christians] in it" (1 Cor. 9:23). Here the gospel is the content in which Paul wants to share (see p. 367 on the gospel or message about Christ as a basis of fellowship); as a result of that Paul gave himself to the advancement of the gospel, so that Gentiles could share in its blessings (Rom. 11:17). Both 1 Corinthians 9:23 and Romans 11:17 use the compound *synkoinōnos*, the *syn-* prefix accentuating the common participation with others in the relation of a community. Among the words Paul uses for his co-workers in the gospel is *koinōnos*, "fellow" or "partner": Titus (2 Cor. 8:23) and Philemon (Philem. 17).

Even as Paul expected Gentile churches who had received spiritual blessings from Jews to share material goods with them (Rom. 15:26-27), so he instructed that "Those who are taught the word must share in all good things with their teacher" (Gal. 6:6).[19] There is a mutuality in which those who receive spiritual blessings impart material blessings to those through whom they come. It is especially in Philippians, where words from the *koin-* root occur six times, that Paul develops the idea of partnership in the advancement of the gospel. At the beginning of his thanksgiving for the Philippians he refers to their "sharing [*koinōnia*] in the gospel from the first day until now" (Phil. 1:5), probably referring to the proclamation rather than the content of the gospel. There is also the implication that they lived the gospel, for Paul goes on to commend them as "fellow partners" [*synkoinōnous*] in God's grace (Phil. 1:7). Their concern for Paul went beyond financial support, but that was one continuing and concrete expression (Phil. 4:15) of their sharing together with Paul in a community founded by the gospel and serving the gospel.

(3) The sufferings of Christ created the Christian fellowship, and having fellowship with him often found expression in sharing in suffering. There is a close connection between the sufferings of Christ and those of the Christian. The advancement of the gospel often meant the experience of suffering. Paul desired "to know Christ and the power of his resurrection and the sharing of his sufferings by becoming like him in his death" (Phil. 3:10f.). The power that goes forth from the resurrection of Christ enables one to endure sufferings and then to receive resurrection for oneself. The Philippians' financial assistance to Paul was a sharing in his afflictions (Phil. 4:14). The Corinthians experienced more directly sufferings with Paul (2 Cor. 1:7). The community

19. "All good things" here refers to material support (cf. 1 Cor. 9:11; 2 Cor. 9:6).

of Christ is defined by common participation in his sufferings. And that participation may contribute to the salvation of fellow believers (cf. Col. 1:24). Christian suffering is not solely the suffering that is common to human beings but what comes because one is a Christian (as in persecution — Rev. 1:9) and what is undertaken because one is a Christian for the sake of others in the service of Christ (cf. Heb. 10:33). Paul's thought about sharing Christ's sufferings in order to attain the resurrection finds exalted echo in 1 Pet. 4:13, "Rejoice insofar as you are sharing Christ's sufferings, so that you may also be glad and shout for joy when his glory is revealed." The sharing in Christ's sufferings has its counterpart in sharing in his glory (1 Pet. 5:1).

(4) All that has been said is caught up in the sharing of a common life together. "[The disciples] devoted themselves to the apostles' teaching and fellowship, to the breaking of bread and the prayers" (Acts 2:42). The meaning of *koinōnia* in this verse has been much debated. It is often taken as referring to the sharing of material goods, according to the common New Testament usage discussed above and on the basis of the description in verses 44-45 following. It might be better to take the word as referring to the broader concept of a common life, the sense of community and brotherly communion, of which the sharing of possessions was a specific expression. The summaries of community life in Acts 2:43-47 and 4:32-35 may be seen as elaborations of this fellowship.

The association together is described in the New Testament in spiritual terms. Even ordinary daily activities are treated as religious. This may be observed especially in the shared meals (Acts 2:46). Out of these grew the practice of the agape or love feast (Jude 12). The social intercourse and association together with the accompanying fraternal feeling are hardly the most distinctive thing to say about fellowship in Christ, since such is possible in human fraternities. Nonetheless, brotherly feeling is all the deeper and more meaningful in view of the spiritual blessings shared. There is a common life in Christ; fellowship does include association with fellow Christians. This is one of the rich blessings of the Christian life.

(5) A specific expression of Christian fellowship is agreement in doing the Lord's work. "When James and Cephas and John . . . recognized the grace that had been given to me, they gave to Barnabas and me the right hand of fellowship, agreeing that we should go to the Gentiles and they to the circumcised" (Gal. 2:9). On the basis of a shared grace, fellowship was acknowledged. The expression of it was the extending of the right hand, a sign of trust and friendship. A handshake

as a sign of agreement was used in concluding contracts. In this passage there is agreement in a division of labor in preaching the gospel.

Some Practical Applications of Fellowship

Fellowship has been found as applying to a relationship with God and a relationship with other believers. The Christian does not want to break either relationship. Just as fellowship with the Lord establishes communion with others, even so attitudes and actions toward others determine the relationship with God. Several passages speak of the priority of personal relations in one's relationship with God.

> Whoever does not love does not know God, for God is love. . . . Those who say, "I love God," and hate their brothers or sisters, are liars; for those who do not love a brother or sister whom they have seen, cannot love God whom they have not seen. (1 John 4:8, 20)

> So when you are offering your gift at the altar, if you remember that your brother or sister has something against you, leave your gift there before the altar and go: first be reconciled to your brother or sister, and then come and offer your gift. (Matt. 5:23-24)

> For if you forgive others their trespasses, your heavenly Father will also forgive you; but if you do not forgive others, neither will your Father forgive your trespasses. (Matt. 6:14-15)

As alluded to above, fellowship with God and with Christ excludes certain other fellowships.

> Do not be mismatched with unbelievers. For what partnership is there between righteousness and lawlessness? Or what fellowship is there between light and darkness? What agreement does Christ have with Beliar? Or what does a believer share with an unbeliever? What agreement has the temple of God with idols? (2 Cor. 6:14ff.)

Sharing in the holiness of God requires separation from sin and forbids association in any activity that would defile body or spirit (2 Cor. 7:1).

The grammatical usage of the *koin-* family of words shows that fellowship is with persons in things. Fellowship is with an individual and has to do with shared activities. Thus, there may be fellowship on one level and not on another; in some things and not in other things.

Fellowship and endorsement, although related, are different things. One can participate with a nonbeliever in activities that are not sinful. One can accept another believer without endorsement of all that he or she does. Acceptance of another neither means participation in everything the other person does nor requires an invitation to participate in everything one does. Fellowship may be applied on an individual level without requiring that one support an organization that promotes something the other person approves but that one does not.

Fellowship is already given in the Lord to baptized believers. Their task is to implement that fellowship, not to create or offer it. Fellowship is God-given, not a human choice. As one is born into a human family and does not choose one's brothers and sisters, so in the spiritual family, God places one in a community through the new birth. Within the spiritual fellowship one learns to accept and work with the family of the church.

Only things done after one becomes a Christian can break the existing fellowship established by reason of being in the Lord. A person who enters a congregation and does not make an issue of views that may be divisive should be received into fellowship (Rom. 14:1; 15:7). Respect for the Christian integrity and commitment of others requires this, even if they hold views different from most in the congregation. If the views are promoted in such a way as to become divisive, then division is the problem and not the views themselves. There come times when the fellowship of a body of believers must be refused or withdrawn from a person, and to that subject we now turn, but only after it is placed in a larger context.

DISCIPLINE

"Do not associate with anyone who does not obey our word. . . . Do not regard him as an enemy, but admonish him as a brother." (2 THESS. 3:14-15)

Positive Discipline

Discipline often connotes negative ideas, because it is so often associated with punishment. The word is being used here in a broader sense to refer to the ordering and scheduling of religious acts in meaningful ways as well as to efforts to remove evil from the community. In the positive sense of ordered activities to achieve a desired goal, discipline is recognized as essential to attaining anything worthwhile. Athletes must train (discipline themselves); students must learn the discipline of study; children must learn to be responsible and regulate their behavior. Even so, the Christian life is a disciplined life. As such, it has both individual (self-discipline) and community aspects (the mutual encouragement and admonition of fellow believers). The positive aspects of discipline are related to edification, as discussed in Chapter 5.

The disciplined Christian life should be viewed in this larger context. Developing the positive traits of Christian character requires teaching, admonition, training for service, and the development of self-discipline. If these things are done well, negative or punitive discipline will not be necessary so often and will be more meaningful when administered (as in the "discipline" of a child).

Personal Spiritual Disciplines[20]

The personal spiritual disciplines remain the same that they have been through the ages. Since the purpose of this book is to deal with the corporate life of the church, the individual spiritual disciplines will not be developed here. However, since the corporate and individual so closely affect each other, notice must be taken of the importance of developing a personal spiritual life. The presence of this in the members profoundly affects congregational life, and the group context can greatly encourage and foster personal discipline.

Regular, orderly participation in the activities of prayer, studying the Bible, reading devotional literature, meditation, and undertaking good works on behalf of others is absolutely essential for developing the Christian lifestyle. Discipline means setting aside a fixed time on a daily basis to cultivate these activities. Making them a habit molds the character, personality, and disposition of a person into the likeness of Christ.

Structures for Developing Church Discipline[21]

The following list is suggestive, not exhaustive, of the methods avail-

---

20. Richard J. Foster, *Celebrating Discipline* (San Francisco: Harper, 1978). Although he concentrates on individual disciplines, much is applicable to the church.
21. This and the following section are much indebted to but much modified

able to the local church to raise the standards of behavior within its membership.

(1) Training and examination of prospective and new members. Teaching of new converts should include the moral behavior expected of members as well as the doctrines and practices of the church. Probably too much is assumed and too little done at the crucial time when a person makes the decision to enter the church.

(2) Training and examination of ministers and leaders. The spiritual level of a congregation is set by its ministers and leaders, who must themselves cultivate and practice the spiritual disciplines. The failures of academic institutions to prepare ministers in the practical areas of ministry and in spiritual formation have led local churches to try to do the academic task for which they are not suited. There should be a cooperation between colleges, universities, and seminaries on one hand and local churches on the other. Although not equipped for giving academic training in the theological disciplines, the local churches are where spiritual formation must take place and where the arts and skills of practical ministry are implemented.

(3) Instruction and admonition from the pulpit. Many churches have relied on this method almost exclusively for instruction of the members and setting the standards of the congregation. Its limitation for this task by itself should not lead to its neglect in encouraging Christian living.

(4) Instruction in small groups. Bible classes at various times and settings can communicate Christian truths adapted to individual needs.

(5) Small groups of mutual concern. Particularly in large congregations it is necessary for members to feel a part of a more closely knit group. Small groups can provide discussion of Christian expectations and personalized support in their fulfillment, as well as care for needs in emergencies.

(6) Visitation by individuals in the congregation. A regular program of personal visitation can maintain contact and give encourage-

---

from Carl O. Bangs, "The Search for the Marks of a Disciplined Church," *Chicago Theological Seminary Register* 60 (1970): 10-22. For the forms of moral instruction in the early church see James I. H. McDonald, *Kerygma and Didache: The Articulation and Structure of the Earliest Christian Message* (Cambridge: University Press, 1980), pp. 69-100; A. J. Malherbe, *Paul and the Thessalonians: The Philosophic Tradition of Pastoral Care* (Philadelphia: Fortress, 1987); A. J. Malherbe, "Hellenistic Moralists and the New Testament," *Aufstieg und Niedergang der römischen Welt* II.26.1 (Berlin: Walter DeGruyter, 1992), pp. 267-333.

ment to weak or lonely members. Such visitation should include that done by pastors but not be left to them exclusively.

(7) An active concern by the elders/pastors of the congregation to promote disciplined Christian living, to meet with members as individuals or families to convey concern or admonition, and to teach publicly and privately the biblical message.

Guiding Concerns of Church Discipline

Discipline according to the church polity laid out in the preceding chapter is not imposed from above but grows out of the community. The effectiveness of this approach assumes the members have committed themselves to the community; if not, they will feel the church is invading their rights when it tries to discipline. The other prerequisite is a sense of fellowship in which the members know one another well and in which there is a loving community life. Then there can be creative and redemptive discipline.

Through Christian history competing views of the nature of the church have come into conflict precisely on the issue of church discipline. Is the church a society of the pure, or is it a mixed body? Is it a holy enclave, or is it a hospital for sick souls? There are important elements of truth in both positions. There is a need to maintain both aspects: holiness and spiritual healing. The church always faces strong temptations to accommodate to the standards of the society in which she finds herself. On the other hand, where the impulse to holiness is strong, there is the temptation to withdraw from contact with society and/or to impose arbitrary (nonmoral) distinctions from the society. Holiness in attitudes and conduct, as exemplified in the individual lives and group activities of the members, will not compromise with the world. At the same time, the church must demonstrate what it means to be Christ-like as well as unworldly. The church is a community where redemptive love and saving forgiveness are maintained and practiced without closing the eyes to sin.

A disciplined community is a place where the individual is sustained by fellow believers in unpopular ethical decisions. A person may resent discipline, but another side of the coin is finding one's covenant community standing beside him/her in a morally or physically trying time. It is within disciplined fellowships that closeness and a sense of belonging are developed to the point where this occurs. Christian convictions are costly. A person may want to hold them without this costing anything, but when holding them becomes costly, the support of one's church becomes indispensable.

There is a place for the individual or a local community of believers to accept symbolic disciplines — fasting, rejection of luxuries, nonparticipation in public functions of a questionable nature — as a witness to higher loyalty and to humble faith. These become not token gestures but real self-denial if they truly point to ultimate reality.

Believers confront dangers of legalism on one side and flabbiness in their spirituality on the other (see further pp. 390ff. on Christian liberty). How does a group keep discipline from being legalistic, rigid, and bound to traditions of the past? Confessing their humanness and inconsistencies will help to save a people from legalism without their having to abandon a high standard of ethos and commitment. Discipline must not be external and mechanical, but in order to achieve its goals it must be regular, proper, and internalized.

Discipline is not nonessential. It is a way of life for a church committed to scripture. Even secular movements recognize the necessity of discipline. The very doctrine and nature of the church are at stake in how the disciplines of the Christian life are maintained and carried out.

Efforts to develop a disciplined Christian lifestyle may be considered as related to fellowship. Nevertheless, the positive structures of discipline are not always successful in achieving their purposes.

Negative Discipline — Withdrawal of Fellowship[22]

When positive discipline fails in the life of someone, other steps must be taken, both for the good of the person involved and for the sake of the integrity of congregational life. In the case of flagrant violations of the Christian lifestyle, negative discipline must be exercised by the congregation. The way in which the church does this is to withdraw its fellowship from the offender. Since this practice is not observed in

22. Göran Forkman, *The Limits of Religious Community* (Lund: C. W. K. Gleerup, 1972); Marlin Jeschke, *Discipling in the Church* (Scottdale, Penn.: Herald, 1988); Ingrid Goldhahn-Müller, *Die Grenze der Gemeinde: Studien zum Problem der zweiten Busse im Neuen Testament unter Berücksichtigung der Entwicklung in 2. Jh. bis Tertullian* (Göttingen: Vandenhoeck & Ruprecht, 1989); James Thomas South II, "Corrective Discipline in the Pauline Communities" (Dissertation, University of Virginia; Ann Arbor: University Microfilms, 1990).

many churches, and is abused in others, it seems necessary to set forth in some fullness the New Testament teaching on the subject. Always this negative exercise of discipline must be seen in the larger context of the positive measures discussed above.

Corrective church discipline follows the example and precedent of Jesus himself during his earthly ministry in admonishing, correcting, and rebuking people for their improper attitudes and behavior. Admonition occurs frequently, as in Luke 13:1-5. His correction of wrong teaching leading to wrong conduct may be seen in Mark 7:1-23. A stern rebuke is found in the strong denunciation of the "scribes and Pharisees" in Matthew 23, yet concluding with the compassionate lament of verses 37-39. The most aggressive action by Jesus in punishing wrongdoers was his cleansing of the temple (Mark 11:27-33; John 2:13-25). The correct understanding of John 2:15 has the whip used on the animals, not the people; the tables of the money changers were overturned, but Jesus' physical actions once more were directed at things, not the persons using them. There are instances of physical punishment in the apostolic church, but these were administered by God, not by the human beings who announced the punishment without actually inflicting it (Acts 5:9; 13:11). Christ expects his people to take firm stands against sin and to maintain discipline within their ranks, but this internal discipline is based on moral persuasion and is exercised in a non-violent manner.

Even as God puts redeemed persons in the community, so he sets the standards of remaining in the community. The community of God's people must let God himself determine its membership. God, however, entrusts to the community the implementation of his standards. The community must be careful not to make rules that God has not made; but at the same time it must be conscious of its responsibility as the instrument of God in maintaining the boundaries of the community. Corrective church discipline aims at bringing the conduct of a congregation's members into line with the teachings of Jesus and his apostles; when this endeavor fails, the congregation in order to maintain its integrity must withdraw its fellowship from the offending member.

The Practice: What Is Disfellowship?

What is involved in this exercise of disfellowship? What does it mean to withdraw the fellowship of the church from a person? The fullest description of the practice is found in Paul's instructions concerning the sexual offender at Corinth in 1 Corinthians 5:9-13.[23]

> I wrote to you in my letter not to associate with sexually immoral persons — not at all meaning the immoral of this world, or the greedy and robbers, or idolaters, since you would then need to go out of the world. But now I am writing to you not to associate with anyone who bears the name of brother or sister who is sexually immoral or greedy, or is an idolater, reviler, drunkard, or robber. Do not even eat with such a one. For what have I to do with judging those outside? Is it not those who are inside that you are to judge? God will judge those outside. "Drive out the wicked person from among you."

To withdraw fellowship means "not to associate with" the person. The prohibition of eating with the person[24] requires some explanation in modern American society. In the ancient world sharing a meal together meant acceptance and established close ties of fellowship. That is not often the case in our cafeteria society, where sharing a table in a public place may be no indication of relationship at all. Eating together today might not be a violation of this teaching, but participating in any activity that would give the appearance of approval of the person's unacceptable conduct would be a violation of the teaching.

Other passages fill out the picture. Paul says more briefly, "Now we command you, beloved, in the name of our Lord Jesus Christ, to keep away from believers who are living in idleness and not according to the tradition that they received from us. . . . Take note of those who do not obey what we say in this letter; have nothing to do with them, so that they may be ashamed" (2 Thess. 3:6, 14). "After a first and second admonition, have nothing more to do with anyone who causes divisions" (Titus 3:10). Second John 10-11 provides another statement of specifics that requires explanation because of cultural changes. The instructions concern false teachers who seem to have left the fellowship: "Do not receive into the house or welcome anyone who comes to you and does not bring this teaching; for to welcome is to participate in the

23. G. W. H. Lampe, "Church Discipline and the Interpretation of the Epistles to the Corinthians," in W. R. Farmer et al., eds., *Christian History and Interpretation: Studies Presented to John Knox* (Cambridge: University Press, 1967), pp. 337-361; J. W. MacGorman, "The Discipline of the Church," in Paul Basden and David S. Dockery, eds., *The People of God* (Nashville: Broadman, 1991), pp. 74-84.
24. It may be that 2 Thess. 3:10 refers to an exclusion from communal meals.

evil deeds of such a person." Earlier translations said, more literally, "give a greeting" instead of "welcome." Although the Greek greeting is expressed here, the background is likely the Hebrew greeting, "Shalom," "Peace." The latter in modern Hebrew has lost its original meaning, as has the English "Good-bye" ("God be with you"). The idea being expressed by John is welcoming someone into the home or giving encouragement in such a way as to express approval and full acceptance. The significance of these words in 2 John 10-11 is illustrated by Jesus' instructions to his disciples about bestowing their peace upon the house (family) that welcomed them as they went about preaching (Matt. 10:12-14, 40-42), with the difference that Matthew 10 speaks about the missionary and 2 John speaks about the resident to whose house the missionary comes. In our day to say "Good morning" in meeting on the street, or even to have the person into one's home, would not necessarily go against what is commanded unless the action is construed by the person or others as an endorsement of his/her conduct. As in the case of eating together, some other activity might have the same significance that this action did in the ancient world, and so would be inconsistent with the withdrawal of fellowship.

The picture that emerges from these passages is for the church to have no social or religious intercourse with the person. That is why it is important that the discipline be an act of the whole church (1 Cor. 5:4). The disfellowshipped person is cut off from any association that would seem to give endorsement or encouragement to the practices for which fellowship was withdrawn. The scriptures say, "Have no company or fellowship with the person." Thus one of the greatest earthly joys of the Christian life is to be taken away, the fellowship of the saints. (See further pp. 364ff. on the biblical meaning of fellowship.)

The Persons: Who Are to Be Disfellowshipped?

What individuals are to be disciplined? What are the occasions for the exercise of this withdrawal of fellowship? At least five groups are spoken of in the passages on church discipline as subject to this action.

(1) The immoral. Paul gives a specific list of types of immoral persons in 1 Corinthians 5:10-11, quoted above. This is a representative and not exhaustive list, but it does cover some of the more serious moral failings.

(2) Teachers and followers of false doctrine. As the first category had to do with fundamental moral failings, so the concern here is with

fundamental matters of faith. Second John 9-10 forbids the acceptance of those who deny the foundation of the Christian faith, "the doctrine of Christ."

(3) The disorderly. The specific disorderly ("undisciplined") conduct in 2 Thessalonians 3:6, 14 is idleness and the failure to work to support oneself. There might be conduct not specifically immoral (although with moral implications) nor doctrinally erroneous (although drawing incorrect implications from the doctrine) that calls for disfellowship. Idleness would not be the only conduct that might fall in this category, but whatever it is, it should have serious implications for the life of the congregation and its standing in society.

(4) Those who cause division. Titus 3:10 speaks concerning such persons. Again, the issue might not be moral or doctrinal. There are indications of such moral and doctrinal problems on Crete addressed in Titus. But division can be caused by personalities and relatively trivial differences. Anything that divides a church ceases to be trivial. (See further the last section on Unity.)

(5) Those who leave the fellowship. The false teachers dealt with in 1 and 2 John had left the Christian community (1 John 2:19; cf. 2 John 7). In these cases the faithful simply acknowledge that fellowship no longer exists. Others have departed. If there is fundamental doctrinal error (number 2 above), then a more overt declaration is called for; if others have only drifted away, the readiness to welcome back is more explicit.

The Process or Procedure — How Is Disfellowshipping to Be Done?

There are several passages that refer to an orderly procedure for accomplishing the exclusion of a person from the fellowship of a congregation. This is a last resort, to be invoked only after diligent effort has been made to correct the person's behavior.

Paul's instructions about how to deal with the sexually immoral person at Corinth indicate that the whole local church is to be involved: "When you are assembled, and my spirit is present with the power of our Lord Jesus, you are to hand this man over to Satan for the destruction of the flesh, so that his spirit may be saved in the day of the Lord" (1 Cor. 5:4-5). The formal withdrawal of fellowship is to be ratified in an assembly of the congregation. It is to be an act by the whole local church.[25] "To hand over to Satan" (cf. 1 Tim. 1:20) means to transfer (or perhaps, in reality, to acknowledge the departure of) the person from the realm of holiness represented by the church to the realm of the Evil One, whom the person has chosen to obey. There are only two realms, God's and Satan's, and a person not in God's realm is in Satan's. The "destruction of the flesh" and "his spirit may be saved" are probably to be understood according to Paul's usual contrast of flesh and spirit, according to which flesh refers to the sinful nature, the life lived according to human desires, and spirit refers to the spiritual nature, life lived according to the Spirit of God (cf. Gal. 5:16-25).[26] "Destruction of the flesh," therefore, refers to the elimination of sinful attitudes and practices. The passage thus expresses the hope that the disciplinary action will bring about the change of life that will result in salvation.

Titus 3:10 indicates something of the preliminary steps before this final action of withdrawal of fellowship is taken: "After a first and second admonition, have nothing more to do with anyone who causes division."

The fullest account of the process of church discipline is found in Matthew 18:15-17:

> If another member of the church sins against you, go and point out the fault when the two of you are alone. If the member listens to you, you have regained that one. But if you are not listened to, take one or two others along with you, so that every word may be confirmed by the evidence of two or three witnesses. If the member refuses to listen to them, tell it to the church; and if the offender refuses to listen even to the church, let such a one be to you as a Gentile and a tax collector.

The correct understanding of this passage requires that it be placed in the context of the whole chapter.[27] Matthew 18 has to do with sin in the community and what to do about it. The chapter begins with the teaching of the necessity of becoming humble like children in order to enter the kingdom of heaven (vss. 1-5). Humility is closely related to the

---

25. "The many" of 2 Cor. 2:6 may refer to the action by the assembly, rather than by the "majority," as in the NRSV. So Olaf Linton, *Das Problem der Urkirche in der neueren Forschung* (Uppsala, 1932), p. 193.

26. G. W. H. Lampe, "Church Discipline and the Interpretation of the Epistles to the Corinthians," in W. R. Farmer et al., eds., *Christian History and Interpretation: Studies Presented to John Knox* (Cambridge: University Press, 1967), pp. 350-351.

27. William G. Thompson, *Matthew's Advice to a Divided Community: Mt. 17,22–18,35* (Rome: Biblical Institute Press, 1970).

subsequent verses about obtaining and giving forgiveness, for one must be humble to seek forgiveness and must as a Christian give forgiveness in humility. After this quality is presented, the theme of stumbling (occasions of temptation and sin) is introduced. The chapter proceeds with self-discipline: avoid what harms others and cut off occasions of sin. One is not to do anything that would cause another to stumble (vss. 6-7) and is to take every measure to remove sin from one's life (vss. 8-9). The "little ones" in this chapter are not children, but those who have become "like children," that is, believers (vs. 6), who are as humble as children (so also for vs. 10). What about the person who does sin, who "goes astray"? The parable of the lost sheep (vss. 10-13) describes the effort made by the shepherd and his rejoicing over the recovery of the lost sheep. This parable occupies center stage in the chapter and is the key to its interpretation. "It is not the will of your Father in heaven that one of these little ones should be lost" (vs. 14).

Then follows the passage quoted above. The preceding parable shows that Jesus' teaching in these verses is not to give a mechanical process to be followed in expelling an erring church member but is to emphasize the effort to be made to reclaim that person. The individual goes to the person; a small group goes; then the whole church goes and makes an appeal. The purpose of the activity is pastoral, not punitive. The goal is to save the other person. Only after the person has refused all these efforts is the church to treat the offender as excluded. To be considered "a Gentile and a tax collector" was to be considered as outside the covenant community (for other indications in Matthew of tax collectors and Gentiles as "outsiders" see 5:46-47 and 6:7). This attitude explains the sharp criticism of Jesus for his eating with "sinners and tax collectors" (Mark 2:15-16). His practice was an offer of grace and fellowship to those with whom "scribes and Pharisees" would not eat since they were "outsiders."[28] When those who have once accepted the offer of grace and forgiveness yet turn back to the old way of life, they are once more to be treated as excluded from table fellowship. Since the church is the forgiven people, the position of the person who will not listen to reproof and accept correction is serious.

Whatever the church binds and looses in these matters is so considered in heaven (Matt. 18:18). "To bind and loose" in rabbinic litera-

28. For Jesus' treatment of tax collectors and sinners as that relates to church discipline, see Marlin Jeschke, *Discipling in the Church* (Scottdale, Penn.: Herald, 1988), pp. 94-96.

ture could be used for interpretations of the law and for binding or forgiving sins. The ideas are closely related, but the context indicates more the latter emphasis here.[29] When the person refuses to listen, his guilt is bound; when correction is accepted, there is a release from sin. The agreement by the "two or three" and the presence of Christ (vss. 19-20) have to do specifically with the resolution of disciplinary matters in the community. (On the divine presence in which such actions are taken, see Deut. 19:17; 1 Cor. 5:4.) "Anything you ask" refers to the context of prayer in the decision making. The meeting to resolve matters occurs in the name of Jesus, literally, "with a view toward Jesus." He is the purpose of the gathering; the resolution of the matter is done for his sake. With that understanding, there is no higher authority in disciplinary matters than the church. By the same token, the church has no other weapon against those who do not respect moral authority.

The theme of sin and forgiveness continues in the following verses. If the sinner repents, forgiveness is to be extended an unlimited number of times (vss. 21-22; contrast Gen. 4:24). As the necessity of making every effort to reclaim the erring person was taught by the parable of the lost sheep, so the necessity of forgiveness is reinforced by the parable of the unforgiving servant, which exalts the greatness of God's forgiveness but the punishment of those who are unforgiving (vss. 23-34). The conclusion is, "So my heavenly Father will also do to every one of you, if you do not forgive your brother or sister from your heart" (vs. 35).

All these teachings indicate that the withdrawal of fellowship is not to be hastily done. Every effort is to be made to reclaim the erring. Disfellowship is a last resort; practically speaking, it is the recognition that the person has withdrawn him/herself from the redeemed community and its standards. Presumably the elders as the spiritual leaders of the congregation will take the lead in the procedures, but the action is to be an action by the whole church and so requires the unanimous (or nearly so) backing of the community of believers.

In a polity of congregational autonomy (as presented in the preceding chapter, pp. 344-364), disciplinary action pertains only to the local church, but each church will respect the decisions and action taken by a

---

29. Herman L. Strack and Paul Billerbeck, *Kommentar zum Neuen Testament aus Talmud und Midrasch*, Vol. 1: *Das Evangelium nach Matthäus*, 3rd ed. (Munich: C. H. Beck, 1961), pp. 738-741, 792-793. Göran Forkman, *The Limits of Religious Community* (Lund: C. W. K. Gleerup, 1972), pp. 130-131, suggests the more general meanings of "pronounce sentence" and "verdict of acquittal."

sister church. However, a different congregation in its autonomy is not bound by the decisions of another. That means that a person who feels a given church has acted unfairly has a "court of appeal" by applying for membership in another congregation, which may then reconsider the merits of the action taken by another body of believers or reevaluate the events of long ago that appear differently in a new context.

The Purpose: Why Is Disfellowship Undertaken?

What are the values of withdrawing fellowship? As indicated by the interpretation of 1 Corinthians 5:5 above, discipline does not involve physical punishment but is aimed at the annihilation of the sinful self. The goal is the salvation of the spirit. A less extreme statement in 2 Thessalonians 3:14 indicates a step toward this goal, "so that they may be ashamed." Discipline has a redemptive purpose: "If anyone is detected in a transgression, you who have received the Spirit should restore such a one in a spirit of gentleness" (Gal. 6:1).[30] Thus the purpose of discipline is not to kick a person down lower, or to show how good the rest of the community is, or to get even with the person. The aim must be the person's ultimate salvation. The purpose is pastoral, not penal. Sometimes it takes a drastic measure to get someone's attention and bring that person to a right way of thinking.

Although the person's own salvation is the overriding concern, there are other values from taking this action. Sometimes the person does not want to be saved, so the church must act for other purposes. (1) There is need to maintain the purity of the church (1 Cor. 5:6-7). (2) There is need to preserve the reputation of the church among outsiders (Col. 4:5). (3) The action will maintain respect for the Lord among church members and others (Acts 5:11).

In all these aspects of discipline, it is well to keep in mind the admonition, "Do not regard them as enemies, but warn them as brothers" (2 Thess. 3:15). Even after a person is excluded from fellowship, the door is kept open for repentance and reconciliation.

Some have seen Jesus' parable of the weeds (Matt. 13:24-30) as contradicting the practice of withdrawing fellowship. However, the interpretation of the parable identifies the "field" as the "world" (Matt. 13:38), not the church. The parable is directed against the efforts of those

---

30. On truly redemptive forgiveness, see Marlin Jeschke, *Disciplining in the Church* (Scottdale, Penn.: Herald, 1988), pp. 62-68.

in Jesus' day who sought to bring in the kingdom by force and opposes the use of force in accomplishing God's purposes.[31] In 1 Corinthians 6:1-8 the church is instructed to exercise judgment in its internal matters, but in 5:12-13 the judgment of those on the outside is left with God.

For disfellowship to be effective, there must be *fellowship* to begin with (see the section above). If there is little meaningful fellowship, the "withdrawal of fellowship" is only going through the motions.

Pardon for Erring Christians

Forgiveness, as indicated in the discussion above, is available for the Christian who falls into sin. A notable case of restoration and forgiveness of a person placed under discipline by a congregation is recorded in 2 Corinthians 2:5-11. It is not clear whether the person described is the same as the man in 1 Corinthians 5 or someone who had opposed Paul, but the punishment imposed "by the many" (that is, the congregation, not "the majority," as in the NRSV, although that may in fact be the case) accomplished the desired purpose, and the congregation is now instructed to "forgive" and "reaffirm [their] love" for him. This passage emphasizes the responsibility of the congregation to restore the person whose conduct was unacceptable. Is verse 10, "in the presence of Christ," analogous to 1 Corinthians 5:4 and Matthew 18:20?

As there are certain things to be done in obtaining the initial forgiveness of sins in becoming a part of the people of God, so there are commands given to baptized believers in order for them to obtain forgiveness of postbaptismal sins. Some have called these commands "the second law of pardon."

Repentance

The baptized believer who has surrendered once more to sin is commanded to "repent." Such was Peter's command to Simon the Magi-

---

31. Marlin Jeschke, *Discipling in the Church* (Scottdale, Penn.: Herald, 1988), pp. 154-162. Robert K. McIver, "The Parable of the Weeds among the Wheat (Matt 13:24-30, 36-43) and the Relationship between the Kingdom and the Church as Portrayed in the Gospel of Matthew," *Journal of Biblical Literature* 114 (1995): 643-659, argues the parable is directed to the church but does not contradict Matt. 18.

cian, who had believed and was baptized (Acts 8:13) but then wanted the power of conferring the Holy Spirit (Acts 8:18-19), doubtless to advance his own reputation and influence.

> "Your heart is not right before God. Repent therefore of this wickedness of yours, and pray to the Lord that, if possible, the intent of your heart may be forgiven you. For I see that you are in the gall of bitterness and the chains of wickedness" (Acts 8:21-23).

The discussion of repentance on pages 175-177 applies here as well. Repentance is the way of reclaiming the benefits of the blood of Christ initially received in baptism (cf. pp. 203-204).

Confession

Besides "repentance" or "second repentance," the process of restoration to the church came to be known in early Christianity by the Greek word *exomologēsis*, "confession." Confession of sin is implicit in repentance and prayer (below). If repentance is the inward turning away from sin to God, confession is the outward expression in word and deed. "Confess your sins to one another, and pray for one another, so that you may be healed" (James 5:16). Confession requires that one be honest with him/herself. Honest confession accomplishes inner cleansing. Bringing the sin into the open is an important early step in achieving repentance and reformation of life. Acknowledgment of sin is essential to receiving forgiveness.

Prayer

Prayer is mentioned in both the passages already cited where repentance and confession are commanded. Petitions for forgiveness are frequent in the Old Testament (e.g., 2 Sam. 24:10; 1 Kings 8:27-53; Ps. 32:5; 51:1-17; Dan. 9:3-19). The practice continued in the church. The passages cited include not only the person praying for forgiveness, but others praying for the person who has sinned. Intercessory prayer for forgiveness is in order in most circumstances (for the qualification, see 1 John 5:16).

Unforgivable Sin?

Some passages seem to imply that certain sins are unforgivable. The Synoptic Gospels record Jesus' warning that blasphemy against the

Holy Spirit has no forgiveness but is an eternal sin (Matt. 12:24-32; Mark 3:22-30; Luke 12:8-12). Mark's account makes explicit that the sin in mind was attributing Jesus' power to the ruler of demons rather than to the Holy Spirit. That was to deny the only power that can save. Consequently, blasphemy against the Holy Spirit would not be a sin to be concerned about in daily experience. However, this passage stands as a warning against denial of God's power at work in Jesus and so against rejecting the only means of salvation.

The book of Hebrews gives stern warnings about the serious consequences of apostasy (Heb. 6:4-8; 10:26-31).[32] The impossibility "to restore again to repentance" comes from the rejection of the only means of forgiveness. There is no other sacrifice for sins than the blood of Jesus. Those who reject the means of forgiveness offered in Christ and persist in willful sin have no hope of repentance and forgiveness. The passage does not say that there is no repentance for falling away from the gospel, but that there is no other means of producing repentance and no other source of forgiveness. It is not the offense which is unforgivable but the sinner's attitude.[33] Those who have denied Jesus and his salvation have refused the salvation of God and so have placed themselves in a dangerous position, but the author does not say that it is impossible for them to return to faith and repentance.

The "mortal" or "deadly" sin of 1 John 5:14-17 is probably to be interpreted in the same way. There is sin that places one outside the source of life (the Son of God and the fellowship created by him — cf. 1:7) in the realm of death. The author describes those who have departed from the Son, broken with the Christian fellowship, and rejected the life of love. Such persons have cut themselves off from the source of life. The author does not address the possibility of such persons being rescued from "death" and restored to "life."[34]

These passages, therefore, do not indicate that there are certain, specific "unforgivable sins." They do indicate that it is possible for

---

32. Barnabas Lindars, *The Theology of the Letter to the Hebrews* (Cambridge: University Press, 1991), pp. 8-15, 68-71, 106-108, describes the situation of the recipients of Hebrews as those about to take an irrevocable step, so the author refers to what he fears might happen and accordingly gives a warning against deliberate sin.

33. Göran Forkman, *The Limits of Religious Community* (Lund: C. W. K. Gleerup, 1972), pp. 151-155.

34. Everett Ferguson, *The Message of the New Testament: The Letters of John* (Abilene: ACU Press, 1984), pp. 83-85.

one to place oneself in such a condition as to become insensitive to spiritual concerns (1 Tim. 4:2) and to refuse the means of forgiveness offered by God. If one is concerned about committing an "unforgivable sin," that person certainly has not committed such and is still in a condition to be receptive to God's offer of forgiveness. The treatment of Peter's denial of Jesus in the Gospels contrasts with any claim that apostasy or other sins are, apart from any other considerations, unforgivable.[35]

Discipline and Evangelism

The disciplined Christian lifestyle draws attention to the Christian message and to the Lord who stands behind it and who is at its center. There is a drawing power about a society in which there are clear distinctions between being inside and out. Where there are standards it means something to be a member. Discipline, therefore, can be an aspect of evangelistic outreach.

There is another sense in which discipline needs to be related to evangelism. The disciplining of an erring member should be treated as another way of doing evangelism. Discipline is a way of offering the gospel and forgiveness to those who depart from the Christian lifestyle. As noted above, the withdrawal of fellowship has as its first goal the saving of the Christian who has fallen into sin. If Christians treat discipline as they do evangelism, they will show proper respect and concern for the party subject to discipline. The efforts to restore such a one are aimed at renewing grace in the person's life (Gal. 6:1). The erring brother or sister will be treated with the patience an unbeliever is in order to convert him or her. If the faithful look to themselves and their weaknesses, they may be spared any casuistry and legalism in administering discipline.

As presented here, discipline is an essential aspect of the church. It has to do with the basic direction of life in Christ.

---

35. G. W. H. Lampe, "Church Discipline and the Interpretation of the Epistles to the Corinthians," in W. R. Farmer et al., eds., *Christian History and Interpretation: Studies Presented to John Knox* (Cambridge: University Press, 1967), p. 357.

CHRISTIAN LIBERTY

"For freedom Christ has set us free."   (GAL. 5:1)

Those who have taken church discipline seriously have often made legalistic demands on church members. Therefore, it is appropriate to include at this point a section on Christian liberty.[36] Christian liberty is used here to describe a mean between legalism (binding what God has not bound) and license (loosing what God has bound).

Freedom in Christ

Although the word "freedom" or "liberty" was used in classical Greek mainly for political freedom, this was not the usage of the New Testament. It does use "free" in contrast to the slave, another common meaning of the word in Greek, but this economic and social use was not the main concern of New Testament writers. The New Testament usage may be classified in terms of "freedom from" and "freedom for."

Freedom From

The New Testament speaks most often of freedom in terms of freedom *from sin* (Rom. 6:18, 22). A person is basically unfree in relation to sin: "you were slaves of sin" (Rom. 6:20). Everyone is a slave to either sin or righteousness (Rom. 6:16). "Everyone who commits sin is a slave to sin" (John 8:34). All sin enslaves, not only addictive practices like taking alcohol or drugs, but also pride, envy, covetousness, and lust. The good news is that Christ sets people free from sin and its consequences (Rom. 8:2, 21). The most important consequence of sin from which the Christian is set free is the power of death; death is no longer terminal (Rom. 6:23).

The Christian furthermore enjoys a freedom *from law* as a means of justification and salvation. Galatians 5:1 taken as the text for this unit belongs to the context of the preceding discussion that the Christian is

---

36. A contemporary theological application of the biblical teaching is presented in my essay "Four Freedoms of the Church," *Restoration Quarterly* 35 (1993): 65-69. See also James D. G. Dunn, *Christian Liberty: A New Testament Perspective* (Grand Rapids: Eerdmans, 1995).

not subject to the law of Moses. Romans 7:1-6 teaches freedom from the law, as chapter 6 had shown freedom from sin. One can be free from law only if dead to sin. Instead, the Christian is under law to Christ (1 Cor. 9:21). The Christian is not free from all law, but free from law as a means of salvation. Galatians and Romans were talking about the law of Moses, but the principles set forth there are capable of broader application. The freedom applies to special disciplinary rules concerning ritual conduct and ascetic practices that others would seek to bind (Col. 2:16-23). No system of law is the means of righteousness. Freed from a legal system of religion, the Christian is supposed to advance beyond a religion of "do's and don't's" to a religion of love and of the Spirit, which fulfills the law and goes beyond the law. Out of love the Christian does more than any human law can require.

Freedom in Christ, moreover, is a freedom *from indifferent things,* that is, things neither right nor wrong in themselves but things that hinder the achievement of a greater good. Second Peter 2:19 speaks of those who promise freedom but are themselves slaves of corruption. The author's statement that "people are slaves to whatever masters them" is applicable to more things than sin and immorality. It applies to laws or rules, even good ones. It also applies to habits and things harmless in themselves. Notice the use that Paul makes of the word "free" in 1 Corinthians 9:1-5, 12, and 19. Paul surrendered his rights in order to be more effective as a missionary. Here is the most mature expression of freedom — by one's own freedom to give up freedom. Freedom is not the highest goal for the Christian. Paul instructed the Corinthians (1 Cor. 8:9) to limit their freedom by a charitable concern for others. That has to be a voluntary choice. Another person cannot require me to surrender my freedom; that would bring me to the level of law again. But freedom may not be claimed when another good can be accomplished by not exercising it.

Freedom For

On the positive side, freedom in Christ is a freedom *to serve God.* Here is the real purpose of the Christian. Liberty is not to be a pretext for evil; it is to enable one to serve God (1 Pet. 2:16). Liberation from compulsion to sin opens up the hitherto impossible possibility of becoming righteous (Rom. 6:18). From one standpoint, a person is going to be a slave of something. Where is the greater or true freedom? In serving sin or in serving righteousness? The person of the world sees him/herself as free from righteousness to serve sin (Rom. 6:20); the Christian is free from sin to serve God.

The Christian's freedom *for* is also a freedom *to serve others* in love. As Galatians 5:13 puts it, freedom is not an opportunity to sin but an opportunity to serve others.[37] In Martin Luther's brilliant paradox, "A Christian is a perfectly free lord of all, subject to none; a Christian is a perfectly dutiful servant of all, subject to all."[38]

Sources of Freedom

This freedom comes from the Spirit of God (2 Cor. 3:17). Spiritual liberty is liberty under God and in obedience to his Spirit. Thus James 1:25 and 2:12 can speak of a perfect "law of liberty."

This freedom is attained by the truth: "The truth shall set you free" (John 8:32). This principle is recognized in other areas. In the natural world when truth is known and applied, ignorance, superstition, and bondage disappear. Freedom comes from living in harmony with the truth. A ship without a rudder or a compass is not free, but helpless. Law and truth give the helmsman the freedom to steer the ship. Truth gives the structure in which to be free. Even so, in the spiritual realm God's truth is liberating. In view of usage elsewhere in John, there is likely a special reference in John 8:32 — not abstract truth, but Jesus as the truth (see John 14:6).

Liberty is found in Christ. The Son of God gives freedom (John 8:36). Freedom is found in a personal relationship with him who is the source of all things. Liberation does not lie in human capacities; only the Son can set people free.

Misunderstandings of Freedom

The biblical usage of freedom makes us aware of some contemporary misunderstandings and misuses of the word "freedom." Some call bondage "freedom." The Communists used to do this when they captured a country. Freedom has become such an ideal concept that whatever one does may be called freedom. In the spiritual realm, too,

---

37. John Buckel, *Free to Love: Paul's Defense of Christian Liberty in Galatians* (Louvain: Peeters, 1993).

38. "The Freedom of a Christian" (1520), in, among other places, *Three Treatises* (Philadelphia: Fortress, 1960), p. 277.

we may impose one form of tyranny for another. Since freedom is internal, a matter of the Spirit, one may be internally free under a code of bondage, but that does not make the bondage equal freedom.

Another misuse of freedom is to want freedom for myself but not for others. Freedom is a social or community concept. Society has rights too. My freedom is limited by your freedom, and vice versa. As someone quaintly put it, "My freedom to swing my arms stops at the end of your nose."

Yet another misunderstanding is to confuse freedom with license, with a "do as I please" attitude. Doing whatever I want to do without a sense of responsibility is not freedom. This attitude leads to the slavery of selfishness. This view of freedom is also illusory. In Eric Hoffer's pungent paradox, "When people are free to do as they please, they usually imitate each other."

The columnist Sydney Harris offers this insight, "Most people mistakenly believe that to be 'free' is to be able to do what you want to do; when, in truth, to be free is to be able to do what is best for yourself — and learning what is best for yourself is the only way to get rid of the slavery of self-indulgence." Elton Trueblood seconds that statement: "Freedom does not mean that everyone can do as he likes, but that he can become what he should."

The Place of Rules in the Christian Life[39]

Divine law must be distinguished from human law and tradition (Matt. 15:2-3; Mark 7:8-9). Divine law is inviolable (John 10:35). Yet even within divine law, there is a ranking and priority (Matt. 12:1-8; Mark 2:23-28; Matt. 19:3-9). Certain principles take precedence over the specifics (Matt. 22:34-40; Rom. 13:8-10), but the specifics serve to show how the principles are to be interpreted and applied.

Human laws, on the other hand, should never be made absolute. They are, however, inevitable in human societies in consequence of the need to do things in an orderly way. Human laws and traditions arise, in part, from interpreting the divine law and implementing its performance. These have their place and are to be respected, even as they are kept in their secondary place.

---

39. For a balanced discussion in a more theological context than that found in my following remarks see T. J. Deidun, *New Covenant Morality in Paul* (Rome: Biblical Institute Press, 1981), pp. 150-226.

The Christian does not despise rules, laws, or regulations, but neither is he/she their slave. Human beings can never have a society without rules or laws. Any time persons are together in any kind of interaction there must be "rules" of conduct regulating those contacts in order for relationships to go smoothly and to protect the rights of the individual from abuses by others.

At times, it is true, one must act on a principle and break the rules. (Ordinarily a driver should stop for a red traffic light, but in an emergency to get a sick or injured person to the hospital, society recognizes a higher responsibility than obeying the law about traffic lights.) At those times a person should be sure that the action is indeed taken on principle and not on whim. Such exceptions remain exceptions and do not become the "rule." The rules remain in effect for ordinary circumstances.

Laws are necessary, and a society cannot function without them. Nevertheless, laws have definite limitations. Law cannot change the heart, impart power to keep its requirements, or bring peace of mind. This was true even for the divinely given law of Moses (Rom. 2:25-29; 3:21-31). Good laws or rules may preserve a principle and guide its application, but even the best laws can never completely encompass the principles they are meant to express. This circumstance provides the occasion for Christian liberty to free a person to serve the higher calling of God's truth and will.

The Exercise of Christian Liberty[40]

Actions and Morality

A given act, in and of itself, is nonmoral (Rom. 14:14-17; Matt. 15:1-20; Titus 1:15). The heart (attitude and purpose) of the person doing it and the circumstances under which it is done determine whether the act is moral or immoral. Some examples will illustrate the point. (1) One may take another person's life in a hunting or automobile accident. If there is no criminal neglect or other blameworthy factor, the person is not judged guilty by the law, as would be the case when anger, hatred, or only irresponsibility is involved. This may not make the person who did the deed feel any less remorse for the act, but the point is that the

---

40. I am indebted for this section to Cecil Hook, "The Exercise of Christian Liberty," *Firm Foundation* (Feb. 7, 1961): 88-89.

action itself was nonmoral. (2) Narcotics may be taken for medical purposes under a doctor's care and their use justified, unlike their use for other purposes or under different circumstances. (3) Sexual relations between a married couple are moral and good; the same act outside marriage is immoral. Again, motives and circumstances determine whether the act is moral or immoral; the same act may be either, for it is nonmoral in and of itself.

Principles Limiting the Exercise of Liberty

Christian liberty is to be exercised with self-control. The natural desires are not wrong but may be used in wrong ways; therefore, liberty in their use is limited by the principle of self-control (2 Pet. 2:19-20; 1 Cor. 6:12-13; 8:8). Some examples once more may clarify the point. (1) The desire for food is healthy and normal, but too much of the wrong kinds of food may become harmful to the body. (2) The need to acquire possessions for oneself or one's family may become the sin of greed or covetousness. (3) The instinct for self-preservation may lead to behavior that is fraudulent, deceptive, or unfair to others. As pointed out in the discussion of freedom above, liberty ceases to be liberty when one chooses an enslaving practice.

One should not abuse freedom by losing control of one's actions. On the other hand, the fact that something could lead to sin is not necessarily a reason for not doing it. Many kinds of games can be used for gambling, but that is not a reason necessarily to avoid participating in or observing the games. Excelling in any endeavor can lead to pride, but that certainly does not make a virtue of mediocrity. What something can lead to is not a reason to avoid it; anything can lead to sin, so one would be left in a situation of not being able to do anything. Nevertheless, what something can lead to should serve as a warning lest it become an occasion for sin.

Christian liberty may be limited out of higher concerns. Paul in several passages sets forth the charitable regard for others as a principle guiding the exercise of Christian liberty (Rom. 14:16, 20-22; 1 Cor. 6:12; 10:23; 1 Cor. 8:13). Freedom is not to be exercised in such a way as to lead a fellow believer into sin.

As a specific application of this, practices which tempt others must be avoided. Even civil law recognizes that a person is liable for creating hazards that endanger others. For some simple illustrations: (1) Teasing another person is often fun for all involved, but teasing a temperamental person to the point of anger and loss of temper would be wrong. One is then tempting the person to sin. (2) Immodest clothing, even if not intended to draw sexual attention to oneself, may induce lust and be a temptation to sin. The other person, of course, may be tempted even without provocation, but putting undue strain on him or her would be wrong.

Freedom from the Scruples of Others

Charitable interest in others and concern for not tempting them do not mean that they can bind their opinions on their fellow believers. A person cannot bind his or her scruples on another so as to limit his/her liberty. Texts like 1 Corinthians 8:13 and 10:32 are sometimes taken to mean that a Christian should not do anything that offends another, and then that is further taken by people as a means of imposing their opinions on others by insisting that others should not do what is objected to. Paul actually says in the former passage that he will not do what will cause the brother to "offend," that is, fall into sin, not what "offends" him. A different word is used in the latter passage to say that the believer avoids giving a bad example; at any rate, it is the believer's charitable regard for others, not a scruple imposed by another, that is under consideration.

If Christians were bound by the scruples of everyone, there would be very little in the way of entertainment or anything else left they could do. Charitable concessions can be made without surrender of freedom, but principles cannot be applied with legalism.

Summary

In exercising liberty in Christ, a person is not to come into bondage to (1) an impure heart or wrong motives, (2) any action that involves loss of self-control, (3) a selfishness that does not regard the welfare of others, and (4) the scruples of others.

CHURCH AND SOCIETY

"Conduct yourselves wisely toward outsiders."   (COL. 4:5)

The preceding topics of fellowship, discipline, and liberty center on relations within the community of faith. It is time now to ask, How does the church as the body of Christ relate to society at large? How does ministry deal with the collective evil present in the world, that is, with evil built into the organized structures of the world? The early church was a countercultural movement and remained persecuted and thus alienated from the power structures of the Roman world until the fourth century. Since that time various forms of state-church arrangements prevailed (except for the existence of some sectarian movements) until the process of separating state and church began in some countries in the eighteenth century. Apart from these historical precedents, two principal models present themselves today. Many see the Christian task as converting individuals, who in turn may or may not have an influence on society at large. This approach does not recognize the collective demonic and sees Christianity in individualistic terms. The thrust of this book has been to emphasize the corporate nature of salvation and the Christian life. Does this mean, then, that the biblical approach is represented by the other model: the attempt by the church to transform society?

The New Testament has little explicit to say on these societal issues. Is there, then, an alternative to the dilemma of individualism versus corporate action on the societal level, of converting individuals versus transforming society? There is. The New Testament places corporate action and responsibility in the Christian community and not on the level of the society at large and does not anticipate the use of the state as the instrument of change.[41] Neither a church dominated by the state, nor a state dominated by the church serves the purposes of New Testament Christianity. New Testament moral teaching is directed neither to the individual alone nor to society at large, but to the community of the saved, the church. The New Testament picture is neither of purely individual salvation nor of society as a whole as the corporate expression of the Christian faith.[42] The church fulfills the corporate

41. The position presented here has been most extensively argued by John Howard Yoder in numerous writings: see, e.g., "A People in the World: Theological Interpretation," in James Leo Garrett, Jr., ed., *The Concept of the Believers' Church* (Scottdale, Penn.: Herald, 1969), pp. 250-283; *The Priestly Kingdom* (Notre Dame: University of Notre Dame Press, 1984); *Body Politics* (Nashville: Discipleship Resources Press, 1993). From a different background see Robert Webber and Rodney Clapp, *People of the Truth: The Power of the Worshiping Community in the Modern World* (San Francisco: Harper, 1988).

42. Stanley Hauerwas and Wiliam H. Willimon, *Resident Aliens: Life in the Christian Colony* (Nashville: Abingdon, 1989), chap. 4.

nature of Christianity, not other entities. The church serves her purposes in relation to society when she is the embodiment of what a true society ought to be. Her best contribution to the wider society is made by living by her message and being the community of salvation in the truest sense.

The church presents an "alternative society."[43] Within the disciplined community of believers the new humanity begins to be realized. The church offers an example to society, a vision of a better way. The church is not called to enter the secular arena in order to make a sick world well. She is called to act well and so to serve as a reconciling witness to society. The church does not *have* a social strategy; the church *is* a social strategy.[44] Within the church there is created a fellowship that shatters society's categories. The Christian gospel and manner of life change persons, and thus society indirectly. But this is not simply the individualism of evangelical Protestantism. The individuals are incorporated into a new social organism (the church), and this offers to the larger society an alternative to its social evils.

In addition to presenting the reality of true community, the church has an influence in consciousness changing. This occurs not only through its example, but also through its verbal proclamation. The church aims to change conduct within her membership, but her message reaches outside to change the consciousness of society so that it becomes a conscience to the world. Christians are both prophets and peacemakers.

For the church truly to be the church, a benevolent state is no less threatening than an oppressive state. Indeed, the favorable state may be more threatening, for it tempts the church to rely on the state and its methods for the advancement of the church's programs. The oppressive state, as seen throughout history, strengthens the faith of the church and sharpens its identity. There is a current lament that a greater threat than either oppression or favor to the church is apathy or indifference by the state and society. Only those with the state-church mentality would think so. Whether the problem be indifference or opposition, the church must trust its Lord and follow his ways, which are not the world's ways, in achieving its mission. The church is always in a culture

43. Gerhard Lohfink, *Jesus and Community* (London: SPCK, 1985), p. 56 and passim; "contrast society," p. 66; "counter-society," p. 122.

44. Stanley Hauerwas and William H. Willimon, *Resident Aliens: Life in the Christian Colony* (Nashville: Abingdon, 1989), p. 43.

and cannot altogether escape a culture's influence, but a high degree of cultural accommodation is the biggest threat to the identity of the church.

Those who want to change society, in whatever direction and on whatever scale, often resort to violence. Those who want to maintain order and resist injustice likewise feel justified in using violence. Actually, violence is not radical enough to get at the root of problems in society, whether of injustice or of oppression. Violence is often itself the problem, and adopting it as a means of redress only continues and promotes the underlying human problems. The way of Jesus is that of loving resistance, "returning good for evil" (Matt. 5:21-26, 38-48). To resort to the methods of hate is to succumb to the very evil that needs to be resisted.

The church offers an alternative society, where the methods of Jesus are exemplified in personal and community relations.

UNITY

"Making every effort to maintain the unity of the Spirit in the bond of peace. There is one body and one Spirit."

(EPH. 4:3-4)

An important aspect of the church's witness to the larger society is displaying the unity that is essential to the church and is God's goal for humanity. The theme of the unity of the church is particularly prominent in the Epistle to the Ephesians,[45] but it is much emphasized elsewhere as well.[46]

The images used for the church (Chap. 2) uniformly denote its oneness: body of Christ (he has one body — Eph. 4:4), bride of Christ (the one husband has one wife — 2 Cor. 11:2; Eph. 5:22-33; Rev. 21:9; cf. 1 Cor. 7:2), temple (God authorized one temple, that at Jerusalem — Deut. 12:5, 14; Eph. 2:21), sheep (one flock and one shepherd — John 10:16), nation (one people and one priesthood — 1 Pet. 2:9, based on Exod. 19:5, 6, Israel chosen out of all the peoples of the earth). Moreover,

---

45. Stig Hanson, *The Unity of the Church in the New Testament: Colossians and Ephesians* (Uppsala: Almquist & Wiksells, 1946); Koshi Usami, *Somatic Comprehension of Unity: The Church in Ephesus* (Rome: Biblical Institute Press, 1983).

46. Hans Küng, *The Church* (London: Burns & Oates, 1968), pp. 269-276.

the unity of God is set forth as a figure for the unity of the church (John 17:21).

Exhortations to Unity and Warnings against Division

Several passages show the importance of unity. It was a principal theme of Jesus' prayer the last night with his disciples:

> I ask not only on behalf of these [disciples present] but also on behalf of those who will believe in me through their word, that they may all be one. As you, Father, are in me and I am in you, may they also be in us, so that the world may believe that you have sent me. The glory that you have given me I have given them, so that they may be one, as we are one, I in them and you in me, that they may become completely one, so that the world may know that you have sent me and have loved them even as you have loved me. (John 17:20-23)

The unity of Christ with the Father is set forth as the image and goal of unity among believers. The gifts of Christ (his glory) to his disciples are intended to achieve unity. The purpose stated for that unity is to bring the world to faith in Christ.

Paul made an urgent appeal to the divided Corinthian church for unity in Christ:

> Now I appeal to you by the name of our Lord Jesus Christ, that all of you be in agreement and that there be no divisions among you, but that you be united in the same mind and the same purpose. . . . Has Christ been divided? Was Paul crucified for you? Or were you baptized in the name of Paul? (1 Cor. 1:10-13)

Since Christ is one, the church must be one also. Christian unity derives from the cross of Christ. The crucifixion accomplished the salvation received in baptism. The fundamental Christian experience of salvation in Christ argues against division — doing anything or taking any names that would separate believers and take away from the name of Christ. Other earnest appeals to unity are found in Ephesians 4:1-6 and Philippians 1:1-4, to be considered below in the section on living out the unity that is in Christ.

Division is clearly branded a sin in Galatians 5:19-21. Of the fifteen items listed "works of the flesh," eight have to do with those things that create disharmony or describe division among people: enmities, strife, jealousy, anger, quarrels, dissensions, factions, envy. People are following the flesh and not the Spirit if they allow nationality, color, social status, cultural mores, economic and political doctrines, educational attainments, or personality differences to keep them apart. Brotherhood is based on having the same divine Spirit (1 Cor. 12:13).

Theological Foundations of Unity

The seven "ones" in Ephesians 4:4-6 set forth the basis of Christian unity.[47] We rearrange Paul's list to give a "theological" order.

(1) The one God and Father is the ultimate foundation of unity. The Jewish affirmation of the oneness of God (Deut. 6:4) is repeated in Christianity (Matt. 22:37; John 5:44; 17:3; 1 Cor. 12:6; 1 Tim. 1:17). This God "created all things" (Eph. 3:9) and is the source of "every spiritual blessing" (Eph. 1:3). The church is his (Eph. 3:19, 22). Unity is his goal (Eph. 1:10). The one God chooses one people as his special possession (Eph. 1:14). God the Father comes last in the Ephesians list, for the last and deepest ground of unity is the one God, creator and redeemer.

(2) The one Lord (Jesus Christ) is the instrument of God's creation and redemption and the one in whom God's people is called in the new dispensation. The "one God, the Father . . . and one Lord Jesus Christ" are put together in 1 Corinthians 8:6 (cf. "one God" and "one mediator . . . Christ Jesus" in 1 Tim. 2:5). Paul's appeal for unity at Corinth is made "in the name of our Lord Jesus Christ" (1 Cor. 1:10, 13). Christians offer their services to the "same Lord" (1 Cor. 12:5). God's goal is to unite all people in Christ (Eph. 1:10). Christians have one Savior. They acknowledge allegiance to one Lord. Not to keep the unity of church means to deny that there is one Lord and that loyalty is only to him.

(3) There is one Spirit, who unites all in baptism (1 Cor. 12:13), gives gifts (1 Cor. 12:4), and seeks to fill believers (Eph. 5:18). Christians have received their knowledge of Christ and salvation from one Spirit (Eph. 3:5; 6:17), were sealed with this one Spirit at baptism (Eph. 1:13-14; 4:30), and all share this one Spirit of God as the life-principle of the body (Eph. 2:22; 3:16). The Holy Spirit is particularly set forth in the

---

47. I draw in this section on my discussion of this passage in the context of Ephesians published in "Theological Foundations of Unity," *Mission* 6 (Nov. 1972): 140-143, a journal no longer in publication.

New Testament as the source and principle of unity (Eph. 4:3). Many things may divide human beings from one another; out of their diversity the Spirit creates a unity. The one Spirit as the theological basis of unity is brought out in the emphasis in 1 Corinthians 12:4-11 on the "same Spirit." Diversity of gifts comes from the one Spirit and is not to be divisive. To the Corinthian congregation that so much needed unity, Paul stresses that they cannot use the Spirit and his gifts as an excuse for division, for all comes from "one and the same Spirit." The church is one people because it is filled with the one Holy Spirit of God. The Spirit effects a reconciliation of those divided. "For through Christ both of us [Jews and Gentiles] have access in one Spirit to the Father. . . . In Christ you also are built together in the Spirit into a dwelling place for God" (Eph. 2:18, 22). No differences in the modern world are greater than the cultural and religious differences between Jews and Gentiles in antiquity, but the Spirit creates unity out of differences. On the other hand, to create divisions is to be devoid of the Spirit (Jude 19) and so be unworthy of the calling to which Christians have been called.

(4) There is one body in which all in Christ are placed (Rom. 12:4-5; Col. 3:15; 1 Cor. 12). The one body goes naturally with the one Spirit (1 Cor. 12:13). The one body is the church (Eph. 1:22-23; 4:12, 16; 5:30). Instead of speaking of a "body of Christians" or a "body of believers," the New Testament speaks of the "body of Christ." That is, biblical thought starts with unity, with oneness and wholeness. From the one Lord is created the community or oneness of his people. The situation is not of human communities where a plurality of individuals come together to form one organization. Christians are not one body because they decided to unite, but they are together because of being incorporated into Christ. Reconciliation to God is in this one body (Eph. 2:16). This may be the physical body on the cross (Col. 1:22), but if so, it virtually includes the church, for the body on the cross produces saved men and women. Jew and Gentile, and by implication all people, are made one in the church (Eph. 2:15). Christ saves the church — he loves, cleanses, and sacrifices himself for it (Eph. 5:23, 25-26). The church is the initial realization of God's goal of unity (Eph. 1:10).

(5) There is one faith confessed by the people called by God (cf. 1 Cor. 15:1-11). The content is supplied by the message about Christ that is preached, a message that is appropriated by personal trust and confessed at baptism. Christ is the object and goal of faith (Eph. 1:15; 4:15). Believing in him comes by hearing the word of truth, the gospel of salvation (Eph. 1:13), and that faith is the means of salvation (Eph.

2:8). Not only the initial salvation but the continuing relationship with Christ is dependent on faith, for it is the means of his abiding presence (Eph. 3:17) and his working in a person's life (Eph. 1:19). The Christian faith is ultimately one (Eph. 4:13). The sphere of unity is faith and knowledge. The common faith and the instruction that enables people to grow in a common knowledge are related to "the Son of God." The one central confession that Christians make, that "Jesus is Lord" (Rom. 10:9), unites them. Division is a sin against the fundamental affirmation of Christianity.

(6) There is one baptism administered in the name of Christ (1 Cor. 1:13). Baptism creates the unity of Christians. It is connected with the one Spirit and the one body (1 Cor. 12:13) and with the one Lord and one faith (Gal. 3:26-27). It makes all who receive it "one in Christ Jesus" (Gal. 3:28). At baptism there is confessed the one faith in the one Lord, and the person is sealed with the one Spirit and introduced into the one body. In baptism Christ cleanses his people to be his bride, "by the washing of water with the word" (Eph. 5:26); by the accompanying "word" I mean the confession of faith. Christians are united by virtue of having experienced a common act of obedience in which they declared their allegiance to Christ, received his Spirit, and were made a part of his people. Paul in 1 Corinthians 1:13-17 protests against any view of baptism which would make it a badge of distinction among Christians instead of a unifying act. Baptism is intended to be a foundation of Christian unity.

(7) There is one hope toward which Christians strive and which sustains them. Reference to faith and baptism reminds one of the calling or summons which came with the hearing of the gospel (Eph. 1:13; Col. 1:5). Believers are called to a specific hope (Eph. 1:18). Christ is the object and basis of hope (Eph. 1:12). The condition of those apart from Christ is to be without hope (Eph. 2:12). Hope is pointed toward eternal salvation (Eph. 6:17; cf. 1 Thess. 5:8; Rom. 8:24f.). In the present, believers are to live a life worthy of the calling to hope received in Christ (Eph. 4:1). The common goal or purpose provided by the Christian hope unifies believers.

These seven items are part of the "givens" of Christianity. Unity is already provided by God in the most important things. Sharing these fundamental things gives a broad and strong basis for unity. In view of what unites, the things that divide seem less formidable. They may be important in themselves. It is important to try to be "right" on any issue. But the things that divide believers are not nearly so important as what unites — one God, one Lord, one Spirit, one body, one faith, one baptism, one hope. In a sense, to be divided is to say God has not done enough to produce unity; it is to minimize the most important aspects of the Christian faith. These doctrinal unities should encourage the expression and application of unity among Christians.

Expressions of Unity

There may be many expressions of unity, but we select here only a few items especially related to the life of the church. These are matters that both unite and express unity.

(1) The one bread of the eucharist, or Lord's supper. We noted in the discussion of fellowship that sharing the cup and the bread establishes a communion with Christ that in turn is the basis of unity among participants (1 Cor. 10:16-17). Paul reverses the normal order of bread-cup to cup-bread so as to elaborate what is said about the bread, probably because the associations of breaking bread with fellowship and community better lent themselves to emphasizing the unity that he wanted to stress. "Because there is one bread, we who are many are one body, for we all partake of the one bread" (1 Cor. 10:17). This one bread is related both to the one body of Christ on the cross and the one body of believers.[48] The manner in which the Corinthian church observed the Lord's supper expressed social and economic divisions among the members (1 Cor. 11:17-22). Hence, Paul gives instructions that will make it possible for the observance better to express the unity inherent in the remembrance of a common salvation (1 Cor. 11:23-26) and the mutual regard involved in the shared act of breaking bread together (1 Cor. 11:27-34).

(2) The one voice of common worship. The one bread is part of the larger participation in one worship. To unify Christians at Rome who observed different customs, Paul wrote: "May the God of steadfastness and encouragement grant you to live in harmony with one another, in accordance with Christ Jesus, so that together you may with one voice glorify the God and Father of our Lord Jesus Christ" (Rom. 15:6-7). Paul's words may have a wider application than congregational worship, particularly if "one voice" is being used as a metaphor for

---

48. Commentators and others are divided over the meaning of 1 Cor. 11:29, the physical body of Christ or the spiritual body of the church.

unity in general; however, one use of the phrase (literally, "one mouth") was for unison singing, and so it was used by Christians for what they did in church. Living together in harmony makes possible and finds expression in united worship. This unity is "in accordance with Christ Jesus."

(3) The one heart and one soul of life in community. The early chapters of Acts give a picture of the unified expressions of joy and service in the common life of the early believers. "Now the whole group of those who believed were of one heart and soul, and no one claimed private ownership of any possessions, but everything they owned was held in common" (Acts 4:32). "All who believed were together and had all things in common" (Acts 2:44). These passages are often taken as describing a complete community of goods after the fashion of modern communism. This appears to claim too much for the description in the text. There was selling of property and placing the proceeds in a common fund administered by the apostles (Acts 4:34-37). But the complete divestment of private ownership was not required (Acts 5:4). The emphasis was not on creating common production and equal distribution of property but on providing for those in need (Acts 2:45; 4:34). The thought seems to be that owners of possessions did not "say" or "claim" these things were their own but made them available to others as there was need (Acts 4:32). Glad and generous hearts (Acts 2:46) expressed their unity of heart and soul by sharing their possessions as part of sharing a new life in the community of faith. This new life together included as well shared worship (Acts 2:42, 47), shared meals (Acts 2:46), and support of the apostles' preaching (Acts 4:33). The resurrection of the Lord Jesus that was the theme of the apostles' testimony gave power to and found expression in this unified community life.

(4) The one attitude of a unified faith. There needs to be a will to unity, as Paul instructed the Corinthians. "Now I appeal to you, brothers and sisters, by the name of our Lord Jesus Christ, that all of you be in agreement and that there be no divisions among you, but that you be united in the same mind and the same purpose" (1 Cor. 1:10). Where the will to unity is absent or weak, nearly anything can be divisive. Where the will to unity is strong, even major disagreements can be resolved or handled in such a way as to avoid division. Paul's appeal is "by the name of the Lord Jesus Christ"; where the Lord is kept uppermost, there is a strong incentive to express unity in him through a common mind and purpose.

Living Out the Unity

The application of unity to the daily Christian life and the congregational activities of believers requires certain attitudes and actions. God's
aim is to bring all things to unity in Christ (Eph. 1:10). The unity is
already given by the Lord as part of what he has done for human
salvation in order to achieve an eternal community. The human task is
not to achieve unity among themselves, but to keep the unity already
created: "Making every effort to maintain the unity of the Spirit in the
bond of peace" (Eph. 4:3). The attitudes necessary to maintain unity are
spelled out in the preceding exhortation of Ephesians 4:1-2: "I therefore,
the prisoner of the Lord, beg you to lead a life worthy of the calling to
which you have been called, with all humility and gentleness, with
patience, bearing with one another in love."

Philippians 2:1-4 offers another important statement of how unity
applies to behavior. On the basis of the "givens" in the Christian understanding, "If then there is any encouragement in Christ, any consolation
from love, any sharing in the Spirit, any compassion and sympathy" (vs.
1), comes Paul's personal appeal for unity, "make my joy complete: be of
the same mind, having the same love, being in full accord and of one
mind" (vs. 2). Then Paul describes the attitudes necessary to achieve this;
or, in other words, how the unity is to be lived out in personal relations:
"Do nothing from selfish ambition or conceit, but in humility regard
others as better than yourselves. Let each of you look not to your own
interests but to the interests of others" (vss. 3-4). Such attitudes and
conduct will go a long way toward making unity effective in congregational life, a need in the Philippian church (Phil. 4:2) as elsewhere. Even
if to exemplify these qualities does not solve the problems of unity in
every case, it is very important to individuals to maintain this behavior.

Other passages that relate Christian life to unity will only be mentioned here. Colossians 3:5-15, with much material parallel to Ephesians,
connects the moral instructions to "love, which binds everything together
in perfect harmony," and continues with reference to the "peace of Christ
. . . to which you were called in the one body" (Col. 3:14-15). The moral
teachings of Romans 12:3ff. follow on the reference to the "one body"
(Rom. 12:4). Similarly, in 1 Corinthians 12, the gifts flow from the one God
and one Lord (vss. 5-6), are activated by the one Spirit (vss. 4, 11), and are
to be used for the "common good" (vs. 7) of the "one body" (vss. 12-27).

"United and pursuing unity" describes the situation of members
of Christ's body, the church.[49]

Contemporary Observations

Unity may helpfully be contrasted with two concepts that stand on either side of it: uniformity and union. Uniformity means everything or everyone alike. Members of the military, a band, or athletic team wear a uniform. The result is that they all look alike; there are few or no differences. Some people think of Christian unity in these terms: everybody must look, think, and sound alike. There is a certain core of beliefs and practices in which there is a uniformity, although even these may often have variations in expression at different times and places; but to expect a large degree of uniformity is to deny individuality and uniqueness of personality.

On the other side, many hope only for a loose sense of union in which people or groups come together in their diversity for limited objectives and a limited degree of unity. Members of a trade union keep their individuality but unite to achieve certain economic goals of common benefit. The American colonies in the eighteenth century came together to create a federal government, "to form a more perfect union," in order to achieve certain political purposes, but the intention was to maintain a high degree of autonomy for the participating states. The term "union" may fairly describe many organizational expressions of the ecumenical movement. Such organizational entities as the World Council and National Council may provide a framework in which the participating bodies may grow closer together, but the most that is achieved, by and large, is a loose federation of churches.

Unity may share some aspects of union (a coming together for a common purpose) and uniformity (certain things held or observed "identically"), but its essential quality is elsewhere. Unity requires solidarity and loyalty. Even where there are differences, there is a commitment to remain together. There is a sense of being "one people," who share a loyalty to the same principles and to one another.

There is room within unity for a diversity that seeks to maintain unity; there is no place for a diversity born of party spirit. Division is a denial of salvation, since the goal in Ephesians 1:10 is uniting all in Christ. Saying that these things are not enough to unite people is a denial of the fundamentals of Christianity.

The program of this book has been to concentrate on the central

49. Rudolf Schnackenburg, *The Church in the New Testament* (New York: Herder and Herder, 1965), p. 128.

affirmations of the scriptures, then to work out from these core concepts to other less clearly or frequently stated matters until those points clearly opposed in scripture as wrong are reached. Perhaps the same procedure can be applied to matters of Christian unity. If believers will concentrate on that which unites, then work out from this to other clear matters, and not be too quick to draw lines of fellowship or division in the fringe areas that are judgmental matters, perhaps some clarity of perspective will be achieved. And if, in particular, an emphasis is given to the attitudes and qualities of life associated with the "way of Christ," then even divisive matters will not injure personal relationships.

Before despairing over the institutional church, the reader would do well to recall the original perspective of this book. Every topic is intimately related to Christ. The same is true for unity. Unity is to be found in Christ. Moreover, remember the example of Christ. He died for his people, the church (Eph. 5:25). When viewed from the standpoint of its human members, the church will never be perfect; otherwise there would be no need for the life, death, and resurrection of Christ and no need for human ministry. There is no way to love Christ and not love his church. And with that love go obligations of service.

Hymn of At-one-ment

Thou God of all, whose spirit moves
    From pole to silent pole;
Whose purpose binds the starry spheres
    In one stupendous whole;
Whose life, like light, is freely poured
    On all men 'neath the sun;
To Thee we lift our hearts, and pray
    That Thou will make us one.

One in the patient company
    Of those who heed Thy will,
And steadfastly pursue the way
    Of Thy commandments still;
One in the holy fellowship
    Of those who challenge wrong,
And lift the spirit's sword to shield
    The weak against the strong.

One in the truth that makes men free,
  The faith that makes men brave;
One in the love that suffers long
  to seek, and serve, and save;
One in the vision of Thy peace,
  Thy kingdom yet to be —
When Thou shalt be the God of all,
  And all be one in Thee.

                                           John Haynes Holmes[50]

Selected Bibliography on New Testament Ethics

Deidun, T. J. *New Covenant Morality in Paul.* Rome: Biblical Institute Press, 1981.

Furnish, Victor P. *Theology and Ethics in Paul.* Nashville: Abingdon, 1968.

Hauerwas, Stanley. *A Community of Character.* Notre Dame: University of Notre Dame, 1981.

Hauerwas, Stanley, and William H. Willimon. *Resident Aliens: Life in the Christian Colony.* Nashville: Abingdon, 1989.

Hays, Richard B. *The Moral Vision of the New Testament.* San Francisco: HarperCollins, 1996.

LeMaster, Philip. *Discipleship for All Believers: Christian Ethics and the Kingdom of God.* Scottdale, Penn.: Herald, 1992.

Lohse, Eduard. *Theological Ethics of the New Testament.* Minneapolis: Fortress, 1991.

Manson, T. W. *Ethics and the Gospel.* New York: Scribner, 1961.

Marshall, L. W. *Challenge of New Testament Ethics.* New York: Macmillan, 1964.

Marxsen, Willi. *New Testament Foundations for Christian Ethics.* Minneapolis: Fortress, 1993.

Meeks, Wayne A. *The Moral World of the First Christians.* Philadelphia: Westminster, 1986.

Meeks, Wayne A. *The Origins of Christian Morality: The First Two Centuries.* New Haven: Yale, 1993.

Schnackenburg, R. *The Moral Teaching of the New Testament.* Freiburg: Herder, 1965.

Schrage, Wolfgang. *The Ethics of the New Testament.* Philadelphia: Fortress, 1988.

---

50. Quoted in James Dalton Morrison, ed., *Masterpieces of Religious Verse* (New York: Harper, 1948), pp. 67-68.

Scott, C. Anderson. *New Testament Ethics: An Introduction.* Cambridge: University Press, 1934.

Verhey, Allen. *The Great Reversal: Ethics and the New Testament.* Grand Rapids: Eerdmans, 1984.

Wiebe, Ben. *Messianic Ethics: Jesus' Proclamation of the Kingdom of God and the Church as Response.* Waterloo: Herald, 1992.

Yoder, John H. *The Politics of Jesus.* Grand Rapids: Eerdmans, 1972.

Yoder, John H. *The Priestly Kingdom.* Notre Dame: University of Notre Dame, 1984.

Selected General Bibliography

Basden, Paul, and David S. Dockery, eds. *The People of God: Essays on the Believer's Church.* Nashville: Broadman, 1991.

Bouyer, Louis. *The Church of God, Body of Christ, and Temple of the Spirit.* Chicago: Franciscan Herald Press, 1982.

Cerfaux, L. *The Church in the Theology of St. Paul.* New York: Herder & Herder, 1959.

Flew, R. Newton. *Jesus and His Church.* London: Epworth, 1956.

Giles, Kevin. *What on Earth Is the Church? An Exploration in New Testament Theology.* Downers Grove: InterVarsity, 1995.

Hanson, Paul D. *The People Called: The Growth of Community in the Bible.* San Francisco: Harper & Row, 1968.

Harrington, Daniel J. *God's People in Christ: New Testament Perspectives on the Church and Judaism.* Philadelphia: Fortress, 1980.

Hort, F. J. A. *The Christian Ecclesia.* London: Macmillan & Co., 1897.

Johnston, George. *The Doctrine of the Church in the New Testament.* Cambridge: University Press, 1943.

Küng, Hans. *The Church.* London: Burns and Oates, 1968.

Lohfink, Gerhard. *Jesus and Community.* London: SPCK, 1985.

Moltmann, Jürgen. *The Church in the Power of the Spirit: A Contribution to Messianic Ecclesiology.* New York: Harper & Row, 1977.

Robinson, William. *The Biblical Doctrine of the Church.* St. Louis: Bethany, 1955.

Schnackenburg, Rudolf. *The Church in the New Testament.* New York: Herder and Herder, 1965.

Watson, David. *I Believe in the Church.* Grand Rapids: Eerdmans, 1978.

Subject Index

Aaron, 4, 37
Abraham, 3, 5, 8, 9, 10, 11, 17, 18,
  56, 65, 74, 78, 79, 81, 82, 84, 91,
  104, 165, 167-68, 171, 175, 197, 221
Acclamations, 262, 263, 264
Adam, 46, 82, 94, 139, 140, 141, 142,
  145, 148, 199
Amen, 263, 342
Angels, 116, 118, 120, 209
Anointing, 21, 36-37, 39, 41, 56, 102,
  118
Apostles, xviii, 12, 47, 48, 56, 59, 66,
  67, 85, 107, 112, 124, 125, 128,
  162, 175, 218, 224, 246, 267, 283,
  291, 292, 298, 299, 301-6, 307, 308,
  309, 310, 312, 313, 314, 319, 327,
  330, 332, 334, 336, 337, 345, 367,
  371, 378, 405
Assembly, 30, 58, 130-33, 211, 216,
  219, 226-79, 288, 341-44, 381
Atonement, 11, 14, 44, 120, 126, 127,
  129, 148-63, 191, 215-17, 220, 223,
  236, 254, 255, 281, 299, 408-9
Autonomy, congregational, 344-46,
  385

Baptism, 10, 34, 64, 66-67, 108, 109,
  118, 169-70, 173, 174-75, 179-203,
  250, 262, 264, 318, 349, 353, 357,
  373, 386, 387, 400, 401, 402, 403,
  404; administrator, 194; of Christ,
  41, 73, 93, 100, 105, 108, 117, 180;

immersion, 174, 186, 191, 201-3;
  Jewish, 179, 180, 201-2; subjects,
  195-201
Beloved, 72, 87, 99, 100-101
Benevolence, 223, 274, 275, 277, 282-
  83, 287, 288-90, 293, 297, 298, 299,
  300, 301, 313, 333, 336-37, 340-41,
  345, 360, 369, 405
Bible. See Canon; Scripture
Birth, new, 84, 108, 118, 164, 188-89,
  373
Bishop, 297, 299, 311, 317, 319, 320,
  322-27, 330, 335, 336, 339, 340, 341
Blessings, 5, 37, 63, 99, 126, 201,
  250, 256, 259, 276, 314-16
Blood of Christ, 10, 11, 61, 66, 83,
  84, 136, 151, 154, 155, 159-60, 183,
  185, 201, 215, 219, 251, 253, 254,
  259, 260, 358, 368, 387, 388
Body of Christ, 71, 72, 91-103, 107,
  121, 124, 126-27, 135, 153, 192-93,
  194, 204, 218, 250, 251, 259, 260,
  284, 295, 298, 345, 350, 359, 368,
  399, 402, 403, 404, 406, 407
Breaking bread, 67, 251-52, 258-59
Bride of Christ, 115, 360, 399
Brothers and sisters, 99, 115, 119-21,
  233, 256, 369, 373
Building, 47, 52, 124-25, 127, 129-30,
  287

Calling by God, 79, 85-86, 87, 88,

411

Scripture Index